MR. LINCOLN GOES TO WAR

MR. LINCOLN
GOES TO WAR

William Marvel

Houghton Mifflin Company

BOSTON • NEW YORK

2006

For information about permission to reproduce selections
from this book, write to Permissions, Houghton Mifflin Company,
215 Park Avenue South, New York, New York 10003.

Visit our Web site: www.houghtonmifflinbooks.com.

Library of Congress Cataloging-in-Publication Data
Marvel, William.
Mr. Lincoln goes to war / William Marvel.
p.   cm.
Includes bibliographical references and index.
ISBN-13: 978-0-618-58349-2
ISBN-10: 0-618-58349-1
1. United States — History — Civil War, 1861–1865. 2. Lincoln,
Abraham, 1809–1865. 3. Lincoln, Abraham, 1809–1865 —
Military leadership. I. Title: Mister Lincoln goes to war. II. Title.
E471.M37 2006
973.7'1 — dc22   2005020046

Book design by Melissa Lotfy

PRINTED IN THE UNITED STATES OF AMERICA

MP 10 9 8 7 6 5 4 3 2 1

To that covey of close companions who
gathered atop South Mountain
on the afternoon of August 10, 2002

Contents

LIST OF ILLUSTRATIONS AND MAPS   ix

PREFACE   xiii

PART I ❖ WE CANNOT SEPARATE

1. Songs for a Prelude   3
2. Flags in Mottoed Pageantry   36
3. The Banner at Daybreak   63

PART II ❖ AND NOW THE STORM-BLAST CAME

4. Behold the Silvery River   93
5. Where Ignorant Armies Clash   120
6. The Crimson Corse of Lyon   155

PART III ❖ THE ERA OF SUSPICION

7. The Despot's Heel   185
8. By Cliffs Potomac Cleft   216
9. Shovel Them Under and Let Me Work   247
   Epilogue   281

APPENDIX 1: Orders of Battle 289

APPENDIX 2: Biographical Sketches 292

NOTES 304

BIBLIOGRAPHY 340

ACKNOWLEDGMENTS 363

INDEX 368

List of Illustrations and Maps

All illustrations are courtesy of the Library of Congress except as noted below. Present-day photographs are by the author.

FOLLOWING PAGE 62

South Carolinians firing on the *Star of the West*
The steamer *Marion* leaving Charleston
Cartoon lampooning the Crittenden Compromise
Cassius Clay's battalion at the White House
Charles P. Stone with his daughter
Senator Edward Dickinson Baker
Lincoln and Buchanan entering the Senate
Lincoln's first inauguration
Caricature of Winfield Scott as a bulldog
Lincoln confronting a secessionist
Secretary of State William H. Seward
Secretary of War Simon Cameron
Alexandria, Virginia, viewed from Maryland
The Marshall House in Alexandria
The 71st New York at rest in Alexandria
Ellsworth's funeral in the White House

FOLLOWING PAGE 154

New Jersey soldiers digging entrenchments
Hayfields, John Merryman's plantation
President Lincoln and General Scott reviewing regiments
Major General Irvin McDowell
Pierre Gustave Toutant Beauregard
Mutinous Garibaldi Guards surrendering
Officers and men of the 1st Rhode Island, spring of 1861
The 8th New York Militia at Arlington, June, 1861

Planning the advance to Manassas
Major General Robert Patterson
Ambrose Burnside's brigade at Bull Run
The remains of the Cub Run bridge
Major General Sterling Price
Major General George B. McClellan
Colonel Frank Blair of the 1st Missouri Volunteers
Captain Nathaniel Lyon
Lyon's success at Boonville
Colonel Franz Sigel at Carthage
John C. Frémont in 1861
Company H, 3rd Arkansas *(General Sweeny's Museum, Republic, Missouri)*

FOLLOWING PAGE 246
Slaves escaping to Fort Monroe
The ransacking of a newspaper office in Bridgeport, Connecticut *(Bridgeport Public Library Historical Collections)*
The cover of *Harper's Weekly,* September 7, 1861
First Lieutenant Nathan G. Evans *(South Caroliniana Library, University of South Carolina, Columbia)*
Eppa Hunton, commander of the 8th Virginia *(Gil Barrett Collection, U.S. Army Military History Institute, Carlisle, Pennsylvania)*
A picket post along the Potomac, early October
Union troops at Fairfax Court House, October 18
The farmhouse on Harrison's Island
Lock 25, at Edwards's Ferry, on the Chesapeake & Ohio Canal
Henry Harrison's house in Leesburg
Margaret Jackson's house, Ball's Bluff
George Washington Ball's manse, Springwood
The Potomac between Harrison's Island and Ball's Bluff
Skirmishing at Edwards's Ferry on October 22 and the retreat on the night of October 23
A modern view of the scene of the October 23 retreat
Vigilant pickets on the Potomac after Ball's Bluff
Body of a Ball's Bluff casualty dragged from the Potomac
Union soldiers celebrating McClellan's promotion in front of his home
Senator Zachariah Chandler of Michigan

MAPS
Theater of War, 1861   7
Maryland and Northern Virginia   65
Bull Run Campaign   115
Missouri and Wilson's Creek   160
Leesburg and Poolesville   203
Ball's Bluff   228

Arm'd year — year of the struggle,
No dainty rhymes or sentimental love verses
   for you terrible year.

— WALT WHITMAN,
"Eighteen Sixty-One"

Preface

The accepted role of the historian is to explain what happened, rather than to guess what might have been, but the most intently objective historical studies sometimes adopt an unintentionally narrow perspective through a reluctance to address alternatives available to the participants. Historians unwilling to consider the conditional past tend to present historical developments as the only possible results of immutable chains of events. In professional circles the examination of alternatives is associated with futile, lowbrow speculation, and indeed the genre of "counterfactual" history often descends to ludicrous levels of political science fiction. Nonetheless, the refusal to weigh actions and events against some measure other than what they actually wrought leaves the historian functioning too much like an annalist and too little like an analyst.

In the study of the American Civil War that trend is exacerbated by the near-unanimous agreement that the conflict yielded the most desirable results, and the principal beneficiary of that phenomenon has been Abraham Lincoln. Credited with winning a war that ended slavery and reestablished the boundaries of the original United States, Lincoln is generally portrayed as having accomplished all that he set out to do — and often as having done so with commendable genius. Even the incisive historian T. Harry Williams ameliorated his token admission that Lincoln "sometimes . . . made bad mistakes" by offering abundantly sympathetic explanation, and Williams ignored the most serious gaffes of 1861.[1] Lincoln is so revered that foundations have been established to reward scholars who interpret his presidency, and laudatory biographies continue to pour from both commercial and university presses. Proponents of particular ideologies have begun to take aim at him, but fourteen decades after

his death he remains the one major figure in Civil War history whose popular image has escaped substantial revision by mainstream historians.

That collective generosity is not difficult to understand, especially in
light of the deathblow that Lincoln's war dealt to slavery. In offhand remarks at Independence Hall, on his way to Washington, the president-
elect hinted ambiguously at his hope for ultimate equality of opportunity
for all men, but — if his overt contemporary statements on the subject
can be believed — the chance to strike a blow at slavery did not motivate
him in the least to begin the war. Even if it had, any citizen of average intellect and contemporary values who could have foreseen the dreadful
cost should have questioned why that end could not have been achieved
less destructively. Had Lincoln himself known how much blood and
treasure his war would ultimately consume, it seems certain that he
would not have pursued it for the sole purpose of emancipating the country's slaves, if he had pursued it at all.

The preservation of the Union remained Lincoln's principal focus
throughout the entire first year of the conflict, and at his inauguration he
stood willing to consign the nation's four million slaves and all their de-
scendants to perpetual servitude to maintain that union. For him, as for
millions of other Americans, the United States formed the white man's
foremost bastion of democracy and liberty — two concepts that popular
thought had come to blend promiscuously. Lincoln represented those
who did not differentiate between the landmass over which the Constitution held authority and the constitutional principles that protected
democracy and liberty. He viewed his sworn duty to "preserve, protect,
and defend the Constitution" as a responsibility to retain all the unwilling members of that union by force, if necessary, and he insisted on doing
so even if it meant arbitrarily reinterpreting or blatantly violating the
Constitution he had sworn to defend. In arrogating such extraordinary
authority to the executive branch, he created precedents that permanently jeopardized the liberty the Constitution promised to all Americans, and most of those precedents predated any hope that they would be
offset by the freedom his actions would incidentally provide for the en-
slaved minority.

Having been liberated from antiquated ideology about race and slavery, the modern student finds it irresistible to condemn the Southern advocates of secession because of the obnoxious institution that underlay
their impulse. The byproduct of the war, emancipation, has come to dom-
inate the memory of the conflict so thoroughly that no contradiction now
seems apparent in the establishment of federal power to impose universal, involuntary military service as a measure for ending involuntary
servitude. If that anachronistic appreciation can be suspended, the ques-

tion of constitutionality next intervenes: did (or, for that matter, does) any state or group of states ever have the right to withdraw from the Union? Former Confederates devoted long passages of their histories and memoirs to polemics on that point, noting that it was the self-righteous Federalists of New England who first considered secession, during the War of 1812. In the victorious North some of their postwar counterparts highlighted the self-contradiction inherent in any constitutional provision for secession, but most of them tended to cite the success of federal arms as sufficient authority to decide the matter. The prevailing Unionist opinion during the secession crisis suggested the difficult condition that a state could secede only if a majority of the other states agreed to the separation, but the rhetoric of 1860 and 1861 insinuates that most Unionists denied the legality of secession under any circumstances. With perfect but unintended irony, the framers of the Confederate constitution acknowledged the flaw in the prosecession argument by implicitly prohibiting secession for any member state in their "permanent" new nation.

Let us suppose there were no grounds for secession. If it was unconstitutional, did the opponents of secession have the right to combat it with equally unconstitutional measures? Was the president's subsequent response any less illegal than the actions of the secession conventions, merely because his excesses followed theirs chronologically? Beyond the question of right, was it wise to meet secession with extralegal force? Was the preservation of the national borders worth the precedent of the chief executive unilaterally initiating warfare, arbitrarily suspending civil liberties, jailing thousands on suspicion or political whim, using the military to manipulate elections, and even overthrowing the legitimate governments of states? Perhaps most relevant then and now, especially considering the potential for the repetition and expansion of those infringements under increasingly numerous and nebulous emergencies, is the question of whether those infringements were even necessary. Did the permanent weakening of America's best protection against tyranny not exceed the violence done to the Constitution by the secession of seven states, and might that fundamental document not have survived in firmer health with the remaining twenty-seven states adhering to it all the more strictly?

For that matter, would the bifurcation of the United States have been worse than the war waged to prevent it? The instinctive reply (after requisite reference to the abolition of slavery) asserts that the precedent of secession would have led to further divisions, until the former nation had been thoroughly Balkanized; Lincoln himself alluded to that potential fragmentation in his first inaugural.[2] Yet the very choice of the pejorative term "Balkanized," which is so often employed in that argument, carries an assumption that a continent of smaller republics would not have been preferable. Nationalist advocates can and have produced abundant evidence of economic and social development under the reconstructed United States, but that evidence does not necessarily suggest that equivalent development would have been impossible under another political and geographic configuration. Although it would likely have increased internal tension in the North, unopposed secession in 1861 ought, at least initially, to have eased the conflict between the sections — rather than aggravating it, as "Balkanization" implies. Disunion would have made slavery a pervasive national issue within the Confederate States, rather than a divisive sectional problem within the United States, thereby eliminating what Arthur M. Schlesinger Jr. considered one of the foremost impediments to a peaceful, internal solution for that evil.[3] The obstacles to proving any hypothesis of separation as a viable alternative apply equally to any assertion of it as an unacceptable solution.

There was a point at which Lincoln would have yielded to the Southern states on the right of secession. He occasionally intimated that he would have to give up the fight for national integrity if the combination against him grew too formidable, and he might have reached this conclusion by April of 1861 had he not so badly underestimated Southern determination and border-state sympathies. In our age of nine- and ten-digit populations, and particularly with the advantage of our enlightened perspective on slavery, we who did not pay any of the cost of the Civil War may not fully appreciate a toll of some 620,000 dead. In the early twenty-first century that is less than the population of Lake County, Illinois, and barely that of Hudson County, New Jersey. In 1861, however, that number reflected about 4 percent of the country's entire male population. On average, one family in nine would bury a father or a son. A proportionate casualty rate in World War II would have been 2.7 million Americans killed — seven times as many as actually died. About 3,600,000 Americans would have to have perished in Vietnam — providing names enough to fill sixty memorial walls rather than one. An equivalent price from the nation's present population would require the sacrifice of about 6 million American lives, with millions of others maimed.

If Lincoln considered the issue of secession negotiable at some point on a scale of increasing resistance, it seems that such devastating mortality would have figured fairly high on that scale. Had he been able to foresee the harvest of death his choices would yield, anyone as reasonable as the sixteenth president might understandably have opted against the carnage and accepted the departure of seven fractious provinces in return for a smaller but more peaceable federation. Of course he owned no such foresight: the resort to arms seldom fails to inflict far greater suffering than either belligerent expects, but it took a peculiar blend of circumstances to turn the American Civil War into an unpredictable bloodbath. Southern intransigence derived from similar ignorance and contributed most of the propellant to the pyre: the tempest over the innocuous coastal forts would have subsided, for instance, had the Confederates simply ignored them. It was Lincoln, however, who finally eschewed diplomacy and sparked a confrontation when he fully understood the volatility of the situation. Although he avoided the political blunder of firing the first shot, he backed himself into a corner from which he could escape only by mobilizing a national army, and thereby fanning the embers of Fort Sumter into full-scale conflagration. Lincoln's misjudgments of 1861 are overshadowed in the public memory by the results of 1865, which seem to validate his earlier decisions, but those ancillary results do not diminish the essential recklessness of his actions at the time he undertook them.

More than half a century ago Kenneth Stampp produced an exceptionally thorough and insightful study of the buildup to the Civil War, and especially of Lincoln's part in it. Although he concluded with a substantially complimentary assessment of Lincoln's performance, Stampp began his book by noting that, like leaders of any period who face the prospect of war, the politicians of 1861 enjoyed the perennial alternative of compromising their respective demands in the interests of peace. Southerners could have risked the perceived threats to their slave-based economy by simply declining to secede and relying upon their political strength in the U.S. Senate; Northerners might have allowed the Southern tier of states to withdraw and form their own government. Such selfless decisions would have earned their authors "a fame unique in the history of statesmanship," Stampp noted, but instead they made what he called the "usual" choice, pitting their populations against each other in a devastating collision. That distinction between political craft and inspired statesmanship implies a mediocrity that seems to have afflicted Lincoln as much as it did Jefferson Davis, in whom it has been more often recognized. Stampp cautioned against harsh judgment of those who brought their countrymen the fury of civil war. They should, as he noted, be measured only against "common standards of statesmanship."[4] It might be added that they should also be judged by the moral standards of their own time, rather than by the values of future generations. Collectively and individually, however, their statesmanship proved altogether too common, and they should not be celebrated for genius — as Lincoln has often been — for adopting a singularly destructive and unimaginative course.[5]

The enormous dimensions of the problems he faced make it difficult to treat Lincoln unsympathetically, even while considering his deadliest errors. Thanks to his native intelligence and political skills honed on lesser planes during half a lifetime, his executive performance developed apace. His reputation might not shine so brightly had he lived through the crucible of Reconstruction, but the second half of his administration merits many of the accolades associated with his name. Understandably, he committed his worst mistakes at the outset of his presidency, but they launched an irretrievable flood of misery, and at times during the brutal conflict that followed he must have wondered whether war had been the wisest choice. That question poses more relevance for future generations than it would have for Lincoln, who had already committed himself to the sword, but asking it within a valid context requires struggling with nearly a century and a half of accumulated biases and ideological evolution.

This book divides the first year of Mr. Lincoln's war into three partially overlapping epochs. Those periods are defined in the hope of illuminating perspectives that might address some of the points raised above.

First came the period of political posturing, before both sides abandoned any hope of being heard by the other. Optimism lingered in surreptitious diplomacy and informal truce even after the guns opened on Fort Sumter, ending with abrupt finality at the close of May and the beginning of June in a string of bloody little affairs.

Then commenced open warfare against the rebellious Confederacy, and rigorous military coercion of doubtful authorities in the loyal border states. As pressure mounted for a quick resolution, Lincoln abandoned his implied promises that he would not invade Confederate territory. He also subordinated the very concept of popular government to his aggressive policies, further alienating political factions within the states that had not seceded. Federal defeats in Virginia and Missouri dampened the dream of an early conclusion to both hostilities and repression.

Finally, as conservative Unionist Democrats like George McClellan rose to national prominence, radicals of ulterior motive turned on them in a partisan crusade, initiating a vicious internal struggle. No matter how devoted they might be to the cause of national unity, Democrats lacking sufficient enthusiasm for social change found themselves pursued and persecuted in a shameful display that echoed the treacherous intensity of the Reign of Terror. This was the period that Bruce Catton called the Era of Suspicion, when paranoia saturated the public psyche. Representing as it did the logical conclusion to a year of growing distrust and antagonism, it stands as an appropriate metaphor for the entire tragic episode.

PART I

WE CANNOT
SEPARATE

1

Songs for a Prelude

❖ IN CULTURE AND CLIMATE, Washington City belonged to the South, and as 1861 opened many feared that it might become part of a Southern confederacy, as well. Those who deplored the prospect ruefully observed that the government of the United States held power there only by popular assent: except for a few Marines and an ordnance company, no organized troops stood by to enforce federal authority. An armed mob could have driven congressmen and senators from their respective chambers, evicted the president from the executive mansion, and forced the United States government into exile north of the Mason-Dixon Line. That January there would have been little anyone could have done to prevent it. Most of the army manned outposts scattered along the Southern coast or across the western frontier, weeks or months away from the smoky saloons and hotel rooms where statesmen and scoundrels negotiated the nation's future.

As the new year progressed and Abraham Lincoln prepared to assume the presidency, key officials began to worry about an armed assault against the federal presence on the Potomac. Terrified that the election of a Republican president threatened their slave-based agricultural economy with containment and extinction, political barons in the Deep South had convinced five state conventions to renounce their ties to the Union by January 19, and most of the remaining slave states had begun debating the expediency of their own withdrawal. The secession of one slave state only encouraged others to follow, for with that initial secession the South's balance of power in the United States Senate evaporated. Appalled at the desertion of their Dixie comrades, border-state senators proposed complicated compromises and constitutional conventions with the hope of forming a still-more-perfect union, but hotter heads prevailed.[1] On January 9 South Carolina volunteers had fired on the *Star of the West* when that unarmed vessel tried to supply the federal garrison of Fort Sumter, in Charleston harbor, and an infuriated North had risen in a nonpartisan outcry for blood. The commander of New York's associated veterans of the War of 1812 even offered the services of his superannuated comrades in defense of the government, and he may have intended more than a symbolic gesture, considering that the seat of government lacked any practical protection. Striving to maintain peace in his final weeks as president, James Buchanan declined to redress the national insult. His inactivity allowed the crisis to abate, but then Southern militiamen aggravated the offense when they began seizing United States forts and arsenals in the seceded states. On January 24 hundreds of Georgia troops compelled the garrison of the Augusta Arsenal to surrender; on that same day, the commanding general of the U.S. Army made arrangements for at least token reinforcements in the federal capital.[2]

Winfield Scott — himself one of those 1812 veterans — had donned his first uniform before president-elect Lincoln was born. He had held the rank of general for nearly half a century, and that of commanding general for two decades, and he was the only lieutenant general the United States Congress had ever created, even by brevet. At seventy-four the towering commander had grown so stout that he could no longer mount a horse or lead troops in battle, but he was the man who had conceived and conducted the brilliant campaign against Mexico City only fourteen years before. For all the pomposity of his prose and plumery he remained a sharp strategist, and he inspired and demanded energy from subordinates even if he did not own much of it himself. Until recently he had been saddled with a secretary of war of dubious integrity: John Floyd, of Virginia, who seemed more loyal to the slave South than to his national obligations. In December, 1860, the resignation of that politico had brought a new and more decidedly loyal secretary into office — Joseph Holt, an unflinching Kentucky Unionist who ignored anonymous death threats and pushed the administration to aggressive federal policy.[3] With the trustworthy Holt behind him, late in January General Scott outlined a plan to introduce more soldiers into Washington gradually, to avoid the inflammatory impression that he was amassing troops to march against the insurgent states.

A couple of batteries of artillery reached the capital by February 1, coming from as far away as West Point. By then, Texas and Louisiana had also seceded. The withdrawal of each state removed two more Southerners from the U.S. Senate, where equal numbers from slave and free states had balanced a fragile truce over the issue of slavery since 1820, and the increasing majority of free-state senators spelled the ultimate end of slavery in whatever was left of the United States. That only heightened the anxiety of plantation aristocrats in the remaining slave states, so secession fever ran epidemic from Annapolis, Maryland, to Fort Smith, Arkansas. In January the stars were falling from the flag so quickly that it seemed no slave state would stick to the Union, and even seasoned army officers whose states had not yet seceded, like Major George Thomas of Virginia, began casting about for alternative employment.[4]

Those Southern-born officers frequently found their allegiance to the Union doubted, both by devoted loyalists who feared their treachery and by authorities in their home states who coveted their services. Major Thomas applied for a post at the Virginia Military Institute; instead he received an invitation to serve as chief of ordnance for the governor of Virginia, and he declined, but others lacked his constancy. At least two artillery captains who brought their batteries to Washington would soon wear the stars of Confederate generals, and one of them briefly commanded all the troops in the city.[5]

The few companies that reached Washington in late January and February numbered barely four hundred men, doubtful officers and all. The presence of even that many soldiers raised questions in Congress, which sent President Buchanan a special inquiry on the subject when the capital garrison had been augmented to only 653 soldiers. Southern representatives who believed in the right of secession but had not made use of it worried that the president intended to bring the Union back together by force. For their part, Northern congressmen wanted to know if the reinforcements indicated that the administration had gotten wind of a conspiracy to seize the capital before Lincoln could be inaugurated; prominent Republicans had been warning of such a plot since the end of December. Bellicose talk among Southern-leaning militia companies in the district fueled widespread anxiety of armed revolt, and citizens took to sleeping with loaded revolvers handy.[6] That anxiety thickened in February, when delegates from the seven estranged states joined together at Montgomery, Alabama, to organize as the Confederate States of America. They elected a president and, on the last day of that month, made provisions for an army.

That potential new market for arms and matériel elicited a sheaf of proposals from Northern manufacturers. A Milwaukee man offered his revolutionary breechloading cannon; a New York firm touted its military and naval telescopes; another New York company sent an agent hawking its percussion caps. Kentucky breeders who wished to supply the Confederate army with horses and mules sent their cards to Montgomery, and a Washington inventor who had produced breechloading carbines for the

U.S. Army stood ready to make as many as the Confederacy might desire.[7] Experienced soldiers, practicing physicians, and common citizens from all over the free states and border states offered their services to the new nation, often without any evident sense of impropriety.[8]

The establishment of a skeleton army by a new government augured no particular ill, for every nation must provide for its own defense: peaceful resolution still seemed possible, especially since the new Confederate Congress authorized the president to appoint a peace commission as soon as he took office.[9] Some Northerners who harbored abundant devotion to their government, and to the nation it represented for them, viewed the voluntary departure of the seceded states with unmitigated relief. One thoughtful and sophisticated New Yorker felt satisfied to bid the Gulf states and rabid South Carolina goodbye — if only Maryland, Virginia, Kentucky, Tennessee, and Missouri would remain (although he seemed not to care either way about Arkansas). Some even wished that those sisters in slavery would follow the Deep South out of the Union. An Ohio attorney who would one day occupy the White House saw no threat in the abrupt division: he stood ready to let the whole South go, assuming that a smaller nation without slavery might be preferable to an "unfortunate union of thirty-three States" that permitted it. A young veteran of the free-state fight in Kansas told the folks back home in Pennsylvania that he greeted the secession of slaveholding states with "much pleasure."[10]

While the formal organization of a Confederate government and army posed no imminent danger to Washington, it excited the advocates of secession in Virginia and Maryland, for the new government at Montgomery might act as a magnet toward other states whose citizens wished to see slavery specifically protected. That attraction pulled strongest on the states that shared a border with the new nation, but even in Virginia, where Union sentiment still throve, most citizens' allegiance would have faltered or fallen at the first sign of hostile intentions toward the Confederacy. If that opposition translated into overt rebellion, fewer than a thousand soldiers and Marines could hardly have defended so large and open a city as Washington. General Scott planned to protect the Capitol and the president's mansion, along with the most defensible department office buildings around the White House. In case of alarm he assigned one company (under one of those future Confederate brigadiers) to garrison the Treasury Department building as a final retreat where he, the president, and every soldier left standing would barricade themselves and hold out as long as they could.[11]

Charles Pomeroy Stone served as one of Scott's chief collaborators in the defense of the capital. Stone had wanted to be a soldier all his life: growing up in western Massachusetts, he was told that his grandfather

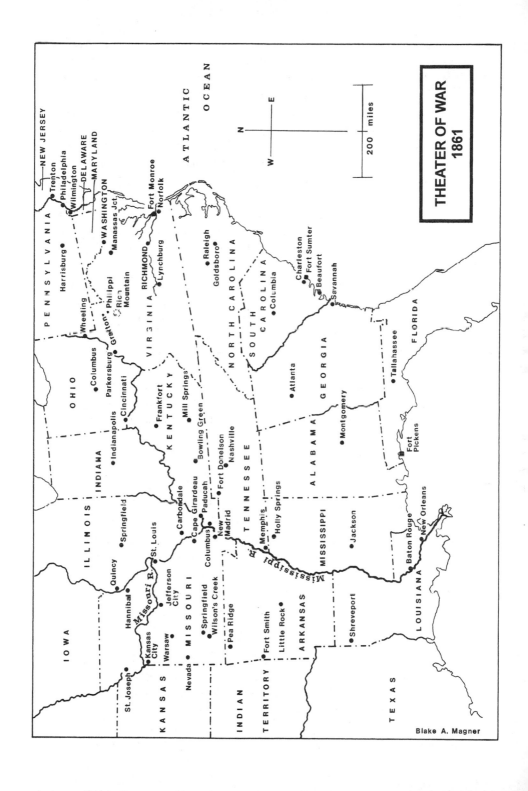

THEATER OF WAR
1861

200 miles

Blake A. Magner

had stood with the militia at Lexington Green and Bunker Hill, and he was only six months past his fifteenth birthday when he first applied to West Point. Numerous testimonials to his scholarship and irreproachable conduct failed to win the appointment that time, but a different secretary of war granted his wish the next year.[12] Stone graduated seventh in the class of 1845, alongside more than a dozen future generals. His intellect and energy inspired confidence from the beginning. After teaching geography, history, and ethics for a term at the academy, he had served Scott as an ordnance officer on the campaign to Mexico City, coming out of that war with two brevet promotions for his conduct at Molino del Rey and Chapultepec, and he had remained in the army for nearly another decade. For two years he had toured Europe and the Levant, observing an assortment of armies. He had spent several years as chief of ordnance on the West Coast, but his career track promised so limited a future that in 1856 he had resigned to go into banking. After less than a year he accepted a survey contract with the Mexican government, mapping the topography and exploring the resources of Sonora and Baja California. By 1860 he had completed that contract and had brought his wife and daughter to Washington. They lodged with Mrs. Stone's father, Captain Robert Clary, a well-heeled army quartermaster, while Stone prepared his Mexican observations for publication.[13] On the last day of that year, shortly after the changing of the guard at the War Department, Stone paid a social call on General Scott, evidently with the ulterior aim of reminding the old general that he was available for service.[14]

Scott's esteem for Stone manifested itself in a commission as colonel and an assignment as inspector general for militia in the District of Columbia, in which capacity Stone immediately began assessing the loyalty of the various uniformed companies in Georgetown and Washington.[15] Stone's surveillance only heightened Scott's concern for the safety of the capital when he found that at least a quarter of the militia seemed sympathetic to the Confederate cause. High on his list of suspicious organizations stood the better part of the National Rifles, a well-armed company under a Baltimore native named Frank Schaeffer. Schaeffer had served as an infantry captain and ordnance officer in the Mexican War before migrating to California, where he finagled an appointment as a second lieutenant in the 3rd U.S. Artillery.[16] He had never reported for duty, though; his regiment had carried him on the rolls as absent without leave for months before he bothered to resign. Later Schaeffer secured a more agreeable position as a clerk in the Interior Department, and in that capacity he had returned East.[17]

Schaeffer's troubles began when he declined a promotion to major rather than take a new oath that would have pledged his fealty to the federal government. Like many Tidewater natives, Schaeffer seemed more devoted to the cause of state sovereignty than to secession, but uncompromising Unionists acknowledged little distinction between the two. Colonel Stone and Roger Weightman, the aging commander of militia in the District of Columbia, confronted Schaeffer in the library of the U.S. Patent Office on February 5, where they asked him certain questions about his loyalty. Schaeffer recalled that they wished to know whether he would take up arms against either Virginia or his native Maryland if those states seceded, and he instantly replied that he would not. As Stone and Weightman recalled it, they wanted to know whether he would defend the capital if those states should attack it, to which he responded that he would not. In any event, he indicated that he could not submit to the oath he would be required to take if the district militia were called into federal service, and on that pretext alone they felt justified in stripping him even of his captain's commission.[18]

Stone apparently marked his man well, for within four months Schaeffer would abandon his federal clerkship and lead scores of Washingtonians over the river to fight for the Confederacy. In his place Stone appointed a captain of the Regular service.[19]

Under the moribund administration of James Buchanan, the government offered precious little resistance to secession, waiting instead for the outcome of congressional and private compromise committees and the accession of the new president, whose election had brought so much trouble. To maintain the loyalty of the remaining slave states, Buchanan wished to avoid the least hint that Washington might contest the right of any state to withdraw, but he fell short of acknowledging the secession itself. The day after Texas voted itself out of the Union, a battery of light artillery unlimbered near the Capitol and fired a salute of thirty-four guns to celebrate the admission of Kansas. A Southern-leaning man who bothered to count the number of discharges might have found something ominous in his tally, noting one round for the new state and thirty-three for the old — including the seven that had opted out of membership.[20]

Symbolic salutes meant little against the events that Buchanan dared not prevent. His policy of placating Southern Unionists cost the army a great deal: most of the manpower still lay scattered on the frontier, and Buchanan failed to concentrate those forces when he had the opportunity, leaving them vulnerable to piecemeal destruction. He also left Texas under the command of David Twiggs, a native Georgian of duplicitous intent, who surrendered all the troops and facilities there as soon as Texas forces asked for them, taking a Confederate general's commission in return. Had Buchanan reassigned Twiggs as soon as Georgia seceded, the Texas command would have fallen to a Connecticut colonel of unquestioned loyalty. Instead, by the time Abraham Lincoln made his appearance in Washington on February 23, the perfidy of General Twiggs had neutralized one-sixth of the U.S. Army, and nearly every fort in the insurgent states had been seized.[21]

On his way across Indiana and Ohio Abraham Lincoln hinted that the government had the right to hold or recover such property by force, but he disavowed any desire to subdue the South and questioned the validity of the crisis, hailing the common cause of South and West. On a loop through New York and New Jersey he said little, but in Philadelphia he stopped at Independence Hall. There, on the day before he reached Washington, he let slip his belief that the Declaration of Independence promised ultimate equality for all, and although he seemed to regret the remark as "something indiscreet," he added that "if this country can't be saved upon that principle . . . I would rather be assassinated on this spot than to surrender to it."[22]

That very night the threat of assassination convinced Lincoln to enter the capital as surreptitiously as anyone might who stood eight inches taller than the average man of his era; he negotiated Baltimore in the wee hours to avoid a plot that Colonel Stone's operatives thought they had detected. Mrs. Lincoln and the rest of the retinue came in on an afternoon train, and the family reunited at the rambling, six-story hotel of the Willard brothers at the corner of Fourteenth Street and Pennsylvania Avenue.[23] The indecorous midnight passage marred Lincoln's introduction to the nation, sparking widespread speculation on his personal courage at a time when such things mattered to people. The safe conclusion of his journey merely initiated ten more anxious days for Stone and Scott, who anticipated further attempts on Lincoln's life prior to the inauguration, perhaps as part of a general revolt. Lowering skies and howling winds buffeted the capital city on the Lincolns' first full day in Washington, setting the tone for their entire sojourn there.[24]

Lincoln spent his final days before the inauguration corresponding with cabinet candidates, perambulating hallways jammed with the office seekers who had descended like locusts upon Willard's, and circulating about the city, introducing himself to the notables who would be his associates. A so-called Peace Convention of representatives from Northern and border states met behind closed doors at Willard's through most of February, and a Missouri delegate who encountered Lincoln there lamented his ascendance: Lincoln impressed him as "a man of no intelligence, no enlargement of views, as ridiculously vain and fantastic as a country boy with his first red morocco hat." That critic spoke from deep hostility to Lincoln's party, but such impressions troubled loyal Republicans as well. Many found the lanky westerner naive, and supposed that he would be ruled by one of his more commanding cabinet officers. Some expected the executive power to be exercised by Ohio's Salmon P. Chase, whom Lincoln wanted to head the Treasury Department, but the real odds went to Senator William Henry Seward, whom Lincoln had chosen for his secretary of state. One fellow senator considered Seward "a coward & a sneak," but Seward viewed himself as the leader of the Republican Party and felt that he had deserved the presidential nomination far more than Lincoln had.[25] Slave-state Democrats who served in the Senate with Seward openly shared his image of himself as the power behind the throne, ultimately to the detriment of Lincoln's relationship with that faction.[26]

Working independently of the executive succession, the Peace Convention forwarded a feeble attempt at reconciliation. From their secret conclave at Willard's the delegates proposed a constitutional amendment specifically prohibiting congressional interference with slavery inside the existing states, and they assumed that they had disposed of the thorniest problem — slavery in the territories — simply by resurrecting the old Missouri Compromise boundary between slave and free territory.[27] The resolutions resembled the elements of the doomed compromise that Kentucky senator John J. Crittenden had proposed the previous winter, which ultimately failed precisely because it ignored the widespread hostility to the territorial expansion of slavery. The convention proposal nonetheless inspired momentary hope on both sides. Reports that the House of Representatives had accepted the resolutions brought some strained rejoicing, including a hundred-gun salute, but the initial euphoria had not abated before most people sensed the futility of such belated measures. The resolutions died in the Senate by a margin of four to one on the eve of the new president's inauguration.[28]

Foreboding over plots of assassination and revolt deepened as inauguration day drew near. At last, on Monday morning, March 4, Benjamin Brown French appeared at City Hall in the role of parade marshal for the inauguration ceremony. French was one of those perennial Washington political appointees, and the role of chief marshal — like most of the positions he had held in government employ — carried less authority or responsibility than the title implied. It would be military men who choreographed the day's events. The participants in the procession and the order of their march had been decided the day before, in General Scott's office. Regular infantry would precede the presidential carriage and double files of District of Columbia volunteers would flank it, freshly mounted and equipped as cavalry, while more district militia followed on foot. Colonel Stone would ride alongside the carriage, among his mounted volunteers, while a detachment of the 1st U.S. Cavalry cleared the way and guarded each intersection.[29] Stone trusted the loyalty of few men in these times, expecting trouble from any quarter, and not without cause. Each shift in the political winds scattered men's sympathies, and today's ally might be tomorrow's enemy. The little cavalry detachment, for instance, responded that morning to the orders of a second lieutenant of good pedigree — Lunsford Lomax, the son and grandson of career army officers, who would end a long family tradition of military service four years hence as a major general in the Confederate army.[30]

A dripping rain threatened the festivities early in the morning, but it gave way to clear skies and cool air. The column left City Hall shortly after eleven o'clock and lined up along Pennsylvania Avenue with the leading elements abreast of Willard's Hotel. The committee of arrangement and assorted assistant marshals fussed with the alignment while everyone waited for President Buchanan, whose last cabinet meeting ran late because his secretary of war, Mr. Holt, had received unsettling news from Fort Sumter. Inside the hotel, Lincoln spent his last hour as a private citizen in the company of his old friend from the Illinois legislature, Edward Dickinson Baker. Lincoln had known this English immigrant for nearly a quarter of a century, and had grown so fond of him in their youth that he had named a son after him. Baker had moved to the West Coast nearly a decade before, but now he was in Washington as one of Oregon's U.S. senators, and Lincoln relied on him as a barometer of political sentiment in the Pacific states. When Buchanan called at the hotel room that noon, the white-haired Baker joined them in the barouche waiting at the door, along with a Unionist Democrat from Maryland. The carriage pulled into line, a band began blaring, and the leading horses lurched toward the Capitol, dragging the rest of the parade after them.[31]

Over the east steps of the Capitol hovered a temporary platform guarded by more of Stone's district volunteers, and marksmen occupied most of the windows in the building. Between there and First Street milled an immense throng, waiting to hear what the new leader would have to say in the way of firmness or conciliation on secession. They numbered so many thousand that few of them could expect to hear the actual words, and for all the hope they expressed to each other they showed little enthusiasm for the new president. The more observant of the spectators lining Pennsylvania Avenue might have offered some speculation on the thrust of Lincoln's address, though, for in the presidential parade rolled a float conspicuously labeled "Constitution," bearing one young lady for each of the thirty-four stars in the national flag.[32]

Lincoln, Buchanan, and Baker dismounted at the north entrance and entered the Senate chamber to watch Hannibal Hamlin take the oath of office as vice president. Then they emerged on the front steps, mounted the platform, and Lincoln turned to his audience. Over the heads of the multitude, on the far side of First Street, loomed the gloomy brick building known as the Old Capitol, where Congress had convened in 1814 after the British burned Washington. To the right of that, as Lincoln scanned the horizon, stood the three-story row house where he and his wife had boarded during his term in the House of Representatives. Barely thirteen years before, in the building right behind him, Lincoln had argued the legitimacy of the Mexican and Texas revolutions, contending that "any people anywhere, being inclined and having the power, have the *right* to rise up, and shake off the existing government, and form one that suits them better."[33]

Now had come a new emergency — and, perhaps, a new perspective on popular revolt. In his remarks Lincoln resumed the soothing homilies of his February pilgrimage, assuring the protection of slavery where it existed and implying that he would not use military force to bring the errant states back into the Union. Reading from the Republican Party platform, Lincoln reminded his listeners that "we denounce the lawless invasion by armed force of the soil of any State or Territory, no matter under what pretext," and he offered support for constitutional amendments like that proposed by the Peace Convention. He warned, though, that he lacked any power to negotiate a separation of the Union, and claimed that no state had a right to secede without the consent of the others. Summarizing the entire dispute as a disagreement over the extension of slavery into the territories that could be resolved peacefully, he asserted that he considered the various secession ordinances legally void and the Union unbroken, insisting that "we cannot separate."[34]

With that Lincoln took the oath of office from Roger B. Taney, the octogenarian slaveowner who served as chief justice. Afterward Lincoln and Buchanan returned to their carriage and drove back to the White House amid their heterogeneous escort of troops, who saluted both of them as they entered the executive mansion. Then the soldiers, including Colonel Stone, turned home for some well-deserved rest while the cavalcade of girls climbed down from their festooned float and filed into the White House to meet President Lincoln. The gangly westerner asked to kiss each of the thirty-four, irrespective of the states they represented, and they all consented.[35]

No violence had marred the day, and in their nervous relief many Washingtonians drew more encouragement from the inaugural address than it ought to have warranted, flavoring their conflicting interpretations with partisan hope. That day's issue of the *Washington Evening Star* printed the entire speech, and residents scanned it by gaslight. Parade marshal French, a New Hampshire native and a convert to the Republican Party, judged it exactly what Union men wanted — conciliatory and peaceable "but firm in its tone." Lieutenant Lomax's mother and several of her Virginia friends concurred on the moderation of Lincoln's rhetoric, albeit for different reasons. Halfway across the continent, in her hovel upon the Kansas prairie, a hopeful woman writing a letter at the hour of the inauguration thought she could sense the relief, for a driving snowstorm suddenly abated and the sky began to clear. As the snow started melting on the ground she predicted that "mad rebellion and blustering secession will subside and melt away under the more genial influence of Republican rule." A Missouri newspaper with a more Southern perspective remarked with grim sarcasm that the address Lincoln read was "not the one that Seward wrote."[36]

New Yorkers who actually read the new president's inaugural speech greeted it, as well as the safe installation of Buchanan's successor, with the same enthusiasm as the residents of Washington. A Wall Street lawyer named George Templeton Strong recorded majority approval among his associates, though he noted that the stock market fell with the news. For his part, Strong complained only of Lincoln's acknowledgment of Northern moralizing on the matter of slavery, which could only hurt Southern Unionists as they tried to dissuade their neighbors from secession. "We Northerners object to slavery on grounds of political economy," wrote Strong, "not of ethics."[37]

Lincoln's address drew more ominous reaction across the South. Moderate newspaper editors strained for hopeful interpretations, but the *Richmond Dispatch* read it as a declaration of war because of the implied threat of coercion. South Carolinians reading galley proofs of the speech on bulletin boards outside the Charleston *Mercury* office translated Lincoln's denial of the right of secession and his refusal to yield federal facilities as a solemn promise to subjugate the Confederacy. With the guns of Fort Sumter glistening over the entrance to their harbor, those Southerners seemed to express relief at the prospect of an armed contest, or even to welcome it.[38]

Abraham Lincoln began his first full day as president by entertaining Joseph Holt, the erstwhile secretary of war. Holt brought fresh news from Major Robert Anderson, the commander of Fort Sumter, indicating Anderson's doubt that the Confederate batteries around the harbor could be successfully overcome by fewer than twenty or thirty thousand troops. Holt went to great length to assure Lincoln that this was a complete surprise to him, and that Anderson had long described the construction of hostile fortifications without the slightest hint that they would be so formidable. The information posed a serious challenge to the promise Lincoln had just made to hold the Southern forts.[39]

Thus did Fort Sumter emerge as the symbol of the secession crisis in the first hour of Lincoln's active administration, but he neither took action nor outlined any, perhaps fearing an incompetence at diplomacy that he confessed to the minister from Bremen on March 6. Ten days into the new presidency, disappointed Unionists like Holt entertained a fear precisely the opposite of the South Carolinians' — namely, that there would be no confrontation at Charleston. Buchanan's former attorney general, Edwin M. Stanton, shared that apprehension. Recognizing that the new president's indecision might allow the Confederacy to establish itself beyond recovery or reconciliation, Stanton speculated with the retired chief executive that the first steps were being taken toward "a strictly Northern non-slaveholding confederacy."[40]

Others nonetheless saw the trouble coming and chose their sides. Samuel Cooper, a New York native who had served as adjutant general of the United States Army for nine years, had developed tenacious Southern associations when he married the sister of a Virginia senator, and even though Virginia had not seceded he resigned three days after Lincoln took office. A fortnight later, Cooper pursued the same occupation in a different army, sitting behind a desk in Montgomery. Pierre Gustave Toutant Beauregard, a brevet major from Louisiana who had spent five days in January as superintendent of the U.S. Military Academy, had already gone South for a commission as brigadier general in the Confederacy's provisional army. At the time of Lincoln's inauguration Beauregard commanded the Confederate troops surrounding Charleston harbor, and Cooper relayed War Department instructions to him about coastal defense. In Charleston Beauregard encountered several other comrades from the old army, including Major Nathan G. Evans (recently Captain Evans of the 2nd U.S. Cavalry), who now acted as adjutant general for the army South Carolina had mobilized. North Carolinian William Dorsey Pender, whose state also still clung to the Union, resigned his commission as lieutenant of artillery and began gathering volunteers for Confederate service from among the more zealous secessionists in Baltimore, sending them to Charleston for Beauregard to swear in.[41]

With defectors of Sam Cooper's seniority and antecedents, and with Confederate officers recruiting troops at Washington's back door, Charles Stone's postinaugural respite came to an abrupt end. The national forces that would have been called on to protect the capital grew daily weaker with the resignation of trained, experienced officers, and no one seemed to do anything about it — even, as in Pender's case, when one of those officers repaired to a loyal state to raise men for a foreign army. No one seemed immune to disaffection: some of the most prominent soldiers in the country contemplated a course they might have considered treasonable a few months before. Rumor impugned the loyalty of Captain Franklin Buchanan, commandant of the Washington Navy Yard; the president himself stood in to give the captain's daughter away at her wedding, but in the end the old sailor would abandon the flag. Escalating tension over Fort Sumter amplified the apparent danger. Each passing week offered greater opportunities for an incendiary incident, and opponents of the government grew increasingly bold as the crisis heightened. Stone drilled his district volunteers more earnestly than ever, and he wanted some of them mustered into federal service to bolster Washington's defenses, especially after the administration concluded to send a relief expedition to Sumter.[42]

Winfield Scott, who had wished to reinforce the Southern forts long before, informed Lincoln one week into his administration that the opportunity had passed. It would be impossible to mount a sufficient force before the Fort Sumter garrison starved to death, he argued, echoing an opinion current among officers inside the fort itself. Scott's inspector general from the Mexico City campaign concurred, advising immediate evacuation of the fort: Ethan Allen Hitchcock lived in St. Louis at the time, and he pronounced both the city and Missouri safe against secession, but he noted that anxiety over Fort Sumter ran high. He expected that voluntarily abandoning the fort would secure the border states by demonstrating the government's willingness to avoid war, and that it might conciliate even the citizens of the seceded states, while attempts to supply the place would only invite hostilities. "'Tis true," Hitchcock warned Scott, "the fault would be the Seceders; but that would not make the calamity less."[43]

In mid-March Lincoln polled his cabinet members on the wisdom of sustaining the fort, and they responded with lopsided opposition. Secretary of State Seward discouraged the idea because it would require such a fight that it would inevitably start a war, which he urged Lincoln not to incite at that particular moment. Attorney General Edward Bates replied that he, too, would surrender vulnerable Sumter "rather than be an active party in the beginning of civil war." Bates would defend the Gulf forts and resist aggression, but he wished to court Southern Unionists rather than alienate them, and he cautioned against "any act which may have the semblance, before the world of beginning a civil war, the terrible consequences of which would, I think, find no parallel in modern times." Gideon Welles, the secretary of the navy, found the proposal foolhardy from both military and political perspectives. The secretary of the interior, Caleb Smith, thought it might be possible to accomplish, but foolish to undertake, considering "all the circumstances." Simon Cameron, chief of Lincoln's War Department, reflected the generally dismal prospects predicted by all the senior army officers and the officers of Sumter as well, and he considered it "unwise." Salmon Chase, the treasury chief, gave his qualified assent in a way that only revealed his ignorance of the situation: he said he would be against it "if the attempt will so inflame civil war as to involve an immediate necessity for the enlistment of armies," but he deemed it "highly improbable" that it would have such consequences. Only Postmaster General Montgomery Blair, the Unionist firebrand of Lincoln's cabinet, offered unconditional approval, insisting (with a level of misunderstanding fully equal to Chase's) that loyal Southerners looked only for firmness from the government to encourage them against Confederate usurpers.[44]

His inaugural promises about holding all the forts notwithstanding, the president seemed discouraged by that weight of opinion, and he continued to vacillate while Sumter's stores dwindled and the garrison started showing signs of dysentery.[45] Perceiving Lincoln's readiness to pursue a less provocative course, Blair composed his resignation, but his father intervened. Old Preston Blair, a former newspaper editor and personal advisor to Andrew Jackson, fervently pushed the contention that giving up Sumter would be viewed as treason. Harried as he was from early morning until late into the night by the appeals of importuning office- and favor-seekers, the exhausted Lincoln appeared vulnerable to abrupt changes in mood, and the elder Blair's exhortation seemed to invigorate him with a sudden pugnacity. Eventually Lincoln conveyed that combativeness to most of his cabinet.[46]

Late in the game Lincoln asked two personal friends to make their way into Charleston and assess public sentiment there. On March 22 Stephen Hurlbut, a Charleston native who had met Lincoln after migrating to Illinois, accompanied the president's occasional bodyguard, Ward Hill Lamon, on the night train south. Their train passed ominous flatcars full of heavy-artillery shells below Richmond, and piles of similar ammunition bordered the depot in Charleston. They secured lodging at the Charleston Hotel and then separated to interview different residents: Lamon mingled among strangers, while Hurlbut sought out old acquaintances. Hurlbut looked for the strongest Unionists he remembered, including the surviving loyalists whom Andrew Jackson had depended upon to fight secession during the nullification crisis of 1832; he found that even they had now shed their devotion to the federal government. There seemed but one Unionist left in Charleston, and he described his neighbors as harboring an astonishingly unanimous attachment to the new nation. Hurlbut concluded that the seceded states, or at least those east of the Mississippi, were "irrevocably gone" from the Union.

After spending less than forty-eight hours in the city, Hurlbut returned and advised Lincoln that any effort to send even provisions into Fort Sumter would meet resistance. He suggested giving Sumter up while it was still possible to do so without an affront to national honor, instead holding Fort Pickens, off Pensacola, Fort Taylor on Key West, and Fort Jefferson on Dry Tortugas if the president intended to assert federal authority with an effective military presence. He warned, though, that any effort to enforce United States law would precipitate war, and that the South would meet it with a united front that the Northern states would lack. The lost states could never be recovered, he believed, except as conquered provinces, with every disadvantage that usually accompanied forcible annexation. For all the aggressive advice that his message entailed, Hurlbut's collective predictions argued implicitly for peaceful separation.[47]

Hurlbut's subtle hint met with an unreceptive audience. Nationalistic appeals for firmness and force had been pouring in to Washington from all over the North since January, filling the pigeonholes of the government's foremost Unionists. Bellicose editorials had echoed those demands, insisting on federal coercion against any state that attempted to secede. Lincoln continued to receive many such letters, including one that promised him political oblivion for his evident weakness. "Give up Sumpter," wrote an anonymous correspondent, "& you are as dead politically as John Brown is physically." A Cincinnati man advised him that anything could be borne but peaceful separation: supply Sumter at any cost, he suggested, and reinforce it, although he finally admitted that it would be better still if the Confederates attacked it and slaughtered the garrison. The ferocity of such comment, if not its volume, reassured many Republicans in Washington that their political survival required a stubborn stance against compromise, which would in turn fuel charges that party interest ultimately trumped national interest. Historians have since cited political necessity as at least partial explanation for the attitude that led Lincoln to adopt a course that might best be described as passive aggression.[48]

Forgotten in the latticework of factors that Lincoln faced that spring is the growing support for the uncontested separation that Hurlbut had backhandedly advised. Since the early weeks of secession, newspapers of different political persuasions had either hailed the withdrawal of the slave states with glee or had reluctantly conceded that they should be allowed to form their own government.[49] Variations on that viewpoint gained momentum with the failure of the Peace Convention, in March. On March 20 Senator James Bayard, a Delaware Democrat and no friend of the administration, introduced a resolution to his colleagues authorizing the president to recognize the Confederacy and make peace. Innumerable editors of more moderate tenor shared that opinion, including many who had supported Lincoln in November, and the call for peaceful separation blossomed with the first flowers of spring.[50]

"It cannot be denied," conceded the *New York Times* on March 21, with vernal candor, "that there is a growing sentiment throughout the North in favor of letting the Gulf States go." That same day the *Philadelphia Inquirer* called for popular elections in the seceded states to determine the true measure of public sentiment, with peaceful division to follow a positive outcome, while the *Daily National Intelligencer* in Washington City endorsed a national convention of the remaining states to bless the de facto division. The following day Washington's *States and Union* employed an assortment of conjugal and filial metaphors to illustrate the wisdom of allowing the dissatisfied states to take their portion of the nation's wealth and depart, rather than holding them by force in a union founded on mutual devotion. On March 23 the *Cincinnati Daily Commercial*, which had backed Lincoln, acknowledged growing popular acceptance of the Confederate government and urged letting the South have its experiment in independence. Even the editor of Lincoln's friendly hometown newspaper, the *Illinois State Journal*, regretfully concluded by early April that "the sooner we cut loose from the disaffected States, the better it may be for all parties and for the nation."[51] Delaware's independent *Smyrna Times*, which had stood firmly for the Union for four months, finally agreed that the South ought to go in peace if it could not be held by persuasion. Echoing the resolution proposed by Senator Bayard, the *Delaware Gazette* advised outright diplomatic recognition of the Confederacy. Republican newspapers in Philadelphia and Harrisburg soon followed with further recommendations for acknowledging secession as the least costly and least dangerous solution. Later — only hours after shells had begun bursting over Fort Sumter — another Lincoln paper in Hartford corroborated an apparent public preference for formal recognition of the Confederacy.[52]

Earlier calls for peaceful separation had carried debilitating conditions for formal negotiations and statewide plebiscites in the seceded states, like those the *Philadelphia Inquirer* had suggested. Confederate leaders had no intention of coming to Washington hats in hand for permission to secede, but they had sent peace commissioners who had never been recognized, and they viewed their state conventions as indirect expressions of popular will. Only by dispensing with obstructive conditions and accepting secession could the Washington government accommodate a peaceful division of the sections, and that washing of hands would surely have gratified Southerners enough to allay the soaring tension. Significantly, most of those numerous new editorial appeals seemed to describe precisely that sort of unconditional acquiescence.

So fully had the Southern Confederacy developed as an independent nation by then that a violent collision could only have been avoided if Lincoln had relented on the notion of separation, but he refused even to consider it. Lurking support for a second or third secession, meanwhile, could only have tempered his resolution against any form of secession. There had been much discussion of a new alliance between the states of the old Northwest, and advocates of a central confederacy between North and South had engaged in private correspondence with border-state governors since December. In March the governor of Maryland, Thomas Hicks, admitted that he had officially approached seven other governors on the subject of a mid-Atlantic confederation, and by the middle of the month newspapers as far north as New Brunswick, New Jersey, espoused such a buffer nation between the Carolinas and New England.[53] In late March most Republicans still favored a firm hand against the seceded states, but that opinion had begun to slip even among Lincoln's primary constituency, and certainly among Democrats. With scattered entreaties for further secession and alternative reconfigurations, the pace of national disintegration seemed likely to accelerate without some annealing executive action.

In light of weakening resistance to secession, Lincoln may have seen Stephen Hurlbut's warning against provisioning Sumter as more of an opportunity than a peril. Hurlbut submitted his report on March 27. The next morning Lincoln received a plan for landing supplies and troops at Sumter from Gustavus V. Fox, a former naval officer who had visited Charleston a couple of weeks before to assess the chances of relieving the fort under fire. Fox included drafts of orders to army and navy officers for the appropriate signatures, and announced that he would leave that afternoon for New York to fit out the expedition. That day — significantly, the day that the U.S. Senate finally adjourned for the session — Lincoln appears to have made at least a tentative decision to force the issue at Charleston. On March 29, at the suggestion of his attorney general, he again polled his cabinet on a proposal to supply Fort Sumter and Fort Pickens, and to reinforce Pickens. This time a majority concurred, including Gideon Welles, who frankly doubted that Sumter could be provisioned peacefully; only Seward disagreed.[54] That evening Lincoln, Seward, and Scott interviewed Montgomery Meigs, an engineer captain whom they intended to lead the Pickens expedition, and Meigs spent the next few days developing his own plans.[55]

So dark a spirit did Washington City harbor that spring that a damp and dismal April Fools' Day passed without humorous recognition. Presidential policy still seemed nebulous, both inside and outside the White House, and on that day Secretary Seward presented Lincoln with a somewhat impertinent letter noting the void in policy and essentially offering to address the deficiency himself. He focused particularly on the issue of Fort Sumter: based on the cabinet discussion of mid-March, Seward had secretly assured a delegation of Confederate peace commissioners that the fort would be evacuated, and now he made another effort to divert his chief from the relief expedition to Charleston. Having been recently liberated from the possibility of interference by a contentious Congress, Lincoln did not intend to surrender any authority to an overweening advisor. He declined to change his decision on the fort, and reminded his presumptive proxy that it was the chief executive's place to determine policy.[56]

The president and his cabinet fully expected that the naval missions would either settle the crisis in a twinkling or initiate great slaughter, and many of them at least pretended to hope for a peaceful result. Welles dismissed the potential for armed conflict with the consolation that, if it came to pass, the blame would fall to the Confederates. One of Lincoln's secretaries, meanwhile, scoffed at the prospect of anything worse than "a little brush at Charleston or Pensacola," and he assured his sweetheart that he had "not the least fear" that the expeditions would spark a more general or prolonged conflict.[57] Yet the firing on the *Star of the West* had demonstrated that the relief of Sumter could not be accomplished without violent resistance, as Hurlbut had so confidently predicted. The White House attitude reflected an incredibly naive assessment of public sentiment in the South: only psychological distraction or obstinately wishful thinking could have prevented Lincoln from recognizing that such an incident would initiate open hostilities. Certainly he had seen enough evidence that military action had the potential to drive many of the eight wavering slave states to side with the Confederacy, vastly complicating any attempt to impose national authority.

At the same time, though, Lincoln surely remembered that the few harmless shots fired at the *Star of the West* had ignited a conflagration of nationalistic indignation across the country, momentarily infuriating even many of those who had wished the seceded states good luck or good riddance. The example of that popular furor may have provided his principal purpose in dispatching the ships. More than two weeks before the

Sumter expedition cast off, the surgeon at Fort Sumter denounced the idea of continued occupation as "suicidal." From the enforced seclusion of his besieged dispensary the doctor sensed that any attempt at supply would only split the country more violently, and he supposed that it could not be accomplished unless "the administration means to bring on a war." Once apprised that the effort would be made, the surgeon received the news as a declaration of war, and his implied accusation bore some merit. Fort Sumter stood for the most volatile element of a delicate crisis, and Lincoln chose to handle it aggressively rather than diplomatically: he gambled on provoking a war to assure the dominance of federal authority when he could not have misunderstood that his policy weighted the odds overwhelmingly against a peaceful outcome.[58]

Later Lincoln would claim that he meant only to keep Sumter in order to "maintain visible possession" of federal property until "time, discussion, and the ballot-box" could resolve the sectional dispute. If that had been his true aim, he could best have achieved it at Pickens and the other Florida forts, as Seward advised; the decision to push the issue at Sumter strongly suggested a readiness to provoke an armed clash. Probably he envisioned the relatively limited conflicts of the nation's past: the deadly mix of improved ordnance and outdated tactics was largely unforeseen by the generals who would fight the war, as was the impact of infectious disease on massive military operations. Lincoln's attorney general had predicted that a civil war between North and South would bring "terrible consequences" that would "find no parallel in modern times," but even that apprehensive solicitor could have had no idea how devastating Mr. Lincoln's war would be.[59]

The novice president made such fateful decisions under extraordinarily debilitating physical and mental strain, as a relentless procession of supplicants devoured his energy and diverted his attention from the national crisis with their demands for clerkships and offices. The president interested himself in the most minor patronage of his cabinet members, annoying his attorney general by interfering even in the assignment of rural federal marshals.[60] The secretary of state perceived the negative consequences of the new chief executive's preoccupation with such trivia, and sought to ameliorate the danger of his apparent shift from indolence to reckless activity. Seward had spent the first weeks of the Lincoln administration attempting to act as a surrogate president, communicating clandestinely through intermediaries with Confederate officials and offering them unauthorized assurances, intruding in the affairs of other departments, and dealing with details that he thought Lincoln had overlooked. He still tried desperately to subvert what he considered an inflammatory and futile attempt to hold Sumter, lobbying vainly for Fort Pickens and other Gulf Coast installations that promised a better chance of success and less potential for war. Seward himself had conceived the term "irrepressible conflict" that others would cite as evidence of the inevitability of civil war, but now he seemed to have changed his mind, and he took extraordinary measures to avert hostilities. Neither the president nor subsequent historians ever accorded the secretary's proposed course much consideration, but, whether it would have accomplished more desirable results or not, it could hardly have wrought more carnage than did Lincoln's.[61]

Because Lincoln rejected Seward's cautious counsel, the secretary's meddling only destroyed the administration's ambassadorial credibility and intensified the volatility in Charleston harbor. Civilian and military leaders in that city had all willingly accepted Seward's injudicious guarantee (relayed by informal conduit to the Confederate commissioners) that Sumter would be abandoned without a fight. The secretary of state was, after all, the administration official who would logically communicate with a foreign power, which is what the Confederates considered their government. As Lincoln's policy toughened, the increasing deviation from Seward's covert assurance impressed Confederate authorities as a campaign of deliberate duplicity, thereby extinguishing the last flicker of hope for peaceful settlement. In the end, the mistrust that Seward had engendered would contribute materially to the very disaster he had wished to avoid.

Part of the Pickens fleet set sail from New York on April 2, and more followed the next day; the last vessels left on April 6. A steady drizzle began falling in Washington the next morning, but off the coast the storm whipped into a gale that raged for four days. The worst of it came during Monday evening, April 8, yet most of the Sumter relief expedition departed that day and the next.[62] Rumors of the impending expeditions leaked out more by surmise than by word of mouth. The mere news that the ships had sailed, along with the inevitable rumors of their probable destination, aroused a flurry of laudatory correspondence from obstinate Unionists in the Northeast, but those accolades smothered beneath an outpouring of wrath from Confederates and Confederate sympathizers who had expected Fort Sumter, at least, to be surrendered. The fleets sparked intense excitement among the cadets and staff at West Point, and brought another round of resignations from the army, including more senior field officers — one of whom hailed from still-loyal North Carolina.[63]

In the border states, where moderate Unionists had resented the Deep South for abandoning them, the sense of betrayal now turned toward the Lincoln administration. A newspaper in Wilmington, Delaware, declared that if the expedition brought war Lincoln would go down in history as a "monster" who should have been assassinated before he worked his evil. Another flock of Marylanders flew south; the manager of Baltimore's Continental Opera House impetuously presented himself to the Confederacy for service in any capacity in which he might be useful. The relief expeditions enraged Democrats in the North, as well. One agitated man from New Hampshire chose the occasion to apply to the Confederate War Department for a commission, and he promised to raise five hundred New Englanders who still breathed "a true spirit that Modern Republicanism cannot blot out." On April 6, perhaps in expectation of border-state reaction, General Scott named Charles F. Smith, a Philadelphian and an old soldier of indisputable loyalty, to command all the troops in Washington, replacing a Virginian appointed only two days before. With the sailing of the fleets, anti-administration fury spread so palpably through the city that a dispassionate functionary in the Patent Office anticipated an imminent public rising against the government.[64]

Knowing the intense excitement that the naval expeditions would arouse, Seward, too, pondered the chances of open revolt inside the District of Columbia. On the morning of April 5 he spoke with Colonel Stone on the subject, and Stone quickly compiled a report from his own informal intelligence network. Using sources a step or two removed from Jefferson Davis, the colonel collected two bombastic and indirect suggestions of Confederate ambitions to capture Washington City as well as Maryland. From a young Georgetown hotspur and an unemployed clerk in a Washington drugstore he heard of an alleged conspiracy among local secessionists to rise up and seize the government, holding the president and cabinet until a Confederate force could arrive to secure those prizes. The reported appearance in various portions of Virginia of renowned Texas Ranger Ben McCulloch seemed to confirm those boasts. McCulloch had led the troops that wrested Texas military posts from U.S. forces the previous February, and those who remembered his Mexican War exploits cringed at the rumor, understanding that he would be just the type to lead such a raid. Stone's report could not have failed to increase apprehension within the cabinet, but it failed to divert the president from his chosen policy, and the very next evening Seward suffered a rebuke for his haughty intrusions into the navy and war departments.[65]

Torrents of rain pummeled the capital Sunday and particularly Monday evening. At times water ran a foot deep in the streets, and persistently leaden skies continued to reflect the mood of the city. With the two seagoing expeditions likely to inflame Virginians and Marylanders alike, Lincoln prepared for military mobilization. He approved militia training in Pennsylvania, sending a drill officer into the state, and he instructed Scott to reorganize the militia in the District of Columbia.[66] At last, on April 9, he consented to Colonel Stone's request for mustering some of his district volunteers into federal service, and the next day a Regular Army major began administering the oath of allegiance to the first of them on the lawn north of the War Department. As many as half the members of some companies refused to take the oath and were allowed to go home, but by April 11 nine companies had been sworn in, totaling more than six hundred men, and the mustering continued from there.[67]

An aging militia colonel pushed himself on the president as the rightful commander of those new battalions, but Colonel Stone and General Scott protested. Stone argued that the new companies had no connection to the former militia organization in which the old colonel held his commission, while Scott contended that no field officers were necessary because the new companies would be serving independently, rather than in battalions. In fact, the volunteer companies had grown so numerous that they very badly needed a field officer, but there may have been no senior officers in the district militia whose fidelity Scott could count on. In the end he appointed Stone to command them himself.[68]

These were the first militia companies sworn into federal service during the war that was to come, and the excuse for that war arose less than forty-eight hours after the first man of them raised his hand to utter his oath. At the anxious prodding of his obtrusive secretary of state, President Lincoln had sent an officer and a State Department clerk to apprise the governor of South Carolina that a relief expedition was on its way to Fort Sumter to land provisions only, but that if the supply ship was fired on, reinforcements would be unloaded that would quadruple the fort's garrison. The pair reached Charleston on April 8, and when they delivered their message the governor called General Beauregard into the room to share the information. In light of Seward's conniving, governor and general both naturally considered the resupply effort a breach of faith. In view of that apparent treachery the two officials turned from nervous courtesy to chilled anger. Thanks to Seward, the Confederates doubted Lincoln's promise to land nothing more than food, suspecting it for a ruse to disguise reinforcement of the fort, and that behooved them to reduce Sumter and its formidable batteries before the relief expedition arrived.[69]

For the next few days Beauregard arranged his guns to bear precisely where the relief vessel would unload its supplies. He ordered out local reserves, and holiday soldiers who had savored the comforts of Charleston during the long siege swaggered out to the batteries, shouldering aside the men who had toiled to build them. On the night of April 11 Beauregard sent a boat to Sumter with a demand for surrender addressed to Major Anderson. Southern tempers on both sides showed even less restraint than Lincoln had: Anderson, a Kentuckian who had trained Cadet

Beauregard in the use of artillery at their common alma mater on the Hudson River, refused to surrender even though he admitted that his rations had essentially run out. In reply, a mortar round from one of the shore batteries exploded over Sumter's parade ground before dawn the next morning, announcing that the months of anxious uncertainty had come to an end.[70]

"Treason is in our midst," wrote a government clerk on April 12. "One hardly knows whom to trust." Little did he even suspect that in less than a fortnight surrounding the Sumter crisis, one of his neighbors entertained no fewer than four future Confederate generals who still wore the blue uniforms of the United States Army.[71]

Colonel Stone's district militia patrolled most of the city's public buildings, augmented by Regular Army detachments as they arrived from posts in the West. Senator James Lane of Kansas organized a mixed company of easterners and Kansas Jayhawkers to guard the White House, where they barracked in the East Room. Cassius Clay, a Kentucky abolitionist whom Lincoln had recently appointed minister to Russia, raised a battalion of similar dignitaries and prominent citizens for the same purpose, marshaling them at Willard's Hotel in their top hats, frock coats, and muskets before marching them onto the grounds of the executive mansion with a dozen rounds per man.[72]

The Fort Pickens expedition landed with anticlimactic ease the night of April 12, leaving the public eye fixed on Fort Sumter. Conflicting stories about events in Charleston prolonged the tension: first Washington heard that provisions had reached Sumter without incident, and then came the information that a bombardment had begun. Speculation that the fort had surrendered spread along Pennsylvania Avenue on April 13 (faster than the story could have carried from Charleston), only to be contradicted the next day by a report that the outnumbered garrison continued to resist. Alongside that rumor traveled news that President Lincoln intended to raise an army to put down what he had finally begun to characterize as a rebellion.[73]

Only this last fragment of gossip reflected what was actually issuing from government offices. Lincoln operated behind a dense mist of uncertainty about affairs in the South in general and conditions at Fort Sumter in particular. He still had not learned how to spell the name of the fort correctly, which may have hinted at the secondhand nature of his information to that point, but now he groped for reliable details. By April 13 he received unconfirmed reports of the bombardment; he interviewed the last messenger from Charleston the next day, and, once convinced that Southern guns had really opened fire, he did not wait for an announcement of Sumter's surrender to make his next move. A hostile Confederate response gave him the public relations advantage that he had been waiting for: the opportunity for such political symbolism had, after all, been the most obvious purpose of maintaining a grasp on the otherwise obsolete bastion. In a private note to Gustavus Fox a couple of weeks later, and in a conversation with an old friend two months after that, Lincoln revealed that he considered the assault on Sumter an especially successful conclusion to the expedition.[74]

Sumter surrendered on April 14. That evening Lincoln's rival for the presidency, Stephen Douglas, stopped by the White House to tell him that, as much as he might resist Lincoln's overall political agenda, he stood squarely behind him on the principle of maintaining the Union. Douglas may have interrupted Lincoln as he began composing a proclamation appealing to the individual states for seventy-five thousand militia for three months of federal service — the maximum allowed by law. Such firm support from so conspicuous an opponent lent credence to Montgomery Blair's expectation that decisive action would cultivate latent loyalty even in the border states, and it was probably with that hope that Lincoln's proclamation went out to the country the next morning. With it came a call for Congress to meet in special session, but not until July 4: for the present, Lincoln intended to make all the decisions himself.[75]

The president sorely misjudged the upper South if he expected his martial gesture to arouse Unionism there. His proclamation instantly cost him half the remaining slave states and vastly augmented the Confederacy in both population and territory, not to mention political sympathy. The editor of the *Southern Literary Messenger* told an old friend from Baltimore that, in Virginia alone, the militia levy had induced as many devoted Unionists to turn against the federal government as Lincoln had called out to defend that government. State authorities in Virginia, North Carolina, and Arkansas immediately resumed the seizure of federal forts and arsenals within their respective jurisdictions. For a few frantic days it seemed that all eight border states might bolt to the Confederacy: the governors of Virginia, North Carolina, Kentucky, Tennessee, Missouri, and Arkansas flatly refused to send a single soldier in answer to Lincoln's call. The governor of little Delaware declined, too, on the grounds that he lacked authority to order Delaware militia into federal service, although he allowed that individual companies could do as they chose. Even in northern Delaware, just a few dozen miles from Philadelphia, otherwise faithful citizens commiserated with the seceded states and deplored Lincoln's decision to use force.[76]

Benjamin Franklin Perry, a South Carolina Unionist who had resisted the secession movement from the start, instantly converted to the Confederate cause at the mere suggestion that federal troops might invade the South. Even Northern immigrants who lived or worked in the South understood how the burning resentment of federal aggression inspired a virtually unanimous spirit of resistance.[77]

John Minor Botts, a staunch Virginia Unionist to the last, firmly believed that the Northern and border states would emerge far stronger without the seceded states, since their departure would eliminate the perennially divisive issue of slavery expansion. A week before the clash in Charleston he traveled to Washington in a vain mission to convince Lincoln of the border-state viewpoint. After the fall of Fort Sumter Botts informed his old Whig Party friend Edward Bates that Lincoln's choice of military force "reduced the question to this — Shall we have dissolution without a bloody Civil War — or war first and dissolution afterwards." Of those two unappealing options Botts sadly accepted the former — to the astonishment of Attorney General Bates. Forgetting his earlier prediction of "terrible consequences" with "no parallel in modern times," Bates now expressed doubt that any bloodshed would ensue, and on that actual or pretended misconception he gave the president's coercive policy his strong endorsement.[78]

Governor Thomas Hicks of Maryland admitted that he was no Republican, but he described himself — without complete candor — as a Union man, adding that he wished to rid his state of its "corrupt horde of Democratic incumbents."[79] He nevertheless hesitated on the matter of militia until Secretary of War Simon Cameron promised him (with a sly caveat typical of Cameron) that Maryland militia would not be employed outside that state and the District of Columbia. In the face of federal coercion Maryland seemed more likely to leave the Union with this second tide, and Confederate officials organized a supply of arms for prospective Maryland recruits.[80]

The 6th Massachusetts Militia reached Baltimore on April 19 in answer to the president's call, and as the regiment shuttled between train stations a crowd of civilians lined its route. The crowd evidently reflected the Southern city's heavy proportion of sentiment against coercion, but it did not appear to have been organized for resistance: five companies of unarmed Pennsylvania militia had, after all, marched through the city under police escort the previous day with little incident. This time, though, a few dissidents dragged anchors across the railroad tracks and poured sand over them, forcing the soldiers to dismount from their cars to traverse the city. Mayor George Brown arrived and removed some of the obstructions with his own hands, but to no avail. Shouts turned to violence, and the civilian rage soon expressed itself in a hail of paving stones. The first gunfire apparently came from a Massachusetts private who shot a citizen for supposedly throwing a stone, and from there the regiment cleared a path for itself with volleys of musketry that left dead and wounded scattered along Pratt Street. A few civilians responded with pocket pistols, bringing down a couple of soldiers, and at least one man wrestled a rifle away from one of the militiamen, but the troops clearly held the edge in firepower. Police threw themselves at the mob and the soldiers alike: some drove back the crowd, while one police lieutenant put his pistol to the head of a Massachusetts officer and offered to blow his brains out if he did not order his troops to cease firing.[81]

The riot ended when the soldiers reached the next station and left Baltimore, but the city still seethed. Uniformed militiamen galloped in from the countryside, mimicking the Minutemen, who had congregated on another April 19, and that evening many a Marylander arranged his personal affairs to take up arms for the Confederacy. Some Northern-born residents threatened to join them: one businessman who hailed from Boston raged privately against Lincoln and the Massachusetts militia, blaming the troops for the bloodshed and accusing them of shooting down even innocent bystanders, including a personal friend of his. Governor Hicks and Mayor Brown telegraphed to Washington, imploring Lincoln not to send any more troops through their furious community, and late that night they dispatched a committee of citizens to petition the president. The emissaries missed Lincoln that evening, but they caught him the next morning as he descended the White House steps to greet General Scott's carriage, and Scott allayed their anxiety with the suggestion that the troops could avoid Baltimore altogether by taking steamers to Annapolis. That satisfied the delegation for the moment, but the government offered the expedient about twelve hours too late to satisfy officials back in Baltimore.[82]

April 19 had closed with news that more troops were on their way through Baltimore from Philadelphia. Doubting that the government would grant their delegation's plea, Baltimore officials met with the governor the night of the riot and determined to protect the city from further unrest by isolating it. As the mayor and the police chief told the story the next day, Hicks was spending the night at the mayor's house, and they approached him as he lay in bed. They presented a proposal to burn the principal bridges leading into the city. The anguished and weak-willed governor objected plaintively, but finally he twisted the sheet over his head and turned his face to the wall, telling the mayor to do whatever he thought necessary. Within the hour the armory bells tolled in some of the local militia. Under police marshal George P. Kane and Isaac Trimble, a railroad engineer and West Point graduate, the militia and the police headed out of the city with a supply of camphene and matches. By morning they had burned at least four of the major spans. Then they returned to Baltimore and began organizing against an expected assault by federal forces; within a few days the city's combined militia and volunteer "associations" numbered about twenty-five hundred men.[83]

The United States flag disappeared from Baltimore, to be replaced by the state flag and the Confederate Stars and Bars. One hardware dealer who employed a number of Massachusetts men instructed them to hide even the U.S. flag that stood in their office, and warned that they might be ordered to leave the city if the mob discovered their origins. Two days after the riot, some communicants took their weapons to church with them. Citizens brandished rifles, pistols, and shotguns at every hand, and accidental discharges wounded a number of men in the militia companies.[84]

At the outset of hostilities more men went south from Maryland than rallied to the national banner, especially from the angry streets of Baltimore, and Governor Hicks managed to recruit only one of the four regiments the president required under his initial proclamation. The state stood strong for the Union, however, especially among yeoman farmers and abolitionist enclaves like the Quaker meetings, where even some confirmed pacifists organized for military drill. Anti-administration outrage among the more educated and affluent momentarily overcame nationalist sentiments, though; the exercise of federal military might so incensed many young Maryland men that they turned a deaf ear to friends and relatives, forsaking their homes — and sometimes their families — to cast their lot with the beleaguered Southern Confederacy.[85]

Like most Marylanders, the majority of Virginians had hoped for a peaceful resolution that would allow their state to remain in the Union. A hard-line Unionist had even been elected to preside over the secession convention, which had just sent a committee to Lincoln asking his intentions toward the Confederate States. Implicit in that inquiry lay the question of whether he would attempt the use of military force to drag the seceded states back into the Union. Lincoln answered on April 13 that, if United States garrisons were driven from places like "Fort-Sumpter" by an unprovoked assault, he would use troops to regain possession of not only the fort that was attacked but any other installations that had been seized before he took office. As it happened, the Virginia delegation did not need Lincoln's formal reply, for on April 15 he vociferously answered the salient question with the announcement of his militia levy.[86]

Two days later, the erstwhile-Unionist Virginia convention voted overwhelmingly to forward a secession ordinance for ratification by the state's voters. Every member of the peace committee that had just visited Lincoln signed the ordinance, as did John Janney, the strong Union man who had presided over the secession convention: the call for troops forced their hands. Intransigent Unionists like Janney managed only to secure the condition of that statewide referendum, scheduling it five weeks later in hopes of giving tempers time to cool, but for all practical purposes Virginia lurched into the void on April 17, and many of the most vocal Unionists among the convention delegates went home to start raising troops.[87] As an afterthought the convention reminded Virginia governor John Letcher to offer state army or navy commissions to those native Virginians still serving as officers in federal forces, and Letcher sent a special courier to deliver those invitations. The envoy pitched the governor's offer to old General Scott, who indignantly rejected the suggestion, but Colonel Robert E. Lee did not wait to be asked: he had already resigned, and he accepted command of all Virginia's forces on April 22.[88]

The secession of Virginia sundered families and friendships in numbers that Deep South states had not seen. Colonel Philip St. George Cooke, a native of Leesburg, clung to the army in which he had served for nearly four decades while most of his family, including his only son and a devoted son-in-law — one J.E.B. Stuart — sided with their native state. George Thomas chose his oath of allegiance over his family, who disowned him. William Terrill stuck with the Union while his brother James became a Confederate, and both would die as generals. A Shenandoah Valley farmer exchanged affectionate correspondence with his brother, who had migrated to Illinois, into the final days of mail service: they announced in their last letters that they were raising companies for opposing armies.[89] One Eastern Shore student at the University of Virginia had voiced passionate sympathies for Southern rights all winter, and he hesitated as long as possible before taking leave of his friends to seek a commission in the U.S. Army; a classmate expressed relief at the outbreak of a war that would soon claim his own life, observing as early as April 15 that some students had already gone home and others were packing to leave.[90]

Only hours after Virginia's tentative secession vote, a lieutenant of United States mounted rifles torched the armory at Harper's Ferry that John Brown had tried to seize eighteen months before, and by the light of the blazing buildings he led his troopers north of the Potomac. The governor of Virginia, John Letcher, hoped to avoid a similar calamity at the Gosport navy yard, opposite Norfolk, and he appointed a military commander there to isolate the place until enough troops could arrive to capture it. Federal authorities anticipated him, though, and on the evening of April 20 a U.S. warship unloaded some Massachusetts militia at the yard, where soldiers and sailors began stripping the place of anything salvageable and destroying what they could not transport. They gathered all the loyal personnel remaining at the yard and fled before dawn the next day, leaving behind a roaring inferno of ships and warehouses. The incendiaries spared only the scuttled hulk of the ancient *United States:* in 1843, in the Marquesas Islands, that frigate had shipped a stranded whaler by the name of Herman Melville, and the germ of *Moby Dick* had matured as he trod her decks, but now she did not seem worth enough turpentine to light her afire. Within days Virginians began pumping the old tub out, though, to serve as a receiving ship for Confederate sailors.[91]

Governor Letcher answered Lincoln's proclamation with a new round of military appointments, the assignment of generals to command the new frontier, and provisions for border defense, particularly along the Potomac. By the end of the war's first weekend he had confiscated munitions belonging to Northern concerns, seized the federal building in Richmond, authorized the recruiting of volunteer brigades, and warned the president of the Baltimore & Ohio Railroad that he would take possession of the expansive Virginia portion of that line if it were used to transport federal troops or supplies.[92]

North of the Mason-Dixon Line and the Ohio River, Lincoln's proclamation drew an opposite but equally enthusiastic reaction. As Lincoln had evidently hoped it might, the attack on Fort Sumter launched a patriotic frenzy — fueled in large measure by fear — that yielded astounding support for the administration. The Northern interpretation of the dispute translated the bombardment of a single offending installation into the first blow in an imagined offensive against the entire North. National indignation festooned whole cities in flags; even the *New York Herald* office sported a pair, if only to deflect accusations of disloyalty over its hostile editorial slant.[93] Perceived reluctance and insincerity led Unionist mobs to descend on dissident businesses and individuals, demanding nationalistic demonstrations. Pennsylvania mobs destroyed the offices of dissenting newspapers, forced business owners to adorn their buildings with flags, and intimidated political figures into public expressions of Unionism. In New York City a resident described an absolute "despotism of opinion" in which considerations of personal safety discouraged any unflattering remarks about the Lincoln administration or government policy.[94]

Patriotic meetings filled town squares, county courthouses, and country schoolhouses from the Atlantic to the Mississippi, where listeners came to have their hearts steeped in hatred and speakers competed for the most venomous denunciations of all things Southern. Common citizens telegraphed the president to describe for him a public response that sounded very much like mass hysteria.[95] In Milwaukee the German immigrant Carl Schurz noted that "all the world wants to march," as volunteers by the hundreds gathered there. Those that had advocated peace changed their tunes, or fell prudently silent. Patriotic rallies in the West inspired the same tyrannical fervor that disgraced so many comparable demonstrations in the eastern cities, and on the night of Lincoln's call for militia Schurz saw a mob narrowly deterred from destroying the offices of opposition newspapers. That same evening, in Cincinnati, a lawyer who had recently wanted to let the Confederacy go its own way joined in the martial celebration, observing that any who dared to disagree risked physical violence. A woman in rural Massachusetts noted similar intolerance to any difference of opinion.[96] Rare was the town like Wilmington, on the Illinois River, where an observer could still count more advocates of peaceful separation than proponents of civil war. Quincy, Illinois, on the Mississippi River, raised seven companies of home guards in a single evening, and the next day most of the populace turned out to send a company of volunteers off to the state rendezvous with adulation, prayer, and endless patriotic serenades.[97]

Every Northern governor complied with the appeal for troops, some of them almost instantly, and most of them offered more troops than the president had demanded. On April 15 the governor of Indiana promised to supply twice as many men as Lincoln had asked of his state, and that same day his counterpart in Ohio pledged to furnish more troops than any other governor, adding that there was "great rejoicing here over your proclamation." In towns along the lower Ohio River, where Southern heritage predominated, the drum beat and the fife shrilled all day long, calling men to newspaper offices and storefronts where amateur captains took the names of eager recruits. Even there, more volunteers came forward than the government could accept.[98]

Congressman Daniel Sickles, a Tammany Hall Democratic, promised Simon Cameron support from the city of New York. Sickles had lately waxed critical of the administration, but now he hoped for a general's star, as he hinted in another note two days later. With the exaggerated verve of a sudden convert, Sickles told Cameron that "Democrats are no longer partisans. They are loyal to the government and the flag."[99]

For all those comforting words, no state troops arrived in Washington for three full days after the proclamation went out. The document itself had already tipped the government's hand, inviting the wrath of those most fervently opposed to the federal use of force, and a military attack or a coup d'état seemed both logical and likely. Newspapers reported wild rumors that the Virginia secession convention had ordered state troops to seize Washington, and those rumors soon fermented into active propaganda. As far away as Kansas, one Republican sodbuster who had opposed Lincoln's coercive policy three weeks before Sumter applauded military action a month later, and only because he believed the paranoid prattle about a Confederate invasion.[100] Indeed there were those in the South (and sympathizers as far north as Massachusetts) who advised a swift raid to secure Washington and capture Lincoln, and Confederates would later have occasion to regret that squandered opportunity, but advocates of a purely defensive strategy soon gained control of the government at Montgomery. Insurgent forces came nowhere near Washington, and nothing resembling a fifth column rose within it. News reaching the city on April 18 of Virginia's conditional secession nevertheless sparked rumors of an attack from that side of the Potomac. The civilian population grew skittish, prompting some residents and flocks of office seekers to leave the city.[101]

That night the first few hundred ninety-day men came into the capital — the five militia companies from southeastern Pennsylvania that had enjoyed safe conduct through Baltimore. They braced public morale little, for they came unarmed, clad in a variety of ragged uniforms, and they reached the city so late at night that most citizens slept through their arrival.[102] Reports of the destruction at the Harper's Ferry arsenal spawned even more insistent tales of an imminent assault throughout Friday, April 19, and then came word of the riot in Baltimore. Fresh from that fracas, the 6th Massachusetts spilled out of the cars at the Washington depot a few hours later, their grey overcoats buttoned against the cool evening air, and their march to the Capitol girded the loyal population with a more visible and impressive reinforcement.[103]

Even as the 6th Massachusetts bedded down on Capitol Hill, 1,050 men of the 7th New York dozed fitfully in their seats as their train rattled over New Jersey rails. This regiment carried a reputation as the best-drilled militia unit in the country, and even the news of its departure had inspired considerable hope. The weary travelers pulled into the Philadelphia terminal at two o'clock on Saturday morning, but there they sat for nearly eight hours while their officers fruitlessly tapped the telegraph key for news from Baltimore. Finally they decided to bypass that tinderbox altogether, embarking their men on a steamer for Annapolis, and that was the last anyone heard from them for two days. Aware by then of the Baltimore bottleneck, three more New York regiments left for Washington on Sunday, and another four on Tuesday, April 23.[104]

With Maryland impeding the passage of troops and Virginia mobilizing, Lincoln's government seemed to lie between a hammer and an anvil. Telegraphic communication had been cut beyond the Patapsco and the Potomac; no news came into the city save the discouraging reports from Baltimore, where it seemed that Lincoln's call for troops had turned the entire state against him — Union men and all. Because of the interrupted wires, no one in Washington knew whether the rest of the troops coming from the North had made their way around troublesome Baltimore by sea: for all Lincoln and his cabinet knew, the mob on Pratt Street had succeeded in turning back all the capital's other reinforcements. So ubiquitous and infectious did secession sentiment seem that government leaders occasionally doubted even the troops that were already in the city, and especially the district companies; there passed chilling moments when the intimates of Lincoln's official family wondered if they might not find themselves staring down the muzzles of the very weapons they had given to those volunteers. Sometime during that week Lincoln might well have regretted his bellicose course, but he postured boldly nonetheless, announcing a naval blockade of Southern ports on April 19.[105]

With too few vessels at his disposal he would not be able to enforce that boast for some time to come, but, like the call for troops, the mere announcement of the blockade produced its own consequences. At that moment the steamboat *Alonzo Child* churned up the Mississippi River under the guidance of a Missouri-born pilot named Samuel Langhorne Clemens, who had never wished for any higher calling than that of riverboat pilot, but the president's announcement nominally sealed the mouth of the Mississippi. Within a few weeks Clemens would see the river closed to commercial traffic, and that forced him to cast about for interim employment until affairs settled down.[106]

2

Flags in Mottoed Pageantry

❖ FROM THE TIDEWATER TO TEXAS, Southerners came alive to resist Yankee aggression. Lincoln had said he would do no more than retake occupied federal property, but — like the denizens of Washington — Confederate strategists anticipated an invasion from the other side of the Potomac, and professionals like General Beauregard expected that the attack would come sooner rather than later. Recruiters had been signing up companies in the seceded states for some time, and the Confederacy had already called for as many as three thousand men from each of its governors, but now that request more than doubled. The same appeals went out to the newly allied border states, including those that had not formally seceded. Volunteers from states outside Confederate authority proffered their services, as well, including a regiment of Kentuckians whom the war had found residing in Louisiana.[1] A native Tennesseean living in Connecticut estimated that he could raise a couple of companies among New Haven's Democrats, if that was acceptable. In Carbondale, Illinois, a resident soon learned that men from an adjoining county had gone into Kentucky to raise troops for a sympathetic insurrection at home.[2] Another man living at the southernmost tip of Illinois started collecting recruits there, accurately predicting that he could find enough exasperated citizens to fill an entire company. A West Point graduate from western New York petitioned Jefferson Davis's secretary of war for a commission, while one furious Democrat from New Hampshire asked a prominent senator of his party to help him enlist in the Confederate army.[3]

The day after Virginia's secession convention passed its tentative ordinance, the government at Montgomery celebrated the state's admission to the Confederacy with a salute of eight guns — without waiting for popular ratification. President Davis offered Governor Letcher any help he might need. All in Montgomery viewed Virginia as the likely battleground, so there the troops concentrated. On April 22 the secretary of war called for one, two, or three additional regiments from the governors of each Confederate state as well as Kentucky, which had not taken the first step toward secession and never would. The secretary directed all these troops to Richmond, Lynchburg, or Harper's Ferry.[4] The next day new regiments began unloading at the Richmond depots in such numbers that the price of groceries started climbing precipitously, and citizens speculated that either the Yankees planned an attack on Richmond or the Confederate government intended to take Washington.[5]

Mississippi governor John J. Pettus responded immediately. On the very day of the War Department's request, a hundred men in the vicinity of Holly Springs, Mississippi, mustered into state service as the Confederate Guards. A few miles to the south, at Sarepta, a university senior by the name of William L. Duff enlisted a contingent of his classmates and neighbors for the Magnolia Guards.[6] At the state capital in Jackson, where rows of ramshackle houses hid behind the oversized columns of their pretentious porticoes, Mississippi's state auditor Erasmus Burt quickly collected enough men for a company: they elected the forty-year-old Burt as their captain and voted to call themselves the Burt Rifles. Governor Pettus's son numbered among Burt's recruits, but in the frontier tradition the boy was expected to make his own way in the army, and his lineage earned him no special privileges beyond a warrant as corporal.[7]

Young men, and some not so young, flocked to the Confederate cause, and across Dixie new military organizations sprang to life fully (if badly) armed. Even in the deepest of the South, a significant number of those who so impetuously shouldered muskets and strapped on sabers had struggled to prevent secession and to avoid war. In Shreveport, Louisiana, a fervently Unionist lawyer apprised his father on Monday, April 22, that the news of hostilities had changed everything. Accepting the new Confederate nation as his own, he felt that he had to fight for the South or against it, so he joined some friends in a local company, heading for New Orleans and war. At that first call another reluctant Confederate in eastern Louisiana put his name down with 150 other men from his parish, and a few days later he bid farewell to his sweetheart before boarding the cars for New Orleans with them.[8] The governor of Arkansas could order no troops into Confederate service before his state seceded, but he passed that duty on to a colonel who made arrangements to supply his own regiment. Missouri's governor lacked both the authority and the arms to send a regiment, but he promised that the men would rendezvous wherever they could be equipped and put to use. Georgia volunteers began pouring into Savannah the day after Lincoln launched the federal mobilization, and the flood intensified a few days later, when Lincoln announced his blockade of the Southern coast.[9]

In time the blockade would strangle a region so deficient in manufacturing capacity. The South imported most of its durable goods from Northern or European suppliers, and that dependency had never seemed so obvious as it did when it came to arms, uniforms, and field equipment. Even so well-stocked a city as Richmond could not supply another yard of cadet-grey cloth four weeks into Virginia's war, and many a company had to settle for cheap, baggy cloth with an odd homemade tint.[10] Southern women came immediately to the rescue, gathering in homes and churches with needles and thread to blister their fingers in military production. They stitched haversacks, havelocks, and battle shirts with big pockets, and when they could get them from the tract societies they slipped Bibles into those pockets for both practical and providential protection. The inaugural battle would not pass without producing the war's first sentimental tale of a bullet striking that token of faith — although the abridged testament allowed the bullet to penetrate and kill the youthful patriot anyway, after ten days of agony.[11]

The volunteers desperately wanted experienced officers in addition to equipment, and the former were on the way, as well. On the far side of the continent a Pony Express rider brought the news of Fort Sumter into San Francisco, and a few days later a party of Southern U.S. Army officers took ship for the East Coast with their resignations in their pockets. Commissioned officers streamed away from the army's line regiments, opening coveted vacancies for those who stood by the flag.[12]

A demanding government afforded few of its servants the cold comfort of personal neutrality. Naval officers returning from the Far East on the old frigate *Congress* heard their first news of the war as they anchored off Boston on April 23. The navy yard presented them with a new oath that would have forced several of them to pledge themselves against their native states, and nine of them declined. Ordered off the ship immediately, they found themselves under military arrest until they could be dismissed from the service, after which they eluded the police and made their way homeward. Having already been declared enemies because they would not serve as allies, most of them eventually entered Confederate service.[13]

Brevet Major Larkin Smith, a West Point graduate from Virginia, had been included in the surrender of U.S. troops in Texas, and under the liberal provisions of that surrender he left the state with his troops. He delivered nine companies of infantry and cavalry to the coast for passage back to Washington, then composed his resignation from the army. Explaining that he preferred retirement to "raising my hand against my people,"

he pleaded that his faithful quarter-century of service might not be re-
warded with the dishonorable dismissal that the navy and Marine Corps
accorded its reluctant officers. Southern nationalism and rigorous Confederate conscription later persuaded Smith to serve as a Confederate
quartermaster and tax official, but he proved as true to his word as the
times allowed, never taking the field against the old army.[14]

In Loudoun County, Virginia, on the banks of the Potomac River, the
presidential vote had revealed a three-to-one majority of Unionist citizens in November, but Lincoln's militia call reversed the proportion of
sentiment even in that conservative shire. A Quaker returning from an errand to Philadelphia witnessed an agitation among his countrymen that
he had never before detected, even in the wake of John Brown's raid: instantly he understood both that war had become inevitable and that his
home county sat on the contested frontier. A young lady in Leesburg, the
county seat, told a Richmond cousin that the sudden Southern nationalism of her neighbors surprised her: "They will live and die for the Confederacy," she reported. The more radical of Leesburg's two newspapers, the
Democratic Mirror, announced the first Confederate appeal for troops
on April 17, and within two days the county provided a company called
the Hillsboro Border Guards that included a twenty-year-old boy named
Flavius Osburn.[15] The unmarried, thirty-year-old editor of the *Mirror*
(who also served as Leesburg's postmaster) vociferously favored Virginia's
alliance with the Confederacy, and he would come to snarl about the
"Hessian" hordes that would despoil fair Loudoun. He played the classic
incendiary, though, and his outrage never drove him to take up arms in
defense of either home or country, although he had been healthy enough
to serve as orderly sergeant of a gentlemen's militia company before the
war.[16] Meanwhile, his more moderate conditional-Unionist counterpart
at the *Washingtonian* abandoned his own newspaper office at the first
threat of Northern coercion, leaving a large family behind in order to lead
another company of his neighbors to the front.[17]

Many of those companies had been meeting for a week or more, from
the moment the word of Fort Sumter brought the prospect of war to their
communities. Anticipation led the more mobile residents of the border to
emigrate, thinning the population visibly, and menfolk went for soldiers
in droves. Between the refugees and the recruits, the churches soon echoed with skeleton congregations of a Sunday morning, especially after
the women started flocking to the camps to admire all the uniforms and
banners.[18]

Traveling through the South on assignment for the *Times* of London,
William Russell found the populace inordinately mesmerized by the little
circle of stars and the broad stripes of the new Confederate flag. "These

pieces of coloured bunting seem to twine themselves through heart and brain," the Briton noted as he traversed North Carolina. As early as April 15, the day of Lincoln's provocative call for troops, he saw a motley array of militia gathered at the Goldsboro train station under an inebriated "general" who teetered about in an old blue frock coat with a red sash. His troops wore little in the way of uniforms and carried ancient flintlock muskets, for the most part, but they exuded a boisterous brand of self-assured patriotism as they gathered for a campaign against two unmanned forts near Beaufort. In a lusty collective baritone they cheered their flag, the train, the intermingled ladies, and themselves, and when the cars pulled away from the depot they sent up a piercing falsetto keen that foretold the eerie rebel yell of more serious battlefields. Russell noticed that alcohol seemed an essential ingredient in these military preparations, as it did in most aspects of Southern men's lives.[19]

Despite the sprawling territory and the hundreds of thousands of potential enemies represented by the loss of border states like Virginia and Tennessee, little Maryland posed the most crucial immediate problem. The governor nominally remained behind the Union, but he had been swayed by the argument that the transit of federal troops would ignite civil strife in the state, and the sentiments of the people seemed even more questionable. A Philadelphia newspaper that had ignored its own city's Unionist mobs reported Southern sympathizers roaming the streets of Baltimore, demanding that passersby participate in their denunciation of the federal government.[20] Rioters had challenged the passage of troops through Baltimore, and, with or without official authority, saboteurs had cut the telegraph to Washington, burned bridges, and torn up the railroad leading from there to Annapolis, where the troops had been diverted. A troubled lieutenant on the faculty of the U.S. Naval Academy, the grandson of a United States president and a nephew of the Confederate president, submitted his resignation as soon as Massachusetts militia started crowding the docks at Annapolis. On his way home he found the country people between there and Annapolis Junction boiling with rage over the invasion. Maryland army officers were resigning their commissions along with Virginians and North Carolinians, and looking for positions with the new government. In Baltimore, a West Point alumnus who had worn the shoulder straps of a captain of United States cavalry until Friday morning tore them from his coat that evening, after learning that the 6th Massachusetts had fired on his fellow citizens. By Monday he had recruited enough men for Southern service to request several hundred of the firearms salvaged from the Harper's Ferry arsenal, and he was signing himself as the major general commanding the "First Light Division, Maryland Volunteers."[21] Baltimore native Frank Schaeffer, the onetime captain of

District of Columbia militia whose loyalty Colonel Stone had doubted, gathered the greater part of his former militia comrades (mostly Marylanders themselves) and fled Washington City for Virginia. There they enlisted in a body, with Schaeffer as their captain once more.[22]

It was Colonel Stone to whom General Scott entrusted the task of restoring rail service between Washington and Annapolis Junction, where the branch road turned for Maryland's capital. Stone marched his district volunteers to the Washington depot of the Baltimore & Ohio, where he commandeered a train and persuaded two companies of his volunteers to board it for a destination beyond the limits of the district. He sent them out under a Regular Army captain, and when they reached Annapolis Junction they found the tracks to Annapolis dismantled as far as the eye could see. At the junction they learned that the troops at Annapolis were rebuilding the road from the other end, and this they reported to Stone when they got back to Washington. Stone returned the National Rifles to garrison the junction until other troops arrived from Annapolis, remaining in charge of the line until the War Department assigned a professional railroad manager.[23]

The weather grew nearly as warm as the political climate during the week of Washington's isolation; the mercury climbed high into the eighties on Tuesday and Wednesday. Several hundred Marines disembarked at the navy yard on Tuesday, but no mail or any other form of communication had come into the city since the Baltimore riot on Friday, leaving the citizens and soldiers free to imagine hordes of Maryland and Virginia secessionists poised to descend on the capital from north and south. Officers of the 7th New York fretted that the capitol would "go to smash" before they arrived. Still protected by the likes of Jim Lane and Cassius Clay, who strolled nonchalantly about the White House with three revolvers and a bowie knife strapped on, President Lincoln found it difficult to disguise his growing despondency. On Wednesday morning he greeted some of the ambulatory wounded from the 6th Massachusetts, who stopped by to see him, but after the handshaking and pleasantries he lapsed into a confessional reverie.

"I don't believe there is any North," he told them. "The Seventh Regiment is a myth. R[hode] Island is not known in our geography any longer. You are the only Northern realities."[24]

Then, at noon on Thursday, April 25, Charles Stone's commandeered train pulled into the Washington depot and the 7th New York climbed out, still wearing the dust of an exhausting march from Annapolis to the junction. Hailed by cheering crowds, the regiment marched down Pennsylvania Avenue to the White House, where it circumnavigated the grounds while the president and his family looked on. After that bit of ceremony the tailored grey uniforms dispersed into avenue hotels for the more important matter of a square meal before mustering in front of the National and marching up to the Capitol, where privates made camp beneath the desks of absent congressmen. The 6th Massachusetts turned out on the Capitol grounds that afternoon, partly to drill and partly to entertain the spectators, who that day included Mr. and Mrs. Lincoln, the secretary of state, and the secretary's wife and son.[25]

Reduced by guard details left along the way, the 7th Regiment added barely eight hundred men to the sixty-five hundred or so Regulars, Marines, district volunteers, and militiamen who stood ready to defend the city. Somehow, though, those eight hundred men, sporting the close hairstyle of that spring's militia fashion, tipped the scales between despair and confidence. The 8th Massachusetts and half of the 1st Rhode Island came in from Annapolis the next day, and the 5th Pennsylvania the day after that. A government clerk who made the rounds of the regimental parades noted that the populace breathed a little more easily among all those glistening bayonets, and by April 27 at least one of Lincoln's department secretaries considered the capital sufficiently safe to begin thinking about offensive operations.[26]

The arrival of the 7th New York may have offered a similarly disproportionate air of security to the chief executive, and just in time to allow him a moment of forbearance that he and the country both desperately needed. The Maryland legislature was scheduled to meet in special session at Frederick the next day, out of sight of both Baltimore rowdies and federal troops. Ben Butler, a Massachusetts militia brigadier commanding the troops concentrated at Annapolis, pressed Lincoln to let him arrest the legislators before they could declare themselves against the government. Butler was a sly politician and an unsavory opportunist who reveled in the exercise of power, but the president actually considered his suggestion. It may have been the recent experience of watching the best-known militia regiment in the country march past the White House that afforded Lincoln the latitude to reject such an outrageous infringement of the democratic process — at least for the present. Writing to General Scott, he reasoned that if the Maryland solons turned secessionist, as he fully expected they might, then he now enjoyed the luxury of subduing them with military force. And, he added ominously, he could suspend the right of habeas corpus in Maryland by his own hand, with all the arbitrary arrests and summary imprisonment that such a drastic action implied.[27]

Habeas corpus represented the fundamental element in the tapestry of law that had always protected American citizens against tyrannical government. Without it, the rights of speedy trial on specific charges by a jury of the defendant's peers meant nothing, for the arresting authority could not be forced to present such charges or provide such a trial. It was all that stood between traditional constitutional freedom and the sinister variety of repression that threatens long imprisonment at the whim of unscrupulous authorities. In the history of the United States only one person had ever pretended to suspend it on his own authority: Andrew Jackson had declared martial law in New Orleans during the War of 1812, and had refused to recognize a writ of habeas corpus for a citizen he had arrested. Constitutional commentators disagreed over the legality of Jackson's actions, the most prominent arguing that in suspending the process of civil law Jackson had usurped a right belonging only to Congress, and that analyst opined further that even Congress could not interrupt habeas corpus except in cases of rebellion or invasion. The Whigs and Republicans with whom Lincoln had associated throughout his political life generally abhorred Jackson's highhandedness, and particularly his suppression of civil authority, but now Lincoln considered emulating it if the rebellion came.[28]

The arrest of the Maryland legislature at that sensitive juncture could very easily have driven Kentucky and Missouri from the Union, just as the mere call for troops had propelled four more states toward secession. It could also have provoked intense resentment in free Northern states where reverence for the United States Constitution ran deep. Despite the rioting and sabotage, official Maryland had not even suggested that it would pit itself against the government. Southern sympathizers and Democrats held the majority of the legislative seats, but when they met in Frederick they took no action more hostile to federal authority than passing resolutions recognizing the theoretical right of secession and preparing to mediate the dispute between the two sections. Lincoln had played that particular hand well, but within forty-eight hours he risked squandering his victory by secretly authorizing the army to "suspend" habeas corpus anywhere on the railroad line between Washington and Philadelphia if resistance threatened "the public safety." Maryland had been saved from rebellion, and no hint of invasion hovered near the District of Columbia: yet Lincoln nevertheless assumed a power the experts had said he did not have, in order to avert a danger that seemed already on the wane.[29]

By surreptitiously delegating the suspension of habeas corpus in a loyal state, Lincoln temporarily eluded the popular wrath and judicial censure that would have followed an official announcement. Perhaps he hoped it would never come to light, for he must have recognized the furor that such autocratic action would incite, especially in so delicate a political environment as Maryland. He may also have understood that by arrogating such power to himself he conveyed to any less scrupulous successors a handy precedent for the first step toward an American dictatorship.

Slim hope for peace still lingered in a few hearts, and one of those hearts beat in the breast of William Seward. The Confederate vice president, Alexander Stephens, arrived in Richmond on April 22 as the Confederacy's special commissioner to Virginia, and reports of his presence soon reached Washington.[30] Through other former Whigs Seward probably understood how friendly Stephens had been with Abraham Lincoln during Lincoln's congressional term, and he may have sensed a rare opportunity for good-faith communications. An offer of intercession by the minister from Bremen came just in time to exploit that opportunity. In a brief interview with the president and Seward on April 24, Dr. Rudolf Schleiden examined the potential for compromise. Lincoln told him that he intended no aggression against the South, insisting that the seventy-five thousand militia were only meant to protect Washington against a Confederate threat such as Colonel Stone's investigation had revealed. The militia levy might have passed for a defensive measure, but Lincoln's proclamation of a naval blockade implied unmistakable aggressive intent, and most Southerners saw it as an effective declaration of war; a reciprocal Confederate proposal for privateers to operate against United States maritime commerce had aroused similar animosity in the North. Hoping to prevent the commercial repercussions of an American war, Schleiden sought to disarm those two most controversial issues by suggesting mutual repeal of the contending proclamations, but Lincoln would commit to nothing. Though pessimistic, Schleiden boarded the southbound train that night on a pass issued by Seward, bearing no proposals from the White House and no authority to negotiate.[31]

Schleiden reached Richmond the next afternoon. In a meeting only hours after Schleiden's arrival, the diminutive Stephens assured the German intermediary that the Confederacy had no plans to attack Washington, and that any belligerent utterances to the contrary could only represent the idle boasts of individual citizens. Schleiden explored the notion of a three-month truce, until the special session of Congress convened, but Stephens resisted such formalities, preferring "tactful avoidance of an attack on both sides" to a declared armistice. He doubted that war could be averted: Lincoln's stated aim of putting down rebellion seemed synonymous with forcing the Confederate states back into the Union, and the South would never submit to that without a "most bloody" fight. He could only promise Schleiden that the government at Montgomery would respond favorably if Lincoln gave some early and official sign of a willing-

ness to negotiate — if he were to receive the Confederate peace commissioners, for instance, or if he opened the special session of Congress on
July 4 with a recommendation to seek a swift diplomatic adjustment of
the differences between the two countries. The following day the two exchanged written versions of their discussion, and Schleiden took the resulting correspondence to Washington, where it was immediately dismissed as unworkable.[32]

The mobilization continued without pause. By the end of April, some
ten thousand volunteers had reached Washington.[33] With the exception
of the 7th New York dandies, who had committed themselves for only
thirty days, they all came as three-month men under the provisions of
Lincoln's April 15 call — trained militia and hastily organized volunteers
alike. From Maine to Kansas, Lincoln's proclamation would eventually
draw 101 regiments and a few scattered battalions of these short-term
troops, although many of them would reorganize for longer service by
the time their initial enlistments expired. One regiment of loyalists even
sprang from the little arm of Virginia wedged between Pennsylvania and
the Ohio River, in defiance of a governor they repudiated.[34]

Though impelled in many cases by an outraged sense of nationalistic
spirit, most of them had impetuously signed on for an exciting thirteen-
week adventure in an age when adventure customarily required a much
longer commitment. Except for the Baltimore riot, hostile fire had injured
no one by the time the last of them enlisted, and they had come to the capital with every reason to suppose they might spend the time strutting
around Washington in their sundry uniforms, staring secession down by a
show of arms before returning home to a hero's welcome. At the very
least, they would do some traveling and see some sights, avoiding the te-
dium of farm or factory for at least a season. To encourage them, many
employers offered to continue their salaries and keep their places open
for them.[35]

As the troops teemed into Washington the city assumed a carnival atmosphere. Regiments amused themselves, the populace, and occasional
honored guests with drill exhibitions, gymnastics, theatrical productions,
and musical programs. Lincoln attended a concert at the navy yard fea-
turing the band and choir of the 12th New York, calling for an encore of
"Le Marseillaise." Spectators gathered for a colorful display every time the
regiments mustered. Uniforms varied mightily in both cut and color:
many, like the 7th New York, wore cadet-grey, often with red piping, while
others chose some shade of blue and a few opted for less traditional colors, like green. The 71st New York Militia arrived on April 27, wearing
long frock coats and carrying grey cardigan jackets for fatigue duty. The
next day the 12th New York appeared in dark blue, hip-length jackets,

light blue caps of the French pattern, and baggy grey trousers gathered into brown gaiters. The 1st Rhode Island sported a grey dress uniform with similar gaiters, but for fatigue duty the regiment stood out in long, loose overshirts, called "Burnside" blouses in honor of the regiment's colonel, who had designed the garment.[36]

In the months before the war there had developed, in the private armories of the uniformed militia, an intense fascination for the Zouave uniform worn by French troops in North Africa. Zouave fashion included short, ornate jackets, extraordinarily baggy pantaloons contained at the ankle by wrapped puttees or buttoned gaiters, and a fez or turban in place of the hat or cap, all in the brightest possible colors. The Zouave also carried a rifled weapon, sometimes of abbreviated length, with which he was expected to operate more independently than regular infantry. Myriad American versions of Zouave companies copied certain elements of the outfit, often modifying the oriental appearance with varying degrees of occidental detail. Washington residents caught their first glimpse of a complete regiment clothed in such apparel on the evening of May 2, 1861, when the 11th New York Fire Zouaves pulled into the depot from Annapolis. Clad in gold-trimmed grey jackets and trousers, red shirts, and red caps, they imitated the 7th New York by marching down Pennsylvania Avenue to the War Department. There they drew their quarters assignment, returning to the Capitol and squeezing in with the three thousand other occupants while the man who had recruited them dropped in at the White House for a chat with the president.[37]

Elmer Ellsworth had raised the Zouave regiment within five days of Lincoln's appeal for militia by organizing an assortment of New York City's volunteer fire companies. Now, barely a week after his twenty-fourth birthday, he appeared before the president as colonel of the regiment. The diminutive Ellsworth enjoyed Lincoln's particular favor, having studied law in his Springfield office, but he never progressed far in the study of law, for he had long since succumbed to a boy's passion for the pomp and grandeur of all things military. In Illinois he had put together a company that he dubbed the United States Zouave Cadets of Chicago, a collection of athletic young men with whom he had toured the country and gained considerable renown. The Fire Zouaves packed revolvers and shouldered Sharps breechloading rifles; the "Zou Zous" reputedly exceeded the average soldier in size, strength, and agility, but, despite Ellsworth's puritan demands for their deportment, they pursued the same diversions preferred by most of New York's rough-and-tumble fire companies. Within five days their appetite for liquor and loose women tainted their reputation in the capital, and a rumor of gang rape even flourished briefly, until the alleged victim offered to withdraw her claim for a gratuity of twenty-five dollars. They redeemed themselves to a certain extent at the end of their first week, when, substituting their acrobatic agility for ladders, they expertly extinguished a fire that threatened to devour Willard's Hotel.[38]

For all the military merits of the Fire Zouaves and the thousands of other militia regiments trooping into Washington, even the tardiest of them would pack up and go home before the end of August. In the same proclamation that had spawned this hodgepodge army, Lincoln had warned the seceded states to renounce rebellion within twenty days, and that ultimatum came due on May 5. If the president had expected his militia mobilization to kindle enough reflection for any Southern state to heed his demand, it was clear by the beginning of May that none would, and that the insurgent region would probably not respond to anything short of a significant confrontation of arms. Preparing for such a contest would take months of training, during which the militia would serve no effective offensive purpose. Acting again without congressional approval, on May 3 Lincoln called up another forty-two thousand volunteers for three years of service. At the same time he expanded the Regular Army by nearly twenty-three thousand men, and to implement his promised blockade of Southern ports he also authorized eighteen thousand more sailors for the navy.[39]

This latest proclamation added eight new regiments of infantry to the Regular Army, and one each of cavalry and artillery, allowing Lincoln to appoint hundreds of company-grade officers and distribute nearly three dozen new field commissions to the most deserving officers. After a few days of consultation he compiled a list of colonels to command the new regiments, dating all ten appointments the same day, and in offering those coveted eagles he did not forget the man who had done so much to protect the capital since the beginning of the year. On May 14, Charles P. Stone became the youngest colonel in the Regular Army at the age of thirty-six.[40]

Those forty-two thousand volunteers would represent thirty-nine more infantry regiments from the individual states, apportioned according to the population of those states and the number of regiments each had already provided. Some, like New York and Pennsylvania, had already sent so many troops that the War Department expected no more from them. Many regiments that had begun recruiting for the three-month service immediately reorganized for three years, especially in Ohio. Like their ninety-day predecessors, many of those who so blithely signed on for three years supposed that the Confederacy would fall apart as soon as any real fighting began, and that they would be discharged within weeks or months, anyway.[41]

Still, the extension from three months of duty to three years revealed the limits of many men's devotion. In Trenton, New Jersey, the vast majority of one gathering regiment balked when faced with the ultimatum, opting for discharge rather than longer service. "I done all I could," lamented their would-be colonel, "but they would not go into it for three years. . . ." The three-year obligation momentarily dampened martial enthusiasm even in Cincinnati, Ohio, which had seen some of the nation's most conspicuous expressions of nationalistic fervor in mid-April. Recruiting picked up again before the end of the month, however — after Governor William Dennison announced additional state incentives that included support for soldiers' families.[42]

New Hampshire had originally been asked to provide one regiment of ninety-day infantry. Enough men for two regiments had come forward, but not a soldier had left the state by mid-May. Secretary of War Cameron conveyed to the governors his desire that the remaining three-month regiments be converted to three-year service, with any reluctant recruits being replaced with men who would sign on for the longer period. The New Hampshire governor passed that request on to the colonel of his one complete regiment, who bristled indignantly at the suggestion. Changing the terms of service would destroy the organization of the 1st New Hampshire, said the colonel, but if the government would accept the regiment under the ninety-day proclamation he had little doubt that it could be persuaded to remain in the field at the end of its term, had the war not ended by then. "Patriotism and self-respect will compel them to see the thing through," he asserted.[43]

Ultimately the government did accept the New Hampshire regiment for the ninety-day service, but neither patriotism nor self-respect compelled the men to remain in the field at the end of their term, and the colonel made no effort to persuade them to stay on; in fact he went home himself, for the duration of the war. Many of the veterans of the 1st New Hampshire did eventually reenlist in combat units, while others sought shorter or safer military service, but the three-month campaign taught one-third of the men in the regiment only that they never wanted to wear a uniform again.[44]

Once his first regiment had started for Washington the New Hampshire governor informed Secretary Cameron that he could immediately provide a second one, for he already had nearly twelve hundred additional recruits gathered in camp at Portsmouth, with more coming in every day. Cameron insisted that this second regiment would have to enlist for three years, much to the dismay of the new recruits, who had expected the same brief stint as their comrades in the first regiment. When faced with a demand for three years of their lives in return for a chance at martial glory, more than seven hundred of them turned on their heels and made for home; two complete three-month companies from the town of Keene could not retain enough three-year recruits to muster the minimum number for a single company. The would-be colonel of the regiment also decamped with his men, as did many of the officers who had raised the various companies. Just over two thousand New Hampshiremen had responded to the ninety-day call within two weeks, but after the government imposed the three-year requirement state authorities had to spend four more weeks recruiting the last five hundred men for New Hampshire's second regiment.[45] The delay illustrated an overwhelming preference for the three-month lark, at least in the Granite State. Even many of those who did submit to the three-year demand did so under the popular assumption that they would not have to serve so long: "You can be pretty sure the war will not last many months," one compliant swain assured his sweetheart.[46]

Political reluctance may have slowed recruiting in New Hampshire, where nearly two-fifths of the state legislature voted against military appropriations and signed a petition denouncing Lincoln's war on state sovereignty.[47] Farther south in New England, where industrialization had drawn a firmer grip on local and regional economies, recruiting for longterm regiments proved less challenging. Broad industrial markets left the inhabitants of industrial communities more vulnerable than ever before to the economic consequences of sectional strife, and the political tension that provoked a war simultaneously produced enough economic tension to help prosecute it. The shoemakers of Massachusetts provided the foremost example of that phenomenon in their state.

Boot- and shoemaking had become the largest single industrial occupation in Massachusetts by 1860, but over several decades the independent craftsman had been lured out of his home and into a factory. Initially, merchants transformed many of those cobblers into subcontractors, supplying them with materials and marketing the finished products. Then came the manufacturer, who could better monitor the waste of material and control the efficiency of production, selling cheaper footgear that priced most independent cordwainers out of the market. From that day, the shoemaker became entirely dependent on the manufacturer.[48] Increased efficiency in shoe production came at the price of inadequate wages for the operatives, and the work entailed frequent layoffs for people who could barely survive on their income at full employment. By 1860 shoemakers in northeastern Massachusetts complained that the $2.75 to $3.00 weekly cost of board ate up most of their wages, while rents averaged $50 to $150 a year. In February they went on strike, seeking higher wages and the recognition of a union, and for weeks their struggle captured national attention. Southern journals remarked with grim satisfaction on the plight of factory operatives in Massachusetts, where abolitionists fulminated sanctimoniously about the inhumanity of Southern slavery. By the estimates of the day, one person in twenty-four was engaged in some aspect of shoe manufacturing there — something like forty thousand people — and about twenty thousand of them joined the strike.[49]

The shoemakers were so destitute that they could not hold out long enough to realize their demands, and before March closed their leaders called an end to the strike. Their return to work availed them little, though, for nine months later secession robbed the industry of its customary surge of December and January orders. Sales began dropping from there as Southern nationalism inspired boycotts of Northern goods, and business remained especially slow into March. Only the worsening political situation crowded news of the recession from the pages of shop-town newspapers.[50]

Shoemakers fared the worst in the downturn, and they composed the most impoverished class of workers in Massachusetts when Lincoln issued his appeal for militia. Few of them belonged to the uniformed peacetime militia, which demanded commitments of leisure time and personal expenditure that they could hardly afford, so the ninety-day militia regiments that responded to the initial call harbored comparatively few shoemakers. The 1st Massachusetts, for instance, which was founded on five existing militia companies, carried only seventy-eight shoemakers on its rolls, and many of them may have enlisted as last-minute substitutes for regular members who preferred to stay home.[51]

The practice of providing a substitute flourished in the antebellum militia organizations, and any member offering a proxy could decline active service without the opprobrium of his comrades. In the factory town of Lawrence, one boy who was not yet eighteen years old took the place of a reluctant soldier in the 6th Massachusetts Militia. With that regiment Luther Furber saw some of the Baltimore riot, after which he expected that the rebellion would dissolve. He soothed his widowed mother with the promise of relative comfort, reminding her that the state of Massachusetts would pay him two dollars a day until he was mustered into federal service, and he had been led to believe that thereafter he would earn twenty dollars a month, plus his keep. "I have plenty of money and some to spare," he assured her, and he assumed that she was also taking advantage of their city's appropriation of two dollars per week for the care of soldiers' families. If the regiment remained in uniform for its entire three-month stint, he calculated that he would come home with the astounding sum of forty-nine dollars.[52]

The state of Massachusetts may have paid its soldiers that generously for active duty, but young Private Furber found the federal government a little stingier. Lincoln's May 3 proclamation nevertheless aroused considerable enthusiasm among shop laborers, for in addition to the pay and allowances of the Regular Army it provided the promise of a hundred-dollar bounty, to be drawn at discharge or paid to the soldier's heirs. Shoemakers providing their own keep on $20 a month or less found relative generosity in a private's pay of $11 (and later $13) a month and a clothing allowance of $2.50, especially since the army would feed them and house them, after a fashion. Community organizations and municipal agencies also began raising funds against a promise to help support the families of needy soldiers, dangling even more bait before the fathers and sons of hungry families. Not surprisingly, therefore, the first Massachusetts regiment of new three-year volunteers attracted 326 shoemakers out of just over a thousand men.[53] The second such regiment, designated the 9th Massachusetts Volunteer Infantry, went to war with 373 shoemakers in its ranks, representing more than 36 percent of the enlisted men in the entire regiment, and recruits ultimately swelled that figure to 481.[54]

This trend continued as recruiting expanded. In mid-May local leaders began raising a regiment from Worcester County, on the western edge of the Bay State's shoemaking region. Local militia companies formed the foundation of that regiment, but when federal officers mustered it for service no fewer than 232 shoemakers and bootmakers raised their hands with the rest; a company of attached sharpshooters included 38 more in the shoemaking trade, and another 91 joined later. The 19th Massachusetts, raised during the summer around an existing militia battalion, eventually drew 351 shoemakers. Even the 20th Massachusetts, renowned for its core of Harvard-affiliated Brahmins, recruited 236 shoemakers. The 22nd Massachusetts, which carried only 58 percent as many names on its rolls as the 20th, enlisted at least 189 shoemakers: even the original colonel of the 22nd, U.S. Senator Henry Wilson, had begun his working life as a shoemaker.[55]

Many of the recruits in each of those regiments specified no occupation when they enlisted, evidently because they had no jobs to claim, and a large proportion of those men would likely have been shoemakers. Even without counting those who had remained idle for so long, though, shoemakers flocked to those early regiments in numbers five to ten times their representation in the general population. Considering that the shoemaking industry had begun to rely heavily on women and older children, the disproportion of adult male shoemakers who rushed to the recruiting offices rises even more sharply. So unequal a representation from so demonstrably destitute a class of citizens speaks to the frequency with which economic desperation drove men into uniform even at the outset of the war, when unrestrained patriotism is supposed to have wrought its greatest influence on recruiting. This enlistment pattern implies that financial distress played a much greater role than ideological considerations in filling Massachusetts regiments in 1861, unless raw patriotism or antislavery principles actuated the poorest citizens at ten times the rate of their more affluent neighbors. Many of Boston's sophisticates also served, to be sure, but often in short-term regiments or in rear-echelon sinecures, and almost always as officers. For every Charles Francis Adams Jr. or Garth Wilkinson James who finally enlisted, there was a Henry Adams, a William James, or a Henry James who never seriously considered it; for each Revere or Abbott family that would sacrifice two sons to the cause, several other Beacon Hill families would provide none at all.

The industrial slump of the secession winter had also slowed or silenced the textile mills of eastern Massachusetts, and those factories disgorged thousands more employees who suddenly found the army financially enticing. It was the same in southern New Hampshire, where an oversupply of finished material fulfilled the military demands for weeks. That, and then a shortage of cotton, silenced textile mills in Manchester, Milford, and Dover through July and August. Prospective officers who swung through those mill towns looking for potential soldiers found fertile ground. Manchester recruiters advertised exaggerated interpretations of army pay and benefits, including an outdated offer of 160-acre land grants — inducements that yielded eight companies from that city by early August. Later that month two men organizing an artillery battery gleaned a hundred men in a week from the spinners, weavers, and mechanics of Manchester's sluggish textile industry, and new infantry companies attracted scores more.[56]

Inadequate wages, underemployment, and unemployment had afflicted shoemakers and textile workers for some years, but the recession of 1860 and 1861 struck indiscriminately through industrial New England as factory closings spread unemployment to suppliers and supporting trades. Amos Stearns, a machinist in a Massachusetts mill town, donned a uniform in September of 1861. Recording his decision to go to war a quarter of a century later, he remembered only a sense of intense patriotic devotion, noting that he had suffered "the war fever" from the outbreak of hostilities. He had buried his wife and only child shortly before he enlisted, so personal despair may have played a part, but his admission that he had been "out of work most of the time that summer" betrayed another significant factor in his motivation.[57]

The military record of New Hampshire's population, like that of Massachusetts, revealed a remarkable disparity in apparent patriotism, as manifested by enlistment, between upper and lower classes. In the town of Conway, on the eastern border with Maine, the poorest residents of rocky hill districts enlisted earliest, and in far greater proportions than their wealthier neighbors. One lone three-month soldier volunteered from the town's largest and most prosperous village during the entire war, while the two poorest hill districts respectively provided 31 percent and 22.2 percent of their eligible males, of whom 33.3 percent and 37.5 percent died in service. Antiwar feeling ran high in Conway, where Democrats predominated, and except in those indigent neighborhoods the town endured a chronic deficiency in its volunteer quotas until the selectmen began offering extremely high bounties, late in 1864. Bounties totaling more than a thousand dollars finally convinced some of the more comfortable population to serve abbreviated terms, and the town as a whole ultimately saw nearly one-sixth of its eligible men go into uniform. Disproportionately high casualties among the poorer recruits yielded an overall death rate of 25 percent among Conway's soldiers.[58]

Meanwhile, military pay and bounties exerted little appeal to the less needy alumni of Dartmouth College, on the opposite side of the state: they enlisted with far less frequency and suffered a much lower rate of mortality. Of the 1,381 surviving graduates from 1837 to 1864 who fell between the military ages of eighteen and forty-five during at least one year of the Civil War, barely 10 percent entered any kind of military service. That reflected a slightly subdued enthusiasm, compared to the overall response nationwide, and the martial ardor of the alumni waned more sharply as the brutality of the war intensified. More than 26 percent of the class of 1860 and 19.5 percent of the class of 1861 eventually served, as well as just over 18 percent of those who graduated in 1862, and 13 percent of the recruits from those three classes perished in the line of duty. The carnage in the second half of 1862 chilled Dartmouth recruiting abruptly: only three 1863 alumni enlisted (without a single fatality), and not one of those who graduated in 1864 appears to have borne arms. Thirty-five students and alumni joined a cavalry company for three months of bloodless frolic in the summer of 1862: only three of them ever reenlisted — briefly — and then only in the navy, or with sedentary militia companies. Most of the Dartmouth graduates who did volunteer selected short-term units or sought staff positions as surgeons, chaplains, paymasters, or quartermasters, so of the 142 who did serve, the war claimed the lives of only 21 — and mostly from disease. In contrast to that quarter of Conway's soldiers who perished, Dartmouth's death roll did not reach 15 percent of its volunteers (at least on the Union side: four of the five Dartmouth graduates who fought for the Confederacy died in its service, including three killed in action). Even more striking is the difference in overall wartime mortality among those who might have served: Conway buried 3.9 percent of its eligible working-class citizens, but only 1.5 percent of Dartmouth's predominantly professional graduates died in the war.[59]

The glaring imbalance in sacrifice between rich and poor suggests either that the well-educated and the working classes did not share the same ideological devotions or that ideological impulses did not play a paramount role in attracting recruits. Political inclination may have produced a patriotic sentiment that moved some of the poor more often than it did the affluent and sophisticated, but evidence from different regions and populations also testifies to an abundance of economic pressure behind the rush to the colors. Especially in the first months, the poor provided so large a portion of the Union army because so many of the working class remained unemployed, and because the modest emoluments of military service provided a viable alternative to absolute want.

The federal military machine's absorption of tens of thousands of indigent workmen seemed to confirm the prediction of one slavery apologist who, in the wake of the Massachusetts shoemakers' strike, had warned that the paupers of Northern industrial society "will demand to be fed out of the public treasury." That same critic had also charged that Northerners wanted to use the federal territories as a relief valve for their surplus unemployed population, and indeed Horace Greeley had specifically offered his famous advice to "Go West" as a solution to the poverty among northeastern factory workers. The land that he advocated giving away through a homestead act would, he supposed, lure hundreds of thousands of penniless shoemakers and other industrial poor out of the cities and lead them into agricultural pursuits.[60]

As Greeley's observation illustrated, New England had not suffered alone. Recession had blighted most industries of the mid-Atlantic in 1860 as employment dropped off and manufacturers trimmed wages. The labor situation in New York had not eased by April of 1861, and that gave recruiters the same pool of jobless men that their Massachusetts counterparts exploited. The *Journal of Commerce* reported that the sectional crisis had thrown as many as twenty-five thousand of the city's factory operatives out of their jobs by the end of November, 1860; by the first of April the *New York Times* was posting two and a half columns of advertisements for "situations wanted" against fewer than a dozen "help wanted" ads. Appeals from the unemployed expanded daily until the eve of the attack on Fort Sumter, when "situations wanted" filled nearly a full page of the eight-page daily. That section began to shrink dramatically as soon as Lincoln announced his call for troops.[61]

Saturday, April 20, would have been a workday for most of those with jobs, but thousands of New Yorkers found the time to attend a patriotic rally at Union Square, where the defenders of Fort Sumter sat beneath their garrison flag. Orators harangued a hybrid crowd of gentlemen and workmen who filled the square, spilling over into Broadway and Fourteenth Street. Lincoln's old friend, Senator Edward Baker, addressed the crowd. Baker, who had raised and commanded an Illinois regiment during the Mexican War, informed his audience that he also intended to fight in this war. He urged the men in that massive throng to join him, and they applauded lustily. The next day the *Times* carried not a single advertisement from the unemployed, instead publishing an invitation for all former Californians and Oregonians to come join the "1st California Regiment," which Baker intended to fill with as many westerners as he could find. On Monday morning the "situations wanted" section returned, but it took up less than two columns, and all but seventeen of the ads had been placed by women. Over the next week, while company after military company filled with recruits, no more than a couple of dozen men sought employment through the newspaper on any given day.[62]

Timothy O'Meara, a young Irishman of Fenian proclivities and no apparent means of support, lived in a boarding house in New York City's Fourth Ward.[63] He responded instantly to the call for three-year volunteers, appearing at a Long Island rendezvous on May 3, and he showed such administrative capacity that the commander of the camp immediately appointed him adjutant of the regiment. With that rank he began drawing pay that allowed him to support his crippled brother and their widowed mother.[64]

Another unemployed Irish immigrant named Thomas McDermott enlisted alongside O'Meara in Lincoln's army. After knocking around New York and northern New Jersey for a long while he had worked for a couple of years as a laborer on a railroad tunnel near Bergen, and when that project petered out he had drifted back to New York City. The city offered few jobs in the winter before the war, and a lack of funds doubtless helped him to conquer a drinking habit early in February. He finally found relief when the federal government offered pay, board, clothing, and — early in May — the $100 bounty. An offer of partial pay in advance seems to have proven decisive, and on May 8 he turned himself over to a recruiter who took him out to the rendezvous of the so-called Tammany Regiment, at Great Neck. There he found hordes of other jobless Irishmen, waiting to sign the roll.[65]

George Geer was an out-of-work laborer who lived in a New York tenement with his wife and two children. He faced a small mountain of debts. At last he enlisted in the navy, primarily for ready income but also with the hope that he could learn a marketable trade. Eventually he would draw an assignment to the USS *Monitor*, on which he served during all eleven months of its service. Occasionally he encouraged his wife with a reminder that he was "fighting for his country," but he alternated such remarks with admissions that he was considering desertion, which only tinged his patriotic assertions with a note of strained insincerity. More convincing are his revelations that he had enlisted primarily to raise money and secure a profession. In one of his earliest wartime letters Geer cursed the navy agent's refusal to give his wife the advance pay he had been promised, and worried that she would have to subsist by further borrowing. At least one of Geer's fellow recruits, a steam ferry engineer, had also shipped as a means of supporting himself and his family: Geer told his wife that this fellow had "lost his place and came here from necessity." Similar desperation had apparently compelled most of the rest of the *Monitor*'s enlisted crewmen to volunteer, judging by the endemic indigence that Geer described among them.[66]

Alfred Wheeler, an unemployed and unskilled Connecticut youth, informed his brother just a few days before the war broke out that a common friend had gone to Manchester, where the factories were still reported to be running full-time. "See if you can get me a job in the Box shop," Wheeler implored his brother, "or any where els [sic] you can." When his brother failed to secure him a position, Wheeler sought work in New York City and Philadelphia, but he found none there, either. Almost every manufacturing firm in Philadelphia had sharply reduced its work force or its hours, and by the fourth week of February an estimated 40 percent of the city's factory operatives lacked enough income to support themselves or had lost their jobs altogether. In Philadelphia Wheeler finally abandoned his quest for civilian employment and enlisted in a company that ultimately composed part of Colonel Baker's California regiment. That solved his immediate financial plight, although it would eventually cost him his life.[67]

Well into June a minister in New York City still observed that "immense numbers of men are unemployed." Even skilled, experienced men could find no work, he noted, and they were "now ready to enlist in the war because they cannot earn their bread." One New York City patriot with business commitments hesitated to enlist in part because "there were men enough out of employment who considered it a privilege to enter the army because they had no other means of support."[68]

The soldiers themselves emphasized how influential financial incentives had been to their enlistment when government agencies failed to come across with the economic inducements they had promised. John Gilbert, a forty-year-old family man who enlisted from Cornish, New

Hampshire, in the summer of 1861, howled at his town selectmen when they denied his wife her portion of the state aid for soldiers' families. Rather than paying her the stipulated allowance, he complained, they doled out driblets of flour and firewood, as though she were a town pauper. Gilbert, who would eventually die on the battlefield, had obviously enlisted with the understanding that his military service would yield his family an adequate income. Marshall Phillips, a middle-aged Maine shoemaker whose town had reneged on promised support for his family, wrote a scathing editorial from the front when his town started offering lucrative enlistment bounties. A Massachusetts recruit who encountered the same broken promises frankly confessed that he had only enlisted in order to provide for his wife with both army pay and state aid.[69]

Recruits in a rendezvous on Staten Island had also been assured of generous public support for their families in that first flush of nationalistic zeal, but by June some of them discovered that it would not all be forthcoming. A few of them therefore refused to be mustered into federal service, preferring the humiliation of being drummed out of camp. When it appeared that the Union Defense Committee would not provide his wife and child with promised funds, another New Yorker who had just survived his first battle concluded that he had done enough for his country only two months into his enlistment. "I Dont see how you are to get along," he mourned, adding that every man in his regiment already shared his readiness to quit the war; a serious mutiny in his regiment two weeks later corroborated his assertion.[70]

Town assistance posed the foremost priority for a reluctant Massachusetts recruit named Fred Clark, who would disgrace himself the first time he came under fire. His wife had vacated their living quarters and sold their surplus possessions, moving into smaller accommodations with a roommate, and Clark had barely reached camp before he started asking whether she had begun collecting her state aid. On his first payday Clark sent most of his money home, and he told his wife that the majority of his compatriots did the same. It came easier to save money on a soldier's paltry pay, he explained, than while providing his own keep from wages of two dollars a day. Clark's first sergeant, who had enlisted in hopes of improving his social position and economic condition with a commission, gave most of his own pay to support his mother and sisters. The 2nd New Hampshire sent over twelve thousand dollars of its second payroll to the Suffolk Bank of Boston, which honored checks written by anyone the soldiers authorized. That averaged more than fifteen dollars per man — well over half of a private's pay for the two-month period.[71]

Where work could be had at decent wages, recruiting suffered. One Indiana youth — and a Quaker, at that — conceded that he would enlist if he ran out of work, but he told an acquaintance that so long as his employment lasted he would not. A bored farm lad from New York's Ontario shoreline enlisted early, only to learn that most of his friends preferred to spend their time logging; his brother made one halfhearted attempt to enlist, but the prospective company failed for lack of recruits. Meanwhile, a more fragile economy in the western states encouraged enlistment for regular pay, public assistance, and seemingly generous bounties. The Panic of 1857 had hit hard in wheat country, and farmers there had been among the last to see any sign of recovery, which came with a sudden European demand for American breadstuffs in 1860. Railroad cars full of wheat from north of the Ohio and west of the Mississippi started rolling eastward that summer, and for a few months the road to prosperity seemed to have reopened, at least for western farmers. Then came secession and the closing of the Mississippi, choking off another vast market.[72]

By the spring of 1861, those who could find work in wheat country considered themselves lucky to earn a salary of sixteen dollars a month. At the minimum monthly pay of eleven dollars and found, the army thus seemed an attractive economic option. The appeal of the military alternative only improved when Congress raised a private's pay to thirteen dollars a month and western communities began imitating the eastern cities' promises of support for the dependents of volunteers. One lieutenant serving in Missouri had evidently enlisted for the summer campaign in lieu of working a troubled farm in western Illinois, for his finances had sunk so low by July that when the paymaster failed to show up he coached his wife on selling their last hogs for grocery money.[73]

A prominent Kentucky Unionist confessed to a federal officer in early May of 1861 that money was the most important inducement for recruits in Louisville, where he noted that there were "a great many workingmen there out of employment" who needed army pay to support their families. Cincinnati, the largest city west of the Alleghenies, began the war by giving as much as three dollars a week to soldiers' dependents, and that helped draw thousands of volunteers. As the conflict ground on, though, and the cost of supporting soldiers' families rose, communities grew less liberal: six months after Fort Sumter, Cincinnati capped support at two dollars per week, per family. That slowed recruiting dramatically, illustrating the significance of economic incentives in the Ohio soldier's decision to enlist. By the end of the war, 84 percent of Ohio soldiers' families were drawing aid — which, since that aid was distributed on a determination of need — suggests a predominance of poor men among Ohio volunteers.[74]

Few of the men who enlisted that bright spring and early summer anticipated the cataclysmic battles and disease-ridden encampments that would kill so many of them. "After all," wrote a well-educated young officer who would die in battle two years later, "when you look at it coolly there is not much more danger in war than in peace. . . . There are comparatively few men who are killed."[75] The first three months of the war corroborated that view, for more regiments suffered fatalities from railroad mishaps and accidental shootings than from actual combat.[76] Illustrated newspapers with their appealing engravings of nattily uniformed soldiers inspired visions of strange lands, adventure, and a touch of glory in the minds of young men who were bored, broke, or both. Some joined for reasons even less altruistic, like one harried New Hampshire husband who enlisted as a means of escaping his scolding wife.[77]

While abstract notions of patriotism or principle clearly played a more superficial part in enticing volunteers into uniform in 1861 than the memoirs of the survivors admit, even the rationalizations that many of them provided their loved ones at the time seem strained. An Irishman who ended up in a Massachusetts regiment left a written record of one man's effort to transform and glorify the more mercenary motive behind his enlistment. Peter Welsh, a native of Prince Edward Island, lived with his wife in New York City; he made a visit to relatives near Boston that ended with a drunken binge in which he spent every cent that he owned, and in his shame and destitution he enlisted. Welsh did not inform his wife until after he reached Washington, admitting to her that "there is hundreds of men here who got in to it in the same way as i did." Reminding her of the "relief money" offered by the state, he consoled her with the logic that at least he would be able to support her, which he had been unable to do by his erratic and infrequent work as a carpenter. After nearly five months in the army, however, he dismissed the immediate cause of his enlistment as "one grain of sand to all on the sea shore compared with the cause in which we are engaged." In words that he had evidently borrowed from the *New York Tribune* and the Catholic bishop of New York, Welsh argued the case against secession at considerable length in a hybrid political and theological brief, with Saint Paul as his principal authority. He acknowledged that his wife would probably not swallow his logic (and she never did), but he had evidently convinced himself. Had he survived the war, he might have joined those legions of veterans who relentlessly recounted the intense patriotism that propelled them into the army, forgetting the more pressing pecuniary factors.[78]

Years afterward, many veterans fulminated against a class of soldiers they called bounty men. They applied that term to those who enlisted after the imposition of a national draft, late in 1863, when the federal bounty jumped to $300 and local bounties rose to $800 and $1,000. The men who went in at the beginning, or even as late as the autumn of 1862, considered themselves much more principled and patriotic than their tardier comrades, whom they ungenerously characterized as mercenary misfits. Frank Wilkeson, a New York veteran who enlisted early in 1864, wrote an unconvincing memoir that depicted him as the only recruit in his detachment who had enlisted for anything but cash. Wilkeson claimed that he never received a penny in bounty money (an assertion flatly contradicted by his service record); he insisted that every other recruit at the rendezvous intended to desert with as much of his bounty money as town, state, and federal governments were willing to pay in advance.[79]

Wilkeson's provocative memoir greatly exaggerated the dishonesty among later volunteers. Early in 1864, for instance, a New Hampshire sergeant initially described one levy of recruits for his regiment as "a rougher & more abandoned set of men than I had supposed could be collected outside the penitentiaries of the U.S." A corporal in the same company shared that dismal first impression, but hoped that time would prove their mettle, and his hope came to a certain fruition, for nearly 10 percent of those recruits found soldiers' graves.[80]

To be sure, a great many of the men who took large bounties planned to abscond rather than fight, and many succeeded. The same was true among substitutes, who signed up in place of men who had already been drafted. The drafted man had to pay the substitute a negotiable fee that usually fell within range of the prevailing bounties; the substitute had to be ineligible for the draft — as the sole support of a large family, by virtue of foreign nationality, by being over or under the limits of draft age, or through some other exemption besides physical disability. Thousands of opportunists took such money and deserted, or made miserable soldiers, but many thousand more teenaged boys, recent immigrants, prolific fathers, and destitute farmers accepted the cash for the support of their families and went on to serve creditably.

A significant percentage of those later recruits — both bounty men and substitutes — now lie in the national cemeteries near where they died. New Hampshire, which kept precise statistics on its troops, provides a good example of the relative sacrifice of the "bounty" men. The state raised seven three-year infantry regiments in 1861, amounting to 6,810 officers and men, of whom just over 24 percent eventually died an honorable death in uniform. Between 1862 and 1865 those same seven regiments received 6,798 recruits who accepted increasingly larger bounties, of whom slightly more than 12 percent died in the line of duty. Considering that the recruits served, on average, less than half as long as the men who originally filled those regiments, they actually endured a higher annual mortality rate than the 1861 volunteers who made a point of looking down on them. The bounty man and the substitute provided the old regiments with raw material just as good as the soldiers of 1861, many of whom turned out to be unsatisfactory. Those later recruits also showed more grit than their predecessors by signing up after the war had begun to wreak its worst carnage, for the earliest volunteers had enlisted — almost to a man — without any expectation of such extensive slaughter.[81]

Neither did the bounty men display much greater greed than their predecessors, in light of wartime inflation. However nationalistic they may have felt, a heavy proportion of the men who flooded Northern recruiting offices in 1861 suffered from straitened circumstances, and for them the smaller compensation of that period proved nearly as alluring an incentive at the time as the bigger bounties did for later recruits. The army absorbed a substantial number of the impoverished that first year, and war production put many of the rest back to work at more reasonable wages. Only then did government agencies have to start spending larger quantities of inflated greenbacks to find enough men willing to participate in what had become a far more deadly adventure than the early volunteers had bargained for.

A fortnight after the surrender of Sumter, a farmer in Minnesota observed that the swarming volunteers lacked only a galvanizing principle to fight for. He innocently suggested that the abolition of slavery might serve the purpose, but he concluded that in the absence of something so grand the soldiers would be killing each other only as a means of determining "whether our government is good for something." For some who enlisted then, the sense of national insult (so effectively exploited by the government and its editorial-page supporters) may have been sufficiently compelling. Many, if not most, required more direct and personal incentives to drive them into the army, either in conjunction with or independently of such ideological impulses. Economic benefit stood prominently among those incentives.[82]

Recruits' personal motivations reflected the general economic influences underlying the collective resistance to secession. As noble as Unionist newspaper editors and politicians might try to paint their cause, commercial considerations played a significant — and perhaps paramount — role in their support for the war. Momentarily abandoning its campaign to smear Southern secession as a "pro-slavery rebellion," the blatantly partisan *Daily Whig and Republican* of Quincy, Illinois, let slip the less admirable purposes of Lincoln's supporters just four days after the president asked for an army. The value of the South to the nation lay in its capacity for commercial expansion (argued the Quincy editor), and as a protective buffer for the commerce of the North and Midwest, for its coastal forts guarded against foreign incursion. The hostility of the Southern people posed no impediment to forcible reunion, for the population of the South did not matter to that Republican. "They may go to the isles beyond the sea," he concluded, "taking their niggers with them, and we will help them off, but the union must stand."[83]

A *Harper's Weekly* engraving of South Carolinians firing on the *Star of the West* at the entrance to Charleston Harbor.

The steamer *Marion* leaving Charleston with the families of the Fort Sumter garrison, which fires a salute at their departure, as depicted in *Frank Leslie's Illustrated*.

A CURE FOR REPUBLICAN LOCK-JAW

A political cartoon lampooning efforts to force the Crittenden Compromise (too big a pill to swallow) down the throat of an uncompromising Republican Party.

Cassius Clay's impromptu battalion of presidential bodyguards in front of the White House, April of 1861.

Charles P. Stone, Inspector General of District of Columbia Militia and brigadier general, U.S. Volunteers, with his daughter Hettie, about 1863.

Senator Edward Dickinson Baker of Oregon, whom Lincoln befriended in the Illinois legislature and who accompanied him on the ride to his inauguration.

Lincoln and Buchanan portrayed by *Harper's Weekly* as they entered the U.S. Senate to witness the inauguration of Vice President Hannibal Hamlin.

Lincoln's first inauguration, March 4, 1861; Colonel Stone's sharpshooters lurk in the open windows at right.

why dont you take it?

Winfield Scott, caricatured as a bulldog, daring the slinking Confederate cur to take the city of Washington, from an 1861 print.

I am glad, I am out of the scrapes! Just in time! Now or never. This is the way we serve all Traitors! I'm ready! Copyright secured.

Cartoon of Lincoln wielding a stick against an armed planter, while James Buchanan skulks away and Winfield Scott directs U.S. soldiers toward the insurgent.

William H. Seward, Lincoln's ambitious and intriguing secretary of state.

Lincoln's first secretary of war, Simon Cameron, who lasted barely ten months.

Alfred Waud's drawing of Alexandria, Virginia, from the Maryland side of the Potomac, showing the Confederate flag flying from the roof of the Marshall House.

The Marshall House at the corner of King Street and Pitt, on the third floor of which Elmer Ellsworth and James Jackson both died, with its bare flagpole.

The 71st New York, sketched by Waud as it rested in the streets of Alexandria.

Waud's depiction of Ellsworth's funeral in the White House, attended by the president, his cabinet, General Scott, and a mournful throng.

3

The Banner at Daybreak

❖ FROM THE UPPER FLOORS of Washington's boarding houses and government buildings it was possible, through most of May, to catch a glimpse of a Confederate flag fluttering over a hotel just down the Potomac River in Alexandria, Virginia. President Lincoln could see it with a telescope. On May 2 Robert E. Lee, commanding the Provisional Army of Virginia, consigned Alexandria to the care of a lieutenant colonel with the poetic name of Algernon Sidney Taylor.[1] Colonel Taylor had been born in Alexandria when it still lay inside the District of Columbia boundaries, but he had spent more than two decades away from the town as a company-grade officer in the United States Marines Corps. He remained officially a U.S. Marine even as he assumed his Confederate command at Alexandria, for the commandant of the corps refused his tardy resignation, and on May 6 he would be dismissed as a deserter. By then he would also find himself in deep trouble with Virginia authorities.[2]

The mobilization of Northern troops only fueled Virginians' suspicions that the U.S. government planned to invade their state. For them, Northern anxiety about a Confederate attack on Washington seemed merely the fruits of incendiary propaganda designed to gain support for that invasion. On May 3, the same day Lincoln appealed for three-year volunteers, Governor Letcher authorized the activation of Virginia militia in the northern counties. For the defense of his native town, Colonel Taylor was allowed 414 of those militiamen, including 70 cavalrymen, 8 of whom needed horses. Forty of the cavalry owned sabers and carbines, for which they could find little ammunition. Of Taylor's infantry, 135 men either lacked arms altogether or shouldered ancient smoothbore muskets, converted from flintlocks, for which they had not been issued a single live round. The remaining 209 infantry had been armed with new percussion muskets and some rifles, but they carried an average of fewer than five cartridges per man. To further disable this incongruous legion, all but one small company came from Alexandria, and the men lived at their respective homes rather than amid the discipline of a concentrated bivouac.[3]

An intercepted communication persuaded Taylor to anticipate a dual amphibious assault on Alexandria, from the waterfront and from behind, in the vicinity of Mount Vernon. He expected the attack as soon as Lincoln's twenty-day ultimatum of April 15 expired, and if it came he would not have a chance. On the evening of May 5, perhaps with more reflection on the fate of captured deserters than on his duty as a soldier, he gave his first and last order as the field commander of an armed body of troops. Without sighting a single enemy, without so much as a hint to his immediate superiors, and in direct violation of orders he had received that morning, Taylor evacuated Alexandria and pulled back along the Orange & Alexandria Railroad eight miles or so, to Springfield, bringing with him all the militia who would come. The brigadier commanding Taylor's department flew into a fury when he found Alexandria so timorously abandoned: he called for Taylor's arrest, but in the end the evacuation caused no harm except to Taylor himself. He avoided arrest, but his precipitate flight prompted inevitable questions about both his judgment and his courage. His loyalty may have suffered some scrutiny, too, not so much for his tardy departure from federal service as for his family connections: reports would eventually emerge that his brother had come out vociferously for the Union. After six months in a backwater assignment, Taylor resigned his field commission to take an even less glorious appointment as a supply officer in the Confederate Marine Corps.[4]

No Union soldiers had molested Alexandria while Taylor left it defenseless, and most of the garrison came back willingly enough, probably because their homes stood there. With no ammunition they offered little protection against an organized attack, but the mere presence of pickets along the Potomac could discourage a Union foray, even if those pickets paced their beats with empty weapons. Richmond sent up Colonel George Terrett, another of those former Marine Corps officers, to command the town and guard the river as far upstream as Georgetown. His cavalry videttes ranged well beyond Arlington Heights, where sat the home of Robert E. Lee.[5]

With the rank of major general, Lee served as the commander of Virginia's little army and navy in the weeks after his state seceded, while the land forces evolved from a ragged agglomeration of militia into organized companies and regiments of one-year volunteers. At the time he held no commission from the Confederate government, but Confederate troops

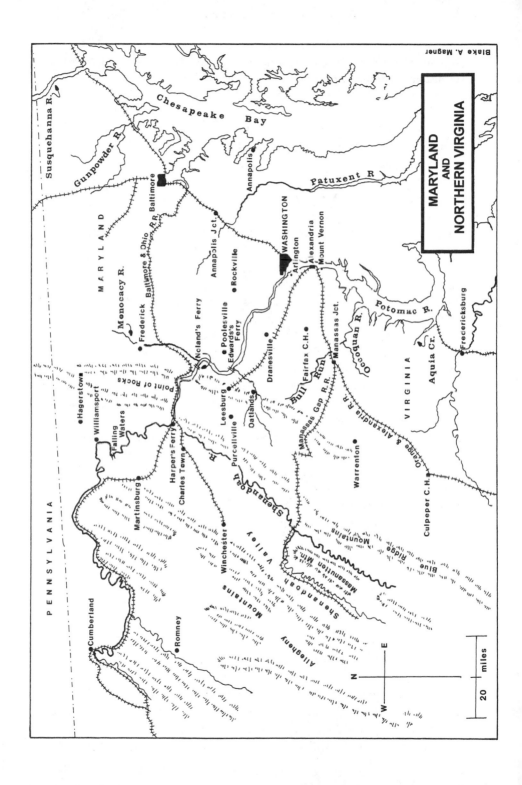

Blake A. Magner

MARYLAND
AND
NORTHERN VIRGINIA

Chesapeake Bay

Susquehanna R.

Gunpowder R.

MARYLAND

Monocacy R.

Baltimore & Ohio R.R. Baltimore

Frederick

Annapolis

Patuxent R

Annapolis Jct.

Rockville

WASHINGTON

Arlington

Alexandria

Mount Vernon

Noland's Ferry

Poolesville

Edwards's Ferry

Dranesville

Fairfax C.H.

Manassas Jct.

Occoquan R.

Potomac R.

VIRGINIA

Fredericksburg

Aquia Cr.

Point of Rocks

Hagerstown

Williamsport

Falling Waters

Leesburg

Oatlands

Purcellville

Bull Run

Manassas Gap R.R.

Orange & Alexandria R.R.

Warrenton

Culpeper C.H.

Harpers Ferry

Charles Town

Martinsburg

Winchester

Shenandoah R.

Shenandoah Valley

Blue Ridge Mountains

Massanutten Mtn.

PENNSYLVANIA

Cumberland

Romney

Alleghany Mountains

N
E
W
S

20 miles

had been filtering into Virginia from South Carolina and elsewhere, and on May 10 a telegram reached Richmond from Montgomery, giving Lee temporary command over those forces. For the moment he kept the out-of-state Confederate troops near the capital and funneled thousands of Virginia volunteers to central locations along the interior rail line, where they could be trained, equipped, and shipped to vulnerable points on the state's borders. When Lynchburg filled with troops he directed the surplus to Culpeper Court House. Some of those at Culpeper he ordered on to Manassas Junction, where the Orange & Alexandria met the Manassas Gap Railroad. From there they might quickly reinforce either Alexandria or Harper's Ferry by rail, and in their encampment at Manassas Junction they would conveniently block the main highway and rail routes from Washington to Richmond.[6]

To most people North and South, all of this looked enough like war, yet the official policy of both Virginia and the Confederacy decreed that hostilities would result only from aggression by the United States. That aggression seemed imminent on land, and it had already begun at sea in the form of the rudimentary blockade, but it was not until May 6 — a few days after the failure of Rudolf Schleiden's one-man intervention effort — that the Confederate Congress and president finally acknowledged the existence of a state of war. A week later news of this congressional resolution had evidently not spread to the new national border, for one of Colonel Terrett's company commanders fumed indignantly when marksmen on the Maryland shore fired at his mounted pickets near the Georgetown aqueduct of the Chesapeake & Ohio Canal. The cavalry captain collected enough sabers, carbines, and revolvers to arm a delegation of five troopers, and with that escort he stomped across the aqueduct to demand an explanation from the corporal of the guard on the Georgetown side. The Union corporal explained that his men had not fired at anyone, and he allowed the captain to send a message to the mayor — who apologized, promised to punish the malefactors if he could find them, and said he would see to it that the troops in Georgetown were relieved of their long-range ammunition. Thus satisfied, the Virginia captain and his retinue strode back into the Confederate States of America and resumed their posts.[7]

This was all play-acting, and few doubted that there would have to be a bloody fight somewhere before the federal government resigned itself to the loss of nearly half its territory. Shooting started soon enough. A Union vessel replied to warning rounds fired when it entered the York River on May 7, launching a brief exchange of harmless shells with a land battery of Virginia artillerymen just below Yorktown. On May 10, in faraway St. Louis, a riot ensued when U.S. Regulars and Unionist volunteers arrested

hundreds of Missouri militiamen on the grounds that they harbored secessionist intentions — despite the Stars and Stripes flying from their
flagpole. Firing erupted, a score or so of people died (most of them civilians), and as usual each side claimed that the other had fired first. Another confrontation between St. Louis citizens and Unionist volunteers
the next day led to the deaths of several more civilians.[8]

Ben Butler, the political general from Massachusetts, risked another
riot in Baltimore on May 12 when he put most of the 6th Massachusetts,
half of a New York regiment, and two field guns aboard railroad cars and
headed them all for Baltimore. For him it constituted a well-calculated
gamble unimpeded by qualms about bloodshed. If there were any resistance, he intended to simply crush it, but he knew that the city lay defenseless against him. Officials there had succeeded in isolating their city,
but that isolation had begun to pinch: food and coal had grown scarce,
and business had begun to suffer from pressures that no one had anticipated. A week after the burning of the bridges, for instance, one private
school lost more than a third of its boarding students: fearing that transportation would be severed permanently, parents took the first opportunity to bring their children home. With no prospects of further unrest by
the first week in May, the mayor and the police commissioners had instructed "Colonel" Isaac Trimble to disband his assorted companies, announcing that it was time for Baltimore to return to normal.[9]

News of the city's voluntary disarmament had convinced Ben Butler he
could pull off his small-scale invasion. In a bombastic letter to the colonel
of the 6th Massachusetts he promised that if Baltimore did not "ignominiously surrender" he would join the colonel at the head of his regiment
and "march over" the city. Butler unloaded his troops at one of the infamous depots of the April 19 affair and marched them right up Federal
Hill, overlooking the harbor, lodging them in an assortment of public and
private buildings while he took more comfortable lodgings at the Gilmor
House. He arrested Ross Winans, the city's wealthiest citizen, as a disloyal
person, planning to imprison him in Fort McHenry, of "Star-Spangled
Banner" fame. He issued a proclamation prohibiting display of the flag of
any seceded state, or of anything remotely reminiscent of a Confederate
flag, and he declared all assemblages of citizens illegal save for the police
and those military companies he recognized as loyal militia. As though
trying to bait Baltimore into another violent demonstration, Butler ordered a platoon of two dozen infantry into the city to demand a store of
municipally owned weapons, and that detachment returned safely largely
because the chief of police cooperated, keeping a mob of indignant citizens at bay with a cordon of officers. All of this Butler did without orders
and without warning. Winfield Scott scolded him for the rashness of even

entering Baltimore, considering it "a God-send" that he had not set that tinderbox ablaze again, and he immediately arranged Butler's removal to a less delicate command.[10]

Scott intended the transfer as a punitive gesture, but Butler came out the winner with a promotion to major general, for his credentials as a prominent Democrat made his support indispensable to Lincoln. Scott had relieved him for reckless disregard of the chain of command, however — not for his disregard of either public safety or the constitutional rights of Baltimore citizens. What mattered to the government then was the military situation, and Butler's unauthorized sally demonstrated that Baltimore's secessionist element lacked the means of resistance, so the troops remained on Federal Hill. Maryland's position north of the Potomac and the conservatism of its legislature had apparently discouraged the state's less-committed secessionists, while the more determined of them had struck for Virginia to take up arms. The departure of those zealous advocates of states' rights only weakened Maryland's secession faction further. The supposedly disloyal police commissioners even dismissed some officers for insubordination when they refused to enforce Butler's edict against secession flags.[11]

Butler's more-benign successor, George Cadwalader, also ruled with a blind eye to the Bill of Rights. Within days, Cadwalader invoked the authority to suspend habeas corpus that Lincoln had secretly arrogated to himself. Lincoln had issued a formal proclamation suspending the writ in the faraway Florida Keys on May 10, but that order had received no more publicity than had his informal authority to suspend it between Philadelphia and Washington. The first public notice of military repression in Maryland came after General Cadwalader arrested a Baltimore County militia lieutenant named John Merryman. Based on the vague claims of a couple of Pennsylvania officers that Merryman had "uttered and advanced secession doctrines," Cadwalader locked him up and refused to turn him over to civil authorities.[12]

Union soldiers surrounded Hayfields, Merryman's spacious plantation home north and west of Cockeysville, at two o'clock on the morning of May 25. Rousing him, his wife, and his large brood of children, they transported him to Baltimore and confined him in Fort McHenry. Though a relatively young man, Merryman had achieved considerable prominence in his community and in the state: he had served as president of the Maryland State Agricultural Society for several years. As a substantial citizen, he sought substantial legal assistance. Chief Justice Roger Brooke Taney of the U.S. Supreme Court, who was both a Marylander and a federal district judge in that circuit, issued a writ of habeas corpus directing

Cadwalader to produce Merryman and explain the grounds for his detention. Cadwalader refused, revealing that President Lincoln had given him authority to suspend citizens' rights to habeas corpus. Noting "the present trying and painful position in which our country is placed," Cadwalader suggested to Taney that one loyal government official should not interfere with another "by reason of any unnecessary want of confidence in each other. . . ."[13]

A pervasive and unnecessary want of confidence seemed to be precisely the problem, however, and especially in eastern Maryland. Baltimore and Annapolis correspondents of New York newspapers reported rumors of suspected spies as though the suspects had already been condemned, and they portrayed rampant disloyalty among public officials. It was such suspicion that had led Lincoln to arbitrarily remove a basic constitutional right, and it was suspicion that had sent John Merryman to an American bastille, at a time when Maryland's relative calm cast grave doubt on the necessity of those extreme measures. From the prestige of his position as chief justice, Taney replied that the president had issued no formal declaration of the suspension, and that any such proclamation would have required a previous vote of Congress. He noted that Thomas Jefferson had sought congressional authority to suspend habeas corpus to contain the conspiracy led by Aaron Burr, and that at that time no one, including Jefferson, felt that the presidency included such unilateral power. Taney concluded that the exclusive authority of Congress on that subject was not even open to question.[14]

At eighty-four, Roger Taney was a decade older than the Constitution itself, and he held to the beliefs of a bygone era. He had supported Andrew Jackson so tenaciously that Jackson had appointed him to succeed John Marshall as chief justice, but Taney seemed not to share Jackson's authoritarian devotion to the preservation of the federal union. Although evidently not a secessionist himself, he clearly considered the maintenance of civil liberties more important than the retention of individual states, especially by force, and his argument on the legal technicality seemed perfectly sound. Lincoln had not bothered to consult with his attorney general before assuming authority to suspend the writ, but Taney's challenge sent the president looking for that cabinet officer.

Instead of instructing Attorney General Edward Bates to examine the question and offer his unbiased opinion, Lincoln told him specifically "to present the argument for the suspension of the Habeas Corpus." Somewhat disingenuously, Lincoln then promised Congress, when it finally reassembled, that Bates would issue an "opinion" on the subject. On the president's direct instructions, Bates composed a specious defense contending that Lincoln had the right to disregard the U.S. Constitution precisely because he had taken an oath to "preserve, protect, and defend" that document. Bates mentioned that the Constitution refers only once to the suspension of habeas corpus, but he conspicuously overlooked the location of the single reference within the article enumerating the duties of Congress; instead he insinuated, without citing any authority, that the executive branch shared that power. After so awkwardly evading the legal impediment, he then confronted the complaint that the power to suspend so basic a right posed a dangerous potential for abuse. He illustrated the partisan nature of his brief when he questioned why the potential for abuse would be any less in the hands of the judicial or legislative branches of government than in the hands of the executive.[15]

In arguing that it would be no more dangerous for a single head of state to exercise the power to suspend habeas corpus than to vest this power in the collective representatives of the people, Bates demonstrated an inability or a refusal to recognize the basic nature of dictatorship. As unlikely as it was that so flagrant a flaw could have escaped Lincoln's lawyer, this was the reasoning he offered.

Regardless of legal propriety, the government was able to keep John Merryman as a political prisoner because it could level enough bayonets to defy the law. That put Maryland's constitutional proponents in an impossible position. If they aired their objections through petitions or editorials, their petitions would be ignored and their more critical newspapers would be suppressed for "aiding and abetting the rebellion." If they rose up in vocal public protest, they would probably be arrested or fired upon as a rebellious mob, and the government would use their demonstration as evidence that the constitutional restrictions were warranted. If they did nothing, the government would assume that the populace accepted such presidential usurpation. The very restrictions they might have wished to protest left them no effective means for that protest, and the resulting paucity of public outcry encouraged Lincoln to more frequent suspensions.

Merryman finally emerged from Fort McHenry in July, on bond, and after many months the government dropped its case against him. He remained at home throughout the war, serving in neither the Confederate nor the Union armies. That was the case with thousands of border-state citizens who, on the one hand, remained devoted to the U.S. Constitution but, on the other hand, recognized the right of secession for those who chose to exercise it through the democratic process. Taney immortalized the Cockeysville planter with his denunciatory brief, *Ex parte Merryman*, which soon earned fame as a primary citation for later complaints about executive abuse and usurpation of authority. In 1864 the grateful citizen tried to reciprocate, and a few weeks after Taney's death Merryman's sixth son came into the world as Roger Brooke Taney Merryman.[16]

Amid the debate about implied powers and the intent of the framers of the Constitution, no one remembered to conduct an objective examination of whether Merryman was actually guilty of any crime. He did belong to the militia, and like many other militiamen he appears to have turned out to confront what he considered the illegal transgressions of federal agents. Witnesses testified that Merryman personally ignited the bridge over the Little Gunpowder River, but if so he did it under the official authority of the governor, who was his commander-in-chief. He may also have fulminated against Lincoln's coercion of the Confederacy, or against the imposition of martial law in his home state, but the government seemed unable to provide conclusive evidence that he had done anything more than exercise his First Amendment right to disparage government policy.[17] Many dissenting citizens landed in prison for weeks or months as the administration and the army grew more brazen in the suspension of civil liberties. Abridging the rights of free speech and assembly aided the federal government in reaching still further beyond its constitutional authority in order to prosecute the war. Without that repression, later war measures, like the imposition of direct federal conscription for military service, might not have survived public opposition to become fixtures contradictory to a free society.

Suspending habeas corpus did the administration no perceptible good in Maryland, and it made enemies of important citizens who had steadfastly resisted secession. Lincoln responded to the public outcry with more severe repression, rather than less, and with more audacious examples of it. Soon he would grow sufficiently confident to wield unilateral authority and military might against the most fundamental elements of democracy, imprisoning duly elected representatives of the people, arresting opposition candidates, and "monitoring" elections with soldiers who refused dissident voters access to the polls. It became evident that he would suspend not only habeas corpus but the entire democratic process in order to preserve federal authority, and that only made his job more difficult. In contrast to Maryland, he applied no excessive measures in Kentucky, where secessionists also represented a vocal minority, and Kentucky remained neutral for months; when it did throw its weight into the fray, it came in on the side of Lincoln. The Baltimore riot notwithstanding, Maryland might have done the same without the arbitrary suspension of constitutional rights, and even then the legislature rejected secession. The tardy and redundant exercise of martial law initiated a cycle of increasing resentment and repression that Lincoln could have avoided by permitting the expression of displeasure in a province he had all but won.

His maladroit performance there produced no more obvious effect than the outrage of tens of thousands of Marylanders, including the man who would eventually murder him.

Lincoln's uncharacteristically clumsy response is better explained by psychological impulse than by political imperative. The survival of Washington City as the seat of national authority depended on Maryland, for the secession of that state would have forced either a siege or a retreat of the federal government. Washington symbolized everything the president stood for, including the continuation of the Union itself: with the specter of insurgent mobs at his back and Confederate banners across the river, he lived in an atmosphere of exaggerated vulnerability that produced excessive reactions.

Lincoln's militia demand had flung a gauntlet at the feet of all Virginians, large numbers of whom would have preferred to remain in the Union if not asked to take up arms against the seceded states. The Virginia convention had voted only tentatively to secede, pending ratification by the public at large, but the disdain that Lincoln's mobilization showed for states' rights had so infuriated Old Dominion citizens that they voted overwhelmingly to leave the Union. The referendum left no doubt of the popular will: only in some of the westernmost counties did Union sentiment prevail. Secession won by lopsided margins in the interior counties, and particularly in Southside Virginia, where some counties voted unanimously to leave the Union. Even in border regions like Loudoun County, where heavy concentrations of Quakers, loyal Germans, and conservative Whigs formed a substantial Unionist stronghold, secessionists outnumbered the Union faction better than two to one. The implied threat of invasion by federal troops decided the question for Clinton Hatcher, the only child of an older couple who farmed a place near Purcellville. This towering young man had come home from college in the District of Columbia at the news of Lincoln's militia proclamation, and within a month his correspondence had assumed a relentlessly hostile tone. On May 23 he participated in his first election, voting in favor of the secession ordinance. Then, after persuading his mother to withdraw her objections, he backed up that vote by signing the roll of a local rifle company. Scores of his neighbors had already enlisted; they did their voting in military encampments around the county.[18]

So certain had Virginia's ratification seemed that the various precinct scrutineers had not even certified their district ballot totals before Lincoln directed his military advisors to seize a sizable foothold on the opposite bank of the Potomac. Winfield Scott and his old friend, Joseph K. F. Mansfield (whose promotion to brigadier general Scott had just arranged), devised a plan to seize a long strip of the Virginia shore by a sudden, simultaneous dash from three different points. Acutely conscious of the Southern sympathizers lurking among district residents, they exercised a secrecy in their arrangements that later led to confusion among some of the principal participants. Mansfield assembled eleven three-month regiments of militia and volunteers, added a battery of Regular artillery and a couple of companies of cavalry, and requested a steam sloop and some transports from the Washington Navy Yard. After midnight on May 23 all the troops formed at the riverside: three regiments at the Cheapeake & Ohio Canal aqueduct at Georgetown and seven at the so-called Long Bridge, which was really two tandem bridges for rail and wheeled traffic stretching a full mile across the Potomac from the end of Fourteenth Street. The last infantry regiment, Ellsworth's Fire Zouaves, boarded the navy steamers at Giesboro Point with orders to land at the Alexandria waterfront.[19]

General Mansfield remained at the Washington end of the Long Bridge. The three-month men would march under the nominal direction of Charles Sandford, one of those inflated militia generals, but the two columns crossing on the Long Bridge and the aqueduct would proceed, respectively, with a colonel and a captain of the Regular Army staff who exercised actual command. Another Regular led a third column across the river: Colonel Stone had once again culled his District of Columbia battalions for volunteers willing to serve outside the district, and just after midnight he trotted a mounted squadron of them across the river on the Chain Bridge, well upstream of Georgetown. Galloping cross-country, he took the Virginia end of the Long Bridge from its guards, who might have set fire to it if they had heard the rumble of so many hooves from the Washington side of the bridge. This was the most delicate part of the plan, on which everything else depended, and in undertaking it Stone earned the honor of commanding the first troops ever to invade Confederate territory. Later he felt quite proud of that distinction, but at the time he made no reference to the precedent, perhaps because his political perspective did not yet allow him to acknowledge such a thing as Confederate territory.[20]

At 2:00 AM the infantry stepped off. Colonel Stone sent some of his mounted volunteers ranging a mile ahead to clear the roads and warn of any organized resistance, but none materialized. Meanwhile, he waited at the head of the Long Bridge and greeted the main column as it debouched onto what Southern newspaper editors so persistently called the "Sacred Soil" of Virginia. Climbing out of the marshy river bottom in bright, eerie moonlight, the column divided: one regiment turned southwest on the Columbia Turnpike, toward their comrades who were crossing at the aqueduct, while the rest continued southeast, along the railroad that led to Alexandria. They moved so quietly that the residents of the nearest houses slumbered right through the invasion. The main body stopped at Four Mile Creek, about two miles short of the city, to coordinate the advance with a signal to Ellsworth's steamers.[21]

The three regiments that traversed the aqueduct split into three detachments: one regiment stopped to fortify the Virginia end of the aqueduct, while two others pressed on to Ball's Crossroads. The staff captain leading that wing advanced two companies of New Yorkers from there to the Loudoun & Hampshire Railroad, four miles from the aqueduct. This column included a few dozen pioneers drafted from Brooklyn's Zouave regiment, the 14th New York State Militia, who wore garish scarlet pantaloons and matching bands around their caps. Before the morning train came through, these dudes pulled off their embroidered jackets and set to work to stop it, burning a couple of bridges and tearing up some track. When the sun rose Major General Sandford, of the New York Militia, rode around looking at what the staff captain had accomplished, nodding approvingly and pretending to be in charge. On his way to another such perfunctory mission with the other column, Sandford stopped by the mansion called Arlington — the home of Robert E. Lee — and deemed it a worthy location for his headquarters. The grounds of the estate rolled gently away in the open land between the two invading columns.[22]

Less than seventy-two hours before, that same General Lee had assigned Milledge Bonham to the department that encompassed Alexandria and Lee's own plantation. Bonham had recently held the rank of major general as Lee's counterpart in South Carolina, but now he was just a brigadier general in the Confederate States Provisional Army, with two regiments of South Carolina troops. Bonham posted himself at Manassas Junction, taking command of all the Virginia volunteers there, and Colonel Terrett remained at Alexandria with his disparate local garrison. Terrett smelled something in the wind by one thirty in the morning, when Captain Dulany Ball raced into town: Ball, a schoolteacher who was just beginning his thirtieth day as commander of a cavalry company, brought news from an observer who had watched Stone's troopers cross the Chain Bridge. Terrett gathered his men, though he knew not against what.[23]

While the main columns tramped across the Long Bridge and the aqueduct, Colonel Ellsworth's Fire Zouaves boarded their steamers and set off for Alexandria. With them went the *Pawnee*, with its battery of nine-inch guns, and as the troop transports hove in sight of the waterfront the commander of the *Pawnee* endured an irresistible twinge of service rivalry. Although he, too, had been sworn to secrecy and knew that the operation depended on surprise, he landed an officer on the wharf to demand the surrender of the city in the name of the U.S. Navy. He claimed that he did so "about daylight," to avoid a bombardment that would have jeopardized the women and children he saw darting frantically about the streets, but the officer he landed received his orders at 4:20 AM, before the first glimmer of dawn.[24]

Lieutenant Reigart B. Lowry strode up from the dock and asked for the local commander. It took only a few minutes to find him, and Terrett came out to meet Lowry in the street. The lieutenant evidently recognized him as the erstwhile captain of U.S. Marines: when Terrett said he would not surrender, Lowry reminded him that "no one knows better than yourself what would be the result" if the *Pawnee* opened fire with so many people about. Terrett offered no hint of bravado, but he had participated in Scott's campaign to Mexico City, and doubtless witnessed the mass execution of American deserters there, so he probably shared Algernon Taylor's fear of capture. He offered instead to evacuate the city, estimating that he could be out of town by 8:00 AM. Lowry lacked authority to grant a reprieve such as that, more than three hours long, but he urged Terrett to make haste, supposing that if the Confederates did not put up a fight the national forces would not fire first.[25]

Lowry jogged back to the *Pawnee*, passing little squads and companies of armed and half-armed Virginia militiamen who had already taken up a line of march out of town. He reached the waterfront again just as Terrett's pickets snapped a couple of rounds at the approaching troop transports. Ellsworth's Zouaves returned a rattling fire, sending the pickets flying back to join their retreating comrades while the Zouaves poured onto the wharf. Lowry recognized Colonel Ellsworth and told him how things stood. Ellsworth promised not to fire on anyone, but he quickly formed his regiment in the street with banners unfurled. Lowry later familiarized Ellsworth with important locations like the telegraph office, and when Lowry joined a detail of sailors and Marines from the *Pawnee* Ellsworth advanced a portion of his men up King Street from the wharf.[26]

Like the commander of the *Pawnee*, Ellsworth itched to rush in and grab the glory. His transports had seen the signal of the main land force while they steamed downriver, and according to the plans the ships should have slowed down to wait for that infantry, but instead they had steamed impetuously toward the docks. Now Ellsworth jumped the gun again. At the corner of Pitt and King Street he found a three-and-a-half-story brick hotel with a rambling wooden addition in the rear. The Marshall House, a favorite stopping place for weary travelers, advertised its "true Southern style" of hospitality, and from an oversized flagpole on its roof flew the Stars and Bars of the Confederacy. In the grey light of the coming dawn Ellsworth spotted it. There fluttered the very flag that had so galled Washington's Unionists for the past five weeks, and at sight of it Ellsworth forgot all his orders and promises to respect private property. Followed closely by a reporter from the *New York Tribune,* he collected several officers and noncommissioned officers, and with that escort he burst into the hotel. He encountered a citizen clad in pants and under-shirt and asked him about the flag, but the man professed ignorance of it, explaining that he was only a boarder in the hotel. Ellsworth — perform-ing gallantly for the newspaperman at his heels — sprinted up the stairs. He posted guards at each floor, then found his own way out on the roof, where he cut down the flag with a borrowed knife and started back down. As he descended the stairway he folded the big banner, probably thinking how pleased his White House patron would be to receive it.[27]

The incursion had wakened a number of hotel guests, who kept to their rooms, but in the dim morning light of the third-floor landing an armed civilian confronted the intruders. He was a clean-shaven man of thirty-eight, with a thick shock of black hair, and he had pulled his suspenders over his nightshirt in obvious haste. At least one of Ellsworth's compan-ions thought this was the same timid fellow who had earlier identified himself as a boarder, but that man would not have been able to slip past the guards with his weapon. Besides, there was nothing timid about this man. He was James W. Jackson, leaseholder of the Marshall House. Well known in Alexandria as an ardent secessionist, he had spent the previous night celebrating Virginia's formal withdrawal from the Union, and he had slept through the commotion in his second-floor bedroom until a servant awakened him with a warning about all the "Lincoln men" in the house. Unlike the citizen-soldiers who were abandoning their town in such haste, Jackson had the courage to single-handedly face down a squad of armed men in his home, even with an entire regiment of their comrades within hailing distance.[28]

The proprietor did not posture for a moment, nor did he offer any boasting threats: without a word he leveled his shotgun at Ellsworth's midsection and pulled the trigger. As the buckshot tore through him, the little colonel slammed into the wall; then his body plummeted face-first to the landing. The corporal ahead of him parried the muzzle of the shotgun and pointed his Sharp's rifle at Jackson's face, blasting a bullet through the bridge of his nose and out the back of his head. For a pointless and perhaps vengeful coup de grâce, the corporal stood over the body and thrust his sword bayonet through the Virginian's torso, driving the tip deep into the floor. The incensed Yankees cared tenderly for Ellsworth's body, but they left Jackson's corpse pinned to the floor until nearly noon, despite the keening of his widow and three young daughters.[29]

The killings at the Marshall House threw the Zouave regiment into sudden confusion, but by then the troops from Four Mile Creek had reached the outskirts of town, coming down Washington Street with a brilliant sunrise glaring before them. Thanks to Ellsworth's deadly diversion and to the premature arrival of the *Pawnee,* Colonel Terrett managed to escape with most of his command. He marched his infantry out Duke Street, loading them on trains of the Orange & Alexandria that he had stopped outside of town. As the troops hurried past the depot to the waiting cars, Captain Ball turned with his cavalry troop toward King Street, to stop at his own quarters. At their parting Terrett told Ball to follow his train and report on any pursuit, but Ball lingered injudiciously. The leading Union regiment on Washington Street, the 1st Michigan, caught Ball and his cavalry troop just as they prepared to leave. The last of the horsemen had their toes in the stirrup, ready to swing into the saddle, when Colonel Orlando Bolivar Willcox bade his Regular artillerymen to unlimber a field piece and called on the Confederates to surrender. Ball gave up meekly enough, though later he complained about a violation of their "truce" with the naval commander. Willcox added insult to injury by locking the would-be cavaliers in Alexandria's slave pen.[30]

Thus ended Alexandria's five-week incarnation as a Confederate city. So sudden a change dazed the more rebellious of the residents, for whom the Confederacy might as well have collapsed altogether. Even Captain Ball took the oath of allegiance to the United States to get out of the slave pen: he had no complaint with the U.S. Constitution, after all, but only with the Republican president who seemed so scornful of it. This justification might have satisfied most of Ball's neighbors before April 15, but in the intervening weeks of furious ferment Southern nationalism had come to demand nothing less than utter contempt for the old country. Ball's more resolute comrades took his defection as a sign that he had harbored sympathy for the Union all along, and that he had perhaps delivered his cavalry troop to the enemy as his part in a conspiracy. He tried to renounce the oath afterward, and labored mightily to regain the confidence of his countrymen.[31]

As the senior surviving officer in the city Colonel Willcox assumed command, resuming old friendships among citizens he had known from an earlier sojourn as an army lieutenant at Fort Washington. Many of his former acquaintances also took the oath so they could resume normal business. After a few days Colonel Stone took charge of Willcox's brigade and of Alexandria, securing the eastern end of a line of Union outposts that stretched from there to the Chain Bridge, occupying the first few square miles of insurgent territory. The objectionable banner had disappeared from Washington's horizon.[32]

Federal engineers soon constructed a bastion anchoring the defensive line on the Alexandria end, out between the Leesburg and the Little River turnpikes, and they called it Fort Ellsworth. Suddenly, that name turned up everywhere. In his final seconds of life Mr. Jackson had supplied the North with its first real martyr: a few soldiers had perished in riots and accidents here and there, but they had all been enlisted men whose incidental passing seemed to warrant no widespread public grieving. Ellsworth's death elevated him, at least temporarily, to an approximation of brevet sainthood. For a time now he would be nothing less than "the gallant Ellsworth," and his name provided the rallying cry that American troops appeared to require for war in the nineteenth century. His body lay in state for a day in the East Room of the White House before starting for home. Thousands passed through to view it, and General Scott sat nearby. As they solicited public sympathy, Ellsworth's eulogists took pains to vilify the assassin who had dared to defend his home, painting the late Mr. Jackson as a representative serpent in a demon Confederacy.[33]

"Thus the tragedy commences," noted a Southern-leaning Washington resident who would supply sons to both armies. "Where will it end?"[34] Eventually the conflict would supply a number of caskets for the East Room, and the last of them would be Lincoln's.

A few optimistic souls had held out hope for a peaceful resolution of the differences between North and South, but with the seizure of Alexandria and a small strip of Fairfax County, that door slammed shut in abrupt finality. The invasion that Confederates had anticipated had now come to pass, confirming what most Southerners suspected all along about Northern aggression, and the violation of Mr. Jackson's home bespoke a medieval disregard for individual rights. If any in Virginia doubted Northern savagery, they had only to read New York newspapers published at the time of Colonel Ellsworth's funeral, which called for an army of street toughs to subjugate the South in a "vindictive, fierce, bloody and merciless" campaign. New York City bid farewell to its celebrated soldier on Sunday, May 26, with a sea of lugubrious mourners standing grimly by. The corporal who had dispatched the hotelkeeper sat on the hearse, still carrying the rifle and the bloody bayonet with which he had earned his footnote in history, and then the body went to Saratoga County for interment.[35] The nationalistic flavor of the funeral betrayed its orchestration as the opening of another recruiting drive. As far away as the Midwest Colonel Ellsworth's death rejuvenated martial enthusiasm, bringing enough men into the camps to fill companies that even the prospective captains had given up any hope of completing. Volunteer organizations here and there incorporated the dead drillmaster's name in the informal titles they adopted, and more than a thousand New Yorkers rallied under the banner of the People's Ellsworth Regiment.[36]

Virginia newspapers undertook less fruitful efforts to canonize Mr. Jackson, the first victim of the vandal horde of that "monstrous tyrant" in Washington, who seemed "prepared to bathe this whole land in blood, in the vain attempt to subjugate a free and independent people." Neighbors brought the body of "the first martyr in the cause of Southern independence" back to Fairfax County, where they buried it in the family plot at the old plantation — which now belonged to an absent Unionist. There flourished the brief but inevitable spasm of public sympathy, and admirers lobbied for popular subscriptions to raise a monument, support the fatherless family, and buy back the family farm for their benefit. None of those initiatives survived long.[37]

Having opened hostilities against Virginia on the hour of the state's official secession, Union forces launched a number of actions around the state. The earliest, most ambitious, and most dangerous came from the northwest, along the Ohio River. There a young major general named George McClellan had gathered an army of troops from Indiana, Ohio, and loyal Virginia — although many of those "Virginians" actually hailed from Ohio or Pennsylvania. Late on the same Sunday afternoon that Elmer Ellsworth's casket went into the grave, McClellan learned that Confederates near Grafton had started burning bridges of the Baltimore & Ohio Railroad. The next morning he directed four of his western regiments to converge on Grafton from Wheeling and Parkersburg, and those twin columns plunged deep into the Virginia mountains on railcars; McClellan phrased his orders as though he sent the Northern regiments merely to assist the nominal Virginians in quelling an unlawful gathering. The Confederate commander, Colonel George Porterfield, had wished to cut those tracks to forestall just such a rail-borne incursion, but Porterfield's force amounted to less than a regiment of intermixed cavalry and infantry companies: instead of fighting, he fled to a little village called Philippi, on the banks of the upper Tygart Valley River. Union troops three or four times his own number occupied Grafton by May 30, providing another little victory for the newspapers to amplify.[38]

The next blow issued from Ben Butler, on the same day that McClellan's troops first crossed the Ohio. In his new assignment as commandant of Fort Monroe, Butler sent a couple of regiments to establish a mainland base at Newport News. He had dispatched a reconnaissance near there on May 23, even as the inhabitants voted on the secession referendum, but in that uncertain political atmosphere the Confederates had again met the intruders with formal complaint instead of gunfire. The defenders initially set fire to a bridge that the Yankees needed, but on the assurances of the federal commander that he bore no hostile intent the outnumbered Virginians cordially aided their nominal enemies in dousing the fire. Like the Englishmen who had settled that same peninsula a quarter of a millennium before, Butler's troops took full advantage of the inhabitants' grudging acceptance of their passage, forcing a permanent lodgment from which they intended to take the field and subdue all Virginia.[39]

Then, two days later, came a naval assault on a Confederate battery protecting the railroad terminus where Aquia Creek spilled into the Potomac. At first a couple of small steamers swung in to throw a salvo at the gunners, testing their range and caliber. The land battery responded with two or three rounds per gun and the vessels pulled away. On the first of June they came back with the bigger *Pawnee,* and the three ships lobbed shells at the battery for four hours from a range of more than a mile. Reports of two troop transports behind those federal warships alarmed the colonel commanding at nearby Fredericksburg, who could muster only a single Tennessee regiment and a few half-organized companies of Virginia volunteers. He logically supposed that Fredericksburg was to be the next Alexandria and that he was about to be overrun, but in the afternoon the barrage ended and the Union steamers again pulled off.[40]

As though to emphasize the unpleasantness attending the Alexandria operation, McClellan exultantly reported that the capture of Grafton did not cost a single life. Newport News likewise fell without violence, and the hundreds of rounds exchanged at Aquia Creek shed no more than the few drops of blood that a shell splinter drained from the hand of a Virginia artilleryman. The fighting had begun, though, and when opposing troops encountered each other thereafter there would be no filing of officious objections.

Before midnight on May 31 a company of the 2nd U.S. Cavalry left the Union lines near Arlington to reconnoiter the Confederate outposts. The scouts picked their way so cautiously that they did not approach Fairfax Court House, fifteen miles away, until about 3:00 AM on June 1, but on the outskirts of town they found their first enemy. They swept up five pickets on the periphery and then galloped into the town — firing left and right at sharpshooters they thought occupied the courthouse, the church, and the hotel before disappearing out the other end of the village. The defense of Fairfax Court House fell to Lieutenant Colonel Richard Ewell, who had been a captain of U.S. cavalry less than a month previously, and Ewell called out every armed man at his disposal. Only one company of riflemen from Warrenton stood near: with the help of a former Virginia governor who had been sleeping in the hotel, Ewell put them in line across the road after the federal horsemen passed by. Soon the cavalrymen returned and again tried to charge through, but a volley from the Confederates sent them reeling back. They rallied and gave it another attempt, but revolvers and sabers failed to dislodge the Virginians. Ultimately the Yankees broke cross-lots and escaped north of town, leaving a number of dead horses and abandoned weapons, including the sword of an officer who had been shot in the foot. The only armed cavalry that Ewell could raise came from too far away to catch the marauders. Among the defenders the captain of the infantry company lay dead, Colonel Ewell nursed a pistol wound in the shoulder, and one of the Warrenton riflemen had been shot in the chest. Each commander reported himself outnumbered by the other, though each had fielded about fifty men. Relying on the perjured testimony of a Virginia clergyman and a Union skulker (who claimed to have been momentarily a prisoner), each also greatly exaggerated the casualties he inflicted on his opponent, but here, at last, had flared a real skirmish.[41]

A more serious confrontation came two days later, in western Virginia, when parts of three Union regiments marched all day and through a pitch-black night in a vicious storm to descend on the Confederate encampment at Philippi. For all the expectation that the enemy would come down from Grafton to attack him, the patrician Porterfield had failed to post guards in the torrent. No one in Philippi knew of the encroaching danger until Union artillery opened on them just before dawn. Fewer than eight hundred Virginians could have fallen in to face twice their numbers if they had had a little warning, but even then they lacked enough ammunition for much of a fight. As it was they fled in some haste, leaving behind a handful of killed and wounded. The only noteworthy casualty on the Union side came when Benjamin Kelley, the fifty-four-year-old colonel in charge of the assault, rushed into close combat: a Confederate officer dropped him at pistol range with a bullet in the lung. For a time it seemed that Kelley would die, but he enjoyed his reputation as the winner of the war's first land battle for another thirty years, and before long he became a general. Colonel Porterfield soon retired to civil life, and bore the shame of his failure for more than half a century.[42]

On either side the tidy victory at Philippi drew disproportionate attention from a nervous public. In the South, where so many imagined their defenders endowed with a natural military superiority, the humiliating defeat brought momentary shock and immediate faultfinding. For a Northern population hungry to read of progress against Southern traitors, the reduced scope of the confrontation meant little; all that mattered was that the enemy had fled precipitously before national troops. The "Philippi Races," as an Ohio newspaperman dubbed the battle, seemed to remove the fear that an initial Confederate success in the mountains might influence the allegiance of the undecided population there. The euphoria of that triumph lasted precisely one week.[43]

Ben Butler administered his own little kingdom at Hampton Roads, earning the enmity of all his subordinates — volunteer and Regular, army and navy. Fort Monroe, where he commanded several thousand Union troops, sat on the sand spit known as Old Point Comfort, at the extreme tip of the peninsula between the James and the York rivers. Within a few months operations here would make that marshy strip of land famous as *the* peninsula, as though no other peninsula existed. In June of 1861, though, it was just three hundred square miles of alluvial plain, swamps, and serpentine rivers, with little apparent significance to anyone but historians. There English settlers had carved out their first successful community on the new continent; there colonists had established the first legislature; there George Washington had trapped a British army at Yorktown and won his country's independence.

At first Butler had resisted his reassignment from Baltimore to the far reaches of the Virginia Tidewater, but with his penchant for insubordinate, authoritarian behavior, he soon found the isolation of Fort Monroe inviting. The place afforded him an arena for the exercise of his will, as in the matter of runaway slaves. For fear of antagonizing Southerners with wavering loyalties, President Lincoln avoided any interference with slavery as he waged war against secession, but Butler almost immediately defied him by liberating the slaves of rebellious Virginians. Employing his aptitude for argumentation, he excused himself with the imaginative pleading that slaves who participated in the construction of enemy fortifications became contraband of war, which served both political and military purposes remarkably well.[44]

Less fortunately for the Union cause, Butler also used his new post as a theater for experimenting with his dubious talents as a military tactician. Colonel John Bankhead Magruder commanded Confederate forces in the area, and when Butler occupied Hampton and Newport News, Magruder withdrew about ten miles up the peninsula's main road, building an earthwork on the north side of a substantial stream at a place called Big Bethel Church. He manned the fort with the 1st North Carolina and some Virginia field artillery directed by Thomas Jefferson's grandson, leaving Colonel Daniel Harvey Hill of the North Carolina regiment in overall command. Butler composed a complicated plan for separate detachments to converge on the Big Bethel road from the east and west, meeting behind a suspected Confederate outpost at Little Bethel and capturing it before turning on the larger encampment at Big Bethel. The base map for the raid consisted of an amateur local chart more than four decades old, and all the marching was to take place in darkness, for Butler wanted to make a dawn attack such as the one that had worked so well at Philippi. To avoid a collision between friendly forces he issued secret watchwords, as well as orders for one of the commands to wear "something white" on their arms.[45]

Those precautions availed nothing, and a mistake of identity eliminated the plan's best chance for success. Crashing through the tangle of forest and vines, two columns of New Yorkers stumbled into each other in a spot where neither expected to find friends, and one contingent opened a fire that sent some of the other bolting instantly for the rear. Their officers rallied them, though, and retreated a short distance until the error could be sorted out. More than a score of men had been shot, and the noise had alerted the Confederates. Butler had given command of the combined detachments to Ebenezer Peirce, a brigadier of Massachusetts militia who, as it turned out, had never been mustered in and lacked any federal authority to command troops. Peirce decided to continue the operation anyway, and in this he was supported by Major Theodore Winthrop, who had come out with the 7th New York Militia in April and stayed on as a staff officer to General Butler.[46]

Not a Confederate remained at Little Bethel, although two civilians turned up with shotguns in their hands. The Yankees burned the settlement and took these men prisoner in the absence of other prizes, then proceeded to Big Bethel, where Colonel Hill waited behind the entrenchments with his regiment. Hill's call for help brought a few hundred Virginia infantrymen and another battalion of artillery, but even when they arrived his total force did not amount to more than fourteen hundred men. All or part of seven Union regiments, totaling well over three thousand men, came at them at about 9:00 AM under the direction of the unaccredited General Peirce. Peirce found the bridge over the river branch protected by an advanced entrenchment to the left of the road and by dense woods and the marshy bank of the branch on the right. With a complete absence of tactical imagination he simply divided his troops on either side of the road and motioned them forward, into the least vulnerable faces of the Confederate position.[47]

Uniforms on both sides varied wildly, with alternating grey, blue, and other combinations making identification difficult. Inside the fort, the Confederates had prepared for the fight by basting white strips of cloth around their caps, much as Butler had advised his troops to wear something white around their arms. Abram Duryée's 5th New York Volunteers needed nothing to distinguish them beyond their uniforms, which featured baggy scarlet pantaloons, gaiters, and a fez swathed in a turban. Less than a week before, a visitor to Fort Monroe from New York City had judged Duryée's "red-legged devils" one of the best regiments he had ever seen — and he felt the same about the 1st New York, from Troy — but that observer had not seen many regiments yet. Duryée's Zouaves led the assault with skirmishers across the whole front, and the Troy regiment went in right behind them.[48]

The Yankees had brought a few field pieces with them, and with these they began a bombardment of the Confederate works from alongside the road, a third of a mile away. The swamp east of the road prevented any progress by the Zouaves there. On the west side, fewer than three hundred Virginians and a single howitzer in the forward entrenchment held back their assailants until a flanking movement by the 3rd New York forced the Virginians to fall back to the main entrenchments. A primer wire had broken off in the howitzer vent, meanwhile, disabling it and forcing its crew to toss it into a ravine, but only the Zouave skirmishers took advantage of that retreat and scrambled into the abandoned fort. The Union flanking force recoiled almost literally in fear of its own shadow: one company of the 3rd New York lost its way in the woods, emerging in such a position that the New York colonel mistook it for a Confederate detachment that had outflanked him. At that he ordered everyone back where they had come from, allowing Magruder to retake his fort. A company of North Carolinians dashed in and drove out the Zouaves, after which Magruder sent the battalion of Virginians back in with a new howitzer.[49]

Federal skirmishers continued to annoy the fort from a cluster of little buildings around a blacksmith shop, but a party of North Carolinians volunteered to dash forth and try to burn them out. One of those volunteers took a bullet in the forehead, becoming the only Confederate fatality of the entire day, and his comrades failed in their mission, but artillery finally destroyed the blacksmith shop and the Union sharpshooters fled. That concluded the Union effort west of the road.[50]

On the east, Theodore Winthrop prodded a makeshift regiment of three-month men from Massachusetts and Vermont to slip around the Confederate left. They crossed the branch at a ford well downstream and reached a vulnerable point in the earthwork, but a few companies of North Carolinians discouraged them with a slow, accurate fire that killed three of the Yankees and wounded a few more. Major Winthrop climbed a fence and waggled his sword at the fort to coax his men onward, but the three-month men had not bargained for such danger, and those light casualties dissuaded them from moving any farther forward. A Carolina marksman completed their demoralization by putting a bullet through Winthrop's heart, and the major dropped from the fence with pointless finality. His life bought nothing but the admiration of his enemy, Colonel Hill, who remarked that Winthrop "was the only one of the enemy who exhibited even an approximation of courage during the whole day."[51]

The patchwork brigade of New York and New England troops outnumbered the Carolinians and Virginians three to one, but they displayed far less determination on the attack than the Confederates did in defense. Despite the reports of Union officers who attributed their repulse to the vigor and rapidity of the Confederate fire, the Southerners actually expended very little ammunition, taking deliberate aim and making every shot count from both infantry and artillery. One rifled field piece provided the most effective Confederate fire at the front of the earthwork, and shortly after the collapse of Winthrop's attack a round from that rifle killed the Regular Army lieutenant who directed the Union battery in the main road. General Peirce thereupon decided that he had been whipped and called everyone in. He started his troops back on the road to Hampton much more expeditiously than they had come, with Duryée's "exhausted" Zouaves nimbly leading the disorganized flight. They loaded their dead and wounded into the few wheeled vehicles they could commandeer in the vicinity, but a hundred Virginia cavalrymen pursued them at an accelerating pace and the Yankees threw away thousands of dollars worth of accoutrements to speed their escape. Eventually they discarded even the bodies of their dead, reaching safety only after burning the New Market Bridge, more than halfway back to Hampton.[52]

Big Bethel demonstrated the military advantage of the tactical defensive, as well as the superior morale that inspires troops protecting their homeland against an invader. It also proved the value of training and experience, for both Magruder and Hill had graduated from West Point and fought in the Mexican War, where between them they won five brevet promotions for conspicuous battlefield performance. None of the senior Union officers at Big Bethel had ever been under fire before, and none could claim any formal training, any more than the major general who had sent them out there. No more than five thousand men took part in the battle, which cost Butler fewer than eighty casualties against only seven for the Confederates — plus a dead mule. This was the bloodiest clash since the beginning of hostilities, though, and like Philippi the fight elicited inordinate measures of dejection and glee North and South. A friend and recent comrade of Theodore Winthrop from the 7th New York Militia sank into gloomy reflection on the major's untimely demise, in part because the friend himself had enlisted in another regiment and now faced a similar prospect. A New York lawyer who understood the depth of Big Bethel's effect on public sentiment ranted about "that miserably managed skirmish." News of the fight reached the armed camp at Washington with lurid details of extensive slaughter by the Confederate artillery, initially demoralizing the troops, and a government clerk lamented the loss of both battle and lives.[53]

In contrast to that distressed federal clerk, one of his counterparts in the Confederate War Department rejoiced over the victory more enthusiastically than the circumstances warranted. Similar elation penetrated the Confederacy at least as far as the Mississippi River, where the battle erased the momentary shame of Philippi and resurrected faith in the invulnerability of Southern arms. Edmund Ruffin, an elderly Virginia planter who doubted overblown reports on the extent of the Confederate victory, nevertheless conceded that it marked a significant accomplishment against superior forces, whether the enemy had lost thirty men or three hundred.[54]

At the same time, Ruffin acknowledged that the Yankees had gained some laurels of their own, particularly in the mountainous counties of western Virginia. They controlled the Baltimore & Ohio Railroad deep into the state, he noted, and the citizens in that region could not be depended on to repel them; instead, they abetted the invasion or at least stood by and allowed it to sweep around them. Worst of all, perhaps, the federal troops in those western counties were led by George McClellan — the officer whom Robert E. Lee was rumored to consider "the ablest of all the commanders under Scott."[55]

Considering the caliber of the men who did command troops under Scott in June of 1861, McClellan may well have been the best of the lot, and of all people Lee should have had a fair estimate of him, for they had served alongside each other in the Mexican War. McClellan had graduated from West Point just fifteen years before, serving with distinction in the Corps of Engineers and as a member of Winfield Scott's staff in Mexico. Like his West Point contemporary Charles Stone, McClellan undertook a tour of European armies, and he participated in the survey of western territory. Also like Stone, he resigned from the army after eleven years to accept more remunerative civilian employment, coming back into uniform only with the outbreak of war. At the age of thirty he had been a captain of cavalry; at thirty-four he wore the stars of a major general in the Regular Army, with no one to outrank him in the entire country except General Scott himself. With that extraordinary expression of official confidence McClellan would win a series of minor battles in his bailiwick, largely because he fielded more troops with better arms than did the Confederates there, and because he enjoyed greater support from the inhabitants. Incidental as his triumphs might be in a strategic sense, they glowed with the illusion of brilliance against the dismal defeats suffered by the commanders of other departments.[56]

Meteoric promotion likewise brought Irvin McDowell's name to millions of men's lips that volatile spring. After graduating with mediocre standing in the West Point class of 1838, Lieutenant McDowell stayed on at the military academy, teaching tactics to cadets like Stone and

McClellan. While those two went to Mexico City with Winfield Scott, McDowell served on the staff of John Wool, in the less-glamorous northern campaign. He had spent the better part of 1859 in Europe, observing the military practices of the old monarchies, and that experience lent him the illusion of relative sophistication in his profession, but in twenty-three years as an army officer McDowell had never held a field command. When the sectional crisis came to a head he occupied an office in the War Department as an assistant adjutant general. He had only risen to the pay grade of captain, although he exercised his duties under a brevet commission as major and was known by that honorary rank. It was he who had sworn in Colonel Stone's District of Columbia volunteers.[57]

McDowell had served so long as a staff administrator that he had developed the bureaucrat's acute instinct for self-preservation, but he also harbored enough ambition that fellow officers found him calculating and devious when he saw a chance for higher station. With as little opportunity for promotion as peacetime staff service offered, those unsavory qualities appear to have escaped detection, and in the spring of 1861 his superiors suddenly deemed him valuable to the country's cause. As an Ohio native without family or business connections in the Confederacy he posed no obvious risk of disloyalty, and his assignment with the adjutant general's office had brought him the acquaintance of all the senior officers of the army. Amid the Regular Army appointments that President Lincoln signed that May, Major McDowell vaulted from relative obscurity to accept a volunteer appointment as brigadier general. Then, just a few days later, he took command of the entire state of Virginia east of the Allegheny Mountains with the exception of a sixty-mile perimeter around Fort Monroe, which the War Department preserved for Ben Butler's temporary exile. The assignment encompassed all the territory in which the principal armies were expected to meet for a grand, decisive battle, and quite evidently the government intended to field McDowell as its champion.[58]

On the same day that McDowell drew his first military command, President Jefferson Davis quietly left his quarters in Montgomery, Alabama, for the long rail journey to Richmond, Virginia. There, at the behest of Southern congressmen and against the wishes of the president, would the Confederacy relocate its national capital. War Department business came to a standstill through early June, while clerks found office space and arranged furniture, and when Davis reached Richmond at 7:25 on the morning of May 29 he called for General Beauregard to meet him there. Evidently unlike the administration at Washington, Davis preferred only the most celebrated commanders to protect the seat of government, and the foremost military figure of the season remained the hero of Fort Sumter. Beauregard left Charleston that afternoon, and the following day he conferred with Robert E. Lee and the president. On the last day of May they placed him in charge of the so-called Alexandria Line that Colonel Terrett and General Bonham had commanded, which no longer included the city of Alexandria. Beauregard repaired to Manassas Junction on the first of June and immediately started to complain about the vulnerability of his position, calling for reinforcements amounting to several times more troops than he had on hand and warning that any attack would probably force him to retreat. His troops showed good spirit, he noted, but there were too few of them and they lacked sufficient arms for an effective defense.[59]

Beauregard had graduated from West Point with Irvin McDowell, although well ahead of him academically. Like McClellan and General Lee, Beauregard had spent his career in the engineers and served on Scott's staff in the campaign against Mexico City. His vanity was at least equal to his talent, and he lived a life of relentless romanticism. Introducing himself to the male citizens of Prince William, Fairfax, and Loudoun counties, he reminded them that their homes lay before and beneath the boot heel of "a reckless and unprincipled tyrant," but he promised to protect them to the full extent of his power. Adjuring them that their own honor and that of their wives and daughters depended on Confederate success, he called on them to join him in "the sacred cause of constitutional liberty" and help him to expel the invader by providing timely information about enemy movements. As always, he signed himself G. T. Beauregard, dropping his first name, Pierre, and demonstrating a preference for the Southern practice of identifying himself only by his initials and patronymic.[60]

Such lofty rhetoric appealed to the Deep South tastes that Beauregard knew best, but Virginians had acquired a more pragmatic perspective than people did in cotton country. Although they might resent an overbearing federal government, and (like James Jackson) even resist tyranny forcibly, this close to the Potomac political loyalty often depended on whether the Confederacy could defend its territory, its people, and their property. Beauregard had no sooner taken charge in northern Virginia than certain citizens belabored him with reports of disaffected neighbors, and when he investigated the charges they proved accurate. Residents felt widespread loyalty to the U.S. flag, even if they entertained no hostility to the Confederacy; they merely wished to be left alone.[61]

Such ambivalence toward the new government spread through much of Virginia. The Confederacy's secretary of the navy, Floridian Stephen Mallory, puzzled over the apparent indifference of so many Virginians, considering them "supine & inert" in the face of invasion. "Va. is almost asleep," he observed, "& one could hardly bleeve [sic] that the foe is upon her soil. . . ." Observing Virginians both administratively and directly from his sweltering office off the corner of Richmond's Capitol Square, Mallory concluded that they demonstrated the least enthusiasm of all the Confederate citizens he had encountered.[62]

Conflicting allegiances muted the fighting spirit in Leesburg, thirty miles north and east of Manassas, although a Confederate presence precluded much display of disloyalty. Colonel Eppa Hunton commanded there, with eight companies of infantry composed largely of local Loudoun County citizens still dressed in civilian clothing. None of those companies mustered a full complement, and the more influential officers and sergeants remained out of camp, scouring the county for prospective recruits. Those eight companies represented the organized portion of Hunton's 8th Virginia Infantry, to which he temporarily added two more Loudoun companies: one of artillery and one of cavalry, as well as a company of cavalry made up of sympathetic Marylanders.[63]

With the wheat nearly ready to harvest, Loudoun farmers feared the enemy would come swooping in from Arlington just in time to destroy or appropriate their crops and impress their horses for the Union army. Hunton shared that fear, sending Beauregard a petition from concerned citizens and asking him for another twenty-five hundred men. The high command at Richmond had recognized Leesburg's vulnerability as early as May 24, when the assault on Alexandria sparked concern about a general advance against Leesburg and Harper's Ferry. To prevent the enemy from dashing toward Leesburg from Alexandria, General Lee ordered Hunton to burn the bridges of the Loudoun & Hampshire Railroad as far down toward Alexandria as he could venture; to avoid a foray against either Leesburg or Harper's Ferry, Lee instructed him to interrupt the Chesapeake & Ohio Canal on the Maryland side of the river. Since then Lee had directed Hunton to establish an advance outpost at Dranesville, midway between Leesburg and Manassas, and to extend his picket posts far enough to connect with Ewell's, who were ranging up from Fairfax Court House. For the moment, though, Lee could offer no reinforcements beyond a lone lieutenant colonel to help Hunton organize his unfinished regiment.[64]

PART II

AND NOW THE STORM-BLAST CAME

4

Behold the Silvery River

❖ SOUND INTELLIGENCE lay behind Colonel Hunton's June 9 appeal for reinforcements. A Leesburg parson returning from the Maryland side of the Potomac had just informed him that barges full of provisions and ammunition could be seen at the Georgetown end of the Chesapeake and Ohio Canal, obviously as part of the preparation for an expedition upriver. Military men of the time usually put undue credence in the information obtained from clergymen, perhaps supposing them more honest or intelligent than the average citizen, but this preacher apparently knew what he was talking about. Only the day previously, Winfield Scott had assigned a sizable brigade to Colonel Stone, giving him instructions to march it up to Edwards's Ferry, on the canal, and (if it were feasible) to cross over the river and take Leesburg. At least a portion of the supplies on those barges was intended for Stone's column.[1]

Stone's brigade consisted of four battalions of his District of Columbia volunteers, along with three regiments of volunteers and militia from New Hampshire, New York, and Pennsylvania. They were all three-month troops, wearing a Napoleonic array of uniforms, with grey predominating. For trained, reliable men Stone could count only on a company of Regular cavalry and a couple of gun crews from the 5th U.S. Artillery. In a suffocating Potomac heat wave he started two battalions up the canal toward Great Falls and the aqueduct at Seneca Creek, but the rest he took overland to Rockville, the county seat of Montgomery County. The first of Stone's soldiers to enter the town heard that a mounted band of "Secession Cavalry" had left there the day before. The citizens of Rockville struck one Pennsylvania sergeant as mainly loyal, but the sergeant's brigade commander did not share that opinion.[2]

Maryland had scheduled a special election for June 13, and the federal government wanted troops in as many polling places as possible, especially after raising Marylanders' ire with military repression in Baltimore. To encourage loyalist voters in that city, Lincoln appointed Major General Nathaniel Banks, an ardent Massachusetts Republican, to supersede the Democrat Cadwalader. Banks took command of the department two days before the election. He promised the mayor of Baltimore that if the police maintained order he would keep his troops out of the city during the election, with the exception of Maryland soldiers who had a right to vote there, but he warned that any unrest might bring dreadful consequences.[3]

In 1861, when a Union general referred to "unrest" in conjunction with an election, he was usually talking about the shouting matches, demonstrations, and scuffles that might attend enthusiastic campaigning by Democrats. As was customary in that era, crowds of partisans often surrounded the polls, intimidating voters who held opposing views, and officials in the Lincoln administration intended that any such intimidation worked to their own advantage. Accordingly, the most notable election-day incident in Baltimore consisted of an assault on Henry May, a constitutional-Union candidate who, with a party of friends, fell victim to an attack by unconditional-Unionist rowdies.[4]

That disturbance erupted even though Banks had broken his promise and sent troops into the city. The 6th Massachusetts stayed in the town all night, one private told his mother, practicing maneuvers and marching ostentatiously through the streets — to the utter terror of the female inhabitants, he noted smugly. A battery of artillery later joined them. Such armed support for their cause could hardly have discouraged the pro-Union mob that assailed Henry May's party.[5]

Colonel Stone reported that the presence of his brigade at Rockville freed loyal citizens to vote openly for Union candidates without pressure from adherents of the states'-rights party. Perhaps his troops exerted greater influence than he realized, for Union candidates prevailed by a substantial majority despite Stone's observation that Rockville voters were "about one-half rabid secessionists," but Stone may have underestimated Maryland loyalty as badly as his president. Aside from the implied intimidation of the nearby encampments, the June election passed without active military interference — unlike the rest of Maryland's elections during this war — and in that last relatively free plebiscite, Union candidates of one stripe or another won every congressional seat and most other offices. These results should have offered more assurance that Maryland posed no threat of secession. Colonel Stone felt comfortable enough that he returned a collection of uniforms and guns to a local militia captain whose equipment had been confiscated in fear of his company's Democratic majority.[6]

The June election did reveal a growing dissatisfaction with federal repression, though, at least in Baltimore. In the Fourth Congressional District there, Henry May beat his unconditional-Unionist opponent by a majority four times as great as the one his district had given to John Breckinridge, the most vehement states'-rights candidate in the presidential election.[7]

While Stone lingered at Rockville, Colonel Hunton sent a few of his Virginians over the Potomac to Edwards's Ferry with the intention of destroying the lock at that point, but the lockkeeper convinced them to leave it intact, instead offering to drain the water out of the canal there. This alternative satisfied the Confederates, who may not have understood that it would take only a few hours to refill that section of the canal enough to float Stone's barges. By then Stone's battalion on the canal had reached the Seneca Creek aqueduct, eight miles below Edwards's Ferry. To dissuade Confederates from inflicting permanent damage on the canal, Stone made conspicuous inquiries about the road to Frederick, as though that were his destination. Then, with the election concluded, he started a regiment and his artillery toward Poolesville early on June 14, before the day turned oppressively warm. The rest of his infantry lingered at Rockville until the worst heat of the day had passed, but Stone rode out with the cavalry soon after breakfast.[8]

Poolesville, a straggling village with a few brick houses and 150 or so inhabitants, sat at the hub of all the roads leading to the river between Seneca Creek and Point of Rocks. It lay nearly equidistant between Edwards's Ferry, south of Leesburg, and Conrad's Ferry, north of that town, and Stone reconnoitered both of those crossings that day, finding no Confederate presence on the Maryland side of the river. In peaceful times Edwards's Ferry had plied between Lock 25 of the Chesapeake and Ohio Canal and the mouth of Goose Creek, on the Virginia shore. Goose Creek ran deeper and wider than its name implied, and it carried canal traffic of its own, transporting grain from mills farther inland. Stone learned that the enemy in Leesburg had burned the Loudoun & Hampshire Railroad bridge over the creek the day before, in belated obedience to General Lee's three-week-old orders. Even in the face of military necessity, the destruction of such vital improvements as railroads and canals came hard to a Virginia gentleman — especially under the gaze of investors like Henry Harrison — and Lee had had to send Hunton a reminder before he carried out the order.[9]

Hunton had refrained from burning a locomotive and some freight cars belonging to the Loudoun & Hampshire line, hoping he might be able to save them for service elsewhere, but he did pile enough firewood and tinder around them that he could ignite them in an emergency. On Saturday night, June 15, the first of Stone's troops marched down to Edwards's Ferry with the intention of establishing a picket post there, but Confederates on the Virginia side thought them more ambitious. Hunton's company of Maryland cavalry watched the crossing that night, under Captain George Gaither of Baltimore. Gaither dispatched a rider to inform Hunton of the enemy's appearance, adding that it seemed the Yankees meant to cross the river. At short intervals Gaither sent a series of messengers with increasingly alarming news, until finally he reported that the enemy was coming over in large numbers and was about to overwhelm his little company. At that Hunton rose from his bed, gathered his entire command, and marched down the road to the ferry, lighting off the freight cars as he left town. On the riverbank he found Gaither and his company unmolested. Not a Union soldier could he see, save perhaps for the sentinel who contentedly paced his beat on the far shore, while from Poolesville Colonel Stone wondered at the glow on the horizon to the west, where the freight cars blazed needlessly. Evidently Gaither had imagined the entire episode from the shadows and sounds carrying across the river in the darkness. Hunton's disgust with the Maryland captain, whom he judged "absolutely worthless as a military man," overcame his wish to keep Gaither's company, which he deemed an admirable body of men. He peremptorily ordered Gaither to lead his troop to Harper's Ferry, to join the army there under Joseph Johnston.[10]

Johnston, lately quartermaster general of the United States Army, had come to Harper's Ferry in May to take command from Colonel Thomas J. Jackson, who had served until April as an instructor at the Virginia Military Institute. He found there a collection of companies displaying an independence approaching mutiny, led by men intriguing against each other for the field commissions in proposed regiments. By the middle of June Johnston and Jackson had gathered, armed, and trained about six thousand of those dubious troops, most of them Virginians, but Johnston found their location entirely indefensible. Harper's Ferry occupied a triangular peninsula between the Potomac and Shenandoah rivers, with soaring heights on two sides from which (as Colonel Jackson particularly noted) an enemy might easily bombard the place into submission. Besides, the site of the ruined arsenal lay so distant from main roads that it virtually removed Johnston's diminutive army from effective operations. By June 14 Johnston knew that a federal force had taken Romney, sixty miles to the west, and he mistakenly supposed that this heralded the vanguard of McClellan's army. He also learned from informants that another Union army at Chambersburg, Pennsylvania, had begun moving against him, and by the morning of June 15 the leading elements of that column had reached Hagerstown, Maryland, fifty miles north by road and only half that distance on the map. He responded to the capture of Romney by sending a couple of regiments in that direction, and he addressed the Hagerstown threat by evacuating Harper's Ferry altogether.[11]

The Pennsylvania column consisted of a substantial collection of three-month regiments under Major General Robert Patterson of the Pennsylvania militia. Patterson, an old man prone to bravado, intended to feign an attack against Harper's Ferry from the Maryland side of the Potomac while driving most of his troops toward Martinsburg to cut off Johnston's escape. Patterson doubted the engineer captain who reported Harper's Ferry already evacuated, but Johnston sat astride the turnpike from Martinsburg to Winchester by the time the first Union soldiers splashed across the Potomac. The federal spearhead dug in on the Virginia shore at Falling Waters, unaware that they outnumbered the Confederates two to one and fearful that the Confederates outnumbered them. Union sympathizers among the local citizenry offered wild reports crediting Johnston with as many as fifteen thousand men, whom those informants insisted had been seen marching through Martinsburg on their way to attack the Yankees at Falling Waters. In reality Johnston and his six thousand men remained ten miles below Martinsburg, furiously entrenching themselves against an enemy whose numerical superiority they had more accurately assessed, but Patterson lost his nerve and shrank back into Maryland. At that Johnston withdrew to Winchester, thirty-five miles below the Potomac by the Shenandoah Valley Turnpike and about the same distance east of Romney, equidistant between the two vulnerable portals of his domain and handy to a railroad that could carry him to Beauregard, at Manassas Junction. The Romney incursion turned out to have been a mere raid from a single regiment, so Patterson's army posed the only imminent danger, and with Patterson in command, the danger remained minimal.[12]

Back in Poolesville, Colonel Stone heard repeated rumors of Johnston's withdrawal from Harper's Ferry, but not a word could he get from Patterson, whom he supposed to be in possession of the town. He yearned to cross over and take Leesburg, especially if Patterson held the Virginia side upstream, for that would have enabled him to return the canal to full operation and protect it from further depredations. Without assurance that Johnston had been driven from Harper's Ferry, though, Stone dared not venture across the river, for Johnston could either fall on his right flank or cross the river into Maryland, behind him, and make a dash for Washington. On the afternoon of June 16 Stone detected larger numbers of troops guarding the two ferries on his front, and through his telescope he could see workmen digging entrenchments on top of the tallest hill between Leesburg and Edwards's Ferry. He supposed these might be part of the Harper's Ferry garrison, but still he could learn nothing conclusive about that town. The next morning the Confederates at Conrad's Ferry opened up with an old six-pounder smoothbore on the New Hampshire regiment camped on the Maryland side, doing no real harm. When they had tired of loading their field piece the Virginians came down to the riverbank and dared their foes to cross, impugning their masculinity with an assortment of invective. Stone estimated quite accurately that Hunton's command on the opposite bank did not exceed eight hundred men, and he interpreted such pointless annoyance as a diversion, but no attack developed elsewhere. The next day the same number of men — amounting to everyone Hunton could have mustered — demonstrated downstream at Edwards's Ferry, while Conrad's Ferry fell quiet; clearly Hunton was shifting his troops about for maximum visual effect. Coming so soon after Patterson's upstream crossing of the Potomac, such theatrics may have been designed to discourage Stone from making a similar foray over the river, but Stone remained ignorant of affairs upstream and dared not cross in any case.[13]

General Scott had pondered bringing a healthy portion of Patterson's idle army down to Stone, to take Leesburg and unite with troops from the Alexandria line for further operations, but Patterson's tentative crossing of the Potomac disarranged that rudimentary plan. Not until late on June 20 did Stone learn the real story of Johnston's inaugural contest with Patterson, and he only gained that information by sending his own intrepid messenger upriver to investigate personally. His scout determined that Harper's Ferry had been abandoned by Johnston but had not been garrisoned by federal troops. Until Patterson moved across the Potomac in force, occupying Johnston's attention, it seemed too risky and too unproductive to capture Leesburg, though Stone guessed that the initial taking of it might not cost much. A few days later the ripening wheat crop increased his anxiety to occupy the town and secure the county, but such a movement required cooperation from, and communication with, General Patterson, who remained silent from a distance of fifty miles over relatively friendly territory. For the nonce Stone satisfied himself with putting the canal back in operation, though without control of the Virginia shore its protection would weigh heavily on his manpower.[14]

Finally, on June 23, a letter from army headquarters apprised Stone that General Scott was trying to prod Patterson forward. Stone applauded Scott's effort, supposing that a federal military presence would cultivate the loyal sentiments he believed existed on the Virginia side. At least one refugee fled into Union lines to avoid enforced service with the Virginia militia, which had recently been called out, and some of the pickets across the river offered congenial conversation with their opposite numbers. Stone described one pair of opposing pickets at Conrad's Ferry who waded into the middle of the river to shake hands and drink each other's health. The colonel put great faith in the Confederate sentry's professed disinclination to fight, but he may have mistaken the Virginian's peaceful disposition for reawakening Unionism. It was true that Governor Letcher's militia levy had angered many Virginians, who viewed it as inefficient and disruptive of internal commerce, but except for the militia most Virginia soldiers at that date had enlisted voluntarily, and with the goal of repelling foreign invaders from their native soil. Their return to their homes would probably have been predicated on the return of the Union soldiers to theirs, and on the cessation of federal efforts to force Southern states back into the Union.[15]

Comprehending at last that General Patterson was not going to communicate with him, Stone decided to make his own reconnaissance up-river. Taking a couple of staff officers and a dozen cavalry, he left Poolesville at 3:00 AM on Monday, June 24. His party crossed the Monocacy River in the first grey hint of light, riding into Point of Rocks at daybreak. He dispatched one officer and a couple of men up the railroad on a handcar as far as Sandy Hook, opposite Harper's Ferry, where he encountered Patterson's engineer captain and exchanged information with him. Stone's officer returned to Point of Rocks early in the afternoon, giving him his first reliable information in nine days of Joe Johnston's whereabouts. Since Johnston could no longer sneak behind him on a raid or flank movement, Stone decided to extend his pickets up to Point of Rocks, for the river was dropping quickly in the hot, dry weather, opening potential new troop crossings every day.[16]

During his day at Point of Rocks Stone learned that Leesburg had been reinforced. As usual, his information proved accurate, coming from one of the many loyalists who lived in and about Loudoun County. A man who had just come across the river on his way from Leesburg told Stone that 950 South Carolina troops had arrived during the night — and so they had, marching from the main body at Manassas Junction. The South Carolinians came equipped with their own colonel, a young man of ample social status and doubtful military ability, so Beauregard had assigned Major Nathan Evans to "conduct" the regiment to Leesburg. Evans, also a South Carolinian, had spent thirteen years in the United States Army; his plebe year at West Point had corresponded with Charles Stone's last year there, although Stone was eight months younger. Confederate authorities hoped that Evans's experience might prove useful to the volunteer colonels, for "Shanks" (as his family and his friends in the old army knew him) had spent years on the plains with the 2nd U.S. Cavalry, from which eventually came thirteen Confederate generals. He had engaged in active campaigns in New Mexico and Texas, and less than three years before he had personally killed a pair of Comanches in a fight along the Washita River. Evans exuded confidence, and conducted himself with such manifest capacity that the volunteer colonels of the 8th Virginia and the 4th South Carolina both agreed to take orders from him. Weeks later the Confederate War Department would issue Evans a commission as a colonel in the provisional army, but from that first assignment at Leesburg he assumed the duties of a brigadier general while wearing only the single star of a staff major.[17]

The South Carolinians, or rather the acting general who directed them, brought a new brand of warfare to the Leesburg front. In contrast to the companionable Virginians, the Carolinians introduced themselves by sniping at Stone's pickets. They drew no blood, and invited return fire that quickly discouraged them, but their sharpshooting established a more hostile presence on the right bank of the river. If this posturing was intended to tighten security on the Virginia shore, it failed. Stone continued to relay surprisingly accurate intelligence to Washington, including far better estimates of the size and position of Confederate forces in front of Patterson than Patterson himself could gather. Patterson thought himself actively beset by twenty-five thousand rebels assembling for a massive assault just beyond his outposts, while Stone accurately gauged Johnston's force at ten thousand men acting on the tactical defensive. Patterson's horror of an ambitious assault by ghost legions prevented him from detaching any of his troops for such projects as guarding the downstream river crossings, guarding vital canal features like the magnificent Monocacy River aqueduct, protecting the loyal citizens from malicious insurgents, and severing the passage of mail and recruits into Virginia through the gap between Point of Rocks and Harper's Ferry. Stone therefore pleaded for more artillery or infantry on his end, to undertake those duties himself. General Scott, who perceived the sense and energy behind Stone's repeated applications, urged Patterson to either attack the enemy in his front or cooperate with Stone against Leesburg, and ordered him to open communication with Stone, but still Patterson ignored his younger ally at Poolesville. Finally Scott realized that the mountain would have to come to Mohammed, and he instructed Stone to take his volunteers, his cavalry company, and his artillery section up to Williamsport to join Patterson.[18]

Although reluctant to abandon his horseshoe of the Potomac between Seneca Falls and the Monocacy River, Stone obeyed with an alacrity that was not instinctive with civilian soldiers like Patterson. Stone started his Pennsylvania volunteers on the march on the afternoon of July 1, a few hours after Scott's order reached him. The Regular cavalry and artillery and his District of Columbia volunteers he ordered back to Washington, for the volunteers' time had almost expired, but he left some of the district men at Edwards's Ferry in hopes of holding the place until another command was sent there. This skeleton detachment bluffed the Leesburg Confederates for the next couple of weeks with disproportionately loud morning drumrolls and an occasional threat to cross the river.[19]

The grey-clad 1st New Hampshire followed Stone's long wagon train upriver as rear guard, still enjoying the holiday atmosphere of the campaign despite oppressive heat. The excruciating pace of the passage left those New Hampshiremen sitting all through Independence Day under a sweltering sun at the mouth of the Monocacy, and some of the soldiers and teamsters dove into the river for relief. Confederate pickets on the far shore did the same, and shouted greetings began floating over the water. A Granite State private and a teamster from one of the stalled wagons eventually swam across for more direct conversation, but that exceeded the limits of Southern conviviality. The New Hampshire soldier, who could have expected to go home in barely five weeks, instead spent the next year in a Confederate prison, and the teamster went with him.[20]

Hundreds of Maryland volunteers had been filtering into the Confederacy via the unguarded length of river above Point of Rocks — not so many as Virginia and Maryland secessionists had hoped, and too few for military significance, but enough to attract political notice. Baltimore's George Steuart, who had ambitiously identified himself as the major general of an imagined "light division" of Marylanders less than ten weeks before, now commanded a battalion of Maryland infantry under Johnston. Well over a thousand men, principally from the eastern half of Maryland, had formed Confederate infantry or cavalry companies in the first month after Lincoln's call for troops, and hundreds more expressed a wish to serve. Francis Thomas, the adjutant general of Maryland, had gone over with them. He tried to organize them into a brigade with the authority of a provisional commission as colonel, but many of the Maryland volunteers had balked at serving under him out of loyalty to other would-be field officers. Thomas therefore decamped for Richmond with those Marylanders who would follow him. He had shorn his hair close to his head and adopted the blue Zouave uniform of the antebellum Maryland Guard: jacket heavy with embroidery, baggy pantaloons, and a jaunty little cap. Old Edmund Ruffin remarked admiringly on Thomas's "Turkish dress," but while he may have impressed officials in Richmond he failed to attract many more recruits from his own state. His remaining companies went to fill other regiments from Maryland or Virginia, and Thomas consigned himself to General Johnston as a volunteer aide.[21]

Colonel Thomas calculated on May 22 that 2,500 Marylanders wanted to fight for the Confederacy. He counted about 1,150 who had already organized for service, but the other 1,350 failed to materialize, at least immediately. Thomas may have overestimated their temper toward the states'-rights cause, or they may simply not have seen enough of federal repression.[22]

The presence of Union troops impeded defection across the Potomac, as well, but it also launched a new wave of even more ardent Confederate sympathy that may have neutralized the immediate military advantage of keeping a few hundred recruits out of the Southern army. For many Marylanders hovering on the political edge, the appearance of federal bayonets on Federal Hill and the ensuing military arrests made all the difference, transforming opponents of administration policy into enemies of the United States government. Recruiting officers put together several more companies of expatriate Marylanders in Virginia that summer and fall, as young men who had struggled to keep their state neutral converted to the cause of active disunion.[23]

In addition to political repercussions like citizen disaffection and grist for Confederate propaganda, the military occupation of Baltimore may have exerted another insidious influence on the Lincoln government in the form of what might best be characterized as executive guilt. Knowing that their previous repressive measures had infuriated wavering citizens, administration officials found the most alarming rumors of Maryland disloyalty increasingly credible, which only continued the cycle by convincing them to take even more repressive action. One radical agitator demonstrated how easily the government could be excited to such counterproductive behavior.

Worthington Snethen, a relentless Republican partisan who had long worked for that party's dominance in Maryland, served Horace Greeley as his Baltimore correspondent to the *New York Tribune*.[24] Snethen's distorted observations painted his city as an enclave of secessionists from city hall to city line, where the disloyal element waited only for federal authorities to turn their backs before bursting into open rebellion. From the secure medium of his New York newspaper Snethen denounced Baltimore's Democratic officials and citizens as secessionists and traitors, calling for their arrest by the federal government, and he spread a false alarm about election-day riots that had brought the gleam of bayonets to the polls. After the election he accelerated his personal campaign against both Baltimore and the *Baltimore Sun,* his professional and political rival. Shamelessly exaggerating citizen animosity toward the federal government, he reported "on the best Secessionist authority" that lurking insurgents held ten thousand modern weapons with which they intended to take control of the city. No one — including General Scott and Secretary of War Simon Cameron, to whom Snethen personally carried his wild tale — seemed to question how a journalist so openly hostile to the Confederacy could have been privy to secessionist planning. Snethen apparently enjoyed a certain intimacy with the Union military, for he had predicted Ben Butler's "liberation" of Baltimore two days before it happened, and he used that familiarity to convince Cameron and the general-in-chief with his contagious blend of fearmongering fables. Scott not only believed him, but selected Snethen to present General Banks with an order for the arrest of Baltimore's city marshal, George P. Kane, and the entire board of police commissioners — all of whom Snethen had implicated in the imagined takeover plot.[25]

So it was that at an early hour on June 27, 1861, a detachment of troops marched through Baltimore's streets under a gibbous moon and appeared at the door of Marshal Kane's home. The police chief greeted the hundreds of soldiers with grim humor, remarking that he would have responded just as readily to a written summons, and he stepped voluntarily into the hack they had brought for him. Within the hour Kane arrived at Fort McHenry, where guards led him to the same cell as John Merryman. The new prisoner certainly did sympathize with secession, at least as a constitutional concept, and Confederate visitors to the city considered him and his police "with us." Kane also admitted material participation in the official sabotage of bridges that prevented federal troops from reaching Baltimore, although he insisted that the governor had approved the action as a means of saving Baltimore from another riot. He had also conducted the Sixth Massachusetts through the riot of April 19, however — sailing into the mob and knocking heads together, appealing to the crowd personally, and directing city police to protect the soldiers and make way for them. However reluctantly, he had cooperated with military authorities. No one could name a law that he had broken, and he had apparently kept faith with his oath of office by observing municipal authority, despite any personal hopes he may have nourished that Maryland would secede. Eventually he would go south himself, but his decision to do so may have originated during the seventeen months of imprisonment at the hands of a government he viewed as having forsaken its own constitution. His imprisonment may also have sent his sons into Confederate service.[26]

At General Scott's suggestion, Banks replaced Kane with a provost marshal, selecting the colonel of the 1st Maryland Volunteers. The police commissioners responded by discharging the entire Baltimore police force, and the provost marshal began replacing those officers with hundreds of new men willing to accept military authority. A search of police headquarters yielded a cache of arms and ammunition, and Banks insisted that the weapons had been "secreted" in such a way as to imply illicit intentions, but the mayor easily explained the "concealed arsenal," as Banks called it. According to His Honor, the assortment of weapons had been collected over the years, many of them by his decidedly Unionist predecessor, to arm the police in case of an emergency, and in spite of recent disturbances there were not even enough to supply the entire force. Some guns had also been confiscated in the April troubles, including a couple of military rifles that rioters had evidently taken away from Massachusetts soldiers.[27]

As plausible as the mayor's report sounded, federal authorities and their civilian supporters looked on the discovery as proof of police collusion in the "plot" to seize Baltimore. Snethen persisted in his private war against dissenting Democrats, continuing to raise the specter of treasonous insurrection through the *Tribune* and lobbying General Scott privately to ensure that the new provost marshal did not forget to gather in the police commissioners, too. Two days after Snethen's reminder, Banks sent out twenty companies of infantry on another dark-of-night mission. When the sun rose over the Eastern Shore on July 1, all four commissioners lay in the dank dungeon of Fort McHenry, including one innocent tubercular who had only recently returned to Maryland after a long and unavailing search for a salubrious climate. Soldiers by the hundreds strode Baltimore's streets with their bayonets fixed that morning, and citizens who dared to express disagreement with their government felt the teeth of martial law.[28]

For all Snethen's blather about impending insurrection, it was only after this latest affront to Baltimore's civil authority that planning appears to have begun for a domestic uprising of Maryland citizens against the federal government. That plan developed in Richmond, with the expectation that a prominent Baltimore Democrat would agree to disseminate strategic details to the appropriate conspirators. Even with the despot's heel grinding a little deeper into Maryland's shore, however, the prospective Baltimore collaborator seems not to have responded.[29]

The United States Congress convened three days after the arrest of the commissioners and questioned the seemingly highhanded action taken against public officials of a loyal state. Knowing that Lincoln had already ignored judicial demands in such matters, the police commissioners bypassed the legal system to petition their congressional representative for relief, and twenty days into its session the House of Representatives adopted a resolution requesting the president to provide grounds and evidence for the arrests. Lincoln declined to cooperate. Citing what would become the favorite excuse of future administrations seeking to invoke a dubious prerogative, he informed the elected representatives of the people that it was "incompatible with the public interest at this time" to release that information. Some of the commissioners remained in confinement for months, and Marshal Kane was not released until November of 1862, but for the rest of the war and thereafter, revealing the reason for their detention remained incompatible with the public interest.[30]

Lincoln had played no overt role in the arrests, but a copy of Snethen's remarks to Scott made its way into the president's papers, and he must have known that the roundup was going to take place. If there was any question of his support for Scott's action, Lincoln answered it the day after the commissioners landed in Fort McHenry by extending the territory in which Scott might suspend habeas corpus all the way to New York City.[31]

The beginning of July found Lincoln busily refining his message to Congress, which he had called into special session for Independence Day. Military matters intruded, though, and one of the details he had to consider was an appropriate assignment for John Charles Frémont. Frémont, a disputatious former army officer known as "the Pathfinder" for his western explorations, had stood as the Republican Party's first presidential candidate five years before. He had just returned from London, bearing another of Lincoln's commissions as major general. Salmon P. Chase, the bold, bald secretary of the treasury, took it upon himself to talk with Frémont about taking command from the hesitant General Patterson and going after Joe Johnston at Winchester while McDowell assailed Beauregard at Manassas. Then, Chase casually figured, after those two had been trounced, Frémont could assemble both Patterson's troops and McClellan's for a grand expedition through neutral Kentucky, into the Unionist stronghold of East Tennessee, and straight down to the Gulf of Mexico, cleaving the Confederacy in two. The role seemed sufficiently conspicuous to attract the proud Frémont, and he showed interest, although some in the administration expected that he would decline the commission altogether.[32]

As it happened, Lincoln and his postmaster general, Montgomery Blair, wanted Frémont for a department that would include Blair's former home state of Missouri; Frémont had been socializing with the Blair family since his arrival from Europe. General Patterson further confounded Chase's plan when, after days of argument and stalling and promises of immediate activity, he finally barged across the Potomac near Williamsport.[33]

Early on the morning of July 2, at the place called Falling Waters, on the same loop of land where his earlier advance had dug in, some of Patterson's Pennsylvanians emerged from the river and scattered into a rye field to cover the crossing of their comrades. Johnston had posted a substantial outpost between Martinsburg and the river, and Colonel Jackson stood by to greet the Yankees as they proceeded into Virginia. With fewer than four hundred Virginia infantrymen and a single field piece, he belatedly contended their passage in a violent exchange that produced a couple of dozen casualties, but then Jackson fell back and left a battalion of Virginia cavalry to monitor Patterson's advance. Lieutenant Colonel J.E.B. Stuart, who led that mounted detachment, cut off and captured more than four dozen of the leading Yankees, including three officers, who had fallen out to rest beneath the shade of an ancient tree. A few of those soldiers tried to flee, but horsemen ran them down and killed them, including one who was shot to death by the black servant of a Virginia captain. When Patterson reported to Washington on his crossing of the river he forgot to mention that unpleasant detail, but he did offer the estimate of sixty enemy dead, which he evidently founded more on hope than hard evidence, for neither Jackson nor Stuart reported a single man killed.[34]

General Scott had been prodding Patterson to act more aggressively, as a means of holding Johnston in Winchester. At the behest of the administration, and against his own judgment, Scott intended to send Irvin McDowell's command against Beauregard. He informed Patterson of the decision in confidence on July 1, implying that if Patterson could prevent Johnston from reaching Manassas Junction, McDowell could muster a respectable numerical superiority, offsetting the disadvantage of taking the offensive. McDowell complained that his troops were green; although the same was true of the Confederate troops, equal inexperience benefited the defending army, which could potentially avoid the type of maneuvers that would tangle the feet of an attacking force. More time would only allow the enemy the opportunity to prepare, though, and political considerations militated for a rapid movement against Richmond. Public opinion, chiefly as it was represented or manipulated by the *New York Tribune*, demanded prompt action — and, as the proponents of an immediate advance noted, the Confederate Congress was expected to convene in its new capitol building on July 20. If Richmond fell before the initial session began, the Confederacy might just crumble. Then there were the sixty regiments of three-month troops serving in Virginia and Maryland that would begin going home by the end of July: they matched or exceeded the three-year volunteers in training at that point, for most of them had been in service longer. The Confederate armies, meanwhile, had mostly enlisted for a year of service, so Beauregard's and Johnston's ranks would still be growing when McDowell's force shriveled to half its size and Patterson's disappeared altogether.[35]

Patterson, who had already accumulated more than fourteen thousand troops, marched into Martinsburg at noon on July 3. There he remained for twelve days, a good twenty miles from Johnston's picket line, allowing the Confederates plenty of time to dig in for stiff resistance; Johnston took full advantage of that opportunity, for collaborating citizens kept him informed of Patterson's burgeoning command. Scott ordered two new Wisconsin regiments to Patterson's aid, as well as a three-year regiment from Massachusetts, and Charles Stone joined him at Martinsburg on July 8 with three regiments and part of another; that day and the next, four more regiments of New York militia arrived from Washington. By July 9 Patterson exercised authority over some twenty-two thousand men. Even with fresh reinforcements, Johnston could raise fewer than half that number, save for a mob of untrained, ill-uniformed, and poorly armed militia from the border counties whose loyalty no Confederate general could trust. One of the Pennsylvania prisoners from Falling Waters doubted that Johnston ever had as many as thirteen thousand men at Winchester altogether, though Patterson judged his enemy closer to twenty thousand strong at the outset and mightier all the time, crediting him finally with over thirty-five thousand.[36]

Scott initially planned for McDowell to make his move against Manassas early in the second week of July. The old general would rather have gathered one immense national army and sent it down the Mississippi, to complete the strangulation of the eastern Confederacy by the naval blockade, for his thoughts inclined to grand strategy: the blockade, after all, was the product of his imagination. General McDowell earned no favor with Scott when, in a cabinet meeting, he disparaged the Mississippi operation as too risky and unworkable. He had already twice displeased the commanding general, once by having the good fortune to earn a briga-

dier's star ahead of so many of his erstwhile superiors, and again by accepting the command of the army forming around Arlington Heights. In
order to solve a seniority conflict involving a militia general, Scott had
asked McDowell to decline that particular plum when the War Department offered it, but McDowell would not even consider refusing the first
field command of his career.[37]

McDowell may have lacked his chief's vision, but he did not lack ambition, and an advance into Virginia from his department would entail
more certain notoriety for Irvin McDowell than would a campaign down
the Mississippi. His argument (and that of Horace Greeley) for a movement in the direction of Richmond carried. The haggling over strategy
consumed valuable time, though, and half of the second week of July had
already passed before McDowell began gathering his division commanders and brigadiers to explain the routes he expected them to follow.[38]

He distributed his fifty-two regiments and battalions among thirteen
brigades, then gathered those brigades into five divisions. Seniority presented a problem in the selection of commanders for those divisions, and
McDowell had to give two of them to men holding state commissions as
brigadier general. One of those two, Daniel Tyler of Connecticut, had long
ago graduated from West Point, and he drew the biggest division, but
McDowell assigned the other general to a reserve division composed entirely of New Jersey militia and volunteer regiments that had arrived only
days previously. The other three divisions went to Regular Army colonels
who had seen long but undistinguished service. None of the three would
greatly improve his reputation in the new post, and for Colonel Dixon
Miles the opportunity merely revealed how thoroughly his fondness for
the bottle had destroyed his fitness for command. Except in the reserve
division and the one under Miles, though, most of the brigades enjoyed
professionally trained and experienced leaders.[39]

Those five divisions, including attached Regulars and a battalion
of U.S. Marines from the Washington barracks, gave McDowell more
than thirty-four thousand men. Confederate strategists would have been
able to estimate McDowell's strength with reasonable accuracy, thanks to
newspapers that published a complete breakdown of his army by brigade
and regiment. Certainly Beauregard scanned Northern newspapers for
that sort of intelligence; he feared the Yankees culling similar military information from the more indiscreet of the Southern journals.[40] By the
time McDowell began to move against him, Beauregard had accumulated
a force approaching twenty-two thousand men of all arms. Dispensing
with the division level, Beauregard preferred to handle eight separate brigades directly; with his high regard for the military academy, which he

had so recently and briefly superintended, he appointed West Point graduates to all but one of those brigades. The eighth brigade went to Brigadier General Bonham, who had commanded troops during the Seminole and Mexican Wars. Although both armies were larger than any that had ever roamed the continent, neither would include any soldier so exalted as a major general.[41]

The Confederates had been expecting a significant attack from the direction of Washington since the day Union soldiers seized Alexandria and Arlington Heights, but at that moment the attention of Confederate Virginia had turned west, over the Alleghenies. There, where Union sentiment crippled the Confederate cause, George McClellan won an unquestionable victory over a weaker opponent. In a sharp fight and a rear-guard skirmish in which a local resident guided his troops into position, McClellan outmaneuvered and routed the overmatched army in his front there, killing its commander and forcing his way over Rich Mountain. The campaign brought him one more river valley closer to the Shenandoah on the main road to Staunton, alarming the rest of Virginia and offering momentary psychological advantage to McDowell's expedition.[42]

Up on the Potomac, Union soldiers sweltered in their sprawling, sunroasted camps, enduring a cacophony of axes, hammers, saws, singing spades, pounding drums, neighing horses, and the endless shouts and murmurs of a greater multitude than any of them had ever seen. Amid this din they caught scraps of headquarters gossip that foretold of imminent movement to a variety of destinations, and a battle likely. With only a couple of weeks left to serve, some of the ninety-day troops on Arlington Heights thought they would be excused from any such excursions. In their letters to the folks at home they occasionally professed enthusiasm for a fight, but they spent those waning days buying souvenir pistols and knives to take home with them. Grumbling about unpleasant conditions and perhaps regretting their extended commitment, the new three-year men in particular seemed earnestly hopeful of a quick confrontation so they could go home, although some of them took special precautions. When they drew their pay — all of it in bright gold coin — most of the officers of the 2nd New Hampshire immediately bought plain field uniforms identical to those of their enlisted men, to avoid attracting undue attention on the battlefield.[43]

For all of General Scott's concern for confidentiality, as early as July 9 the Washington newspapers alerted their readers — Unionist and secessionist alike — that McDowell would advance that week. Those reports represented the intentions at army headquarters accurately enough, but they ultimately proved overoptimistic: a shortage of fresh horses delayed the advance for nearly another week. Not until the afternoon of July 16 did four of McDowell's divisions fall in and begin moving south and west across a front ten miles wide, converging near Fairfax Court House.[44]

The four columns took the road in light marching order, without tents or knapsacks and with only three days' rations in their haversacks. Each man rolled his extra socks and a handful of possessions inside his blankets, tied the ends of the blankets together, and lifted the resulting loop over one shoulder, letting the tied ends hang beneath the opposite arm. Save for a dozen or so wagons to carry the cooking equipment of each brigade, no baggage train followed: McDowell wanted the roads clear for his ammunition train and ambulances. Thanks to a Washington informant and a Virginia courier, Beauregard knew almost the instant that the first Union regiment stepped off from its camp. With a typically romantic flourish he broadcast that intelligence through an order to his troops, admitting that they faced a more numerous foe but adjuring every man from general down to private to stand firm at his post, meeting the intruder with cool courage and careful aim.[45]

Beauregard may not yet have learned that excited Northern troops had already begun to fulfill his predictions of plunder, ransacking private property even as they gathered on the fringes of their camps for the grand offensive. They left those camps with their flags flying, not only to demonstrate that they brought back federal authority but to avoid a clash between friendly forces, or worse. At Falling Waters a captain of the 14th U.S. Infantry had allowed Confederates to level a dangerous volley at his men when he mistook the grey uniforms of a Virginia regiment for those of the 1st Wisconsin, and regional variations of that blunder invited another similar accident. An alarming number of McDowell's troops also wore the traditional grey of antebellum militia organizations. State authorities had equipped both the 2nd Wisconsin and the 2nd New Hampshire in nearly identical uniforms of light grey material with red trim, and both looked almost precisely like the uniform that was becoming the standard among Confederate volunteers. Those grey uniforms were still common state issue for Union soldiers in late July.[46]

Regiments seemed to compete with each other for distinction in dress. "It was," remembered a Boston newspaper reporter who accompanied McDowell's army, "more like a grand masquerade than anything I have ever seen." The 39th New York, informally known as the Garibaldi Guard, outfitted itself in an Italian uniform of beryl green. The regiment wore hats with rounded crowns and broad, flat brims, and most of the men decorated these alien chapeaus with peacock feathers. The flags of the Garibaldi Guard bore nationalistic Italian slogans, and they marched under field officers named D'Utassy and Ripetti.[47]

Seven major languages reputedly dominated different companies of the Garibaldi Guard, and the only officer who could understand all seven was the colonel. On the parade ground he shouted his orders in French, whereupon the captains would turn on their heels and repeat the commands to their companies in a volley of Indo-European babel. Many of the officers boasted extensive classical education and expensive tastes: the field and staff kept a chef at a salary of fifty dollars a month, and they livened their headquarters table with lager beer and vintage French and Hungarian wines. Once, when unexpectedly ordered to duty away from their camp, the Guard marched off with loaves of bread impaled on their bayonets. Officers and men alike tended to insubordination, leading to the early mutiny of one entire company. McDowell assigned that hybrid regiment to Colonel Louis Blenker, a Hessian with service in a German legion, whose brigade absorbed so many foreign troops that it brought the flavor of continental Europe to rural Virginia. Blenker's other three regiments were composed largely of Germans, including his own grey-clad 8th New York, which styled itself the 1st German Rifles; the only history of that regiment, a little pamphlet produced a year after this campaign by one of its former captains, would be published in German. When Blenker rose to brigade command he relinquished the regiment to Julius Stahel, a Hungarian veteran of the Austrian army. His other regiments, the 29th New York ("1st German Regiment") and the 27th Pennsylvania, were led respectively by Adolph von Steinwehr and Max Einstein.[48]

If all had gone according to McDowell's plan, this polychromatic, polyglot force would have joined and won the battle of Manassas within forty-eight hours of the Tuesday afternoon departure. Events rarely transpire according to plan in war, however, as those novice campaigners learned before the first sunset. Tyler's division advanced toward Vienna, where Confederates had waylaid a trainload of Ohio recruits a month before with bloody consequences; the survivors of that ambush were marching with Tyler, so the troops proceeded with exaggerated care, especially after the light began to fade. One brigade left its camps near Georgetown at 3:00 PM, crossing the Potomac on the Chain Bridge, and even on a smooth, clear road those four regiments had made only eleven miles when they lay down to sleep eight hours later, exhausted and footsore. The Confederates had prepared ahead of time to slow any invading army by dropping trees across the roads in windrows, and the columns stretched and bunched like a concertina as patrols scouted every fallen tree for another of those masked batteries made infamous by the Vienna ambush. Whenever a regiment closed up to halt it would lose scores of men who scattered for fresh water, or for the blackberries that sprouted abundantly in that vicinity. The roads grew especially narrow below Alexandria, with thick woods pressing from either side to heighten the sensations of claustrophobia and vulnerability.[49]

The pace slowed even more the following day. Men unaccustomed to walking any great distance woke at sunrise on Wednesday with blistered feet and stiff shanks, and the leading units of each column moved with increasing caution as their march took them closer to the enemy. A daylight glimpse of trees scarred in the Vienna ambuscade gave Tyler's men a reminder of the danger they might find ahead, which hastened them not at all, and the troops marching from Alexandria found their comrades in the lead plodding dreadfully. Distractions again interfered, this time in the form of abandoned property thought to belong to disloyal citizens. In Vienna some of Tyler's Michigan troops rifled a "secession grocery," stealing everything in it that men could carry — and destroying whatever they could not remove.[50]

Milledge Bonham's South Carolina brigade held Beauregard's forward outpost, at Fairfax Court House. McDowell hoped to capture it, but Beauregard's early warning robbed him of the opportunity. McDowell's schedule called for three of his divisions to fall on Fairfax Court House about the time the Confederates were finishing breakfast, but the dilatory march of those divisions (and particularly Tyler's division, as McDowell saw it) gave them until lunchtime. That was all they needed. Bonham prepared to clear out as soon as Union infantry and artillery drove in his pickets, first waiting long enough to determine that he faced a superior force.[51]

Standing on the spot Richard Ewell's pickets had occupied during the June 1 cavalry raid, Bonham turned his gaze toward Flint Hill — where the Union cavalry had fled that night — and when he saw Tyler's infantry sweeping down the slope toward the village he knew it was time for him to leave. As it was he lingered longer than some thought prudent, leaving behind an unnecessarily bountiful trove of supplies. A Michigan soldier particularly remembered one pile of blankets and jackets that he supposed would fill two wagons, and a New England quartermaster thought there was enough plunder to equip legions of Yankee peddlers. Such a wealth of legitimate booty seemed only to whet the winners' appetites, and the first troops into the shire town began walking into private homes and businesses, helping themselves to whatever struck their fancy. One returned to his regiment with a family Bible under one arm and a portrait of George Washington under the other, while some of his more malicious comrades demolished a parlor piano and tossed the remnants into the yard.[52]

Richard Ewell, now a general as well, fell back from his post on the Orange & Alexandria Railroad at the same hour. Due, probably, to Bonham's tardy departure, one of Ewell's regiments failed to get the word in time and punctuated its escape with a lively skirmish. By dint of some tall marching in the deadly heat the South Carolinians escaped unscathed, but one of McDowell's more eager brigade commanders captured a forgotten squad of Alabama soldiers in Ewell's camp, as well as some camp equipment and a blue silk banner abandoned by an Alabama regiment. These were the first, and ultimately the only, Confederate prisoners taken in the campaign, and the only flag.[53]

One mile beyond Fairfax Court House on the Little River Turnpike, the humble village of Germantown lay in the fork where the Warrenton Turnpike veered toward Centreville. Here lived a number of mechanics and laborers too poor to have taken much part in the secession dialogue, but if any of the unoffending families remained when the first federal soldiers arrived, they soon departed, and it was well for them that they did. Here senseless looting deteriorated into outright pillaging. As though intent on fulfilling Beauregard's predictions of Northern savagery, the leading troops stole whatever came handy and set fire to the houses. Troops who followed them a few hours later found only chimneys and smoldering wreckage. Every resident became a refugee, and from that day Germantown ceased to exist. Passing through three days later, British journalist William Russell remarked reproachfully on the embers of "what once was Germantown," and an officer in one of Tyler's regiments returned on another campaign the next year, noting that his company camped "near Germantown, or where Germantown was." A brigade commander who saw the destruction remarked that "henceforth we ought never to hope for any friends in Virginia."[54]

In another demonstration of their lack of discipline, the Yankee pillagers had consumed all their rations one day early, but they had no intention of going hungry if they could help it. They would not, as their commander later complained, deny themselves anything: they seized pigs, chickens, and milk cows from barnyards and pastures while the terrified owners looked on helplessly. One impertinent cluster of Minnesotans demanded salt from local farmers to flavor the meat of their own slaughtered cattle.[55]

Bonham's Confederates lay waiting for the exuberant Yankees at the next village, Centreville, just a few miles ahead, but the sacking of Germantown marked the end of their day's advance. With the greater part of McDowell's army, Tyler's men camped near the ashes of Germantown that

night beneath a bright, almost-full moon. During the night, when it became clear that the Yankees would not accommodate him by stumbling
into his ambuscade, Bonham retreated again. In the morning McDowell
sent Tyler forward to seize Centreville, and Tyler selected the same brigade that had burned Germantown. Colonel Israel Richardson, a freshly
married West Pointer with an admirable Mexican War record, threw out a
heavy screen of skirmishers and prowled forward three miles at barely
one mile per hour. As McDowell had surmised when he wrote his morning orders, Richardson found Centreville empty. A mile out of town General Tyler rode up to the front with a troop of cavalry. Richardson selected
a couple of infantry companies, and together they ranged ahead to find
out where the Confederates had gone. As they approached a place that
their maps called Blackburn's Ford they detected part of an artillery battery and a little infantry waiting for them — just as local citizens had informed Tyler — along "a creek called Bull Run."[56]

Milledge Bonham's brigade of South Carolinians lay just upstream,
at Mitchell's Ford, and the infantry Tyler saw on the main road were
his pickets. The battery consisted of a section of the Alexandria Artillery, composed of men who would have been acquainted with Mr. Jackson, the martyred hotelier. The gunners fired a few rounds as soon as the
Yankees topped the rise, and then they limbered up and slipped back
across the creek. Downstream from this more visible presence, hidden
amid thick vegetation, waited a brigade of four Virginia regiments under Brigadier General James Longstreet, lately a paymaster in the U.S.
Army. McDowell's orders for the day directed Tyler to maintain the illusion of a direct attack on Manassas from Centreville, but he cautioned Tyler to provoke no engagement, for McDowell wanted time to slide a column around Beauregard's right flank and attack him from the side or
rear. Tyler thought it would be worthwhile to at least learn the strength of
the Confederate position, so he brought a pair of long-range guns up to a
crest overlooking the ford. The brace of rifles elicited no initial response,
and Richardson sent the 1st Massachusetts down into the creek bottom.[57]

On either side of Bull Run here, a series of hills stepped down to the
creek like giant stairways, pitching finally into a ribbon of alluvial plain at
the edge of the stream. Woods filled the steeper slopes, intermixed with
less precipitous fields, and thick brush lined the opposing plains. Two
companies of the 1st Massachusetts, G and H, scurried ahead of their regiment as skirmishers, ferreting Confederate pickets out of some modest
farmhouses and outbuildings that stood before the wood line. Then they
started down the forested hillsides toward the creek.[58]

Company G, the Boston Fusiliers, took the lead. The Fusiliers included
some very young men from Boston and Brighton: at least one boy in that

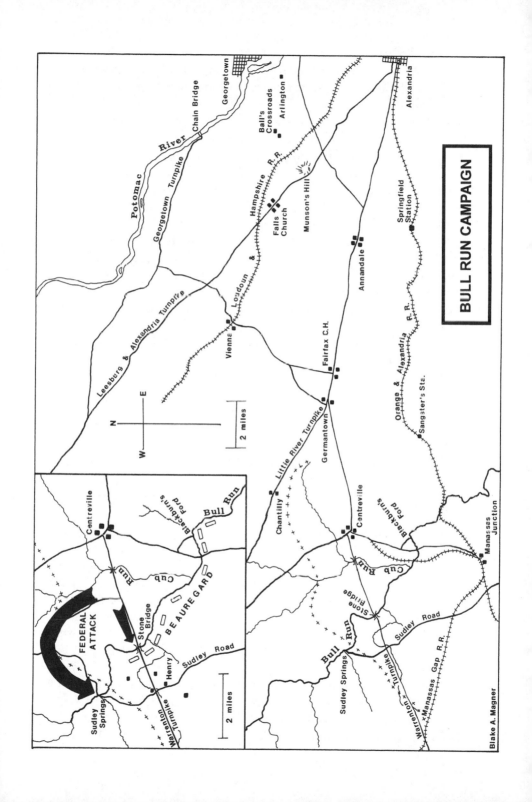

BULL RUN CAMPAIGN

Blake A. Magner

company, Eugene Stimson, had not yet turned seventeen. Adventuresome teenagers littered the regimental roster of the 1st Massachusetts: Company H included a youth from Chelsea named Albert Wentworth, whose father had abandoned his family. As the youngest son, Albert had been supporting his mother with a small salary as a conductor on the city's horse-drawn trolleys. He had fallen victim to the war fever, though — or to the prospect of regular army pay, which he promised to send his destitute mother — and the recruiters had accepted him although he was only sixteen. When he strode into the thicket along Bull Run he was only twenty days past his seventeenth birthday.[59] Like the rest of the 1st Massachusetts, he and his companions wore cadet-grey uniforms, and when they approached the brushy bottom they encountered some strangers wearing clothing of a similar cut and the same color. Lieutenant William Smith of the Fusiliers thought them Michigan troops, and he hailed the newcomers to avoid a deadly mistake, announcing himself as a Massachusetts man. "We know who you are," shouted one of the strangers, and a rattling volley peppered Smith's skirmish line, killing him instantly.[60]

Though stunned by the volley, the novice skirmishers put their heads down and plowed deeper into the brush. Searing fire from a heavy Confederate skirmish line across the creek fell with increasing accuracy, dropping men every few minutes. One of the Fusiliers stumbled when a bullet pierced his left foot near the ankle, but he remained standing and even fired another couple of rounds until a second slug blew off part of his right heel. Company H came up to join their outnumbered comrades, but they fell just as quickly: the Confederate skirmish line overlapped theirs, and flank fire gradually forced them into the mouth of a ravine that ran perpendicular to the run. The steep walls of that ravine trapped them there, leaving them no way to move except back the way they had come. As they fell back they ran into other troops from their own brigade, wearing blue uniforms, who had come to join them in the assault. The meeting provoked another near-tragic case of mistaken identity, and the Massachusetts skirmishers scrambled out into the open so they could see where they were going. The South Carolinians on Bonham's right could now see them, too, as could Longstreet's infantry and some of his artillery, and all those Confederates opened up on the two harried companies. Finally they withdrew up the open slope to the topmost hill, where they fell in behind Tyler's pair of big guns.[61]

In fifteen minutes the hundred or so men in those two companies of the 1st Massachusetts lost more than a dozen men killed and mortally wounded, including Lieutenant Smith; the flags of Boston would drop to half-staff for them when the casualty report reached the State House. A member of the Fusiliers noted that thirty-two of his company had retreated to the ravine with him, and only eleven of them came out. Several wounded, like the man shot through both feet, fell behind for the enemy to collect, but when they did not emerge from the wood their comrades feared the worst. The casualty rate betokened far more ferocious fighting than any that had passed before. A Brighton private whose friend had congratulated him on the opportunity for free travel in the army replied "I think it's paying pretty dear to see the country."[62]

There was even more hot work to be done that day. In what he claimed was merely an effort to force the enemy to reveal his strength and position, General Tyler ran some artillery down close to the creek, selecting a pair of howitzers from the 5th U.S. Artillery, under Captain Romeyn Ayres. To support them he ordered up some more Regulars: a company of the 2nd U.S. Cavalry that had, until recently, been chasing Comanches through West Texas. Colonel Richardson, meanwhile, realigned his infantry for another effort, guiding the 12th New York into line to the left of the artillery section. He aligned the regiment for a charge, and sent them in while Ayres threw his brace of guns into battery and loaded them with canister. The New York regiment flung a string of skirmishers along the edge of the stream, where they traded shots with riflemen of the 1st Virginia who wore dark jackets and light trousers almost identical to their own. Then Richardson started back to arrange the rest of his brigade on the right of the guns: at that moment his two Michigan regiments remained on top of the hill, supporting the rest of the artillery, and the Massachusetts colonel was still putting his regiment back together. Canteens filled that morning were running dry by then, and the heat and humidity had grown so oppressive that men had begun passing out under the blazing sun. Heavy blanket rolls and jackets littered the countryside as sweltering men stripped down to their sweat-drenched shirts.[63]

The guns on top of the hill directed their fire at the Confederate battery upstream, convincing Bonham that they intended to force their way over Mitchell's Ford, but Ayres turned his muzzles toward Blackburn's Ford, where so far they had only heard from skirmishers. While Richardson readied his three other regiments, Ayres began blasting canister blindly into the foliage, showering the enemy with branches. At that the forest began to disgorge deafening volleys of musketry as Longstreet responded to an apparent full-scale attack on his ford. Some of his men quailed under the hail of canister, but Longstreet rode out into the storm of iron with a cigar clenched in his teeth, waving his Virginians back into line and encouraging them with his own indifference to the danger. The brunt of the New Yorkers' charge fell on the 17th Virginia, including a company led by the Leesburg newspaper editor who had, until Lincoln's mobilization, preached peace and union. When Longstreet saw the New Yorkers closing in, he sent those Virginians spilling over the banks of the creek in a countercharge. Three companies splashed across the run with fixed bayonets, and at sight of those glittering blades most of the New York regiment crumbled. The men fled shamelessly back out of the woods, and when Richardson saw them streaming away he sailed into them, calling for their officers to rally them, but none of the officers were present and no one could tell him where any of them were. The fugitives never slowed down until they had put more than a mile between themselves and Bull Run.[64]

In their brief fight the New Yorkers had suffered nearly three dozen casualties, and — suspiciously enough — the list of killed and wounded did not name a single officer. In the same period Captain Ayres had lost four men from his two gun crews, as well as half a dozen horses. Up on the hilltop, where McDowell's chief engineer had been heckling General Tyler about exceeding his orders, that old brigadier decided to pull all the infantry out of the fight when he saw the New York regiment disintegrate. His guns continued to punish the Confederates from the high ground, but by 4:00 PM even they fell silent, and the defenders of Blackburn's Ford congratulated themselves on having beaten back the invaders.[65]

The repulse of a single brigade in McDowell's army reversed Confederate humiliation over the defeat at Rich Mountain. The next morning the Richmond newspapers, which had expected a decisive fight on July 18, jubilantly announced Confederate victory in the "Great Battle of Manassas." The enemy had been "completely routed," they reported, gleefully passing on mythical estimates of a thousand or fifteen hundred Union casualties. Their recent apprehensions about McClellan's victories notwithstanding, the Richmond editors revealed not the slightest surprise at so complete a victory: they held most Northern soldiers in contempt, after all. Judging, probably, by the Pennsylvania prisoners Jackson had taken at Falling Waters, the *Dispatch* had reported only the day before that the federal government had filled its armies with foreign mercenaries, most of whom seemed to be Germans. The rosters of many Virginia regiments were also sprinkled with German names, but the Pennsylvania Germans frequently preferred the ancestral language reminiscent of the alien armies that King George had hired to help him quell the Revolution.[66]

For all the hopeful reports of dead Yankees, neither side tallied more than six dozen killed and wounded in the fierce contest at Blackburn's Ford. On the Confederate side quite a few officers had been shot, including a battery commander and two field officers, reflecting their more conspicuous personal presence on the firing line. The opposing armies had

had too little contact with each other to learn what manner of men they faced; after the violation of James Jackson's home and the sacking of Fairfax Court House and Germantown, the Confederates had every right to assume that victory would only encourage the invaders to further depredations. In this first clash with troops they now commonly characterized as "Hessians," the Virginians therefore showed unusual desperation to prevail.[67]

5

Where Ignorant Armies Clash

❖ MCDOWELL'S SUCCESS at Manassas would depend in great measure on what Robert Patterson did fifty miles to the northwest, and what Patterson did depended largely on his personal confidence — in which the old general seems to have been unusually deficient. For nearly a fortnight Patterson had lain at Martinsburg, twenty miles from Johnston's entrenchments, while his own army swelled from fourteen thousand to well over twenty thousand. Among the troops that augmented his force was the militia brigade under Charles P. Stone, who arrived in Martinsburg with it on July 8. Four more regiments and a battery of four guns reached Patterson over the next couple of days, and a fifth regiment marched in on the night of July 12. Johnston, meanwhile, managed to add only about twenty-five hundred unreliable militia to his regular troops, who numbered fewer than eleven thousand, of all arms, but Patterson imagined him with twenty-six thousand men and two dozen big field guns. At first, Winfield Scott had urged his old friend to trounce Joe Johnston's Winchester force or chase him away, and Patterson issued orders for his various brigades to advance on July 9, but he suspended those orders when his senior officers began muttering against the move. The old man offered further evidence of his flagging self-assurance by calling a council of war in lieu of the advance, and then deferring to the more timorous opinions of his Regular Army staff officers. Those officers feared that Johnston meant to lure Patterson away from his source of supply until he could pounce on him with reinforcements from Manassas: they concluded that instead of marching directly against Winchester, Patterson should move obliquely, toward Charles Town, where he could draw supplies from Harper's Ferry with less danger of interruption.[1]

Patterson attended to his correspondence with Washington little more conscientiously than he had communicated with Stone, and in his crippling anxiety about spies, disloyal officers, and intercepted dispatches he sometimes employed a confusing, cryptic style when he did write to Scott. As soon as he decided against driving deeper into Virginia he wrote a long letter to the general-in-chief, informing him of his new plan to march on Charles Town, from which place he could move parallel to the Potomac and take Leesburg. In the copy of his letter that went to Washington, Patterson then asked Scott to let him know when he ought to move against "Leesburg," suggesting that the day could be named in a coded telegraphic message beginning "Let me hear of you on . . ." Scott received that July 9 dispatch by courier three days later, and by telegraph he immediately replied "Let me hear of you on Tuesday," meaning July 16.[2]

The secretive references to place names created needless confusion. Patterson later contended that his original dispatch to Scott asked when he should move against Winchester, rather than Leesburg, as though he had not given up aggressive intentions. Years later both Patterson's adjutant general and his military secretary (who happened to be Patterson's own son) concurred that Winchester was the implied target. The officer who supervised publication of Union and Confederate records stood by the Leesburg reference of the printed version, but a quarter of a century after the war a special search for the original document failed to uncover it. A march on Leesburg fit the context of the July 9 dispatch better, but — even if a headquarters scrivener did not err in his transcription — the doddering Patterson may have meant instead to promise a stab at Winchester on his way to Charles Town.[3]

Still hesitating at Martinsburg on July 13, Patterson opened a hand-carried dispatch from Scott that had passed his in the mail, and it corroborated the fears of the Regulars on Patterson's staff. According to a reliable, confidential communication that had landed on Scott's desk, the Confederates intended to draw Patterson beyond the possibility of retreat and destroy his army with a rapid concentration of forces before turning on McClellan's mountain force and then doubling back to Fairfax Court House to deal with McDowell. The warning could have come from a sympathetic idler about Beauregard's headquarters, for it provided a slightly garbled description of a plan the Creole general actually was polishing for Jefferson Davis's consideration. The contents of that message confirmed Patterson in his caution, and he informed Washington that he "would rather lose the chance of accomplishing something brilliant" than risk defeat by bold maneuver. Wallowing in self-doubt, though, he begged Scott to "let me be instructed" if his passive attitude did not meet with approbation.[4]

Patterson's obvious trepidation disturbed Scott all the more as the time neared for McDowell to strike at Beauregard, and the aging conqueror of Mexico City immediately wired back with more direct instructions. If Patterson felt himself too weak to beat Johnston immediately, he should at least offer an aggressive demonstration that would force Johnston to prepare for his own defense. That would theoretically prevent him from slipping away to join Beauregard, but if even that failed then Patterson should hasten down the Potomac through Leesburg to aid McDowell.[5]

With his fluctuating delusions about Johnston's strength, Patterson clearly felt himself too weak to challenge the Winchester Confederates in open battle. The professionals in Patterson's army understood, and doubtless conveyed to their commander, that the best threatening demonstration they could make would be to move up to Bunker Hill, halfway between Martinsburg and Winchester. The advance would stretch their tenuous supply line another ten miles, so Patterson decided to seize Bunker Hill only in passing. Providing his men with enough rations to march to Bunker Hill and then on to Charles Town, he arranged for a new, more secure supply depot at Harper's Ferry.[6]

In Patterson's defense, he had been assigned a most ticklish job, at least in light of his disinclination to fight a pitched battle. Holding Johnston without attacking him required enough aggressive behavior to keep him alarmed, but not enough to frighten him away. As Charles Stone and Fitz John Porter later told a congressional committee, such theatrics were probably not going to dissuade Johnston from going to Beauregard's aid in any case. Patterson might have accomplished his purpose more effectively by marching around Johnston's right flank, interposing himself between the two Confederate forces and blocking the mountain gaps. The move would have put him in a dangerous position, but it was the maneuver that Jefferson Davis feared most of all. Months after the fact Patterson's senior subordinate, the New York militia general Charles Sandford, said he was willing to take that chance with only eight regiments and a couple of batteries. Barring that, the only other option for detaining Johnston consisted of an actual assault on Winchester, and Patterson enumerated several impediments against that. To begin, there was his inflated estimate of Johnston's numbers, which would have given Johnston an overall advantage if they had been accurate. Then came the supply issue, which created universal concern so early in the war, before bolder generals were allowed to provision their armies from the enemy's countryside. Finally there was the morale and condition of his troops, and on that point he probably found his most justifiable reason for avoiding an assault — on Winchester, Leesburg, or any other position Confederates chose to defend.[7]

When the well-drilled 2nd Massachusetts marched into Martinsburg under a veteran West Pointer on July 12, a lieutenant in that regiment found the rest of Patterson's army particularly wanting in discipline. The troops' laxity bespoke both inexperience and neglect. With the exception of some of their officers, almost none of the infantry at either Martinsburg or Winchester had served more than three months in uniform. The men's greenness would have worked to Patterson's disadvantage if he went on the attack. Attacking troops had to perform cumbersome maneuvers under fire while the defenders could often stand in place, sometimes behind protective earthworks that promised fewer casualties, less disorganization, and much less opportunity for panic. Johnston drilled his militia reinforcements feverishly, and kept them busy building breastworks beyond Winchester, where they might be expected to put up a better fight against assailants with little more experience.[8]

The most experienced men on either side belonged to the earliest regiments of Patterson's three-month militia, and he had thousands of them, but it was these men whom he doubted most of all. As early as Independence Day he predicted that few of them would reenlist for the three-year service. Ten days later, on the ninetieth day after Lincoln's call for those troops, Patterson warned headquarters that the militia had begun to grouse about the possibility of not being allowed to go home when their enlistments expired; most of the captains of the 6th Pennsylvania had petitioned their colonel against even a short extension. Of his Pennsylvania regiments alone, eighteen were due to be discharged by July 24: reinforcements in comparable numbers could not reach him in so short a time. Discouraged by reports of campfire grumbling, Patterson made no patriotic appeals for the men to remain on duty until the campaign ended. In many cases their shoes and britches had worn through and they had no means of replacing them, limiting the troops' usefulness even if they had been willing to waive a timely discharge.[9]

When Patterson relayed his concerns about the militia, Winfield Scott pointed out that the week of service those regiments had remaining offered plenty of time to attack Johnston, but Patterson had already convinced himself that he would be soundly defeated in any attack. He considered his army crucial to the protection of both McClellan and McDowell, against either of whom Johnston could throw his weight with Patterson out of the way. Unless Scott sent him a direct order to attack Johnston, Patterson thought it best to pussyfoot around the perimeter. Scott persisted in urging him to take action, but did not feel he could order him to the attack after all the dire warnings Patterson had sent his way.[10]

Scott's telegram asking Patterson to "let me hear of you on Tuesday"

left Patterson supposing that Tuesday, July 16, would be the day of Mc-
Dowell's long-awaited attack on Beauregard. He therefore advanced
from Martinsburg on July 15, chasing Confederate pickets from Bunker
Hill and camping his own men in their place. For about forty-eight hours
Johnston was tied to Winchester while McDowell's various columns
started rolling toward Fairfax Court House. On the appointed Tuesday
Patterson sent a sizable reconnaissance toward Winchester under Colonel
George Thomas — the Virginia Regular who had applied for a post at the
Virginia Military Institute the previous winter, before he opted to stick
with the federal government. Thomas scouted the roads and frightened
some of Johnston's troops into line of battle, but that appeared to be all
the threat Patterson dared to pose: in expectation of making no more
than a semblance of an attack, he had encumbered his men with only
a two-day supply of food. On July 17 his brigades began filing to the
east, away from Winchester and toward Charles Town, where he could re-
plenish their rations from Harper's Ferry. He anticipated that McDowell
would have achieved his objective by that point, relieving him of the need
to forestall Johnston any longer, but he learned his mistake shortly after
midnight on July 18, when a courier delivered the latest telegram from
Scott.[11]

Scott began with a reprimand. He had instructed Patterson to report
frequently while on the march, but he had heard nothing from him for
three days, and had only learned of Patterson's movement toward Harper's Ferry through Philadelphia newspapers. After lecturing him about
letting Johnston deceive him with a detachment while he repaired to
Manassas with his main body, Scott announced that McDowell had just
driven the Confederates out of Fairfax Court House, and that he would
probably attack Manassas "tomorrow." The telegram was dated 9:30 PM
on Wednesday, July 17, and it was not yet four hours old when Patterson
read it.[12]

In Winchester, more than twenty miles away, another courier delivered
another telegram to another general at about the same moment. Relaying
information from Manassas, the War Department in Richmond warned
General Johnston that Beauregard was under attack and needed the help
of Johnston's army, if he could get away. Johnston already knew that
Patterson had sidled away to Charles Town, perhaps with the intention of
sliding up the Blue Ridge to seize those gaps or to make an attack from
below. In either case, Johnston concluded, he could and should go to
Beauregard's aid immediately, and he put his troops on the march for the
Manassas Gap Railroad. There he boarded his infantry on cars, meanwhile directing Colonel Stuart's cavalry and the artillery overland. The

railroad could take only a few regiments at a time, with nearly as many men on top of the cars as inside them, and while the first contingent shuttled off the rest turned to an impromptu banquet prepared by local citizens. Some seventeen hundred of Johnston's men remained behind in Winchester, afflicted by the epidemics of minor ailments that proved so deadly to country boys. To defend the town, Johnston left the remaining militia in their entrenchments under the local militia general.[13]

Patterson telegraphed back to Scott early that morning, asking if he should attack even though some regiments had warned him they would not remain an hour beyond their ninety days. An exasperated Scott replied that he had certainly been expecting Patterson to fight, and to win, or to at least maintain the feint of an attack, while Patterson had instead allowed Johnston to slip away to Manassas Junction. If the three-month militia should forsake him, said Scott, Patterson could simply dig in before the enemy and wait for reinforcements. Patterson's reply revealed both the depth of his own irritation and the inadequacy of his military intelligence. He denied that Johnston had stolen a march on him (even as Johnston's troops streamed out of Winchester), and he congratulated himself on holding back an army that was even then on its way to reinforce Beauregard. Finally, he came close to chastising the general-in-chief for expecting so much from him against "an enemy far superior in numbers," when in fact Patterson outnumbered Johnston about two to one, excluding the ragtag Virginia militia.[14]

The news that McDowell was now making his attack alone failed to invigorate Patterson. He called a general formation for the afternoon of July 18, during which he intended to ask the militia regiments to stay on, but before that assembly he sent home two of the five Pennsylvania companies that had first answered Lincoln's April 15 call. He also ordered more of his troops to Harper's Ferry, still farther from Winchester, signaling the abandonment of the campaign against Johnston, and that only dampened the response to his appeal. In all, just three regiments agreed to a ten-day extension of their terms. The rest insisted on immediate discharge. Although some of the officers in those departing regiments assumed that their men would reenlist after a few weeks at home, many of them never reentered the army.[15]

The three-month militia and volunteers may have been anxious to go home, but Patterson's inaction confused and dismayed some of his three-year men. Officers in the 2nd Massachusetts had expected to march on Winchester from Bunker Hill, and their diversion to Charles Town perplexed them. When Patterson sent their regiment ahead to garrison Harper's Ferry, they felt "sheepish," as one of them said, about leaving

Johnston free to maneuver. After they heard rumors of bad news from Manassas and suspected that their army had caused the trouble by failing to prevent Johnston's march, outright mortification began to set in.[16]

For a couple of days Patterson lingered at Charles Town, discharging his three-month regiments and sending Washington ridiculous reports that Johnston still held Winchester, with troops coming in every night to reinforce him. Finally, on July 20, he laconically announced that Johnston had, after all, escaped with "a portion of his force" on July 18. Taking the word of a Confederate colonel's brother, who had recently visited Winchester and apparently wished to bluff the Yankees, he estimated Johnston's total strength at 35,200 men — nearly three times as many as Johnston ever had there. The next day Patterson removed his headquarters to Harper's Ferry, where he gave up on the rest of the ninety-day men and calculated his effective force as half a dozen three-year regiments, three artillery batteries, and some Regular cavalry. As though abdicating his command altogether, he asked army headquarters if he should evacuate Harper's Ferry and come to Washington with that oversize brigade. Not until July 23 did a disgusted Winfield Scott wire back that "your force is not wanted here." Later that day Patterson discovered by way of an army order published in a newspaper that he had been abruptly discharged from the army and replaced as commander in the Shenandoah vicinity by the Massachusetts politician Nathaniel Banks.[17]

Still later that same night, Scott sent Banks information from a loyal newspaper editor indicating that Winchester contained valuable arms, artillery, ammunition, and equipment, with only about five hundred raw militia to defend it: evidently Patterson's withdrawal had convinced many of the Virginia militiamen that it was safe to go home. Patterson still retained actual command, so naturally the message fell into his hands the next morning, and in his last official communication with headquarters he remained as contentious and defensive as ever. There were three thousand Confederates at Winchester, he insisted — probably relying on the same stale, inaccurate information that had hobbled his entire campaign. They might be militia, he admitted, but that was more men than he could put in the field. Besides, he added, if he took that many men from Harper's Ferry the place would be helpless. He maintained that he needed twenty thousand men: the daily departure of the three-month men had so weakened him that he could not defend the town, yet his command was "too large to retreat with if forced to evacuate." There no longer seemed to be any place in Virginia where Patterson felt secure. Two days later Banks arrived and Patterson bade a formal farewell to the troops of his command — most of whom had already left for home ahead of him. That concluded his military career, save for another few months of wrangling about his record with Scott, the secretary of war, and anyone else who would listen.[18]

Years later, a distinguished veteran of the three-month regiments would challenge Patterson's assertions about their reluctance to serve beyond their terms, but at the time Patterson had plenty of cause to doubt their enthusiasm. A captain with the ninety-day militia sent Patterson a letter on July 17 corroborating that many of the men in his regiment and even some of their officers blatantly refused to serve one hour beyond their time. The disappointing proportion of those men who immediately reenlisted confirmed both the captain's warning and the old general's concerns.[19]

Some officers who served with Patterson later alleged that the three-month troops grew discouraged only after it became clear that their commander's want of combativeness had foiled the foremost object of their campaign, but the contention rings false.[20] McDowell found his own three-month men demanding their discharges at the same juncture, and they hovered menacingly before the enemy at the time. On the very eve of what many expected to be the great battle to decide the fate of the Union they refused their superiors' every entreaty to stay and fight.

Army headquarters logically marked the three-month commitment from the day the various regiments had been mustered in by federal officers. The men who carried the rifles took a more personal perspective, and they had been counting off the days since they marched away from their homes. In McDowell's army the troops closest to the end of their militia terms belonged to a battery that had come out with the 8th New York. The artillerymen, who had always marched proudly as the 1st Troop Washington Grays in New York City parades, insisted on going home the moment they heard about the bloody clash at Blackburn's Ford. They had organized for service on April 19, four days into an orgy of nationalistic infatuation, and apparently the prospect of being maimed or killed had not occurred to them: they calculated the end of their contract on July 18, and the immediate presence of the enemy only whetted their impatience to be gone. The 4th Pennsylvania had organized at Harrisburg on April 20, and on the ninetieth day of their service the men of that unit felt the same way.

McDowell did not press the point about the dates they had been mustered in, which left both units with a few more days of service due, but he did ask them to stay on a little longer to see the army through the impending battle. The colonel of the Pennsylvania regiment made a more personal appeal, and so did Simon Cameron, the hawk-faced secretary of war: Cameron had come out with his brother, who commanded the predominantly Scottish 79th New York, and he begged the Pennsylvanians to uphold the honor of his native state. McDowell offered to send the unwilling back to Alexandria, and then he called for those who would stay, but only the colonel stepped forward. On the sweltering morning of Saturday, July 20, the entire 4th Pennsylvania started back for Washington under the lieutenant colonel, and every man of the Washington Grays left with them. The Pennsylvania colonel offered himself to his brigade commander as an aide-de-camp, and some volunteers from one of Louis Blenker's German regiments appropriated the abandoned guns of the New York battery.[21]

The disaster at Blackburn's Ford had disrupted McDowell's plans by forcing him to bring up the rest of his troops immediately, rather than leaving them behind to collect rations from his inadequate supply train, but it may have wrought even more damage to his army's morale. They had come out from Washington and Alexandria with the news of McClellan's mountain victories still ringing in their ears, and the sheer size of their own force had lent an atmosphere of invulnerability to their march. This confidence gave way to despondency among many of those who took part in the fight of July 18, and the tale of the 12th New York's shameful flight circulated through the camps of the army, dousing the ardor of some who had thought the vast array of uniforms and ordnance irresistible. It helped little to rejuvenate the enthusiasm of Richardson's brigade when their dead and wounded were recovered the next morning, for the artillery had mangled some of the bodies horribly.[22]

There also arose a chilling report that the rebels had bayoneted the wounded. Fueled by deliberate propaganda from partisan newspapers, groundless rumors of that nature pervaded the coverage of early battles, but this one originated on the battlefield itself the following morning. True or not, it may have come from the testimony of wounded who survived, or merely from the discovery of apparent bayonet wounds on the bodies of the dead. One of the Massachusetts skirmishers told friends at home that he heard a wounded comrade in the distance begging for his life, but that a Southern voice replied "Bayonet the son of a bitch."[23]

As fraudulent as most reports of atrocities may have been during that period, the Massachusetts skirmishers who ventured closest to the creek suffered an unusually high percentage of killed. The two companies lost no fewer than sixteen men, of whom four were captured (at least three of them wounded, and one by bayonet), while eleven of the others were killed on the field. Battles with muzzleloading weapons usually left more men wounded than dead, at least initially, and often the wounded outnumbered the dead by at least a factor of two or three. The regiment that faced the 1st Massachusetts, for instance, lost one man killed and fourteen wounded.[24]

Three missing Massachusetts soldiers did return from captivity months later, but others — including young Albert Wentworth — were never seen again. They evidently died on or near ground traversed by the three Virginia companies that later splashed across the run to disperse the 12th New York. An eyewitness recorded that those men, members of the 17th Virginia, forded the creek with fixed bayonets. The 17th Virginia hailed from the northern counties of the state, some of which McDowell's army had already desecrated. The first company over the creek, in fact, was Company A, from Alexandria, where Yankees had inaugurated their invasion: Company A may have included the husband and brothers of an Alexandria woman recently murdered by a straggler from McDowell's army. The ferocity of the Virginians' counterattack illustrated a literal effort to deliver their homes and families from a vicious enemy. Such fury might well have propelled decent men to forget themselves as they rushed headlong toward a far more numerous foe, and the suspiciously high proportion of killed in the Massachusetts detachment suggests that some of them may have succumbed to that savage impulse. At that stage of the war, nervous Yankees needed only an instance or two of such indiscretion to conclude that the despicable traitors could be expected to give them no quarter.[25]

McDowell faced not only a crisis in the morale of his troops, but the spontaneous reorganization of his plans, as well, for while Tyler battered one of his brigades against Blackburn's Ford McDowell had reconnoitered the terrain on Beauregard's extreme right. Finding that he could not easily launch a flank attack in that direction, he had to select another option with the clock ticking toward the discharge of nearly one-third of his army. McDowell did not know it, but the time it took to develop and deploy for another attack posed an even more critical disadvantage for him, because the passage of every hour brought Joe Johnston's army closer to a junction with Beauregard's. General Scott had promised that Patterson would either keep Johnston occupied in the Shenandoah or follow him to Manassas if he got away, leaving Union forces with numerical superiority in either case, but throughout July 19 the vanguard of Johnston's reinforcement rumbled slowly eastward on the Manassas Gap Railroad. His leading brigade, under the same Thomas Jackson who had confronted Patterson at Falling Waters, reached Manassas Junction that evening. The train started back right away for another brigade, returning the next morning. Johnston himself arrived on the field by noon of July 20. Though his date of rank made him senior to Beauregard, Johnston waived that prerogative on the grounds that Beauregard knew the field much better than he did.[26]

Beauregard called in all the additional troops he could wring from Virginia. From Fredericksburg he ordered up two infantry regiments — one from Tennessee and one from Arkansas — and a battery of artillery. From Richmond he requested the newly arrived Hampton Legion, a combined regiment of infantry, cavalry, and artillery led by the wealthy South Carolinian Wade Hampton.[27] From Leesburg he brought down Eppa Hunton's 8th Virginia, which left that town July 18 and filed into line by noon on the following day.[28] Before he departed Leesburg Hunton called out the Loudoun militia to picket the river, man the empty entrenchments, and herd the army's stock of fat cattle to safety at the foot of the Blue Ridge.[29] Beauregard had already recalled the 4th South Carolina from Leesburg, along with Nathan Evans, the staff major who was still masquerading as a brigadier general. Evans had asked for higher rank in the provisional army, but he would fight the upcoming battle without official promotion. Beauregard separated the 8th Virginia and the 4th South Carolina when they came in from Leesburg, assigning Hunton's regiment with some other Virginia troops. He continued Evans as an ersatz brigadier, giving him the South Carolina regiment, a battalion of Louisiana Zouaves, a troop of cavalry, and part of an artillery battery.[30]

Hunton's 8th Virginia joined the brigade of Colonel Philip St. George Cocke, who had served as a general in Virginia's military organization but had, like many other state officers, been dropped a grade when he entered the Confederate service. Cocke had been the original Confederate commander in this region, and more than two months before he had proposed precisely the plan that Richmond was now putting to work: one large force at Manassas and another at Winchester, each prepared to aid the other over the intervening railroad. With his brigade he held three local fords just south of the Warrenton Turnpike, near Beauregard's left flank. Before Hunton reported, Cocke had already gathered three Virginia regiments and three companies of another new one, besides two four-gun Virginia batteries. Also under Cocke's command, forgotten by historians and by every Confederate except Colonel Cocke, were three companies of expatriate Marylanders and Virginians who had recently resided in the District of Columbia. They had rallied to the Confederate cause under Captain Frank B. Schaeffer, the district militia officer for whom Charles Stone had refused a field commission the previous winter. Two of Schaeffer's companies supported one of Cocke's batteries on the right bank of the creek while the third had waded across and taken position as advance skirmishers behind the left bank, using the natural embankment as a breastwork.[31]

Beauregard gave Cocke nominal command of Evans's demi-brigade as well, but Evans acted as though he considered Cocke more of a colleague than a superior. Evans took the extreme left of the Confederate line, guarding both the stone bridge that carried the Warrenton Turnpike over Bull Run and another small ford upstream.[32]

McDowell's senior engineer scouted the fords north of the Warrenton Turnpike for much of July 19, searching for an avenue of attack. He turned back as soon as he rode into Confederate videttes, but he had already satisfied himself that a flanking column could follow existing roads all the way to Sudley Ford, three miles upstream as the creek meandered. That night another engineer party went out to confirm the details of the route, but it ran afoul of Colonel Cocke's skirmishers, as did two other officers who tried to examine the situation downstream. Still, McDowell felt compelled to make some kind of attack, and to make it soon, for they could hear the locomotives running into Manassas Junction and supposed that each one brought Beauregard more troops — perhaps even from Johnston. McDowell therefore composed a plan based on nothing more than his chief engineer's abbreviated reconnaissance, and on Saturday evening he called his various division and brigade commanders to his headquarters tent, a mile east of Centreville.[33]

In pugilistic terms, McDowell proposed a couple of feigned jabs followed by a roundhouse haymaker from his right. The feints would come from Israel Richardson, on his left, who would repeat his Thursday assault against Blackburn's Ford with his brigade, and from General Tyler, who would deploy the rest of his division in the center against the stone bridge on the turnpike. Neither would attempt an immediate crossing: David Hunter's division would lead the real blow from the right, diverging from the turnpike behind Tyler to follow a wagon track leading around the Confederate left in a wide arc, fording Bull Run in the shallows at Sudley Springs. As Hunter swept back down the right bank of the creek he would uncover a crossing for Samuel Heintzelman's division, which would ford Bull Run and join him, and their five brigades would all hit the Confederates on their left flank, driving them away from the bridge. Then Tyler would cross, adding the weight of three more brigades and assuring the destruction of Beauregard's army. An entire division of New Jersey regiments had stayed behind to protect McDowell's communications, and that left only one other division at his disposal on the battlefield. Just in case Beauregard should offer an attack of his own, McDowell ordered that last division, commanded by the dipsomaniac Dixon Miles, to lie in reserve on the imposing ridge near Centreville.[34]

Everything depended on an early start, especially in the case of the flanking column, so McDowell directed the commanders of his divisions to be on the road between two and two thirty on Sunday morning. That would allow the men who had the most ground to cover to make their march before the oppressive midday heat, and the darkness would shield most of their movement from the eyes of vigilant Confederates. After explaining his marching instructions to the division commanders he dismissed them to their commands, where they relayed instruction to their brigade and regimental commanders. The news soon reached individual campfires, where men wrote boastful letters home, burnished their muskets, and arranged little arsenals of dirks and pocket pistols. In some regiments chaplains gathered their men for abbreviated sermons and a brief prayer before everyone turned in for what sleep the momentous circumstances might allow.[35]

As it happened, Beauregard did entertain aggressive intentions, and his battle plan mirrored McDowell's almost precisely. Anticipating an attack on his immediate left, somewhere in the vicinity of the turnpike, he supposed that McDowell would have weakened his own left to make that attack, so that was where he aimed to hit him. Most of his reinforcements had reached the field: he expected the Hampton Legion from Richmond momentarily, and a few thousand of Johnston's men still rumbled along the road from Winchester, so he could throw in every man he had and still accumulate a satisfactory reserve. By Saturday night he calculated his effective force at more than twenty-nine thousand men, and he began massing the majority of them on his right for an assault that he planned to launch on Sunday morning, July 21.[36]

The men who would have to make McDowell's flank march arose two hours after midnight, assembling without bugle or drum tap near the fading embers of their campfires. They carried nothing but blanket rolls, haversacks full of hardtack, canteens, and cartridge boxes with forty rounds of ammunition. It was, thought a seventeen-year-old private from Vassalboro, Maine, "a beautiful cool morning." Five brigades lined up under a bright moon: fourteen regiments of amateurs, a battalion apiece of Regular infantry, cavalry, and Marines, and two dozen cannon — all but three of which would belong to the Confederates before another twenty-four hours had passed.[37]

The punctuality of those five brigades gained nothing. Ahead of them marched Daniel Tyler's division, which, in an acute lapse of logic, McDowell had directed to proceed first. From his camp behind Cub Run, Tyler needed to advance barely three miles to keep his appointment for a daybreak assault. Until he covered half that distance he would block the entrance to the roundabout wagon track that Hunter and Heintzelman had to follow, which veered off to the north at an old blacksmith shop. The different regiments in the flanking column faced a march of ten to twelve miles from their campsites, and ought to have started first, but McDowell apparently expected that Tyler would be out of the way before the flanking column even reached that intersection.

Tyler disappointed McDowell for the third time in four days. First, his leading brigade dawdled beyond the deadline, and then, fearing an ambush behind every tree, it crept forward into the territory that McDowell's engineers had not been able to reconnoiter. The brigade had with it a battery of oversized Parrott guns, including a thirty-pounder rifle — a behemoth that could throw its massive projectile for miles — and the lieutenant in charge of this ponderous piece feared that it would collapse the wooden bridge over Cub Run. The entire column thus came to a halt while the lieutenant shored up the bridge. Between the delay of Tyler's infantry and the wait for the thirty-pounder, Hunter's division stood restlessly in formation or squatted along the roadside not far from its camps for two solid hours. From the private in the ranks to Hunter himself, everyone wondered why they could not move. The brigade of Ambrose Burnside edged up behind Tyler, inching forward. Commanding the brigade behind Burnside, Colonel Andrew Porter grumbled about the delay with his adjutant, mistaking it for Burnside's fault. The adjutant, future brigadier general William Averell, held it against Burnside ever afterward.[38]

The problem, as Averell recognized at the time, was the absence of overall direction: "a lack of headquarters," as he phrased it. General McDowell had eaten something that did not agree with him, and he slept late on that crucial morning, hoping to face the day as fresh as possible. Five o'clock had nearly come when he finally roused, mounted a horse, and rode up through a tangle of troops lounging in the road, to investigate the congestion. Tyler's first brigade had still not passed Cub Run bridge. McDowell urged Tyler's men on, but the last of them had not shuffled out of Hunter's way until 5:30 AM, by the watch of McDowell's engineer. The watches in this army disagreed by as much as an hour, but nearly three hours had been lost: Tyler was about ready to begin his part of the program when the flanking column turned down the wagon track with another eight miles to march.[39]

This deep into Virginia, Union officers could still find numerous loyal citizens, and one of them — a New Jersey native who worked nearby as a farm laborer for a New York immigrant — conducted Hunter's division down the wagon track. The guide warned against a more direct route that would have saved a couple of hours, arguing that it would have revealed the column to the Confederates, but that precaution proved both pointless and costly. The sun rose soon after the head of Hunter's division passed the intersection. Burnside's four regiments led the way, spurred by the occasional booming of the Parrott battery behind them as Tyler tried to distract the enemy at the stone bridge. More than five hundred of these men would never see another sunset, yet a holiday atmosphere prevailed; they joked with each other as they marched, dropping out again for black-berries when the whim struck them, despite stern new orders to the contrary. This would be the last march of the storybook war, and even then many of the men along that wagon track may have expected their campaign to end with bands, banners, and no serious bloodshed. With the sun came the stifling July heat, and the column began alternately bunching and stretching, forcing men who had been brought to a complete halt to break into a sprint. They sweat profusely and began shucking blanket rolls, jackets, and even haversacks to lighten their loads.[40]

A Minnesota private in Heintzelman's division, halfway between the head and tail of the flanking column, could neither see the ends of it nor guess its magnitude. "The road seemed like a living river of soldiers," he remarked a few days later.[41]

With daylight, too, came the early detection that the Confederates would have been denied by the timely departure of McDowell's flank march. Beauregard's weight lay primarily on his right at that hour, along Mitchell's Ford and Blackburn's Ford, where he prepared to launch his own surprise attack while Colonel Cocke held the stone bridge against McDowell. In positioning his troops for that assault James Longstreet waded his Virginia brigade over Bull Run early in the morning, running into Israel Richardson again as Richardson came forward to perform his diversion. Still intent on spearheading the offensive, Longstreet threw out skirmishers and arranged his regiments under desultory artillery fire, but then he sent a pair of Texans who were serving him as volunteer aides to examine the enemy lines from a nearby hilltop. One of the Texans climbed a tree, and with the aid of full daylight he spotted Hunter's troops circling around toward the undefended fords upstream.[42]

Not long thereafter, Beauregard's signal officer also noticed the movement of troops near Sudley's Ford as he read messages through his telescope, and he reported that the enemy was flanking the army farther up Bull Run. Beauregard and Johnston had just taken position behind Mitchell's Ford to watch their army fall on McDowell's flimsy left flank, but now they realized that the firing at the stone bridge did not represent McDowell's main effort. They called Longstreet back over Bull Run and started shifting troops to the extreme left to meet what they expected would be a heavy blow. Nathan Evans (Major Evans, as the supercilious Colonel Cocke insisted on calling him) had anticipated them, and as the commander of the nearest troops he decided to confront the threat on his own hook. He informed Cocke that he was leaving four companies to cover the ford, and he turned to meet the vanguard of Hunter's division with two field pieces and fewer than a thousand South Carolinians and Louisiana Zouaves. A Virginia doctor led him over local roads, advising him to take position on a hillside along the Sudley Road, forming his skirmish line parallel to the turnpike.[43]

It was now midmorning. Stopping on high ground before he reached Bull Run, Andrew Porter and his staff fixed their binoculars on dust clouds that seemed to be moving up the creek on the other side, toward Sudley's Ford. Porter led the other half of Colonel Hunter's division, following Burnside's brigade, and he suspected that the dust could have been raised by Heintzelman's troops, who might have taken another route to a lower crossing. A glimpse of blue trousers seemed to corroborate that, but at least some of Evans's Confederates must have been wearing blue pants, for it was his men Porter saw. When Porter rode ahead to the ford to confer with Hunter, he mentioned the sighting. Colonel Hunter, who was celebrating his fifty-ninth birthday that morning, seemed to know that it could not be Heintzelman — that it had to be Confederate troops, and he galloped ahead of his division to select the ground where he would have to fight. With him rode William Sprague, the rich young man who had just been elected governor of Rhode Island. A slight figure in spectacles, Sprague had initially attempted to act the part of a brigadier over the two regiments from his state, but now he attached himself to Burnside's staff with all the fervor of a boy playing at war. Then came Burnside at the head of his brigade, quickly peeling off the 2nd Rhode Island and its attached battery of artillery to deal with his old West Point comrade, Evans. The South Carolinian opened with his artillery first, and when the infantry came within range he put up such a fight that the Yankees thought him much stronger than he was. One of the first Federals to turn for the rear, wounded, was David Hunter, who left Burnside in charge of the division until Porter, the senior colonel, could reach the front.[44]

Evans stalled the 2nd Rhode Island, then sent the Louisiana Zouaves flying into them in an impetuous charge, and when the Rhode Islanders reeled backward Burnside ordered the 2nd New Hampshire to their support. A lieutenant in that regiment, formerly a schoolteacher, drew the grim duty of posting skirmishers ahead of the regiment. The main body of the New Hampshire regiment managed to tangle itself into a knot as it executed complicated commands under fire. The novices did finally stumble into some semblance of a firing line, but they turned shaky the moment Evans's skirmishers started pecking away at them; their equally amateur field officers hardly knew how to steady them, and soon they broke and ran back over the crest to safety. Burnside then called on the 71st New York Militia behind them to come up and fill the void, but they, too, fell into confusion when artillery drivers plowed through their ranks with limbered guns, so the frustrated colonel whisked his own 1st Rhode Island Militia into line and sent them ahead. The two Rhode Island regiments pushed forward together, though the men who led them both went down with their death wounds within minutes.[45]

Eventually some of the company officers in the New Hampshire Volunteers re-formed most of it. The New York militiamen also pulled themselves together, and the two regiments resumed their places on the line of battle, but the inexperienced 2nd New Hampshire began firing wildly, without orders. Soon a Confederate bullet found the colonel of that regiment, fracturing his shoulder. He reined for the rear without assistance, where a surgeon bound his wound, and then he returned gamely to the fight with his arm in a sling. An orderly led his horse while the colonel groaned his way through a speech intended to encourage the troops, but the sight of their grimacing leader did little to improve the spirit of the men. One of his lieutenants admired the colonel's pluck but admitted that "he was useless as a commander when he was unwounded."[46]

Out front, on the skirmish line of the 2nd New Hampshire, the embattled schoolteacher saw one of his former students knocked to the ground and struggled to remain at his post rather than go to the boy's aid. Then, as the Yankees seemed to be making some progress, the first Confederate reinforcements reached the field. They came from Barnard Bee's brigade of Johnston's army — courtesy of Robert Patterson. Two regiments from Alabama and Mississippi braced Evans as he backed down the hill, and then they stepped ahead of his battered command to take over the fight. Porter's brigade appeared in time for Burnside to appeal for the Regulars who accompanied it, while part of Francis Bartow's Georgia brigade strode in to help Bee and Evans. The Federals had already made a tiresome march, but the newest Confederate troops had enjoyed only one night of sleep during the previous three days, and for a full day they had lain under the broiling sun without tents. Awkwardly the weary men trotted into place; each of the battle lines grew slowly wider, then deeper, and the roar of the battle began to bellow across three counties.[47] The Georgians ran into fire that swept their ranks like a murderous hailstorm, smashing into musket stocks, tugging at hats and clothing, and dropping men at an alarming rate. Officers suffered severely: the colonel of the 8th Georgia crumpled with a broken leg, and his adjutant fell with a bullet through the chest, breathing his last in Union hands.[48]

Twenty miles to the east, London newspaper correspondent William Russell rode toward the anticipated battle in a rented rig when he heard the distant rumbling of artillery. Somewhere between Alexandria and Fairfax Court House he encountered a pathetically disheveled column of uniformed men marching resolutely to the rear. Russell called his driver to a halt so he could interview one of their officers, who identified the dusty procession as the homeward-bound 4th Pennsylvania. The Briton asked the Pennsylvanian why his men were marching away from the sound of the guns, and the officer replied simply that the regiment's term had expired. "We have had three months of this sort of work," he said, "and that's quite enough of it." His former comrades on the right bank of Bull Run might have said the same thing at about that time.[49]

For all the threat to his left, Beauregard still hoped to strike McDowell from the south, at Centreville. He ordered three brigades out to make the assault, and they moved into position again, but the aide who carried the specific instructions fell behind when his horse gave out. The three brigades sat waiting for orders until nearly ten thirty, when Beauregard judged that the opportunity had passed and called them back. McDowell had directed Dixon Miles to dig in against the very angle of attack that Beauregard had envisioned, but the ten Confederate regiments might still have been a match for the eight Union ones — at least so long as they remained under the command of the increasingly intoxicated Miles.[50]

McDowell would not have been available to direct the defense of his Centreville headquarters had Beauregard hurled those brigades against it. By then the Union commander had cantered after his flanking column with his adjutant and his chief engineer, passing Heintzelman's division on the way. When he rode up behind the wounded Hunter's division he found some overheated troops from Porter's brigade still lingering at the creek, drinking and filling their canteens. The portion of the division out on the battlefield was faltering, and McDowell sent back to Heintzelman for a couple of regiments to bolster the line. From the ferocity of the fight and the tall clouds of dust coming toward him he realized that Beauregard was bringing up too many troops for his flanking column to overcome alone. Tyler would have to force his way over the bridge rather than wait for Porter and Heintzelman to clear it for him, and a courier galloped off toward Tyler with orders to that effect.[51]

McDowell examined some prisoners when he found a free moment, and only then did he learn, beyond doubt, that some of Johnston's troops had reached the field: he had not yet seen a telegram from General Scott relaying Patterson's belated admission about Johnston's escape. Until then he trusted Scott's assurance that Johnston would be detained, but even after the confirmation of his worst fear he seemed undaunted.[52]

As far as McDowell could observe, the delays and the bad news about Johnston had not brought much harm. Once the last of Hunter's division fell in, under Burnside now, the flanking column fielded the equivalent of nine full regiments on the Confederate side of Bull Run, including fifteen companies of Regulars, a battalion of Marine recruits, and fourteen guns. Even with the reinforcement of one small brigade and one regiment from another, the Confederates suffered from a severe disadvantage in both men and metal. That disadvantage only worsened as the first of Heintzelman's eleven fresh regiments trotted up and filed into formation, tossing off blanket rolls that would, in most cases, never be seen again by their original owners. One youth whose mother had carefully lined his blanket for him felt a peculiar pang of homesickness as he threw that final token of maternal affection on the ground.[53]

The uneven contest drove the defenders down to the turnpike and beyond, allowing two of Tyler's brigades to wade Bull Run and stiffen the pressure, but McDowell appeared not to use his superior numbers very effectively. The Union assault came in such driblets that a few hundred South Carolinians were able to stem the tide for a while longer. The infantry of Wade Hampton's South Carolina legion had just arrived from Richmond that morning, and he led them into action on the hilltop south of the turnpike. There sat the humble residence of eighty-five-year-old Judith Henry, who still occupied it with her family. The little frame dwelling stood out so prominently that the soldiers fighting there came to think of the spot as "the hill with a house on it," although that would have described numerous other parts of the battlefield as well.[54]

Hampton formed his legion under a blood-red banner embroidered with South Carolina's trademark palmetto and crescent; its heavy silver thread hinted at Hampton's slave-bought wealth. In the valley below stretched a ragged Union battle line that struck one of Hampton's nervous foot soldiers as miles wide. Armed with smoothbores that could do little damage from their distance, they swept down Henry Hill toward the turnpike six hundred strong, and stronger still for the integrity of their line. The 27th New York sprang forward to confront them, but for a critical moment the New Yorkers mistook the South Carolinians' uniforms for those of the 8th New York Militia — which, like most of the early South Carolina regiments, clothed its enlisted men in grey and its officers in blue. The confusion gave the Hampton Legion the first volley, which scattered the New Yorkers. Having momentarily blunted the Union juggernaut, Hampton backed slowly up Henry Hill, covering the retreat for refugees from the other shattered commands. The 8th New York and the 14th New York Militia, in its own distinctive blue and scarlet uniforms, trotted down the Sudley Road to the turnpike to threaten Hampton's flank, an objective that could have best been accomplished by crossing the turnpike and simply facing left to fire a volley. Instead, the two regiments spilled into the turnpike, exposing their own flank to the Confederate artillery on top of Henry Hill, which pelted them viciously for a few moments. Unstrung, both regiments disappeared down the turnpike toward safety, where the fastidious 8th New York Militia disintegrated completely, despite having endured barely two dozen casualties. The regiment mustered out twelve days later, leaving those few ignominious moments to stand as its entire record of battlefield service.[55]

The diversity of uniforms, and in some cases the outright absence of uniforms, caused deadly hesitation at numerous junctures that day. At least four regiments in Hunter's division had taken to the field in grey, or in alternating combinations of grey and blue, and the 14th New York had become famous for those blue jackets and red trousers. The Rhode Island regiments had been issued the tall-crowned, broad-brimmed black hats of the Regular Army, which differed little from the slouch hats of many Confederates, and especially those from the Deep South. The 2nd New Hampshire sported grey forage caps with leather brims, while the caps of the 14th New York combined broad splashes of dark blue and red. In Heintzelman's division, the 11th New York — Ellsworth's Fire Zouaves — wore grey trimmed in yellow and scarlet, and searing heat drove many of them to peel off their jackets, uncovering bright red shirts. Most of the 1st Minnesota went into the fight with black trousers and red or blue flannel shirts, without a coat in the ranks. On the other side, two companies of the 11th Mississippi also lacked jackets, fighting instead in their dark, plastron-fronted "battle" shirts. The Minnesotans and Mississippians faced each other at one point, and a Mississippi officer questioned whether the blue shirts he was about to fire on belonged to other Confederates: he ran forward to inquire, only to find himself a prisoner. No officers at any level seemed to require their men to don a "uniform of the day," and some Southern units fought with no uniforms at all. Individual soldiers only worsened the confusion by stripping down to fight in their shirtsleeves, creating a kaleidoscope in flannel and calico every time they changed formation.[56]

Federal infantry and artillery had sprawled across to the western side of the Sudley Road, outflanking the Southern brigades and driving them to the east, toward Bull Run, as well as south, away from the turnpike. Two of the best artillery batteries in federal service — with rifles accounting for ten of their twelve guns — stood together on Dogan Ridge, west of the Sudley Road, dueling Confederate guns along the wide crest of Henry Hill and punishing the remnants of the troops who had held off the flanking column all morning.[57]

As the battered Confederate line backed up the north face of Henry Hill, a fresh Virginia brigade marched up the low southern slope to meet it. The five regiments belonged to Thomas J. Jackson, the former Virginia Military Institute professor who had met Patterson at Falling Waters nineteen days before. He held a new commission as brigadier general but wore no insignia to indicate that rank. In fact he adhered to the colorful chaos of the day with his old blue VMI uniform and a faded antebellum cap, not unlike the one he had worn in the Mexican War. His variegated brigade reflected the same reliance on local sartorial supply. At least a portion of the 4th Virginia marched in loose flannel battle shirts of light grey, with dark blue caps (closely resembling the 71st New York that day). Some companies of the 27th Virginia retained the dark blue jackets favored by the Old Dominion militia before the war, and at least a fair proportion of one regiment wore blue shirts and pants, with straw hats. No style approached a standard within the brigade, and some companies stood out from the rest of their regiments, while individual officers sported custom-tailored uniforms wildly different from those of their men. One teenage VMI student donned his cutaway cadet "coatee" to lead a company of the 27th Virginia, but instead of lending him an air of martial authority the ornate jacket left him looking more like a drummer boy.[58]

Jackson had come toward Henry Hill in response to Colonel Cocke's appeal for support at the stone bridge, but before he could reach the bridge the Yankees had swept across the turnpike and threatened to swarm up over the crest. Control of that hill would have allowed McDowell to roll up the Confederate line and finish things in short order, so Jackson forgot about the bridge and veered his brigade to the hilltop, distributing the regiments out of enemy sight just behind the crest. Aligning his artillery in front of them, including the three surviving guns of a retreating battery that he had picked up on the way, he waited for the battle to come to him. In relative safety his men stood, shoulder to shoulder, while the scorching summer sun soared beyond its zenith.[59]

From his roving headquarters above the turnpike, Irvin McDowell knew nothing of Jackson's line, lurking just over the opposite hill. He saw only the disorganized retreat of three Confederate brigades and the Hampton Legion up the slope of Henry Hill, and that pleased him so greatly that he failed to capitalize on his advantage. He seemed unable to wield his army as a whole, instead concentrating on one or two brigades at a time. It was a problem he had anticipated long before: he had tried to practice maneuvering larger units with brigade reviews back on Arlington Heights, but when those reviews grew to include eight regiments General Mansfield had jealously rebuked him for making an ostentatious display. With his enemy falling away in disorder, and plenty of his own troops on hand to seal the victory, McDowell did not seem to know quite how to arrange his forces for a decisive stroke.[60]

Erasmus Keyes, who had led one of Tyler's brigades over the creek, tried to follow Tyler's instructions to carry the guns on Henry Hill, but neither he nor Tyler apprised McDowell of the attempt. The assault therefore proceeded without the support of any of the numerous other United States troops on the field. It required Keyes to plow through the Hampton Legion, which had been shrinking back from the Union guns on Dogan Ridge, and Keyes sent the 2nd Maine and the 3rd Connecticut up the hill at a trot. The legion had been reduced to little more than five hundred men by then, but Evans and Bartow gathered enough of their weary survivors to help Hampton disperse that threat. The South Carolinia legion lay down in a sunken farm lane offering such effective protection that Keyes mistook it for a line of prepared breastworks. The two Union regiments lost heart after a few vicious volleys and a few dozen casualties, tumbling back down the hill, and with that single effort Keyes seemed to think that he had accomplished enough work for one day. His brigade retired to safety at the foot of the hill while Hampton and the jumbled remnants of Bartow's and Evans's troops pulled back over the top and took shelter behind Jackson's brigade.[61]

To McDowell the withdrawal seemed to signal the end of Confederate resistance, and he needed only to bend the Southern line back enough to separate it from Manassas Junction and the road to Richmond. For that coup de grâce he turned to the dozen guns that had wrought the worst punishment on Beauregard's troops, giving his chief of artillery instructions to send the pair of Regular batteries up on Henry Hill itself, presumably to fire over the brow of the height at the fleeing enemy. This would be the last grand mistake of the day, and one for which McDowell would assiduously avoid responsibility, reporting the disastrous outcome in the passive fashion of a mere observer. Artillery chief William F. Barry, newly promoted to major after nearly a quarter-century of active duty, dutifully transmitted McDowell's order to the captains of the two batteries — Charles Griffin and James Ricketts. Griffin immediately complained that his battery would sit fully exposed in the very face of the enemy, with no support, but Barry promised him that he would have infantry support from the 11th New York. Griffin scorned the Fire Zouaves, doubting their tenacity. Barry insisted that the advance was the commanding general's order: Barry had finished a few numbers ahead of McDowell in the West Point class of 1838, and had served with him on the Canadian border; he knew him well enough to obey without hesitation. Griffin finally consented to go, but he predicted that the Zouaves lacked the discipline to support him effectively; from their bullyragging of civilians, Griffin had marked them for a collection of cowards.[62]

The best-known alumnus of West Point's Class of '38 cantered his horse back and forth on the lee shoulder of Henry Hill as Griffin limbered up his guns. General Beauregard inspired every Confederate who could see him with a conspicuous disdain for flying lead and iron, furiously building a new front by rallying the infantry and adding artillery to the line that Jackson had begun. Barnard Bee, an academy classmate of Charles Stone, still wore the blue jacket of the U.S. Army: as he put his brigade back together, Bee alluded to Jackson's regiments standing "like a stone wall" (thereby anointing "Stonewall" Jackson with eternal fame), and directed his own men to form behind them. Colonel Francis Bartow and a few other patrician officers of little formal military training tried to lend their influence to the confused mass.[63]

Griffin started up the hill with five of his guns, leaving behind one with a cartridge jammed in the tube, but his first lieutenant led the battery astray, and the time it took to correct his mistake allowed Ricketts to reach the crest first with his six rifles. At such close quarters the rifled guns lost all the advantage they had enjoyed at longer distance over the Confederate smoothbores. Ricketts had no sooner dropped his guns into battery than he began to lose men and horses from small-arms fire, and he blamed it on sharpshooters he supposed hidden in Mrs. Henry's house. Turning his pieces on that frail frame dwelling, he riddled it with shell, incidentally blasting old Mrs. Henry out of her bed with wounds that would kill her in a few hours: born with the beginning of one Revolution, she perished with the commencement of another.[64]

Griffin brought his five remaining guns up and fell in to the left of Ricketts while Major Barry personally led the 11th New York up the sunken Sudley Road to support the batteries. Having recovered their courage, the red-legged 14th New York followed, along with 350 Marine recruits and the 1st Minnesota. Leaving the infantry as it marched up the hill, Barry galloped over to talk with Griffin, who was starting to shift pieces to the other side of Ricketts's battery. Their guns were all firing generally toward Jackson's patient line; the shells soared over swales big enough to hide whole regiments before exploding harmlessly in the woods on the far side of the crest. Griffin saw a sizable battalion come out of those woods off to his right, and he began turning pieces to scatter it when Barry interfered. Barry — who denied it afterward — cautioned Griffin not to fire, assuring him that those were the Zouaves who had come to support him. Griffin doubted it, but their promiscuous dress confirmed nothing: General Heintzelman, who was leading the 1st Minnesota toward that mysterious formation from farther up the Sudley Road, found their apparel so varied that he took it for citizens' clothing.[65]

The newcomers, probably the half-organized 33rd Virginia backed by three companies of the 49th, filed left and right while Griffin watched nervously. He saw someone trot out in front of their line, perhaps to inspire them with the requisite harangue, and then to his horror they abruptly leveled their rifles in the direction of the eleven guns. The first volley felled so many gunners and horses that Griffin could neither return fire nor evacuate most of his battery. Behind him he saw his Zouave supports, sitting as though stunned. Farther to his right the 1st Minnesota suffered the same uncertainty about uniforms until those strangers began tattering their ranks with musketry. Both the Minnesotans and the Zouaves staggered backward with heavy losses, and at that critical moment J.E.B. Stuart burst out of the woods and into the Sudley Road with about 150 horsemen, bearing down on the right flank of the entire Union line.[66]

Stuart, too, had questioned whether he faced friends or foe, thinking perhaps that the red shirts of the Zouaves belonged to the Louisiana Tigers or some other Southern Zouaves whom he had not yet encountered. Once he spotted the U.S. flag among them, he spurred his little squadron into a full gallop in a column of fours, and the Virginians rode right into the Fire Zouaves with revolvers barking left and right. Muttered tales of a Confederate command known as the "Black Horse Cavalry" filled Union soldiers with absolute terror — much like the ubiquitous "masked batteries" that federal troops so dreaded, as though their firepower somehow exceeded those of guns standing in the open. The appearance of a few dozen mounted men therefore turned Ellsworth's startled heroes to jelly. A few of them did find enough courage to turn around and fire into the backs of Stuart's passing troopers, knocking a few of them out of the saddle, but the New York firemen apparently felt more comfortable terrorizing civilians than holding up their end of a fair fight. Regular Army officers met them in midflight and beseeched them in the name of their martyred colonel to stay and fight, but they bolted for the rear, leaving the Minnesota regiment little choice but to follow.[67]

The most severe musketry that Ricketts had ever experienced killed his executive officer and toppled Ricketts from his horse with a wound that would cost him a leg. Those crewmembers who escaped the first volley sprinted away, and the Confederates pitched forward to claim the artillery. Griffin managed to get one gun and a caisson away, but ten pieces remained abandoned on the field.[68]

Confederate infantry surged forward in disconnected lunges, and with a fearful loss in actual and acting general officers. General Bee fell with a fatal wound as he guided a fragment of his battered Alabama regiment toward the guns. A bullet pierced Colonel Bartow's heart as he led one of his Georgia regiments in a headlong charge, flag in hand. Colonel Francis Thomas, the adjutant general of Maryland and Johnston's ordnance chief, died leading the stragglers of numerous regiments back into the fight. Then Jackson's Virginians swept forward, as did Cocke's, who had come up from the stone bridge. Sixty-three-year-old William Smith, a former and future governor of Virginia, brought up a few companies of his incomplete regiment to bolster the Confederate left; he was joined by a new regiment of North Carolinians, who soon lost their colonel.[69] Confederate generals knew no more about maneuvering large commands than their opponents did, and they repeated the mistake of throwing their force into action a regiment or two at a stroke, thus prolonging the contest as long as one side retained fresh troops.

There still remained plenty of Union regiments crowded in the Sudley Road where it climbed Henry Hill, protected by the towering banks of the road cut. They threw themselves at Beauregard's line in rapid succession, but without central authority they wasted their blood and valor, and in some cases valor was in short supply: two Massachusetts regiments made a dash at the guns, but some of the Bay Staters threw down their weapons and ran before the first shot, and the rest followed them at the opening volley. The 14th New York marched into the fusillade three separate times, making little headway, until after the third repulse the demoralized survivors melted back into the road and down the hill in a blur of blue and red. The Marines went with them despite the best efforts of their officers; one unlettered captain who had boasted of his Marines' conduct at Fairfax Court House confessed their abysmal performance on Henry Hill. Orlando Bolivar Willcox successively led two wings of his 1st Michigan against Confederates who had overrun the batteries, but without coordinated support neither attempt succeeded, and a bullet through the forearm disabled Willcox enough to make him dismount. A Confederate countercharge swallowed him up, along with an officer who had stopped to assist him.[70]

William Sherman brought all four of his regiments into action, but not simultaneously. First he sent the 2nd Wisconsin over the tall roadbank toward the hill, but the Badgers' grey uniforms brought them trouble and they came reeling back amid cries that they were being fired on by friendly forces. A second attempt fared no better, so Sherman replaced them with the 79th New York Highlanders, under Simon Cameron's brother. The Highlanders also fell back under a deadly mixture of rifle and artillery fire that cut down one man in eight and one officer in four, tearing at least one captain's body completely apart. Colonel Cameron and thirty of his men lay dying on the hillside as the survivors streamed back to the Sudley Road. The Irish 69th New York tried next and held on a little longer near the Henry house until they faced a countercharge from Eppa Hunton's 8th Virginia. The Virginians had been rushed to answer this emergency after surrendering their canteens to a detail that had departed to fill them, and they broke from the dense woods in a ragged line, half-crazed with thirst, but they raised a roar, tilted their bayonets, and hurtled into the Irishmen. Their sheer velocity shivered the 69th, the fragments of which poured to the rear; the 13th New York kept up a steady fire from the left of Sherman's front, but even without approaching the hilltop that regiment endured a few dozen casualties.[71]

The retreat of the 69th marked the exhaustion of Sherman's brigade. By midafternoon the impressive superiority of fresh troops that McDowell had accumulated in the morning had been reduced to a single brigade. Fatigue and disorganization now afflicted the rest of his command on the right bank of Bull Run as badly as they did the Confederates, and he had to recall some of his less-battered regiments to go back into the fight. Ambrose Burnside's 2nd New Hampshire, which had run like rabbits in the morning, filed toward Henry Hill with a chance to redeem itself in support of the beleaguered Union right, but without further direction the Granite Staters huddled behind the embankment where the Sudley Road cut deepest into the side of Henry Hill. There they lay, without firing a shot, while artillery and musketry splintered the rail fence at the top of the cut. Nor did all of them even answer the call: on the opposite hillside, near the scene of the morning's fight, a Rhode Island captain from the same brigade encountered a shaky New Hampshire lieutenant with a score of his men, plodding dejectedly for their distant camp. The lieutenant lamented that his demoralized platoon represented the last survivors of a regiment that he presumed had been utterly destroyed.

"Thus," grumbled a disgusted subaltern in that regiment, "did the *Gallant New Hampshire 2nd Regiment* acquit itself on Sunday the 21st of July Anno Domini 1861." The disgruntled officer would soon abandon his volunteer comrades for a commission in the Regular Army.[72]

The one uncommitted brigade at McDowell's disposal belonged to Oliver Otis Howard, whose four Maine and Vermont regiments had been marching, shuffling, and standing in the intense heat for about nine hours with insufficient water. Howard's brigade glided down to the turnpike west of the Sudley Road and parallel to it, extending the Union right much as the New Hampshire regiment had been expected to do. Howard arranged a two-regiment front and led the first rank forward, opening fire just as Milledge Bonham's South Carolina brigade reached the field from the other end of Beauregard's line. Bonham's infantry and an artillery battery spread out to reply, their color bearer waving a palmetto flag the size of a pillow sham, and there they might have deadlocked had it not been for two more Confederate brigades within easy marching range of the Sudley Road. Howard's first line kept up a steady fire while he advanced the second, but the fresh Confederate battery began gnawing away at his exposed flank. Then came the unexpected pressure of a new Confederate force, in the form of the last brigade of Johnston's Valley army, just arrived by railroad. Arnold Elzey's brigade — three regiments from Maryland, Virginia, and Tennessee — hit Howard on his flank as his men were already wavering, pushing the last cohesive Union brigade on the field inexorably backward into the muddled mass of McDowell's battered army. This final assault varied little from any other attack that day, save that McDowell had no reserves with which to respond. The entire Union army now staggered backward.[73]

United States forces irrevocably lost the battle from that moment. The retreat became total as individual soldiers turned, tired and thirsty, for the springs and creeks that lay toward the rear. They spilled down the hills and ridges west of the Sudley road into the valley of the Warrenton Turnpike, where hundreds of stragglers had already accumulated, and then they swarmed up the hills that Evans, Bee, and Bartow had so stubbornly yielded that morning. All the long way back to Sudley Ford they fled, ignoring importunate officers, while here and there small groups tried to make a stand. General McDowell appeared on the ridge where the day's fight had begun and ordered an impromptu rear guard formed around the battalion of Regulars, whose well-trained officers held their recruits as steady as any veterans.[74]

A squadron of Regular dragoons fanned out to cover the troops as even the rear guard began backing away, but then the bulk of Burnside's brigade finally came up out of the ravine near Bull Run where it had been resting. They were now the freshest infantry on that part of the field, and Burnside formed them behind the cavalry. The Confederates followed deliberately, holding the advantage in artillery, and all it took was one frightened officer galloping by with an agitated report of the enemy's imminent approach to scatter Burnside's men like chaff. They were the last Federals to splash across Bull Run at the ford, and they left behind nearly three hundred wounded men who lay in and around Sudley Church, too badly injured to bear movement. Then started a race back to Centreville, and Burnside's brigade began dissolving as each man sought to save himself. Those at the rear fled the imagined pursuit, and those at the front envisioned Confederates advancing from the stone bridge to cut them off at the turnpike junction. A mile from Sudley Ford Burnside stopped and reorganized his command, but the men had intermingled so thoroughly with other troops and lost so many officers that the best Burnside could do was cluster little mobs of survivors around the regimental flags. For the next few miles the commander of the Regular cavalry repeatedly frightened Burnside's troops into greater haste with warnings that they might soon find themselves surrounded.[75]

Most of Tyler's troops crossed at the stone bridge — including the brigade under Erasmus Keyes, which only half an hour before had lain on the east slope of Henry Hill, waiting to charge up behind Stonewall Jackson's brigade. Those who traversed the circuitous road by Sudley Ford did so with greater haste than they had in the morning, though, and dusk had not yet come when they emerged onto the turnpike on the other side of Bull Run. Bonham's South Carolinians moved down into the turnpike, where Delaware Kemper's artillerymen from Alexandria shelled the Yankees with as much glee as they had at Blackburn's Ford three days before, and with even more satisfaction, for this time they used one of the Parrott rifles captured on Henry Hill. Tyler's brigades pulled away toward Cub Run just as the first fugitives from Sudley Ford poured back onto the turnpike. The merging traffic choked the bridge, preventing some of the batteries from bringing their guns across. Impatient soldiers began veering around the bridge and wading waist-deep Cub Run, leaving the rest of the army to take care of itself.[76]

The South Carolinians pursued cautiously, waiting for permission to chase the enemy, and that pause allowed the Union retreat to continue in relative calm, if not in good order. Had he been able to push eastward on the turnpike in time to intercept the retreating flank force, Beauregard might have done much worse damage to McDowell's army and vastly increased his tally of prisoners. As it was, the tail of the flanking column reached the turnpike unmolested, save by a couple of Captain Kemper's shells. A few companies of hastily gathered Virginia cavalry forded Bull Run below the turnpike and lashed at Tyler's Yankees near the little wooden suspension bridge over Cub Run, coming away with the flag and the colonel of the Irish 69th New York. Then Kemper rolled his guns ahead and opened on the Cub Run bridge from a distance of half a mile. His first shell exploded right over the bridge, so frightening the horses that an ambulance collided with the hospital wagon of the 2nd New Hampshire and knocked it over, blocking the bridge completely. Aiming carefully, Kemper fired about a dozen rounds, taking off the legs, arms, and fingers of a number of men in the 2nd New Hampshire and cutting a Rhode Island captain neatly in two with one shot.[77]

Those few shells turned the disordered retreat into absolute mayhem. Men flung their rifles and muskets into the woods or simply dropped them and ran. Ambulance drivers abandoned their vehicles and left the wounded to clamber out and make their own way. Artillerymen deserted their guns, which could never negotiate the steep banks of Cub Run, and even the big thirty-pounder Parrott that had begun the day's work remained behind as a Confederate prize. Officers fled their companies or lost them in the mob surging toward Centreville: two New Hampshire officers flanked the color bearer of their regiment, beseeching their comrades to stand and fight, but one of them observed that he might as well have "shouted to the winds."[78] Another spate of atrocity rumors only accelerated the flight, and many a willing soldier disgraced himself that evening, tormented by a vision of relentless rebel bayonets.[79]

McDowell's army was finished. After every Yankee had bolted across Cub Run, the real Black Horse Cavalry finally made its appearance to salvage the prizes. That single troop — Virginia horsemen of no particular distinction — trotted up, dismounted, and untangled ten rifled guns from the vicinity of the bridge alone, collecting their caissons and nearly a dozen four-horse teams with harnesses. Rifles eminently superior to Confederate muskets lay all along the road, complete with cartridge boxes.[80]

The sun set before the last refugees reached Centreville, and in its place rose a pale full moon. Some of McDowell's subordinate officers thought that he should stay where he was, arranging his troops on the ridge at Centreville to repel the inevitable Confederate attack in the morning: at least that is what those officers said months later to inquiring congressmen. That Sunday night, though, McDowell had to consider the extreme demoralization of his command, the heavy losses of artillery and small arms, his depleted ammunition, and the impending hunger of an army that had thrown away much of its last issue of food. Even worse, the besotted Colonel Miles had withdrawn from Mitchell's and Blackburn's fords, jeopardizing the army's left flank. McDowell decided to continue the retreat all the way back to the Potomac, and it was well that he did, for a substantial portion of his army had decided to do just that anyway; many of them were already well on the way. Some, including an extraordinary number of Ellsworth's renowned Zouaves and several officers of the 2nd New York State Militia, did not stop until they reached New York City.[81]

J.E.B. Stuart's Virginia cavalry battalion slept under the stars and the brilliant moon that night, a few hundred yards from Sudley Church. Nearby lay the battle's most critically injured Union soldiers, many of them left outside for lack of room in the church, and heaps of amputated arms and legs lay piled about the perimeter of the ghastly bivouac. The wounded moaned and cried out piteously, provoking the sympathy of Stuart's sergeant major, who speculated that one glimpse at the day's work might pacify the most belligerent of the war's advocates.[82]

Washington City had fairly quivered with excitement all that Sabbath, for the residents could clearly hear the booming of artillery twenty-five miles away. President Lincoln sat nervously at his desk, reading dispatches as they came in at the rate of four an hour from Fairfax Court House. The telegraph operator there could send nothing more reliable than his own interpretations of the sound of battle as it drifted his way, and in the afternoon the president grew so frustrated that he ambled over to ask General Scott for his assessment of the information. Scott rose from a nap long enough to explain the vagaries of wind and echo that made such auditory evidence useless, and then lay back down as the president left. A couple of hours later the reports remained favorable, and Lincoln went out for a ride. While he was out, Secretary Seward burst in with news of McDowell's headlong retreat and a telegram warning Scott to save the capital. Excitement soared when the troops remaining around the city began marching across the river and into Virginia. The lights blazed in every hotel as gossipmongers speculated on the outcome. A vanguard of frantic civilian spectators reached the city before midnight, and curious multitudes pumped them for information about the battle. Some roused their families with warnings to pack and leave the city, for the grand army of the republic had been destroyed. McDowell confirmed that the routed troops refused to rally.[83]

If anyone still doubted the catastrophe, the proof came the next morning, accompanied by an appropriately dreary rainstorm. Soldiers in various degrees of disarray started plodding up to Arlington Heights, singly and in groups mingled indiscriminately from different commands. Those who thought to evade the provost-marshal details continued across the Long Bridge into the city, where men who retained any cash invaded the hotels and restaurants for food and drink. Most had no money. Some carried weapons, but some did not. Officers wandered about with empty holsters and scabbards, or no scabbards at all, having dropped or discarded their side arms. A few offered excuses for the losses: one lieutenant in a company that ran away from the first enemy fire at Henry Hill told his family that his sword had been "bent double by a cannon shot," and two officers whose regiment crumbled with unseemly haste both claimed that their revolvers had been stolen on the retreat. Many had lost their headgear; a few had replaced their hats and caps with piratical bandannas.[84]

Ninety-day men predominated among the stragglers who filled the streets. Their pilgrimage had muddied some of them up to their shoulders, and hundreds of them filled Pennsylvania Avenue. Already at work on a searing account of the retreat for the London *Times,* an exhausted William Russell glanced out his window at Willard's and saw the demoralized cavalcade proceeding, he thought, toward the Capitol — as though for the advice of their congressmen. He failed to consider that the rail depot for northbound trains also lay in that direction.[85]

Ellsworth's Zouaves figured prominently among the heralds of the rout, most of them regaling eager audiences with tales of the slaughter and vying with each other for the most shocking account of casualties.

There were only 250 survivors of Ellsworth's valiant 1,100, said one, while another contended that only 150 of them remained. Indeed, the lieutenant colonel commanding the regiment had been wounded, and ten dozen of his men with him — but not a single other officer. Most of the survivors appear to have deserted: ten days after the battle their brigade commander could not find three-quarters of the men who wore Ellsworth's distinctive uniform, yet they were seen everywhere on the streets immediately after the fight.[86] Citizens who had befriended certain soldiers, or even whole companies of them, invited the stragglers in to dry off and have some tea. Their guests warned them that the worst had not come; later in the day rumors sprang forth that the enemy had dogged McDowell's trail every step of the way and lay only five miles from Alexandria. A new crop of atrocity stories fanned the terror: the rebels were said to have blown up Sudley Church and murdered all the Union wounded there. Postmaster General Blair's sister found the occasion of the retreat an opportune moment to visit Philadelphia for a few days, and at least one gentleman of Southern sympathies expected President Lincoln to slip out of Washington as secretly as he had entered it.[87]

Had Confederates in the ranks had their way, the pursuit would have continued with far more vigor. Confederate cavalry did advance as far as Fairfax Court House, but by no means did it hound the ragged rear of the beaten foe, as cavalry was expected to do. A New York officer snagged by the Confederates supposed that his captors had taken pity on McDowell's terrified rabble, reflecting that it was no fault of Union officers that the carnage had not been worse. General Keyes attributed the weak pursuit to a "striking want of generalship" on the Southern side, but it was mainly a want of cavalry that had prevented the capture of more of the beaten army.[88] Johnston and Beauregard did not have two full regiments of horse between them, and most of those companies had been parceled out for scouting duty to the various brigades. One good mounted brigade might have cut off thousands of frightened Federals after Confederate artillery initiated the chaos at Cub Run, or driven the laggards in on their own friends to compound the panic.

Beyond that, the last Confederate opportunity to capitalize on the surprise victory ended when the prey escaped behind Centreville. McDowell's reserve division lay just a few miles farther east, and thousands of reinforcements came down quickly from Washington, far outnumbering Johnston's fresh troops and nearly matching his entire army. The victory gladdened secessionists and their sympathizers, but the whole state of Virginia did not contain enough Confederate troops to turn that enthusiasm into conquest of the federal capital. Distorted perspectives obscured the limits of the victory, and a relieved Southern population rejoiced as though at complete deliverance, although some harbored peripheral anxiety that the invaders had not been permanently discouraged.[89]

The Southern clergy used the victory to corroborate the sense of divine protection that had, since the first shot at Sumter, given Confederate civilians across the country the confidence to confront so much more numerous a foe.[90] One minister deemed it significant that their victories had come on fields bearing biblical names like Bethel and Manassas. Richmond newspapers satisfied themselves with endless crowing about "another victory," and since their exaggerated accounts had already labeled the fight at Blackburn's Ford as the definitive-sounding "battle of Bull Run," they called the more decisive confrontation of July 21 the "battle of Stone Bridge." More than a week later they finally lighted on the more specific reference to Manassas, which — perhaps because of those biblical implications — became the traditional Southern name for the engagement.[91]

By Tuesday the news of the Confederate victory had reverberated as far west as St. Louis, where Unionists braced needlessly for an uprising by jubilant Southerners. On its return march up Broadway, less than a week after the battle, the battered 69th New York brought tears to the eyes of spectators, who supposed not only that the Confederacy had won its independence but that it might now assume the offensive against a defenseless capital. Back in Washington, though, the fear had begun to abate by then; those stricken by the tidings of apocalyptic catastrophe rebounded after hearing that the casualties had not been so severe nor the panic so devastating as originally reported. Troops that had bypassed their camps at Arlington began showing up for rations, and credible intelligence allayed the anxiety of an immediate attack.[92]

Tireless proponents of Abraham Lincoln's war quickly reinterpreted the defeat as a lesson that had been necessary to rededicate the North to more strenuous military effort. A Massachusetts woman fervent in the abolition movement reasoned that so embarrassing a reverse would inspire patriots to enlist while it dissuaded the timid, and it might lead the government to cull incompetent officers from the army. Opponents of slavery used the defeat as another excuse to promote abolition as a war policy, arguing that it would chill foreign sympathy for the Confederacy and simultaneously reinvigorate the army with more and better recruits by offering a stronger moral incentive.[93] Conscientious opponents of human bondage had criticized the mere preservation of the Union as an inadequate motive from the outset, or had hoped that the war would incidentally end the peculiar institution. Even Quakers who opposed the war altogether had noted that in his prosecution of it Lincoln did not seem to address the fundamental political problem behind disunion — slavery. After the debacle at Bull Run one Quaker newspaper expressed the hope that the "turmoil" would at least eliminate that evil. Translated from the pacifistic parlance of an apolitical sect, the statement represented an appeal for a more aggressive administration policy on emancipation.[94]

The war's first military catastrophe brought the inevitable process of assigning blame, with the usual failure to affix it justly. General Patterson had already been discharged before the battle started, but the tardy announcement of his removal implied that he bore responsibility for the defeat. McDowell had to go, as well, whether the fault were actually his or not, and on Thursday he toppled from public view in the traditional backhanded bureaucratic manner. The new Division of the Potomac swallowed McDowell's Department of Northeastern Virginia, and Major General George B. McClellan, the engineer or nominal director of most of the little victories in western Virginia, assumed command of the Potomac army.[95]

There arose mutterings that McDowell had deliberately lost the battle, but the rumor of his disloyalty gained no official consideration. It was Colonel Dixon Miles, the tippling old Regular who abandoned his position at the lower fords, who drew the sharpest personal censure. Miles's action had uncovered McDowell's left flank, and McDowell cited that circumstance as his principle reason for continuing the retreat all the way to the Potomac. A court of inquiry later concluded that Miles was, in fact, drunk on the evening of the battle, but the consumption of alcohol permeated both military and civilian society in that era, and the court prescribed no penalty for an inebriated officer.[96]

Numerous officers, both professional and volunteer, assigned responsibility for the disaster to the general absence of competence and courage throughout the army. From all over the field came complaints that Union soldiers had shown the white feather: in their role as aggressors they had undeniably performed a lot less valiantly than the Confederates had in defense of their homeland. William Tecumseh Sherman observed that "our men are not good Soldiers — they brag, but don't perform — and a march of a few miles uses them up." Judging from the stampede of the 12th New York at Blackburn's Ford and the conduct of his own brigade on Henry Hill, Sherman considered the army's volunteers a craven lot. West Pointer William Averell lamented the overall lack of discipline among the volunteers after witnessing several New York militia regiments dissolve under relatively light punishment, while one lieutenant in the 5th Massachusetts commented candidly on the cowardice of the entire army, including the men of his own regiment and company.[97] Another Bay State lieutenant concurred that "the men of some of the regiments acted like

Cowards," and he apparently counted his own brother among them.[98] A New Hampshire lieutenant who expressed disgust with his regiment seemed to find the most fault with his fellow officers, and especially the field officers. A Rhode Island captain evidently concurred, remarking with an understatement typical of his Quaker forebears that "some of our officers were not quite up to the times."[99]

The shameless conduct of many volunteer officers attracted widespread notice, at least in Washington City. On the day following the retreat, a gathering of citizens and soldiers at the House of Representatives heard a sober witness describe officers hightailing it ahead of their men, and even throwing away their swords and cutting team horses out of harness to facilitate their flight. Residents estimated that two-thirds of the first few hundred fugitives who poured into the city wore shoulder straps. Back in their home states, unfounded reports briefly credited the volunteer regiments with far better behavior than they had actually exhibited. New Yorkers heard, for instance, that Ellsworth's Fire Zouaves had "fought specially well," but a visit to the capital quickly cured that delusion.[100]

Civilians north of the Potomac gave more credence to the talk of incompetent officers than to the pervasive tales of sheer cowardice among both commissioned and enlisted defenders of the Union. Many criticized the premature advance of an untrained army: some suspected McDowell of wishing to preempt McClellan's glory, but others faulted the newspapers (and specifically Horace Greeley's *Tribune*) for impatiently demanding action against Richmond. Some in the government assigned the onus to Lincoln's cabinet, absolving Greeley, Lincoln himself, and General Scott. With conspicuous examples like Colonel Miles, editors in the Northern religious press easily concluded that intemperance had led a divine omnipotence to decide the battle in favor of the enemy; neither did it help for the generals to undertake an attack on a Sunday, many of them added.[101]

President Lincoln owned an indirect but ironic share of the responsibility. His decision to subdue secession by force of arms had made fighting inevitable, of course, but more to the point his April 15 appeal for militia had given the Confederacy the very troops that won the first battle. Bull Run had been decided by nothing more complicated than which army held the final reserve. The tide had washed first one way and then the other, even after the batteries of Griffin and Ricketts had been eliminated, but it was Arnold Elzey's Blücher-like arrival that had finished things. Elzey's attack, after the assault of McDowell's last fresh brigade, blotted out the final hope of Union victory and precipitated the hasty retreat that evolved into rout and panic. One Union soldier who was driven away by that final counterattack recognized as much, and he illustrated its effectiveness when he credited Elzey with a division twenty thousand strong.[102] In fact Elzey may not have fielded one-tenth that many troops, but his brigade consisted of the 1st Maryland, the 3rd Tennessee, and the 10th Virginia — three regiments that would never have belonged to the Confederate army had Lincoln not chosen a military course. Without the demand for troops after the bombardment of Fort Sumter, Tennessee and Virginia would probably still have belonged to the Union, and few Maryland citizens would have found cause to turn against their own government. Reluctant border-state secessionists under Stonewall Jackson had stalled the Union juggernaut on Henry Hill, and reluctant border-state secessionists under the Marylander Elzey had sent it packing.

Havelock-draped New Jersey soldiers digging entrenchments at the Virginia end of the Long Bridge, from a Waud sketch that did not make the newspapers.

John Merryman's plantation home, Hayfields, outside Cockeysville, Maryland, in a photograph taken seventy-five years after his arrest there.

President Lincoln and General Scott reviewing one of the new three-year regiments along Pennsylvania Avenue.

Irvin McDowell as a major general, months after he relinquished command of what became the Army of the Potomac.

Pierre Gustave Toutant Beauregard, McDowell's classmate at West Point and his opponent at First Bull Run.

A mutinous company of the Garibaldi Guards (39th New York) surrendering to a detachment of Regular cavalry in June of 1862.

Officers and men of the 1st Rhode Island drawn by Waud in the spring of 1861, wearing the poncho and "Burnside blouses" designed by their commander.

The 8th New York Militia at Arlington in June of 1861. The officers wear blue and the enlisted men grey, as though in imitation of South Carolina troops. This regiment disintegrated almost as soon as it came under fire at First Bull Run.

Planning the advance to Manassas, as drawn by Waud: General Scott among his senior aides.

Major General Robert Patterson, apparently in his Mexican War uniform.

Waud's drawing of Ambrose Burnside's brigade engaged on Matthew's Hill at Bull Run.

The remains of the Cub Run bridge, which delayed McDowell's flank attack on the morning of July 21 and impeded the retreat that afternoon.

Sterling Price, the former governor of Missouri and president of its secession convention, pictured later in the war as a Confederate general.

Major General George B. McClellan.

Frank Blair, Missouri congressman and colonel of the 1st Missouri Volunteers.

Nathaniel Lyon as a captain of infantry, a few months before his death.

Lyon's success at Boonville, Missouri, caricatured by an artist who had obviously never seen any images of Claiborne Jackson or Sterling Price.

Colonel Franz Sigel heroically portrayed on the battlefield of Carthage, Missouri, where his rashness led to an abrupt defeat.

John C. Frémont as he looked on his return from Europe in 1861.

Company H, 3rd Arkansas, dressed in civilian clothing and mismatched uniforms typical of Confederates who fought at Wilson's Creek. Their captain, at lower right, is distinguished only by his sword.

6

The Crimson Corse of Lyon

❖ THE PEOPLE OF MISSOURI, like those of Maryland, remained predominantly loyal at the outset of hostilities, but — also as in Maryland — heavyhanded federal authority angered and alienated many of the more moderate state residents. Slavery did not pervade the culture and economy as it did in Dixie: all but 3 percent of Missouri's 116,000 blacks remained in bondage, but whites composed nine-tenths of the state's population. Immigration and railroads had gone a long way toward diluting Missouri's river-borne associations with the slave South since 1850, and a significant proportion of state residents felt stronger ties of blood and economic interest with New York than with New Orleans. In the presidential election of 1860 and in the choice of delegates to a secession convention the following February, Missouri demonstrated overwhelming opposition to secession, showing even less sympathy with the Deep South than Marylanders did. A fortnight after Lincoln took office, the convention delegates voted three to one to abide with the Union.[1]

In August of 1860 Missouri voters had elected Kentucky-born Claiborne Jackson as their governor. Jackson represented the slaveholding Southern element, but he had attracted many votes through his support of Unionist presidential candidate Stephen Douglas. He favored secession when the question arose, but even among most of those Missouri politicians who supported withdrawal from the Union there lingered hope for future reconciliation.[2] Lincoln's expedition against Fort Sumter disgusted the defenders of states' rights, though, inspiring the birth of at least one new anti-administration newspaper in St. Louis, and the presidential militia call only further stiffened Southern sympathy in Missouri, eliciting a torrent of editorial criticism. A newspaper in Southern-leaning

Liberty had been advertising its nationalist views with a banner motto proclaiming "One Union — One Country — One Destiny," but the editor suddenly asked, on April 17, if Missourians would murder their brothers merely to sustain the abolitionist aims of the Republican Party. In some secession communities, intolerant proclamations announced that "those who are not for us are against us." The militia levy also brought Governor Jackson's resounding refusal to send a single soldier, but the dominant statewide sentiment continued to oppose secession. The plurality of citizens, and perhaps the majority, seemed to prefer remaining neutral. A well-attended conditional-Union rally in Columbia adopted resolutions calling for the protection of Missouri soil "against invaders of hostile interference from any quarter whatever," including from the federal government. Even in the northeastern corner of the state, where Southern feeling ran particularly strong, the plea for neutrality drew a significant following.[3]

Missourians had reason to suppose that they could maintain neutrality if the sections went to war. Maryland might find difficulty doing so because it sat directly in the corridor of troop travel and so close to the national capital, but Kentucky refused to take sides for twenty tumultuous weeks even though it straddled the centerline between North and South. Missouri lay on the fringes of the likely battleground, and (despite Lincoln's remark that an armed neutrality amounted to "disunion completed") both sides might have welcomed a neutral Missouri to protect their western flanks.[4] The civil strife that would torture Missouri through and beyond the coming war need not — and might not — have happened, but for the actions of two zealots.

The lesser of the two fanatics was Governor Jackson. Though privately supportive of Missouri's prompt secession in his private communications with editors, local politicians, and Confederate officials, Jackson overtly adhered to his constitutional limitations. He convened the state legislature to decide on measures for the state's general protection, and assembled the state militia for annual training, presumably to prepare for defense against any external or internal threat. One of Jackson's aides later alleged that the governor and the commander of the St. Louis militia district conspired to seize the United States armory in that city for the state's use. A St. Louis citizen had already advised Confederate officials to take the armory, promising thousands of local recruits, and the Confederate government provided a couple of dismounted pieces of artillery, ostensibly to aid that effort.[5]

On the other side was Nathaniel Lyon, a captain in the 2nd U.S. Infantry and an insubordinate, self-righteous psychopath. Lyon's erratic record reflected his unstable personality: his posting to St. Louis in March,

1861, represented his third assignment in three months, and his seventh in three years, but in the secession crisis he found his purpose in life. With the help of Francis P. Blair, another unconditional Unionist whose brother served as Lincoln's postmaster general, Lyon rid himself of his department commander in order to exercise what he perceived as his divine duty. Lyon and Blair doubted the loyalty of Brigadier General William S. Harney because of both his Southern birth and his restraint toward secession proponents, and the influence of Blair's brother helped secure Harney's recall to Washington. That left Lyon with a free hand at St. Louis, at least temporarily, and when the Missouri militia gathered at Lindell's Grove, on the western edge of the city, Lyon began arming volunteers to confront them.[6]

As it happened, there no longer existed any need for a confrontation at Camp Jackson, as the militia called their bivouac at the grove. At Lyon's suggestion the arsenal's ordnance had largely been transferred to safer hands in Illinois, and Frank Blair appealed to the Illinois governor for some of those weapons to arm Unionist companies in Missouri. Attorney General Edward Bates, a citizen of St. Louis, confided to the U.S. attorney there that the removal of those arms had eliminated any temptation for the state troops to seize the arsenal, and Bates assured him that the city was now "safe, at least, from actual war."[7]

That same U.S. attorney, James Broadhead (Frank Blair's brother-in-law, and one of his closest allies), admitted that the militia included plenty of loyal citizens: one officer who later commanded a Union regiment served with the militia at Camp Jackson. The U.S. flag flew prominently over the camp, where the men had all taken oaths to serve both the state and federal governments. In any case, the militia lacked the strength to take the arsenal by force. With the complicity of the Lincoln administration, Lyon and Blair had already skirted state officials and federal law to arm several regiments, and those troops — primarily German residents of St. Louis — stood ready to defend federal property before the militia even reached its muster ground. The German volunteers elected Lyon as their brigadier general, and Lyon immediately began acting in that capacity, although no one outside the German-language press seemed to recognize his promotion.[8]

Despite displays of Southern and even Confederate feeling, the encampment passed most of its statutory six-day muster in the relative quiet of company and battalion drill, offering sightseers a pleasant military display. In their encampment at Lindell's Grove the militia received that pair of large-caliber cannon tubes from Confederates downriver, but they had not mounted the guns and evidently had no intention of using them. Lyon knew of their arrival, though. In fact, he probably knew about them before they were even delivered, and refrained from interfering lest he lose his only excuse for the attack that he proved so eager to make.

Two factors appear to have driven Lyon to provoke a needless incident. First, the militia was scheduled to disband on May 11, which would have robbed him of a theater in which he might perform. Second, the order for General Harney's removal had been revoked, and the judicious old soldier would be returning imminently to relieve the impulsive captain. On Saturday afternoon, May 10, Lyon threw his illegal St. Louis volunteers into line with two companies of Regulars and marched them to Camp Jackson by different routes. Their divergent paths brought them into positions surrounding the camp, whereupon Lyon presented Brigadier General Daniel Frost with a demand for the capitulation of his legitimate state militia. Frost, a New York native and West Point graduate who would later offer the Confederacy lukewarm service, protested Lyon's unlawful assault on a statutory body, but Lyon's full brigade left him no choice beyond surrendering his few hundred unprepared militiamen. As he had demonstrated in confrontations with Indians and contentious enlisted men, Lyon ignored all legal and moral impediments when he held power over an adversary.[9]

In his report of the affair, Lyon mentioned almost incidentally that "a mob attacked our force" as he started his prisoners toward the arsenal. To justify the bloodbath that followed, Union partisans usually took Lyon's cue in telling the story afterward — implying or even asserting that the disarmed militiamen or their civilian supporters started the shooting.[10] It was actually Lyon's amateur troops who shot first — firing recklessly into a crowd composed largely of women, children, and peaceable onlookers whose politics leaned in every direction.

Among those standing in the line of fire in that "mob" were two future Union generals — William Tecumseh Sherman and his brother-in-law, Charles Ewing, and Sherman's little boy accompanied them. Sherman blamed the tragedy on the nervous German volunteers. The Regulars who led the procession presented their bayonets to ward off the throng, and the people fell back and made way for them despite some catcalls and hooting. Then came the German troops, who responded to the taunts with a shot, and then another, and finally with reckless, rolling volleys that killed at least a dozen people — civilians and soldiers alike — and wounded scores more. One woman and a fourteen-year-old girl died, as well as a handful of young boys. The shooting created a stampede that caused additional injuries; one woman who was knocked to the ground by a fleeing citizen rolled beneath the wheels of a buggy, coming away with severe bruises but no broken bones. The slaughter filled Lyon's prisoners with anger and dread: one militiaman stared forlornly at his own house as his captors marched him past it, never expecting to see it again. The massacre sparked partisan rioting that continued through the rest of that Friday, although the actual rioters seemed few in number and a downpour dampened their ardor. On Saturday one man in a jeering crowd fired on a detachment of new German troops as they marched through the city — or at least so said the officers in command of those soldiers, after their men fired several volleys down the street and killed a few more civilians.[11]

This was precisely the sort of provocation that General Harney had sought to avoid. As in Baltimore, the massacre of civilian protestors and spectators by skittish federal volunteers only created more enemies for the government. One woman who considered herself a "strong Republican" ranted against the "Dutch" soldiers whom she held responsible for the killing, to the astonishment of her closest friends. Even citizens with entirely Northern family and business ties turned scornfully from the federal government, and some of them never recovered their former loyalty.[12]

In direct reaction to Lyon's attack on Camp Jackson, the state legislature reorganized the militia into a more hostile incarnation known as the Missouri State Guard, handing Governor Jackson virtually complete control over it and appropriating all the money he needed for immediate mobilization. Many of the companies gathering in Jefferson City hailed from solidly secessionist counties, including some from the upper Missouri who came armed with weapons seized from the smaller U.S. arsenal at Liberty, but the crime against St. Louis brought Missourians of all stripes to the state's defense, including some firm Unionists.[13] More conspicuous were the conditional Unionists, who decided by the thousands that the requisite conditions for union no longer existed in Missouri, and they joined the State Guard even if it meant rebellion against the federal government. Among the latter came Congressman John B. Clark, a veteran advocate for slave interests but a hopeful Unionist. With him appeared former governor Sterling Price, the president of the state convention that had so recently rejected secession. Barely a week after the Camp Jackson affair Price went to Jefferson City to take command of the State Guard as its major general, and Clark assumed command of one of its divisions — for which Frank Blair sponsored Clark's expulsion from the House of Representatives. The highly respected Price brought immense prestige to Governor Jackson's administration, and his strenuous efforts to keep the state in the Union provided a large measure of legitimacy as well.[14]

General Harney resumed command in St. Louis the day after Lyon's deadly excursion to Lindell's Grove. On his way to Washington he had been captured by Confederates who stopped his train at Harper's Ferry, and they had sent him to Richmond, where he indignantly refused an offer of a Confederate commission. Authorities there had returned him to

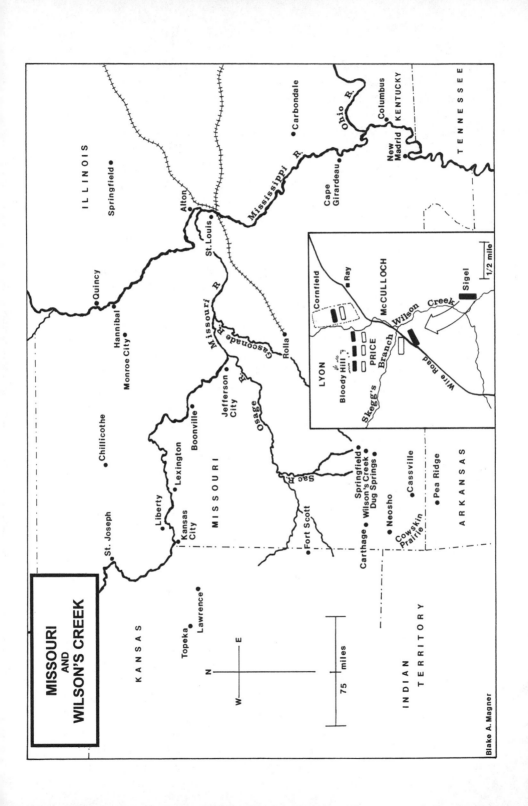

MISSOURI
AND
WILSON'S CREEK

ILLINOIS

Springfield•

Alton

St.Louis•

•Quincy

Hannibal•

Monroe City•

•Carbondale

Mississippi R.

Ohio R.

Columbus

New Madrid

Cape Girardeau

KENTUCKY

TENNESSEE

Missouri R.

Gasconade R.

Rolla•

Jefferson City•

Boonville•

•Chillicothe

Lexington•

Liberty•

Kansas City•

St. Joseph•

MISSOURI

Osage R.

Sac R.

Fort Scott•

Springfield•
Wilson's Creek•
Dug Springs•
Carthage•
•Neosho

•Cassville

Cowskin Prairie•

•Pea Ridge

ARKANSAS

KANSAS

Topeka•

Lawrence•

INDIAN   TERRITORY

N
W—E
S

75 miles

Blake A. Magner

Cornfield

•Ray

McCULLOCH

Sigel

1/2 mile

LYON

PRICE

Bloody Hill

Skegg's Branch

Wilson Creek

Wire Road

his own lines, and this indisputable evidence of his loyalty had probably secured his reappointment. Harney immediately tried to blunt Lyon's antagonism when he returned to command, issuing a proclamation that subtly censured Lyon's impetuosity, although the same document reiterated the evidence of disloyalty that had prompted the raid on Camp Jackson. Harney denounced the secessionist takeover of the Liberty arsenal and the legislature's creation of the State Guard, which he called "an indirect secession ordinance," but he reminded state citizens that he, too, lived in Missouri and shared the interests of his fellow citizens. He sought to remove the German home-guard regiments from the city to expunge the specter of class warfare that the Southern-leaning native population feared, but Frank Blair warned him that the home guards would ignore any such order. Harney therefore promised St. Louis citizens, through his proclamation, that he would eschew the assistance of the home guards if he could, instead calling only on the Regulars in the event of trouble.[15]

Lyon lodged the prisoners from Camp Jackson at the arsenal, but Harney soon released most of them. They gained their freedom by signing a parole not to engage in hostile action against the United States, although at first they all refused on the grounds that they had done nothing to require such an extraordinary oath. Some of those who later violated the oath may understandably have considered it null and void, since it was administered under duress after illegal arrest and detention, but only one officer refused to accept the required parole. Emmet MacDonald, captain of a cavalry company, put his faith in the same legal recourse that John Merryman pursued. Hoping perhaps to illustrate the unconstitutionality of Lyon's actions with his own case, MacDonald had an attorney file a writ of habeas corpus. The government had found brute force preferable to the embarrassment that might result from observing the legal requirements, however, and General Harney sent the solitary prisoner into Illinois, where he had no jurisdiction. On that technicality he avoided the legal issue, which evaporated in the subsequent unfolding of events.[16]

A couple of days after he assumed command of the Missouri State Guard at Jefferson City, Sterling Price traveled downriver to St. Louis to meet with Harney. Blair and his influential coterie of unconditional Unionists were pressuring Harney to accept nothing less than dissolution of the State Guard and the resignation of Claiborne Jackson and his administration, but Harney understood the impossibility of such demands. After a few hours the two white-haired generals came up with an agreement that would theoretically allow Missouri to sit out the war. Price promised to maintain civil order with his state troops, which implied that he would also prevent further depredations against United States property. In return, Harney assured him that U.S. troops would not intervene as they had under Lyon.[17]

Radical Unionists like Frank Blair and Nathaniel Lyon suspected that this was merely a ploy to allow Claiborne Jackson time to raise an army, and they regarded every step to organize the Missouri State Guard as an effort toward that duplicitous end.[18] Yet if Price were to maintain order in so large and volatile a state, he would have had to call on a well-organized militia. The informal peace treaty served federal interests as well, for the longer U.S. troops could be kept from such forays as the Camp Jackson fiasco, the less antagonistic the people of Missouri would feel toward the Washington government. Governor Jackson admitted privately that he expected Missouri to ally itself with the South at some point, and in April he had expected that alliance to come within a month, but by late May he seemed less ardent. He may have been content to wait for the Confederacy to achieve independence first, in which case his approval of the Price-Harney accord reflected a conditional sincerity similar to Abraham Lincoln's early promises not to invade the seceded states.[19]

Lieutenant Governor Thomas Reynolds, whose agitation for Missouri's secession set him in conflict with the suddenly patient governor, viewed the Price-Harney agreement as the triumph of those who favored the state's neutrality. On a visit inside the Confederacy, however, Reynolds met secessionist refugees from Missouri who saw the agreement as proof that Price had defected back to the Unionists. Such alternating suspicion testified to the moderation of Price's course. Reasonable men on both sides of the political question expressed confidence that both Price and Harney had acted in good faith, although some partisans on either side seemed to doubt the capacity of their own man. Price the conditional Unionist meant what he said, and General Harney did as well. With those two pointedly honorable elders in charge of the potentially belligerent forces, Missouri's various factions might conceivably have been placated indefinitely.[20]

The imperious Nathaniel Lyon would not hear of peace when he saw so rare an opportunity to fulfill his apocalyptic personal destiny. He and his principal patron, Frank Blair, had sent proxies to Washington who persuaded General Scott to write an order placing Harney on leave of absence. President Lincoln dreaded the impression of apparent indecision that would accompany three changes of command in less than a month, and — given Harney's personal influence in St. Louis — he feared making an enemy of the general. Lincoln therefore wrote to Blair, to whom the order for Harney's relief had been sent, to ask that he withhold the order unless its delivery became "indispensable."[21]

Although it caused much grumbling among his angry troops, Price started almost immediately to demobilize the State Guard, in accordance with his promise to Harney.[22] He retained the St. Louis troops as an active command for the present, perhaps partly to avoid worsening the tension in that city by sending them back into it. Minor incidents marred the peace in Springfield, St. Joseph, and southeastern Missouri as secessionists took matters into their own hands; they demonstrated special contempt for loyalists in Kansas City, abusing foreign immigrants in particular. Those events mirrored (and may have been meant to avenge) the more formal oppression of Southern sympathizers in Union strongholds like St. Louis. Harney forwarded all accounts of secessionist misconduct to Price, along with one report that Confederate troops were gathering in Arkansas for an invasion of Missouri. Price investigated each complaint, and assured Harney that he would repel any invasion, urging him not to send U.S. troops toward Arkansas lest they raise the ire of Missouri citizens. Washington officials heard from radical informants that loyal Missouri citizens were being driven from their homes "in great numbers" by secessionist mobs, but Harney found such tales groundless. His faith in Price exasperated Blair, who seemed convinced of all the rumored indignities and offenses, and within ten days of receiving Lincoln's discretionary letter Blair deemed it "indispensable" to send Harney away.[23]

Blair's Washington influence only made matters worse, for his brother, the postmaster general, had finagled a promotion for Lyon into the order relieving Harney. As the old man faded out of history, the explosive captain rose to brigadier general of volunteers, which gave him undisputed control of the department. Lyon gleefully assumed that command on the last day of May.[24]

Lyon immediately warned army headquarters that General Beauregard had arrived in Memphis with plans to invade Illinois, and that another column in Arkansas had positioned itself for a move against southwestern Missouri. By the time that message reached Washington, officials there probably knew that Beauregard had taken command at Manassas Junction. The apparent inaccuracy of Lyon's intelligence and the urgency of his message may have alerted General Scott to the new brigadier's unstable temperament, but public confidence precluded a fourth change of commanders in barely six weeks. Scott therefore redrew the boundaries of the Department of the West, stripping Missouri from it and adding it to George McClellan's massive Department of the Ohio, which already stretched from the Allegheny Mountains of Virginia to the Mississippi River. Scott then moved the headquarters for the Department of the West from St. Louis to Fort Leavenworth, Kansas, thus evicting the unpredictable General Lyon from Missouri without any change in his assignment.[25]

McClellan had recently aggravated abolitionists with a proclamation assuring slave owners that he had no intention of interfering with their chattel property. That proclamation had won McClellan much popularity in Kentucky, where he proposed a neutrality agreement not unlike the one between Price and Harney.[26] The order redrawing the Department of the West did not leave army headquarters for over a week, though, perhaps because the administration wished to see whether General Lyon could restrain himself — and, possibly, because of reservations about McClellan's Harney-like suggestions for Kentucky. News of the impending change may, however, have traveled to St. Louis through the conduit of the Blair brothers' personal correspondence, in which case Lyon could have known about it as early as the morning of June 10. The knowledge that he was about to be robbed of his personal opportunity in Missouri (along with his natural inclination to dictatorial bullying) would offer some explanation for Lyon's inflexible behavior in a meeting that he agreed to hold with Governor Jackson and General Price.

Jackson and Price entered St. Louis under safe-conduct passes and lodged at the Planters' House. Lyon arrived there on the morning of June 11, accompanied by Frank Blair. Jackson and Price had come to ascertain whether Lyon intended to continue General Harney's agreement, but they must have realized early in the course of their hours-long interview that he had no intention of doing so. The governor offered to disarm the State Guard and to waive his rights to activate the militia under the legislature's recent authorization, which federal authorities found so objectionable. He promised to repel any invasion by Confederate forces with militia alone, and to call on U.S. troops for assistance if militia proved inadequate. He outlined a treaty far more deferential to the federal government than the one Lincoln observed in Kentucky about the same time, and all he asked in return was that Lyon dismantle the predominantly German home-guard regiments that he and Blair had raised. The proposal amounted to complete demilitarization of all but U.S. Regular troops.

Jackson's aide recalled that Lyon abruptly interrupted the parley with the announcement that he would see every man, woman, and child in Missouri dead before he allowed state officials to tell federal officers where their troops might or might not go. Without waiting for a reply, he then delivered the announcement that he had probably intended to make all along: that Missouri and the United States were now at war. He gave Jackson and Price one hour to get out of his lines, whereupon he turned on his heel and left the other conferees — including Blair — sitting in stunned silence. To satisfy the ambition of one sadistic martinet, some twenty thousand Missourians would have to die.[27]

Lyon would likely have pounced on any excuse for war. He may not have known that he was about to be relegated to the more placid plains of Kansas, but his history of reprimands and reassignments by dissatisfied superiors had probably conditioned him to anticipate his removal from a new command almost as soon as he assumed it. Had he missed that first opportunity to commit his new department to military action, he might not have seen a second.

The day after the Planters' House conference, while Lyon marshaled troops to attack the state forces, Governor Jackson repaired to Jefferson City and called out fifty thousand militia to face Lyon's invasion. Citing military repression and arbitrary arrests echoing the travails of Maryland, Jackson still pointed out that, like Maryland, Missouri suffered such outrages from the national government while remaining a loyal member of the federal union. In formal proclamation, at least, Jackson expected both Unionist and secessionist Missourians to come to the defense of their state against the oppression of "the military despotism that has enthroned itself at Washington." That argument did attract at least some Northern men, including a few recent immigrants.[28]

Thus began the mobilization of the West. U.S. Regulars, home guards, and volunteers took one side and the Missouri State Guard the other. The Unionists hypocritically called their foes in the State Guard "rebels" — although it was the Unionists who intended to overthrow the duly elected state government and the state troops who vowed to defend it. The State Guard troops had not become Confederates yet, either, as willing as they might be to accept aid from the Confederacy. Through the summer of 1861, most of those who took up arms with the State Guard saw themselves for what they really were: citizens of the United States and champions of legitimate state authority against federal troops bent on overpowering state sovereignty.

Sterling Price burned his bridges in more ways than one, first cutting the rail and telegraph lines to vulnerable Jefferson City: a special detail that included Governor Jackson's son burned the Gasconade River bridge of the infant Pacific Railroad. Then Price ordered his State Guard district commanders to begin reassembling their regiments in encampments of their own choosing, save for one division that he directed to Boonville, midstate on the Missouri River, where he hoped he could safely relocate Jackson's government. Southern sentiment lay thickest along the river and north of it, for there sat the plantation land tilled by most of Missouri's slaves. Now that Nathaniel Lyon had forced him to choose sides, Price found it vital to maintain contact with that northern third of the state.[29]

The second military district of the State Guard occupied the northeastern strip of the state, hard against the Mississippi River from the mouth of the Des Moines River to that of the Missouri. Lyon's entire force stood between that region and Price's army, which delayed the distribution of Price's mobilization order there by a week to ten days. To avoid interception, recruits for the State Guard had to congregate cautiously in that divided district. The river town of Hannibal raised a full company of Unionist home guards, and at high noon on June 12 the steamer *Black Hawk* docked there to unload a battalion of Illinois volunteers. A regiment of Iowa troops came down from Keokuk on the *Jenny Deans* and landed on Hannibal's upper levee the next day. The young men from that village who sided with Sterling Price slipped out of town by dark of night, in platoons. According to a Hannibal correspondent for the *State Journal* who signed himself only as "Sam," several dozen State Guard recruits left town in the days following Lyon's declaration of war, and plenty more itched to follow. "Sam" may have joined them, in fact, for he wrote to the *Journal* no more after the middle of June.[30]

That *State Journal* correspondent could well have been Sam Clemens, the Mississippi riverboat pilot whose employment had been terminated by the hostilities. Two dozen years later Clemens provided a wry rendition of his escapade with a handful of would-be Confederates who decamped from Hannibal late one night in June. Armed principally with battered mantelpiece shotguns, the self-styled Marion Rangers slunk by darkness from one sympathetic farmer to another, trying to find the rendezvous chosen by their district chief, Brigadier General Thomas Harris. Harris had designated a spot on the upper Salt River. They migrated that way by a circuitous route, suffering miserably as a result of bad weather, periodic panics, and indifferent guides, until by early July, in the vicinity of Clemens's Monroe County birthplace, they began to meet other squads and companies bound for the same rendezvous. A few hundred Illinois and Iowa volunteers and the Hannibal home-guard company pursued those roving bands, capturing suspected insurgents and a number of homemade flags, including one that combined a Revolutionary-vintage rattlesnake coiled beneath the South Carolina palmetto. The mere news of the Yankees' coming convinced Clemens and half of his comrades to retire from the war before the antagonistic contingents clashed. Shortly afterward the Union detachments scattered the remainder of the aspiring State Guardsmen, a large percentage of whom evidently followed Sam Clemens out of the war.[31]

Similar impediments discouraged others in that region who might have taken up the states'-rights cause, significantly reducing both Harris's strength and that of the State Guard, and the summer had nearly ended before Harris managed to join Price's army with what men he did muster. By then the situation had changed dramatically.[32]

Union regiments materialized much more quickly. The German volunteers already waited, uniformed and equipped, in St. Louis, and the surrounding states had also raised troops that poured in to sustain Lyon's impetuous campaign. Kansas, less than six months into statehood, had already organized two complete regiments that perched on Missouri's northwest border, and Iowa had three poised on its northeast corner. Eight Illinois regiments hovered on their side of the Mississippi opposite Missouri, and five more started for the river shore as soon as Lyon called for help. Even sparsely populated Nebraska Territory began raising an infantry regiment the moment that Lyon committed his country to war against Missouri.[33]

Hard times seem to have aided the federal recruiting effort west of the Mississippi, just as they had in New England and the mid-Atlantic states. Business had come to a virtual halt in St. Louis that spring of 1861. One man who would eventually find a satisfactory position as a chief quartermaster in the Union army rejoiced at having found a subordinate job with the post office, where he could "finally" earn some money again. A woman informed her absent brother that the political crisis had so interrupted commerce that many businessmen were losing not only their investments but their houses, and rivermen could find almost no employment. Poverty rivaled political considerations in persuading Union recruits to come forward, as one State Guard soldier discovered early in July. That soon-to-be Confederate, a Northern man with an extensive New England education, interviewed a throng of prisoners taken from one of the city's German regiments at Neosho, asking them why they had signed up to make war against the state. He may have posed the question with genuine curiosity, in anticipation of a political debate, but their uniform reply — "Nothing to do in St. Louis" — suggested that they had been driven into the army by a moribund economy.[34]

The Panic of 1857 had crippled the Kansas economy, and residents had not even begun recovering when the worst drought in memory dried up the rivers and parched the prairie. Brutal heat and unusually violent dust storms in July of 1859 signaled the worsening of a long period of light precipitation, and the close of summer saw the virtual end of rain for that year. No snow fell during the following winter, either. The spring of 1860 continued dry, with late frosts in May that killed any hope for a fruit crop. Ominous dust storms returned in July, and by mid-September of 1860 no perceptible precipitation had yet fallen, prompting a correspondent of the *Lawrence Republican* to compose a poem subtitled "A Prayer for Rain."

Virtually every crop in the state failed, leaving farmers as short of cash as the general community had been during the Panic.[35]

Bad roads in southern Kansas caused near-starvation in January of 1861, just as the territory became a state, for relief provisions could not reach the isolated districts. The public and private charity that too many Kansans had come to expect from eastern benefactors could barely provide enough staples for immediate needs, let alone compensate for so devastating an economic and agricultural failure. Farm families abandoned their fields and set out in search of wage labor, but few potential employers had any money to pay them with, and seldom for more than a few days' work at a time.[36]

Six days after Lincoln appealed for militia to suppress the rebellion, a young farmer north of Topeka informed his Pennsylvania family that "times are very hard and scarcely any money [is] in circulation." Not surprisingly, he also noted that three military companies were forming in his vicinity, even though the president had evidently forgotten to call on Kansas for a single man. In fact, every county in the newest state was raising at least one company, for every county had plenty of men suffering from a shortage of cash; even in the newly settled town of Salina, halfway to Colorado, aspiring soldiers convened to elect officers and begin drill. By then the drought had spread financial ruin to all the industries subsidiary to agriculture, and unemployed tradesmen who had joined farmers in their prayers for relief saw those prayers answered by the army's offer of bed, board, and pay. So many destitute Kansas farmers and farm hands joined the army that the vigorously pro-Union *Lawrence Republican* editorialized against their enlistment, instead pointing to the many thousands of unemployed businessmen, tradesmen, and mechanics who could find occupation by filling the ranks. The farmers might finally expect to realize some profits, the editor predicted, and it was their duty to "cultivate the last acre of ground" to provide sustenance for the army's commissaries and quartermasters. The *Fort Scott Democrat* took the argument a step further, contending that the drought had left Kansas too poor to sustain a war, but three weeks later that struggling newspaper lost its editor, pressroom foreman, journeyman, and printer's devil to the army. At the end of June a bountiful wheat crop started coming in for the first time in two years, and the Kansas economy began recovering enough that many of the recruits from early May found the ninety-day service sufficient to satisfy their patriotic impulses.[37]

Iowa had fared little better than Kansas. Late frosts, early frosts, pest infestations, and an overabundance of rain and snow (which may have reflected the same shifting weather pattern that robbed Kansas of precipitation) had ruined three straight years of crops even in longer-settled eastern Iowa. Poor crops, deep snow, and arctic temperatures killed hogs and cattle or left them too lean to butcher. Debts accumulated far beyond mere insolvency for the hardest hit, and those were usually the tenant farmers. One such debt-ridden leaseholder, hearing of the brief wheat boom farther west, tried to squeeze in on that deal in the fall of 1860, planning to cultivate sixty acres the next spring, but before spring came the secession crisis sent crop prices plummeting again.

"If we had the money for what we raised last year at Eastern prices," his wife insisted, "we should be independent." Local banks began devaluing their money as they had in the Panic less than four years before, and she lamented that what produce she did save for market brought paper money that might be worthless before she could redeem it. Even military service could not solve their financial troubles, for her husband had mangled his right hand in a farm accident.[38]

Little wonder, then, that a Dubuque newspaper reporter who accompanied the 1st Iowa on its three-month campaign found it so full of the indolent, indigent, or underemployed — despite a healthy leavening of professionals and industrial tradesmen. For all his intimate acquaintance with those men, he could name few who had taken up arms from especially altruistic motives. "I knew the young men who responded to the call —" wrote Franc B. Wilkie, of the *Dubuque Herald*, "knew them by hundreds."

They were clerks on small salaries; they were lawyers with insufficient business; they were young men with no occupation and anxious for employment; they were farmers' boys disgusted with the drudgery of the soil, and anxious to visit the wonderful world beyond them. To these were added husbands tired of the bickering of domestic life, lovers disappointed in their affections, and ambitious elements who saw in the organization of men opportunities for command. Others, differing but little from the last named, scented political preferment, and joined the popular movement.

Physicians with limited practice were early and numerous in their applications for permission to enter the service; clergymen with unappreciative parishes, small incomes, and unsympathetic social environments, came to the front and proffered their assistance. Young men well to do, with virile physiques, anxious for adventure, with their hot blood thrilling in response to the sudden clamors of the drum and the shrill invocations of the fife, thronged with eagerness the recruiting stations and wrote their names in bold characters on the list.

There was not one man in a hundred that believed there would be any war or fighting. All were unanimous in the conviction that the

South would not fight, and that if the North put armies in the field, the terrified secessionists would hasten to seek shelter from the storm they had invoked. It was a picnic, a pleasure-trip, a triumphal jaunt through Dixie, with flying banners and beating drums, with all the pleasure of a free excursion, sight-seeing, new faces and places, and pay, food, and clothing during their absence. Some there were who saw loot as they contemplated the wealth of Southern plantations; there were romantic dreamers who caught glimpses in the distance of dark-eyed women with raven hair; and others, idlers by nature, who enjoyed in anticipation the languid delights of the orange groves, the flowering hedges, the beauty of the magnolia blossoms, and the genial air of the "sunny South."[39]

Such were the troops that Lyon sent or called into the interior of Missouri. He claimed that he invaded the state in response to Jackson's June 12 proclamation, which he considered "a declaration of war," but that was obviously not true. His response came so quickly that he must have planned all the details of his campaign even before the conference at the Planters' House, and he implemented that plan with impressive speed. By the morning of June 12, as Illinois troops reached Hannibal, Kansas City was occupied by a substantial phalanx of U.S. Regulars consolidated from various frontier garrisons. The 1st and 2nd Kansas Volunteers marched to join them the next day, ready to settle old border-war scores with Missouri's "ruffian element"; even the governor of Kansas remarked that "Missouri must be taught a lesson." Within a day or two, vengeful Unionist citizens of Kansas City were enthusiastically badgering suspected "traitors" and driving them out of town.[40]

With the same deference to Regular Army officers that seemed to prevail in St. Louis, the colonels of those Kansas regiments accepted Major Samuel Sturgis, of the 1st U.S. Cavalry, as their overall commander. While Sturgis pressed the state forces from the west, Lyon sent three St. Louis regiments toward Rolla, below Jefferson City, under the command of another Regular, Captain Thomas Sweeny. As that little brigade made its way to Rolla, Lyon steamed up the Missouri River to the state capital with Frank Blair's regiment. One of the German regiments (the one that had caused all the trouble at Camp Jackson) followed him there, and Lyon started after Jackson and Price with those two regiments alone.[41]

Price had not managed to recall as many troops to the field as he had mustered before his agreement with Harney: despite a widespread assumption that he had negotiated the armistice to gain time for organizing troops, his faithful observation of that truce had actually worked to his disadvantage. A few hundred State Guard troops tried to defend Boonville, but Lyon vastly outnumbered and outgunned them. His two regiments took possession of the town on Monday morning, June 17. Governor Jackson and the State Guard fled farther upriver toward Lexington, where Price tried to concentrate his forces, but at that town Lyon and Sturgis could have easily converged to cut them off from their only organized allies, in Arkansas. They had but one route of escape and that was south, which separated them once again from those thousands of potential adherents north of the Missouri River. They began a frantic retreat before the week ended, heading for the southwestern corner of the state. Price's main body marched or rode due south from Lexington in a long, disorganized hegira, picking up rustic recruits from isolated hamlets and losing fainter hearts who had not yet signed their names. The governor accompanied the division of Monroe Parsons on a parallel route farther east. Parsons had a thousand or so men, with one four-gun battery and a baggage train of about two dozen vehicles — several of them stage coaches. The manager of the Overland Mail Company station at Warsaw showed his allegiance by giving Jackson ten teams of horses, but many of them drowned in the crossing of the Osage River.[42]

Lyon ordered Sturgis south in pursuit of those two bands, and sent Sweeny's column from Rolla toward Springfield, both to intercept their flight and to interpose a force between the State Guard and the Arkansas Confederates. Meanwhile, Lyon remained at Boonville to collect transportation for his own overland journey. On June 20, while he lingered there, he acknowledged official receipt of the order removing Missouri from his department and giving it to George McClellan, but in his reluctance to leave the scene of action he claimed on June 22 not to understand whether that was what the order really intended.[43]

The Blair machine once again went to work on Lyon's behalf. In Washington, Montgomery Blair solicited treasury secretary Salmon P. Chase, McClellan's friend in the cabinet, to have the order rescinded. Chase appealed to General Scott, arguing that McClellan did not understand Missouri affairs and considered the additional responsibility a burden, but Scott declined to interfere because, as he understood it, Attorney General Bates wanted McClellan to have the post. Blair then leaned on Bates, pointing out that Lyon was older than McClellan by some years and had seen much more service. Eventually Blair had his way, but not to the degree he had hoped. A fortnight later McClellan, who looked on Missouri as an impossible addition to an already cumbersome department, interpreted the original order in a completely different way — as having relieved Lyon from the Department of the West altogether, leaving him in command of nothing beyond the troops he led in the field. By then, unbeknown to McClellan, the Blair intrigue had succeeded in bypassing him. Frank Blair had arrived in Washington, abandoning his regiment to take his seat in Congress, where he entertained high hopes of becoming Speaker of the House. Brother Frank's presence abetted the postmaster general's request, and it was then that Lincoln assigned John Charles Frémont to the Department of the West. McClellan's interpretation of Scott's gerrymandering carried into Frémont's administration, however, so Lyon retained control of the little army that he had gathered. At least (as the Blairs would have viewed it) if General Lyon must work beneath a superior officer, that officer would be an antislavery Republican; besides, the postmaster general considered Frémont "a man of genuine native military talent."[44]

By the end of June scores of State Guard companies, amounting to several thousand half-equipped and ill-uniformed adventurers, had gathered in a broad swath of prairie bivouacs between the ardently Confederate towns of Nevada and Neosho. So far did that archipelago of State Guard campfires stretch that it encompassed the birthplaces of three of Missouri's four most famous sons. Neosho sat barely a dozen miles from the borders of both Kansas and the Indian Territory, and only a couple of dozen miles above the Arkansas border, where lurked Ben McCulloch with a brigade of Confederates from Arkansas and Louisiana. Sweeny's Union brigade raced toward them from Rolla, with a St. Louis regiment under German-born Franz Sigel far in the lead. Sigel marched right into the midst of that tatterdemalion host with about six hundred men and proceeded to maneuver himself between the Missouri troops and their friends in Arkansas.[45]

Lyon started south from Boonville early in July, but Sigel — who shared Lyon's impetuosity — would not wait. Part of another St. Louis regiment reinforced him, and on July 5 he flung himself at the Missouri State Guard with a thousand men and eight guns. The much larger state force simply wrapped itself around Sigel's bold front, threatening to gain his rear and seize his supply train, and he had not advanced very far when he decided that he had better turn back. Sigel retreated through the town of Carthage, whence he had come, but Governor Jackson's troops still lacked the arms, ammunition, and organization to give Sigel a sound thrashing. The Germans escaped without serious losses, although some of McCulloch's Arkansas cavalry dashed up to Neosho during the battle and captured an overgrown company that Sigel had left to garrison the place.[46]

Sigel's report of the repulse caught up with Lyon a few days later, soon after he had combined with Sturgis and as he tried to negotiate the Osage at its junction with the Sac River. Sigel conveyed frantic visions of impending annihilation, but Lyon expected that it would take two or three more days just to ferry his trains over the river. He offered Sigel the redundant advice that he should call on Sweeny for aid, but the majority of Sigel's men made it safely back to Sweeny's camp at Springfield on the very day that Lyon dispatched his message. Knowing nothing of that, Lyon thought better of waiting for his trains. Taking what provisions he could carry, he forged ahead to Sigel's aid with Sturgis's cavalry and half his infantry, leaving the rest of the column to be prodded along by a Regular Army lieutenant, who was to bring it across the river and follow as soon as he could.[47]

Whichever political faction enjoyed the security of a sympathetic military presence seemed to terrorize the other, and Union men along the Kansas border feared for their lives when they heard that Sigel had been "all cut up." Anticipating that pro-slave ruffians from the border war would take the opportunity to adjust accounts, thousands of refugees left their homes in southwestern Missouri and southeastern Kansas and took the road to Fort Scott, where hundreds of armed men milled about as though in search of a commander. Doubting the assurances of Governor Jackson and General Price that Missouri would fight only to repel invasion, Kansans camped outdoors in fear of punitive raids, and volunteer lookouts kept constant vigils over the border. Secessionist citizens likewise emptied out of their homes in the path of Lyon's advance, either to join Jackson's forces or to escape Yankee soldiers whom they considered as brutal as any border ruffians. Like McDowell's amateurs on their way to Bull Run, Lyon's volunteers helped themselves to whatever they wanted on the usual pretext that the coveted property belonged to "secesh."[48]

The victory over Sigel disproportionately encouraged state forces and their supporters, but neither the Unionist citizens of southwestern Missouri nor Nathaniel Lyon had to worry about an immediate attack. Until late July the Missouri State Guard remained too short of ordnance and discipline for any significant hostile movement, even against a smaller force. General Price concentrated his diminutive divisions on Cowskin Prairie, in the extreme southwestern corner of the state, only three miles from Arkansas and as close as half a mile to the Indian Territory. There they equipped themselves nearly from scratch, molding their own bullets and, if they were fortunate, patching together uniforms from divers bolts of cloth. For the most part, the Missouri State Guard had gone to war wearing civilian clothing in a scramble of colors, prints, and stripes, with an array of headgear ranging from ancient military caps to top hats and broad sombreros. Each day they drilled for two hours before breakfast and two more in the late afternoon, retreating to the shade of trees in the creek bottoms during the enervating heat of midday.[49]

The heat and humidity caused even worse suffering among those Union soldiers still plodding southward. Most of Lyon's troops wore white linen havelocks draped over their caps and the napes of their necks to prevent sunburn, but those contraptions clung uncomfortably and the flapping corners gave their column the appearance of a drove of flop-eared sheep. The daily temperatures exceeded even those that broiled Irvin McDowell's troops, who gathered for their appointment along Bull Run, a thousand miles away, just as Lyon settled in at Springfield on July 13. Ignoring his nominal department commander, he promptly forwarded army headquarters the same warning that Robert Patterson and McDowell offered from Virginia: his ninety-day men were about to go home, leaving him dangerously understrength in the face of a superior enemy. He needed at least ten thousand more troops if he was to hold his advanced position, and the five thousand or so soldiers he had with him desperately wanted pay and clothing. Both the volunteers' personal wardrobes and the professional soldiers' uniforms hung in rags: one Kansas infantryman remarked that Lyon himself habitually dressed in a shabby coat and pants "much the worse for wear." The commissary of the 1st Iowa brought a new shipment of havelocks into the camp at Springfield, but not a stitch of other clothing for his nearly naked regiment. Even more critical was the shortage of food, although local farmers who smelled a quick profit supplied the hungry soldiers with wagonloads of pies, cornbread, and biscuits at "scandalous" prices.[50]

Lyon received no reinforcements. Worse yet, with real danger imminent his three-month troops complained indignantly of the inadequate attention their government gave them, and they could hardly wait to get out of the army. For all of that Lyon brazenly sat where he was for two weeks, and in the last week of July the combined forces of the Confederacy and the state of Missouri started moving east and north, toward Springfield, with the intention of demolishing Lyon's little army. Ben McCulloch commanded two brigades of Arkansas troops, along with one regiment from Louisiana, with a total strength approaching six thousand men — all well-armed and carrying a moderate supply of ammunition. Price, who subordinated himself to McCulloch for the coming battle, had mustered more than nine thousand men by then, but barely two-thirds of them owned any weapons and most carried shotguns, hunting rifles, or a haphazard assortment of military muskets. McCulloch staked Price to all the ammunition he could spare from his own stores. He and Price met at

Cassville, and by nightfall of August 1 the advance division camped at Crane Creek, just one day's forced march from Springfield.[51]

To McCulloch's surprise, Lyon had come out to meet them halfway with his own legion of fewer than six thousand, pushing his men through enervating heat to the banks of Wilson Creek. Lyon's advance betrayed a boldness (or rashness) uncommon even for him, because he supposed that his opponents marshaled more men than they actually did. He understood that the Missouri State Guard composed the majority of the enemy, and that they lacked decent weapons, but like his protégé Sigel he willingly confronted a much stronger opponent. Lyon surpassed Sigel as a tactician, though, and his daring brought momentary success and vindication. In a spontaneous fray at Dug Springs on August 2 a few companies of Lyon's Regulars routed more than twice their number of Price's Missourians, driving them into headlong flight. The display not only encouraged the Federals, but elicited open and official contempt for the Missouri troops from the Arkansas Confederates who came to their assistance.[52]

The following day Lyon put more pressure on McCulloch's vanguard. He managed to drive it back in one skirmish, although the ninety-day men of his 1st Iowa disintegrated in a panic. Then Lyon began to fear for his supply line, since he had too few cavalry to prevent a raid, and on August 5 he withdrew to the outskirts of Springfield again. McCulloch's division and his Missouri compatriots moved up to the site of Lyon's advanced camp; the next day his command ambled another couple of miles closer to Springfield and settled into Lyon's earlier encampment, on the hills overlooking Wilson Creek.[53]

"Prudence," Lyon wrote on August 4, "seems now to indicate the necessity of withdrawing, if possible, from the country, and falling upon either St. Louis or Kansas," but prudence had never been Lyon's long suit, and he showed less of it with every passing day. He lingered injudiciously at Springfield, and then planned a reckless assault for the morning of August 6. In the darkness he moved some infantry and artillery out in preparation for a general advance, but he dawdled well into the afternoon — when, glancing at his watch, he expressed surprise at how late it was and called the attack off altogether.[54]

Perpetually equivocating about a strategic withdrawal, Lyon still tarried at the extremity of his vulnerable supply line while his enemy drew ever closer with an overpowering force. His well-justified fear of annihilation seemed overshadowed by anxiety that his campaign would seem a failure — or, perhaps, that Frémont might come out to assume command if he abandoned his advanced position. His disdain for the Missouri troops who comprised most of McCulloch's army sustained him, too, and that disdain filtered down to the company officers. So, somehow, did a much less alarming image of the odds against them: in his reports to Frémont the increasingly distracted Lyon represented himself (with seeming sincerity) as outnumbered by more than five to one, yet subalterns in his volunteer regiments more accurately understood the disparity as less than two to one. The Union soldiers shared not only the confidence that they surpassed their enemy in discipline, equipment, and training, but the opinion that Nathaniel Lyon's military capacity equaled that of any general in the country.[55]

With the arrival of a regiment styled the South Kansas–Texas Cavalry, early in August, the allied Southern columns included men from as far north as the Iowa border and as far south and west as the Brazos River. Additionally, the Missouri State Guard harbored a sprinkling of Northern men whose loyalty to their interpretation of the United States Constitution exceeded any they felt for their native section. Missouri remained technically part of the Union, after all, and despite their violent resistance to the tyranny of the Lincoln government many of the troops still slept under the U.S. flag, and apparently perceived themselves less as an army of rebels than as a posse of aggrieved citizens. They used the pleasant interlude at Wilson Creek to recuperate from days of exhausting campaigning, collecting vegetables and fresh meat from the countryside for meals that seemed sumptuous. They cleaned their arms and tended to their meager equipment, with the occasional creature comfort of a bath or an evening of music.[56]

In his pastoral bivouac there, McCulloch estimated his effective force at something under 11,600 men. More than half of that number consisted of cavalry, and of infantry he counted 5,300; four small batteries added about 250 artillerymen. Many hundreds more Missourians tagged along with Price, mounted but without weapons of any kind, and McCulloch considered them "continually in the way." Few of his 6,000 cavalry carried modern weapons, most of them having taken whatever muskets or shotguns they could find at home, and an alarming number of those arms still employed the flintlock firing mechanism that failed so often in wet weather. If there was a bayonet in the entire army it escaped the attention of the commanding general, and some units carried as few as twenty rounds of ammunition per man. Like Lyon, McCulloch exaggerated his enemy's strength considerably, allowing the Federals between 10,000 and 12,000 well-equipped troops, but on Friday, August 9, he nevertheless decided to move against that exaggeratedly formidable foe. He intended to divide his command into four columns, marching all night to bring those wings into position for a dawn attack from four different points.[57]

Lyon's men had known for nearly two weeks about McDowell's defeat at Bull Run. That same information must also have reached Southern ears, though perhaps the story that carried westward bore all the original overtones of Union disaster without any of the subsequent modifications that had alleviated public panic in the East. In that engagement McDowell and Beauregard had composed similar plans that they intended to implement on the same day, and so did the belligerents on the Missouri prairie. Lyon and Sigel concocted a scheme involving a night march to Wilson Creek, where Sigel would take a detachment of St. Louis regiments on a roundabout route to attack McCulloch's rear while Lyon assailed him from the front.[58]

Originally, Lyon intended to slam head-on into McCulloch with his entire command. The plan had satisfied the rest of the senior officers, but Sigel alone prevailed on Lyon to split his smaller army — which seemed all the more inferior to them because they imagined McCulloch to have twice as many troops as he did. The division of forces in the presence of a strong enemy violated one of the cardinal tactical precepts in which Sigel had supposedly been thoroughly educated at a German military academy; although such risks would bring Stonewall Jackson and Robert E. Lee lasting fame, they usually resulted in utter defeat. Lyon nonetheless concurred, illustrating the deterioration of his own judgment, and his regiments began leaving camp before dark on Friday evening. McCulloch had ordered his own army to march at nine o'clock that night, and had drawn most of his pickets in so they could rejoin their commands, but as that hour approached a light drizzle set in, and for a time heavier rain seemed likely. McCulloch had managed to keep his command mobile for the previous couple of weeks in part because of a lack of rain. He feared putting his troops on the road during a downpour, for most of them wore no cartridge boxes, and the paper cartridges in their pockets or the loose powder in their shot bags would not survive a soaking. Thick clouds also shrouded the faint thumbnail of the waxing moon, blotting out the dim light that would have made a night march feasible. The men lay awake long into the night, waiting for a more propitious sky, losing sleep while the enemy slunk, unseen, into position.[59]

With ten dozen Regular cavalrymen and a thousand St. Louis Germans, including one battery of artillery, Sigel swung around the sprawling campfires of McCulloch's army, little troubled by the darkness that had discouraged McCulloch. Lyon marched straight down the Wire Road, as residents called the wagon track that the telegraph followed into Arkansas. He left a big regiment of home guards and a little cavalry in Springfield, as a reserve, and without much hope of a response he called in home guards from fifty miles around. With him went about forty-three hundred men and ten guns, all manned by Regulars. A few miles out of Springfield he veered off the Wire Road to his right, slipping up on McCulloch from the north. An hour after midnight the main Union column halted within sight of flickering fires in the enemy camp, and Lyon's men lay down for a few hours of sleep.[60]

Sigel, too, reached position in good season, looking down on the camp from surrounding hills and waiting for the sound of fighting on Lyon's front. Lyon arranged his line of battle by 4:00 AM, rolling it forward cross-lots even before the sky began to lighten. The fires he had seen evidently belonged to a few men who had roamed far beyond the main encampment, and Union skirmishers drove those outliers back on their friends, tramping rapidly onward through the gloaming for another mile. Splashing across a branch west of Wilson Creek just as the coming dawn extinguished the morning star, the leading Union infantry ran into the same division of the Missouri State Guard that had fled so ignominiously at Dug Springs barely a week before. This time, to the surprise of some Union volunteers, the State Guard mounted stiff resistance. The first unit that came into action faced irresistible odds and fell back fighting to the perimeter of their camp, on a hillside overlooking the creek. Comrades came to their aid until most of James Rains's division faced Lyon's assault. Rains commanded State Guard regiments from all along the state's western frontier below the Missouri River, while the predominantly German 1st Missouri Volunteers of urban St. Louis spearheaded Lyon's attack. Armed mainly with unrifled weapons, those inhabitants of opposite ends of the state hammered each other from point-blank range in a brawl that might have assumed overtones of class and ethnic conflict if the combatants had paused to introduce themselves to each other.[61]

Hearing the echo of that engagement, Sigel pitched in with his artillery downstream, at the southern end of the camp. To the amusement of his Germans, who could see the guns' effect, Arkansas and Missouri cavalrymen sprang from their tents and blankets and bolted from their breakfast fires, streaming northward to the cover of a wooded hollow cut by Skegg's Branch. From that cover they continued upstream, either to join the fight against Lyon or find a hiding place, while Sigel's brigade of infantry sauntered down and occupied the deserted camp.[62]

Lyon brought the 1st Kansas and 1st Iowa into line beside the 1st Missouri, pushing them all into the growing battle for the crest of the hill that dominated the center of the enemy camp. When a four-gun Arkansas battery began sweeping Lyon's line with enfilade fire from a hillside across the creek, Lyon threw four companies of Regulars and a couple of hundred home guards at them. This mixed battalion struck for the battery, and as they crossed the cornfield of one John Ray they encountered the 3rd Louisiana on its way to threaten that flank. The Federals caught the

Louisiana regiment in an awkward formation with their first volley, top-pling a few victims, but the surprised Pelicans deployed under fire and lay down while the bullets skimmed over their heads. The 2nd Arkansas Mounted Rifles fell in beside them. The Regulars in Ray's cornfield, pre-senting fewer than three hundred muskets, also dropped to the ground as Southern rifles accumulated against them, until both the Louisiana and Arkansas regiments rose up, vaulted a fence, and dashed at them, scream-ing like banshees. Outnumbered three or four to one (it seemed to a re-cent recruit like twenty to one) the Regulars jumped to their feet and turned for the rear when the charging Confederates had closed to pistol range. Still, they recoiled in relative defiance considering their position and the dozens of men they had lost. One of Lyon's artillery batteries swung to the left and began lobbing spherical case shot to cover their re-treat.[63]

After the Regulars fell back to the western bank of the creek, most of the Louisiana regiment turned about with other scattered troops and confronted Sigel's isolated fragment at the rear of McCulloch's army. The same confusion over uniforms that had worked against McDowell's troops at Manassas twenty days previously led Sigel to grief, for the Loui-siana regiment wore an array of uniforms dominated by various shades of grey. Most of the Missouri State Guard — the enemy with whom Sigel's troops were most familiar — lacked any uniforms at all, and when they saw the 3rd Louisiana coming at them on the Wire Road they mistook their clothing for the similarly mismatched (but mostly grey) uniforms of the 1st Iowa. Assuming that Lyon had broken through and was coming to meet them, the Germans held their fire and waved the Stars and Stripes in greeting. In reply, two batteries opened on them from left and right, and the supposed friends leveled a volley into their faces. Sigel's infantry and artillerymen alike dispersed like milkweed in a gust of wind, with Texas cavalry and State Guard horse and foot in hot pursuit. Five of Sigel's six guns fell into enemy hands, as did scores of his men. Sigel himself out-stripped all of his command in his anxiety to escape. He wore a light-col-ored western hat, and on that sultry summer day he threw a blanket over his shoulders, which allowed him to pass for a Texan.[64]

From that moment Lyon was on his own, but he knew nothing of Sigel's flight and continued the contest at least partly in the vain hope of contributing to his subordinate's success. He hung on remarkably long, for the surprise of his attack had so shaken his enemy that most of McCulloch's commanders reported fragmentation in their units, with reg-iments breaking into battalions or companies that fought independently. Hundreds simply left the field or huddled in the shelter of swales and creek bottoms. One entire Arkansas regiment never pulled a trigger all day, remaining only nominally under fire on the eastern bank of the creek throughout the fight. Lyon, meanwhile, committed all but a company of Kansas cavalry and the two companies of home guards that had ducked out of the scrap in Ray's cornfield. The Missouri State Guard bore the brunt of Lyon's attack for the first couple of hours, aided by dismounted Texas and Arkansas horsemen whom Sigel had shelled out of their camps.[65]

The opposing battlefronts swept back and forth over the crest of what soon earned the nickname of Bloody Hill. Sterling Price estimated that his State Guard contributed about five thousand men to the firing line there, along with one cavalry regiment each from Arkansas and Texas and a couple of companies that had lost their way from the 3rd Louisiana. Two batteries of U.S. Regulars made up for much of the difference in numbers, mowing Price's men down in swaths every time they surged forward. The scrub oak and underbrush lay thick enough in spots to screen the infantry until it came within twenty yards of the muzzles, which then erupted in canister: artillery and musketry together would rise to a sustained crescendo and then abate as the survivors staggered back the way they had come. A lull intervened between each assault, as though by the mutual consent of dazed and exhausted foes. Bodies, some stilled by death and some writhing in agony, littered the ground in such profusion that Union artillerymen had to move them aside for room to work their pieces, while their assailants stepped carefully to avoid treading on their own wounded comrades. Plenty of Federals also fell beneath the hail of small-arms fire: Frank Blair's 1st Missouri Volunteers, fighting without the congressman-colonel, lost more than a third of its men that morning.[66]

The Texas cavalrymen worked their way around Lyon's right flank, and Lyon stretched his force thin to meet them. The two Kansas regiments each blunted one attack against the center, but in a third assault the 1st Kansas wavered and fell back. Lyon replaced it with the 1st Iowa, but a volley struck that regiment just as the retreating Kansans disrupted their formation, and hundreds of the ninety-day Iowa men melted away. Lyon saw his line unravel there, and before the enemy could exploit the rupture he galloped into the gap with his hat in his hand, calling on the men who swirled about him for a countercharge and offering to lead it. The 2nd Kansas rallied around him, but a blast of musketry announced the arrival of Price's latest assault, and one bullet from that fusillade knocked Lyon out of the saddle. In a few moments he was dead — killed three months too late to save Missouri from the devastation of civil war.[67]

Lyon's death remained virtually a secret for half an hour, until Sam Sturgis learned that he had inherited command of the beleaguered army as the next-ranking Regular officer. Sturgis knew nothing of Lyon's plans, though, and no one else seemed to, either; perhaps he had had no plans, beyond the hope that a simultaneous attack on either end of McCulloch's camp would scatter the Southern forces to the corners of the compass. Neither was there any way to extemporize a plan in conjunction with Sigel, whom no one had heard from all day. Soon another wave of infantry came rolling toward the Union line, but for a time they seemed to be friendly, for their casual dress looked like Sigel's St. Louis soldiers and they carried what seemed like the national flag. Either the Federals mistook the Confederate Stars and Bars for Old Glory or more of Price's Missourians were still fighting under the flag that stood for their shattered constitution, for the approaching line opened fire at close range. Some of the Texas cavalrymen swung around the right flank at the same time, galloping for the Union rear. A couple of hundred Union rifles (home guards, perhaps) and the Regular batteries spun to the right, deflecting the cavalry with a volley or two, then turned back on the worn-out Southern infantrymen, whose charge seemed to wither prematurely. The badly bloodied state and Confederate regiments had lost much of their enthusiasm for the attack.[68]

Sturgis calculated his losses, overestimated the strength of McCulloch's army by the customary factor of two, and observed that his ammunition had begun to run out, whereupon he concluded to retreat. The lull following that final assault offered the perfect opportunity, and when Sturgis's troops shrank back from Bloody Hill McCulloch showed no inclination to take up the chase. McCulloch also maintained his exaggerated count of Union forces, and, given the poor armament and discipline of his command, he considered himself lucky simply to have won a victory that had hung precariously in the balance until the final moments. Some Union soldiers, including officers, saw McCulloch's brigades falling back to regroup, and they mistook the action for an enemy retreat, but Sturgis resisted the urgent appeals of those who wished to resume the offensive. He turned for Springfield, running into several hundred survivors of Sigel's command under the care of a company of the 2nd U.S. Dragoons and the lieutenant who had brought that fragment off safely.[69]

A remnant of fewer than four thousand Union soldiers entered Springfield at 5:00 PM. Around dusk, an ambulance came in under a flag of truce to deliver General Lyon's body, which had been forgotten at the field hospital. Eventually Colonel Sigel turned up and claimed command as the senior officer. Major Sturgis had led the army from the field despite the presence of at least two unwounded lieutenant colonels and Captain Sweeny, who had been elected brigadier general by his brigade of Missouri volunteers, but — to the dismay of most of the professional soldiers under him — Sturgis surrendered control to Sigel. At three o'clock the next morning Sigel began a badly organized and ill-conducted retreat to Rolla, embarrassed by an immense train of civilian refugees. Only the absence of enemy pursuit allowed the fugitives to reach the railhead, for McCulloch did not move his headquarters into Springfield until the third day after the battle.[70]

By the time the first news of Wilson's Creek hit the eastern seaboard it had been contorted into a signal success of Union arms. The *New York Times*, always optimistic at the earliest notice of any engagement and especially anxious to erase the shame and discouragement of Bull Run, announced the battle to its readers as a "Great National Victory." George Templeton Strong, who had gushed with admiration of Nathaniel Lyon when the *Times* reported his "impressive victory" at Boonville, began to understand that such reports carried more wish than truth. Later *Times* accounts mentioned the retreat of the national forces, ameliorating it by reporting the loss of "only a very few guns," but readers comprehended the sudden change of tone.

"If these be victories," Strong remarked, "may we soon enjoy a few defeats!"[71]

PART III

THE ERA
OF SUSPICION

7

The Despot's Heel

◆ A PRECARIOUSLY OVERLOADED stagecoach carried Sam Clemens across the rugged mountains and alkali deserts of northern Nevada while Nathaniel Lyon orchestrated his final effort to crush the defenders of the Missouri state government. As the hybrid armies maneuvered toward the banks of Wilson Creek, half a continent away, Clemens approached the territorial capital of Carson City; he stepped down there four days after the battle. The young man who had grown up in Hannibal had found Missouri more bitterly divided than he could bear, and never again would he call his native state his home.[1]

Missourians had discovered that the mere expression of sympathy for their state government could bring trouble wherever federal troops maintained control, as they did in Hannibal. The *Daily Messenger* reported that the Illinois and Iowa troops who seized control there immediately silenced the local "secession organ," and the *Messenger* moderated its occasionally censorious tone considerably while those troops camped nearby. The Iowans continued inland by railroad and took control of the Macon City *Register*, appropriating the office to put out a single-sheet edition called the *Whole Union* while they rounded up town officials for the provost marshal.[2] The party that had grasped military power equated disagreement with the Lincoln administration to actual treason, and those who impeached the wisdom or legality of administration policy could face dire consequences. Soldiers acting under the orders of their superiors squelched the principal voice of states' rights in Missouri — the *State Journal* of St. Louis — by forcing their way into the office before dawn one morning and removing the paper's printing equipment. The federal district attorney in St. Louis then collected testimony and sought an indictment for treason against the editor, whose principal crime had been to express in print his (and others') outrage at Lincoln's dictatorial policies.[3]

The war to preserve the Union quickly eviscerated the First Amendment. Across the nation, federal agents ordered or allowed Union soldiers to suppress the newspapers of dissident editors, and official disregard for freedom of speech licensed a popular intolerance that led to violence. Ninety-day New Hampshire volunteers, returning to their state capital from their bloodless campaign under General Patterson, led a surly crowd in an attack on the office of Concord's *Democratic Standard*. The newspaper had offended the summer soldiers by denouncing the war generally and reporting specifically on the 1st New Hampshire's depredations against Maryland citizens. In order to prove their courage and defend their honor, the three-month men assaulted the editor and his sons and destroyed their print shop. The newspaper never resumed publication, but no arrests or prosecutions followed. A few days later a mob in Bangor, Maine, demolished the office of that city's *Democrat*.[4]

Republican newspapers expressed sympathy with such mobs, inciting them to further action. The *Daily American* of Manchester, New Hampshire, excused the soldiers who destroyed the *Standard* on the grounds that they "were provoked into it by the offensive character of the paper." A week later the *American* published a list of Northern newspapers that had called for peace or criticized the administration, checking off the *Standard* and the *Democrat* as "suppressed." Prominently featured in that list was the *Advertiser and Farmer* of Bridgeport, Connecticut, which the Manchester editor considered "the most abusive" of the opposition sheets. Inspired by another platoon of discharged three-month volunteers, a massive throng of Union men broke up a peace meeting near Bridgeport a few days later, assaulting at least one speaker. Then they moved on to sack the office of the *Advertiser and Farmer* and drive the editor out of town. Similar mobs put several other administration critics out of business that season, and the threat of such violence convinced even more editors to temper their complaints.[5]

Where mobs failed to do the work of curbing free expression, the government stepped in. A federal grand jury in New York delivered "presentments" against several opposition newspapers in New York City, most prominently the *Daily News* and the *Journal of Commerce*. Postmaster General Blair refused mail service to those newspapers that most vigorously criticized the Lincoln government — including the *News* and the *Journal*. Federal marshals seized any copies that traveled out of the city, and within a month or so they put the *Daily News* out of business. The *Journal of Commerce* also succumbed, though it was allowed to resume its mail subscriptions once the founder and editor agreed to sell out. When the editor of New York's *Freeman's Journal* lived up to his publication's libertarian name and refused to knuckle under, Secretary of State Seward resorted to his extraordinary powers of arrest, throwing the editor into Fort Lafayette. Frequently, officials down the chain of command took it upon themselves to shut down anti-administration newspapers. One of Ulysses Grant's earliest orders as a brigadier general dispatched a detachment of soldiers from Jefferson City to arrest the editor of a defiantly anti-Lincoln Boonville newspaper and confiscate its printing apparatus.[6]

Union officers in Missouri showed the same oppressive tendencies as their Maryland counterparts. One general arrested a state legislator solely because he had served as Speaker in the last session of the Missouri House of Representatives, forcing him to dig latrines all day long in temperatures exceeding one hundred degrees. Troops arrested citizens wholesale on nothing more than secret accusations that they favored secession. The day after he learned of Lyon's death and the flight of his army, John Frémont's response was to declare martial law in St. Louis, and his subordinates responded as though he had invoked it across the entire state. Frémont had read reports of heavy concentrations of secession sentiment north of the city, and growing sympathy statewide, precisely because of the excesses committed in the name of the Union; evidently he feared that news of Lyon's defeat would encourage open rebellion. He wailed for reinforcements, asking the secretary of war to order all the disposable troops in Illinois, Indiana, Wisconsin, and Ohio to St. Louis for his use, and his alarm so rattled Washington that President Lincoln attended to some of the regimental movements himself.[7]

With yet another Confederate victory, Southern confidence fairly soared from the Ozarks to the Atlantic. Wilson's Creek had opened a wonderful chance to recover the state from federal forces, but dissension at headquarters squandered that opportunity. With his loyalty to the Confederate States, Ben McCulloch wanted to secure Springfield as a meeting place for the fugitive state legislature, where it might decide on secession. A vote to withdraw, McCulloch supposed, would create a unified command and bring the full resources of the Confederate government to the conflict in Missouri, absorbing Missouri recruits into a permanent and well-armed organization and securing captured territory against further federal aggression. Sterling Price declined to cooperate. Demonstrating that he still considered secession subordinate to the protection of Missouri sovereignty, Price headed north to liberate his state with its own troops.[8]

Operating with even more limited resources than Price, other Missouri troops cooperated with Confederate forces in southeastern Missouri, harassing large Union contingents on the banks of the Mississippi and among the swamps above the bootheel.[9] Just across the Mississippi from southeastern Missouri lay Kentucky, which had spawned many of Missouri's leaders, including Governor Jackson. Like their Missouri neighbors, the people of Kentucky struggled with conflicting political loyalties. Incensed by Lincoln's appeal for troops, Kentuckians as far north as the Ohio River had offered the Confederacy assistance, including the son of a prominent Unionist newspaper editor from Louisville, where three hundred young men had taken up arms to resist Northern aggression.[10] At Paducah great numbers of men who had previously professed strong Union sentiment turned secessionist after the federal troop levy, and a meeting there on April 18 had raised a troop of cavalry, a company of infantry, and a battery of artillery for the Southern army — all before the first ragtag Pennsylvania militia reached Washington. Sympathy with the slaveholding South carried over to transient Northerners, who developed an antipathy for the Republican Party and the seeming intransigence of the Congress that it dominated, but those animosities did not necessarily preclude personal attachment to the Union.[11] Kentucky's Southern-leaning governor, Beriah Magoffin, refused to participate in the subjugation of Southern states and sent no militia in answer to Lincoln's April call. Magoffin may not have been a thoroughgoing secessionist at heart, but he worked with — and ultimately against — a preponderantly Unionist legislature. Union feelings ran much deeper in Kentucky than they did in Missouri, partly because Kentucky had been a state longer than most of its citizens had been alive and partly because of a long tradition of nationalism that had kept Henry Clay in the U.S. Congress for nearly three decades. Clay had been dead nine years by 1861, but even after the ascension of two Kentucky natives to contending presidencies it was the Virginia-born Clay who came to most Americans' minds as the prototypical Kentuckian.

Alongside the reverence for union with sister states slave and free breathed the spirit of independence that had driven the Kentucky Resolutions of 1798. The Kentucky legislature had embraced this document in defiance of Federalists in Congress whose broad interpretation of the Constitution threatened states rights. Like similar articles adopted by Kentucky's mother state, Virginia, the Kentucky Resolutions insisted that the Union consisted only of a compact between independent states, and that the federal government existed only to provide certain services for those member states. The army that Abraham Lincoln wished to wield against the estranged states would have disavowed the Kentucky Resolutions and crushed the spirit that created it, forever subordinating the will of Kentucky to that of the government in Washington.

From the outset, militia companies of varying political persuasions sprang up in virtually every community, yet most Kentucky residents favored the same neutrality that Missouri espoused. Like the Maryland legislature, the Union-loving solons of Kentucky voted by considerable margins to keep out of the dispute except to provide mediation. Governor Magoffin issued his promise of strict neutrality to all parties on May 20. Unionists initially hailed that pledge for its discouraging effect on secession agitation, but Magoffin's devotion to neutrality eventually provoked suspicion: his even hand prompted radicals on either side to denounce him as unreliable.[12] When he learned of a Southern rights rally scheduled for one of the lower counties, Magoffin dispatched an emissary to present his neutrality proclamation as an alternative to militant action. He responded with complaints and appeals whenever federal or Confederate troops infringed upon his state's borders. The Confederate government, which would realize great benefits from a neutral buffer across its midsection, paid close attention to Magoffin's communications, even ordering back recruiting officers who penetrated the Bluegrass on their own initiative.[13]

Union authorities proved less receptive to Magoffin's entreaties, as befit the tenor of the federal war against proponents of states' rights, but President Lincoln accorded Kentucky tremendous significance. Acknowledging that he had to keep the state loyal in order to hold Missouri and Maryland, he observed neutrality passively, but made no promises. On the sly, however, he treated Kentucky no more deferentially than he did Missouri, allowing pro-Union volunteers to enlist under the guise of home guard companies. Lincoln bolstered those companies with arms, ammunition, and ultimately with the security of a cantonment called Camp Dick Robinson, in the heart of the state, from which they could seize military control on short notice.[14] Governor Magoffin, Congressman (and former senator) John J. Crittenden, and "the most prominent citizens" of the state complained about the encampment, while federal agents professed ignorance. In August Lincoln chose Robert Anderson, the Kentucky native and Fort Sumter hero, to command in Kentucky, and Anderson diplomatically located his headquarters across the river in Cincinnati, where Unionist Kentucky volunteers could rendezvous more openly without inflaming their fellow citizens.[15]

There already existed an official, organized militia to protect the state, but it would have been inclined to resist with force if pushed too far by the federal government. Like the reorganized militia of Missouri, it was called the State Guard, and it was composed of men whose view of federal authority would probably lead them south if they were forced to choose sides. Nominally, though, the State Guard threatened to repel incursions from either army, and for the sake of neutrality a majority of the members were probably willing to meet that responsibility. Those who harbored active hostility to the United States had the option of migrating into Tennessee, alone or in the company of adventurers like Nathan Bedford Forrest, who dashed twenty miles into western Kentucky in mid-August, looking for men to fill his cavalry regiment. Confederate authorities welcomed such refugees, and from the opening guns many hundreds of them crossed the line: one battalion of Kentucky Confederates reached Harper's Ferry as early as May 11. Unionist Kentucky editors nonetheless mistrusted the State Guard as a "camp of instruction for the Southern Confederacy" and hounded the governor to disband it.[16]

The failure of Unionist editors to complain about the home-guard encampment betrayed their willingness, approaching eagerness, to subvert Kentucky neutrality and throw the state into the war on the side of the federal government. Governor Magoffin maintained the middle ground with better faith, objecting to both the home guards at Camp Dick Robinson and the Confederate camps just below the Tennessee line. His correspondence with Jefferson Davis and the Confederate governor of Tennessee remained more cordial than his exchanges with federal authorities, but the Confederate government had not established camps on Kentucky soil and discouraged individual Confederates from transgressions within Magoffin's territory, while the Washington government largely ignored his pleas.[17]

Probably because federal troops committed no overt crimes against the state, as they did in Missouri, most Kentuckians retained their underlying affection for the Union. Congressional elections in June demonstrated overwhelming support for Unionist candidates almost everywhere except in the southernmost counties. State elections in August corroborated federal loyalty, notwithstanding the prevailing preference for peace.[18]

Forgetting the perennial neutrality of Switzerland in the face of global conflagration, many a historian has suggested that Kentucky's neutrality could never have lasted because it lay across so broad and strategic a path between the belligerent sections. In truth, the principal threat to that neutrality originated with aggressive federal ambitions. To the Confederacy, a neutral Kentucky offered an inestimable boon, providing a secure border along 750 miles of the Ohio River without the deployment of a single soldier. To the Lincoln administration, it posed a great roadblock in the path to forcible reunion, for it reduced the Confederacy's permeable borders to hostile Virginia and contested Missouri. Any overland invasion of the insurgent states would face concentrated defenses on those fronts, and ambitious campaigns had already foundered on each of them. Union commanders coveted Kentucky as a field of operations, but the danger of offending wavering factions discouraged them from landing the first army on "the dark and bloody ground."

Toward the end of August General Frémont elicited a sample of Kentucky's political volatility from his headquarters in Missouri. Now that federal troops had deposed the legal government of Missouri, Frémont lamented the lack of civil control and essentially anointed himself provincial viceroy. He extended martial law throughout the state, proclaimed that any Missourians found with arms in their hands would be executed, and declared that the property of the disloyal would be forfeited for public use, while their slaves would go free. Secessionists pounced on that last threat as confirming the abolitionist fervor they associated with Republican nationalism.[19]

In Kentucky the news of Frémont's decree landed on the floor of the legislature with "pretty much the effect of a bomb shell," noted Senator Garrett Davis. The proclamation upset a tide of Union support that had been swelling gradually all summer. "It has caused me despondency for the first time for Ky.," Senator Davis told Lincoln's secretary of the treasury. Joshua Speed, an old friend of Lincoln's from Louisville, feared Frémont's proclamation might have done irreparable damage to the Union cause in Kentucky. He confided to Joseph Holt that "we could stand several defeats like that at Bulls run better than we can this proclamation." Speed warned the president of the unanimous disapproval Frémont's words drew from Union men, and reminded Lincoln that the administration's Kentucky friends had promised their neighbors that the war would not disturb slavery. Some Union recruits from Kentucky threw down their arms and went home, and Lincoln feared that the thousands of guns he had provided for other Kentucky volunteers might end up being turned against the government.[20]

Illustrating the unlimited capacity of Northerners to misunderstand their Southern counterparts, the *New York Sun* applauded Frémont's disregard of the administration's "hush-a-by-baby" policy in the border states. The *Sun* doubted that Lincoln would dare repeal Frémont's draconian pronouncement, and called for similar measures in Kentucky. Lincoln nominally allowed Frémont's controversial threat of execution to stand, but he insisted that the punishment be subject to presidential approval. He also required Frémont to modify the emancipation portion of his proclamation to match the existing policy regarding contraband property. Disappointed abolitionists howled in turn at Lincoln's "fatal order," one of them lamenting how "hopeless" it made the war. "We could bear the defeat at Manassas," he wrote, mirroring Speed's comparison, ". . . better than we can bear this Order of an imbecile President."[21]

One Missouri State Guard commander promised to "hang, draw, and quarter" Union prisoners if Frémont should stoop to his promised executions, but until Lincoln's reproof arrived in mid-September Frémont strutted and puffed all the more exuberantly. Missouri's conservative loyalists turned against him, though, and the Pathfinder's days were numbered. A White House secretary confided to his fiancée that Missouri seemed more inclined to secession than ever, which he finally ascribed to Frémont's disorganized and imperious management. Even the Blairs waited on the president to admit their error in recommending Frémont's appointment. Meeting Lincoln in the presence of two other cabinet officers well after the emancipation threat had been quashed, Attorney General Bates demanded in an uncharacteristically abrupt tone that the president recall Frémont.[22]

Having dealt one spectacular blow to Kentucky's Union cause with his proclamation, Frémont intended to follow it up with another gaffe that might have driven the state into the Confederacy altogether. He had assigned Ulysses Grant to the command of Cape Girardeau, with instructions to take charge of several columns and disperse Confederates concentrating south of there. To help secure the region, Frémont specifically wanted Grant to occupy the town of Columbus, Kentucky, where towering bluffs commanded the Mississippi River above New Madrid.[23]

It required an immense Confederate blunder to simultaneously undo the damage of Frémont's emancipation order and save him from his own designs against Kentucky neutrality, but one Confederate general proved himself equal to the task. Lincoln's best ally in Charleston harbor had appeared in the form of Southern impetuosity, which had incited the entire North against the Confederacy, and Southern impetuosity saved him again in Kentucky. Leonidas Polk, who had doffed the alb of an Episcopal bishop to don the uniform of a Confederate major general, imperiously assumed the mission of preempting the Union occupation. Polk commanded the banks of the Mississippi River from the point where it entered the Confederacy, and Columbus lay just outside the boundary of his domain. Demonstrating equal insensitivity to state sovereignty and ignorance of the value of Kentucky neutrality to the Southern cause, Polk sent Brigadier General Gideon Pillow across the Mississippi on September 3 to fortify the bluffs, and over the next few days he landed more men at Hickman. The governor of Tennessee immediately asked Polk to withdraw, alluding to the pledge that he and President Davis had made to abide by Kentucky neutrality, but Polk obdurately denied any knowledge of such a pledge. Davis's secretary of war ordered Polk out of Kentucky promptly, and directed him to tell Governor Magoffin that his foray was "wholly unauthorized." Southern-leaning Kentuckians visited Polk in Columbus and begged him to retire, lest public support once again swing back to the federal government. Simon Buckner, the commander of the Kentucky State Guard, advised Richmond similarly.[24]

Seizing an irresistible opportunity, Grant steamed troops up the Ohio and landed them at Paducah. As General Buckner pointed out, the deployment neutralized Polk's position at Columbus. Buckner promised that if Polk would pull back to Tennessee he would mobilize the State Guard to confront Grant and drive him from Kentucky soil, if necessary, and perhaps in that way Kentucky's neutrality might be restored. Buckner had, after all, salvaged a similar situation the previous June, when the same impatient General Pillow responded to Nathaniel Lyon's declaration of war against Missouri by trying to fortify the same bluffs. At that juncture Buckner had appealed to Pillow's common sense and his regard for Kentucky's rights, and he had activated a battalion of the State Guard to back up that appeal.[25]

This time there would be no redemption. The Kentucky legislature turned on the initial aggressor in a blind rage, and as that aggressor the Confederate army drew the wrath that could have been Frémont's lot, had Polk waited just a few days. On September 12 the state saw competing war proclamations: the legislature demanded that the Confederates go home and asked for federal aid in the expulsion — despite editorial objections that the Unionist home-guard encampments had long posed a worse violation. That same day, General Buckner denounced the tyranny of a president who had thrown the Constitution aside, and called on liberty-loving Kentuckians to band together against the usurper; a few days later he led Confederate troops into Bowling Green and seized the railroad from there into Tennessee.[26]

Mutual withdrawal might possibly have appeased Kentucky ire, but Union authorities had no incentive to revive the state's neutrality. Federal troops had violated it often enough themselves, and rather than yield their priceless foothold they preferred to see Kentucky embattled — especially at Richmond's diplomatic expense. General Polk had played into the hands of his enemies, alienating the most strategically important state of all for no gain whatever. His pointless excursion to Columbus did more to assure Northern victory than anything that had happened thus far: the long, secure border dissolved into chaos, and Kentucky would provide three Union soldiers for every one who shouldered a musket for the Confederacy. Through a combination of restraint and good luck, Abraham Lincoln had won the state of his birth to the national cause.

The absence of such restraint had cast a much darker cloud over Missouri. Sterling Price still acted as though his state might never leave the Union, and as though its fight with the Washington government did not necessarily require a permanent alliance with the Confederacy. He and his followers imagined that they fought a war against the Republican Party and an overweening despot, and they pursued that fight relentlessly. On August 25 Price gathered up the Missouri State Guard, broke away from Ben McCulloch's Confederate force at Springfield, and struck northward in a wide arc, intending to sweep the state free of federal invaders. Recruits strengthened him all along the way. With a comfortable advantage in numbers he brushed aside a foray of Kansans from Fort Scott, driving them back into Kansas but, partly as a concession to that state's sovereignty, declining to follow them across the border.[27] From there he pressed on to the Missouri River, joining forces with State Guard regiments that had been isolated north of the river all summer — minus such discouraged followers as Sam Clemens. With an overwhelming force of as many as eighteen thousand loosely organized troops, mostly in mufti, Price surrounded a Union brigade at Lexington and captured it in a spectacular battle, advancing his infantry to striking distance behind a rolling breastwork of hemp bales. In less than a month he had reopened communications with the northern counties, positioned himself between Missouri's two principal federal bastions, and nearly doubled the size of his army.[28] Now families known for their Union politics began flocking out of northeastern Missouri in long trains of laden wagons, anticipating retribution for the federal repression of June.[29]

In the spring of 1861 the preponderance of Missouri's population had seemed solidly behind the preservation of the Union, despite a vocal secession faction. As the summer of that year came to an end, an increasingly authoritarian federal government appeared to be losing the sympathy of Missouri's citizens as well as military control of the state. Having botched its handling of affairs west of the Mississippi, and apparently having learned nothing from the experience, the Lincoln administration turned its attention back to Maryland.

The Maryland legislature held an extra session in July, again repairing westward to Frederick, where members would not have to deliberate under the glint of bayonets. There, the persistently Unionist body fulminated against the federal government that it still found cause to support. The legislators passed resolutions denouncing the government's unconstitutional repression in a loyal state, where soldiers were quartered and homes were searched in direct violation of the Third and Fourth Amendments. They excoriated the executive branch for "the oppressive and tyrannical assertion and exercise of military jurisdiction within the limits of Maryland," where legitimate civil authorities were unseated, jailed, and replaced by uniformed minions of the federal government. Despite these grievances, though, they refused to take their state out of the Union.[30]

After all the indignities the federal government had heaped on the Old Line State, and all the resentment Maryland legislators had so plainly expressed, their obstinate refusal to raise the subject of secession offered abundant evidence that the state did not have to be held by brute force. Lincoln and his principal cabinet officers failed to see it that way. Instead, their fear of backlash from earlier repression only appeared to drive them to more: they could not have failed to recognize that employment of the iron fist had created enemies for them, and overt public animosity convinced them that they had to exercise that fist even more vigorously. Now that the vital state of Kentucky had committed itself to the Union, Lincoln felt free to infringe even further on Maryland's sovereignty.

Forgery, intrigue, and obsessive anxiety combined to magnify the extent of dissidence in Maryland. A document of dubious origin circulated in Washington through August, purportedly outlining a two-pronged attack on the national capital by Confederate columns crossing the Potomac above and below the city. The letter alleged a Southern force of more than three hundred thousand in Virginia (an exaggeration wild enough to herald its fraudulence), and it insinuated that the attack would begin as soon as the Maryland legislature passed an ordinance of secession. The legislature would reconvene on September 17.[31]

The letter came into Union hands through pickets under Nathaniel Banks, who had taken over Robert Patterson's command at Harper's Ferry. A Confederate invasion from the upper Potomac had been anticipated since the week after Bull Run, and as early as August 6 Banks had been forwarding intelligence reports of Joe Johnston gathering a powerful army at Leesburg. At first the spectral Southern legions were thought to be aiming for the little army that George McClellan had left in the mountains of western Virginia, but the letter seemed to delineate a plan to capture Washington. Banks sent it to McClellan, who swallowed the tale whole. McClellan credited Johnston with an army three or four times the size of his own, and believed that the only thing saving him from complete destruction was the weather, for heavy rains had transformed the Potomac into a raging torrent. The intercepted document conjured disproportionate alarm, as it seemed to corroborate a popular paranoia. On the same day that the letter reached McClellan the *New York Times* ran a similar story, warning of overwhelming Confederate armies gathering for the envelopment of Washington.[32]

The panic induced by these reports appeared to afflict nearly everyone. The news so agitated Colonel Randolph Marcy (who was McClellan's father-in-law as well as his chief of staff) that he advised the young general to demand immediate conscription of the troops he needed to meet the imagined invasion. "Men will not volunteer now," Marcy grumbled, noting a recruiting slump that followed the Bull Run debacle, "& drafting is the only successful plan." McClellan passed the suggestion on to the president with a favorable endorsement. Simon Cameron ordered a wholesale shutdown of at least the less supportive of Baltimore's newspapers, apparently to prevent them from aiding the civilian uprising that was supposed to accompany the Confederate assault, but Secretary Seward talked him out of the crackdown before the directive left military channels.[33]

The fear of a massive invasion did not subside with the waters of the Potomac River. The nearer the next session of the Maryland legislature approached, the more anxiously all Washington braced for the blow, and through early September McClellan adjured his commanders upriver from the city to watch closely for signs of the Confederate onslaught. Finally, nine days before the session opened, McClellan reassured Secretary Cameron with a report of nearly eighty-five thousand Union troops manning the Alexandria line. He thought he could defend Washington against attack from a greatly superior force by pulling his troops from the upper Potomac into the fortifications around the city, but he supposed that the enemy would aim for Baltimore, to facilitate Maryland's secession and to isolate Washington from the rest of the country.[34]

The rumor of a Confederate invasion reflected nothing more substantial than the wishful thinking of certain high-ranking Southern generals. On September 6 Beauregard had suggested forming a reserve of several brigades for the purpose of threatening Washington, or crossing into Maryland to counter any Union offensive, and Johnston appears to have favored a modified version of Beauregard's plan. Jefferson Davis disapproved, citing a lack of armed troops and the dangers of divided operations, but that did not prevent the rumor from seeping across the Potomac, in addition to gaining credence among midlevel Southern officers. The acting adjutant of a Mississippi regiment bivouacked near Leesburg, for instance, had the opportunity to overhear gossip at regimental headquarters. On September 13 he informed a friend back home that "we are expecting orders any day to march on Baltimore & I suspec we will have some bloody work in crossing the Potomac." A mile away, a Virginia sergeant in Eppa Hunton's regiment anxiously awaited the invasion, hoping to winter in Washington.[35]

The editor of the Frederick *Herald*, whose office would have lain in the path of any column bound for Baltimore, seemed to fear the federal government more than the Confederate army. He congratulated the county convention of the peace party, and under the title "Arrests for Opinion's Sake" he ran an editorial about the now-common despotic abuses of the Lincolnites. Those Lincolnites then convened to confirm the validity of his allegation.[36]

President Lincoln, William Seward, Simon Cameron, and General Mc-Clellan met in grim conclave to determine how they could best thwart the mythical plan they so dreaded, and they concluded that the easiest solution would be to prevent the Maryland legislature from casting any vote at all. That would require forcible interference with the assembly of duly elected representatives of the people, but by September of 1861 the Lincoln administration was growing accustomed to that sort of work, and with Kentucky safely under federal control there remained little incentive for restraint. On September 11 Secretary Cameron instructed General Banks, in whose jurisdiction Frederick fell, to arrest as many legislators as he deemed necessary to foil the anticipated secession vote. That evening the chief of General McClellan's spy network, Allan Pinkerton, traveled to Baltimore with a flock of detectives and with an order for the arrest of several opposition legislators at their homes. Pinkerton stopped at Fort McHenry for additional manpower, but he arrived so late that he and the department commander, John Dix, decided to wait another day.[37]

The delay gave General Dix time to expand Pinkerton's list with the names of several more state senators and representatives, as well as that of Mayor George Brown, two contentious newspaper editors, and one other private citizen. Well after dark on Thursday, September 12, mixed bands of soldiers, detectives, and city police surrounded the men's homes, and around midnight they pounced. Bells rang frantically and doors shuddered under violent pounding; nervous voices asked for identification, which some officers gave, and for arrest warrants, which no one carried. Frightened family members protested helplessly as armed men led fathers and husbands away. Under an eerie quarter moon the carriages lumbered from every quadrant of Baltimore City and Baltimore County toward Locust Point, converging finally at the portcullis of Fort McHenry. As the various passengers recognized fellow legislators among the prisoners they began to understand that, at least for the present, representative democracy had come to an end in Maryland.[38]

By dawn of September 13, nearly a dozen prominent citizens occupied damp cells inside Fort McHenry, and more came in after breakfast. The prisoners included Frank Key Howard, of the *Baltimore Exchange*.[39] Howard's grandfather, Francis Scott Key, had boarded a British ship in Baltimore harbor under similar duress exactly forty-seven years before, and from the deck of that ship he had written a poem about the flag flying over that same fort. His grandson may have observed the anniversary with somber reflection on "the land of the free."

"So much for the middle course," observed William Wilkins Glenn, the editor and principal owner of the *Daily Exchange*. That same day, against the advice of his pressman, Glenn ran one last seething rebuke of the city's new military dictators, and the following morning the soldiers came for him, too.[40]

Out in Frederick, General Banks prepared a similar reception for any delegates or senators who might appear for the special session. He planned for a Wisconsin regiment to invade both houses of the legislature at the same moment, and he gave the colonel of that regiment a list of members who should be detained in addition to all the clerks, secretaries, and presiding officers. He directed the Wisconsin colonel to suppress any resistance by force, "whatever the consequences." Alerted as they were by the Baltimore arrests, numerous members failed to arrive for the opening gavel, so Banks did not collar a quorum of the body, but patrols combed the legislative districts for several more representatives over the next few days. There was no September session of the legislature at Frederick, and in the course of his sweep Banks apparently also extinguished the most likely source of local complaint: the *Frederick Herald* never published another issue.[41]

In Baltimore, a throng of Lincoln supporters celebrated the suppression of their state legislature with a bonfire fueled by thirty thousand copies of the general assembly's summer pamphlet complaining about the administration's earlier excesses. A Catholic priest who had suffered the Know-Nothing prejudice against immigrants observed that the "Lincolnite" mob consisted largely of Plug Uglies and other gang members who had terrorized the city in antebellum days, before Marshal Kane's police brought them under control.[42]

Kane and each of the new prisoners sought to learn the cause of his incarceration, but without success. A statement attributed to Abraham Lincoln appeared in the pro-administration *Baltimore American* two days after the arrests, assuring the public that every arrest had been made for "substantial and unmistakable complicity with those in armed rebellion against the Government of the United States." According to that statement, the government had not imprisoned Maryland's public officials on "mere suspicion, or through personal or partisan animosities," but had secured "tangible and unmistakable evidence" of such complicity, "which will, when made public, be satisfactory to every loyal citizen." The government never released any such evidence, and apparently none existed beyond the very "suspicion" and "personal or partisan animosities" that the president disingenuously denied.[43] Even after having chosen sides, otherwise loyal Kentuckians worried about that blatantly partisan repression; one Unionist friend of Joseph Holt's acknowledged that Lincoln was guilty of unconstitutional usurpation, and thought it weakened him in the public eye.[44]

State Department clerks later jotted down informal charges alongside the records of the Maryland legislators' arrests and imprisonment, for the prisoners all became the responsibility of Secretary Seward. The Speaker of the Maryland House of Delegates, for instance, was arrested on the grounds that he was a "dangerous secessionist": General Dix said so. Senator Charles Macgill, of Hagerstown, was charged with "disloyal sentiments and purposes" on the basis of a single purported utterance. Alongside most of the other names Seward's scribes added vague allegations that the prisoners were "disloyal members of the Maryland Legislature" or that they belonged to a conspiracy to pass an act of secession.[45]

After depriving the citizens of Maryland of their constitutional representation, and depriving those representatives of their liberty, Pinkerton's detectives and Dix's soldiers ransacked the homes and offices of the arrested men for evidence to justify the arrests. All they found — or said they found — was a questionable petition supposed to have been in the possession of Frank Howard, calling for recognition of the Confederacy and for Maryland to leave the Union if Virginia should do so. The wording of the petition suggested that it was more than four months old if it was genuine at all, but many of the signatures had evidently been written in the same handwriting — and sometimes very labored handwriting, at that. Evidently even State Department officials doubted the document's authenticity.[46]

George McClellan, seemingly convinced of the conspiracy between the Maryland legislators and the Confederacy, steadfastly refused to apologize for having participated in the arrests. The legislators themselves denied any conspiracy to secede. Speaking for himself, the reputed mastermind of that conspiracy disavowed any personal intention to support secession: in defense of his fellow legislators, S. Teackle Wallis pointed out the legislature's lopsided votes against secession even as it passed resolutions denouncing a tyrannical federal administration. The detained delegates entertained no doubt that the motive behind the coup d'état lay entirely in party politics. The arrested legislators were all Democrats, and they believed that the Lincoln government confined them in order to prevent them from campaigning for the November 6 election, as well as to intimidate peace candidates and anti-administration voters from participating.[47]

It does seem that, having despaired of winning free and open elections in Maryland, Lincoln's collaborators determined to retain power there through forceful intervention. Correspondence between William Seward and a Baltimore informant tended to corroborate the government's political motive for the arrests, and the secretary admitted as much to the British consul in Washington two days before the election. Seward confirmed that private remark with public action immediately after the polls closed, when his department began offering to release those prisoners who were still willing to sign a compulsory oath of loyalty to the federal government.[48]

Despite the apparent political manipulation, army headquarters suffered genuine anxiety about a Confederate invasion through the long gap between the army around Washington and the Harper's Ferry garrison under Nathaniel Banks. Early in August General Scott had intended to plug that void with a division under Major General Charles Sandford, of the New York militia, but Sandford wished to go home when his three-month term expired, and he suggested Charles Stone for the job. Stone's militia brigade had dissolved by then, but McClellan recommended him for an appointment as brigadier general of volunteers, gave him more troops, and assigned him responsibility for the unguarded portion of the upper Potomac. After a brief reunion with his wife and daughter in Washington, Stone started back to his old encampment at Poolesville.[49]

Stone took a battery of Regular artillery with him on his way out of Washington: that is, he took all that was left of the battery that James Ricketts had led to its doom at Bull Run. In Rockville and at the aqueduct over Seneca Creek, Stone stopped to collect the four regiments that formed his new brigade. Unremitting rain and rookie quartermasters turned the thirty-five-mile march into a four-day slog, and he reached Poolesville on August 15. There, in the spirit of his instructions to watch the swollen river crossings, he established the headquarters of what he called the Corps of Observation.[50]

At the behest of the War Department, General Banks moved a regiment downriver to Point of Rocks, with pickets reaching toward Stone to within a couple of miles of the Monocacy. From that last picket to the Seneca Creek aqueduct, nearly twenty-two miles downstream, the river became Stone's responsibility, including a great concave arc that ended at the "clump of dirty houses and a few shops" known as Edwards's Ferry. He stretched his picket posts another four miles below Seneca Creek to meet those sent up from George McCall's brigade, at Great Falls.[51]

To cover twenty-six miles of the Chesapeake and Ohio Canal towpath and the Potomac River, Stone could field no more than about a hundred men to the mile, but for the first week the river surged so high that the shortage mattered little. The 1st Minnesota, which he posted at Edwards's Ferry, had taken a vicious beating at Bull Run, but the survivors seemed reliable. The 2nd New York State Militia had suffered considerably less from casualties at Bull Run, but it had lost a lot more in morale, and the battle had revealed some glaring deficiencies in its leadership. Stone found the regiment generally demoralized, depleted by excessive absenteeism, and virtually useless, so he sent it up to the relative quiet of the

Monocacy. He left the 34th New York at Seneca Creek, and positioned the 42nd New York — the Tammany Regiment — near Conrad's Ferry. A few companies of each regiment stood picket in little squads along the tow-path, half a mile apart, drowsing by day but alert by night. The rest camped around Poolesville, from which roads radiated to each of the crossings like spokes leading from the hub of a wheel. Here the remnants of the artillery battery came back to life with new guns, caissons, teams, and recruits, while the infantry turned Maryland cornfields into neat, well-drained campsites at the season when the trees in adjoining or-chards hung heavy with fruit.[52]

On August 16, exactly two months after he had first trained his binocu-lars on the mouth of Goose Creek, Stone stood once more at the Maryland side of Edward's Ferry and scanned the Virginia landscape as Confederate field guns innocuously shelled a canal boat making its way down the Chesapeake & Ohio. Freshly returned from the scene of his glory at Ma-nassas, Nathan Evans again commanded the troops on the other side. Now officially a colonel in the Provisional Army and awaiting a promised promotion to brigadier general, Evans had brought along the 13th, 17th, and 18th Mississippi regiments, the latter two of which had "behaved badly" in the battle of July 21. Eppa Hunton had come back, too, filling out the infantry of the command with his 8th Virginia; a battery of the Richmond Howitzers served as the brigade artillery. Jealous Virginians secretly scorned both Evans and the Mississippians, yet morale improved throughout the command. After weeks on the Manassas plain, where ex-pansive camps and earthworks ravaged the landscape, Mississippian and Virginian alike regarded Leesburg as a paradise with its clean brick build-ings, rolling piedmont pastures, cool groves, and broad, picturesque river. Like their foes across the river, the men in the ranks particularly appreci-ated the abundance of fresh campsites and clear drinking water. Faced with enemy troops only three miles away, local citizens treated the Con-federate soldiers as saviors, lavishing every imaginable kindness on them. The sick, of whom the Mississippi regiments harbored many, found haven in churches and private dwellings, while Leesburg ladies volunteered as nurses under the tutelage of regimental surgeons.[53]

With his four slightly experienced regiments, Evans was expected to keep watch over more than thirty miles of the Potomac River. Unlike Stone, he operated without immediate support on either flank. The only aid he could reasonably expect would come from Manassas, a day or more away.

On Stone's left, General McCall's Pennsylvania Reserves — a full divi-sion, now — covered the river from Great Falls down toward Washing-ton. On his right, Colonel John Geary occupied the extremity of General

Banks's line with his 28th Pennsylvania Infantry. Geary, a pompous brag-
gart who had resigned as territorial governor of Kansas because he perceived enemies at every hand, brought a similar paranoia to the line of the
Potomac. Thoroughly convinced of the existence of a Confederate multitude lurking just over the river, he impressed Stone as an alarmist before
their respective commands had spent a week alongside each other.

"I fear there is too much nervousness on my right," Stone warned
McClellan, " — that is, in the command of Col. Geary, at Point of Rocks."
Stone explained that Geary's frantic ambulance drivers had just come
swarming into Stone's camp at Poolesville, fleeing from an imaginary attack that Geary had anticipated the previous evening.[54] Geary belatedly
sent Stone an overheated announcement that he was about to be assailed
by superior forces, but that he intended to fight tooth and nail. Stone replied that he had received both Geary's message and his ambulances, although not in that order. With condescending irony, Stone complimented
Geary on his determination to resist an enemy crossing, remarking that
"it would be very hazardous of them to attempt such a movement in the
face of a fine regiment." He nevertheless assured the Pennsylvania politician that the Confederates posed no threat that night, with the Potomac
still running so high. Stone's subtle sarcasm eluded Geary altogether, and
that evening Geary adopted a tone of combative disappointment when he
complained in a private letter to his wife that "the enemy would not give
us battle."[55]

Letters intercepted on their way over the Potomac almost all alluded
to a ponderous Confederate force waiting to roll across the river sometime in August. The reports of loyal Virginians contradicted the notion,
though, and except for nervous amateurs like Geary the senior officers on
the upper Potomac doubted any imminent danger. Stone consistently reported a single brigade in his front, accurately estimating it at no more
than four regiments.[56]

Despite so manageable an opposing force and the availability of nearby
support (or perhaps because that support consisted of the unpredictable Colonel Geary), Stone still felt the need of more troops. He asked
McClellan for a couple of specific regiments, including the 15th Massachusetts, which had just arrived in Washington. The 15th came entirely
from Worcester County, in central Massachusetts. Men who listed their
occupations as shoemakers or bootmakers composed a quarter of the regiment, reaffirming the disproportionate attraction that military employment exerted on the lower working class. Such desperation may have
served as a common impetus for enlistment, but it failed to assure a recruit's qualifications: Colonel Charles Devens, the Worcester lawyer who

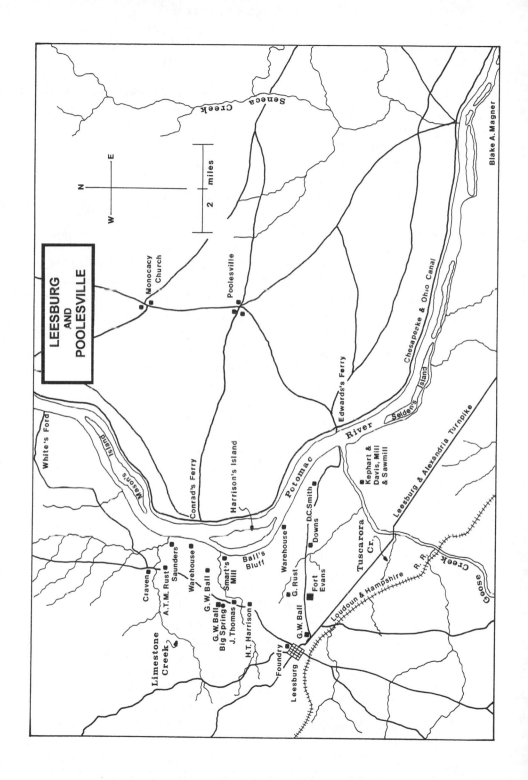

LEESBURG AND POOLESVILLE

Seneca Creek

N W E S

2 miles

Monocacy Church

Poolesville

White's Ford

Mason's Island

Conrad's Ferry

Harrison's Island

Edwards's Ferry

Potomac River

Selden's Island

Chesapeake & Ohio Canal

Craven

A.T.M. Rust

Saunders

Warehouse

G.W.Ball

Big Spring

J.Thomas

Smart's Mill

Ball's Bluff

Limestone Creek

H.T. Harrison

Foundry

Leesburg

G.W. Ball

Warehouse

G. Rust

Fort Evans

D.C.Smith

Downs

Kephart & Davis, Mill & Sawmill

Tuscarora Cr.

Loudoun & Hampshire R. R.

Leesburg & Alexandria Turnpike

Goose Creek

Blake A. Magner

commanded the 15th Massachusetts, conceded before the regiment left the state that he was "much depressed" over the caliber of both the officers and the men.[57]

Enough new regiments had begun flooding into Washington to fulfill Stone's request, and the 15th Massachusetts left its camp on Kalorama Heights on the last Sunday in August. On Tuesday the newcomers arranged their tents alongside those of the Regular battery, on the village common in Poolesville. Another artillery unit that would become the 6th New York Battery (just then it was known as Company K of the 9th New York State Militia) set up camp on the common a few days later.[58]

The heart of General Stone's jurisdiction and concern lay along the five miles of river between Edwards's Ferry and Conrad's Ferry, and especially at the two ferries themselves. Between, on the Virginia side, the shoreline climbed sharply along most of that distance. At Goose Creek the heights bordered an alluvial plain several hundred yards wide, but steep bluffs rose from the water's edge along the two miles of river that flowed closest to Leesburg. Downstream, nearest the floodplain above Goose Creek, the bluffs towered as much as a hundred feet over the water, brick-red and unassailable. Colonel Evans saw no need of pickets there.

Directly opposite Leesburg, the terrain grew even more complicated. There the largest island in the Potomac River divided the watercourse. The local people originally called it Black Walnut Island, in allusion to the trees that covered it and the adjacent riverbanks, but when the Swann family owned it cartographers began labeling it Swann's Island. It occupied about two miles of that concave arc of river, amounting to nearly five hundred acres, and the Swanns turned it into a farm, complete with a big brick house and a slave crew. Thomas Swann nearly lost it all to the Bank of the United States in 1835, but his son reclaimed it and finally sold it, in 1850, to Henry T. Harrison. Thenceforth it became Harrison's Island to nearly everyone — although the river islands in that vicinity often assumed the names of the farmers who leased them. Just below Edwards's Ferry lay what the maps called Selden's Island, known in the war year of 1861 as Young's Island because of Samuel Young, a Marylander who raised grain there in partnership with a Poolesville doctor. Harrison also leased his island to a farmer, but the tenant did not reside in the house there, at least by the time Stone's troops settled in.[59]

Harrison, one of Leesburg's more prosperous citizens, lived in an elegant Georgian manse in town, but he collected farms in the vicinity. He owned another one on the Leesburg side of the ridge that screened the town from the river; he had patched it together from the subdivided shards of Jacob Stoneburner's old estate, which Stoneburner had bequeathed to his many children. Most of that patriarch's progeny had migrated westward, leaving behind one widowed sister: Margaret Jackson, née Peggy Stoneburner. The departed siblings sold their fragmented shares of the family tract, mostly to outsiders, but a few signed their property over to Mrs. Jackson, who accumulated a little more than forty acres of rocky, ravine-rippled land running down to the precipitous bank of the river. In piecing the rest of the former estate back together, Squire Harrison paid one of the illiterate Stoneburner daughters for land that she had already given to her sister Peggy, so as the widow Jackson struggled to provide for ten children she also contended with a clouded title to her home.[60]

On her hardscrabble farm Mrs. Jackson kept a few cows, a couple of dozen hogs, and a fair-size flock of chickens for both sustenance and income. Most of her land remained in timber and scrub growth, except for a sizable clearing that overlooked the river. The estates of retrenched gentry surrounded her. South of the Jackson parcel sat Exeter, the seventeen-hundred-acre home of General George Rust, deceased; the half of Exeter nearest to Mrs. Jackson now belonged to one Horatio Trundle — who, though no grandee, seemed comfortably wealthy. To the north of her humble homestead lay Springwood, the sprawling demesne of George Washington Ball, who as a boy had fallen heir to one of the county's greater fortunes.[61] Ball's grandfather, Burgess Ball, had claimed blood relation and personal friendship with the first president; young Ball's father, Fayette Ball, had married into the Mason clan of Tidewater renown. George Washington Ball himself continued that patrician custom by taking a Randolph as his wife.[62]

Burgess Ball's home had stood alongside an enormous spring on the road to Point of Rocks (Big Spring, and thus Springwood), but by 1861 his grandson had replaced it with a Victorian manse that faced the river from a distance of a mile. George Ball — a tall, gangly young man with the classic Celtic traits of black hair and blue eyes — still owned more than seven hundred acres in a wide swath reaching all the way to the river. He had sold off portions of the family land, but with the proceeds of those sales he accumulated more modern investments, doubling his nominal worth to nearly a hundred thousand dollars. Most of that appreciation had come in a decade when half a dollar bought a day's labor from someone like Mrs. Jackson's sons, but inflation accounted for much of the increase. A significant portion of Ball's wealth lay in the twenty-one human beings whose labor he could command for nothing, which helped to explain the economic disparity between Ball and the Jackson boys.[63]

Big Spring created a substantial stream that crossed the Ball land on its way to the Potomac, dumping into the river near the upper end of Harrison's Island. Early in the century an entrepreneur in the Ball clan had diverted part of the stream into a millrace to feed a tall brick gristmill that he constructed along the riverbank. John Smart, a miller from Jefferson County, bought the mill in 1834, just as the Chesapeake and Ohio Canal passed that reach of the river. Later Smart established smaller gristmills and at least one sawmill along Goose Creek, sending the resulting lumber and flour down that stream as locks made it navigable. He still owned them all as 1861 opened, along with a couple of dozen slaves to work them, but he left most of the daily operations to junior partners. Smart was approaching his seventieth winter, and had made a halfhearted attempt to retire to his little house in town.[64]

George Ball's grandfather had once held title to all the land in the vicinity of Big Spring, including everything that belonged to Henry Harrison and Margaret Jackson at the outbreak of war. The echo of Burgess Ball's ownership lingered — and still lingers — in the name of the near-vertical cliff where Mrs. Jackson's land met the river. Ball's Bluff, a 150-million-year-old fold of dolomite, looms more than a hundred feet over the water, almost a mile below Smart's Mill and opposite the center of Harrison's Island. Cut by streambeds on either side, the wall of stratified rock stands a light or medium grey in the sunlight, but rain transforms it into a glistening green. Accumulated millennia of erosion have exposed it so prominently that the predominant regional substratum is known as Ball's Bluff siltstone.[65]

Occluded as it was from the Maryland shore by the island, Ball's Bluff did not particularly concern General Stone. As the near-tropical rains of August abated and the river subsided, Stone turned his attention back to the ferries and the fords. The persistent anxiety over a rebel invasion demanded unusual vigilance, but fog and drizzle sometimes prevented a clear view of the Virginia side for days at a time. To assure timely response for any threat, Stone wanted cavalry — preferably experienced troopers, and in the summer of 1861 that meant Regulars. One such company had been sent, and then detached elsewhere, but in its place McClellan promised a couple of troops of volunteers. McClellan also promised that as soon as enough new volunteers came in he would send eight more regiments of infantry to Poolesville, which would elevate Stone's command from a brigade to a division. Stone asked if he might have his own 14th U.S. Infantry among the eight, to serve as an example for the volunteers, but the army's Regular regiments lay scattered through the country by companies and battalions. Until his final weeks as a U.S. soldier, three years later, Stone never saw the regiment that he nominally commanded assembled in any one location; he had probably never even laid eyes on a portion of it when he first requested it for his command.[66]

The Confederates on the far shore did not initially pose Stone's greatest concern. The volunteers in his brigade caused trouble enough, like those at Seneca Creek who had hardly pitched their tents before they began hiding fugitive slaves from their Maryland owners. Those troops belonged to the 34th New York, the "Herkimer Regiment," from upstate, and in their refusal to distinguish between secessionists and loyal slaveholders they reflected the more general confusion surrounding the aims of the war. It was still August, before the government's worst affronts to Maryland sovereignty, so Stone saw no irony in chastising the New Yorkers for disregarding the laws of a state that yet clung, however discontentedly, to the Union. Even after Lincoln trumped the common soldiers' disdain for Maryland by imprisoning its legislators, though, Stone continued to remind his troops that they had come to suppress rebellion, rather than to free slaves — or, as he appeared to fear even more, to encourage those slaves to insubordination. Massachusetts men who frowned when Stone allowed a young lady to cross the river and marry a Confederate officer scowled all the more fiercely when they heard that one of their own officers had been discharged for shielding a runaway from a Maryland plantation.[67]

The more frequent complaints of pillage and wanton destruction by Union soldiers disturbed Stone as much as the freelance slave-stealing. In their encampment south of Poolesville the Minnesotans had appropriated a cornfield for their tents, parade ground, and latrines. Quartermasters arranged payment for the damage to that field, but the enlisted men had also wandered into the adjacent cornfield to help themselves to fresh corn, and they stripped the stalks so clean that the owner called the crop a total loss. The troops had also dismantled thousands of feet of split-rail fence to feed their campfires, rather than traipse into the forested ravines for greener wood that they would have had to chop and haul.[68]

Camped nearby was the perennially unruly 2nd New York State Militia, the officers of which controlled their men no better than they controlled themselves. Privates casually robbed local farmers of whatever they wanted, while their superiors divided their time between filing charges against brother officers and composing applications for furlough. The brigade inspector specifically cited that regiment for its "mania for leaves of absence to officers, and furloughs to the men," which he judged "intolerably embarrassing to the public service," and he observed that the worst offenders came from New York City. General Stone had to approve most of those leaves of absence, but when he denied them, or refused to extend them, officers in the 2nd New York often either resigned or simply remained at home without leave until Stone asked for their dismissals.[69]

Good officers seemed a scarce commodity that summer of 1861. General Stone thought he had one in the person of a notorious English aristocrat who had assumed the name of Charles Stewart. At the tender age of twenty-five Stewart already claimed a record of service in the British army, but fortune had found him in Maryland that spring, and he had served as an aide to Stone during the summer. Stone asked for him as his assistant adjutant general, and army headquarters seldom refused Stone anything so easily given.[70]

President Lincoln also thought he had located a good officer when he included Frederick West Lander in a mass appointment of brigadier generals on August 6. Lander, an engineer well known for his frontier survey work, could claim no military experience except the few weeks he spent in the mountains of western Virginia as a volunteer aide to McClellan, with the honorary title of colonel. Lander distinguished himself all around, though, and with McClellan's recommendation he took command of his own brigade straight from civilian life. In the panic surrounding the anticipated Confederate invasion a confusion of orders first sent Lander toward the Alexandria line on September 12, and then brought him back and put him on the road to Poolesville, to reinforce Stone.[71] After three days of hard marching in dreadful Potomac humidity, his vanguard arrived there on Saturday, September 14, amid groundless rumors that a massive Confederate cavalry raid had been launched against them from the far shore. That afternoon the 19th and 20th Massachusetts regiments and the 1st Massachusetts Sharpshooters company spilled into fields around Poolesville and made temporary camp; those reinforcements included some five hundred more of their state's destitute shoemakers. Battery B of the 1st Rhode Island Artillery rode into town right behind the Massachusetts regiments, and the 7th Michigan Infantry trailed in the next day.[72]

The arrival of Lander's brigade elevated General Stone to division command. Willis Gorman, the colonel of the 1st Minnesota, earned his own commission as a brigadier about that time, and at Stone's request he was allowed to remain near Poolesville with his brigade. Gorman and Lander soon fell into a dispute about overlapping jurisdictions that boded ill for their future cooperation.[73]

The bucolic splendor of the Potomac Valley only fueled the romantic reveries of these newcomers, for whom the novelty of war had not yet subsided. They crawled from their tents at night and slept under the stars, shaking off the soaking dew at dawn to admire the mist that hung over the river. The men from Northern forests, farms, and factory towns marched by companies through sleepy, fog-wrapped rural hamlets to the canal and out on the riverbank for their first sight of the hostile Virginia shore and their first tour on picket. Then, with a quickening of the pulse, came the inaugural glimpse of a Confederate soldier on the opposite bank, the surprised relief when he declined to fire, and perhaps the sharp lilt of a strange dialect if he shouted a greeting across calm water. In the late summer of 1861 the recruit could hardly have found a more idyllic war than the one waged along that length of river.[74]

Maryland's rolling landscape differed from anything most of those men had ever seen, especially in the ravines and the tropical vegetation along the canal and river, but it was the slaves who lent the region a truly alien atmosphere. Many of the Northern soldiers confused slave ownership with secessionist sentiment, and perhaps with some reason, for the wealthier slaveholders seemed the most unfriendly toward them. More slaves lived in the area than even the better-informed officers had supposed, and they wandered about with an apparent liberty that made them all the more visible. Paul Revere, the major of the 20th Massachusetts and grandson of Boston's nightriding silversmith, might have startled his Brahmin brethren had he confessed how benevolent the Potomac version of slavery seemed to him. He conveyed such observations only to his wife, to whom he confided that freedom would probably prove more demanding to the slave than the Maryland brand of bondage.[75]

Some found it difficult to believe that such rustic languor could erupt in bloodshed, yet apprehension lingered. Into late September, the Confederates camped around Leesburg still shared their Union counterparts' expectation of an imminent battle as the opposing pickets at the fords and ferries traded rumors across the Potomac. They supposed, perhaps because they saw no activity among their own command, that the fighting would come downriver. The rank and file under Evans also guessed, correctly, that anxiety over the safety of Washington would prevent the Yankees from initiating any offensive operations from the Maryland shore, and as summer waned they enjoyed the last pleasant interlude they would know in the army. They devoured a bountiful harvest and a delicious landscape, patronizing struggling homesteaders for rare treats like eggs and butter and roving the hills for spectacular views of the Blue Ridge or a glimpse of the growing enemy encampment at Poolesville. Confederates who had sickened in the early camps began trickling back from the Culpeper hospital, while those who had more recently fallen ill recovered in the comfort of nearby homes, nursed by their comrades and local citizens. Romances blossomed between lonely Southern soldiers and Loudoun County girls as young as fifteen, sowing the seeds of autumn weddings or winter heartbreak, and verdant visions of live oaks and magnolias helped the Mississippians prevail in their occasional courtship competition with native Virginians.[76]

Bad intelligence and gullible commanders sparked one last alarm along the embattled river toward the end of the month, on the night following a daylong deluge of cold rain. Again, the stir originated with Colonel Geary. Back in the middle of August it had been Geary who originally intercepted the bogus letter about the Maryland invasion. Now, on the word of a paid informant calling himself Frank Buxton, Geary dispatched a courier who woke General Stone hours before dawn on a Saturday morning. According to Buxton, Joe Johnston had reached Leesburg at the head of twenty-seven thousand men, with whom he was about to force a crossing near Noland's Ferry. Geary certified that Buxton (an Englishman using a nom de guerre) had just crossed over from Leesburg, affirming that there could be no doubt about what he had to say. Stone doubted the report nonetheless, for his own trusted information network had detected nothing of the kind. He asked Geary to send Buxton down for an interview, but the spy disappeared back into Virginia, where he may have been feeding Confederate authorities with reports of Union dispositions. For the second time in a fortnight Geary terrified his wife with a letter ending in the melodramatic announcement that he was going out to fight an enemy vastly superior in numbers, promising a detailed account of the carnage — if he should be spared.[77]

As usual, no carnage ensued, at least in Geary's sector. It happened that the Confederate high command was just about to consider, and reject, the idea of invading Maryland, or raiding across the river to destroy the Monocacy aqueduct, but that conceptual discussion coincided with Buxton's information only by accident. Johnston remained in Centreville, and not a regiment had reinforced Leesburg.[78]

Buxton's misinformation did help provoke a bustle of confused activity down on the lower Potomac. Just as Geary sent out his frantic appeal, the Confederates drew back from their advanced positions opposite McClellan's Alexandria line. The troop movement would have prompted some investigation in any case, but Buxton's tale of strong Southern legions in Leesburg heightened the sense of urgency. Another of those new brigadiers, William F. Smith, made a hasty reconnaissance toward Munson's Hill, on the Leesburg Turnpike, perhaps testing whether Johnston's army was actually on the move toward Leesburg or simply falling back. Smith made a botch of it, though, failing to coordinate with surrounding commands engaged in the same enterprise: at least a few officers suspected that he might have been the worse for drink. On Smith's verbal orders two Pennsylvania regiments ventured out into the darkness, the leading one wearing grey uniforms left over from the spring, and they ran into a line of their own advance infantry at the edge of a wood line. A ripple of rifle fire invited volleys in return, and for a couple of minutes the troops blazed away at each other at ranges as close as twenty feet, throwing enough muzzle flash into the night to illuminate the Pennsylvanians' grey clothing. A score of them had gone down before their officers stopped the shooting, and then everyone went back to camp. The next day those regiments and the rest of their brigade started on the march for Poolesville, to reinforce Stone's Corps of Observation.[79]

Although the men who took part in the exchange of friendly fire had enlisted mainly in Philadelphia and New York, and their battle monuments would all bear the designations of Pennsylvania regiments, they were then known as the 1st and 2nd California Infantry. There was a third California regiment too, with a fourth in the world, and they traveled under the command of Colonel Edward Baker — the same white-haired Oregon senator who had ridden with Lincoln to his inauguration. Baker had started raising men for his first regiment with the great patriotic rally in Union Square, in New York City, only days after the surrender of Fort Sumter, advertising for adventurers who had spent time on the West Coast during or after the Gold Rush. So many men responded that he kept adding to the standard ten companies until he had sixteen. With the addition of the second and third regiments the size of his command called for a more exalted commission, and his friendship with Lincoln should have secured it, but Baker might have felt obliged to resign his seat in the Senate if he accepted any rank higher than colonel. As it was, he had spent much time away from his troops on legislative business: he did not even appear to have been with them in the tragic nighttime fracas near Munson's Hill.[80]

Baker did follow his brigade to Poolesville, though, marching into camp on October 3. Stone sent the brigade out five miles on the road to the Monocacy aqueduct, where the "Californians" began irritating the local farmers as successfully as the 2nd New York State Militia had. Politician that he was, Baker tried to curb the depredations by setting limits rather than imposing punishment, allotting each company an allowance of ten fence rails for all its campfires. Old soldiers that they had suddenly become, they collected ten rails at a time until they had picked the countryside clean of fences.[81]

The 1st California discarded its deadly grey uniforms shortly after reaching its new camp, trading them for the sky-blue trousers and dark blue jackets and caps that had become standard for the volunteer service. Colonel Baker's influence may have contributed to an issue of French "chasseur" overcoats, made with fancy braid and a waterproof cape, but he found it more difficult to supply his brigade with enough blankets. The days remained unseasonably warm, but the nights turned surprisingly cold with the first of October, and the thick woolen clothing worn on the Maryland shore shamed the more shabbily attired pickets on the Virginia side.[82]

In the Confederate camp, companies and parts of companies lacked any uniforms at all. A Virginia captain who resided in Loudoun County still sought homemade uniforms for some of his men when October frosts began nipping, and none of the Virginians owned any overcoats. Every man in the 17th Mississippi Infantry still wore the clothing in which he had enlisted the previous spring, or replacement apparel that had been sent from home since then. Officers went hunting for appropriate uniform material in early September, but the goods had to travel all the way to the different companies' home counties for family manufacture, and eight weeks passed before the first partial installment of uniforms reached Leesburg. Most of the Mississippians did not don Confederate grey until the better part of their initial one-year enlistment had expired.[83]

Mississippi could not afford to send off well-clad regiments, and in any case the climate of the Gulf states demanded lighter dress than the regulation uniform ultimately adopted by the Confederate army. Most photographs of Mississippi troops in the first year of the war show them wearing loose cotton shirts, usually without vests or jackets, and pants from their personal wardrobes in stripes, checks, or a broad assortment of plain shades. Their hats display little uniformity save in an apparent preference for wide brims to ward off the broiling Southern sun, and similarly diverse headgear typified the daily musters in most regiments even after government clothing had been issued.[84]

Some of the civilian-clad defenders of Leesburg refused to even be fitted for uniforms, betraying an individuality that may have sprung from a deeper cultural independence. Especially on the frontier, where Mississippi might still have been said to lie in 1861, Southern society observed a cult of honor that frowned on the concept of a mercenary military, particularly in defense of the homeland. This backwoods Bushido meant that early Union recruits who accepted the hundred-dollar bounties were regarded as avaricious vandals. From the outset of the war the Southern press characterized Northern soldiers as Lincoln's "hirelings," and editors from the Occoquan to the Osage found "Hessians" a useful slur for Union volunteers, harking back to the Germans who fought in the pay of the British during the Revolution. Some Southerners so scorned the concept of fighting for pay that they refused to enlist, instead marching off to war at their own expense without formal muster. Several such "independents"

accompanied the Mississippi regiments and the Virginia cavalry companies of the Leesburg garrison, and their prominence on the casualty lists
would soon demonstrate the depth of their commitment to the cause.[85]

Except for returning convalescents, Nathan Evans accumulated no additional troops while Stone's division grew. He lacked both the strength
and the incentive for any raids across the river, and could barely hope to
repel a determined assault, against which he continued construction of an
expansive earthen battery that Colonel Hunton had begun the previous
June, on top of the most prominent hill alongside the road from Edwards's Ferry; ultimately it would bear his name, as Fort Evans. General
Stone arranged his own rifled battery on a corresponding hill overlooking
Edwards's Ferry. For all the weakness of his enemy, Stone feared an attack
every few nights — or so he informed his troops, testing their readiness
with frequent midnight musters and forced marches to vulnerable points
along the river. His most veteran troops had served only five months thus
far, and the Poolesville common became a parade ground for three hours
every morning and three more in the afternoon as officers who knew only
the rudiments of close-order drill tried to instill it in soldiers who knew
even less.[86]

Musketry practice tattered the afternoon quiet, interrupted by the frequent failure of ordnance; the locks of the Union rifles caused an inordinate amount of trouble, often because the nipples had been cast too large
for the percussion caps, or because the caps themselves had been made
too small. Whole regiments suffered from malfunctioning weapons: the
Enfields of the 20th Massachusetts would not work well except with a
certain kind of cap, while the rifles of the 7th Michigan (either Belgian
imports or flintlocks subjected to the "Belgian" conversion process)
needed some gunsmithing modifications to rectify persistent misfiring. A
French servant to one of the Massachusetts captains remarked that the
guns of the 15th Massachusetts were not worth a great deal, perhaps referring to the age and short range of the smoothbore muskets with which
most of that regiment had been armed.[87] The 1st Minnesota carried a
combination of Springfield rifles and 1841 "Harper's Ferry" muskets, converted from flintlocks; the muskets posed little threat to anyone across
the river, despite the bravado of men who represented themselves to the
home folks as skilled marksmen. The only sure shots in Stone's division
were the Massachusetts sharpshooters, each of whom had brought his
own cumbersome telescopic rifle, and most of whom could hit a man-size
target with reasonable frequency at half a mile.[88]

Despite their dubious weaponry, the men of Stone's command felt confident that their training would bring them victory in the next encounter
and allow them to avenge the shame of Bull Run. Like most others in the

country, they had come to view their July defeat as a blessing in disguise: with the help of newspapers and clergymen who beat that drum incessantly, they convinced themselves that it had taught them humility and illustrated the extent of the work that lay before them, all at relatively little cost.[89]

With the reinforcement of Baker's brigade Stone dared to expand his observation posts early in October, ferrying a few companies over to the islands in the middle of the river. He issued orders against open campfires, fearing the exposed detachments might be captured by a raid or mauled by artillery, but compliance diminished as the temperature dropped. With only a couple of diffident slaves in residence, Massachusetts and Minnesota pickets soon managed to strip Selden's Island of Mr. Young's fence rails, for which Stone assessed the regiment collectively for restitution of $124. Discipline suffered throughout the division with the sudden influx of men, and Stone had to dispense reprimands and punishment liberally. He chastised Colonel Baker for letting his Californians wander indiscriminately about the countryside, evading duty and finding liquor enough to cause trouble, and he promised to prosecute them for desertion if he caught any more of them. The Rhode Island battery commander and the cavalry companies invited Stone's censure for racing their horses to lameness and ruin. The regiment at Seneca Creek undertook some petty marauding that landed some of them in irons; pornographic books surfaced in Lander's brigade and filtered into Gorman's.[90] Then Stone learned that the lackadaisical quartermaster of Baker's 1st California, Francis Young, had been engaged in some creative contracting during his frequent sojourns to Washington. Acting as the brigade quartermaster, Young had arranged with at least one of his Washington suppliers to resell provisions that Young had nominally bought for the brigade.[91]

This upsurge of misbehavior might have been expected with the tripling of the garrison between Seneca Creek and the Monocacy, simply due to the presence of a larger population. With the exception of Quartermaster Young, however, boredom may also have had a hand in it. Even the added picket details on the islands could not occupy all the time of so large a force, and the inactivity bred mischief.

The lack of action affected visiting newspapermen adversely, too, and they spiced the dull rendition of daily events with speculation and imaginative details. Stone complained to McClellan of a reporter named Underhill, who stopped at Edwards's Ferry without permission and published a false report indicating that Stone had retracted his outposts because of Confederate pressure. Stone suggested that the correspondent of the *New York Tribune* had so breached the boundaries of truth that he ought to be arrested for treason. The *Tribune* reporter suffered no repercussions, thanks partly to his editor, Sam Wilkeson: Wilkeson ingratiated himself with powerful Republicans through promises of favorable treatment, and in return his dispatches earned the secretary of war's personal exemption from either censorship or suppression. Common folk enjoyed much less freedom, to Stone's dismay.

"Harmless farmers and laborers in our vicinity are frequently arrested," Stone indignantly reminded his commanding general, "and made to explain for far smaller offences, and on *suspicion* of communicating intelligence."[92] The country had not yet seen the last of such arbitrary arrests, or the worst that a climate of rampant suspicion could bring.

8

By Cliffs Potomac Cleft

❖ FRANK BUXTON, the freelance spy, surfaced again at John Geary's headquarters on October 6, offering a suggestion that may have contributed to disaster. Referring once again to those twenty-seven thousand Confederates at Leesburg, he proposed a plan to snare the phantom army. Buxton supposed that if McClellan moved his entire force forward, with an attendant feint at Occoquan Creek, Joe Johnston would draw all his outposts back to the Centreville line. That would open up the Leesburg Turnpike, whereupon coordinated movements against Leesburg from Falls Church and from Stone's division might capture the entire Leesburg garrison.[1]

It seemed as though McClellan acted on Buxton's advice when, three days later, he pushed George McCall's division of fourteen Pennsylvania regiments across the Chain Bridge into Virginia and turned them in the direction of Leesburg. That movement simply represented another increment of McClellan's creeping occupation of the Virginia side of the Potomac, however. He stopped McCall just beyond Langley, where he settled his division into camp on the Georgetown Pike, extending the right flank of McClellan's permanent line another four miles upriver. That put Union soldiers within twenty-five miles of Leesburg — as close to that town as the main Confederate army at Centreville. In conversation with President Lincoln, McClellan revealed that he considered the movement a fine day's work, even though it took him two days to complete it.[2]

The Yankees struck closer still on the far side of Leesburg. Half a dozen companies of Massachusetts and Wisconsin infantry and a pair of guns crossed into Harper's Ferry to raid the neighborhood for stored wheat, prowling Jefferson County for several days within the jurisdiction of Lieutenant Colonel Turner Ashby, the quintessential Virginia cavalier. Then came Colonel Geary, who added four companies of his Pennsylvania regiment and another gun to the raiding party. Ashby could raise only three hundred militiamen, carrying antique flintlocks, and four companies of cavalry, so he sent to Evans for help. Evans dispatched parts of the 8th Virginia and 13th Mississippi, along with a section of the Richmond Howitzers, but while those reinforcements were still negotiating rough mountain roads Ashby launched an attack without them. He struck on the morning of October 16, the second anniversary of John Brown's raid, and the memory of that uprising may have aggravated the ardor of the local militiamen who faced the invaders. With the help of Ashby's cavalry those untrained and ill-equipped militia gave a little better than they got, killing a few of Geary's men and driving them out of their breastworks. The Yankees came back and fought them to a standstill, but Geary pulled his whole force back to the Maryland side that night, claiming to have inflicted fifteen times as many casualties as the Confederates had actually suffered. When he returned to Point of Rocks he composed a long letter to his wife, describing his glorious victory over a foe six times his number.[3]

With McCall's division uncomfortably close on his right flank, Colonel Evans reacted with justifiable apprehension to the confrontation at Harper's Ferry, on his left. The din of Ashby's fight drifted into Leesburg and Poolesville over two intervening mountain ranges in a confusing echo; at least some of Leesburg's defenders thought the sound came from the southeast.[4] Rumors of an imminent attempt against Leesburg had been circulating for at least a week, even among Union officers. The major of the 2nd New York State Militia left for a furlough on October 10, but when General Stone ordered him to return by October 18 the major assumed that the invasion would start then, with a crossing of the river about October 20. Newspapers went so far as to announce that General Stone would lead the army's advance into Virginia.[5]

Evans evidently feared that the activity on either side of him marked the commencement of that campaign, and that he might be cut off by a dash from McCall below the town. Then, when General Stone strengthened his picket posts on Harrison's Island, a rumor floated over to the Confederate shore that he, too, was preparing to cross the river. Shortly after midnight on October 17, before word reached Leesburg that Geary was evacuating Harper's Ferry, Evans used a dense cover of fog to pull the main body of his brigade south of Leesburg, below a plantation known as Oatlands. The new campsite put him within an hour's march of the Little River Turnpike, offering shorter and safer contact with the army at Centreville. Evans informed General Beauregard of his withdrawal only after he had completed it, and Beauregard chastised him for leaving the road open for a junction of McClellan's army with Stone and Banks. He insisted that Evans at least keep an outpost at Leesburg.[6]

The thick weather prevented Stone's pickets from detecting the disappearance of the opposing forces until that evening, when he reported it to McClellan. As it happened, Johnston had again contracted his own lines on that same day, retreating this time all the way to the entrenched Centreville line, with only a cavalry picket camped at Fairfax Court House. General Stone had forwarded McClellan a report from an escaped prisoner in the 34th New York who had seen almost no entrenchments at Fairfax, where he said the Confederates kept their baggage packed for a withdrawal to more intricate fortifications at Manassas.[7] Alerted to an apparent Confederate withdrawal on October 16 by his spy chief, Allan Pinkerton, McClellan confirmed that movement the following day through the free-flight of an army balloonist and subsequent ground reconnaissance.[8]

Now McClellan saw an opportunity for at least a theatrical facsimile of the lunge toward Leesburg that Buxton had outlined, although he preferred to avoid the battle that would be necessary to capture the Leesburg garrison outright. McClellan would have been happy to simply maneuver Evans out of his position and capture the town, for he was beginning to feel some pressure to produce results after nearly three months at the head of the army. Instead of driving aggressively toward Leesburg with McCall's division and crossing Stone's division to complete the envelopment, McClellan ordered McCall to feel his way as far as Dranesville, within fifteen miles of Leesburg, and to stop there. McCall accordingly started from Langley on the morning of October 19, with twelve thousand men and three batteries of artillery.[9]

At Dranesville McCall dispatched an assortment of reconnaissance parties, mostly in mounted squads. Some of them, including an infantry detachment, stumbled into Confederate videttes along the Loudoun & Hampshire Railroad and exchanged a few shots with them.[10] Reports of those encounters failed to reach Evans in a timely fashion. On Beauregard's instructions to position himself between McClellan and Banks, Evans sent William Barksdale's 13th Mississippi up to guard the lower reaches of Goose Creek; the Mississippians parted glumly from their comrades, feeling certain they would be swallowed up by converging Union columns. Then, having learned from the troops returning from Harper's Ferry that the enemy was gone from there, Evans directed the 17th and 18th Mississippi back toward Leesburg. They came into town on King Street that evening, swinging right through and camping a mile or two north.[11] Across from the courthouse on Market, just a few doors from King Street, sat the Loudoun Hotel, where on October 19 a man by the name of Ellis lodged, on his way to Richmond. Ellis worked for McClellan's spy chief, Pinkerton, and he had just come across the river from Maryland; he could not help but note the passage of troops and artillery beneath his window, though the mud from that day's rain muffled the noise of their march.[12]

Long after dark that Saturday night some local citizens came into Barksdale's camp with news of McCall's big division barging up the Leesburg Pike — or the Alexandria road, as some knew it from the Leesburg end. According to the civilian reports, McCall lay within eight miles of Goose Creek (in fact, his farthest advance did come within ten miles of the creek). Barksdale extended and doubled his picket line and hurried word to Evans, who sent the rest of his brigade midnight orders to march for Goose Creek. Several hours passed before those orders awakened the scattered regiments, and daylight had come on Sunday before they made their way through Leesburg again; Pinkerton's spy passed the 17th Mississippi as it traversed the town in its grimy clothing, noting them as "the most shabby, reckless, and ugly body of men I ever saw." The bridge on the turnpike had been destroyed early in the summer, during another scare from the Alexandria line, but Evans arrayed his men at the ruins of that burned span and in the dense foliage along the most fordable lengths of Goose Creek.[13]

Colonel Winfield Scott Featherston of the 17th Mississippi, a former congressman, attempted to fortify his men against the overpowering foe with oratory; perchance he invoked the legendary career of his namesake, who had vanquished larger armies on numerous fields. Colonel Barksdale, who had followed Featherston into Congress, doubtless offered some soaring prose of his own. Perhaps so did Erasmus Burt, the colonel of the 18th Mississippi, for he had been a legislator before becoming Mississippi's state auditor and must have known how to deliver a stump speech. Then General Evans bellowed a brief address to the brigade as a whole, probably unnerving as many men as he encouraged when he offered to die right there with them.[14]

By then the townspeople recognized that the shuffling of troops signaled no ordinary march. The 8th Virginia had returned to its main camp on the Old Carolina Road, a mile or so south of Leesburg, and that morning the regiment strode up King Street, trailing a section of the Richmond Howitzers on their way out to the burned bridge. Scores of hometown boys filled those ranks, including Corporal Flavius Osburn of the 8th Virginia; he had known the streets of Leesburg all of his twenty years. Sergeant Clinton Hatcher lived just the other side of the mountain where Leesburg's evening sun set. With the enemy thought to be bearing down on them, the loyal Confederates among the Leesburg residents poured into the streets to greet the Virginia troops with waves and an occasional invitation to refreshment. Girls darted like birds from one doorstep to another to admire the soldier boys (or so a romantic veteran remembered years later), and handkerchiefs flurried from windows all along the streets. Then the column turned up Market Street, and all those familiar faces were gone — some of them, like those of Corporal Osburn and Sergeant Hatcher, gone forever.[15]

General Stone had reported evidence of the Confederate exodus from Leesburg on Thursday, and Friday evening he slipped an officer and a couple of men across the river on a reconnaissance that detected some enemy concentration between Leesburg and Edwards's Ferry. Evans had replaced a few of his pickets by Saturday afternoon, from whom Stone's pickets at Harrison's Island secured a recent Richmond newspaper, but by that evening the lack of enemy baggage wagons and tents left Stone convinced that Evans had reduced his presence at Leesburg to an outpost. The bad weather since Thursday had denied Union lookouts any clear views of the extensive troop movements from the signal station on Sugar Loaf Mountain, some fifteen miles away in Maryland.[16] That Sunday morning the sky finally cleared, although apparently not until the last Confederate infantry had settled into position. The signalmen trained their glasses on Leesburg, finding the town, the old encampments, and the more prominent earthworks abandoned: Evans had unwittingly fooled them by arranging his available forces under the cover of wooded bluffs and creek bottoms. The erroneous signal report went first to General Banks and then straight to McClellan, and it convinced the youthful general that McCall's expedition had succeeded in its bluff. McClellan wired Stone his first description of the situation, telling him that McCall held Dranesville and was scouring the countryside with "heavy reconnoissances [sic]." He asked Stone to watch the Virginia shore closely for signs of an evacuation, suggesting that if Evans had not yet been frightened away a "slight demonstration" from Stone's Corps of Observation might do the trick.[17]

Such a demonstration might not have pried Evans out of Leesburg, in light of Beauregard's orders to "make a desperate stand" against any but the most overwhelming adversaries, but Evans would have stood his ground in any case, after the gift that came to him on Sunday morning. Cavalrymen he had sent down the pike to scout McCall's progress came back with one of McCall's couriers, complete with his dispatch pouch and orders for nothing more aggressive than examining the roads around Dranesville. Greatly relieved, Evans understood that McCall had no intention of attacking Leesburg. Now it was just between him and Stone.[18]

Stone probably suspected that Evans would not retreat without a fight. The day before, he had carefully interviewed a black teamster who had deserted from one of the Mississippi regiments. The man carried valuable information that he had allegedly overheard at headquarters, and Stone tested his story by asking for descriptions of the celebrity Confederates the teamster claimed to have seen. The deserter predicted that Evans would first fight at Leesburg, but if forced to he would fall below Oatlands to favorable ground along Goose Creek and make another stand. Only if defeated in both places would the Confederates retreat to Manassas, said the man, whose account matched Stone's other observations so closely that the general believed him.[19]

For all that, Stone dutifully began the desired demonstration. McClellan's telegram arrived at Poolesville sometime after 11:00 AM, and by 1:00 PM Stone was on his way to Edwards's Ferry with four regiments of infantry and three troops of volunteer cavalry. The rifled guns of Battery I, 1st U.S. Artillery, opened up from their lofty position on the heights over the ferry while two more infantry battalions, one full regiment, and a pair of Rhode Island guns headed upriver for Harrison's Island and Conrad's Ferry.[20]

From his hilltop Stone could see that Evans had not completely abandoned Leesburg, for Union binoculars had focused on at least one Southern regiment marching out of town and into the growth along Goose Creek, near the turnpike. The Regular battery lobbed shells and case shot into every thicket near Edwards's Ferry without effect, and General Gorman's infantry paraded back and forth as though preparing to cross. A few hours of such histrionics failed to budge the Confederates, so Stone took his demonstration a step further late in the afternoon, telling Gorman to send a couple of companies across the river. A hundred Minnesotans and their officers clambered into three of the new flatboats that Stone had ordered built the previous week; the passengers stood upright, and some of them manned poles to push their way over. The water flowed calm and not very high, bringing the first of the boats to the Virginia bank in four minutes, just as the sun sank into the Blue Ridge beyond them. The first men to scramble up onto the floodplain leveled their rifles at the Virginia cavalrymen who stood watch there; the horsemen turned away without firing a shot and galloped for the bluff that loomed in the distance. The trespassers browsed that fringe of alien territory in brief pantomime of an invasion, then returned to their boats. Once back on the Maryland side they marched up the hill to their camps and cooked their dinners in darkness, some of them speculating that their brief sojourn on enemy soil foretold a more serious incursion on the morrow.[21]

When the Union guns fell silent General Evans suspected the enemy might be moving over the river, and he sent his field officer of the day from his headquarters at the burned bridge to investigate the situation at Edwards's Ferry. The road did not run directly to the ferry landing, instead cutting back toward Leesburg until it intersected the ferry road from town. In the last glimmers of light Evans's field officer, Lieutenant Colonel John McGuirk of the 17th Mississippi, found Colonel Burt and his regiment lounging in the roadway and shielded from enemy view by woods, just short of the ferry road. In the name of Colonel Evans, McGuirk told Burt to move his troops down to the plantation of one Aaron Dailey, on the last open, high ground before the bluffs. Then, in darkness, he led a skirmish line toward the ferry until he met one of the cavalry videttes who had watched the flatboats cross, who claimed he had seen two Yankee regiments land. McGuirk transformed the cavalryman into a courier, sending him to Evans with his story, while McGuirk made the final approach to the ferry with a squad of infantry and a local citizen as a guide. The moon rose early, bright, and nearly full, allowing him to tell where the flatboats had landed and retaken their passengers. It appeared that there would be no incursion, at least that night, but on the exaggerated and stale information of the mounted picket Evans had already sent the 17th Mississippi down to bolster Burt's regiment.[22]

Except for a few couriers and videttes, Evans had scattered most of his four cavalry companies along the pike, in the direction of McCall's position at Dranesville. In light of what seemed an imminent crossing by the enemy, he appealed to Beauregard for the use of that cavalry, and sometime that evening Beauregard dispatched four mounted companies from his own command to replace the screen in front of McCall.[23]

Along with the troops he had sent upriver, General Stone had dispatched orders to Colonel Charles Devens, of the 15th Massachusetts, to transfer half of his regiment to Harrison's Island, where there had previously been only a picket detail. The order found Devens visiting outside of camp, and he did not return for more than an hour, but when he came back he directed Church Howe, his quartermaster, to transfer another pair of new scows from the canal into the river and ferry the companies over. Later, Stone instructed Devens to land a platoon on the Virginia shore from Harrison's Island and send it scouting toward Leesburg. Stone expected him to complete the reconnaissance before dark, but for some reason Devens waited until after sunset before he even began.[24]

The rest of the regiment fell in for the sunset parade several miles away, blissfully unaware of their comrades' expedition. Captain Chase Philbrick and a score of his Worcester County men made their way across the river, shrouded by shadows, and with the colonel's permission Quartermaster Howe accompanied them. Philbrick had been snooping around the Virginia side the previous Friday, on General Stone's order, but he still seemed unfamiliar with Ball's Bluff. In the hour between sunset and moonrise he missed an established path a couple of hundred feet downstream, and a swollen creek discouraged him from seeking a much milder incline that lay a few hundred yards north. Philbrick's men scaled the bluff near the most difficult point, much as James Wolfe's army had ascended the Plains of Abraham a century before. Once on the top they prowled forward through that conspicuous clearing on the outer extremity of Margaret Jackson's patchwork freehold, sliding past her place through the woods south of her house. Light timber and scrub growth covered the ridge that ran between Leesburg and the river, ending near the crest at least three-quarters of a mile from the bluff. Had they only come two hours earlier, as Stone had wished, the scouts might have seen all the way to the spires of Leesburg; such a view would have revealed no evidence of military occupation, for Evans had taken his last available soldier with him. As it was, the same orange moon that lighted Colonel McGuirk's way down at the ferry distorted the images on the plain below Philbrick's detachment. Light filtering between a row of trees on Henry Harrison's mainland farm gave the impression of a line of conical tents, suggesting a military encampment. They gazed upon it for some time, those twenty men, their captain, and the quartermaster, and they all concluded that it was, indeed, an isolated camp. Their instructions bade them to withdraw as soon as they saw anything of the enemy, so they turned around and groped their way back through the woods, down the bluff, and across the river with their news.[25]

At the behest of Colonel Devens, Quartermaster Howe mounted a horse and rode down to Edwards's Ferry to present a firsthand report of what he had seen. General Stone had forsaken his headquarters bed that night to sleep on the hill near the Regular battery. When the quartermaster found him and described the supposed encampment, Stone authorized a dawn attack upon it. By firelight he composed detailed instructions for Devens to shift his five companies on Harrison's Island over to the bluff, and for Colonel William Lee of the 20th Massachusetts to replace them with men from his own regiment, taking one company over to the Virginia shore to cover the raiders' retreat. He cautioned Devens not to chase the enemy too far, lest he risk falling into an ambush. After signing the orders, Stone added a proscription that Colonel Devens, the former state senator, would have found painful to enforce against the constituents who composed his regiment: any officer or enlisted man who strayed from his company for curiosity or plunder was to be shot on the spot.[26]

Below Edwards's Ferry, a sergeant roused eight enlisted men from the 2nd New York State Militia, telling them to leave their rifles but bring their blankets. On the towpath he introduced them to a pair of small mountain howitzers and pointed upriver; with two men pulling and two pushing on each piece, they started for Harrison's Island. Ahead of them, orders went flying up to Colonel Baker to bring his 1st California down from the Monocacy to Conrad's Ferry, and to ready the rest of his brigade in case they were needed.[27]

The sabbath had passed into midnight when the long roll drummed the rest of the 15th Massachusetts out of their blankets on the old Poolesville common. At that moment their compatriots on Harrison's Island shucked their knapsacks and overcoats into a pile near the middle of the island and turned, shivering, for the narrow passage on the Virginia side. Stepping gingerly to lessen the echoes of their embarkation, they climbed into a couple of skiffs and a metal lifeboat, pulling away with fewer than three dozen men at a time through the night. Brilliant moonlight glimmered over the rippling water, illuminating their passage in a romantic vignette that defied the danger of the moment. Two trips, and sometimes three, brought a company to the muddy, walnut-littered shelf that bordered the foot of the bluff. While they departed the island, a more capacious flotilla shuttled companies of the 20th Massachusetts from the Maryland shore to replace them.[28]

As the boats and scows transported their men, the field officers of the two Massachusetts regiments convened in the brick house on Harrison's Island. To a couple of fellow Harvard men Colonel Devens seemed unduly gloomy, while Colonel Lee encouraged and advised him. The white-bearded Lee had more than a dozen years on Devens, and a much more extensive military education: he had graduated from Norwich Military Academy, in Vermont, and had attended West Point in the same class as another Lee who held the rank of full general in the opposing army. Among his cautions, Lee offered the observation that victory would be essential in the coming raid, for there would obviously be no retreat from such imposing heights with a river at their backs.[29]

The half of Devens's regiment back at Poolesville gathered into ranks quickly enough, then remained there for nearly two hours before starting off to join their comrades. It was almost four o'clock before they reached the river and marched up to the "center picket" station on the canal towpath, where scows and an old ferryboat carried reinforcements over to the island. By then Colonel Devens had crossed into Virginia, after the last boatload of his first battalion had landed; he had stripped his men to their jackets for the coming fight, but he still wore his own overcoat to stave off the damp autumn chill.[30]

Ball's Bluff rises between two nameless creeks that empty into the Potomac a third of a mile apart, and the Massachusetts men evidently landed toward the upper end. Had they made their way upstream another few hundred feet they could have climbed much gentler slopes, but they turned downstream instead, where the bluff only grew higher and more sheer. Three hundred yards or more down that soggy shelf, just short of the lower creek, Captain Philbrick had finally detected a trail rising — steep, slippery, and narrow — up the perimeter of a precipitous ravine. There the three hundred raiders scrambled to the brow of the bluff: Harvard graduates of impeccable lineage and shoemakers who had left hungry broods at home, alternately clutched sword or musket in one hand and grasped for roots and bushes with the other. They had already disappeared up the slope when their colonel and his headquarters family came looking for them, losing their way in the darkness before doubling back to find the path.[31]

Colonel Lee followed with two companies of the 20th Massachusetts rather than the one company Stone had advised. Their passage required four circuits of the boats, and as they came ashore the officers lined them up in single file on the narrow, slick embankment, but with the last boatload both companies still numbered barely a hundred men. The moon had dropped low enough by then that Lee found it quite dark under the shadow of the bluff and the canopy of sycamores and black walnuts that shrouded the Virginia shore. He led the detachment down to the path and followed it upward until, at the top of the bluff, the track opened to a width of a few feet. Once at the top he could see shadows milling about, and there stood Devens with his battalion, waiting for the first hint of twilight.[32]

While those Massachusetts Yankees found their way up the bluff, Mississippian John McGuirk rode toward White's ford, north of Conrad's Ferry, to check the picket line for activity. The picket detail there consisted of the "Magnolia Guards," the company of the 17th Mississippi commanded by erstwhile university student William L. Duff. Captain Duff's men had stood guard over the Potomac below Mason's Island for many weeks, and they knew that length of river well. Their southernmost post lay at Smart's Mill, the better part of a mile above Ball's Bluff, but the guards there had evidently not spotted the moonlit outline of the Bay State boatmen as they glided over the glistening water; neither had they heard the echoes of clumsy feet on the bottoms of the boats. Colonel McGuirk stopped at the mill, perhaps while the Yankees were still crossing a thousand yards downstream, but the guards reported nothing suspicious there, and all remained quiet at Conrad's Ferry, too. McGuirk continued upstream to White's Ford, at the upper end of Mason's Island, and by the time he reached that crossing daylight had come. He rode up to a prominent height for a better view of the opposite bank, scanning his field glasses over a troop formation across the river, on the canal towpath, that he generously estimated at four regiments.[33] They stood as though awaiting orders, he thought, and so they may have been: he had probably trained his binoculars on the Pennsylvania regiments that made up the rest of Colonel Baker's "California" brigade, assembled in case the mysterious operation downriver developed into something more serious.[34]

On top of Ball's Bluff, the seven companies of Massachusetts men lounged in the rough rectangular glade where some of them would spend eternity. At the first sound of crepuscular birdsong Colonel Devens rose, peeled off his overcoat, and handed it away, never to see it again. Then he whispered his men to their feet and started them into the forest on the far side of the clearing, throwing Captain Philbrick and his company to the front to lead the way over ground he had already traveled.[35]

Back through the woods went the weary Philbrick, following the trail as it wound along the spines of radiating ravines. At the brim of the last ridge they slowed to a halt. Philbrick crept ahead to where the treeline gave way to fields and pointed to the encampment, or to where it should have been, but Devens saw nothing of the kind. The colonel could pick out the conical shapes of light seeping between a line of planted trees, and in the minutes before sunrise he understood how they might be mistaken for a row of tents, but it looked like no camp. In the half-light Captain Philbrick clung to the memory of what he had seen, so Devens wandered forward with him another couple of hundred yards, leaving the battalion under cover of the ridge. The town of Leesburg appeared before them, a mile and a half away, but the growing light betrayed no Confederate camp. They saw only what one of the enlisted men saw when he came over the ridge an hour or so later: the white house and outbuildings of Henry Harrison's "other" farm, where the squire boarded his family's supernumerary livestock.[36]

At that moment Devens might have waved his men back to the boats; it would have saved much misery if he had. General Stone's orders to him had included a reminder to make topographical observations of the vicinity, however, so Devens jotted down some notes from different locations. He could not descry a single Confederate soldier anywhere in the landscape. Returning to his troops behind the ridge, he made a fateful decision not to abandon his mission just yet. Feeling safely concealed in the woods, he dispatched Quartermaster Howe to take another report to Stone, asking for further instructions.[37]

The quartermaster trotted back to the bluff, slid down to the river's edge, and ran to one of the waiting boats. By the time he had crossed the island and the other half of the river, mounted his horse, and started galloping down the towpath, the sun would have cleared the horizon. At an easy gallop he should have been able to cover the three and a half miles to Stone's field headquarters within twenty minutes, but the information he carried to General Stone had probably passed into obsolescence even as he put a heel to his horse.[38]

While waiting for the 15th Massachusetts to return, Colonel Lee had sent scouting parties radiating to the north and south. One of them, under First Sergeant William Riddle, wandered north, toward Smart's Mill. Riddle, a lithographer from Boston whose company commander considered him the best sergeant in the 20th Massachusetts, took three privates and picked his way into the forest. They spread out and left Mrs. Jackson's property as they descended sharply into the ravine cut by the creek on the north side of Ball's Bluff. Then, splashing over that little branch, they climbed the milder slope of the north side onto the old Ball estate, where they mounted another plateau. At the same time, some of Captain Duff's Mississippi pickets started south from Smart's Mill, following the course of some Union soldiers they had seen poling a big flatboat around the island. Major Revere, of the 20th Massachusetts, had ordered that boat from the Maryland side to hasten the passage of troops from the island. Colonel Lee had expected the twenty-five-foot-long scow to be dragged across the island by hand, to reduce the chances of enemy observation, but he had not specifically ordered it. That would have posed a cumbersome project, and Revere instead sent it by the easiest route: upstream and then down. A swift current made the first half of the journey much slower than the second half, and by the time the boat rounded the upper end of the island the approaching dawn disclosed its passage to Duff's southernmost picket post. The blunder forfeited the raid's secrecy.[39]

An officer just behind Sergeant Riddle's patrol guessed that they had proceeded a quarter of a mile from the clearing — they may even have found the Smart's Mill Road — when Captain Duff's inquisitive pickets announced their presence with an abrupt volley. The Confederates drew the first blood of the day, with one bullet smashing Sergeant Riddle's right elbow. Riddle's compatriots emptied their own rifles in reply, then gave chase, but the pickets had fulfilled their duty by firing their weapons and they fled back to report the enemy presence. Riddle stumbled back across the creek and up the ravine to Ball's Bluff, where his captain oversaw the

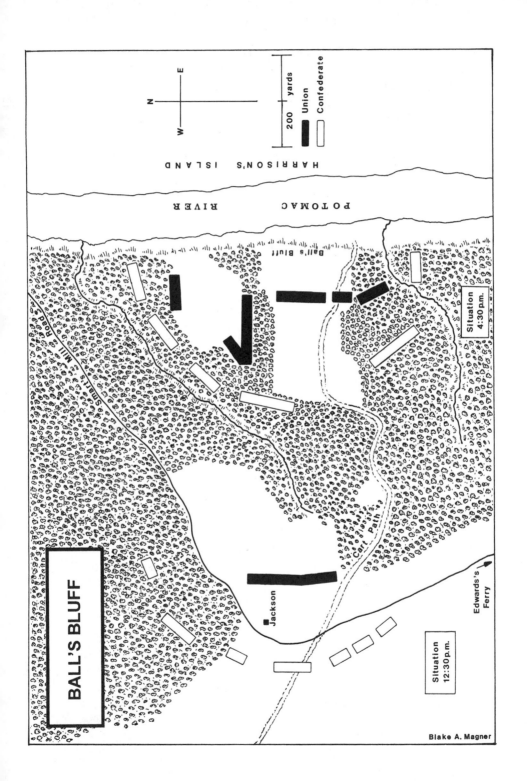

BALL'S BLUFF

N
E
W
S

200 yards

Union
Confederate

HARRISON'S ISLAND

POTOMAC RIVER

Ball's Bluff

Smith's Mill Road

Situation 4:30 p.m.

Cart Path

Jackson

Situation 12:30 p.m.

Edwards's Ferry

Blake A. Magner

bandaging of his arm with a handkerchief and sent him back across the river, not yet ninety days a soldier and now an invalid: the arm came off a few days later.[40]

The brief exchange of gunfire signaled the Federals' last fair chance for a safe retreat to Harrison's Island. Looking back on it later, those who heard the inaugural shots supposed that they erupted sometime before or after 7:00 AM — depending on how their various watches marked local time.[41] Among those who apparently did not hear those seven or eight discharges were Colonel Devens and his men, less than three-quarters of a mile away, and Quartermaster Howe, who must have already passed beyond the bluff on his way to Edwards's Ferry. When Howe reported to General Stone, he did not mention any contact with the Confederates.

The ravines and vegetation that muffled those first few shots allowed Duff time to gather most of his company together and to dispatch an officer to warn Evans of the Yankee crossing. The off-duty portion of his company had spent a cold night on the hard board floor of George Ball's house — probably his father's old home, rather than the new Victorian manor where he now resided; Ball disdained private soldiers, considering them common folk. Most of Duff's men still lingered about the spring at that hour, or at the doors of neighborhood homes, begging breakfast. With about forty rifles at his back the young captain strode briskly downriver. Near Smart's Mill he slowed to a walk, stealing toward the enemy's suspected location through a long hollow, under the cover of the woods where the first clash had flared. As he came out on a hilltop near one widow's little house he could see the Massachusetts men in another widow's yard — Mrs. Jackson's. The blue uniforms clearly outnumbered him by a factor of five or ten, but he dashed south a little farther, interposing his company between Leesburg and the enemy before flinging his civilian-clad cohort into an audacious line of battle on Squire Harrison's farm.[42]

Devens threw two companies out to meet Duff's challenge. One of them tried to flank the Mississippians on their left, but they encountered some slight resistance there and seemed to give up. Captain Philbrick's company came over the ridge at a rattling jog and confronted Duff directly, but Duff fell back toward the main road and lured Philbrick well away from the main body behind the ridge. Like most of the 15th Massachusetts, this company carried old smoothbore muskets, converted from flintlocks, so Philbrick preferred a short-range fight, and when Duff called on him to halt he simply identified his command as "friends" and kept coming. Finally Duff dropped his men to one knee to fire a volley, and when the smoke cleared Philbrick's skirmishers had fallen back in broken squads. They stumbled into position for another try, but a second volley scattered them again. Philbrick rallied his company a third time, but by then it presented a dozen fewer muskets. For some minutes they traded an ineffective fire with Duff's men, who carried rifles, and Devens readied another company to go out and give them a hand.[43]

On his way to Fort Evans the officer who carried Duff's warning alerted Walter Jenifer. One of Charles Stone's less illustrious contemporaries at West Point, the Maryland-born Jenifer had served sporadically as a cavalry officer since the Mexican War, including six years as a lieutenant in the same regiment as Nathan Evans. His life revolved around horses: he enjoyed a good reputation as a horse trainer, he owned a grey Arabian stallion of some renown in the Old Army, and he had invented a cavalry saddle that became notorious for irritating a mount's withers. George McClellan soon designed a better saddle, and at least one fellow officer joked that Jenifer's stallion showed more sense than its owner did. Jenifer held a commission as colonel of a theoretical new Virginia cavalry regiment, but on this field he commanded four independent companies of Old Dominion horsemen unaffiliated with his paper regiment. That October morning he displayed both good and bad judgment, taking the initiative of galloping immediately to Captain Duff's assistance while simultaneously depriving Colonel Evans of every cavalryman in his command. The four companies poured into Leesburg on the turnpike, reining to the right at the courthouse and thundering up King Street, past Henry Harrison's village manse, while the Harrisons and their guests peered out the third-floor windows toward the embattled farm.[44]

The appearance of Jenifer's horsemen convinced Devens to withdraw Philbrick rather than reinforce him, and the blue line shrank back into the woods on the other side of the ridge. There Devens awaited an attack from both horse and foot, but none came. Jenifer satisfied himself with forming a stronger defensive line and gathering in a couple of the wounded Massachusetts men. Those prisoners offered accurate information on the composition of Devens's party, but — perhaps supposing that their entire regiment had come over with them — they inflated his actual strength to about six hundred men.[45]

Meanwhile, knowing nothing of the escalating resistance around Ball's Bluff, Quartermaster Howe reported to General Stone that the raid had not detected a single Confederate soldier on the Virginia side. On the chance that Evans might have abandoned Leesburg, or left it to a skeleton force, Stone decided to expand the reconnaissance. He gave Howe orders for the lieutenant colonel of the 15th Massachusetts to bring the rest of his regiment across the island and land it at Smart's Mill, which could serve as a ready-made fort to protect Devens's right flank. The river also ran shallower there, and once it dropped a little more it would be easy to ford at that point. In addition, Stone detailed a staff captain upriver with ten cavalrymen to act as scouts for Devens.[46]

Stone had already dispatched another three dozen cavalry to scout across the river at Edwards's Ferry. Major John Mix led the detachment, and Stone's adjutant, Charles Stewart, accompanied him. Two companies of the 1st Minnesota poled back over on their scows to establish a picket line on the bluff, and Mix rode his troop through them. The little column cantered more than a mile up the road toward Leesburg — past the Dailey house, past a freshly deserted house, and past a left-hand turn that Mix thought would have taken them to the burned bridge at Goose Creek. The road narrowed there, and the underbrush on either side grew dense. They scared up a Confederate cavalry vidette who scampered out of sight, and Mix stopped to question a slave who said he had seen both infantry and cavalry there just an hour before. As they neared the foot of the hill topped by Fort Evans, Mix could see the tips of bayonets gleaming over the underbrush around a turn, and in a moment they found themselves face to face with most of the 13th Mississippi, which filled the road in a column of fours. Mix spied still more bayonets moving to cut him off. The three-dozen Yankees drew their revolvers and peppered the flanking column, winging one private in the leg. The front squad in the main infantry column let fly at them, dropping one of the horses, but a couple of Mix's officers recovered the dismounted man by an intrepid dash, and the troopers galloped back to safety around a bend in the road. Without much haste they retraced their steps, posting pickets at the deserted house and snagging a Virginia cavalryman who wandered into their path.[47]

Major Mix had expected to come racing back ahead of Confederate cavalry and glide between the Minnesotans, who would cover him while he ferried his men and horses over to Maryland. Instead, when he reached the bluff he saw more of Gorman's infantry disembarking on the Virginia side. Having expanded the reconnaissance from Ball's Bluff, Stone had decided to strengthen the diversion downriver, and for the moment the ruse exerted the desired effect: Evans kept most of his Mississippi troops around Fort Evans and left the 8th Virginia at the burned bridge. He even called Colonel Jenifer back with the cavalry, which he would need to monitor and harass any Union advance from Edwards's Ferry. When Jenifer relayed the intelligence of six hundred Yankees at their rear, though, Evans sent him back with fragments of three mounted companies and a hybrid battalion of Mississippi infantry.[48]

Captain Philbrick's savage skirmish seemed to unsettle Charles Devens. After waiting half an hour behind the ridge near Mrs. Jackson's, the Massachusetts colonel put his five companies into a double file and marched them back down the path to the bluff. Philbrick's wounded had been brought through the clearing shortly before; thinking that Devens had been defeated, Lee had arranged his two companies on either side of the trail to facilitate the retreat. Devens halted his battalion between Lee's two companies, and there he stood as though stunned, offering almost no information and keeping his column on the path, facing the river, while Colonel Lee tried to advise him. After as much as half an hour Devens turned his men around without a word of explanation and marched them back toward the widow Jackson's. Only by that movement was Colonel Lee able to infer that Devens intended to fight.[49]

The peripatetic quartermaster, Lieutenant Howe, climbed back up the bluff a few minutes later. Wrought by fatigue and anxiety, Howe struck Lee as a nervous and unreliable soldier, and the quartermaster did nothing to improve Lee's impression of him when he asked, on behalf of General Stone, what the old colonel thought about the situation. Lee laconically replied that if Stone wished to open a campaign in Virginia they needed reinforcements and provisions. He apparently meant that in the absence of such ambitious intentions it was time to be leaving, but Howe received the remark in a much more optimistic light, and his misinterpretation helped to translate the morning's collection of unfortunate decisions into that evening's deadly disaster.[50]

Howe had not crossed paths with the wounded from Philbrick's fight, and he only learned of the collision when he ventured out again to confer with Devens. He told his colonel that Stone had ordered over the rest of the regiment, as well as a few cavalry to help him reconnoiter. Though relieved to have both orders and reinforcements, Devens worried about the Confederate cavalry — it could only have been Jenifer's — that was concentrating in the distance on his left. He sent Howe yet again to Stone's headquarters with word that they had had a fight, and as Howe traversed Harrison's Island for the sixth time in half a day he met the rest of his regiment coming the other way, under Lieutenant Colonel George Ward. Ward would undoubtedly have pumped Howe for information about affairs over the river, and from their conversation Ward may have deduced that he should forget about crossing at Smart's Mill and go directly to Devens. Afterward, when it began to appear that the Smart's Mill crossing would have been the more judicious choice, Ward remembered Howe telling him that Devens specifically wished him to go to Ball's Bluff.[51]

Whoever made the decision, the remainder of the 15th Massachusetts aimed for the bluff rather than for Smart's Mill. As they crossed the island some of them glanced into the brick farmhouse, where surgeons had established a hospital; the first operations had already splattered the porch and the front room with gore. On their way to the boats the reinforcements encountered more of Captain Philbrick's wounded, including one man who had been shot through both legs and the lower abdomen. A lieutenant looked around his company as it spilled into the boats a platoon at a time, wondering which of them would come back mutilated and mangled, or not at all. He felt sure of his own safety, but then he reflected that those wounded men had begun the day in similar certainty.[52]

The boats veered upstream against the current, then drifted back down to the muddy shelf between the creeks that defined Ball's Bluff. As they planted their feet for the first time on the soil of a seceded state, some of them reinforced the political significance of their landing by muttering "Virginia," while others melodramatically swore aloud never to be driven from that rebellious soil.[53]

At that moment Edward Baker stood with General Stone at his headquarters overlooking Edwards's Ferry, where Nathan Evans expected Stone to make his real attack. Baker reported the arrival of the first battalion of his California regiment at Conrad's Ferry, and Stone familiarized him with the strategic situation, including the presence of McCall's division at Dranesville. The main object of the day's work, as the general explained it to the senator, was to determine the strength and disposition of the enemy's forces. As Baker and a few staff officers stood around him, Stone crouched down, spread a sheet of paper on his knee, and scribbled his orders with a pencil. Baker was to take command of affairs opposite Harrison's Island, including all the troops in that vicinity, and — at his discretion — either funnel reinforcements over there or withdraw both Devens and Lee. Baker's half-century of life had wound down to its last eight hours when he took that scrap of paper, mounted, and spurred his horse upriver with his staff in hot pursuit.[54]

Baker's chaplain rode with him that day as a volunteer aide. Like many of Baker's acquaintances, the chaplain later insisted that Stone had given Baker direct orders to cross the river and capture Leesburg. Some of the senator's military family may have believed as much, including the chaplain, who admitted that he never actually read the written order. According to the chaplain's rendition of a breathless conversation conducted at a gallop on the towpath, Baker made no mention of discretion, instead asserting that Stone had ordered him to take every man he needed and press forward to Leesburg. If the chaplain repeated the conversation faithfully, Baker had either misunderstood his orders or decided to exceed them from the outset.[55]

A few moments later they met Lieutenant Howe cantering down from Harrison's Island to tell Stone of Philbrick's skirmish. Baker inquired of the situation upriver, and Howe conveyed his distorted interpretation of

Colonel Lee's comment, implying that Lee had actually advised turning the reconnaissance into an invasion. If Baker had had any reservations before, that information eliminated them, and he told Howe "I am going over immediately, with my whole force."

Howe went on to Stone's headquarters, giving the general his first warning of any armed resistance in front of Devens. The quartermaster also mentioned that Colonel Ward had redirected the remaining half of their regiment to Ball's Bluff, rather than to the mill. Though puzzled by Ward's disregard of his earlier orders, Stone had given Baker the latitude to manage the right wing, and he declined to interfere in the details.[56]

Once more Lieutenant Howe lifted himself into the saddle and returned to Harrison's Island. Before crossing the island again to rejoin his regiment he approached Colonel Baker for any orders he might wish to give Devens. Baker, who could not yet have learned anything substantive about events across the river, nonetheless praised Devens for noble conduct and told him to stay where he was. In his ignorance of the limited transportation, Baker grandiosely promised to join them shortly with his entire command. Howe found his regiment lounging near the Jackson house, together as a unit for the first time after many weeks of picket duty, and there he briefed Devens on Baker's assignment and intentions, including the comforting fantasy about rapid relief by heavy reinforcements. Midmorning had passed, and they sat down to wait while anxious hours wasted away.[57]

At the sound of Duff's skirmish, several Leesburg citizens and a few soldiers from the hospital strayed out to join the Magnolia Guard. Then came two companies from the 18th Mississippi and William Ball's company of Chesterfield County cavalry, all from the makeshift battalion that Evans had sent back under Colonel Jenifer. Captain Ball dismounted his troopers, and with the infantry they aligned themselves to the west of the ridge where Devens lay. Jenifer himself remained hidden in a ravine to the south with the rest of the cavalry and some infantry from the 13th Mississippi. Later in the morning Evans sent him all but one company of Eppa Hunton's 8th Virginia, bringing them over from the burned bridge, but before Hunton arrived Jenifer doubted that he had many more than 320 men from one end of his thin line to the other.[58]

When the last company of the 15th Massachusetts came up, Devens had twice that many troops, counting the officers, but the trees and brush disguised his advantage. He sent Company C, a rifle company, off to his right, to guard against any threat from roads leading upriver, and he kept another company fanned out before him as skirmishers, five paces apart. That forward line carried smoothbores, though, and from their direction came the infrequent boom of a musket as a Worcester County man tried his luck against a Mississippi marksman. The longer range of Duff's rifles usually settled those duels, sending a man in blue wandering back toward the river in search of the hospital. Most of the forenoon had passed in such lethal leisure when Devens sent his Company B out to relieve the skirmishers. Captain Clark Simonds marched his first platoon over the brow of the ridge and arranged it in an open amphitheater formed by the crescent of woods, leaving his second platoon as a reserve.[59]

Toward Leesburg, Simonds could see a body of infantry marching their way. He focused on that column — likely the 8th Virginia — while his men contended with the Mississippi skirmishers. A private had found a slave lurking in the vicinity and brought him to Simonds, but the captain stared so intently at those distant troops that he not only ignored the prisoner but failed to detect the movement of Jenifer's mixed battalion, farther to his left. The Confederates struck first from the woods on his left flank, where Jenifer had hidden with his cavalry. A thick volley raked the Union skirmish line and the little reserve, and the skirmishers fairly melted away: Simonds waved them back over the hill, then headed for some timber himself, but the cavalry bolted forward at a run into that very timber. That was the last his comrades saw of Captain Simonds that day, and several of his men disappeared with him.[60]

The rest of Company B fell back to the main body of the regiment, on the ridge. There, while their comrades in Company C trotted back from the road to Conrad's Ferry, the Massachusetts men brought Jenifer's assault up short — at least until the 8th Virginia swung into line with him and evened up the odds. The field fell almost silent then, save for the hysterical shrieking of Margaret Jackson and her terrified daughters, who huddled in their little house. With no sign yet of Colonel Baker's reinforcements, Devens used the lull to withdraw from his exposed position, backing toward the river. On their second assault the Confederates pushed into the edge of the woods, where they settled down to punishing the Federals from beyond the reach of their outdated muskets.[61]

Back on Harrison's Island, Major Revere heard the firing and started loading his portion of the 20th Massachusetts into the boats. With three companies detailed elsewhere, he commanded only a couple of hundred men and a handful of officers.[62]

Unlike the 15th Massachusetts, which hailed from a single county, the men of the 20th came from all across the Bay State. Cape Cod fishermen and Nantucket whalemen shouldered into the ranks under Harvard scholars and professors, and most companies inevitably fielded a substantial core of those desperate shoemakers from towns in northeastern or central Massachusetts. Company A alone represented the entire breadth of the state: like many of the officers in his regiment, First Lieutenant Oliver Wendell Holmes Jr. had been raised on the sunnier slope of Boston's Beacon Hill, while Sergeant John Merchant lived in Pittsfield, just short of the New York border.[63]

Merchant, a Scottish immigrant, had been earning a precarious living as a tailor when the war began. His wife had borne their fourth child on the day Fort Sumter surrendered; after watching dozens of his acquaintances enlist, Merchant, too, had chosen the military route to escape poverty and debt. Groups of novice soldiers had been marching to the Pittsfield train depot since spring, waved to war by bands of admiring neighbors like Herman Melville, who observed their departures with a particular sadness. Three Pittsfield men crossed the Potomac that day with Lieutenant Holmes's company, and two of them would never come back; another Pittsfield citizen would sacrifice his arm.[64]

Major Revere brought over every man he could find and delivered them all to Colonel Lee shortly after midday, making a total of some 950 Massachusetts men on top of Ball's Bluff, with a healthier proportion of rifled weapons. Behind Revere, driven by Colonel Baker's instructions for everyone to cross, came the two mountain howitzers dragged by the eight detailed men from the 2nd New York State Militia. Lieutenant Frank French, a mere boy from Maine with a three-week-old appointment in the Regular Artillery, directed the hauling as temporary commander of the section. The mountain guns sacrificed range and velocity to save weight: they rode on much smaller carriages and featured a lighter tube than regular field pieces, measuring less than an inch thick and barely a yard long from muzzle to cascabel. The squad of infantrymen managed to drag them up the arduous path to the bluff with unanticipated ease, for that was precisely the terrain for which they had been invented.[65]

Up on the bluff, the Mississippi companies had begun sidling around the Federal right. Captain Duff, whose men knew that ground best, took the extreme left of the concave Confederate line, and at Colonel Jenifer's instruction Duff sent his morning picket detail back out to investigate enemy activity near their post at Smart's Mill. Two of these men saw the 20th Massachusetts and the howitzers waiting to board the boats, and after firing harmlessly at them they raced back to alert Duff.[66]

From the Maryland side Colonel Baker next pushed the larger half of his regiment toward the bluff under his lieutenant colonel, Isaac Wistar. Wistar, who had been Baker's partner in a West Coast law practice, started crossing men to the island, then went there himself to relay them to the Virginia shore as quickly as he could. With his troops fighting off assailants on the other side of the river, Baker dallied at the canal, apparently giving his personal attention to the rigging of a ferry line and the manhandling of a canal barge over the towpath and into the river.[67]

At his headquarters in the fort that bore his name, Nathan Evans began to realize that the lingering threat from McCall's division at Dranesville had subsided — something Charles Stone would not learn that day. By noon McCall was long gone from that place, making his way back to Langley. George McClellan failed to mention that vital detail to Stone, although he had Stone's report of an engagement across the river, and McClellan's chief of staff gave the impression that McCall remained close at hand when he telegraphed Stone about communicating with "Darnesville." Stone naturally mistook that as an orthographic error for Dranesville, and he took the telegram as a hint that McCall would pitch in against Evans if the Confederate backed away. The ambiguous message really meant for him to maintain a relay of couriers for dispatch to General Banks at Darnestown, Maryland.[68]

The last word Stone had from Baker was Lieutenant Howe's news that he intended to commit his "whole force." On that information Stone had sent even more troops to Gorman's line on the Virginia side of Edwards's Ferry, to further enhance the diversion in Baker's favor, but the guns in Fort Evans discouraged him from making an attack there. Early in the afternoon, with Wistar's battalion of the 1st California gliding from the canal towpath to the island, and then to the walnut-encrusted Virginia shore, and with the Tammany Regiment queued up to follow, Eppa Hunton hurried a messenger to Fort Evans with an earnest request for reinforcements. Evans either suspected that Stone intended no real mischief at the lower ferry or he deemed Ball's Bluff the more vulnerable point — or both — and he decided to shift the greater part of his brigade to the fight for Mrs. Jackson's woods. Thus far he had parceled off only a company or two from each of his three Mississippi regiments, but in response to Hunton's envoy he turned to Colonel Erasmus Burt and told him to march the remaining eight companies of his 18th Mississippi to face the threat behind them.[69]

Burt's arrival would bring Confederate numbers to about twelve hundred, momentarily leveling the odds again. At last, after a company or two of the California Regiment had reached the battlefield, Baker himself finally took the field. He appeared like a vision on horseback behind Colonel Lee, just as that officer was about to go looking for him, and with an air of exaggerated courtliness he bowed low, congratulating Lee "on the prospect of a battle." By the time the last of Wistar's battalion had scaled the bluff, Union soldiers there outnumbered their assailants by about 30 percent, but Colonel Baker's dawdling had thrown them into great jeopardy. Without central authority to either arrange a cohesive defense or mount an advance, the field officers on the scene had cobbled together a faulty deployment through individual preference, and in trying to fix things Baker only illustrated his ineptitude.[70]

At that hour the haphazard Union battle front lay a couple of hundred yards from the water's edge, with the 15th Massachusetts still somewhat advanced. Without even examining the ground in front of him, Baker drew the 15th Massachusetts back and elbowed it awkwardly in alongside the core of Colonel Lee's regiment, at right angles to both friend and foe. It was midafternoon; the mountain howitzers threw a speculative shell into the forest from time to time, but the enemy responded with such desultory sniping that as the California companies scaled the bluff they stacked arms and sat down. Lee suggested to Baker that the enemy would probably attack on their left, for there lay the most vulnerable ground. The nameless creek at the downstream end of the bluff curved southward, and its opposite banks towered almost perpendicularly to a ridge from which an assailant might sweep the bluff with impunity, shredding the left flank of the Union position. Baker consulted with Colonel Wistar when he arrived, and Wistar confirmed Lee's analysis. At that Baker gave his lieutenant colonel full responsibility for the flank, instructing him to "do as you like." Wistar tried to extend skirmishers far enough south, but the ravine plunged more precipitously at his end of the creek than it did farther upstream, and an enemy firing line would still be able to overlap his.[71]

Baker advertised his self-doubt by seeking advice from nearly every officer he spoke to, including a Massachusetts lieutenant who had worn shoulder straps for barely a hundred days. Belatedly, the harried colonel wondered what lay in front of him, and he selected Wistar to find out. With two companies Wistar eased forward through thick brush toward the scene of the morning's fight while a healthy portion of Eppa Hunton's 8th Virginia crept just as carefully from the opposite direction. The two reconnaissance forces surprised each other and blazed away at close range for several minutes. At the first volley scores of Hunton's men bolted ignominiously for the rear, and the Californians briefly snared a platoon of the most impetuous, but enough Virginians remained to overpower the two isolated Union companies. Wistar sprinted back to prepare the main body of his battalion for a standup fight.[72]

Few of Wistar's skirmishers returned uninjured, and most of their covey of prisoners escaped back to their own lines. Confederates rolled in on the heels of the survivors, and now the enemy began pressing the other side of the Union line from the ravine to the north. Baker's slipshod dispositions had left companies orphaned from their regiments and facing in different directions; a significant number of his men, including nearly half the 15th Massachusetts, could not deliver effective fire without hitting their own friends. Those who could find clear shots aimed them generally into the hostile woods.[73]

Baker's dilatory arrival had allowed confusion to develop on the battlefield, and his inattention had created havoc. After supervising incidental details of the crossing that he should have left to his quartermaster (had he had one worth his salt), Baker had abandoned that post without leaving another officer to direct the transportation either from the towpath or from the island. As a result, the commanders of the next two regiments in line found absolute chaos at those two points. The colonel of the 19th Massachusetts took charge on the Maryland side, running a rope from shore to island to regulate the passage of boats, while Colonel Milton Cogswell of the Tammany Regiment left his major to oversee the shuttling of boats between the island and the Virginia shore. Cogswell, a Regular Army captain with West Point credentials, jumped into the flatboat that took his first platoon over. Captain Duff's Mississippi riflemen had come back down to hinder the crossing, throwing a few rounds at the boats, and when Cogswell's first company had gathered on the Virginia side he sent it upstream to root them out. Some dismounted Virginia cavalrymen came to Duff's assistance, however, and it was the New Yorkers who retreated, falling back up the slope of that northern ravine toward their comrades on the bluff.[74]

With Cogswell came another piece of artillery. This gun, a thirteen-pounder James rifle belonging to Company B of the 1st Rhode Island Artillery, came across with a fourteen-man crew; the horses followed in another boat. The Rhode Island captain — the man Stone had earlier chastised for racing his horses to exhaustion — absented himself from his battery on some errand of sudden significance. In his place Lieutenant Walter Bramhall took charge of the James gun, even though Bramhall belonged to the artillery company attached to the 9th New York State Militia. The limber of the James gun came over, too, but the crewmen took it apart and carried it up to the battleground in pieces: they managed the ammunition chest with relative ease because, through the neglect of the missing captain, it held an inadequate supply of ammunition. Even if the path had not been churned into deep muck it rose too steep and narrow for the horses to negotiate, but the gunners found a sufficiently gradual slope where they could persuade those doomed creatures to lunge up the height — probably up the ravine cut by the branch near the landing place. The gun was also too big to roll up the infantry trail, so Bramhall dismounted the tube and dragged it up with ropes; then he dismantled the carriage and gave the fragments to New York infantrymen to lug up by hand. Near the crest he reassembled the parts, buckled his horses back into the traces, and wheeled the gun into the clearing as bullets began whistling overhead.[75]

About then the 18th Mississippi elbowed into the fight on the southern side of the bluff. Conspicuous on horseback, Colonel Burt urged his regiment into action over the rough ground. Evidently he entered the battle with the same hopeful spirit that had allowed him to leave his wife and eight children for war without the precaution of drawing up a will, but there on the banks of the Potomac reality met the colonel's faith head-on. Early in the assault he attracted the attention of some California riflemen, who directed one volley for him especially, and they or someone in the 15th Massachusetts slipped a bullet over the pommel of his saddle that bored through his lower intestine. Sympathetic hands removed him to Leesburg, where he could die in peace, if not without pain, and his lieutenant colonel took over. The new commander of the 18th Mississippi dispatched a couple of companies to flank Wistar's extreme left, in the ravine.[76] In concert with their comrades in front of the enemy, the Mississippians focused a blistering fire on the crew of Lieutenant Bramhall's rifled gun, dropping all his horses in a kicking, shrieking heap and picking off his gunners with alarming rapidity. The limber chest of the James gun lacked canister, which would have proven most effective at shorter ranges, but Bramhall did what he could with the few rounds of shell that the Rhode Island captain had left him. When his piece finally fell silent for lack of able gunners, a volunteer crew of colonels and staff officers jumped to man it for a few more rounds. Even Colonel Baker helped roll it into position, neglecting his command responsibilities again to do the duty of a private.[77]

Out in front of the Union infantry, the pair of mountain howitzers suffered a similar fate. Baker had posted Quartermaster Howe by them with a field telescope, to direct their fire, but the quartermaster could not spot a target in the thick vegetation until the woods erupted with musketry. Disabled by wounds early, Lieutenant French could not prevent his ersatz gunners from flattening themselves on the ground while bullets flew over their heads from both sides, and those who escaped injury soon ran away.[78]

From there the battle descended into a maelstrom of uncoordinated attacks and counterattacks in the arc encircling Ball's Bluff, from the ravine south of the bluff almost to the mouth of the creek that formed its northern limit. Because they occupied the outside of that curve, the Confederates managed to maintain relatively steady organization, concentrating their fire on the ever-condensing crowd of blue uniforms. To Union soldiers the converging bullets and buckshot appeared to fly in sheets, covering every square foot of space, and escape from each onslaught seemed simply miraculous. With the river right behind them the Yankees fought ferociously, as Colonel Lee had predicted they must, trading volleys at a hundred yards and less; now and then bayonets flashed in terrifying proximity beneath the muzzles of empty muskets.[79]

From the wounds they treated, Union surgeons deduced that most of the Confederates carried smoothbore muskets. The Southerners had to move in close to make their fire count, for at longer ranges their charges of buck and ball lacked punch and accuracy; a shortage of rifles could have accounted for the light Confederate fire during most of the day's skirmishing. The volume of fire intensified as the day waned, and an hour into that final stage of the fight a solid ounce of lead knocked the wind out of Lieutenant Holmes, the Boston Brahmin, when it struck him in the midsection. A few minutes later he regained enough breath to lead his company in a close-quarter countercharge, and a second ball plowed through his torso. Like most of those struck by the smoothbores, Holmes recovered completely, but those old muskets could deal death readily enough. As he lay with the wounded on the edge of the bluff, Holmes spied his own Sergeant Merchant: the Pittsfield tailor and father of four lay nearby, silently bleeding to death from a slug that had penetrated his brain. Whenever they could, the defenders fought from prone positions behind trees or irregularities in the ground, and head wounds predominated in the Union field hospitals.[80]

It was primarily the officers who took their wounds standing upright. Lieutenant Colonel Ward, of the 15th Massachusetts, lost a leg when a bullet smashed his shin just above the ankle. In the 20th, Captain John Putnam lost an arm: Holmes later saw that severed arm at the field hospital, lying forgotten on a blanket in a pool of blood. A bullet in the stomach killed Lieutenant William Lowell Putnam; Lieutenant James J. Lowell fell with a wound in the thigh, and Captain George Schmitt suffered three in the legs and one in the back. Colonel Wistar did not leave the field until he had been shot three times — in the thigh, neck, and elbow.[81]

The 18th Mississippi endured the worst of the Union musketry, losing more than seven dozen killed and wounded. The day hit Mississippi state government hard: besides Colonel Burt, the state auditor, the mortally wounded included a former state legislator who had come out as an independent, and Frank Pettus, the governor's son.[82]

Colonel Hunton regrouped his regiment's shaken stragglers and redistributed their remaining cartridges to give each man a few rounds for another charge. The Virginians hurtled into the middle of the clearing between the artillery positions, and with a few stray Mississippi companies they slammed into the latest Federal reinforcements, overrunning the two silenced mountain howitzers. At the head of the Mississippians fell James Ballou, another of those "independents" who scorned enlistment and fought as a civilian; because he had not put his name to any roll, it was not spelled correctly anywhere in the casualty lists.[83]

Hunton's men, most of them natives of that very county, pitched recklessly toward the intruders despite their dwindling ammunition. Towering above his comrades, Sergeant Clinton Hatcher plunged forward as though to make good a private boast of carving dead Yankees into breakfast steaks. Hatcher had passed most of his life ten miles from that spot, and just up the Shenandoah Valley lived a maid who doubtless came to mind when he thought of defending home and hearth. He had just written that girl a letter asking if she could possibly love an oafish romantic like him, but a bullet from the Union lines cut short his ardor, and neither he nor anyone else ever learned the girl's answer. With him perished Leesburg's Flavius Osburn and a handful of their neighbors, but in the end the 8th Virginia backed sullenly into the undergrowth, leaving the enemy holding the brim of the bluff.[84]

The din abated as each assault dissolved, and with his ears ringing from the receding thunder of the fight at least one sergeant in the California Regiment could hear the eerie tooting of a band playing patriotic airs on the Maryland side.[85] Such pauses grew shorter and less frequent, though, and with each new thrust against their fragile line more Federals fled to the rear than returned to drive the Southerners back. Sometimes as few as a score of enlisted men rallied around some intrepid officer or their regimental colors; demoralized comrades crouched behind trees, rocks, or the dead horses of Bramhall's gun, and milling skulkers began adding to the confusion where the brow of the bluff dipped out of range. The flanks contracted inexorably, and the front began to dissolve. Colonel Baker stood in the forefront of the disaster that he had unwittingly created. A volley knocked him to the ground, and he rose unsteadily to his feet but fell again almost immediately with several bullets through him.[86]

With his death Colonel Baker caused the final command confusion of the day. Colonel Lee, who had so vigorously argued the impossibility of retreat, now assumed command and ordered one. He tried to piece together one last battle line at the edge of the clearing, to cover the evacuation of the wounded and the withdrawal of the battered troops, but Colonel Cogswell thought his commission older than Lee's and he objected to the move. Instead, said Cogswell, they should reform all their men and push inland until they cleared the deep ravine on their left, then turn for Edwards's Ferry and try to break out. Lee submitted, and Cogswell gathered his Tammany companies to lead the drive.[87]

In their retreat from the earlier collision with Wistar's California skirmishers some of Hunton's Virginians had forgotten to stop, dispersing into the fields on the Leesburg side of Mrs. Jackson's ridge. Later they and their colonel would blame their unilateral withdrawal on a misunderstanding of orders and physical exhaustion, but they had also exhausted their ammunition and their spirit, so Hunton again called for more help. Listening to the roar of battle behind him, Colonel Evans stripped one more regiment from Fort Evans, sending Colonel Featherston with the 17th Mississippi; that left him only nine companies of Barksdale's regiment to face several times their number above Edwards's Ferry. In the lengthening shadows of late afternoon Featherston hastened his civilian-clad regiment over the intervening two miles, running them at least part of the way and bringing the eight companies into line gasping for breath. He squeezed them in between the 18th Mississippi on his right and a company of the 13th on his left, and they dressed ranks in a broad crescent. In a stentorian baritone Featherston called for the sons of Mississippi to drive the invaders into the Potomac or into eternity. Like the blade of a scythe they swung forward with the receding sun glinting off their bayonets, and Cogswell's bold offensive crumbled before them.[88]

A few stalwart riflemen clung to the brow of the bluff and stalled that final onslaught, but for the men in blue the day had been irretrievably lost. Individually and in desperate bands they slid down the path or tumbled down the rocky face of the bluff: an impromptu battalion of assorted Mississippi infantry denied them the more gradual slope upstream. The fleetest swarmed into the shallow boats, pushing for the island with only inches of freeboard, as bullets began spitting into the water around them. So many men jammed the scow — the one that Major Revere had ordered around in the morning — that water started pouring over the sides. The clumsy craft swamped in midstream, spilling dozens of soldiers — many of them wounded — into the frigid, swollen Potomac, where either their frantic comrades or their sodden woolen clothing dragged most of them to the bottom.[89]

That barge had brought over two fresh companies of the 42nd New York. Their comrades back on the island sensed impending calamity and refused to follow, so these would be the day's last reinforcements. Those few platoons of Tammanies pushed against the tide of fugitives and met their colonel at the foot of the path. Cogswell sent them up to form a skirmish line and cover the retreat, probably recognizing that they would all be killed or captured in the process. The colonel had become friends with Captain Timothy O'Meara, a pugnacious Irishman from New York's vast army of unemployed, and Cogswell put him in charge. In his first battle O'Meara lurched valiantly up the bluff in the fading twilight to show the men how it was done, just as he would lead his own regiment up Missionary Ridge in his last battle, twenty-five months hence. Cogswell led by example, as well, and he assembled a dozen riflemen to confront several Mississippi marksmen who were firing into the helpless mob from the mouth of the downstream ravine. In the darkness the Yankees wandered too far, and the encroaching Confederates surrounded them.[90]

Colonel Devens opted to save himself, and announced to his men that they were on their own. Some of them clung to him anyway, including Lieutenant Charles Eager and Walter Eames, a brawny soldier who had been in the fight since the dawn skirmish. Devens did not swim well, and Eager could not swim at all, but with the help of Eames and a few others they decided to try. Devens cast his sword as far as he could across the river and stripped off everything but his drawers and shirt; Eames stuck his bayonet into the mud and drove his entire musket into the embankment, down to the trigger. Eager and the other enlisted men flung rifles and pistols into the stream and peeled down to the same rustic uniform as their colonel. They wove a hasty raft of branches to aid Devens and Eager, then shoved for the island with bullets spattering around them, for the Confederates had reached the edge of the bluff. At midstream Eames heard a friend calling vainly for help, but instead of swimming to the rescue he stayed with his helpless colonel. When Devens started to struggle Eames twisted a hand in his beard to hold his face out of the water, imploring him to stay afloat until they reached the island.[91] Up and down the channel wounded and exhausted swimmers called for help, for mothers, and for wives, until their cries subsided to gurgling and silence. A lieutenant in one of the German companies of the 20th Massachusetts went to the aid of his stricken captain and countryman, only to drown with him.[92]

Colonel Lee hesitated to join the frenzied retreat. He seemed to believe that surrender alone would prevent the slaughter of his men, who were already dying by the dozen in the river. Thinking him disabled by sheer despair, his adjutant and Captain Francis Bartlett slipped their arms under his and encouraged him down the bluff along with Major Revere and Revere's brother, the regimental surgeon. A glance at the mobbed boats and the rain of bullets on the surface of the water convinced them to struggle upstream until they had left the battlefield behind. Once beyond the range of hostile fire, Bartlett left the party and went back for his own company. He found them, swimmers all, and sent them into the chilling water after they had shed the heaviest of their clothing. Then he collected an assortment of officers and men representing every regiment that had fought on the field, including two derelict privates of the 2nd New York State Militia, from the provisional crew of those mountain howitzers. With these nonswimmers he proceeded upriver, picking up stragglers until a full company trod the bank behind him. Those with weapons threw them into the river, for now that they had passed beyond the killing ground Bartlett planned to surrender to the first Confederates they saw.[93]

At Smart's Mill Bartlett discovered a slave who pointed out a disabled skiff. They dumped the water out of it and improvised a patch to cover a leak, but as soon as they pushed it into the river Bartlett had to draw his revolver to prevent a stampede. He pointed to a few men, who climbed in and started off; then sent the rest to a nearby barn to await his call for another load. It took fifteen or twenty trips before they all reached the island, and Bartlett went with the last boatload — none too soon, for Captain Duff's pickets soon returned to the mill and appropriated the barn for their guard shack.[94]

Colonel Lee and his headquarters party were not so lucky. They had already passed that way, spurning the same leaky skiff before continuing up the riverbank. After a time they wandered inland, and in the moonlight they detected a farm gate on what may have been George Washington Ball's property. There the pilgrimage ended, for as they tried to slip around that gate a cavalry squad surrounded them with a circle of carbine muzzles.[95]

The curtain dropped at Ball's Bluff soon afterward. Elijah White, a cavalry private who lived a few miles upriver, at Spinks's Ferry, had spent that day acting as a volunteer aide and guide for Eppa Hunton, and after dark he performed his most impressive duty of the day. Leading a few dozen Virginians down to the riverbank while a few more stood on the bluff above, White found the demoralized remnant of Edward Baker's mismanaged command. Many of them still held arms in their hands, but when Confederate officers called on them to surrender they seemed to welcome the opportunity, and 325 of them fell in to give up their weapons. Captain O'Meara and the shards of the last two Tammany companies joined them.[96]

While details scoured the riverbank for cowering Yankees, Leesburg citizens brought cooked meals out to Ball's Bluff to reward the weary defenders.[97] Down on the Maryland side of Edwards's Ferry General Stone grew fretful over the lack of news, for if Baker had had any success Stone would have wanted to capitalize on it by pushing forward from his end of the line. He also had to coordinate with General Banks, who stood ready to lend a hand with his division, if necessary. Late in the afternoon, evidently supposing that Baker had made good on his promise to take his entire force over, Stone had apprised Banks that his division had engaged the enemy across the river, and he asked Banks to send a brigade from Darnestown. When Stone finally dispatched a staff officer to interview Colonel Baker, that officer met a detail carrying Baker's body back to the Maryland shore. The day had turned to night by the time Stone learned of

Baker's death. He appealed to Banks for the rest of his division and informed McClellan that Baker had been killed, adding that he was leaving his field headquarters to take care of his right wing. Starting up the towpath at a gallop, he soon met the escort bringing the colonel's body the other way, and reined up respectfully until it had passed. Still he knew nothing of the disaster, though he began to suspect it when, after moonrise, he rode into staggering clutches of half-dressed men — wet, empty-handed, and thoroughly dejected.[98]

As he neared the crossing place Stone saw increasing numbers of men who had just swum back from the island, and when he questioned a few of them they agreed that Evans had been heavily reinforced, perhaps with as many as ten thousand men. A chaplain tending wounded along the towpath reported complete defeat on the opposite shore, with all the Union soldiers killed or captured. Stone left orders for the colonel of the 19th Massachusetts to hold Harrison's Island, collect the refugees, and send back the wounded. Fearing that the oft-reported Confederate horde might have materialized at Leesburg after all, the general reined around and pelted back to Edwards's Ferry, to withdraw Gorman's troops from the Virginia side before they met disaster, too.[99]

Only when he had seen that withdrawal safely under way did Stone telegraph General McClellan with the particulars, characterizing his efforts as "preventing further disaster" and mentioning that he was pulling Gorman back to the Maryland shore. McClellan, who would have to face the political consequences of a repulse after so many weeks of inactivity, wired back twice in rapid succession for Stone to stop Gorman's troops where they were and dig in, demanding that the Federals hold their Virginia foothold "at all hazards." Generals used such words sparingly, and usually only in reference to defending an object or position of vital importance, but the object that McClellan seemed to consider more crucial than Gorman's survival that night was public opinion. Stone naturally complied, but he urged the commanding general to at least order McCall up from Dranesville to threaten the Confederates' right flank. From McClellan's reply — the last communication to come from him that day — Stone learned for the first time that there could be no aid from Dranesville. The strategic supports that Stone had supposed would be available to him all day had marched out of reach before the real fighting at Ball's Bluff ever began.[100]

Slaves escaping to Fort Monroe by moonlight to claim "contraband" status.

Papers and equipment of the Bridgeport, Connecticut, *Daily Advertiser and Weekly Farmer* lie in the street after a pro-union mob ransacked that dissenting newspaper's office and printshop.

The cover of *Harper's Weekly* for September 7, 1861, showing a Baltimore woman flaunting a semblance of the Stars and Bars over her dress as she passes Union soldiers. The image reflected widespread fear of a secessionist uprising in Baltimore.

Nathan G. Evans in the uniform of a first lieutenant, U.S. Cavalry, shortly before the war.

Eppa Hunton, who commanded the 8th Virginia at Ball's Bluff.

Illustration of a picket post along the Potomac from *Harper's Weekly* of October 5, 1861, when the war seemed to have settled back into idyllic leisure.

Union troops scouting the abandoned Confederate position at Fairfax Court House on October 18, 1861, which prompted McClellan to order reconnaissances and demonstrations at Dranesville and Leesburg.

Unoccupied farmhouse on Harrison's Island, used as a field hospital for Union wounded.

Lockhouse at Lock 25 of the Chesapeake and Ohio Canal, on the Maryland side of Edwards's Ferry.

Henry Harrison's village home on King Street, Leesburg.

Margaret Jackson's house on the Ball's Bluff battlefield, with numerous modern additions.

George Washington Ball's Victorian manse, Springwood, near which Captain Duff's pickets established their encampment.

The channel of the Potomac between Harrison's Island, at left, and Ball's Bluff, behind the trees at right. Here some eighteen hundred Union troops crossed in boats, and here dozens of them drowned trying to make their way back.

Double illustration from *Leslie's Illustrated*, November 16, 1861. Above, Regular artillery at General Stone's hilltop headquarters shells William Barksdale's 13th Mississippi during skirmishing at Edwards's Ferry on October 22. Below is the retreat at Edwards's Ferry on the night of October 23, on an imaginary pontoon bridge.

A modern view of the scene of the October 23 retreat, showing Goose Creek entering the Potomac in the center distance; the Union troops landed on (and debarked from) the embankment at right.

In the wake of the Ball's Bluff disaster, *Harper's Weekly* portrayed Potomac River pickets as much more vigilant; this was published November 2, 1861.

Alfred Waud's drawing of Union soldiers dragging the body of a drowned comrade from the Potomac, many miles downstream from Ball's Bluff.

Union soldiers in front of McClellan's Washington home on the night of November 3, 1861, celebrating his promotion to general-in-chief with a torchlight parade.

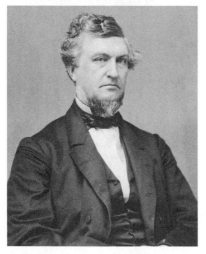

Senator Zachariah Chandler of Michigan, who introduced the resolution for a congressional committee charged with investigating the defeat at Ball's Bluff.

9

Shovel Them Under and
Let Me Work

❖ LATE THAT EVENING Confederate captors herded their growing flock of prisoners into Leesburg by way of King Street, where residents stood gawking and occasionally jeering. Surgeons found shelter for the more seriously wounded. Guards plucked the Union officers from the bedraggled column as it passed the lantern-lighted porch of the Mansion Hotel, escorting two dozen of them upstairs to General Evans's office. Evans stood before a roaring fireplace, brawny and long of limb. In a sympathetic tone he announced that he would permit his commissioned captives to provide themselves whatever civilized accommodations Leesburg offered: they had only to submit an oath to report as prisoners to General Beauregard, at Manassas, and to sign a parole against taking up arms against the Confederate government until duly exchanged. The Union officers declined, and after allowing them to warm their clothing by the fire for a time Evans sent for some wagons to take them away.[1] The hotel proprietor, an early Confederate volunteer (and an early deserter, as well) lost a sizable profit when the Yankee officers filed back out the door.[2]

A chilling drizzle commenced before dawn and soon escalated to a downpour, drenching both prisoners and guards as they plodded muddy roads toward Manassas. The prisoners suffered no more than their escort of Mississippi infantry, and in some cases less, for many of them had surrendered in their overcoats. At least half their guards lacked any uniforms at all, and none had been issued heavy clothing. Red mud lay ankle deep that night on the Little River Turnpike. That was the route the 8th Virginia had taken to Manassas in July, and the cavalcade of prisoners arrived at the Bull Run battlefield at sundown of the next day, sleeping on wet ground along the Warrenton Turnpike at the foot of Henry Hill. The next day they covered the final leg of their march to Manassas Junction, where they waited for the cars to take them to Richmond. In a driving rainstorm a South Carolina regiment, a battery of Louisiana artillery, and a Virginia cavalry company passed their soggy bivouac on their way to reinforce Evans.[3]

Curious rebel soldiers encircled them at the depot, peppering them with the questions common to such encounters — including why such seemingly friendly fellows had joined a war of conquest against the Southern people. Just as Franz Sigel's St. Louis Germans had told their Missouri captors the previous summer, most of the shoemakers and factory workers of Massachusetts, New York City, and Philadelphia replied that they had been "thrown out of employment and had nothing else to do." That seemed to soften the tension between the antagonists, and they chatted easily all day.[4]

Late that night a train pulled in to collect the prisoners in cattle cars, and the next morning they climbed out of the cars at the Broad Street terminal in Richmond. From there they marched through town, flanked by sparse rows of bayonets, to a tobacco warehouse near the banks of the James River. The tattered Bull Run prisoners who greeted them counted 24 officers and 657 enlisted men in their column, making a total of nearly 2,700 Yankees who had entered Richmond as unwilling guests since McDowell's calamitous campaign.[5]

The guards who had marched to Manassas with the Ball's Bluff prisoners lost the opportunity to glean the battlefield for spoils of war, but their comrades outfitted themselves nicely. Southerners who had shivered through the chilly autumn nights scoured the bluff for shoes, blankets, and clothing, including the waterproof chasseur overcoats shed by the California regiment and the thick chesterfields of the 20th Massachusetts, gaudy with scarlet satin linings. Refuse from the fighting clothed and equipped whole companies of Confederates.[6] Most of the booty went to the 17th Mississippi, which dressed itself in blue federal overcoats and forage caps, besides appropriating many of the discarded weapons. Even some of the Confederate officers donned U.S. uniforms to stave off the cold. Once the Federals retreated from Harrison's Island, some of Barksdale's men braved the bitter waters of the Potomac, scavenging for private plunder and diving for rifled muskets to replace their smoothbores.[7] The Yankees lost or tossed away as many as fifteen hundred weapons, the majority of them Springfield, Enfield, or Belgian rifles, and virtually all of them found their way into Southern hands.[8]

Union generals came swooping down on Edwards's Ferry the day after the battle, riding through clusters of disarmed, disheveled, and disrobed survivors who had spent a miserable night on Harrison's Island. Nathaniel Banks arrived early in the morning and took command of the field, bringing the first pair of two-star shoulder straps, but his three brigadiers preceded him. General Lander, who had been enjoying the comforts of Washington while he awaited another command, returned to his brigade a few hours behind Banks. In accordance with McClellan's orders, General Stone had spent Monday night and Tuesday morning shuttling troops across to the Virginia side as fast as they arrived, and Banks had continued the process until they had nearly twice as many men posted near the Dailey plantation as Evans had in his entire brigade. McClellan himself finally arrived at Poolesville that evening, riding out to the ferry after dark, fresh from a mournful interview with the president over Edward Baker's death.[9]

Evans sent Barksdale's lone regiment out to face those thousands of Yankees, for the 13th Mississippi had suffered the least during Monday's bloody work. In the pouring rain of Tuesday afternoon Barksdale brazenly attacked an open flank of the sprawling Union force with two companies. One of his lieutenants and a private died in the assault, but the gambit threw the entire enemy division on the defensive for the rest of the day.[10] General Lander meandered boldly but ineffectively about the field, sputtering and fuming theatrically until a bullet slapped into his boot. Throughout the day the blue host dared nothing more aggressive than skirmish fire from the 1st Massachusetts Sharpshooters, conducted at a distance accommodating their telescopic rifles.[11]

McClellan reached the observation knoll above Edwards's Ferry after dark on Tuesday night, and could not even begin to plan any action until daylight on Wednesday morning. He faced only Barksdale's pickets all day, for Evans withdrew his trains and the rest of his exhausted brigade to the upper reaches of Goose Creek again that morning. The reinforcements from Beauregard met him at the creek, but there they sat while Barksdale continued his bluff.[12]

Hoping for some coup like the capture of Leesburg to counterbalance Monday's losses, McClellan pondered the situation all day Wednesday. Howling winds tore out of the northwest and whipped across the floodplain, roiling the river violently enough to impede retreat, and Beauregard began planning an ambitious attack on the stranded division. Recognizing his plight, McClellan reluctantly ordered his troops back to the Maryland side that night. The windstorm churned the river dangerously, but more than four thousand men poled back to safety without a single fatality or a shot fired. In the end, the smooth withdrawal offered the only success McClellan could cull from the disaster; at least it played better than precipitous flight with the enemy in hot pursuit.[13]

Reports of the fighting at Ball's Bluff swelled to mythic proportions. Each side had committed between seventeen hundred and eighteen hundred men to the battle, but each credited the other with overwhelming force. A man in the 15th Massachusetts told the folks at home that the Yankees had faced "immense odds," and survivors' estimates of Confederate numbers started at ten thousand. Two years later an officer of the 20th Massachusetts met the adjutant of the 18th Mississippi in a Gettysburg hospital (the former missing a hand and the latter an arm), and the Bostonian scoffed at the Mississippian's recollection that there had been no more than two thousand Confederates on top of Ball's Bluff. The earliest reports from Leesburg, meanwhile, led Beauregard's headquarters to telegraph President Davis that Evans had captured a full six-gun battery and driven a dozen Union regiments into the river.[14]

Ball's Bluff dealt the Lincoln family a stunning blow, adding the death of a dear friend to the military reverse and political repercussions. Gone was Lincoln's old ally in the Springfield legislature, his colleague of prairie courtrooms, and his companion at a hundred dinners; Baker had shared Lincoln's last moments as a private citizen and had earned enough regard to lend his name to a son now dead. Observers detected the president's obvious distress — a reporter claimed that he stumbled out of the office, dazed, when the telegraph brought the news — and the first lady retreated to solitary mourning, refusing all visitors.[15]

The battle marked the third consecutive defeat for Union forces in three months, and it shook the national confidence just as hope had begun to revive among civilians and soldiers alike.[16] For a few days the public could find little real news, thanks partly to a government that had assumed arbitrary power over the nation's communications. Edmund Stedman, a correspondent for the *New York World*, rode out from Washington for firsthand information only to happen across Baker's quartermaster, Francis G. Young, and Young's wild version of the battle flavored his entire account. Stedman tried to telegraph Young's apocalyptic casualty estimate to his New York office, only to have the transmission intercepted and stopped by government operators. His report had to travel by mail, so the front-page story reflecting Young's chilling depiction of the disaster did not appear for more than a week, by which time the public had digested the tale in more manageable portions.[17]

As usual, the earliest stories brought vague accounts of victory. The next round of reports portrayed the casualties of October 21 as the required cost of a Virginia foothold on the upper Potomac, and represented the action itself as the beginning of the long-awaited offensive. On October 23 the *New York Times* heralded that offensive under a headline proclaiming "The National Troops Successful at All Points." The report buoyed public sprits briefly, and even encouraged some generals, but the next day the paper referred more soberly to the "important advantages gained by our troops." By the third day the *Times* headlines were admitting the "repulse of the Union forces" with "heavy losses," and news of Wednesday night's withdrawal only deepened the sense of pointless loss.[18] The Baltimore correspondent of the *New York Tribune* (the same individual who had convinced federal authorities to dismantle Baltimore's local government) complained that Ball's Bluff had "operated on the loyal thermometer of our city like an ice bath." Union soldiers waiting to launch a dangerous coastal operation from Hampton Roads fell into deep despair, anticipating for the first time the possibility of defeat. The gloom reached as far as the American embassy in London, where the grandson of John Quincy Adams read the list of casualties among his Harvard classmates, which filled him with an overwhelming sense of waste.[19]

Central and eastern Massachusetts lapsed into panic and grief at the casualty lists. Selectmen dispatched local agents to care for their communities' soldiers, while newspapers covered their front pages with somber headlines and gory elaboration. One man had lost three sons and two nephews at Ball's Bluff, announced a Worcester paper. That same journal, which routinely published grisly tales of workers mutilated in the machinery of local mills, offered a specific description of the painful genital wound suffered by a corporal of the 15th Massachusetts. A Fitchburg weekly speculated grimly that those counted as missing were probably dead, and then aggravated their families' distress by naming them.[20]

The large number of men captured and drowned caused immense anguish, and the wives of missing men besieged their husbands' comrades for information. Bodies washed up farther downstream every day, but time and the river rendered them increasingly difficult to identify. Sentries at the Chain Bridge, just inside the boundaries of the District of Columbia, dragged five bodies out of the water as late as November 2. One decomposing corpse, identifiable only as the body of a Massachusetts soldier, carried a locket bearing miniature photographs of a man and woman. A Boston jewelry company displayed the images in a storefront window until a passing businessman recognized the pair of portraits as a Worcester County man and his wife, now a widow, who had borne a child only days before the battle.[21]

When the extent of the failure finally emerged, Union-loving optimists struggled, as they had after Bull Run and Wilson's Creek, to transmute the blow into another valuable object lesson. A prominent light in the Massachusetts literati regretted the loss of friends in the battle, but he informed his mother that a defeat was "just what we needed. . . ." What he seemed to privately wish — and what many in his intellectual circle explicitly hoped — was that such setbacks might keep the conflict alive long enough to crush slavery as well as rebellion. So hinted the minister who buried Boston's Willie Putnam when he remarked that the death of that promising youth might have more meaning if the cause of Union could be linked to that of liberty.[22]

Newspapers started keening for "responsibility" as soon as they understood the extent of the reverse. Privately, most of those in a position to know put the blame on Baker, including some in Lincoln's official family. Lincoln was said to have offered Baker commissions as both brigadier and major general, and it seems to have been true. In some circles Baker was supposed to have been scheming for his own assignment to overall command of the United States Army, and that theory gained greater currency after the public announcement of Winfield Scott's retirement, on the first of November.[23] The appointment of a militarily inept politician to command the army would not have seemed unreasonable in many circles, especially if the ineptitude remained concealed. Baker had, after all, led a regiment in the Mexican War, and there was always the example of Frémont. Writing to his senior senator, an Ohio Republican lamented that the army had been "whipped at Bull Run — whipped at Ball's Bluff — whipped at Big Bethel. . . ." The only solution, as that abolitionist constituent saw it, was to replace McClellan with an antislavery Republican like Frémont, who could be trusted to go after the enemy with a will.[24]

Massachusetts officers who had arrived on the scene under General Banks, only hours after the disaster, had learned from their friends in the field hospital that the fault lay with Baker. That opinion seemed nearly unanimous, at least at first. One captain in the 2nd Massachusetts concluded that Baker had been so confident of his promotion that he had gone to glory in an effort to win a victory on his own hook, thereby justifying his elevation over McClellan. A lieutenant in the 13th Massachusetts considered Baker fortunate to have been killed rather than enduring the universal reproach he deserved for such costly impetuosity. Both those men had spoken to the wounded officers of the 20th Massachusetts, who had been in the thickest of the fight.[25]

Those were all private conversations. In public debate — on the floor of the Senate and in most newspapers — Colonel Baker's death seemed to have exempted him from censure. The administration still found it productive to cultivate public sympathy from the demise of popular officers, and Colonel Baker went to his grave on the Thursday after the battle in a state funeral that included an impassioned eulogy from his brother. The entire cabinet attended, and government came to a halt for a few hours to bid another new hero farewell.[26]

If the public demanded a responsible party, and Edward Baker had been absolved by virtue of apotheosis, Charles Stone and George McClellan stood next in line, and both were Democrats who showed no sympathy with abolition. *Frank Leslie's Illustrated Newspaper* wondered who had sent Senator Baker into the "jaws of death," borrowing a phrase from Tennyson's "Charge of the Light Brigade" to imply the incompetence of Baker's immediate superior — Stone. The *New York Herald* and Greeley's *Tribune* sowed preparatory prejudice against Stone: the *Herald* suggested that he had acted without orders, while the *Tribune* sought severe consequences for "so deplorable a lack of generalship," and actively promoted Francis Young's account, in which a blundering or duplicitous Stone had sent Baker to certain death.[27]

Taking advantage of the confusion attending the death of his colonel and the severe injury of his lieutenant colonel, Lieutenant Young accompanied the detail that escorted Baker's body to Washington, where he had already spent far more time than his superiors thought necessary. Only three days had passed since Stone had caught Young secretly selling government property; in another week Baker's successor would relieve Young on the grounds that he was "perfectly worthless," and Young would respond by deserting his post and heading back to Washington. In a few more weeks Young would find himself cashiered from the service, but in an effort to forestall that disgrace he used his time at the capital to curry favor with Baker's acquaintances and colleagues, including the bereaved President Lincoln, by spinning fabulous tales of Baker's death. Enthralled with the attention this won him, he composed a laudatory and largely vicarious memoir of Baker's last battle, submitting it directly to army headquarters as an official report and signing it with an exalted staff rank that he never held.[28]

Even before offering that account to headquarters, "Captain" Young (as he styled himself ever afterward) sent it to the *Tribune*, complete with implied criticism of General Stone for ordering Baker to attack Leesburg without the means of transferring enough troops to the Virginia shore. That report went back to Stone, to whom it should have been submitted in the first place. Stone had already seen his purported order to Baker quoted in a local newspaper: the general repudiated it as a "shameless forgery" and characterized Young's description of the battle as the "extraordinary production of a fertile imagination," observing as well that Young had owned the specific responsibility for Baker's transportation.[29]

Stone's refutation did not see the light of day for another twenty years, but its immediate publication would have helped little: the damage had already been done. Scandalous rumors flew through his division. At least one junior officer in the 20th Massachusetts considered Quartermaster Young a liar and a coward whose criticisms merited no credence, yet he still seemed to believe Young's charge that Stone had ordered Baker to cross regardless of feasibility, rather than allowing him the discretion to do so. That lieutenant blamed Stone for giving the command to an incompetent like Baker in the first place, and a few of his fellow subalterns probably concurred. Worst of all, there surfaced in that same regiment an allegation that General Stone had specifically refused to send Baker reinforcements, permitting the men at Ball's Bluff to be slaughtered, and that accusation soon reached hometown newspapers. Among the prisoners in Richmond (who would clearly have had no way of knowing about it) there even emerged a preposterous tale that, in that final hour after dark, Stone had personally ordered the boats to stop bringing men back from Ball's Bluff.[30]

Frank Buxton, the nomadic vendor of conflicting and inaccurate information, threw a dangerous light on such idle gossip in his next communication with General McClellan. Four days after Ball's Bluff, Buxton reappeared at Point of Rocks to report some thirteen thousand Confederates at Leesburg. That amounted to less than half his earlier estimate, but still four times as many men as Evans could have put in the field, even with his recent reinforcement from Manassas. Buxton implied that he had stopped at Manassas, where he claimed to have heard the victors jubilantly boast of sympathetic Confederate agents operating within the United States Army. Juxtaposing his earlier caution about large Confederate concentrations at Leesburg against the bloody repulse of October 21, he remarked in a tardy postscript that Stone "must have acted without proper information."[31]

While it may not have been Buxton's intention to specifically say so, the timing of his observations made it easy to deduce that some of the disloyal individuals of whom he spoke held substantial rank in the Corps of Observation — up to and including the commander of the division. Buxton's reports remained within McClellan's headquarters family, but the notion of traitors in high places — traitors in every possible place, for that matter — seemed to take firm control of the public mind in the autumn of 1861.

Suspicion had, of course, jaundiced political discourse for nearly a year. From the first declaration of secession, extremists on both sides of the issue had interpreted any doctrinal deviation as evidence of outright infidelity. With the outbreak of active hostilities, military oppression, mob violence, and the widespread detention of "spies" emphasized that intolerance. Through at least midsummer, though, outside certain wavering districts like Maryland and Missouri, only the most overt critics of either government had suffered severe consequences for alleged disloyalty; North and South, politically motivated assaults or arrests remained relatively rare. Virginia sheriffs bucked that trend in September, when they started collaring strangers with foreign or Northern accents as "suspicious persons," but at that juncture officials in the Confederacy still resorted to arbitrary arrests much less often than did those in the United States.[32] Mobs and federal soldiers had destroyed or cowed the most vehemently antiwar Northern newspapers by September, but six months into the fighting Southern critics could still denounce their new government. In East Tennessee, where Confederate authorities still governed a sharply divided population, the defiantly Unionist editor of the *Knoxville Whig* reported partisan atrocities and relentless oppression, but he published his stridently antisecessionist newspaper until October 24, when he closed at his own discretion.[33]

Voluntary restraint may have explained the infrequency of retaliation in the South, where the dominant slave culture had long repressed divergent opinion. Below the Potomac, the seeming tolerance of spring and summer began to disperse once the leaves turned color. A week or so before the battle of Ball's Bluff, Nathan Evans had attempted to quash dissension around Leesburg by imposing what amounted to undeclared martial law. He appointed a political inspector by the name of George Ish and empowered him to arrest anyone whose loyalty he questioned. Ish, a Loudoun County native who had just returned from a decade or more on the West Coast, apparently exercised his sudden authority with unbridled enthusiasm, much to the annoyance of many loyal Confederate citizens. On the night of October 18, after Evans's brigade had retreated to Oatlands, Ish deputized several citizens of the surrounding countryside, including at least one soldier from the 8th Virginia, and with that armed squad he proceeded to the farm of Alexander Davis, near Aldie. Davis, who had moved to Virginia from Connecticut about a dozen years previously, did not hide his Union sentiments: he had been one of only five voters in the Aldie precinct who had openly voted against secession. Davis barred the door to his house when Ish ordered him out, but the posse broke in and attacked him when he resisted, injuring him so badly that they did not even bother to take him into custody.

Appalled at such brutality, local justices interceded. County officials arrested Ish and those accomplices they could find, including the soldier from the 8th Virginia, charging them all with burglary and assault with intent to kill. Matthew Harrison, a Leesburg lawyer, wrote directly to the secretary of war, Judah Benjamin, to complain of Ish's injudicious appointment and his highhandedness, which had landed numerous unoffending citizens in jail. Benjamin inquired of Evans, who bemoaned the interference of such "civilian justices" and instinctively reverted to the now-standard accusation leveled against anyone who disagreed with national authority on either side: Squire Harrison was just another "disloyal citizen," Evans insisted, "as I judge by his well-known character." Evidently unaware either that Harrison had supported secession or that he served as a conduit for military intelligence to Richmond, Evans asserted that the attorney had always been a Union man and an opponent of the Confederacy.[34]

The paranoid excesses of a relatively isolated and heavily outnumbered outpost commander like Evans might be understood, if not forgiven, but Northern officials imitated his authoritarian rule. From McClellan's headquarters Allan Pinkerton kept busier than ever that autumn, casually ordering the arrests of Maryland and Washington citizens on the flimsiest of accusations, occasionally arresting the accusers as well, and disabusing prisoners' attorneys of any illusions that the Constitution protected their clients.[35] In Connecticut, one man was arrested as "a noisy secessionist," and another for allegedly uttering a hope that the Confederates would capture Washington. In Boston the U.S. marshal threw one traveler in jail because his trunk contained a "Canadian" army uniform, while a Maine man bound for Canada ended up spending nearly three months in prison for "incidental remarks" of a political nature that he made at a depot in northern New Hampshire. Neither the editors of "disloyal sheets" nor their contributors operated so long in the North as they did within Confederate territory, for the federal government cracked down early on those who disseminated "obnoxious and dangerous principles" or "secessionist teachings." Even women spent weeks confined in improvised distaff dungeons for no greater crime than voicing sympathy with the Southern cause. General Stone had backhandedly complained about unjustified arrests in his jurisdiction as early as October 10, perhaps because of a man who had been brought before him that very day under an absurdly vague charge of having communicated with the enemy.[36]

By late September the pace of arrests had accelerated, and the charges grew increasingly capricious; in many cases no one in the government seemed to know what their prisoners had been accused of. The surge of internment may have reflected broad public outrage over the arrest of Maryland's legislature: provost marshals soon began rounding up a new wave of young Marylanders whom they suspected of sneaking off to the Confederate army, and arrests for disloyal statements spread deep into the interior of the loyal states. The government preferred to keep its political prisoners out of public sight and mind, as well as out of reach, so island forts in various Northern harbors began filling up with citizens who were confined primarily because of their opinions. By the second half of

October a temporary encampment for some of those prisoners sprouted on Bedloe's Island, off Jersey City, where the world's best-known monument to liberty would rise a quarter of a century later.[37]

In October the State Department recorded nearly twice as many arrests as it had in September, and suspicion only deepened with the disaster at Ball's Bluff. An official of the Sanitary Commission who visited Washington at the end of the month considered it a "great misfortune that the North is not yet thoroughly purged of spies and traitors.

"I could name a dozen people in this city," he wrote, "whom I believe fully capable of conveying intelligence to the rebels." The entire North fell into hysteria over enemies lurking within the government and the military. With no more evidence than a nine-month-old anonymous letter offering ambiguous hearsay, Secretary of State Seward ordered a U.S. circuit court judge placed under surveillance, with guards around his residence to monitor his visitors, movements, and correspondence. Seward also stepped over cabinet boundaries again by directing a Treasury Department official to discontinue the judge's salary; that action was specifically prohibited by Article 3, Section 1 of the Constitution, but the president approved it nonetheless.[38]

General Banks and his excitable colonel at Point of Rocks, John Geary, took travelers into custody as far away from the Potomac as Frederick on the bare assumption that they intended to cross the river and communicate with the enemy. Banks arrested one Montgomery County man for writing a private letter to his father, who lived in Virginia, although the son explicitly noted in the intercepted letter that fear of arrest prohibited him from touching on political or military subjects.[39]

The federal government also used arbitrary arrest for more specific political purposes than the wholesale incarceration of potential enemies. Anticipating that the best chance their Maryland friends had of winning the November 6 state election was to steal it, Lincoln and his allies turned their new powers of detainment toward that end. By midautumn it was clear that Maryland would not — and could not — secede: the issue had become the continued prosecution of the war. Friendly newspapers characterized any who opposed the administration as members of the "peace" party, and a plurality of the state's sundry factions seemed to fit that description.[40]

Most of the potential peace candidates had already been lodged in Fort McHenry. An aged veteran of the War of 1812 agreed to run for governor under the main opposition party's standard; in fear that he might win, the administration exerted all the considerable pressure at its disposal. Those opposition newspapers that had not previously been silenced dared not editorialize too vigorously for fear of similar treatment. Roving patrols

of Union soldiers threatened to raid peace party rallies on the grounds
of perpetrating an "act of open hostility to the Government." Most of
Maryland's Union soldiers drew furloughs to go home and vote. Army
headquarters ordered military commanders to post guards at each polling place for the ostensible purpose of protecting the rights of Unionist
voters. More to the point, those guards had instructions to arrest "dis-
unionists" who dared approach the polls, and Unionist citizens stood by
to point out all the suspects — which proved easy enough, since the anti-
administration parties distributed ballots of a different color from those
of the "loyal" parties. Not surprisingly, considering his scruples about pro-
cedure, Charles Stone's troops appear to have made no such arrests, although their presence alone probably influenced the turnout in those pre-
cincts. Elsewhere, soldiers arrested disgruntled Marylanders all day long
before they could cast ballots against Lincoln's war, and Lincoln's favorite
candidates naturally swept the day. The voters arrested on election day
were nearly all released as soon as the polls had closed, for the government had achieved its purpose by preventing them from voting, and
would have found it difficult to levy credible charges against them.[41]

Lovers of liberty would see worse before peace returned, but for those
who cherished the Union above all else these were probably the blackest
days of the war. Every attack on insurgent forces had ended in abject failure, and the repeated discouragement had begun to exact a toll on the
war's most fervent supporters. Headlines had repeatedly announced the
most glorious victories only to revise them into disaster, until the best
news brought little solace. Important strategic victories like the bloodless
capture of Hatteras Inlet, on North Carolina's Outer Banks, barely regis-
tered with a public trained to cynicism. The premature report that Union
forces had reoccupied Lexington, Missouri, in early October only diluted
any reaction to the actual event eleven days later, and in any case General
Frémont's quixotic generalship in that theater disappointed nearly everyone. The enormous Confederate mistake with Kentucky excited far less
attention than the defection of the former vice president of the United
States and other prominent Kentuckians to Richmond, with their promises of thousands of Bluegrass Confederate soldiers. Southern morale
soared, while Northern spirits plunged.[42]

For those who wished to purge the government, the setback at Ball's
Bluff offered a convenient pretext. Some of Edward Baker's Senate colleagues were already drifting back into the capital after a season's absence, wondering why there had been no movement of the army beyond
that disastrous foray and looking for someone whom they might hold to
account. In that atmosphere of pervasive suspicion and faultfinding it
bode especially ill for Charles Stone to find himself even remotely impli-

cated by the sort of gossip circulating within his own division. Vulnerably situated as he was between an ambitious superior and the posthumously revered subordinate who bore the bulk of responsibility for the defeat, Stone offered an enormously inviting target. He realized as much, and he composed an interim defense for McClellan's eyes and for the written record, denouncing the fabrications of Baker's "friends" as well as pointing out Colonel Baker's failures of judgment and tactical transgressions.[43] Along with Stone's denunciation of Quartermaster Young's report, that document disappeared into headquarters correspondence for two decades, emerging for public consumption only after Stone's most powerful critics had gone to their graves.

On Wednesday morning, November 6, fog still hovered over the Potomac after the previous evening's rain when a party of Union officers and civilians approached the landing of Harrison's Island, fluttering a white flag for the observation of Confederate pickets on Ball's Bluff. From the other side appeared a comparable squad of Confederates wearing blue overcoats identical to those of the flag bearers. After mutual acknowledgments, the island band crossed to the Virginia shore in one of the boats that had ferried so many to their doom.

The civilians had come from New York to recover the body of Captain Henry Alden, of the Tammany Regiment, for the comfort of his family. With the assistance of their Virginia guides they scaled the heights in full view of their comrades on the island, for the leaves were falling fast. Heavy rains of the past few days had washed away much of the earth that a harried burial detail had scraped over the captain's body. The weather had not been cool enough to prevent decomposition, and the workmen wasted no time transferring the body to the coffin they had brought with them. The respective commanders of the details exchanged civilities, said their farewells, and by afternoon they had resumed their old positions to become enemies again.[44]

Duty along that length of the river returned to its former monotony, aggravated only by increasing cold and — for the Union soldiers — by the memory of that terrifying and humiliating defeat. Artists for the illustrated newspapers resumed sketching their romantic vignettes of soldier life on the upper Potomac, including one that appeared to be based on Captain Philbrick's ill-fated reconnaissance.[45] For weeks General Stone concentrated on restoring his command to its former efficiency. At his request McClellan sent a West Point brigadier to command Baker's regiments, which shed their spurious California designations for Pennsylvania numerals, and under more professional leadership they would earn renown as the Philadelphia Brigade that met Pickett's Charge. The new brigade commander, William Burns, immediately installed another quartermaster and preferred charges against Francis Young when he absconded to Washington. Young's successor set about repairing the lapses and omissions of Young's tenure — finding healthier campsites, restoring rotted equipment, and replacing the spoiled commissary stores that Young had probably bought in deliberate oversupply for resale at personal profit. General Burns also chastised Thomas Vaughn, the captain of the Rhode Island battery, for failing to equip his limbers with enough primers and shells.[46] Burns made no mention of Vaughn's curious absence at the opening of his first battle, but that circumstance (in addition to the woman who slept in Vaughn's tent, passing as his sister) may have figured in the captain's resignation, barely a month after Burns's reprimand. Throughout the division, the regiments that had suffered worst at the bluff drew better arms, fresh uniforms, and recruits from home. Artificers replaced the captured Rhode Island gun, as well as its horses and equipment, and the artillery company that sacrificed Lieutenant Bramhall to command that gun separated from the 9th New York State Militia to emerge as an independent battery with six ordnance rifles.[47] By November 8 the three brigades had recovered sufficiently to mount a grand review.[48]

While Stone nursed his division back to health, certain officers inside that division cultivated an assortment of grudges against him. Quartermaster Young rekindled the vendetta immediately after he was relieved from duty. Resuming the whispering campaign that he had waged since the battle, Young enlisted the adjutant and one captain of the California Regiment to compose sworn statements that they had read a direct order from Stone instructing Baker to "make a dash at Leesburg." One of the officers (both of whom, like Young, were headed for formal charges and early conclusions to their military careers) swore that the general signed the order with the melodramatically simple signature "Stone." From his absentee lodgings in Washington Young circulated these statements among other officers from Stone's division, indicating that he intended to have them published, and he said that if Stone denied the charge the officers of the California Regiment would produce the original order, which allegedly remained in their camp. With wide circulation by newspapers like Greeley's *Tribune,* Young's libels caught on in many circles, along with the embellishment that Baker had obeyed Stone's order despite considering it his "death warrant."[49]

Disaffection with General Stone began with that conspiracy of New York officers in the California regiment and spread quickly through the New York regiments, mutating as it grew. Late one Saturday night soon after the battle some officers of the Tammany Regiment sat drinking together when, suddenly, a captain lurched into profane soliloquy about Stone's loyalty. In a stage whisper so loud that it carried to the enlisted men's campfires, he denounced not only Stone but his own captured colonel, indicting them both as "God damned secessionist sons of bitches."[50]

Recurring disciplinary problems in the field and staff of the 2nd New York State Militia did nothing to ease Stone's relations with New York officers. Under Colonel George W. B. Tompkins the 2nd New York had behaved with noteworthy cowardice at Bull Run, where its officers set an example for the enlisted men by deserting the field before they even came under fire, and the regiment still harbored numerous fractious and irresponsible officers. The quartermaster of that regiment had proved as unreliable as Francis Young, earning early rebukes for his frequent vacations in Washington, and those absences continued after the battle, despite official disapproval. Colonel Tompkins not only overlooked his quartermaster's transgressions but imitated them, taking the regiment's ambulance with him on his own unauthorized absences, and finally Stone brought him up short. Tompkins failed to offer satisfactory excuses for either his own behavior or that of his quartermaster. When an inspector discovered that the quartermaster had never submitted any of the required accountings of his expenditures, Stone ordered Tompkins to relieve him immediately.[51]

Following Stone's attempt to reform the 2nd New York and its commander, the regiment's major wrote surreptitiously to New York congressman Roscoe Conkling, offering evidence that he hoped could be used against General Stone. Asking for personal anonymity, Major Joseph J. Dimock claimed that a lieutenant in the Rhode Island battery, whose commander had resigned after his dubious performance in the recent battle, was willing to recount how Stone had personally ordered him to cover Baker's crossing with his guns. Such testimony would have supported the damaging fiction that Stone had specifically ordered Baker over the river, thereby helping to shift the blame from Baker's shoulders to the general's.[52] By then Congress had created a joint committee to investigate the prosecution of the war, which provided vengeful subordinates like Major Dimock with a vehicle to use against their military superiors. Conkling passed Dimock's letter along to Ohio's senior U.S. senator, Ben Wade, the chairman of that committee.

Wade, a determined opponent of slavery, wore the grim, thin-lipped visage of a Komodo dragon. He and two other dedicated antislavery senators — Zachariah Chandler of Michigan and Lyman Trumbull of Illinois — returned to Washington well before the December session in order to lobby for another immediate battle with the Southern forces. Those three immigrant westerners, all New England natives, frequently expressed anxiety that the Confederacy would become too firmly established if the disaster at Ball's Bluff was allowed to stand as the last military endeavor before winter settled in. If the Confederacy survived, slavery would persist on the continent, and for those abolitionist solons that would have represented a moral travesty on top of a political tragedy.

Wade spoke with Lincoln and Montgomery Blair on Friday morning, October 25, and Blair arranged a meeting between Wade and McClellan for that evening. They convened at Blair's row house, just northwest of the executive mansion and about a block from McClellan's lodgings, on the corner of H Street and Sixteenth.[53] Chandler and Trumbull came by as well, and late that night they joined Wade to sit down with the young general. McClellan intimated that he, too, wished to bring things to a rapid finish, but with ambitious craft he implied that General Scott stood in his way, and the senators accommodatingly promised to press for Scott's retirement. McClellan probably offered no culprit for the Ball's Bluff affair, and especially not Stone; he had just informed his senior generals of Baker's culpability, but he may have found it inexpedient to point that out to men who had sat on Baker's side of the Senate chamber. McClellan had already taken the position that the troops had crossed the Potomac without his orders, though, and that may have done Stone some preliminary damage in the eyes of Capitol Hill inquisitors.[54]

Parting from the general early in the morning, the trio evidently remained in migratory conclave all weekend. None of them recorded any discussion of Ball's Bluff, but it would have been a difficult subject to avoid in the two or three days after Senator Baker's funeral. At Willard's the next morning, London *Times* correspondent William Russell overheard the first ominous whisperings that General Stone was suspected of treason for ordering Baker over the river. Russell's scathing account of Bull Run had helped to shake public confidence in Northern arms, but, remembering rumors about McDowell after that battle, Russell sardonically remarked that treason became "a common crime of unlucky generals."[55]

Wade, Chandler, and Trumbull appeared at the White House on Saturday night, pushing the president until midnight to remove Scott and encourage McClellan to action, and on Sunday night they met with Simon Cameron. Everywhere McClellan had nourished the notion that Winfield Scott's military usefulness had come to an end, as the president discovered on a late-night visit to McClellan's headquarters that weekend, and through the week he prepared a report on the feasibility of offensive operations. With the help of the radical senators, Scott went into retirement and McClellan ascended to overall command of the army by Friday.[56]

Soon the impatient senators who had collaborated on McClellan's pro-

motion saw reason to regret his rise, for the army lay just as inactive under him as it had under Scott, and because of McClellan's politics and his
softness on slavery, they suspected deliberate delay. McClellan, whose obsessive organizational habits had carried him to second place in his West
Point class, immediately sought to address the haphazard management of
army headquarters, diving into the details of reorganizing the entire army
as energetically as he had with the command that he now called the Army
of the Potomac. In his first fortnight as the nation's senior soldier he familiarized himself with the various departments, selected new commanders for the crucial states of Missouri and Kentucky, examined and criticized the recruiting of surplus cavalry regiments, composed an appeal for
expanding the military academy and establishing a school for staff training, and asked for administrative indulgence in a manner that suggested
he was being badgered to take the field immediately.[57]

The president pestered McClellan with plans and ideas for campaigns,
waylaying him at his headquarters on the corner of Nineteenth Street
and Pennsylvania, and at his home opposite Lafayette Square. McClellan
responded with little more than condescending equivocation, and one
night, while Lincoln and Seward waited for him at his home, McClellan
brushed past them without a word and went to bed. A rare success at Port
Royal, South Carolina, brought a brief surge of optimism shared even
by conservative cabinet members, but McClellan continued to organize
and drill his divisions. In official correspondence, he claimed that the
year's reverses (of which he singled out Bull Run and ignored Ball's Bluff)
demonstrated that Union soldiers owned greater courage than their opponents. In private letters he acknowledged instead the courage and discipline of the enemy's troops, and advised the same deliberate preparations and planning that had brought so much criticism down on his
predecessor.[58]

The public could hardly deny that McClellan had done his best to whip
his amateur army into professional shape. For any who doubted it he
scheduled a grand review near Munson's Hill, on the Leesburg Pike, for
November 20. The day dawned cool but bright — one of those last bit-
tersweet autumn days before the first snowfall. Thousands of citizens
crossed over the Potomac by carriage, horse, and foot to see the spectacle;
a promiscuous traffic jam crawled across the Long Bridge all morning. At
one point the cavalcade came to a complete halt, squeezing against one
side of the bridge as McClellan, his staff, and what one witness described
as "about two miles of cavalry" rumbled melodramatically past. A crowd
gathered a quarter of a mile deep on the perimeter of the massive parade
ground as some sixty-five thousand infantry, cavalry, and artillery prome-
naded this way and that under Irvin McDowell's immediate direction. A

score of field batteries roared salutes that filled the Virginia landscape with smoke. The president and McClellan cantered in review past the divisions (Lincoln's secretary thought his ungainly chief unusually graceful on horseback), and the whole spectacle came off without a hitch before a host of dignitaries foreign and domestic.[59]

The grand review may have demonstrated McClellan's success in organizing and training the army, but the sight of so many troops in full panoply only increased the frustration of those who longed for action against the enemy. Although President Lincoln exercised greater patience than the importuning radicals, and sometimes defended McClellan before them, he was one of those disappointed by McClellan's apparent lethargy. He offered McClellan strong, repeated hints, and about ten days after the grand review Lincoln gave the general a detailed list of questions about his own plan for a dual movement against the Confederates at Centreville from the Alexandria line and an amphibious force landed on the Occoquan River. During the intervening ten days the inaugural snow of the season had fallen — which, along with frost and frequent rain, compromised most of the roads leading into Confederate territory. McClellan considered the president's interrogatory during an unusually warm and dry December interlude, but he anticipated more seasonable weather and offered the idea little enthusiasm. His response alluded to a new plan of operations that would probably surprise both the enemy and "many of our own people," and while Lincoln may have found it encouraging that McClellan was planning anything, that new idea would ultimately leave his army idle through most of the winter.[60]

As he prodded his general for military action, Lincoln sought to appease the radicals of his party with some action of his own on the issue of slavery. On the eve of the congressional session he informed a friendly senator of his intention to attempt compensated emancipation in the remaining border states, and perhaps he hoped that the news would spread through the Senate. The Jacobin Club (as Lincoln's private secretary dubbed the most radical congressmen) seemed ignorant of Lincoln's idea when they concluded that they must take matters into their own hands if the country were to be saved — and saved as they wished. They lacked the authority to change presidential policy or direct the movements of the army, but they did possess the power to investigate and criticize those movements, and through that function they hoped to inspire a more enthusiastic and productive performance, with due regard for abolition.[61]

The Jacobins did not lack support for their radical vision, even in the lower ranks of the army. One first sergeant in a Massachusetts regiment — who had enlisted mainly to improve his social station and who expressed only the mildest reflections of patriotic devotion — nevertheless regretted Lincoln's apparent reluctance to address slavery directly. On reading the president's annual message to Congress, the sergeant sneered that "he don't talk nigger enough. . . . Nigger has got to be talked, and thoroughly talked to[o], and I think niggers will come out of this scrape free."[62]

Lincoln delivered his message to the second session of the Thirty-seventh Congress, which opened on December 2. On that day New York's Roscoe Conkling rose in the House of Representatives to submit a resolution asking the secretary of war to explain what his department had done to fix responsibility for the Ball's Bluff disaster. Later that week Zachariah Chandler suggested that the Senate conduct its own investigation into both Bull Run and "Edwards's Ferry." Ten days into the session, in an official tribute to Edward Baker, Senator Charles Sumner of Massachusetts remarked of Ball's Bluff that there was "a strong desire to hold someone responsible, where so many perished so unprofitably," but Sumner's eulogy reflexively acquitted his late colleague. Others, with grievances in the western theater, wanted the investigative list expanded to include affairs in Missouri, but Chandler resisted that, for it raised the specter of public inquiry into the radical darling, John Charles Frémont. Chandler argued the amendment down on the more judicious excuse of limited time and resources, but he revealed some partisan intent when he remarked on the unpopularity of the war among many army officers, who reportedly viewed it as a "damned black Republican" struggle. Ultimately an amendment suggested a joint committee, with three senators and four congressmen, and that proposal passed handily.[63]

On the morning of December 20 a sharp fight broke out between two brigades at Dranesville, leaving fifty men dead and a couple of hundred more wounded. It ended with the Confederates taking to their heels, but the affair sparked little comment even in nearby Washington. The Dranesville skirmish had no connection with the longed-for advance, and within hours of the victory General McClellan came down with typhoid, taking to his bed until early in the new year. The joint congressional committee convened for the first time that same day, in the Capitol room devoted to the Senate Committee on Territories. Five Republicans dominated the committee, providing it with a thoroughly Jacobin flavor, and Ben Wade took the chair.[64]

The Joint Committee on the Conduct of the War would survive throughout the conflict, but within days of its first meeting the chairman had contorted its errand of military inquiry into a mission to transform administration policy. With the very first witness, whom the committee interviewed on Christmas Eve, Wade began to exceed the limits of the committee's prescribed purpose by fishing for evidence that nothing stood in the way of an immediate attack on the enemy's Manassas fortifications. By the third day of testimony Wade had begun inquiring about the fate of runaway slaves who entered the army's lines.[65] A quorum of the committee met with the president in a New Year's Eve interview that Lincoln characterized as congenial, but an observer recorded that Wade severely reprimanded the president (and by implication General McClellan, who still lay critically ill) for military inaction and the absence of a slave policy.[66] Less than a week later the committee came back to meet Lincoln and his entire cabinet, calling by then for McClellan's outright removal from command; they had even chosen a replacement — Irvin McDowell, who had already testified in warm support of a winter campaign.[67]

McClellan's evident lethargy certainly angered the committee, but the real rub was his adherence to Democratic doctrine on slavery; men like Wade suspected him of avoiding a conclusive military victory that might force emancipation on a defeated South. Their reasoning made little sense, for winning the war quickly would have served as the best assurance against universal abolition, but they came to believe the same of many professional soldiers, and especially the graduates of West Point, whom they considered prone to political sympathy with the South. Senator Chandler stood ready to close the nation's military academy altogether. A more conservative colleague observed that the proportion of West Point officers who opposed administration policies only matched that of their volunteer counterparts, but even he supposed that 80 of the army's 110 brigadiers harbored Democratic sentiments.[68] Under Wade's leadership, the Committee on the Conduct of the War presumed to examine not only the competence of the army's generals, but their loyalty to both nation and party.

Theirs was not the first congressional examination into the politics of public servants. Since the previous summer the House Select Committee on the Loyalty of Clerks, chaired by Wisconsin congressman John Potter, had been sifting the city for traitors. The committee found no real wrongdoing, though it denounced a number of apparently innocent people; it also established a perfunctory examination process for prospective clerks that one applicant considered a partisan "humbug." Even a close friend of the Lincoln family feared the results of his examination because he was a Democrat, and he observed that the examiners needed little reason to reject someone. Potter's committee implicated the White House gardener and a couple of doorkeepers at the executive mansion, all of whom seemed perfectly loyal: after he was dismissed, the gardener volunteered in the army and was commissioned as a lieutenant.[69]

The Committee on the Conduct of the War pursued the same crusade at higher echelons of government service, exercising even greater vigor than Potter's committee but no better discretion, thereby dispensing widespread injustice. Through neither coincidence nor accident, almost all of the blame assessed by that preponderantly Republican body fell on lifelong Democrats.[70]

Ben Wade, and probably a majority of his committee, wanted McClellan deposed early in the game, but because of his relative inaction they could point to no great failure worthy of investigation. Instead, they wove a case for errors of omission by soliciting opinions from every officer who would admit that one or another element of a military campaign could be accomplished in winter as well as in summer. They found Robert Patterson more inviting prey because of his timid performance against Johnston, and by ignoring all the contributing factors (including their own insistence on a premature offensive campaign) the committeemen managed to lay the full weight of Bull Run on him. "The principal cause of the defeat on that day," they conveniently concluded, "was the failure of General Patterson to hold the forces of Johnston in the valley of the Shenandoah."[71]

Patterson's failures made him an easy mark, but in settling the responsibility on him the committee had not touched McClellan. Charles Stone posed a much more appealing prize, for he was not only McClellan's immediate subordinate and his respected colleague, but something of a friend to the commanding general. The committee started grilling other officers about Ball's Bluff two days after Christmas, and with their second witness, General McCall, they opened the matter of fugitive slaves. Knowing that Stone had returned at least a few Maryland slaves to their owners, some committee members apparently intended to entrap him on that issue, and McCall gave them some ammunition by admitting that he sent all contrabands to Washington, as his instructions required. McCall's division occupied rebellious Virginia, however, where contraband status applied, while Stone's camps lay entirely within Maryland, where the Fugitive Slave Law still dictated the return of slaves to their masters.[72]

Congress was wrestling just then with a bill that would bar army officers from restoring slaves to their owners on penalty of dismissal, and that debate involved Charles Stone particularly. Someone in the 20th Massachusetts had complained directly to Governor John Andrew, without resort to the chain of command, that Stone's policy had forced officers of that regiment to surrender fugitive slaves, presumably to Maryland owners. Andrew appealed to Massachusetts senator Charles Sumner, who denounced Stone on the floor of the U.S. Senate and ridiculed him for his recent defeat on the Potomac.[73]

"Brigadier General Stone," Sumner told his presiding officer on December 18, "the well-known commander at Ball's Bluff, is now adding to

his achievements there by engaging ably and actively in the work of surrendering fugitive slaves. He does this, sir, most successfully. He is victorious when the simple question is whether a fugitive slave shall be surrendered to a rebel."[74] Within five days Stone read the speech in the *National
Intelligencer;* it served as his first notice of any discontent on the subject,
and he instantly responded with a fierce personal letter to the senator. Alluding to Sumner's notorious failure to defend himself against an outraged Southern congressman five years before, Stone called the senator "a
well known coward" and accusing him of sniping away "from a safe distance in rear" while Stone was busy facing an armed enemy in the field.[75]

Radicals in and out of Congress had already convicted Stone in their
minds. Horace Greeley, the willing dupe of Quartermaster Young, had devoted his *Tribune* to Stone's condemnation ever since the battle. Now he
worked behind the scenes to impugn Stone's competence, his compas-
sion, and his loyalty, complaining that he had rebuffed requests from survivors who wished to recover the remains of Union soldiers and alleging
that he seemed too friendly with the enemy. In Stone's defense the *New
York Times* explained that after the story on the recovery of Captain
Alden's body Stone had been besieged with appeals for similar favors,
which he had ultimately been compelled to refuse. Much of Stone's correspondence with the enemy, which Greeley touted as evidence of uncertain
devotion to the cause, emanated from just such missions of mercy, but
Greeley would hear none of that. He snipped out the *Times* article and
mailed it to Ben Wade with snide remarks about the refusal of Stone's
"stalwarts" to accept any evidence against their hero.[76]

Asked when it would be convenient for him to testify, Stone objected to
choosing the date. The committee initially suggested December 30, and
Stone replied that one day was as good as another, but the new year came
without a reply. Brigadier General Daniel Harvey Hill, a West Pointer
whom Stone held in high regard both personally and professionally, had
taken over for Nathan Evans at Leesburg. Knowing Hill well, and perhaps
calculating that his deeply religious nature would leave him less likely to
launch an attack on a Sunday, Stone chose the first Sabbath in 1862 to
dash down to Washington for a conference with McClellan. While he was
there he asked the committee to hear him.[77]

In his introductory appearance Stone made no friends. He resisted the
committee's now-routine request for his opinions on an offensive campaign, contending that only the commanding general owned enough information to formulate such an opinion. He denied that he ever gave
Baker a direct order to take his troops across the river, contrary to the numerous newspaper reports that credited Quartermaster Young's account.

He criticized the use Baker made of available transportation, as well as the failure to ferry the reinforcing troops over at Smart's Mill.

Stone vehemently refuted the accusation that he had ever sent refugee slaves back to secessionist owners, calling it a "slander." The topic remained a sore spot with Stone, who explained to the committee that the intrusion of Massachusetts politicians in the matter of fugitive slaves had undermined his authority within the division. He pointed out that state and federal statutes prohibited him from protecting Maryland slaves against recovery by their masters, and at least one of the committee's radicals bridled at Stone's assertion that he would not act otherwise "until you gentlemen change the laws."[78]

The day after Stone's appearance before the committee, Roscoe Conkling vilified him again in Congress. Complaining of McClellan's refusal to launch his own investigation into the defeat at Ball's Bluff, Conkling questioned both Stone's competence and his constancy. In light of the reckless accusations, Stone asked headquarters whether it would not be prudent to ask for a court of inquiry, or to at least offer an analysis of Conkling's "extraordinary batch of misstatements." With far greater concern for avoiding political trouble at headquarters than for Stone's reputation, one of McClellan's staff advised him to keep quiet.[79]

Stone's detractors lined up to volunteer their testimony before the committee, which called a procession of witnesses who had privately evinced dislike for the general, including Major Joseph Dimock of the 2nd New York State Militia. One witness who did not appear, oddly enough, was the Rhode Island lieutenant whom Dimock had conspiratorially offered as a witness on the subject of Stone's orders to Baker, and that lieutenant's absence left it open to question whether Dimock had quoted him correctly. In any case the major delivered lengthy testimony about Stone's correspondence with civilians and soldiers across the river, the crossing of Confederates' wives at the fords, and the passage of slaveowners — with their slaves — to the islands. He described a universal lack of confidence in Stone since the battle, and repeated the comments of officers and men who considered him a traitor. Dimock's most enticing submission, in the view of the Republican committee members, may have been his remark that within Stone's jurisdiction the conflict was a "very civil" war.

"It is conducted upon peace principles on our side?" asked Republican Daniel Gooch, of Massachusetts, in what a judge would have considered a leading question.

"More so than any war I ever before heard of," replied the cooperative Dimock.[80]

George Tompkins, Dimock's colonel, corroborated his major's assertions about Stone's unpopularity within the 2nd New York, with which

Stone and the brigade commander had experienced so much trouble. Tompkins, whom Stone had so recently called to account for his own misbehavior, repeated the "evidence" of Stone's disloyalty by alluding to mysterious communications and civilian traffic. In describing his commander, Tompkins said that "we do not know whether he is what he seems to be," and although he later added that "I cannot say exactly that I doubt his loyalty," he plainly insinuated that he did. He commented suspiciously on at least one riverside encounter between Stone and Confederate officers, and although Tompkins considered himself the senior colonel in the entire volunteer service he professed not to know whether that meeting was appropriate. He did admit that he personally lacked confidence in Stone's ability to handle troops, and as though to support that point he claimed that he had served under a similar officer at Bull Run: "a fine man, but no soldier." It was not clear whom he meant to malign with that remark: it was Tompkins whose regiment had been singled out for particular misconduct at Bull Run — and especially among its officers, some of whom had gone straight home from the battlefield, never to return to duty. The continued bad habits of the 2nd New York suggested that the principal incompetent was Colonel Tompkins himself. McClellan had hoped for months that Stone could encourage Tompkins to resign, offering to drop the accumulated charges against him if he would go home quietly.[81]

In delivering his Parthian volley at the division commander whom he credited with trying to drive him out of the service, Tompkins nearly redeemed his own shattered career. In gratitude for Tompkins's assistance in finding witnesses, and probably at Wade's insistence, the sergeant-at-arms who collected testimony for the committee misinformed the president that Stone had preferred charges against Colonel Tompkins in retaliation for his testimony. In fact the charges against Tompkins had come first, some of them filed by other officers in regard to Bull Run and some for financial misconduct preceding the formation of the committee, but in ignorance of that President Lincoln authorized the secretary of war to make Tompkins a brigadier general. McClellan's report on the colonel's distasteful record nullified the promotion, though, and Tompkins disappeared into well-deserved civilian obscurity that spring.[82]

Eight of the committee's thirty-nine Ball's Bluff witnesses belonged to the hostile 2nd New York State Militia, from the colonel and chief instigator down to a private whom one of the officers had prodded to testify. By far, the 2nd New York provided the most damaging and fanciful testimony against Stone: the private even swore that he had seen General Stone rowed across the river for a clandestine visit inside Confederate lines. At least two of the 2nd New York officers who offered incriminating testimony about Stone had to be released from arrest in order to travel to Washington. In their examination of Ball's Bluff the committee interviewed no more than three men from any other single regiment, including those units that had actually participated in the fighting that the congressmen were supposed to be investigating. Except for a handful of senior officers whom the committee called as a matter of course, most of the witnesses appear to have volunteered themselves.[83]

Among the perjurers who filed in to settle old scores with Stone came Edward Baker's former quartermaster, Francis Young. He had never held any rank higher than lieutenant, but — more than two weeks after he had been dismissed from the army altogether — Young introduced himself to the committee as a brigade quartermaster and commissary holding the grade of captain. In his egocentric perversion of the Ball's Bluff story it was he, rather than Colonel Baker, who received Baker's orders from Stone, and Young characterized those orders as positive verbal instructions to cross troops over the river as soon as firing erupted on the Virginia side. For the better part of one day the committee members listened to Young's heroic saga of his services to his gallant colonel — their lamented colleague — but for all their alleged study of the testimony they never detected the flagrant inconsistencies between Young's account and those of nearly everyone else.[84]

The congressmen did, however, detect the contradictions between Stone's testimony and that of some of his critics, and particularly those from the 2nd New York, but they seemed to account for the discrepancies by doubting Stone's veracity. Since the proceedings remained secret, Stone was not immediately able to learn who had testified, let alone what they had said. That robbed him of the basic right to face his accusers and cross-examine them, and it allowed the witnesses to fabricate whatever they wished. Had Stone been permitted so much as a glance at the witness list, he ought to have been able to force even so biased a panel as Wade's committee to acknowledge that many of those who spoke against him did so from impure motives.[85]

While the committee collected testimony on the Ball's Bluff engagement, Senator Chandler received a letter from one of Stone's former superiors that he could have interpreted as veiled criticism of Stone. Brigadier General Joseph K. F. Mansfield, who had been an officer longer than Stone had been alive, fumed at the promotion of less-experienced soldiers over his head. In what may have been an effort to ingratiate the emerging radical plurality in the Senate, which confirmed the appointment of general officers, Mansfield informed Chandler that now would be a good time to purge the army of all those poor brigadiers that Lincoln had appointed. "In the first place no appointment should be confirmed where a fugitive slave has been sent into the enemies territory by order of our officers," Mansfield wrote. "When I was in command in Washington I would never suffer it." Mansfield was probably responding to reports of such incidents in more radical newspapers, but in his zeal for a war of abolition Senator Chandler might have missed the distinction that Stone was dealing with the slaves of technically loyal owners.[86]

Mansfield wrote his letter the day after the War Department passed into the hands of a new secretary, and that succession seemed to provide the pretext for Mansfield's communication. In his ten months at the department Simon Cameron had presided over increasing inefficiency and some questionable business arrangements that he characterized as "mistakes" or "complications," and his first annual report had earned the president's ire. Other cabinet officers had been expecting Cameron's departure since early December, and before the middle of January Lincoln gently exiled him as the new minister to Russia. He allowed the disgraced secretary to depart as though by Cameron's personal preference, and Cameron initiated some gossip that he had been permitted to choose his own successor, but no truth attended either of those rumors.[87] In his place Lincoln appointed Edwin McMasters Stanton, a lawyer of national repute and a former attorney general in James Buchanan's cabinet. Stanton had been a Democrat all his adult life, albeit an unrelenting advocate for the Union, but if his party affiliation concerned Republicans they soon found him politically sound. Treasury secretary Chase smoothed the way for Stanton, sending his own carriage to arrange one interview for a radical senator who later broadcast his complete satisfaction with the appointee.[88]

Although a Democrat, Stanton stood ready to wage war against slavery as well as against secession. That was the crucial inclination demanded by radical congressmen from the outset, and by increasingly less radical factions as 1862 opened. At mid-January moderate Republican editors were expounding on the transformation of rebellion into revolution, hinting that "the bayonet is pushed only where *ideas* direct." By the end of the month some state legislatures had begun open (if necessarily nonbinding) discussion of universal emancipation as a means of both winning the war and assuring more harmonious reunion.[89]

Such talk thrilled men like Ben Wade. He and Zachariah Chandler joined Stanton for breakfast at Cameron's house the morning that Stanton's nomination was to be presented to the senate, and he recognized the nominee as a potentially powerful ally in the war against insufficiently radical generals.[90] On his first official day as secretary, Stanton called the entire Committee on the Conduct of the War to his office for a long conference. Something said in that meeting may have prompted Wade's committee to return the following day and make an official inquiry about whether the title of general-in-chief then held by McClellan bore any statutory authority, and whether the army could legally offer a higher rank than major general. That gambit toward unseating or superseding McClellan fizzled, but Stanton's influence on the subject may have contributed to McClellan's removal from the position exactly seven weeks later.[91]

The news of Stanton's appointment brought him congratulations from radicals who seemed attuned to his sound attitude on slavery. Worthington Snethen, Baltimore's unswervingly Republican correspondent for Greeley's *Tribune*, sent a fawning promise of unflinching support, and urged Stanton to kill slavery "by the sword," predicting that if he did so "it will die in Maryland by sympathy." Joseph Medill, the *Chicago Tribune* editor who had helped put Lincoln in the White House, sent Stanton a list of generals whom he suspected of political empathy with the enemy — or worse — and his list included Stone.[92]

Stanton almost immediately started belaboring McClellan with instructions to reopen Washington's hampered communications. He wanted the Baltimore & Ohio Railroad cleared, which would have required an aggressive lunge by both Banks and Stone, and he wished to see the Confederate batteries on Chesapeake Bay neutralized, to revive the capital's river transportation. Then, on January 27, Lincoln presented McClellan with a unique document that he called "President's General War Order No. 1," announcing a simultaneous advance of all the armies in Virginia, in Kentucky, and on the Mississippi. Suddenly it appeared that the more demanding Republicans, the president, and the converted Democrat in the War Department were all pulling in the same direction.[93]

The Jacobins made good use of their new friend. One week into Stanton's tenure, Wade sent the three most radical of his committee members to the new secretary's home "to communicate to him additional testimony in relation to General Stone." Stanton instantly called Stone back to Washington, and the general hastened there with the impression that McClellan wanted to discuss a plan that he had devised for capturing the Confederate force at Leesburg. Instead, Stanton informed him that his loyalty had been impeached by witnesses before the Committee on the Conduct of the War, and he sent Stone back to the committee as though to clear the matter up. The secretary had already ordered McClellan to relieve Stone from the command of his division, though, and to place him under arrest — and not the arrest in quarters that officers were usually accorded, but the close confinement of a common criminal. The arrest order bore the date of January 28, only the day after the radical subcommittee came to Stanton's house, and before Stone had arrived to answer the charges. When Stanton handed the order to McClellan he conceded that he had made it out at the solicitation of Senator Wade's joint committee. McClellan did not act on it immediately, leaving Stone ignorant of his intended fate.[94]

Armed only with the general accusations that the senators afforded him, Stone defended his conduct as vigorously as he could. They portrayed his failure to reinforce Baker from Edwards's Ferry as evidence of his disinclination to win the battle, and he invited them to examine the ground before rendering judgment on the feasibility of such a maneuver. Senator Wade waved that plea aside with the remark that none of the committee members were "military men."

"But you judge military men," Stone retorted.

"Yes, sir," Wade admitted, "but not finally." Then he alluded to the allegation that Stone carried on "undue communication with the enemy by letters that had passed back and forth."

"That is one humiliation I had hoped I never should be subjected to," replied Stone. "I thought there was one calumny that could not be brought against me." He reminded Wade that as inspector general of District of Columbia militia and as chief organizer and commander of the district volunteers he had done more than any single man to protect the capital from an insurgent threat. The volunteers that he raised were the only ones in the city until the ninety-day militia started coming in, he pointed out, and he led them as the spearhead of the first federal invasion of Virginia soil. So forcefully did he express his frustration at having to prove his loyalty to a panel of men who had never "exposed a little finger for the defence of the Government" that the stenographer failed to include some of his more pungent comments.[95]

In a controlled rage Stone launched into a voluble defense of every form of communication he had had across the river, from the flags of truce to bury and recover the dead to the passage of comforts and money to those of his wounded who lay in the hands of the enemy. He and his officers made useful observations whenever they carried flags of truce to the other side, he told the committee, and at some length he explained the value of relaying private letters over the river for the information he was able to glean from them: he knew the very house where General Hill lived, he said, and the room that he occupied. Though he made no specific mention of it, he had also detected genuinely disloyal residents on the Maryland side through letters that he examined in passage.[96]

Stone also failed to mention a letter that he had written to C. H. Powell, who lived near Poolesville. Powell had given him an unsealed message to William H. Gray, of Leesburg, for delivery through the picket lines, and Stone had read it as he read all such correspondence. He declined to deliver it for fear that it might compromise Gray with the Confederate authorities, but he wrote back to Powell to applaud him for the tone of his letter, which Stone said "does you much honor for it is loyal and honest and bold." Stone composed that note on the same day that Edwin Stanton ordered his arrest, and it was probably found at his headquarters by his successor. The message landed eventually in the president's papers, and its retention there hints that someone saw evil intent in Stone's correspondence with the acquaintance of a prominent citizen in Confederate Leesburg, despite the general's commendation of Powell's loyal language.[97]

Stone rather handily disposed of an insinuation that he had allowed the enemy to build Fort Evans without interference, but by then the committee showed signs of boredom. Wade concluded the interview in relative haste, considering that Stone was the only witness on that day's schedule.

"I believe we have stated to you all that we deemed of importance," he told Stone, "and of course we are very glad to hear your explanation." Stone seemed unconvinced of their implied satisfaction, and he reiterated some of the details of his defense, prompting Wade to remark that "we have not forgotten your explanation."[98] Stone left the room, whereupon the committee promptly abandoned its pretense of judicious deliberation. Although Stone had refuted every imputation for which they would offer him enough details, Pennsylvania congressman John Covode made a motion for the committee to refer the conflict to Stanton as "a conflict of testimony." As innocuous as that sounded, it amounted to another vague indictment for treason, and the communications between Stanton and the committee reveal that Stone's guilt had been decided before he even appeared for his second interview. Covode had some experience at using committee investigations to discredit Democrats, and in the absence of its most prominent Democrat, Andrew Johnson, the committee concurred without evident dissent, assigning Covode to carry the paperwork to the War Department personally.[99]

Charles Stone's military career had passed its zenith, at least in the United States. McClellan leaked the news that Stanton had chosen Stone for a scapegoat, and when Attorney General Bates learned of it he sent Stanton a belated note to dissuade him from doing the bidding of Wade's committee, but Stanton probably would have ignored Bates in any case.[100] For another week McClellan kept Stanton's order in his pocket, resisting the will of his new superior with unusual nerve, considering that the same radicals who sought Stone's head would have preferred to have his. Then came Jacob Shorb, a Leesburg native who had been apprehended by Colonel Geary's pickets as he tried to slip north of the Potomac.

Shorb rambled interminably about Stone's disloyalty once he deduced what his interrogators wished to know. He described Stone as the toast of the Confederate leadership, who considered him the only gentleman on the Union side of the river — an accurate representation of the sentiment in Leesburg, as it happened, but no sign of treason. Shorb corroborated all the stories that the most venomous witnesses from the 2nd New York had initiated, repeating each tale so mechanically and in such matching detail as to suggest either leading questions or direct coaching; in the process he included an inordinate amount of personal conversation with prominent personalities whom a transient like himself would seldom have encountered. Allan Pinkerton interviewed Shorb personally after he had been in custody for six days, but a captain in Geary's regiment had apparently spent a lot of time with the prisoner beforehand. Although Pinkerton noted that Shorb "did not impress me very favorably," he sent McClellan a report that someone later endorsed as a "full account of Gen. Stone's treachery." McClellan passed that report on to Stanton — who, on learning that Stone was still free, gave McClellan peremptory orders to arrest him immediately.[101]

Still unaware of Stanton's earlier instructions to relieve him of his command, General Stone lingered in Washington awaiting orders to return to his Corps of Observation, which he hoped to lead in a sudden coup against Hill's isolated division. He attended a grand White House party on the night of February 5. After dinner on the evening of February 8 he left his wife and daughter at their apartment in Captain Clary's house and walked over to Willard's Hotel, where he and Colonel Wistar met a railroad man in his room. For at least four hours they discussed the layout of railroads in the Confederacy, presumably in preparation for the grand advance, and when they parted, after midnight, Stone returned home to find Brigadier General George Sykes pacing before his door while a squad of Regulars stood nearby. His pleasure at seeing his old friend soon evaporated when he learned that Sykes had been sent to arrest him. Sykes warned him that he was to be sent to Fort Lafayette, in New York harbor, affording him enough time to gather some clothing and say goodbye to his family before leading him away. At sunrise of February 10 a lieutenant and two detectives turned Stone over to the commander of Fort Lafayette — another old friend from the Mexican War who exploded in astonishment when he recognized the latest prisoner for the administration's dungeon of dissidents. Thus did one of the army's best and most senior brigadiers begin twenty-seven weeks of cold, damp confinement, initially in isolation even from the brother-in-law who attempted to act as his attorney, and without the slightest outline of a specific charge.[102]

Having gained apparent ideological control of Congress and, with

Stanton, a devout convert inside the administration, Republicans intent on turning the war to a radical social agenda now declared war on those Democrats who supported only their nationalist political aims. Henceforth, resistance to abolition would raise questions of loyalty to the government. The Era of Suspicion had begun.

The announcement of Stone's arrest and the publication of amorphous doubts about his loyalty launched a flood of additional volunteers with testimony to offer. Most of the new information came second- and third-hand, often reflecting the suggestions of newspaper accounts. The publicity also attracted a few more witnesses for the Committee on the Conduct of the War, including that private from the 2nd New York State Militia who claimed to have seen Stone cross the river and disappear, alone, into enemy lines.[103]

Stone's arrest shocked the army's professional officers, who respected him greatly and accurately perceived him as a victim of partisan politics. Even Harvey Hill, the Confederate commander in Leesburg, scoffed at the notion of Stone as a traitor to his flag. No old Regulars doubted Stone's absolute loyalty to his government, and many of those men understood from personal experience that national loyalty could easily abide alongside the most vehement disagreement with the administration in power. William T. Sherman attributed the suspicion to Stone's long antebellum friendship with William Whiting, a Confederate general, but he supposed that Stone would never have been singled out had he won the battle of Ball's Bluff. Military mistakes had now become crimes, he noted.[104]

Brigadier General Phil Kearny blamed the Ball's Bluff defeat on McClellan, evidently for having relieved the pressure on the Leesburg Confederates by abandoning McCall's expedition to Dranesville. Kearny, who hated McClellan, concluded that the commanding general had chosen to sacrifice Stone in lieu of enduring an inquiry into his own shortcomings, satisfying political pressure for a scapegoat without jeopardizing his viability as a future presidential candidate.[105]

Colonel Cogswell, who had last commanded Baker's force on Ball's Bluff, returned from a Southern prison a couple of weeks after Stone's arrest and began broadcasting an unequivocal defense of his former commander. He clearly held Edward Baker responsible for the poor disposition of troops on the bluff, and for the ultimate disaster. Cogswell's outspoken defense of Stone surely cost him the hope of promotion to any grade the U.S. Senate would have to confirm, but his comments failed to rouse the curiosity of Senator Wade's committee, which never asked for his testimony.[106] Anything he might have told them would probably have gone unheeded anyway: the congressmen demonstrated much less interest in the inconvenient observations of those who actually fought in the battle than they did in the vindictive fables of skulking malcontents like the officers of the 2nd New York.

Abraham Lincoln's two younger sons lay perilously ill with fever that February, distracting the president from administrative details. His new secretary of war did not disturb him with the information that he had arrested an accomplished and devoted general on evidence that Stanton himself — one of the foremost attorneys in the nation — could not have failed to recognize as pathetically flawed. Such constitutional minutiae had ceased to trouble federal authorities, however, and Stone lingered in confinement in New York for more than six months. He appealed repeatedly for the formal charges that were his due, without official response. A California senator tried to wring some information about his arrest, to no avail, but in the closing days of the session Congress finally took up the subject of releasing political prisoners. Thanks to the California senator, that discussion also yielded a rider to an appropriations bill requiring the release of all army officers who had been in arrest more than thirty days without charges. That bill became law on July 17.[107]

Edwin Stanton kept Stone imprisoned until the last possible moment. The thirty-day limit began only with the passage of the law, and exactly thirty days later, on August 16, the adjutant general issued the order for Stone's release. Stanton refused to restore Stone's reputation, though, asserting only that the army's active campaign in Virginia precluded any trial. The law also demanded that any arrested officer should have formal charges filed within eight days, but Stanton never met that requirement, nor did he supply any excuse for the failure to specify an accusation. *The Rebellion Record,* a popular periodical, did venture to publish "charges" that reflected the rampant innuendo of the Committee on the Conduct of the War, thus convincing many readers that government officials had serious reason to suspect Stone of treachery.[108]

For five more months Stone languished, without orders, at his father-in-law's Washington home. In January Ambrose Burnside, the new commander of the Army of the Potomac, appointed him to preside over a court martial, but a War Department order relieved him from that duty as soon as Stanton learned of the appointment. A few weeks later Burnside's successor, Joseph Hooker, applied for Stone as his chief of staff, but Stanton refused him that post as well.[109]

The Committee on the Conduct of the War invited General Stone for another interview on the night of February 27, 1863. They were about to see General McClellan in the morning, and perhaps they sought ammunition for that encounter. Stone held nothing back, for he deemed McClellan partly responsible for his downfall by then, both for his failure to warn him about McCall's withdrawal from Dranesville on the day of Ball's Bluff and for neglecting to press for a trial after he had been arrested. He kept the appointment reluctantly, for his wife lay dying at home, but he had evidently determined to make the most of his appearance. The details of his testimony imply that he had finally been made privy to the more damaging testimony against him, and he methodically rebutted each and every accusation through a long winter's evening. He returned to the Clary home late that night, only to discover that his wife had died.[110]

In April the joint committee published its reports, testimony, and minutes, which moved the *New York Times* to remark that the injustice Stone had suffered "will probably stand as the very worst blot on the National side in the history of the war." The next month Stone finally drew orders to report to General Banks, down in the Department of the Gulf, and in July Banks appointed him as his chief of staff. In Louisiana he met and married a young Southern woman whose family's politics did nothing to improve his professional standing. After nearly six months of good service in his new position, as he and General Banks were about to begin a major campaign up the Red River, Stone wrote to Abraham Lincoln to ask if there was not something the president could do or say to relieve the cloud over his name. Stone's only answer came in orders from Lieutenant General Ulysses Grant, who had just taken overall command of the army. Grant relieved Stone from his post, and a few days later Stone's perennial tormentor, Edwin Stanton, summarily mustered him out of the volunteer service, depriving him of his general's star and reducing him to his Regular Army rank of colonel. The demotion came so soon after Grant's order as to imply that Grant and Stanton had discussed the sequence. Lincoln may have been privy to it as well, for he began a rather unsympathetic reply to Stone's appeal on the day after Stone was stripped of his volunteer commission. That fragment, which Stone never saw, betrayed that even the president of the United States did not find the evidence against him convincing — yet Lincoln never deigned to interfere.[111]

Late in August of 1864, after two more inactive seasons, Colonel Stone traveled down to the Petersburg front and reported to the Fifth Corps to command a brigade that included his own 14th U.S. Infantry. Barely a week later he took temporary command of his division, but most of the time he worked under his former juniors in rank. As Stanton knew, without at least a volunteer appointment as brigadier Stone had no hope of gaining further distinction. Nearly three years of unwarranted persecution finally took its toll, and rumors soon started circulating around Army of the Potomac headquarters that Stone was losing his mind. It was said that he heard men calling out "Ball's Bluff" as he passed, and that he imagined himself the subject of universal gossip. He wrote a wry note to General Meade, theatrically asking Meade to have him shot for the atrocious crimes that newspapers had even recently credited to him. Three weeks into his last field command, with his fortieth birthday looming to accentuate the obscurity of his assignment, he resigned the permanent colonel's commission that many Regular officers would have sacrificed a limb to secure.[112]

For all the energy he had expended on behalf of an ungrateful nation, Charles Stone finished its greatest conflict as a civilian. Only a foreign power would ever trust him enough to reap the full benefit of his talents.[113]

Epilogue

❖ CHARLES STONE had served his country faithfully and well, but under a government that had dispensed with the rule of law even his stellar record could not save him. Ben Wade, Zachariah Chandler, and the other Radical Republicans who wished to transform a war of national unity into an abolition crusade casually destroyed Stone's reputation as a means of bending Congress, the army, and the country to their will. Edwin Stanton deliberately scuttled Stone's career to win the endorsement of those radicals, and he denied the discredited general a conspicuous post thereafter, as though any visible accomplishment of Stone's would cast implicit reproach on the man who had jailed him. Stanton's vindictive obsession also suggests that Stone's mere survival as a high-ranking officer posed a bitter reminder to that cabinet minister of his own ruthless nature — from which Mary Surratt and others would suffer even more harshly in 1865.[1]

The "very worst blot on the National side," as the *New York Times* called Stone's maltreatment, spread a broad swath of shame across the government and the army, ultimately staining both George McClellan and Ulysses Grant for passively abetting Stanton's truculence. The affair tarnished even Abraham Lincoln, who refused to act. Considering the president's frequent intervention on behalf of less worthy soldiers who were actually guilty of misbehavior, his impassive acceptance of a grievous wrong against so devoted an officer does Lincoln much discredit — which may help explain why so many of the sixteenth president's admiring biographers have ignored Stone's ordeal.[2]

In fact, despite the undeniably difficult responsibilities he assumed in 1861, Lincoln probably deserves a less friendly assessment of his entire first year in office than he is usually accorded. In his zeal to preserve the Union he abandoned statecraft, exploiting the delicate issue of Fort Sumter and committing the nation to a bloodbath far worse than he or any of his advisors ever envisioned. At the time, his belligerent course promised no better result than maintaining the territorial integrity of the United States at the expense of weakening the Constitution, and with no initial hint of eliminating slavery.

In his mission to preserve the nation's geographical boundaries, Lincoln quickly violated his oath to "preserve, protect, and defend the Constitution of the United States." He did so in the executive power that he assumed, in the increased federal authority that he imposed in order to prosecute the war, and in his arbitrary suspensions of constitutional liberties. By sheer military might his proxies deposed the duly elected legislatures of two states of the Union. If he did not resurrect the Roman custom of dictatorship in a time of crisis, he did introduce a modified form of the concept in a republic that would previously never have borne it. Lincoln's relative restraint and benevolence in the application of unconstitutional decrees may bear on the assessment of his character, but such factors have no relevance in determining the basic illegality of his actions. His precedent in the arbitrary curtailment of constitutional rights can only weaken individual liberty by giving more autocratic executives an example to expand upon.

Lincoln gradually arrogated so much authority to his office that his own dominant party dared not pass that power on to a member of the opposition. When the Democrat Andrew Johnson succeeded Lincoln and resisted Radical Republican aims, a Republican Congress and Supreme Court quickly curtailed presidential powers through legislation, judicial interpretation, and political maneuvers, including the first exercise (and the first abuse) of the power to impeach a president. Unfortunately, no retroactive restraint could restore the antebellum intolerance to authoritarian government. In 1919 the Supreme Court ratified the wartime abolition of such inconveniences as the First Amendment in *Schenck v. U.S.*, which Justice Oliver Wendell Holmes Jr. famously summarized with an inept analogy to shouting "fire" in a crowded theater. Fifty-eight years after the allegedly liberal Holmes was nearly killed at Ball's Bluff, he still subordinated his regard for constitutional liberty to his terror of military defeat.

Of course, this was not all Lincoln's fault. Secessionists had circumvented the political process before he ever came to Washington, propelling the two sections toward a collision that the majority of citizens doubtless wished to avoid. Lincoln still might have averted the clash had he been willing to negotiate a peaceful separation, but he represented a nationalist faction only slightly less intransigent than the Southern fire-caters. Culmination of a peaceful settlement would have demanded truly inspired statecraft: instead, Lincoln elected to risk a confrontation at Fort Sumter even though his personal emissary, Stephen Hurlbut, had assured him that it would end in violence. If Lincoln believed that a demonstration of executive will would restore Southern loyalties, he not only ignored Hurlbut's conclusions but made an enormous mistake in political strategy, for his aggressive post-Sumter militia levy crystallized Confederate nationalism more than any other single incident, including his own election. By the end of his first year in the White House he had probably begun to understand the depth of his misjudgment on that point, although he may not yet have begun to imagine how ghastly the consequences would be.

Until the attack on Fort Sumter, loyal citizens across the country considered the withdrawal of the seven recalcitrant cotton states a perfectly satisfactory solution to the persistent national tension over slavery. They clearly supposed that the Union would be stronger for their departure, if smaller; they seemed content to allow the border slave states to remain, if they chose, perhaps because the unsavory institution seemed moribund there.[3] Had the full human cost of enforced reunion been apparent in the spring of 1861, let alone the constitutional price, support for a negotiated separation might have prevailed. Even Lincoln conceded, five months into the conflict, that a peaceful division would be the prudent course if the last of the border states insisted on seceding.[4]

It would be fruitless to speculate on the historical ramifications of that discarded option. There is, however, no convincing reason to expect that it would have proven any more traumatic than the division of the original thirteen colonies from their Canadian counterparts — and especially if an early settlement had limited the Confederacy to those first seven states. A proportional partition of the western territories by latitude, for instance, might have settled the most inflammatory issue — slavery in those territories — by giving each section permanent jurisdiction over its portion. The Missouri Compromise had contained that conflict for a generation with a similar division, only to have the dispute revived by congressional interference, but national division would have made the compromise irrevocable.

The cost to slaves of delayed freedom vastly complicates modern speculation about peaceful separation. Economic studies have long suggested that Southern slavery might have remained viable indefinitely, but those studies tend not to account for the political upheavals that might have attended secession. More peaceful emancipation on some scale seems at least to have been feasible.[5] The withdrawal of Deep South congressmen inevitably threatened the survival of national legislation protecting slave property in the remaining states, and the repeal of fugitive slave laws would have encouraged even more slaves to escape from the loyal slave states, further weakening the institution there. Meanwhile, just as isolation hastened the end of apartheid government in South Africa, the international stigma and external economic pressures of an increasingly enlightened world ought eventually to have driven Confederates, however reluctantly, to a voluntary abolition that internal economics and cultural indoctrination made them resist. Such alternative approaches to emancipation would have allowed decades of further suffering for the four million slaves of 1860, as well as for their future offspring, and the subtraction of such suffering from the saving of about 620,000 lives now poses an insoluble calculation. The prevailing attitudes of 1861 might have made such mathematics easier.

Except for prolonging slavery, a formal political split between the sections of the United States might not have produced unmitigated misfortune. The mere willingness to consider separation would have cooled the crisis. Allowing the most militant slave states a peaceful departure would have allayed the Southern planters' suspicion that the ruling party in the federal government intended to destroy their way of life, thereby offering a foundation for future peaceful relations. The interposition of an international boundary might also have sped the erosion of slavery in the Confederacy by surrounding it with territory in which it could no longer be enforced. Secession by mutual agreement might well have encouraged further division of the country into several smaller republics, as many charged during and after the secession crisis, but those republics might also have recombined in a loose confederation similar to the modern European Economic Union. Such a union could have peacefully wielded still more pressure to discourage the continuation of so primitive a tradition as slavery.

Slavery provided the root cause of national tension, but the real conflict concerned its theoretical extension into the territories. The existing institution in the Southern states played no acknowledged part in the secession crisis, and the emancipation for which Lincoln and his war earned such retroactive credit carried no weight whatever in the decision to fight. Had an unbroken succession of coordinated Northern victories ended the war before its second spring, Abraham Lincoln's name might not now evoke the image of the liberator that he became, almost incidentally, through the stubbornness of Southern resistance. Instead, he would probably be remembered as a nationalist hero, or as a tyrant who trampled on the Constitution, or as a contradictory admixture of the two, depending on the political orientation of the critic.

The real praise for ending slavery is due those Radical Republicans who otherwise deserve censure for their amateur military meddling and disingenuous machinations. Their bullying and posturing smoothed a road over territory that Lincoln would otherwise have found difficult to tread, however willingly he finally did traverse it. Only extremists like them greeted the war from the first shot as an opportunity for ending slavery. The man who eventually proclaimed emancipation explicitly disavowed their abolitionist dream at the outset: on the day he was inaugurated, Abraham Lincoln announced his readiness to perpetuate slavery in return for restoration of the Union. Crediting his pugnacity after Fort Sumter with abolition motive presumes incredible foresight on his part, as well as casting doubt on the sincerity of the assertion he made exactly six weeks before.

In Maryland and Missouri that spring and summer, the excesses of Lincoln and his agents so worsened animosity toward the federal government that Lincoln risked losing those states despite the relative loyalty of their legislatures and their citizens. Injudicious military appointments and oppression only aggravated delicate situations. In Missouri overzealous federal functionaries assailed the legitimate state government, permanently surrendering the moral advantage in order to gain temporary military superiority, and the arrogance of their regime spawned some of the war's worst brutality. In Maryland the imprisonment of potentially dissident legislators and the shadow of bayonets over the ballot box suggested ultimate mistrust in the democratic process, notwithstanding Lincoln's later tribute to government of, by, and for the people.

Before the war had grown very old Richmond authorities began to suppress political freedom and civil liberties in the Southern states, but that hardly absolved the Lincoln administration, which undertook its own repressions prior to and independently of the Confederacy.[6] Each government justified its constitutional infringements in a frantic atmosphere of military peril. Both in Washington and in Richmond, that atmosphere emanated from the initial confrontation in Charleston harbor — which Lincoln chose to exploit rather than defuse — and from his mobilization on the excuse of that confrontation. Lincoln therefore bore considerable responsibility for creating the environment that encouraged repression on both sides, as well as holding primary responsibility for the transgressions under his executive authority. Jefferson Davis sinned similarly, and ultimately exceeded Lincoln in centralizing authority, but his satellite presidency did not produce any precedents that survived the Confederate government, while Lincoln's actions became prominent features in the nation's political tradition.

Any appraisal of Lincoln's decisions in 1861 is deeply influenced by the viewpoint of the observer, for political perspective and personal values bear heavily in balancing considerations of human life, human bondage, and individual liberty. Deliberation on his performance remains incomplete, however, without recognizing that other courses were open to him — whatever Confederate leaders might already have done, or might do thereafter.

While Charles Stone languished in Fort Lafayette, the politically suspect George McClellan trained his army and groomed generals to lead it. Many of those generals either shared their chief's politics or admired him on a level that transcended politics. With his motives questioned and his chief lieutenants doubted at every turn, McClellan gathered the army for the grand spring campaign to Richmond, swinging around Joe Johnston's Centreville line by water to attack the Confederate capital on the right flank. Nathaniel Banks started up the Shenandoah Valley, and John C. Frémont descended into the mountains of western Virginia, combining with Banks to threaten Richmond from its left flank.

The infantry division that General Stone had molded and trained marched into Virginia under a new commander, then doubled back to follow the Army of the Potomac, with which it would establish a bloody reputation and win great glory for those veterans who survived. Abraham Lincoln mourned a dead son, tried to mediate between increasingly polarized factions, and groped for some means of extracting ultimate good from the devastating cataclysm that he had played so significant a part in bringing upon his country. As the struggle entered its second year that ultimate good began to reveal itself, and Lincoln would embrace it to convince the nation that his war was worth the price.

APPENDIX 1

ORDERS OF BATTLE

APPENDIX 2

BIOGRAPHICAL SKETCHES

NOTES

BIBLIOGRAPHY

ACKNOWLEDGMENTS

INDEX

Orders of Battle

First Bull Run, July 21, 1861

Union Forces, Department of Northeastern Virginia, Brig. Gen. Irvin McDowell

First Division, Brig. Gen. Daniel Tyler
  1st Brigade, Col. Erasmus D. Keyes
  2nd Brigade, Brig. Gen. Robert C. Schenck
  3rd Brigade, Col. William T. Sherman
  4th Brigade, Col. Israel B. Richardson
Second Division, Col. David Hunter
  1st Brigade, Col. Andrew Porter
  2nd Brigade, Col. Ambrose E. Burnside
Third Division, Col. Samuel P. Heintzelman
  1st Brigade, Col. William B. Franklin
  2nd Brigade, Col. Orlando B. Willcox
  3rd Brigade, Col. Oliver O. Howard
Fourth Division (not engaged), Brig. Gen. Theodore Runyon
Fifth Division, Col. Dixon S. Miles
  1st Brigade, Col. Louis Blenker
  2nd Brigade, Col. Thomas A. Davies

Confederate Army of the Potomac, Brig. Gen. P. G. T. Beauregard

1st Brigade, Brig. Gen. Milledge L. Bonham
2nd Brigade, Brig. Gen. Richard S. Ewell
3rd Brigade, Brig. Gen. David R. Jones
4th Brigade, Brig. Gen. James Longstreet
5th Brigade, Col. Philip St. George Cocke

6th Brigade, Col. Jubal A. Early
7th Brigade, Major Nathan G. Evans
Reserve Brigade, Brig. Gen. Theophilus H. Holmes

Confederate Army of the Shenandoah, Brig. Gen. Joseph E. Johnston

1st Brigade, Brig. Gen. Thomas J. Jackson
2nd Brigade, Col. Francis Bartow
3rd Brigade, Brig. Gen. Barnard E. Bee
4th Brigade, Brig. Gen. Edmund Kirby Smith
1st Virginia Cavalry, Lt. Col. J. E. B. Stuart

Wilson's Creek, August 10, 1861

Union Army of the West, Brig. Gen. Nathaniel Lyon

1st Brigade, Maj. Samuel D. Sturgis
2nd Brigade, Col. Franz Sigel
3rd Brigade, Lt. Col. George L. Andrews
4th Brigade, Col. George W. Deitzler

Confederate Forces, Brig. Gen. Ben McCulloch

McCulloch's Confederate Brigade, Col. James M. McIntosh
Arkansas State Troops, Brig. Gen. Nicholas Bartlett Pearce
    Missouri State Guard, Maj. Gen. Sterling Price
Third Division, Brig. Gen. John B. Clark Sr.
Fourth Division, Brig. Gen. William Y. Slack
Sixth Division, Brig. Gen. Mosby Monroe Parsons
Seventh Division, Brig. Gen. James H. McBride
Eighth Division, Brig. Gen. James S. Rains

Ball's Bluff, October 21, 1861

Corps of Observation, Brig. Gen. Charles P. Stone

1st Brigade, Brig. Gen. Frederick W. Lander
    19th Massachusetts, Col. Edward Hinks
    20th Massachusetts, Col. William R. Lee
    1st Massachusetts Sharpshooters, Capt. John Saunders
    7th Michigan, Col. Ira B. Grosvenor
2nd Brigade, Brig. Gen. Willis A. Gorman
    1st Minnesota, Col. Napoleon J. T. Dana
    2nd New York State Militia, Col. George W. B. Tompkins
    34th New York, Col. William LaDew
3rd Brigade, Col. Edward D. Baker
    1st California, Lt. Col. Isaac Wistar

2nd California, Col. Joshua Owen
3rd California, Col. DeWitt Clinton Baxter
5th California, Col. Turner G. Morehead
Unassigned Infantry
   15th Massachusetts, Col. Charles Devens
   42nd New York (Tammany Regiment), Col. Milton Cogswell
Cavalry
   3rd New York Cavalry (4 companies), Col. James H. Van Alen
   Putnam Rangers, District of Columbia Volunteers, Capt. George
      Thistleton
Artillery
   Battery I, 1st U.S. Artillery, Lt. George A. Woodruff
   Battery B, 1st Rhode Island Light Artillery, Captain Thomas Vaughn
   Company K, 9th New York State Militia, Capt. Thomas B. Bunting

Confederate Seventh Brigade, Col. Nathan G. Evans

13th Mississippi, Col. William Barksdale
17th Mississippi, Col. Winfield Scott Featherston
18th Mississippi, Col. Erasmus R. Burt
8th Virginia, Col. Eppa Hunton
Virginia Cavalry Battalion, Col. Walter H. Jenifer
1st Company, Richmond Howitzers, Capt. John C. Shields

APPENDIX 2

Biographical Sketches

ROBERT ANDERSON (1805–1871). After his graduation from West Point, in 1825, Anderson served continuously in the artillery, and in 1860 President Buchanan assigned him to the command of Fort Sumter in hopes that his Southern heritage would ease tensions with Charleston secessionists. He adhered to his flag, though, and thus served reluctantly as Lincoln's instrument in transforming the crisis into a war. After the surrender Lincoln made him a brigadier general and gave him command of his native Kentucky, but once that state sided with the Union Anderson retired from active duty.

EDWARD DICKINSON BAKER (1811–1861). Born in England, Baker moved to the United States as a child and befriended Abraham Lincoln while they were both serving in the Illinois legislature. He commanded a regiment during the Mexican War and later moved to the West Coast, where he was elected senator from Oregon as a Republican. He raised a regiment in 1861 and took the field as its colonel while retaining his Senate seat, but he was killed in his first engagement, at Ball's Bluff, where his incompetence contributed substantially to the Union defeat.

NATHANIEL P. BANKS (1816–1894). Banks rose from poverty to become Speaker of the U.S. House of Representatives and governor of Massachusetts. His prominence as a Republican contender for the presidency may have led to his appointment as a major general of volunteers despite his lack of training or experience. He commanded troops in Baltimore and later in western Maryland, where he oversaw the arrest of the Maryland legislature in September, 1861, and came to the aid of Charles Stone's division after the Ball's Bluff repulse. His later military exploits in Virginia and in Louisiana almost all resulted in disaster, and in 1865 he returned to politics.

EDWARD BATES (1793–1869). An early resident of St. Louis and one of Missouri's leading Whigs, Bates became a Republican after the 1856 election and was considered for the party's presidential nomination in 1860. Lincoln appointed him attorney general, and he officially supported the president's arbitrary arrests, but the senseless persecution of citizens like Charles Stone led him into confrontations with more radical cabinet officers. His relatively conservative viewpoint fell out of favor as the doctrine of the Radical Republicans began to prevail, and he resigned after the election of 1864.

PIERRE GUSTAVE TOUTANT BEAUREGARD (1818–1893). This Louisiana native served in the engineers from his graduation from West Point in 1838 until he resigned in February of 1861 to take a commission as brigadier general in the new Confederate army. He oversaw the reduction of Fort Sumter and then commanded in northern Virginia, where with the help of Joseph E. Johnston's Army of the Shenandoah he routed the Union army at First Bull Run. As a full general he later commanded Confederate armies on the field of Shiloh, on the coast of Georgia and South Carolina, and before Petersburg, Virginia.

FRANCIS P. BLAIR JR. (1821–1875). As a young man Frank Blair moved to St. Louis to practice law with his brother, Montgomery Blair. Elected to Congress as a Free Soil Democrat, he later became a Republican. In 1861 he served as the Lincoln administration's principal agent in Missouri, advising the appointment of Nathaniel Lyon and, later, John C. Frémont as commanders there. Blair's underlying social conservatism ultimately led to his defeat by a Radical Republican, but in the meantime he rose to the rank of major general in the army and commanded two infantry corps. He returned to the Democratic fold after the war.

MONTGOMERY BLAIR (1813–1883). Blair graduated from West Point in 1835 but resigned from the army to study law. He practiced and served as a judge in St. Louis before removing to Maryland. Like his brother, Frank Blair, he gravitated from the Democratic to the Republican Party over the extension of slavery, and his support for Lincoln won him appointment as postmaster general. He fell out with the Radical Republicans, though, and resigned in 1864.

SIMON B. BUCKNER (1823–1914). Resigning from the army after eleven years of service and a distinguished career in the Mexican War, Buckner went into business until taking command of Kentucky's State Guard during the secession crisis. He attempted to maintain Bluegrass neutrality, but when his state chose the Union Buckner chose the Confederacy, accepting a commission as brigadier general. His superiors abandoned him at Fort Donelson early in 1862, and Buckner surrendered to his old friend Ulysses Grant.

BENJAMIN F. BUTLER (1818–1893). Until the eve of the Civil War Butler clung to the Southern wing of the Democratic Party, casting a ballot for Jefferson Davis at the party convention of 1860, but at the outbreak of war he took a commission as brigadier general of Massachusetts militia. In that capacity he violated his orders to put Baltimore under military rule, and as a major general of volunteers he established the habit of taking the slaves of rebel owners into his camp as "contraband of war." He ordered the expedition that ended in the defeat at Big Bethel, and later in the war he outraged Southerners with his occasionally draconian rule in New Orleans. In 1864 he demonstrated his ineptitude in the campaign against Richmond and Petersburg, but after the war he took advantage of his conversion to Radical Republicanism, inventing the phrase "waving the bloody shirt" by doing so, literally, in an appeal to Union sympathies.

FRANK LACY BUXTON (dates unknown). A British subject whose real name appears to have been William Saunders, Buxton worked for George McClellan as a spy, but his reports proved wildly inaccurate and he was eventually imprisoned for supplying similar information to the Confederates.

SIMON CAMERON (1799–1889). A machine politician with a history of bribing his way into office, Cameron secured the secretary of war's seat in Lincoln's cabinet by throwing his Pennsylvania delegates to Lincoln during the convention. His management of the burgeoning War Department proved so careless that even if he was not guilty of outright malfeasance it was easy to understand why everyone thought he was. He avoided disgrace by accepting the diplomatic post of St. Petersburg, Russia, and he repaid Lincoln's lenience by delivering Pennsylvania in the 1864 election.

ZACHARIAH CHANDLER (1813–1879). Chandler's political experience was limited to a term as mayor of Detroit until he was elected to the U.S. Senate in 1856, and he achieved distinction only with the emergence of the Radical Republicans. He used his membership on the Joint Committee on the Conduct of the War to further both personal and party ends, and his sudden prominence illuminated dissolute tendencies toward the bottle and bombast. He continued in the Senate until 1875 and was reelected just before his death.

SALMON P. CHASE (1808–1873). Chase was born in New Hampshire and graduated from Dartmouth College, but he gained his reputation in Ohio. He left the Whigs to join the Liberty Party in the 1840s, and in 1848 he helped found the Free Soil Party, under the banner of which he went to the U.S. Senate the next year. As a Republican, Chase was elected governor of Ohio in 1855. Like Seward, he was a major contender for the nomination in 1860, and Lincoln consoled him with the Treasury Department. He often seemed out of his element there, but he used his office to continue influencing military and political policy. When it appeared that Chase might challenge Lincoln for the nomination in 1864, the president appointed him chief justice of the Supreme Court.

PHILIP ST. GEORGE COOKE (1809–1895). A native of Leesburg, Virginia, and an 1827 graduate of West Point, Cooke was better known for his relatives than for his service. While Cooke remained loyal to the Union and was promoted to brigadier general, his son became a Confederate brigadier and his son-in-law, J.E.B. Stuart, rose to major general in the Confederate cavalry service. He should not be confused with Philip St. George Cocke (1809–1861) — another Virginian and West Point graduate, but a Confederate brigadier.

ELMER E. ELLSWORTH (1837–1861). Ellsworth earned some renown as commander and drillmaster of a Zouave company before the war, and he neglected his law studies in Lincoln's office to pursue that avocation. In answer to Lincoln's call for troops he organized several New York fire companies as the 11th New York Zouaves and led them in the invasion of Alexandria on May 24, 1861. At the head of a squad of his men he burst into a hotel there to tear a Confederate flag from the rooftop, and as he returned with that prize the hotel proprietor killed him, giving the North a handy martyr.

NATHAN G. EVANS (1824–1868). Evans (West Point, 1848) served in Texas with the 2nd U.S. Cavalry, resigning at the outbreak of war to accept a staff commission in the army of his native South Carolina. While still a major he effectively commanded small brigades at Leesburg and at Manassas, but his best day came at Ball's Bluff. Thereafter his star dimmed, and although promoted to brigadier general he turned intemperate and insubordinate.

JOHN C. FRÉMONT (1813–1890). Though without military education, Frémont was commissioned in the topographical engineers in 1838 and earned the nickname "Pathfinder" for his explorations of the American West. He mapped not only U.S. territory but Mexican, and when the Mexican War began he was in California, where he played a prominent role in organizing the Bear Flag Republic, but his disputatious conduct led to a court martial and his departure from the army. The Republican Party ran him as its first candidate for president, and his reputation as a radical led to his appointment as a major general in 1861. His administration in Missouri and his later commands in western Virginia all ended in political or military disaster. Frémont threatened to run against Lincoln for the Republican nomination in 1864 but dropped out of the race.

JOHN W. GEARY (1819–1873). After commanding a Pennsylvania regiment during the Mexican War, Geary moved to California, where he became mayor of San Francisco. After an unpleasant tenure as territorial governor of Kansas he returned to Pennsylvania. He raised a regiment in 1861 and was assigned to service along the Potomac under Nathaniel Banks. His pickets intercepted the spurious documentation of a planned Confederate invasion of

Maryland, which precipitated the arrest of the Maryland legislature. Pompous and boastful in oratory, and often downright vicious as a disciplinarian, Geary tended to collapse in panic at the first sign of an enemy attack. In 1862 he was promoted to brigadier general, and eventually he seemed to gain control of his nerves.

HORACE GREELEY (1811–1872). As publisher of the *New York Tribune,* one of the most widely distributed newspapers in the nation, Greeley exercised immense political influence with his strident editorials. He supported Lincoln's candidacy in 1860, then belabored the new president for speedy military action against secession and for a liberal emancipation policy.

THOMAS HICKS (1798–1865). A proslavery Whig until the 1850s, Hicks was elected governor of Maryland as a candidate of the American Party — the Know-Nothings. He held office until 1862, vacillating before the Baltimore mobs of April, 1861, and he reluctantly authorized the destruction of railroad bridges to keep federal troops from inciting further mayhem by traversing the city again. His successor as governor appointed him to fill an unexpired term in the U.S. Senate.

DANIEL HARVEY HILL (1821–1889). After graduating from the military academy in 1842, Hill spent seven years on active duty, earning two brevet promotions during the Mexican War before resigning to become a college professor. He reentered military service as colonel of the 1st North Carolina, in which position he exercised successful field command at Big Bethel and won a promotion to brigadier general. Late in 1861 he took over the defenses of Leesburg. As a major general he commanded divisions under Robert E. Lee, and as a lieutenant general he led a Confederate corps at Chickamauga and Chattanooga. He returned to the field of education after the war.

JOSEPH HOLT (1807–1894). Holt, a Kentucky Unionist, served as postmaster general under President Buchanan until the secession crisis, when he was appointed secretary of war to replace the perfidious John B. Floyd. He conferred with President Lincoln about the defense of Fort Sumter, and Lincoln later named him judge advocate general, in which capacity he bore responsibility for some of the more conspicuous injustices of the military commissions.

EPPA HUNTON (1822–1908). A lawyer, militia brigadier, and delegate to Virginia's secession convention before the war, Hunton raised the 8th Virginia and became its colonel. Despite persistent ill health, he led his regiment at Manassas and Ball's Bluff. He was captured at the end of the war as a brigadier general. In 1873 he entered national politics, serving four terms in Congress and three years in the U.S. Senate.

CLAIBORNE FOX JACKSON (1807–1862). Like Abraham Lincoln, Jackson was born in Kentucky, migrated west, served as captain of his company in the Black Hawk War, and served numerous terms in the legislature of his adopted state. Elected governor of Missouri in 1860, he attempted to maintain a neutral position until Nathaniel Lyon declared war on the state. When Lyon advanced on the capital at Jefferson City, Jackson fled with the army and most of the legislature. The Unionist remnant of the Missouri secession convention then met to declare the governor's chair vacant, installing the brother-in-law of Lincoln's attorney general as provisional governor.

JOSEPH E. JOHNSTON (1807–1891). Johnston, an 1829 graduate of West Point, was quartermaster general of the U.S. Army when he resigned to accept the rank of brigadier in the Confederate service. He was assigned to command of Harper's Ferry in May, 1861, and in July he took his Army of the Shenandoah to Manassas to reinforce Beauregard. After the battle Johnston was promoted to full general and commanded the Confederate army in northern Virginia. He retreated to Richmond to face McClellan's peninsula invasion, and there he was severely wounded, making way for Robert E. Lee to assume that command.

GEORGE P. KANE (1820–1878). As police marshal of Baltimore before the war, Kane subdued the pseudo-political gangs of Plug Uglies that often terrorized city voters. He attempted to halt the riot of April 19, 1861, but to prevent more federal troops from sparking further violence he and his police joined the militia in burning railroad bridges into the city. When Union soldiers took control of Baltimore Kane cooperated with them, but in June he was arrested and confined for seventeen months without charges. After his release he turned wholeheartedly against the federal government, joining Confederate secret service operatives in Canada and later recruiting Maryland volunteers for Southern service. He was elected mayor of Baltimore the year before his death.

JOHN LETCHER (1813–1884). A lawyer, Democratic newspaper editor, and former congressman from Lexington, Virginia, Letcher was elected governor in 1860. He angrily refused Lincoln's call for troops in April, 1861, and apparently viewed Virginia's tentative secession ordinance as sufficient authority to transform the state into a republic. He remained governor until 1864.

LUNSFORD L. LOMAX (1835–1913). Descended from a long line of Virginia soldiers, Lomax graduated from the U.S. Military Academy in 1856, and during the secession crisis he was stationed at Washington, where his widowed mother lived. Late in April, 1861, he resigned and joined the Confederate army. After two years of staff service he was assigned to the cavalry, surrendering as a major general.

NATHANIEL LYON (1818–1861). Lyon graduated from West Point in 1841. He served in the frontier army the rest of his life, with suspiciously frequent transfers and some revealing disciplinary difficulties. In the spring of 1861 he was assigned to command the Department of the West. In the lexicon of a later day Lyon might have been described as mentally disturbed, and his furious, uncompromising temper vastly aggravated the political situation in Missouri. He was killed at Wilson's Creek.

GEORGE B. MCCLELLAN (1826–1885). Graduating from West Point at the age of nineteen (1846), McClellan served on Winfield Scott's staff in the Mexico City campaign and spent eleven years on active duty before resigning to become a railroad executive. He was appointed major general early in the war, and his success in western Virginia led to his assignment as commander of the Army of the Potomac in July of 1861, and as general-in-chief of the U.S. Army three months later. Lincoln relieved him as general-in-chief when he undertook his peninsula campaign, and after his failure there in the summer of 1862 the army was taken from him one corps at a time. He resumed command in September and repelled Robert E. Lee's invasion of Maryland, but he let Lee's much smaller army escape, and for the lethargy of his pursuit President Lincoln removed McClellan from command. In 1864 McClellan ran against Lincoln on the Democratic ticket.

BEN MCCULLOCH (1811–1862). McCulloch took part in the Texan war of independence and served with the Texas Rangers in the Mexican War. With the rank of colonel in the Texas army he administered the surrender of U.S. forces in 1861, and that summer he led a small Confederate army into Missouri, where he defeated a smaller Union army at Wilson's Creek. The following March he was killed at the battle of Pea Ridge, Arkansas.

IRVIN MCDOWELL (1818–1885). After a twenty-three-year career spent mostly in army administration, McDowell was promoted to major general and given command of the army raised around Washington in the spring of 1861. The novice general led his novice army to defeat at First Bull Run, but he retained command of a division and later a corps in that army when George McClellan took it over. Lincoln intended to give him another army in the spring of 1862, but eventually subordinated him to John Pope in the Army of Virginia. A second defeat at Bull Run that summer ended both Pope's and McDowell's service with the eastern army, and they were exiled to the West.

BERIAH MAGOFFIN (1815–1885). As the Democratic governor of Kentucky from 1860 until 1862, Magoffin resisted both secession and war, notwithstanding accusations that he would have preferred secession. He tried to lead a course of strict neutrality between North and South, but Confederate blundering and a thoroughly Unionist legislature frustrated his efforts.

JOHN BANKHEAD MAGRUDER (1810–1871). After thirty-one years on active duty with the U.S. Army Magruder was still only a captain. With his brevet rank of lieutenant colonel he briefly commanded all the troops in Washington during the secession crisis, but in April, 1861, he resigned to follow his native Virginia. As a colonel, brigadier general, and major general he commanded on the Virginia peninsula in 1861 and 1862, winning the battle of Big Bethel and impeding McClellan's peninsula campaign for weeks with inferior forces. In 1863 he recaptured Galveston, Texas, from Union forces, and after the war he joined the imperial Mexican army rather than surrender.

JOSEPH K. F. MANSFIELD (1803–1862). An 1822 graduate of the military academy, Mansfield spent more than a quarter of a century as an engineer officer and nearly a decade on staff duties. At the outbreak of the war he was assigned to the command of Washington, and later of Fort Monroe. He was given command of a corps on the eve of the battle of Antietam, where he was mortally wounded. Though obviously talented, Mansfield harbored an abundance of professional jealousy and was not above political chicanery.

ROBERT PATTERSON (1792–1881). Though born in Ireland, Patterson served in all the major wars of the United States during his lifetime. He was in the Pennsylvania militia during the War of 1812, and he rose to the rank of major general of volunteers during the Mexican War. Although he was in his seventieth year at the outbreak of the Civil War, Pennsylvania governor Andrew Curtin assigned him to command of the state's ninety-day regiments, and he led them through a lackluster campaign during June and July of 1861. His inaction played a substantive role in the defeat of Irvin McDowell's army at First Bull Run, and Patterson was summarily mustered out of service.

EBENEZER PEIRCE (1822–?). As a brigadier of Massachusetts militia, Peirce led Ben Butler's expedition to Big Bethel in June, 1861. Peirce had not been mustered into federal service and so had no authority to command troops outside of his state. By mishandling his greatly superior force he lost the battle and contributed to growing public dismay. He served three more years at the reduced rank of colonel.

GEORGE A. PORTERFIELD, (1822–ca. 1914). Graduating from Virginia Military Institute in 1844, Porterfield served as a line and staff lieutenant in a Virginia regiment during the Mexican War. He later farmed near Charles Town, Virginia, but as a colonel of Virginia forces he oversaw the destruction of railroad bridges on the Baltimore & Ohio Railroad. His negligence contributed substantially to the surprise and dispersal of his troops at Philippi on June 3, 1861, and that failure precluded any further assignments of any significance. Porterfield left the army early in 1862, giving his parole to Union forces and returning to his farm.

STERLING PRICE (1809–1867). Besides managing his Missouri plantation, the Virginia-born Price pursued a political career and a legal practice before commanding a brigade during the Mexican War. He served in the legislature, in Congress, and as governor before chairing Missouri's secession convention in 1861, and after Nathaniel Lyon's attack on state troops he took command of the Missouri State Guard. His peace accord with Union General William Harney dissolved when the volatile Lyon replaced Harney, and thereafter Price, a conditional Unionist, led Missouri forces against U.S. troops. Through most of 1861 he considered the Confederate army nothing more than an ally, but when the fugitive Missouri legislature voted to secede, Price accepted it.

CHARLES W. SANDFORD (1796–1878). As the senior major general of New York militia, Sandford claimed nominally prominent positions during the early days of the Civil War. He led one of the columns that invaded Virginia on May 24, 1861, and commanded a division in Patterson's army before Winchester. In deference to Sandford's seniority General Scott wanted him to command the defenses of the upper Potomac after First Bull Run, but Sandford complained of a leg injury and said he preferred to go home at the end of his ninety-day term. In his place he recommended Charles P. Stone, who was given the command.

FRANK B. SCHAEFFER (ca. 1821–1900). During the Mexican War Schaeffer, a Baltimore native, served as a volunteer captain, and after the war he settled in California. He obtained a commission as lieutenant of artillery in the Regular Army in 1855, but he never appeared for duty and resigned the next year. By 1860 he had obtained a federal clerkship in Washington and was captain of a militia company there, but early in 1861 Inspector General Charles Stone relieved him from duty on the grounds of disloyalty. Schaeffer led three companies of District of Columbia volunteers into Confederate service later that spring, commanding them at First Bull Run, but afterward he secured a staff commission as inspector of ordnance. He surrendered at Galveston, Texas, in June, 1865, and returned to Washington, where for the rest of his life he supported himself on an assortment of minor government appointments and a Mexican War pension.

WINFIELD SCOTT (1786–1866). A native of Virginia, Scott won a brevet as major general by the age of twenty-eight, during the War of 1812. More than thirty years later he led the decisive campaign to Mexico City that ended the Mexican War. In 1852 he ran for president as a Whig, losing to Franklin Pierce, who had served under him in Mexico. As the Civil War opened he commanded the entire U.S. Army, but he was nearly seventy-five years old and his huge frame was turning to fat. Vain and contentious to the end, he demonstrated clear vision that might have led to a less costly conclusion to the war had President Lincoln resisted the political pressure for quick military action. After the third conspicuous military defeat of 1861, Scott retired and was replaced by George B. McClellan.

WILLIAM HENRY SEWARD (1801–1872). In the dozen years before the war this former governor of New York gained fame as an antislavery Whig in the U.S. Senate, where he was also known as a sly operator. He expected to be the Republican Party's presidential nominee in 1860, but his vehement anti-slavery record worked against him. Lincoln chose him as secretary of state, and in that position Seward turned more conservative, trying to act as a de facto prime minister. His intrigues worsened the antagonism over Fort Sumter and irritated his fellow cabinet officers, in whose departments he frequently interfered. He implemented Lincoln's policy of arbitrary arrests and, until early in 1862, became the nation's chief prison keeper. He once advocated initiating a war with England to distract Southerners from secession doctrine and later engaged in a feud with Treasury Secretary Salmon P. Chase, but Seward continued at the head of the State Department until 1869.

FRANZ SIGEL (1824–1902). Although he graduated from a German military academy and spent several years on active duty in the service of his native country, Sigel showed more pugnacity than talent in the United States. At Carthage and Wilson's Creek his impetuosity led to defeat. He redeemed himself sufficiently at Pea Ridge to earn promotion to major general, but his undistinguished career in Virginia ended with an embarrassing defeat at New Market in 1864. His principal value lay in his appeal to German recruits.

CALEB B. SMITH (1808–1864). Easily the weakest member of Lincoln's first cabinet, Smith was appointed to head the Interior Department in payment for his efforts to see Lincoln nominated in 1860. His tenure saw the Sioux uprising in Minnesota, for which much of the responsibility was laid at the feet of negligent or dishonest Interior Department agents. Smith resigned late in 1862 and died barely a year later.

WORTHINGTON G. SNETHEN (dates unknown). The Baltimore correspondent for Horace Greeley's *New York Tribune* described himself as a faithful Republican but only hinted at the radical nature of his Republicanism. His newspaper submissions and his surreptitious reports to Washington officials betrayed a thoroughly jaundiced perspective that helped taint administration impressions and contributed substantially to military repression in Baltimore. He spent his spare time flattering prominent federal officials, persuading them to imprison his political and professional opponents, and lobbying them for political sinecures.

EDWIN M. STANTON (1814–1869). A lawyer of national repute, Stanton offered the first successful temporary-insanity defense to win the acquittal of Congressman Daniel Sickles for the murder of his wife's alleged lover. President James Buchanan appointed him attorney general during the secession

crisis, and Stanton's firm nationalistic stance earned him many admirers outside his Democratic Party. Lincoln named him to replace Simon Cameron as
secretary of war, and Stanton held that office into the Johnson administration, exercising an authoritarian control that became most evident in the
weeks after the president's assassination.

CHARLES P. STONE (1824–1887). A West Point graduate (1845), Stone was
appointed by Winfield Scott as inspector general of District of Columbia militia in January, 1861. He became colonel of the 14th U.S. Infantry in May and a
brigadier general of volunteers in August, but after losing the battle of Ball's
Bluff in October he became the target of Radical Republicans and was imprisoned without charges from February through August of 1862. Secretary of
War Edwin Stanton refused to restore him to duty until the summer of 1863,
and in the spring of 1864 he summarily stripped Stone of his volunteer commission. Stone resigned his Regular Army commission the following September. In 1869 he began a successful career as chief of staff of the Egyptian army.
A few years before his death he returned to the United States to superintend
construction of the pedestal for the Statue of Liberty.

THOMAS WILLIAM SWEENY (1820–1892). Despite losing an arm in the
Mexican War, the Irish-born Sweeny later obtained a commission in the Regular Army. While still a captain in the Regular service, he acted as brigadier
general of Missouri home guards under Nathaniel Lyon, and he was wounded
again at Wilson's Creek. Like Lyon himself, Sweeny showed more passion
than sense. Appointed brigadier general of volunteers in 1862, he served in
the western theater until his violent temper dictated his removal from command. Subsequently he participated in Fenian activities, including a ludicrous invasion of Canada that nearly brought him to grief, but he still managed to secure reinstatement in the army. He served another three years
before retiring on a pension.

ROGER B. TANEY (1777–1864). Appointed chief justice by Andrew Jackson,
Taney wrote the infamous Dred Scott decision in 1857, which inflamed the debate over slavery extension by declaring that a slave remained in bondage
even if taken to a free state by his master. Taney rebuked Lincoln's assumption
of the power to make arbitrary arrests and opposed the rest of his more extraordinary war measures to his dying breath.

ALGERNON SIDNEY TAYLOR (1817–1899). A native of Alexandria, Virginia,
Taylor served in the U.S. Marines from 1838 until 1861. He was still technically a Marine officer when he took command of Alexandria as a lieutenant
colonel of Virginia infantry on May 2, 1861. Three days later he abruptly abandoned that town, which led to his removal. Eventually he secured a commission as captain in the quartermaster department of the Confederate Marine

Corps, but before the war ended he was arrested for allowing the use of government property for private profit.

GEORGE HUNTER TERRETT (1807–1875). Born in Virginia, Terrett spent thirty-one years as a Marine Corps officer, resigning in 1861 for a colonel's commission in the Virginia service. He commanded the garrison that evacuated Alexandria on May 24, 1861, and later resigned to accept the rank of major in the Confederate States Marines. For much of his Confederate career he commanded the Marine detachment at Drewry's Bluff, below Richmond.

BENJAMIN F. WADE (1800–1878). Wade's antislavery fervor won him election to the U.S. Senate from Ohio in 1850, and he retained the seat for eighteen years. In 1861 he was chosen as chairman of the Joint Committee on the Conduct of the War, and in that office he zealously persecuted Union generals who failed to meet his standards on the subject of emancipation. He favored a stern, almost vindictive policy against the defeated South, but he bore a large share of the credit for civil rights gains during Reconstruction.

GIDEON WELLES (1802–1878). An old Jacksonian Democrat, Welles was one of the founders of Connecticut's Republican Party. He chaired the state's delegation to the 1860 convention but seems to have had no other qualifications to be secretary of the navy beyond a conservatism that Lincoln found compatible. He nonetheless served with surprising competence, guiding department policy and grand strategy but leaving the direction of operations to the professionals under him.

FRANCIS G. YOUNG (ca. 1828–?). Young was employed, or unemployed, as an attorney when he was appointed quartermaster of Edward Baker's 1st California in the spring of 1861. By dint of something other than competence he secured Baker's recommendation of him as brigade quartermaster, but the promotion was never made. By then Young's misdealings had become apparent through his purchase of shoddy equipment, private resale of surplus provisions, and failure to balance his accounts. He entered the usual plea of ignorance and error rather than dishonesty, but he was dismissed for the additional transgression of desertion. His fables about the battle of Ball's Bluff helped to ruin Charles Stone, who first detected Young's irregular conduct and prompted his prosecution.

Notes

ABBREVIATIONS

DU: Duke University, Durham, N.C.
KSHS: Kansas State Historical Society, Topeka
LC: Library of Congress, Washington, D.C.
LOV: Library of Virginia, Richmond
MHS: Massachusetts Historical Society, Boston
MDHS: Maryland Historical Society, Baltimore
MEHS: Maine Historical Society, Portland
MNBP: Manassas National Battlefield Park, Manassas, Va.
MOHS: Missouri Historical Society, St. Louis
NA: National Archives, Washington, D.C.
NH Archives: New Hampshire Division of Records Management and Archives, Concord
NHHS: New Hampshire Historical Society, Concord
OR: *War of the Rebellion: A Compilation of the Official Records of the Union and Confederate Armies.* Washington, D.C.: Government Printing Office, 1880–1901.
ORN: *Official Records of the Union and Confederate Navies in the War of the Rebellion.* Washington, D.C.: Government Printing Office, 1894–1922.
RG: Record Group
SHC: Southern Historical Collection, University of North Carolina, Chapel Hill
UNH: University of New Hampshire, Durham
USAMHI: United States Army Military History Institute, Carlisle Barracks, Pa.
USMA: United States Military Academy, West Point, N.Y.
VHS: Virginia Historical Society, Richmond
WHMC: Western Historical Manuscript Collection, State Historical Society of Missouri, Columbia

Preface

1. *Lincoln and His Generals* (New York: Alfred A. Knopf, 1952), 8–9.
2. Basler, *The Collected Works*, 4:267–68.
3. Schlesinger, "The Causes of the Civil War," 969–81.
4. Stampp, *And the War Came*, 3, 284–86.
5. The most recent example of Lincoln idolatry is Perret, *Lincoln's War*, in which every incident seems molded to conform to a bold subtitle.

1. Songs for a Prelude

1. *OR* Series 1, 1:3–6, 327–30 (all citations from Series 1 unless otherwise noted); *The Crisis, and What It Demands!* 14, folder 1, Polk Papers, SHC.

2. Thomas Martin to James Buchanan, January 19, 1861, M-25, Reel 36, Letters Received by the Office of the Adjutant General (M-619), RG 94, NA; *OR* 1:318–21.

3. Unsigned, undated letter marked "January 5" [1861] and Silas Teede to Joseph Holt, January 4, 1861, both in Box 6, Holt Papers, LC.

4. *OR* 51(1):311–13, 343.

5. Ibid., 314, 317, 319.

6. OR 51(1):314; Moore, *The Works of James Buchanan,* 12:152–54; Basler, *The Collected Works,* 4:170–71; Taft diary, January 9 and 20, 1861, LC.

7. A. G. Miller Jr. to Jefferson Davis, February 18, 1861, Semmes & Co. to Leroy Pope Walker, March 13, 1861, F. Goldmark to Walker, March 22, 1861, James N. West to Thomas R. R. Cobb, February 26, 1861, and George W. Morse to Walker, March 11, 1861, Letters Received by the Confederate Secretary of War (M-437), Reel 1, NA.

8. Edward M. Grant to Jefferson Davis, March 11, 1861, John H. Hammersby to Davis, March 2, 1861, Justin Clavé to Leroy Pope Walker, March 16, 1861, G. Weldon Claiborne to Walker, March 12, 1861, George McHenry to Walker, March 21, 1861, Stiles Kennedy to Walker, March 23, 1861, Letters Received by the Confederate Secretary of War (M-437), Reel 1, NA.

9. *OR* Series 4, 1:103.

10. Nevins and Thomas, *The Diary of George Templeton Strong,* 3:95; Williams, *Diary and Letters of Rutherford Birchard Hayes,* 2:2, 4; "The Letters of Samuel James Reader," 27.

11. *OR* 51(1):314; Stone, "A Dinner with General Scott," 532.

12. Charles P. Stone to J. R. Poinsett, March 25, 1840, and to James Bell, March 23, 1841; Alpheus F. Stone to Poinsett, February 16, 1841, and the recommendations of Thomas O. Rice and Luther B. Lincoln, Charles F. Stone file, reel 129, USMA Cadet Application Papers (M688), RG 94, NA.

13. Cullum, *Biographical Register,* 2:117–18; Stone, *Notes on the State of Sonora;* Eighth Census (M-653), reel 102, 403, RG 29, NA.

14. Stone, "Washington on the Eve of War," 9–10.

15. Charles P. Stone to Lorenzo Thomas, February 26, 1861, Reel 54, Letters Received by the Office of the Adjutant General, 1861–1870 (M-619), NA; Cullum, *Biographical Register,* 2:118.

16. Frank B. Schaeffer to Josiah Gorgas, August 22, 1862, Schaeffer file, Reel 220, Compiled Service Records of Confederate General and Staff Officers, and Non-Regimental Enlisted Men (M-331), NA.

17. Heitman, *Historical Register,* 1:863; Third Artillery regimental returns, September of 1855 through March of 1856, Reel 20, Returns from Regular Army Artillery Regiments (M-727), RG 94, NA; Eighth Census (M-653), Reel 102, 553, RG 29, NA.

18. Frank B. Schaeffer to Adjutant General Samuel Cooper, January 16, 1861, and to R. C. Weightman, February 9, 1861; Weightman to Cooper, February 6 and 14, 1861, Reel 54, Letters Received by the Office of the Adjutant General, 1861–1870 (M-619), NA; Samuel Cooper to Joseph Holt, January 20, February 11, and February 15, 1861, Reel 97, Register of Letters Received by the Office of the Secretary of War (M-22), RG 107, NA.

19. Company muster roll for July and August, 1861, Frank B. Schaeffer file, Reel 360, Compiled Service Records of Virginia (M-324), NA; *OR* 51(2):86; John R. Smead to Lorenzo Thomas, March 30, 1861, Reel 55, Letters Received by the Office of the Adjutant General, 1861–1870 (M-619), NA.

20. French, *Witness to the Young Republic,* 341.

21. *OR* 1:524, 586.

22. Basler, *The Collected Works,* 4:195–96, 240–41.

23. Stone memorandum, February 21, 1861, Reel 17, Lincoln Papers, LC. Stone, "Washington on the Eve of the War," 23–24; French, *Witness to the Young Republic*, 342, 343.

24. Nevins and Thomas, *The Diary of George Templeton Strong*, 3:102; John Taylor Wood diary, February 23, 1861, Wood Papers, SHC; Lomax, *Leaves from an Old Washington Diary*, 144.

25. Russell, *My Diary North and South*, 40–41; Alexander W. Doniphan to "My dear Jno [John]," February 22, 1861, WHMC; Benjamin F. Wade to Caroline Wade, October 25, 1861, Reel 3, Wade Papers, LC.

26. See, for instance, the pamphlet entitled *The Crisis, and What It Demands!*, 5, folder 1, Polk Papers, SHC.

27. *New York Tribune*, February 6, 1861; Nevins and Thomas, *The Diary of George Templeton Strong*, 3:103–4; J. W. Crisfield to Henry Page, February 24, 1861, Henry Page Papers, SHC.

28. Laas, *Wartime Washington*, 37; Lomax, *Leaves from an Old Washington Diary*, 144; French, *Witness to the Young Republic*, 343–44; Taft diary, March 1, 1861, LC; *Congressional Globe*, 36th Cong., 2nd sess., part 3, 1405.

29. French, *Witness to the Young Republic*, 348; Stone, "Washington on the Eve of the War," 24–25; Samuel Cooper to Joseph Holt, March 1, 1861, Reel 97, Register of Letters Received by the Office of the Secretary of War (M-22), RG 107, NA.

30. Lomax, *Leaves from an Old Washington Diary*, 144.

31. Heintzelman journal, March 4, 1861, LC; French, *Witness to the Young Republic*, 348; Moore, *The Works of James Buchanan*, 11:156; Basler, *The Collected Works*, 1:89, 138–42, 391.

32. Stone, "Washington on the Eve of the War," 24–25; Taft diary, March 4, 1861, LC; Heintzelman journal, March 4, 1861, LC.; French, *Witness to the Young Republic*, 349; *Harper's Weekly*, March 16, 1861.

33. French, *Witness to the Young Republic*, 348; Kimmel, *Mr. Lincoln's Washington*, 24, 71; Basler, *The Collected Works*, 1:438.

34. Basler, *The Collected Works*, 4:263, 265, 268–69.

35. French, *Witness to the Young Republic*, 349.

36. *Washington Evening Star*, March 4, 1861; Lomax, *Leaves from an Old Washington Diary*, 145; French, *Witness to the Young Republic*, 348; "Letters of Jane and Sarah Everett," 366; *Boonville Weekly Observer*, April 13, 1861.

37. Nevins and Thomas, *The Diary of George Templeton Strong*, 3:106.

38. *North Carolina Standard*, March 9, 1861, *The Daily Picayune*, March 10, 1861, *Richmond Daily Dispatch*, March 5, 1861, quoted in Dumond, *Southern Editorials*, 475–83; Scarborough, *The Diary of Edmund Ruffin*, 1:560.

39. Moore, *The Works of James Buchanan*, 11:157–58.

40. Letter of Rudolf Schleiden quoted in Lutz, "Rudolf Schleiden and the Visit to Richmond," 210; "A Page of Political Correspondence," 474.

41. *OR* 1:35, 265, 277, 279; Hassler, *One of Lee's Best Men*, 10, 12.

42. Stone, "Washington in March and April, 1861," 3, 6; Russell, *My Diary North and South*, 53, 55–56.

43. Scott to Lincoln, March 11, 1861, Reel 18, and Hitchcock to Scott, March, 1861, Reel 19, Lincoln Papers, LC. See also Samuel W. Crawford to "My Dear A.S.," March 19, 1861, Crawford Papers, LC.

44. Basler, *The Collected Works*, 4:284–85; Beale, *The Diary of Edward Bates*, 178–80.

45. Abner Doubleday to Mary Doubleday, April 2, 1861, Reel 20, Lincoln Papers, LC.

46. Beale, *The Diary of Gideon Welles*, 1:13–14, 2:248; John G. Nicolay to Therena Bates, March 20, 24, and 31, 1861, Nicolay Papers, LC; Niven, *The Salmon P. Chase Papers*, 3:55.

47. Hurlbut to Lincoln, March 27, 1861, Reel 19, Lincoln Papers, LC.

48. "A Republican" to Lincoln, April 3, 1861, and J. H. Jordan to same, April 4, 1861,

Reel 20, Lincoln Papers, LC. See an assortment of editorials in Stampp, *And the War Came*, 87, 155–57. Stampp's 1950 book offers a more judicious examination of the sense of Republican imperative than anything since.

49. *New York Herald*, February 5, 1861; *Gazette and Courier*, February 11, 1861; *Detroit Free Press*, February 19, 1861; *Springfield Daily Republican* and *New York Tribune*, February 23, 1861.

50. *Congressional Globe*, 36th Cong., 2nd sess., part 2, 1477–78.

51. *New York Times*, March 21, 1861; *Philadelphia Inquirer*, March 21, 1861; *Daily National Intelligencer*, March 21, 1861; *States and Union*, March 22, 1861; *Cincinnati Daily Commercial*, March 23, 1861; *Illinois State Journal*, April 3, 1861, quoted in Perkins, *Northern Editorials*, 363–79.

52. *Smyrna* Times, April 4, 1861; *Delaware Gazette*, March 22, 1861; Pennsylvania *Daily Telegraph*, April 5, 1861; *Philadelphia North American*, April 10, 1861; *Hartford Courant*, April 12, 1861.

53. John P. Kennedy to Beriah Magoffin, December 25, 1860, and to George S. Bryan, December 27, 1861, Kennedy letterbook, Peabody Institute, Johns Hopkins; *OR* Series 4, 1:152; The Annapolis *Gazette*, cited in Wright, *The Secession Movement*, 59; *New Brunswick Times*, March 14, 1861.

54. Fox to Lincoln, March 28, 1861, Reel 19, Lincoln Papers, LC; Beale, *The Diary of Edward Bates*, 180; Welles to Lincoln, March 29, 1861, and Montgomery Blair to same, undated, Reel 19, Lincoln Papers, LC.

55. "General M. C. Meigs on the Conduct of the Civil War," 299–300 (this includes transcripts of Meigs's diaries, the originals of which, in the Library of Congress, suffer from almost illegible handwriting).

56. Lomax, *Leaves from an Old Washington Diary*, 147; Taft diary, April 1, 1861, LC; Basler, *The Collected Works*, 4:316–18.

57. Beale, *The Diary of Edward Bates*, 181; Welles to Mrs. Welles, April 10, 1861, Reel 19, Welles Papers, LC; John G. Nicolay to Therena Bates, April 7, 1861, Nicolay Papers, LC.

58. Samuel Crawford to "my Dear A.S.," March 23, 1861, and to "My Dear Brother," April 9, 1861, Crawford Papers, LC.

59. Basler, *The Collected Works*, 4:425; Beale, *The Diary of Edward Bates*, 179.

60. John G. Nicolay to Therena Bates, March 24 and 31, 1861, Nicolay Papers, LC; Thompson and Wainwright, *Confidential Correspondence of Gustavus Vasa Fox*, 1:11; Edward Bates to Lincoln, March 27, 1861, and Salmon P. Chase to Lincoln, March 28, 1861, Reel 19, Lincoln Papers, LC.

61. "Papers of Hon. John A. Campbell," 31–35; Beale, *Diary of Gideon Welles*, 1:24–28.

62. Montgomery Meigs diary, April 2 and 3, 1861, Meigs Papers, LC; *ORN*, Series 1, 4:111–12, 243, 249; Taft diary, April 7–10, 1861, LC; Lomax, *Leaves from an Old Washington Diary*, 147.

63. "A Page of Political Correspondence," 475; C. O. Goodell to Gideon Welles, April 5, 1861, James G. Bolles to same, April 6, 1861, and David S. Dodge to same, April 9, 1861, Reel 19, Welles Papers, LC; Sumner, *The Diary of Cyrus B. Comstock*, 229.

64. *Delaware Gazette*, April 9, 1861; Albert Cassedy to "Dear Pres.," April 11, 1861, and Joseph H. Knowlton to "Dear Sir," Letters Received by the Confederate Secretary of War (M-437), NA; *OR* 51(1):317, 322; Taft diary, April 6, 1861, LC.

65. Stone to Seward, April 5, 1861, Reel 20, Lincoln Papers, LC; Taft diary, April 11, 1861, LC; Beale, *Diary of Gideon Welles*, 1:23–25.

66. Taft diary, April 7–9, 1861, LC; Russell, *My Diary North and South*, 64–65; Basler, *The Collected Works*, 4:324, 326.

67. *OR* 51(1):321–24; Lomax, *Leaves from an Old Washington Diary*, 147; *Daily Whig and Republican*, April 11, 1861.

68. Basler, *The Collected Works*, 4:334–35; *OR* 51(1):326.

69. OR 1:13, 250–52, 285, 289–91.

70. OR 1:13–15, 250–51, 289; A. C. Haskell to "Dear father and mother," April 11, 1861,

Haskell Papers, SHC; Crawford diary, April 11 and 12, 1861, and Crawford to "My Dear A," April 13, 1861, Crawford Papers, LC; Lee journal, April 11, 1861, Stephen D. Lee Papers, SHC. See also Younger, *Inside the Confederate Government*, 112–13.

71. Taft diary, April 12, 1861, LC; Lomax, *Leaves from an Old Washington Diary*, 148–49.

72. Taft diary, April 12, 1861, LC; Burlingame and Ettlinger, *Inside Lincoln's White House*, 1–2; "Historickal Crotchets," 183–84.

73. *OR* 1:376; Taft diary, April 12–14, 1861, LC.

74. Thompson and Wainwright, *Confidential Correspondence of Gustavus Vasa Fox*, 1:44; Pease and Randall, *The Diary of Orville Hickman Browning*, 1:475–76.

75. Johannsen, *The Letters of Stephen A. Douglas*, 509–10; Basler, *The Collected Works*, 4:330–32.

76. John R. Thompson to John P. Kennedy, May 16, 1861, Kennedy Papers, Peabody Institute, Johns Hopkins; *OR* Series 3, 1:70, 72, 76, 81, 82–83, 99, 114; *Smyrna Times*, quoted in the *Philadelphia Enquirer*, April 19, 1861.

77. J. L. Petigru to Perry, December 8, 1861, and Perry journal, July 21 and October 27, 1861, Perry Papers, SHC; Platt K. Dickinson to Mrs. John G. Dabney, December 1, 1860 and January 8, February 5, and March 13, 1861, Dickinson Papers, SHC; Frank F. Steel to "My Dear Sister," December 8, 1860 and to "Dear Anna," August 19, 1861, Steel Papers, SHC.

78. Bates to Lincoln (introducing Botts), April 5, 1861, Reel 20, Lincoln Papers, LC; John Minor Botts to Edward Bates, April 23 and May 9, 1861, and Bates to Botts, April 29, 1861, Bates Family Papers, MOHS; Edward Bates to James O. Broadhead, May 3, 1861, Broadhead Papers, MOHS.

79. Hicks to William Seward, March 28, 1861, Reel 19, Lincoln Papers, LC.

80. *OR* Series 3, 1:79–80, and Series 1, 2:773–74; Francis J. Thomas to Isaac Trimble, May 5, 1861, Isaac Trimble Papers, MDHS.

81. "Brother against Brother," 6, 89; *OR* 2:7–21; Marks and Schatz, *Between North and South*, 29; David Creamer diary, June–July, 1861, MDHS. A New York patent attorney sojourning in Washington informed his son on April 18 that the five Pennsylvania militia companies had endured taunts and a few brickbats as they passed through Baltimore "this morning" ("Historickal Crotchets," 184).

82. Elizabeth B. Randall to Alexander Randall, April 20, 1861, Philpot-Randall Family Papers, MDHS; "Brother against Brother," 6–7; John G. Nicolay to Therena Bates, April 19–21, 1861, Nicolay Papers, LC.

83. *OR* 2: 13–15, 17–18; Marks and Schatz, *Between North and South*, 30; Moore, *Rebellion Record*, 2:182; David Creamer diary, June–July, 1861, MDHS; Daniel Murray Thomas to "My Dear Sister," April 21, 1861, Daniel Murray Thomas Papers, MDHS; list of corps and morning report of May 3, 1861, Isaac Trimble Papers, MDHS.

84. Charles H. Eager to Alfred Eager, undated but April 27 and 28, 1861, Eager Letters, Lewis Leigh Collection, USAMHI.

85. William Kirkwood to Robert Kirkwood, April 24, 1861, William Kirkwood Correspondence, MDHS; Mary Davis to "My dear Brother," May 25, 1861, Rebecca Dorsey Davis Papers, MDHS; Isaac Briggs to "Dear James," May 10, 1861, Briggs-Stabler Papers, MDHS.

86. Basler, *The Collected Works*, 4:329–32.

87. *OR* 51 (2):22, and Series 4, 1:223; Hunton, *Autobiography*, 18–24.

88. John Robertson to John Letcher, April 23, 1861, Executive Papers, 1859–1863, Series I, and Executive Journal and Index, January–December, 1861, 114, 120, LOV; *OR* 51(2):24.

89. John P. Welsh to James L. Welsh, May 23, 1861, and James Welsh to John, May 26 and June 2, 1861, Welsh Family Papers, LOV.

90. J. W. Crisfield to Henry Page, January 20 and April 28, 1861, Page Papers, SHC;

Randolph Fairfax to "Dear Mamma," April 15 and August 12, 1861, Fairfax Family Letters, LOV.

91. *OR* 2:21–23, 51(2):16; *ORN* 4:292–96, 402, 405.

92. Executive Journal and Index, January–December, 1861, 107–16, LOV.

93. *Boston Post,* April 17, 1861; John Gill to Lizzie Ingersoll, April 21, 1861, Gill Papers, DU.

94. H. B. Robinson to Hendrick B. Wright, April 15, 1861, Wright Papers, Wyoming Historical and Geological Society; Sidney Webster to Franklin Pierce, April 19, 1861, Pierce Papers, LC. Both of these letters are cited in Wright, *The Secession Movement,* 161, 204, among other evidence of mob violence.

95. *Mercury,* April 25, 1861, and *Rochester Sentinel,* April 27, 1861, both quoted in Tombaugh, *Fulton County, Indiana Newspaper Extracts,* 29, 253; Richard M. Blatchford, Moses H. Grinnell, Richard M. Corwine, and William M. Dickson to Abraham Lincoln, all April 15, 1861, Reel 20, Lincoln Papers, LC.

96. Schafer, *Intimate Letters of Carl Schurz,* 253–54; Williams, *Diary and Letters of Rutherford Birchard Hayes,* 2:9; Meltzer and Holland, *Lydia Maria Child: Selected Letters,* 380.

97. L. J. Gildersleeve to Leroy Pope Walker, April 15, 1861, Letters Received by the Confederate Secretary of War (M-437), NA; *Daily Whig and Republican,* April 17 and 18, 1861; Pease and Randall, *The Diary of Orville Hickman Browning,* 1:462–64.

98. *OR* Series 3, 1:70, 73, 75, 79–81, 87, 88, 93–95, 100; Trueblood diary, April 19–23, 1861, KSHS.

99. *OR* Series 3, 1:72; Daniel Sickles to Simon Cameron, April 17, 1861, Reel 6, Cameron Papers, LC.

100. Taft diary, April 18, 1861, LC; *Philadelphia Enquirer,* April 19, 1861; *Lawrence Republican,* May 16, 1861; "The Letters of Samuel James Reader," 30.

101. M. B. White to Leroy Pope Walker, April 14, 1861, Reel 1, Letters Received by the Confederate Secretary of War (M-437), NA; Lomax, *Leaves from an Old Washington Diary,* 149.

102. *Philadelphia Enquirer,* April 19, 1861; Undated memorial of E. McDonald, James Wren et al., to Simon Cameron et al., filed under April 18, 1861, Reel 6, Cameron Papers, LC; *OR* 51(1):344.

103. Burlingame and Ettlinger, *Inside Lincoln's White House,* 5; Taft diary, April 18–20, 1861, LC.

104. Duncan, *Blue-Eyed Child of Fortune,* 75–76; *OR* Series 3, 1:165.

105. John G. Nicolay to Therena Bates, April 26, 1861, Nicolay Papers, LC; Basler, *The Complete Works,* 4:338–39.

106. Anderson et al., *Mark Twain's Notebooks and Journals,* 1:55–56.

2. Flags in Mottoed Pageantry

1. Russell, *My Diary North and South,* 101; *OR* 52(2):53, and Series 4, 1:217–19, 221–22, 226.

2. *OR* Series 4, 1:216; J. M. Kelly to Lyman Trumbull, April 29, 1861, Reel 11, Trumbull Papers, LC.

3. G. W. McKenzie to Leroy Pope Walker, April 15, 1861, and John A. McClure to same, April 17, 1861, Reel 1, Letters Received by the Confederate Secretary of War (M-437), NA; G. G. Fowle to Hon. J. Lane, April 18, 1861, Executive Correspondence, Record Group 1, Box 26, NH Archives.

4. *OR* 51(2):16–17, and Series 4, 1:231–33.

5. *OR* 51(2):16–17, and Series 4, 1:231–33; Scarborough, *The Diary of Edmund Ruffin,* 2:8–9; J. M. Tompkins to "Friend Sam," April 23, 1861, C.S.A. Archives, Soldiers Letters, DU.

6. Silver, *A Life for the Confederacy*, 21; muster-in roll and record of service, Magnolia Guards, William L. Duff file, Reel 253, Compiled Service Records of Mississippi (M-269), NA.

7. Muster-in roll, E. R. Burt and Frank Pettus files, Reels 264 and 272, Compiled Service Records of Mississippi (M-269), NA; Russell, *My Diary North and South*, 194.

8. Cutrer and Parrish, *Brothers in Gray*, 13–14; Taylor, *Reluctant Rebel*, 29.

9. OR 1:688–90; Myers, *The Children of Pride*, 664, 671–73.

10. William Henderson to Daniel Ruggles, May 15, 1861, Ruggles Correspondence, DU.

11. *Richmond Enquirer*, April 23, 1861; Clift, *The Private War of Lizzie Hardin*, 17–18; *Richmond Dispatch*, July 26, 1861; R. E. Jones to Julia Cain, undated, and James Cain to Thomas Webb or John N. Kirkland, July 30, 1861, Vol. 10, Mangum Papers, LC.

12. Gallagher, *Fighting for the Confederacy*, 28–29.

13. Conrad diary, April 23–25, May 12 and 25, 1861, LC.

14. Larkin Smith to E. D. Townsend, March 28, 1861, and to Lorenzo Thomas, April 22, 1861, Reel 55, Letters Received by the Office of the Adjutant General, 1861–1870 (M-619), NA.

15. *Democratic Mirror*, November 14, 1860, and April 17, 1861; "Sallie" to May E. Sangster, April 19, 1861, Civil War letters, Balch Library; Janney, *Memoirs*, 188; Muster-in roll, Flavius A. "Osborn" file, Reel 471, Compiled Service Records of Virginia (M-324), NA.

16. *Democratic Mirror*, January 4, 1860, April 10 and 17, May 22, and October 30, 1861.

17. *Washingtonian*, February 1, 1861; Eighth Census (M-653), Reel 1359, 54, 66, RG 29, NA; *Directory of Leesburg;* Members of the Loudoun Guard, April 27, 1861, Miscellaneous Lists, Balch Library.

18. McGuire, *Diary of a Southern Refugee*, 9–10, 12; Clift, *The Private War of Lizzie Hardin*, 18.

19. Russell, *My Diary North and South*, 72, 76–78.

20. *Philadelphia Enquirer*, April 23, 1861.

21. John Taylor Wood diary, April 15 and April 19–22, 1861, SHC; OR 2: 596, 740, 773–74, 51(2):24, 34–35, and Series 2, 1:630.

22. Muster roll of July and August, 1861, Frank B. Schaeffer file, Reel 360, Compiled Service Records of Virginia (M-324), NA.

23. Charles P. Stone to E. D. Townsend, April 24, 1861, and to Theodore Talbot, April 27, 1861, Reel 55, Letters Received by the Office of the Adjutant General (M-619), NA; Duncan, *Blue-Eyed Child of Fortune*, 82; OR 2:600.

24. Taft diary, April 23 and 24, 1861, LC; John C. Dalton to Charles H. Dalton, April 20, 1861, Dalton Papers, MHS; Burlingame and Ettlinger, *Inside Lincoln's White House*, 8–11.

25. Taft diary, April 25, 1861, LC; Duncan, *Blue-Eyed Child of Fortune*, 80–82.

26. Taft diary, April 25, 1861, LC; OR 51(1):344; Wheeler, *Letters*, 281; "Letters of Edward Bates," 139.

27. Burlingame and Ettlinger, *Inside Lincoln's White House*, 12; Basler, *The Collected Works*, 4:344. In this source Lincoln suggests suspending habeas corpus only "in the extremest necessity," but in *The Fate of Liberty*, 7, Mark Neely revealed that this was a last-minute emendation to the letter; in the first version Lincoln treated the suspension much more casually.

28. Neely, *The Fate of Liberty*, 4–5.

29. Burlingame and Ettlinger, *Inside Lincoln's White House*, 13; Basler, *The Collected Works*, 4:347.

30. OR 51(2):242.

31. Schleiden's dispatches of April 24 and May 2, 1861, to the committee on foreign affairs in Bremen, quoted in Lutz, "Rudolf Schleiden and the Visit to Richmond," 211–13.

32. Ibid.; Phillips, "The Correspondence of Robert Toombs, Alexander H. Stephens, and Howell Cobb," 563–64.

33. *OR* 51(1):344.

34. Dyer, *Compendium*, 1008–1673.

35. Ai B. Thompson to "My Dear Father," April 18, 1861, MNBP. See, for instance, the *Philadelphia Enquirer*, April 19, 1861, for offers made to employee volunteers.

36. Burlingame and Ettlinger, *Inside Lincoln's White House*, 21–22; *OR* 51(1):344; *Boston Journal*, July 20, 1861; Russell, *My Diary North and South*, 304; Field and Smith, *Uniforms of the Civil War*, 107, 112; Alfred Waud drawing no. 179, LC; Marvel, *Burnside*, 7.

37. Burlingame and Ettlinger, *Inside Lincoln's White House*, 16–17; Taft diary, May 2, 1861, LC.

38. Burlingame and Ettlinger, *Inside Lincoln's White House*, 4, 20, 22; Hay, "Ellsworth," 119–24; Taft diary, May 1, 2, and 7, 1861, LC; Nevins and Thomas, *The Diary of George Templeton Strong*, 3:136.

39. *OR* Series 3, 1:145–46.

40. Ibid., 154–55; Heitman, *Historical Register*, 1:92.

41. *OR* Series 3, 1:203–4; Dyer, *Compendium*, 1497–1506; Luther V. B. Furber to "Dear Mother," April 20, 1861, MDHS.

42. Robertson, *The Civil War Letters of General Robert McAllister*, 32; Williams, *Diary and Letters of Rutherford Birchard Hayes*, 2:19; Holliday, "Relief of Soldiers' Families," 98–99.

43. *OR* Series 3, 1:161; Mason Weare Tappan to Ichabod Goodwin, May 7, 1861, Mason Weare Tappan Papers, NHHS.

44. Ayling, *Revised Register*, 3–23.

45. *OR* Series 3, 1:187; Ayling, *Revised Register*, 1194–96; Ai B. Thompson to "Dear Father and Mother," May 21, 1861, MNBP; Waite, *New Hampshire in the Great Rebellion*, 53–57.

46. Haynes, *A Minor War History*, 5.

47. *Journals of the Honorable Senate and House*, 2:157–211.

48. Faley, "Cultural Aspects of the Industrial Revolution," 372–73.

49. *Haverhill Gazette*, February 24, March 2, and March 16, 1860; *Democratic Mirror*, March 14, 1860; Faley, "Cultural Aspects of the Industrial Revolution," 393.

50. *Haverhill Gazette*, March 30, 1860, March 1, 8, and 15, 1861.

51. *Lowell Courier*, quoted in the *Dollar Weekly Mirror*, March 2, 1861; *Massachusetts Soldiers*, 1:1–68.

52. Luther V. B. Furber to "Dear Mother," April 20 and 23, 1861, MDHS; Catherine McGovern relief voucher, October 3, 1861, Oliver Norcross Papers, MHS.

53. *OR* Series 3, 1:153–54, 860; *Massachusetts Soldiers*, 1:69–145. This was the 2nd Massachusetts; half the companies of the 1st Massachusetts consisted of antebellum militia, and half of volunteers.

54. *Massachusetts Soldiers, Sailors, and Marines*, 1:617–81.

55. *Massachusetts Soldiers, Sailors, and Marines*, 2:131–204, 411–593, 651–710; *OR* Series 3, 1:153–54, 860.

56. *Aegis and Transcript*, September 21, 1861; *Daily American*, July 10, August 9–14, September 7, 10, and 21, 1861; *Dollar Weekly Mirror*, May 11, June 22, 1861; 1st N.H. Battery Enlistment Papers, NH Archives.

57. Stearns, *Narrative of Amos E. Stearns*, 5.

58. Marvel, "A Poor Man's Fight," 33–40.

59. Chapman, *Sketches of the Alumni of Dartmouth College*, 289–470; Ayling, *Revised Register*, 1093–95.

60. "The Union. Its Benefits and Dangers," 3; *New York Tribune*, March 13, March 28, and May 1, 1860.

61. *New York Journal of Commerce*, quoted in Scarborough, *The Diary of Edmund Ruffin*, 1:504; *New York Times*, April 1–20, 1861.

62. *Letters of a Family,* 1:44–45; *New York Times,* April 21–25, 1861; *New York Tribune,* April 21, 1861.

63. Eighth Census (M-653), Reel 789, 968, RG 29, NA.

64. Muster roll of the field and staff, 42nd New York, September 1, 1861, RG 94, NA; affidavits of John Sharkey, John Fogarty, and Michael Fogarty, and Timothy O'Meara to John O'Meara, November 23, 1863, Mary O'Meara pension file, certificate 39332, RG 15, NA.

65. Thomas McDermott to "Dear Mother and Brothers," December 10, 1861, Civil War Letters, Thomas Balch Memorial Library, Leesburg, Va.

66. George S. Geer to Martha Geer, March 18, April 13 and 16, October 25, and November 29, 1862, Geer Letters, The Mariners' Museum.

67. Alfred Wheeler to Alonzo Wheeler, April 4, "1860" [1861], and to "Dear Mother," August, 1861, Alfred Wheeler letters, Civil War Miscellaneous Collection, USAMHI; *Philadelphia Inquirer,* February 22, 1861; muster roll of Co. M, 71st Pa. Volunteers, dated August 6, 1861, and muster roll of Co. H, dated October 31, 1862, Alfred Wheeler service file, RG 94, NA.

68. *Boston Journal,* quoted in *Dover Gazette,* June 29, 1861; Longacre, *From Antietam to Fort Fisher,* 23.

69. John Gilbert to "Dear Sir," February 4, 1862, NHHS; Phillips to unnamed recipient, undated [but July or August of 1862], MEHS; John Peirce to Clara Peirce, June 23, 1864, Peabody Essex Museum.

70. Harris, *Dear Sister,* 3; Johnston, *Him on the One Side and Me on the Other,* 29.

71. Frederick W. Clark to Lizzie Clark, July 22, August 4, and September 16, 1861, Clark Papers, DU; Blight, *When This Cruel War Is Over,* 5, 9–10, 33, 40, 168; *Granite State News,* October 9, 1861.

72. Daniel Wooten to Miriam Green, July 11, 1861, Green Papers, Indiana Historical Society; Rundell, "Despotism of Traitors," 333–34; *New York Tribune,* August 31, 1860; Throne, "Iowa Farm Letters," 79.

73. Diary of Webster W. Moses, March 4 and September 2, 1861, KSHS; *OR* Series 3, 1:402; William L. Broaddus to "Dear Wife," July 8 and August 8, 1861, Broaddus Papers, DU.

74. *OR* 52(1):162; *Cincinnati Daily Gazette,* May 28 and October 19, 1861; Holliday, "Relief for Soldiers' Families," 111.

75. Duncan, *Blue-Eyed Child of Fortune,* 107.

76. See, for instance, Ai B. Thompson to J. H. Thompson, June 25, 1861, Thompson Letters (MNBP), Charles E. Jewett to "Absent brother," June 26, 1861, Jewett Papers (UNH), and David Thomas Copeland to Mattie Adair, June 23, 1861, Copeland Papers (SHC).

77. A. Bickford to Mason Weare Tappan, May 15, 1861, RG 12, Box 8, NH Archives.

78. Kohl, *Irish Green and Union Blue,* 17, 20, 65–67.

79. Wilkeson, *Recollections,* 1–20. The muster and descriptive roll of Wilkeson's detachment of recruits reveals that he received a $60 cash advance against his $302 federal bounty: see roll dated April 9, 1864, Frank Wilkeson service record, 11th New York Independent Battery, RG 94, NA. Wilkeson's memoir is littered with obvious fabrications.

80. Oscar D. Robinson to Mr. and Mrs. E. T. Rowell, January 9, 1864, Robinson Papers, and Elmer Bragg to Mrs. William L. Bragg, December 29, 1863, Bragg Papers, Dartmouth; Ayling, *Revised Register,* 511.

81. Ayling, *Revised Register,* 97, 151, 206, 281, 347, 402, 454.

82. Bowen, *A Frontier Family,* 181.

83. *Daily Whig and Republican,* April 17 and 19, 1861.

3. The Banner at Daybreak

1. Burlingame and Ettlinger, *Inside Lincoln's White House,* 13; *OR* 2:795.

2. *Baltimore Sun,* May 27, 1899; Donnelly, *Biographical Sketches,* 43–44.

3. *OR* 2:26–27, 797–98, 805.

4. Ibid., 2:23–27, 879, and Series 2, 2:1434; Donnelly, *Biographical Sketches*, 44.

5. *OR* 2:25, 796, 819, 842–43; Donnelly, *Biographical Sketches*, 45.

6. *OR* 2:824, 827, 829.

7. Ibid., Series 3, 1:281–85, and Series 1, 2:842–43.

8. *ORN* Series 1, 4:380; *OR* 3:4–9

9. Rebecca Dorsey Davis to "My dear Brother," April 27, 1861, MDHS; "Brother against Brother," 7, 89–90; George Brown to Isaac Trimble, April 25 and May 6, 1861, Trimble Papers, MDHS.

10. *OR* 2:28–32, 639, 640–41; Butler to Edward F. Jones [May, 1861], Jones Papers, MDHS; *Baltimore Sun*, May 14 and 15, 1861; *Frank Leslie's Illustrated Newspaper*, May 25, 1861.

11. *Baltimore Sun*, May 15, 1861.

12. *OR*, Series 3, 1:184–85.

13. Ibid., Series 2, 1:574–76; *Baltimore Sun*, May 27, 28, and 29, 1861; Merryman's petition of May 25, 1861, Merryman Collection, MDHS.

14. *Baltimore Sun*, May 14, 1861; *Frank Leslie's Illustrated Newspaper*, May 25, 1861; *OR* Series 2, 1:578.

15. Basler, *The Collected Works*, 4:390, 431; *OR* Series 2, 2:20–30.

16. *OR*, Series 2, 2:226; Merryman headstone, Sherwood Episcopal Church cemetery, Cockeysville, Md.

17. David Creamer diary, June and July, 1861, MDHS.

18. *Richmond Examiner*, June 3, 1861; Vote on the Ordinance of Secession and Membership of the Loudoun Guard, Miscellaneous Lists, Balch Library; Clinton Hatcher to Mary Anna Sibert, May 29 and October 8, 1861, Evans-Sibert Family Papers, LOV. Hatcher, who had attended Columbian College, was remembered by a classmate as six feet, seven inches tall (Richards, "Ball's Bluff," 32).

19. *OR* 2:37–40; *ORN* Series 1, 4:447.

20. Scott, *Forgotten Valor*, 261–62; *OR* 2:40, 43.

21. *OR* 2:40–41; Scott, *Forgotten Valor*, 262, 263; Heintzelman journal, May 25, 1861, Reel 7, Heintzelman Papers, LC; *Report of the Joint Committee*, 2:427.

22. *OR* 2:38–39, 40.

23. *OR* 2:43, 879–80; *Frank Lelsie's Illustrated Newspaper*, April 25, 1882 (clipping in M. Dulany Ball Papers, Yale).

24. *ORN*, Series 1, 4:478–79.

25. Ibid., 479., and *OR* 2:43.

26. *ORN* Series 1, 4:479–80.

27. Scott, *Forgotten Valor*, 263, 268; *ORN* Series 1, 4:479; *Democratic Mirror*, May 8, 1861; *New York Tribune*, May 26, 1861.

28. *New York Tribune*, May 26, 1861; *Richmond Daily Dispatch*, May 27, May 28, and July 20, 1861; Eighth Census (M-653), Reel 1343, 874, RG 29, NA.

29. *New York Tribune*, May 26, 1861; *Richmond Daily Dispatch*, May 27 and July 20, 1861. Partisan coverage in these two newspapers yields interesting contradictions in the details of this story.

30. Scott, *Forgotten Valor*, 264, 266; *OR* 2:41.

31. *OR*, Series 2, 3:683–87.

32. Scott, *Forgotten Valor*, 274; *OR* 51(1):389–90; Charles P. Stone to James B. Fry, May 29, 1861, Reel 56, Letters Received by the Office of the Adjutant General, 1861–1870 (M-619), NA.

33. *OR* 2:39; Taft diary, May 24 and 25, 1861, LC.

34. Wheeler diary, May 24, 1861, LC.

35. Scarborough, *The Diary of Edmund Ruffin*, 2:36 (with undated clipping of the *New York Herald*); Nevins and Thomas, *The Diary of George Templeton Strong*, 3:147; Augustus Haight to Abraham Lincoln, May 29, 1861, Reel 22, Lincoln Papers, LC.

36. Williams, *Diary and Letters of Rutherford Birchard Hayes,* 1:19; Dyer, *Compendium,* 1420.

37. *Richmond Daily Dispatch,* June 3 and July 20, 1861.

38. *OR* 2:44–45, 49–50, 51–52.

39. *OR* 2:35–36.

40. Ibid., 55–59; *ORN* Series 1, 490–93.

41. *OR* 2:50, 55, 60–64.

42. Ibid., 65–73; *New York Herald,* June 16, 1861; Porterfield, "A Narrative," 90; "A Veteran of Two Wars."

43. Smart, *A Radical View,* 1:15–19.

44. Edward B. Dalton to Charles H. Dalton, July 10, 1861, Dalton Papers, MHS; *OR* 2:641–42, 649–50.

45. Ibid., 77–78, 92–94; *Report of the Joint Committee,* 3:384. Major George Wythe Randolph, of the Richmond Howitzers, had been born at Monticello; later he served as the Confederate secretary of war.

46. *OR* 2:84, 86; *Report of the Joint Committee,* 3:384.

47. *OR* 2:84, 91, 94.

48. Ibid., 84–85, 89; Nevins and Thomas, *The Diary of George Templeton Strong,* 3:156.

49. *OR* 2:84–85, 94–95, 99 and 51(1):4–5.

50. Ibid., 2:92, 96; *Atlas to Accompany the Official Records,* plate 61, map 4.

51. *OR* 2:82, 95; *Atlas to Accompany the Official Records,* plate 61, map 4.

52. *OR* 2:83–84, 85, 88, 89, 95–96.

53. Duncan, *Blue-Eyed Child of Fortune,* 109; Nevins and Thomas, *The Diary of George Templeton Strong,* 3:158; Jordan, *The Civil War Journals of John Mead Gould,* 26; Taft diary, June 12, 1861, LC.

54. Jones, *A Rebel War Clerk's Diary,* 26; Russell, *My Diary North and South,* 193, 197; Scarborough, *The Diary of Edmund Ruffin,* 2:44–45.

55. Scarborough, *The Diary of Edmund Ruffin,* 2:45.

56. Sears, *The Civil War Papers of George B. McClellan,* 1, 24.

57. Cullum, *Biographical Register,* 1:559–60; Basler, *The Collected Works,* 4:411; *OR* 51(1):321–23.

58. Sparks, *Inside Lincoln's Army,* 46, 53; Eby, *A Virginia Yankee,* 36; *OR* 2:653.

59. Jones, *A Rebel War Clerk's Diary,* 19, 21, 22–24; *Richmond Daily Dispatch,* May 30, 1861; *OR* 2:896, 901–2 and 51(2):119–20.

60. *OR* 2:907.

61. Reports of James L. Preston and John L. Manning, June 9, 1861, Beauregard Papers, DU.

62. Stephen Mallory diary, June 21 and July 9, 1861, SHC.

63. Hunton, *Autobiography,* 25–26; Clinton Hatcher to Mary Anna Sibert, Evans-Sibert Papers, LOV.

64. Hunton, *Autobiography,* 24–27; *OR* 2:872, 894, 915–17.

4. Behold the Silvery River

1. *OR* 2:104, 915.

2. Athearn, *Soldier in the West,* 45; *OR* 2:106. For the heat wave see Taft, diary, June 10–15, 1861, LC.

3. *OR* 2:106–9, 675, 681.

4. *Baltimore Sun,* June 14, 1861.

5. Luther V. B. Furber to "Dear Mother and Sister," June 15, 1861, MDHS.

6. *OR* 2:106–7; Laas, *Wartime Washington,* 47; M. Viers Bowie to Charles P. Stone, February 7, 1862, Letters Sent and Received, Entry 3812, RG393, Part II, NA.

7. *Baltimore Sun,* June 14, 1861.

8. *OR* 2:107–8.

9. *St. Paul Pioneer*, August 18, 1861, quoted in *History of the First Regiment*, 62; *OR* 2:108, 917; Laas, *Wartime Washington*, 48.

10. *OR* 2:108; Laas, *Wartime Washington*, 48. Hunton's account of this (*Autobiography*, 25, 27–28) comports with Stone's reports and the sketch of Gaither's company in Goldsborough, *The Maryland Line*, 249.

11. *OR* 2:123, 471–72, 684, 687. For evidence of the rivalries between officers, see the exchange between Kenton Harper and William S. H. Barlow, May 24, 1861, Kenton Harper Papers, SHC.

12. Ibid., 472, 685–86, 689, 698, 701, 934.

13. Ibid., 109–11, 120; William N. Berkeley to Cynthia Berkeley, June 18, 1862, Berkeley Letters, Balch Library; Athearn, *Soldier in the West*, 48; Louis Bell to his wife, June 20, 1861, Bell Papers, UNH.

14. *OR* 2:112–14 and 51(1):404.

15. *OR* 2: 114–15, 805; *Richmond Daily Dispatch*, July 18, 1861.

16. *OR* 2:115–17.

17. Ibid., 116; Clinton Hatcher to Mary Anna Sibert, June 21, 1861, Evans-Sibert Family Papers, LOV; Pierre G. T. Beauregard to Nathan G. Evans, June 21 and 26, 1861, quoted in Silverman et al., *Shanks*, 60–61, 75–6; Cullum, *Biographical Register* 2:225; Hunton, *Autobiography*, 28 29.

18. *OR* 2:116–19, 717, 725, 726.

19. Ibid., 119; Clinton Hatcher to Mary Anna Sibert, July 17, 1861, Evans-Sibert Family Papers, LOV.

20. *OR* 2:119; *New Hampshire Patriot*, July 24, 1861; Ayling, *Revised Register*, 23.

21. *OR* 2:472, 856, 896, and 51(2):35–36, 101–2; Scarborough, *The Diary of Edmund Ruffin*, 2:54–55. McHenry Howard described the Maryland Guard uniform in his *Recollections*, 9.

22. *OR* 51(2):101. Eleven Maryland companies entered Confederate service that spring: eight in the 1st Maryland Infantry, one in the 21st Virginia Infantry, one in the 1st Virginia Cavalry, and the 1st Maryland Artillery (Goldsborough, *The Maryland Line*, 10, 160, 249, 259).

23. Goldsborough, *The Maryland Line*, 275, 296, 319, 329–33. See also, for instance, the memoir accounts of McHenry Howard (*Recollections*, 13–15) and George Booth (*Personal Reminiscences*, 8–9), although both, writing decades later, may have exaggerated the influence of military repression on their decisions.

24. For Snethen's party bias see his letter to Lincoln, March 25, 1861, Reel 19, Lincoln Papers, LC.

25. *New York Tribune*, May 7, 8, 9, 10, and 13, June 12, 13, 21, and 22, 1861; *OR* 2:138–39. It was Dean Sprague who first illuminated the depth of Snethen's intrigue in *Freedom under Lincoln*, 46–49. See the *New York Tribune* of May 10, 1861, for Snethen's remark that "we are on the eve of our deliverance. . . ."

26. *Baltimore Sun*, June 28, 1861; *OR* 2:20, 139–41, Series 2, 1:628–31, and Series 4, 3:717; Hassler, *One of Lee's Best Men*, 12; Kane to James A. McMaster, October 24, 1861, McMaster Papers, Notre Dame.

27. *OR* 2:18–19, 139–40; *Baltimore Sun*, June 28, 1861.

28. Snethen to Scott, June 29, 1861, quoted in Sprague, *Freedom under Lincoln*, 53; *OR* 2:140, and Series 2, 1:622–23, 627.

29. *OR* 51(2), 155–57.

30. *OR* 2:145–56.

31. Basler, *The Complete Works*, 4:419.

32. Basler, *The Complete Works*, 4:397, 420; Niven, *The Salmon P. Chase Papers*, 3:79, 108; *Report of the Joint Committee*, 2:238.

33. Niven, *The Salmon P. Chase Papers*, 3:108; Basler, *The Complete Works*, 4:419–20; Laas, *Wartime Washington*, 53–54.

34. *OR* 2:157, 185–86, 717, 724–26, 728–30, 732–35, and 3:390; James R. McCutchan to Rachel Ann McCutchan, June 28, 1861, McCutchan Family Papers, Washington and Lee University; Report of Colonel Kenton Harper, July 2, 1861, Pendleton Papers, DU; Trout, *With Pen and Saber*, 14.

35. *OR* 2:157, 166; *Report of the Joint Committee*, 2:36, 242; *New York Tribune*, June 26, 1861.

36. *OR* 2:157–59, 163, 172, 187, and 51(1):412; *Report of the Joint Committee*, 2:55–56, 226–27, 229; William Brooks to "Dear Sister," July 8, 1861, Brooks Family Papers, University of Virginia.

37. *OR* Series 1, 51(1):369, 387; *Report of the Joint Committee*, 2:37.

38. Scott, *Forgotten Valor*, 281.

39. *OR* 2:314–15, 438–39.

40. *OR* 2:309; *Boston Post*, July 19, 1861; Robert B. Rhett Jr. to Beauregard, undated [but July, 1861], Beauregard Papers, DU.

41. *OR* 2:487, 568.

42. Sears, *The Civil War Papers of George B. McClellan*, 56; *Richmond Daily Dispatch*, July 16, 1861; Trueblood diary, July 11, 1861, KSHS; Jones, *A Rebel War Clerk's Diary*, 32–33; Scarborough, *The Diary of Edmund Ruffin*, 2:68.

43. Enoch George Adams to "Dear Mother & Brother," June 26, 1861, Box 10, folder 21, Adams Family Papers, UNH; Lewis F. Cleveland to "Dear Will," July 8, 1861, Cleveland Collection; James J. Gillette to "Dear Mother," July 14, 1861, and to "Dear Father," July 15, 1861, Gillette Papers, LC; Ai B. Thompson to J. H. Thompson, July 15 and 16, 1861, MNBP.

44. Charles Dow to James Butler, July 10, 1861, quoted in Otis, *The Second Wisconsin*, 133, 136; *OR* 2:161, 303–4.

45. *OR* 5:928, and 51(2):175, 688; Thomas Leaver to "My Dear Mother," July 23, 1861, Leaver letterbook, NHHS; Henig, "Give My Love to All," 25.

46. *OR* 2:184, 305, 369, and 51(1):419; Charles Dow to James Butler, July 10, 1861, quoted in Otis, *The Second Wisconsin*, 135–36; *New Hampshire Patriot*, May 1, 1861; Reid-Green, *Letters Home*, 7.

47. [Coffin], *Stories of Our Soldiers*, 18. Examples of the Garibaldi Guards uniforms, and of the regimental flag, can be found in Davis, *Touched by Fire*, 2:213.

48. Diary of Mrs. Edward Bates, August 15, 1861, Bates Family Papers, MOHS; John G. Nicolay to Therena Bates, July 7, 1861, Nicolay Papers, LC; Theodore Kruger to "Dear Madame," June 24, 1861, Box 1, folder 20, Maurice Family Papers, SHC; Alfred Waud drawing no. 17, LC; OR 2:427; Struve, *Das 8 Regiment N.Y. Freiwilliger*.

49. Sears, *For Country, Cause & Leader*, 50–51; *Report of the Joint Committee*, 39; Charles C. Perkins diary, July 17, 1861, quoted in Davis, *Battle at Bull Run*, 97; Samuel P. Heintzelman journal, July 18, 1861, LC.

50. Thomas B. Leaver to "My Dear Mother," July 23, 1861, Leaver letterbook, NHHS; *Report of the Joint Committee*, 39; Sears, *For Country, Cause & Leader*, 51; Scott, *Forgotten Valor*, 284.

51. *OR* 2:449–50; *Report of the Joint Committee*, 2:39.

52. *OR* 2:449–50; Cutrer, *Longstreet's Aide*, 25; Sears, *For Country, Cause & Leader*, 51; John S. Godfrey to "Bro[ther] Horace," July 26, 1861, Godfrey Papers, NHHS; Rhodes, *All for the Union*, 25; Roelker, "Civil War Letters of William Ames," 90–91.

53. *OR* 2:309–10, 450, 459–60, 537; Scarborough, *The Diary of Edmund Ruffin*, 2:70–71; Scott, *Forgotten Valor*, 284, 287; Theodore Kruger to "Dear Madame," July 19, 1861, Box 1, folder 20, Maurice Family Papers, SHC; Samuel P. Heintzelman journal, July 20, 1861, LC.

54. Heintzelman journal, July 19, 1861, LC; Sears, *For Country, Cause & Comrade*, 51–52; Meagher, *The Last Days of the 69th*, 6; *Rochester Union and Advertiser*, July 24, 1861, quoted in Hennessy, *The First Battle of Manassas*, 8; Russell, *My Diary North and South*, 264; Otis, *The Second Wisconsin*, 46; Simpson and Berlin, *Sherman's Civil War*, 125.

55. *Winona Republican*, August 7, 1861, quoted in Moe, *The Last Full Measure*, 45; *Report of the Joint Committee*, 39.

56. Scarborough, *The Diary of Edmund Ruffin*, 2:71; Cutrer, *Longstreet's Aide*, 25; *OR* 2:310–11, 312–13, 314; *Report of the Joint Committee*, 2:199.

57. *OR* 2:311, 312; *Report of the Joint Committee* 2:39–40.

58. *Boston Journal*, July 20 and 23, 1861; George D. Wells to "Dear S.," July 19, 1861, Wells letterbook, Joyner Library, East Carolina University; George H. Johnston to his wife, undated letter fragment (but July, 1861), MHS.

59. Affidavits of Julia Gibson, Drusilla Hobbs, and Frances L. Wentworth, all dated April 13, 1864, and affidavit of E. S. Julius, December 16, 1864, Susan Wentworth's mother's pension file, Record Group 15, NA; Albert Wentworth gravestone inscription, Ossipee Village Cemetery, Ossipee, N.H.

60. *Boston Journal*, July 19, 20, and 23, 1861; Charles Bowers to Lydia Bowers, July 19, 1861, Bowers Papers, MHS.

61. Richard P. Rowe affidavit of January 16, 1862, in his invalid pension file, Record Group 15, NA; George H. Johnston to his wife (July, 1861), MHS; *OR* 2:314, 454; Sears, *For Country, Cause, & Leader*, 52.

62. Frederick W. Clark to Lizzie Clark, July 22, 1861, Clark Papers, DU; Richard Smart to "Dear Friends," July 19 and 23, 1861, MNBP; George D. Wells to "Dear S.," July 19, 1861, Wells letterbook, Joyner Library, East Carolina University. Richardson underreported losses in the 1st Massachusetts: see *OR* 2:314, against *Massachusetts Soldiers, Sailors, and Marines*, 1:40–46; individual pension records reveal that even the latter source missed a number of the wounded.

63. *OR*, 1:584, 2:311, 313; Potts diary, June 27, 1861, LOV; Sears, *For Country, Cause, & Leader*, 53–54.

64. *OR* 2:311, 313, 462, and 51(1):33–34; Potts diary, July 27, 1861, LOV; Cutrer, *Longstreet's Aide*, 26; *Report of the Joint Committee*, 2:20.

65. *OR* 2:314, 329, 373, 462; *Report of the Joint Committee*, 2:162.

66. *Richmond Daily Dispatch*, July 17, 19, and 20, 1861.

67. Ibid., June 3, 1861; *OR* 2:462–63 and 51(1):34.

5. Where Ignorant Armies Clash

1. *OR* 2:159, 161–64, 187, and 51(1):412, 415, 418; Duncan, *Blue-Eyed Child of Fortune*, 112; *Report of the Joint Committee*, 2:84, 87, 185.

2. *OR* 2:162–63, 165.

3. *Report of the Joint Committee*, 2:87; Livermore, "Patterson's Shenandoah Campaign," 25–26, 48.

4. *OR* 2: 164–65, 485; *Report of the Joint Committee*, 2:87.

5. *OR* 2:166.

6. *Report of the Joint Committee*, 2:73–75, 154.

7. Ibid., 56–57, 74–75, 87, 155; *OR* 2:977.

8. Duncan, *Blue-Eyed Child of Fortune*, 113; Trout, *With Pen and Saber*, 18.

9. *OR* 2:158, 166, 167, 169–70; *Report of the Joint Committee*, 2:141–42.

10. *OR* 2:167–68.

11. Ibid., 2:165–66; Duncan, *Blue-Eyed Child of Fortune*, 114–15; *Report of the Joint Committee*, 2:106, 156.

12. *OR* 2:167–68.

13. Ibid., 473, 478, 982; Robert Grant to "Dear Mother," July 24, 1861, MNBP.

14. *OR* 2:168.

15. Ibid., 169–70; *Report of the Joint Committee*, 2:141.

16. Duncan, *Blue-Eyed Child of Fortune*, 115, 118.

17. *OR* 2:170–73; *Report of the Joint Committee*, 2:107, 141.

18. *OR* 2:173–79; *Report of the Joint Committee*, 2:78–142.

19. Livermore, "Patterson's Shenandoah Campaign," 56; *Report of the Joint Committee*, 2:142. For a handy illustration of the high percentage of men in one ninety-day regiment who reenlisted much later or not at all, see the roster of the 1st New Hampshire in Ayling, *Revised Register*, 3–23.

20. Livermore, "Patterson's Shenandoah Campaign," 50; *Report of the Joint Committee*, 2:40, 51, 113.

21. *OR* 2:168, 308, 406, 745, 769; Dyer, *A Compendium of the War of the Rebellion*, 1403; Samuel P. Heintzelman journal, July 20, 1861, LC.

22. *Report of the Joint Committee*, 39; Sears, *For Country, Cause & Leader*, 54.

23. *Boston Journal*, July 22, 1861; *OR* 2:313; Sears, *For Country, Cause & Leader*, 54; Richard Smart to "Dear Friends," July 23, 1861, MNBP.

24. *OR* 2:314, and 51(1):33–34; *Massachusetts Soldiers*, 1:40–46; Richard Smart to "Dear Friends," July 23, 1861, MNBP; affidavit of November 15, 1907, Eugene K. Stimson invalid pension file, RG15, NA.

25. Horatio Roberts affidavit of December 18, 1864, Susan Wentworth's mother's pension file, RG15, NA; *OR* 51(1):33–34; Cutrer, *Longstreet's Aide*, 25–2; Daniel White to "Friend Marie," August 3, 1861, White Letters, Vermont Historical Society.

26. *Report of the Joint Committee*, 2:39, 40; *OR* 2:330, 473, 486; Conrad diary, July 18–19, 1861, LC; Robert Grant to "Dear Mother," July 24, 1861, MNBP.

27. *OR* 2:565–66; Isaac Hirsh diary, July 19 and 20, 1861, LOV.

28. *OR* 2:545, 558; Clinton Hatcher to Mary Anna Sibert, July 27, 1861, Evans-Sibert Family Papers, LOV.

29. Thomas Jordan to A.T.M. Rust, July 19, 1861, Reel 2, Beauregard Papers, LC.

30. Evans to Robert E. Lee, July 6, 1861, and pay voucher dated October 24, 1861, Nathan G. Evans file, Reel 88, Compiled Service Records of Confederate General and Staff Officers, and Non-Regimental Enlisted Men (M-331), RG 109, NA.

31. *OR* 51(1):26–27.

32. Ibid., 27, 32.

33. Ibid., 330–31; *Report of the Joint Committee*, 2:162, 207; Samuel P. Heintzelman journal, July 20, 1861, LC.

34. *OR* 2:318.

35. Ibid., 318, 326; Samuel P. Heintzelman journal, July 20, 1861, LC; Charles E. Jewett to "My dear brother," July 20, 1861, UNH; Samuel Burnham to "My Dear Mother," August 12, 1861, Burnham/Stearns Family Papers, NHHS. Orlando Bolivar Willcox later noted that McDowell furnished none of his subordinates with a written copy of the orders (Scott, *Forgotten Valor*, 289).

36. *OR* 2:487.

37. Ibid., 394, 397, 407, 417, and 51(1):23; Ai Thompson to J. H. Thompson, July 24, 1861, MNBP; Henig, "Give My Love to All," 23; John Robertson to "My Dear Wife," July 27, 1861, Robertson Letters, MHS.

38. *OR* 2:362, 383; *Report of the Joint Committee*, 2:212; John C. Robertson to "My Dear Wife," July 27, 1861, Robertson Letters, MHS; Eckert and Amato, *Ten Years in the Saddle*, 295.

39. *Report of the Joint Committee*, 2:41–42, 214; *OR* 2:331. The artillery officers who first fired from Tyler's front recorded doing so at "5 AM exactly," but the staff officer McDowell ordered to note those opening rounds put them precisely one hour later (*OR* 2:362; *Report of the Joint Committee*, 2:42). Across Bull Run, Nathan Evans heard the same sound at 5:15 and Colonel Cocke at 5:30 (*OR* 2:558 and 51[1]:28).

40. *OR* 2:329, 331; Eighth Census (M-653), Reel 1343, 965, RG29, NA; Rhodes, *All for the Union*, 26; Henig, "Give My Love to All," 23. The guide, Mathias C. Mitchell, bore no relation to the Mitchells of Michell's Ford.

41. *Winona Republican*, August 7, 1861, quoted in Moe, *The Last Full Measure*, 47.

42. *OR* 2:543; Cutrer, *Longstreet's Aide*, 27.

43. *OR* 2:474, 488, 561.

44. *Report of the Joint Committee*, 2:212; *OR* 2:395; Pease and Randall, *The Diary of Orville Hickman Browning*, 1:479–80.

45. *OR* 2:395–96 and 51(1):23; Samuel Burnham to "My Dear Mother," August 12, 1861, Burnham/Stearns Family Papers, NHHS; Ai B. Thompson to J. H. Thompson, July 24, 1861, MNBP; Albert G. Bates to Edith Bates, July 23, 1861, Wiley Sword Collection, USAMHI.

46. Ai B. Thompson to J. H. Thompson, July 24, 1861, MNBP.

47. *OR* 2:396, 559; Samuel Burnham to "My Dear Mother," August 12, 1861, Burnham/Stearns Family Papers, NHHS; Robert Grant to "Dear Mother," July 24, 1861, MNBP.

48. Thomas L. Wragg to "My dear Papa," July 23, 1861, LC; Hamilton Branch to "My dear, dear Mother," July 23 and 25, 1861, Sexton Papers, University of Georgia.

49. Russell, *My Diary North and South*, 262–63.

50. *OR* 2:491, 536–37, 543.

51. *OR* 2:319, 331, 402.

52. *Report of the Joint Committee*, 2:40; *OR* 2:746.

53. *OR* 2:390, 392–93, 402, 559; Henig, "Give My Love to All," 25.

54. *OR* 2:566; Thomas B. Leaver to "My Dear Mother," July 23, 1861, Leaver letterbook, NHHS.

55. James Singleton to "Dear Cousin Mattie," July 26, 1861, University of Virginia Library; Richard Habersham to "Dear Father & Mother," July 26, 1861, Habersham Family Papers, LC; *OR* 2:389, and 51(1):18; *Report of the Joint Committee*, 2:214–15.

56. *Report of the Joint Committee*, 2:30, 171; Searles, "The First Minnesota," 83, 85–86; *New York Times*, August 2, 1861. "The Last Roll," 180, includes two 1861 photographs of recruits in Company F, 11th Mississippi, wearing their dark "firemen's" shirts in lieu of complete uniforms.

57. *OR* 2:346, 394.

58. *OR* 2:481; *History of the 71st Regiment*, 160; Barton, "Stonewall Jackson," 283. Individual uniforms of the 4th and 27th Virginia are represented in photographs of William Ott and Charles Norris held by Manassas National Battlefield Park, which also preserves Norris's original jacket, and in Reidenbaugh, *27th Virginia Infantry*, 121, 122; Charles Griffin, commander of a battery that faced Jackson at close range, testified to the blue uniforms and straw hats (*Report of the Joint Committee*, 171).

59. *OR* 2:481, 492; *Daily Courier*, July 29, 1861.

60. *Report of the Joint Committee*, 2:38.

61. *OR* 2:353, 566–67; Richard Habersham to "Dear Mother & Father," July 26, 1861, Habersham Family Papers, LC.

62. *OR* 2:320, 347; *Report of the Joint Committee*, 2:144, 168–69, 174; Cullum, *Biographical Register*, 1:554.

63. *OR* 2:492–93; James Singleton to "Dear Cousin Mattie," July 26, 1861, University of Virginia Library; *Richmond Daily Dispatch*, August 17, 1861. Among those who noted Bee's blue uniform was the surgeon in Jackson's brigade (Conrad, "History of the First Battle of Manassas," 89–90.)

64. *Report of the Joint Committee*, 2:168–69, 243; Gravestone of Isaac and Judith Carter Henry, Henry Family Cemetery, MNBP.

65. *Report of the Joint Committee*, 2:30, 143, 145, 169.

66. Ibid., 146, 169; *OR* 2:403, 483, 552, and 51(1):21; Letters quoted in Casler, *Four Years in the Stonewall Brigade*, 35–38, credit the 33rd Virginia with annihilating Griffin's battery.

67. *OR* 2:347, 483, and 51(1):21; Trout, *With Pen and Saber*, 22; *Report of the Joint Committee*, 2:30–31, 146–47, 243.

68. *Report of the Joint Committee*, 2:243; *OR* 2:347.

69. *OR* 2:492–93, 495; *Richmond Daily Dispatch,* August 17, 1861; Thomas L. Wragg to "My dear Papa," July 23, 1861, Wragg Collection, LC.

70. *OR* 2:385, 392, 406; Charles E. Bowers to Lydia Bowers, July 26, 1861, Bowers Papers, MHS; *Report of the Joint Committee,* 2:175, 246; William Cartter to "Dear Mother," July 20 and 25, 1861, Cartter Family Papers, LC; Scott, *Forgotten Valor,* 293–95.

71. *OR* 2:369–71, 545, 547, and 51(1):17; Johnston, *Him on the One Side,* 27–28, 33; *War Letters of William Thompson Lusk,* 58–59; Clinton Hatcher to Mary Anna Sibert, Evans-Sibert Family Papers, LOV.

72. *OR* 2:396; Ai B. Thompson to "My Dear Father," July 24, 1861, MNBP; Haynes, *A Minor War History,* 14; Isaac P. Rodman to "My Dear Sister," August 15, 1861, George Hay Stuart Collection, LC.

73. *OR* 2:418, 496, 522; Henig, "Give My Love to All," 24; Marshall, *A War of the People,* 37, 39; Moore, *The Rebellion Record,* 2(Documents):42–43.

74. *Report of the Joint Committee,* 2:217–18; *OR* 2:320, 385, 390–91.

75. *OR* 2:396–97, 497; Rhodes, *All for the Union,* 34; Samuel Burnham to "My Dear Mother," August 12, 1861, Burnham/Stearns Family Papers, NHHS.

76. *OR* 2:525, 535; Henig, "Give My Love to All," 24.

77. *OR* 2:497, 525; Scarborough, *The Diary of Edmund Ruffin,* 2:88–89; Samuel Burnham to "My Dear Mother," August 12, 1861, Burnham/Stearns Family Papers, and Thomas B. Leaver to "My Dear Mother," July 23, 1861, Leaver letterbook, both in NHHS; Ai B. Thompson to "My Dear Father," July 27, 1861, MNBP; affidavits of Isaac W. Derby, invalid pension certificate 9589, and George S. Chase, invalid pension certificate 9492, RG 15, NA; Rhodes, *All for the Union,* 34; Roelker, "Civil War Letters of William Ames, "16–17.

78. *OR* 2:328, 525; Scarborough, *The Diary of Edmund Ruffin,* 2:89–90; Samuel Burnham to "My Dear Mother," August 12, 1861, Burnham/Stearns Family Papers, NHHS.

79. More tales of murdered wounded flourished in the days following the battle: see, for instance, Sears, *For Country, Cause, and Leader,* 58, and Morrell, *Seymour Dexter, Union Army,* 37.

80. *OR* 2:534; Scarborough, *The Diary of Edmund Ruffin,* 2:89–90.

81. Russell, *My Diary North and South,* 275; *Report of the Joint Committee,* 2:27; *OR* 2:321, 322, 351.

82. Trout, *With Pen and Saber,* 18, 19; Barnes, *Medical and Surgical History,* Part 1, 1(appendix):8.

83. John Nicolay to Therena Bates, July 21, 1861, Nicolay Papers, LC; Taft and Wheeler diaries, July 21, 1861, LC; *OR* 2:746–48; Russell, *My Diary North and South,* 275–76; French, *Witness to the Young Republic,* 366.

84. Samuel Burnham to "My Dear Mother," August 12, 1861, Burnham/Stearns Family Papers, NHHS; Sears, *For Country, Cause & Leader,* 58–59; Theodore Kruger to "Dear Madam," July 23, 1861, Box 1, folder 20, Maurice Family Papers, SHC; Charles E. Bowers to Lydia Bowers, July 26, 1861, Bowers Papers, MHS; John C. Robertson to "My Dear Wife," Robertson Letters, MHS.

85. Pease and Randall, *The Diary of Orville Hickman Browning,* 1:485; Russell, *My Diary North and South,* 277–78.

86. Taft and Wheeler diaries, July 22, 1861, LC; *OR* 2:404–5.

87. Taft diary, July 22, 1861, LC; John C. Robertson to "My Dear Wife," July 27, 1861, Robertson Letters, MHS; Laas, *Wartime Washington,* 68–69; Wheeler diary, July 22, 1861, LC.

88. Bennett Taylor to "My Dear Sue," July 31, 1861, Soldiers Letters, Army Miscellany, C.S.A. Archives, DU; James Gillette to "Dear Parents," August 8, 1861, LC; *Report of the Joint Committee,* 2:151.

89. Beale, *Journal,* 59.

90. W.G.H. Jones to unidentified recipient, July 21, 1861, Barbour Family Papers,

VHS; Robert Lewis Dabney to Elizabeth Randolph Dabney, April 25, 1861, Dabney Family Papers, VHS; Sarah Wadley diary, April 18, 1861, SHC.

91. Armstrong, *"The Hand of God Upon Us,"* 12–15; *Richmond Daily Dispatch,* July 22, 24, 25, and 29, 1861.

92. Philander Draper to Sarah Draper, July 23, 1861, Reel 1, folder 10, Draper-McClurg Family Papers, WHMC; *Letters of a Family,* 135–36; Nevins and Thomas, *The Diary of George Templeton Strong,* 3:169.

93. "The Advantages of Defeat," 363–64; Meltzer and Holland, *Lydia Maria Child: Selected Letters,* 391; Norton and Howe, *Letters of Charles Eliot Norton,* 1:237–38; Looby, *The Complete Civil War Journal and Selected Letters of Thomas Wentworth Higginson,* 224; *Independent,* August 22, 1861.

94. Bowen, *A Frontier Family in Minnesota,* 181; *Christian Advocate and Journal,* May 2, 1861; *Friend's Review,* July 20 and 27, 1861.

95. *OR* 2:171, 174, 763, 766.

96. *Boston Journal,* July 26, 1861; Henig, "Give My Love to All," 24; *OR* 2:321, 438.

97. Simpson and Berlin, *Sherman's Civil War,* 121, 124; *Report of the Joint Committee,* 2:215, 217, 218; Charles E. Bowers to Lydia Bowers, July 26, 1861, Bowers Letters, MHS.

98. George H. Johnston to "Dear Wife," July 23, 1861, Johnston Papers, MHS.

99. Ai B. Thompson to J. H. Thompson, July 24 and 30, 1861, MNBP; Isaac P. Rodman to "My Dear Sister," August 15, 1861, George Hay Stuart Collection, LC.

100. French, *Witness to the Young Republic,* 366–67; Nevins and Thomas, *The Diary of George Templeton Strong,* 3:169, 174.

101. Hammond, *Diary of a Union Lady,* 39–42; Sumner, *The Diary of Cyrus B. Comstock,* 234; Pease and Randall, *The Diary of Orville Hickman Browning,* 1:485; *Christian Recorder,* July 27, 1861; *German Reformed Messenger,* July 31, 1861; *Independent,* August 1, 1861; *Christian Advocate and Journal,* August 15, 1861.

102. Charles A. Jewett to "Sarah," July 28, 1861, Jewett Papers, UNH.

6. The Crimson Corse of Lyon

1. Benjamin F. Massey to John F. Snyder, May 31, 1861, Snyder Collection, MOHS; Resolutions of the Missouri State Convention, March 22, 1861, Reel 19, Lincoln Papers, LC. Demographic details are taken from an unpaginated appendix tipped into the *Journal of the House of Representatives of the State of Missouri, at the First Session of the Twenty-first General Assembly.*

2. See, for instance, *The Crisis, and What It Demands!,* 13–14, folder 1, Polk Papers, DU.

3. *Boonville Weekly Observer,* April 20, 1861; *Clay County Flag,* April 17, 1861; Confederate proclamation, WHMC; Rollins, "The Letters of George Caleb Bingham," 514; *Daily Messenger,* April 17 and 19, 1861. The rabidly hostile *State Journal* began publication that month.

4. Lincoln made that remark in his message to the special session of Congress on July 4. Basler, *The Complete Works,* 4:428.

5. Jackson to J. W. Tucker, April 28, 1861, James O. Broadhead Papers, MOHS; Jackson to David Walker, April 19, 1861, WHMC; *OR* 1:688, 690; Snead, "The First Year of the War in Missouri," 264; Lawrence B. Richmond to Leroy Pope Walker, April 18, 1861, Reel 1, Letters Received by the Confederate Secretary of War (M-437), NA. The evidence most often cited for Governor Jackson's duplicity was his letter to Tucker, which U.S. Attorney James Broadhead used to incriminate both men. It bears a signature similar, but not identical, to other examples of Jackson's (see, for example, his letter to George B. Hunt, August 1, 1861, Civil War Collection, MOHS). Witnesses familiar with the governor's hand differed in their opinions of the authenticity of the Tucker letter: see the testimony of James H. Britton, Isaac Rosenfelt Jr., John M. Krum, and "Mr. Robinson," in Broadhead's notes

for "Prosecution for Treason, *U.S. vs. Tucker*," Broadhead Papers, MOHS. Those same notes include the testimony of Deputy U.S. Marshal Ephraim Tunncliff, who claimed that he had pulled the letter from Tucker's desk during a raid on the newspaper office. Tunncliff evidently voiced concerns that he might be accused of having been bought by the government, perhaps because he had previously been indicted for bribery, but Broadhead assured Tunncliff that he "needn't talk to me about criminal prosecutions."

6. Cullum, *Biographical Register*, 2:11–12; *OR* 1:658, 669–71; Frank Blair to Montgomery Blair, April 19, 20, and 25, 1861, Reel 2, Blair Family Papers, LC; *St. Charles Demokrat*, May 16, 1861; *Daily Messenger*, May 22, 1861. For an insightful study of Lyon's disturbing personality see Phillips, *Damned Yankee*.

7. *OR* 1:667, and Series 3, 1:80–81; Frank Blair to Richard Yates, April 29, 1861, Blair Family Papers, MOHS; Edward Bates to James O. Broadhead, May 3, 1861, Broadhead Papers, MOHS.

8. *OR* 1:675, and 3:7–8; Broadhead to Montgomery Blair, May 22, 1861, Broadhead Papers, MOHS; John Knapp to his wife, May 10, 1861, Knapp Family Papers, MOHS; *St. Charles Demokrat*, May 16, 1861.

9. *OR* 1:669 and 3:4–7, 369. Christopher Phillips describes Lyon's cruelty toward helpless opponents in *Damned Yankee*, 33–35, 68–70, 88–90.

10. *OR* 3:5. For the more biased Unionist version of the fracas see *OR* Series 2, 1:107; *Lawrence Republican*, May 16, 1861; "Memorandum of Matters in Missouri" by Montgomery Blair's law partner, in the F. A. Dick Papers, LC; Krug, *Mrs. Hill's Journal*, 13–14; and the German-language *St. Charles Demokrat* of May 16, 1861. In *Civil War St. Louis* (108), Louis Gerteis quotes an eyewitness who claimed that the German soldiers fired without any provocation except verbal insults, but Gerteis does not cite the original source of that eyewitness testimony.

11. *OR* 3:5; Simpson and Berlin, *Sherman's Civil War*, 80–82; Bek, "The Civil War Diary of John T. Buegel," 310; *Daily Missouri Republican*, May 11, 12, 13, and 14, 1861; *Daily Missouri Democrat*, May 13, 1861; *Westliche Post*, May 15, 1861; Alice E. Cayton to Alexander Badger, May 12, 1861, Badger Collection, MOHS; [Lucy B. Hutchinson?] to "My Dear Brother," May 22, 1861, Civil War Collection, MOHS. Decades later, Sherman remembered a drunken citizen starting the riot by firing his pistol at the soldiers (Sherman, *Memoirs*, 1:201–2), but he made no mention of this man in letters at the time.

12. "Sarah" to "Dear Friends," May 13, 1861, John Stillman Brown Family Papers, Kansas State Historical Society. See also the diary of Elvira A. W. Scott, in the WHMC. Mrs. Scott was an Indiana native living in Miami, Missouri; her merchant husband felt no connection to the South or slavery, yet the excesses of the Lincoln administration and its agents transformed the entire family into Confederate sympathizers.

13. *Journal of the House of Representatives of the State of Missouri, at the Called Session of the Twenty-first General Assembly*, 54–55; *Journal of the Senate of Missouri, at the Called Session of the Twenty-first General Assembly*, 33, 76; *Daily Missouri Democrat*, May 13, 1861; Allen P. Richardson to James O. Broadhead, May 24, 1861, Broadhead Papers, MOHS.

14. John B. Clark to Bedford Brown, March 20, 1860, and John W. Cunningham to Clark, December 20, 1860, Brown Papers, DU; *OR* 53:686; *Congressional Globe*, 37th Cong., 2nd sess., 116–17.

15. *Daily Times*, April 30, 1861; *OR* 3:371, and Series 2, 1:111; Frank Blair to Montgomery Blair, May 20, 1861, Blair Family Papers, LC.

16. Irwin, "Missouri in Crisis," 152; *Daily Missouri Democrat*, May 13, 1861; *Daily Missouri Republican*, June 1 and 2, 1861; *OR* Series 2, 1:114–16.

17. *OR* 3:375; James O. Broadhead to Edwin Draper, May 21, 1861, Broadhead Papers, MOHS.

18. Richard C. Vaughn to James O. Broadhead, May 30, 1861, Broadhead Papers, MOHS; Frank Blair to Montgomery Blair, May 25, 1861, Reel 2, Blair Family Papers, LC.

19. Jackson to David Walker, April 19, 1861, WHMC.

20. Reynolds, "Price and the Confederacy," 23–24, MOHS; Thomas T. Gantt to Montgomery Blair, May 21, 1861, Reel 2, Blair Family Papers, LC; Richard Marshall Johnson diary, May 26, 1861, MOHS; Barton Bates to Edward Bates, June 3, 1861, Bates Family Papers, MOHS.

21. OR 3:374; Basler, The Collected Works, 4:372–73.

22. Allen P. Richardson to James O. Broadhead, May 24, 1861, Broadhead Papers, MOHS; Daily Missouri Democrat, May 24, 1861.

23. Rollins, "The Letters of George Caleb Bingham," 513–14; [Lucy B. Hutchinson?] to "My Dear Brother," May 22, 1861, and [Euphrasia Pettus?] to "Dear Sister," May 20, 1861, both in Civil War Collection, MOHS; Barton Bates to Edward Bates, June 3, 1861, Bates Family Papers, MOHS; OR 3:376, 378–81, 383, and 53:689–90.

24. Montgomery Blair to Frank Blair, May 17, 1861, Reel 2, Blair Family Papers, LC.

25. OR 3:382, 384.

26. OR 2:48–49; Sears, The Civil War Papers of George B. McClellan, 30–31.

27. Snead, "First Year of the War in Missouri," 267; OR 53:697. Dyer's Compendium, 1301–43, documents 13,632 deaths in Missouri's Union regiments during the war, although no fatalities are reported for some units that served for long periods. Assuming that Confederate troops from that state suffered proportionately, total Civil War deaths among Missourians easily exceeded 20,000, without even counting extensive civilian and guerrilla mortality.

28. OR 53:696–98. See Easley, "Journal of the Civil War in Missouri," 12–14, for the difficulties that a Yale- and Amherst-educated Philadelphian endured in order to join Price's army.

29. James O. Broadhead's notes on the testimony of Martin Loughlin and Michael H. Cohen, "Prosecution for Treason, U.S. vs. Tucker," Broadhead Papers, MOHS; OR 3:592–93.

30. OR 3:40 and 53:750–51; Daily Messenger, June 13, 14, and 20, 1861; William L. Broaddus to "Dear Wife," June 12, 1861, Broaddus Papers, DU; James H. Guthrie diary, June 13–16, 1861, KSHS; William W. Branson diary, June 13, 1861, WHMC.

31. OR 3:40–41; William L. Broaddus to "Dear Wife," June 15 and 16, 1861, Broaddus Papers, DU; Daily Messenger, June 23, 1861. Under his nom de plume of Mark Twain, Clemens recounted his brief service in fictionalized form as "The Private History of a Campaign That Failed," which is analyzed against the historical record in Marvel, "Fortnight as a Confederate."

32. OR 3:684.

33. Dyer, Compendium, 1046–53, 1164–65, 1186–87, 1345.

34. Richard Marshall Johnson diary, May 11, 1861, and Alice E. Cayton to Alexander Badger, May 12, 1861, Badger Collection, MOHS; Easley, "Journal of the Civil War," 19.

35. Malin, "Dust Storms," 133, 137–40; Lawrence Republican, May 10 and 17 and September 13, 1861.

36. "Letters of John and Sarah Everett," 365, 368, 369.

37. "The Letters of Samuel James Reader," 29; Luke F. Parsons diary, May 7, 13, and 29 and June 1, 1861, KSHS; "The Diary of James R. Stewart," 360, 363–93; Lawrence Republican, June 6 and 27, 1861; Fort Scott Democrat, May 4 and 25, 1861.

38. Throne, "Iowa Farm Letters," 74–76, 77–81.

39. Wilkie, Pen and Powder, 14–15.

40. OR 3:11; Daily Times, June 12, 1861; Lawrence Republican, April 18 and June 13, 1861; C. C. Gilbert to "Dear Cousin," July 15, 1861, Box 1, folder 2, Gilbert Papers, LC; Charles Robinson to Sara T. D. Robinson, June 17, 1861, Reel 1, Robinson Papers, KSHS; Hatcher and Piston, Kansans at Wilson's Creek, 24.

41. OR 3:11–12, 15.

42. OR 3:11–12; Easley, "Journal of the Civil War," 14–15; Central City and Brunswicker, June 29, 1861.

43. Rollins, "The Letters of George Caleb Bingham," 521; OR 3:11–12, 385.

44. Montgomery Blair to Edward Bates, June 19, 1861, Reel 2, Blair Family Papers, LC; Sears, *The Civil War Papers of George B. McClellan*, 48; Laas, *Wartime Washington*, 52, 54; Niven, *The Salmon P. Chase Papers*, 3:108; "Letters of Edward Bates and the Blairs," 140.

45. *OR* 3:16; Easley, "Journal of the Civil War," 16; Simpson diary, June through July 16, 1861, WHMC. Harry Truman, George Washington Carver, and the painter Thomas Hart Benton were all born within range of the sprawling State Guard encampments.

46. *OR* 3:17–19, 38–40; Easley, "Journal of the Civil War," 17–19; Bek, "The Civil War Diary of John T. Buegel," 311–12; *Arkansas True Democrat*, August 1, 1861.

47. Lobdell, "Civil War Journal and Letters," 449–50; Lyon to Sigel, July 10, 1861, WHMC; Bek, "The Civil War Diary of John T. Buegel," 312.

48. *Fort Scott Democrat*, July 13, 1861; *Daily Conservative*, August 4, 1861; Lobdell, "Civil War Journal and Letters," 453; Latimer, *Love and Valor*, 43, 47.

49. Easley, "Journal of the Civil War," 20–21. An extensive collection of photographs owned by General Sweeny's Museum of Republic, Missouri, adjacent to the Wilson's Creek National Battlefield visitor center, demonstrates this variety of attire.

50. Latimer, *Love and Valor*, 42, 47, 50; Poole diary, August 1 and 3, 1861, Wilson's Creek National Battlefield; *Dubuque Weekly Times*, August 8, 1861; *OR* 3:394; Hatcher and Piston, *Kansans at Wilson's Creek*, 51; Branson diary, July 22, 1861, WHMC.

51. *Davenport Daily Democrat & News*, August 8, 1861, quoted in Hatcher and Piston, *Wilson's Creek*, 132; *OR* 3:408, 622–23; Easley, "Journal of the Civil War," 20–21.

52. Poole diary, August 1 and 2, 1861, Wilson's Creek National Battlefield; *OR* 3:47–52; Branson diary, August 4, 1861, WHMC; Lobdell, "Civil War Journal and Letters," 22–23.

53. *OR* 3:47–48, 57; Lobdell, "Civil War Journal and Letters," 23; Easley, "Journal of the Civil War," 21–22.

54. *OR* 3:48; Lobdell, "Civil War Journal and Letters," 23–24.

55. *OR* 3:57; L. L. Jones to "My Dearest," August 8, 1861, Herbert S. Hadley Papers, MOHS; C. C. Gilbert to "Dear Cousin," July 15, 1861, Box 2, folder 1, Cass Gilbert Papers, LC.

56. *OR* 3:74, 99; Easley, "Journal of the Civil War," 22.

57. *OR* 3:99, 104; Easley, "Journal of the Civil War," 22.

58. Lobdell, "Civil War Journal and Letters," 457; *OR* 3:60, 86.

59. Lobdell, "Civil War Journal and Letters," 25; *OR* 3:94, 104; Randolph Harrison Dyer to "Dear Sister," August 12, 1861, WHMC; Cutrer and Parrish, *Brothers in Gray*, 40.

60. *OR* 3:65; Lyon to William B. Edwards, August 9, 1861, Lyon Collection, MOHS; Lobdell, "Civil War Journal and Letters," 28.

61. *OR* 3:86, 100, 127, and 53:751; Lobdell, "Civil War Journal and Letters," 28–29; L. L. Jones to "My Dearest," August 9, 1861, Hadley Papers, MOHS. The best military, social, and political study of not only Wilson's Creek but the war in Missouri in 1861 is Hatcher and Piston, *Wilson's Creek*.

62. *OR* 3:86–87, 109–10, and 53:425; Bek, "The Civil War Diary of John T. Buegel," 312.

63. *OR* 3:65, 72, 111, 113, 121; Lobdell, "Civil War Journal and Letters," 29–30; Cutrer and Parrish, *Brothers in Gray*, 41; James H. Wiswell to "Dear Sister," August 31, 1861, DU.

64. *OR* 3:66, 87–88, 113, 119, and 53:425–26; Larimer, *Love and Valor*, 16; Cutrer and Parrish, *Brothers in Gray*, 41. Sigel, who was widely criticized for abandoning his troops, admitted donning the disguise in "The Flanking Column at Wilson's Creek," 305.

65. *OR* 3:121–22, and 53:425.

66. *OR* 3:72, 100–101, 113–14, and 53:429–30; Lobdell, "Civil War Journals and Letters," 30–31; Easley, "Journal of the Civil War," 22–23.

67. *OR* 3:63, 67, 81, 118–19; Lobdell, "Civil War Journals and Letters," 30–31.

68. Lobdell, "Civil War Journals and Letters," 31; *OR* 3:67–68.

69. *OR* 3:68–69, 104; Lobdell, "Civil War Journals and Letters," 31, 34; Hatcher and Piston, *Kansans at Wilson's Creek*, 77; "A Texan at Wilson's Creek," 46–47.

70. Bek, "The Civil War Diary of John T. Buegel," 313; *OR* 3:63-64, 94-98, 107; Lobdell, "Civil War Journals and Letters," 36-37; Branson diary, August 11, 1861, WHMC; Poole diary, Wilson's Creek National Battlefield.

71. Harris, *Dear Sister*, 4; *New York Times*, August 14 and 15, 1861; Nevins and Thomas, *The Diary of George Templeton Strong*, 3:160, 175. The battle of August 10 is traditionally known as Wilson's Creek, although the stream for which it is named is called Wilson Creek.

7. The Despot's Heel

1. Branch, *Mark Twain's Letters*, 1:122.

2. *Daily Messenger*, June 14, 1861; *South Danvers Wizard*, June 26, 1861.

3. *Daily Missouri Republican*, July 13, 1861; "Prosecution for Treason, *U.S. vs. Tucker*," James O. Broadhead Papers, MOHS.

4. *Daily American*, August 9, 1861; *Boston Evening Transcript*, August 9, 1861; *New Hampshire Patriot*, August 14 and 21, 1861; *Laconia Democrat*, August 11, 1861; *Democratic Standard*, uncertain date, quoted in the *New York Times*, August 11, 1861; *New York Tribune*, August 13, 1861.

5. *Daily American*, August 16 and 26, 1861; *New York Tribune*, August 25, 1861; *New York Times*, August 25, 1861.

6. Nevins and Thomas, *The Diary of George Templeton Strong*, 3:175; *New York Times* and *New York Tribune*, September 15, 1861; *Journal of Commerce*, September 5, 1861, quoted in Sprague, *Freedom under Lincoln*, 145; *OR* Series 2, 2:802; Simon, *Papers of Ulysses S. Grant*, 2:139.

7. *OR* 3:433-34, 439, 442, 459; Basler, *The Collected Works*, 4:485.

8. Grimball journal, August 19, 1861, SHC; Sarah Wadley diary, August 21, 1861, SHC; *OR* 3:747.

9. *OR* 3:658, 660, 667, 680, 698-99; M. Jeff Thompson to Gideon Pillow, 6:30 PM August 31, 1861, Pillow Papers, DU.

10. H.A.M. Henderson to Leroy Pope Walker, April 15, 1861, Clarence J. Prentice to same, April 17, 1861, and M. A. Quarles to same, April 16, 1861, Reel 1, Letters Received by the Confederate Secretary of War (M-437), NA.

11. John Clay to Simon Cameron, April 19, 1861, Reel 6, Cameron Papers, LC; Frank F. Steel to "My Dear Sister," December 8, 1860, and August 19, 1861, Steel Papers, SHC; Marshall, *A War of the People*, 22-23.

12. C. F. Burnham to James S. Rollins, April 22, 1861, Rollins Papers, WHMC; R. M. Robinson to John J. Crittenden, April 20, 1861, Reel 13, Crittenden Papers, LC; Moore, *The Rebellion Record*, 1:264-65; *Louisville Journal*, May 21, 1861.

13. Magoffin to John M. Johnson, May 24, 1861, Magoffin Letters, LC; *OR* 4:183-84, and 52(2):69, 102-3, 106-7.

14. Basler, *The Collected Works*, 4:532; Burlingame and Ettlinger, *Inside Lincoln's White House*, 24; *OR* 52(1):141-42, 161-62; Niven, *The Salmon P. Chase Papers*, 3:77, 80-82; *Kentucky Yeoman*, May 25, 1861, quoted in Coulter, *Civil War and Readjustment*, 90; George Morrison to "Dear Sir," August 1, 1861, Container 217, Breckinridge Family Papers, LC.

15. Magoffin to Isham G. Harris, August 12, 1861, Magoffin Letters, LC; William Nelson to Crittenden, August 16, 1861, Reel 13, Crittenden Papers, LC; Basler, *The Collected Works*, 4:368-69.

16. *OR* 4:367, 374, and 52(2):46; Neal, *The Journal of Eldress Nancy*, 3-4; Muster-in rolls of Companies A through F, 1st Kentucky Infantry, Reel 21, Records of Confederate Movement and Activities (M-861), RG 109, NA; *Commonwealth*, July 15, 1861.

17. *OR* 4:378, 396-97, and 52(2):102-3, 106-7; Magoffin to Isham G. Harris, August 12, 1861, Magoffin Letters, LC.

18. Evans, *Confederate Military History*, 11:25.

19. *OR* 3:466–67; *An Address to the Citizens of the State of Missouri,* folder 1, Thompson Papers, SHC.

20. Joshua F. Speed to Joseph Holt, September 7, 1861, Book 30, Holt Papers, LC; Niven, *The Salmon P. Chase Papers,* 3:92–95; Basler, *The Complete Works,* 4:532.

21. *New York Sun,* September 3, 1861 (clipping in Book 30 of the Holt Papers, LC); Basler, *The Complete Works,* 4:506, 517–18; Elizur Wolcott to Samuel Wolcott, September 17, 1861, Letters to Samuel Wolcott, Yale.

22. *OR* 3:693; John G. Nicolay to Therena Bates, September 11 and 17, 1861, Nicolay Papers, LC; Montgomery Blair to Frank Blair, September 27, 1861, Reel 5, Blair Family Papers, LC.

23. *OR* 3:141–42.

24. *OR* 4:179–81, 185, 188–90, 191–92; Welker, *A Keystone Rebel,* 25–26.

25. *OR* 4:189–90, 196–97; Moore, *Rebellion Record,* 2:164.

26. *Louisville Journal,* September 16, 1861; *Kentucky Yeoman,* September 10, 1861, quoted in Coulter, *The Civil War and Readjustment,* 110; Moore, *The Rebellion Record,* 3:127–29; Neal, *The Journal of Eldress Nancy,* 4.

27. J. T. Hughes to R. H. Miller, August 29 and September 4, 1861, Mosby Monroe Parsons Papers, DU; *OR* 3:163–65.

28. *OR* 3:185–93; Isaac Hockaday to "Dear Mother," September 26, 1861, WHMC; Samuel Churchill Clark to Meriwether Lewis Clark, November 5, 1861, Clark Family Papers, MOHS.

29. *The Republican,* August 29, 1861, quoted in Nevins, *The War for the Union,* 1:331.

30. *Resolutions of the General Assembly,* 4; *Protest of the General Assembly,* 4; *Report of the Police Commissioners.*

31. Unsigned and undated letter, quoted in Sprague, *Freedom under Lincoln,* 184, and cited as in the Lincoln Papers, LC. A manual search of the Lincoln Papers in 2004 and an electronic search in 2005 failed to produce the letter.

32. Simpson and Berlin, *Sherman's Civil War,* 125; *OR* 5:554, 555–56, 567–68; Sears, *The Civil War Papers of George B. McClellan,* 86, 87, 89; *New York Times,* August 18, 1861.

33. Randolph B. Marcy to McClellan, August 20, 1861, with McClellan's endorsement, McClellan to Lincoln, same date, and Seward to Lincoln, August 22, 1861, all on Reel 25, Lincoln Papers, LC.

34. Seth Williams to Charles P. Stone, September 4, 1861, Letters and Telegrams Sent and Received, Entry 3812, RG393, Part II, NA; *OR* 5:585; Sears, *The Civil War Papers of George B. McClellan,* 95–97.

35. *OR* 5:833–34, and 51(2)275–76; E. A. Miller to "My Dear Vic," September 13, 1861, South Caroliniana Library, University of South Carolina; Clinton Hatcher to Mary Anna Sibert, September 13, 1861, Evans-Sibert Family Papers, LOV.

36. *Frederick Herald,* September 3, 1861.

37. Sears, *The Civil War Papers of George B. McClellan,* 99; *OR* 5:193, 195–96, and Series 2, 1:679.

38. *OR* 5:196, and Series 2, 1:667–75; *Correspondence between S. Teackle Wallis, Esq. of Baltimore, and the Hon. John Sherman,* 3; Sangston, *The Bastiles of the North,* 7–8.

39. Sangston, *The Bastiles of the North,* 8–9.

40. Marks and Schatz, *Between North and South,* 36–37.

41. *OR* Series 2, 1:667–74, 681, 684–85.

42. Father John McCaffrey to Archbishop John Purcell, September 26, 1861, Archdiocese of Cincinnati Papers, University of Notre Dame.

43. *American,* September 15, 1861, quoted in Basler, *The Collected Works,* 4:523.

44. E. T. Bambridge to Joseph Holt, September 18, 1861, Book 30, Holt Papers, LC.

45. *OR* Series 2, 1:667–75.

46. *OR* Series 2, 1:676–77.

47. Sears, *The Civil War Papers of George B. McClellan,* 565; *Correspondence between*

S. Teackle Wallis, Esq. of Baltimore, and the Hon. *John Sherman,* 4–7; Sangston, *The Bastiles of the North,* 4–5.

48. *OR* Series 2, 1:667–75, 679–80; *New York Times,* March 1, 1862.

49. E. D. Townsend to Stone, August 3, 1861, and Charles W. Sandford to Winfield Scott, August 6, 1861, Charles "B." Stone Papers, Box 5, Generals' Papers, Entry 159, RG 94, NA.

50. *OR* 5:557–58, 559, 560, 567.

51. *OR* 5:560, 562, 567; *Boston Journal,* October 25, 1861.

52. *OR* 5:560, 567–69; Cutrer, *Longstreet's Aide,* 50; letters to the St. Paul *Pioneer* dated August 18, 1861, and to the *Winona Daily Republican* dated August 24, 1861, quoted in *History of the First Regiment,* 62–64.

53. *OR* 5:567; pay account dated October 24, 1861, Nathan G. Evans file, Reel 88, Compiled Service Records of Confederate General and Staff Officers, and Non-Regimental Enlisted Men (M-331), NA; George N. Newlon to "Dear Parents," July 28, 1861, Newlon Family Letters, LOV; John R. White to "My Dear Mollie," October 31, 1861, McDonald Papers, DU; Silver, *A Life for the Confederacy,* 51; James M. Holloway to "My Dearest Wife," August 29 and September 19, 1861, Holloway Papers, VHS.

54. *OR* 5:578.

55. *OR* 51(1):454–55; Blair, *A Politician Goes to War,* 11.

56. Nathaniel Banks to Abraham Lincoln, August 22, 1861, and to Simon Cameron, August 28, 1861, Reel 25, Lincoln Papers, LC.

57. *OR* 5:569; *Massachusetts Soldiers, Sailors, and Marines,* 2:131–204; Looby, *The Complete Civil War Journal and Selected Letters of Thomas Wentworth Higginson,* 224.

58. Stowe journal, August 25–27, 1861, USAMHI; Coco, *From Ball's Bluff to Gettysburg,* 17; *OR* 51(1):467.

59. Deed Books STS4, 498–500, 503–5, and TD5, 308–11, Montgomery County Courthouse. For reference to Young and his island enterprise see *Report of the Joint Committee,* 346–47, 497; Ira Grosvenor to Charles P. Stone, December 30, 1861, and H. W. Hudson to Stone, January 8, 1862, both in Letters Sent and Received, Entry 3812, RG 393, Part II, NA.

60. Loudoun County Land Book, 1860, reel 488, Balch Library; Deed Books 5C, 90–91; 5D, 29–30; 5G, 231–32; 5L, 170–71, 5O, 211–12; 6A, 178, 189–90, Loudoun County Circuit Court; Seventh Census (M-432), Reel 957, 310, and Eighth Census (M-653), Reel 1359, 42, 79, RG 29, NA. A cursory title search done for the Northern Virginia Regional Park Authority overlooks Mrs. Jackson's ownership of the central portion of the battlefield.

61. Deed Books 5O, 328–29, 6N, 123–24, and 6P, 409–10, Loudoun County Circuit Court.

62. George Washington to Burgess Ball, August 4, 1793, February 3 and July 18, 1794, Ball Papers, LC; headstone inscriptions, Ball Family Cemetery, Routes 15 and 740, Leesburg, Va.

63. George Washington Ball's oath of allegiance, Reel 56, Case Files of Presidential Pardons (M-1003), NA; Seventh Census (M-432), Reel 957, 330, and Eighth Census (M-653), Reel 1359, 78, and Reel 1393, 15, RG 29, NA; Loudoun County Land Book, 1860, Reel 488, Balch Library.

64. Deed Book 4B, 382, Deed Book 5I, 205, and Will Book 2Q, 325–26, Loudoun County Circuit Court; Loudoun County Land Book, 1861, Reel 489, Balch Library; Eighth Census (M-653), Reel 1359, 40, and Reel 1393, 7, RG 29, NA. A Union officer described Smart's Mill in *Stories of Our Soldiers,* 74.

65. Deed Book Y, 132–34, Loudoun County Circuit Court; Lee and Froelch, *Triassic-Jurassic Stratigraphy of the Culpeper and Barboursville Basins,* 16–18. Topographical maps give the crown of Ball's Bluff a height of about 120 feet above the river, but the steepest portion of the bluff begins to level off about a hundred feet above the shelf of the riverbank.

66. *OR* 5:592–93, and 51(1):463; Edwin V. Sumner Jr. to George Thistleton, September 16, 1861, Letters Sent and Received, Entry 3812, and Charles P. Stone to Seth Williams, September 10, 1861, Letters Sent, Entry 3804, both in RG 303, Part II, NA.

67. Stone to "Col. Le Duc," August 17, 1861, Letters Sent, Entry 3804, and General Order No. 17, September 23, 1861, General Orders, Entry 3814, both in RG 393, Part II, NA; Crosby diary, October 11 and 24, 1861, Yale.

68. Stone to Stephen Miller, August 19, 1861, Letters Sent, Entry 3804, and "Capt. Smith" to Stone, October 12, 1861, Letters Received, Entry 3808, both in RG 393, Part II, NA.

69. Charles Stewart to Thomas Poole, October 17, 1861, and Willis Gorman to Charles Stewart, October 19, 1861, Letters Sent and Received, Entry 3812, and Charles Devens to Stone, October 17, 1861, Letters Received, Supplemental, Entry 3810, all in RG 393, Part II, NA. For specific examples of charges, countercharges, requests for leave, and resignations in the 2nd N.Y.S.M., see also John H. Wilcox to Stone, September 2, 1861, G.W.B. Tompkins to Stone, September 17, September 20, October 2, and October 20, 1861, James Brady to Stone, September 20, September 26, and October 24, 1861, and Charles E. Robinson to Stone, August 25, 1861, all in Letters Received, Entry 3808, RG 393, Part II, NA, and Special Orders No. 85, 87, and 88, Special Orders, Corps of Observation, Entry 3816, RG 393, Part II, NA.

70. *Report of the Joint Committee*, 2:391–92; Stewart to Adjutant General, September 17, 1861, Letter S-1015, Reel 58, Letters Received by the Office of the Adjutant General, 1861–1870 (M-619), NA; *OR* 5:115.

71. *OR* 2:66, 207, 218, 288, and 51(1):478.

72. *Roxbury City Gazette*, October 10, 1861; Nathan Hayward to "Dear Father," September 15, 1861, Hayward Letters, MHS; William Bartlett to "Ben," September 15, 1861, quoted in Palfrey, *Memoir*, 7–12.

73. *OR* 5:592–93; Gorman to Charles "Stuart," September 26, 1861, Letters Sent and Received, Entry 3812, RG 393, Part II, NA.

74. Coco, *From Ball's Bluff to Gettysburg*, 20, 22–23; Nathan Hayward to "Dear Father," September 15, 23, and 26, 1861, Hayward Letters, MHS.

75. Athearn, *Soldier in the West*, 49; Paul Revere to "My Dear Lu," October 8, 1861, Revere Family Papers, Reel 4, MHS.

76. Edwin C. Myers to "Dear Father," September 24, 1861, Myers Letters, University of Mississippi; Silver, *A Life for the Confederacy*, 57–58, 60–62; James Montgomery Holloway to "Dearest Wife," September 19, 1861, Holloway Papers, VHS; Lack diary, November 26 and December 9, 1861, and Miller diary, November 15, 1861, both in Balch Library.

77. Blair, *A Politician Goes to War*, 10, 14–15; *OR* 5:606, and 51(1):489–90; Geary to Stone, September 28, 1861, Letters Sent and Received, Entry 3812, RG 393, Part II, NA. See Edwin Fischel's sketch of "Buxton," an apparent double agent, in *The Secret War for the Union*, 86–88.

78. *OR* 5:884–87; Cutrer, *Longstreet's Aide*, 47.

79. Cutrer, *Longstreet's Aide*, 47; *OR* 5:218–20; Acken, *Inside the Army of the Potomac*, 21–26; Bombaugh, "Extracts from a Journal," 304–5; Alfred Wheeler to "Dear Mother," October 8, 1861, Wheeler Letters, Civil War Miscellaneous Collection, USAMHI.

80. *Berkshire County Eagle*, October 24, 1861; Bates, *History of Pennsylvania Volunteers*, 2:801–28; *New York Times*, April 22, 1861; Bombaugh, "Extracts from a Journal," 305; *OR* 5:217.

81. Alfred Wheeler to "Dear Mother," October 8, 1861, Wheeler Letters, Civil War Miscellaneous Collection, USAMHI; Acken, *Inside the Army of the Potomac*, 27.

82. Acken, *Inside the Army of the Potomac*, 28, 37; Baker to Charles P. Stone, October 14, 1861, Letters Sent and Received, Entry 3812, TG 393, Part II, NA; Daniel Schambert to "Monsieur," October 12, 1861, Box 1, Winthrop Family Papers II, MHS; *Berkshire County Eagle*, October 24, 1861. Civil War soldiers typically misspelled "chasseur" when

they intended the French word for a light-infantry soldier; the popular American spelling "chausseur" is the French word for a merchant of footwear.

83. William Berkeley to Cynthia Berkeley, August 30 and October 1, 1861, Berkeley Letters, Balch Library; Silver, *A Life for the Confederacy*, 56, 74, 88.

84. For examples of such photographs, see Davis, *Touched by Fire*, 1:168–73.

85. Silver, *A Life for the Confederacy*, 54–55; "List of Killed, Wounded, and Missing in Battle of Ball's Bluff," Consolidated Report, Reel 5, Confederate Casualty Lists (M-836), RG 109, NA; Miller diary, November 15, 1861, Balch Library.

86. *Cambridge Chronicle*, October 12 and 19, 1861; *The Villager*, October 24, 1861; John McEwen to "Cousins Maggie & Jennie," October 18, 1861, McEwen Papers, LC. Fort Evans still survives: see Balicki and Owen, *Documentation*, 54.

87. Nathan Hayward to "Dear Father," September 26, 1861, Hayward Letters, MHS; *Report of the Joint Committee*, 2:333, 340, 406; Daniel Schambert to "Monsieur," November 1, 1861, Winthrop Papers, MHS. Schambert remarked that "le 15iem Mass. V. est trés mal armé, leurs fusilles ne vallent [sic] pas grand chose."

88. Matthew Marvin to his brother, August 1, 1861, Minnesota Historical Society, and Joseph Spencer to his sister, September 1, 1861, Wisconsin Historical Society, both quoted in Moe, *The Last Full Measure*, 77; Groat, *Pages Clothed in the Plainest of Dress*, 16; *Chelsea Telegraph and Pioneer*, October 12, 1861.

89. John McEwen to "Cousins Maggie & Jennie," October 18, 1861, McEwen Papers, LC; Robert Askew to "My Dear Bro.," September 16, 1861, Askew Family Letters, Bowling Green State University.

90. *OR* 5:493; Charles Devens to Stone, October 19, 1861, Letters Received, Supplemental, Entry 3810, RG 393, Part II, NA; "Captain Smith" to Stone, October 12, 1861, Letters Received, Entry 3808, RG 393, Part II, NA; H. W. Bunting to Stone, October 13, 1861, Charles Stewart to Gorman, October 13 and 16, 1861, Stewart to Robert Parrish, October 15 and 16, 1861, Stewart to C.W.C. Baxter, October 17, 1861, all in Letters Sent and Received, Entry 3812, RG 393, Part II, NA.

91. Charles Stewart to T. Harvey, Young to Baker, and Baker to Stewart, all October 19, 1861, Letters Sent and Received, Entry 3812, RG 393, Part II, NA.

92. Stone to "My Dear General," October 10, 1861, Letters Sent and Received, Entry 3812, RG 393, Part II, NA; Wilkeson to Lyman Trumbull, November 6, 1861, Trumbull Papers, LC. For Wilkeson's special War Department dispensation, see Starr, *Bohemian Brigade*, 69–70.

8. By Cliffs Potomac Cleft

1. *OR* 5:613.

2. Sears, *The Civil War Papers of George B. McClellan*, 106; Woodward, *Our Campaigns*, 42; *OR* 51(1):496; Burlingame and Ettlinger, *Inside Lincoln's White House*, 24–25.

3. *OR* 5:239–48; William Noland Berkeley to Cynthia Berkeley, October 16, 1861, Berkeley Letters, Balch Library; Hill diary, October 15 and 16, 1861, Mississippi Department of Archives and History; Fisher, "The Travels of the 13th Mississippi," 291–92; Richmond Howitzers Order Book, 28, VHS; Hodijah Lincoln Meade to Jane Eliza Meade, October 30, 1861, VHS; Blair, *A Politician Goes to War*, 18.

4. Charles P. Stone to Randolph Marcy, 10 PM October 16, 1861, Reel 20, Telegrams Collected by the Secretary of War, Unbound (M-504), NA; Hill diary, October 16, 1861, Mississippi Department of Archives and History.

5. Joseph J. Dimock to "My dear Sister Jennie," October 12, 1861, Dimock Family Papers, Emory University; *Baltimore Commercial Advertiser*, October 7, 1861.

6. Fisher, "The Travels of the 13th Mississippi," 292; *OR* 5:292, 347.

7. *OR* 5:347, 621; Blackford, *Letters from Lee's Army*, 48–49; Stone to McClellan,

2:30 PM October 15, 1861, Reel 20, Telegrams Collected by the Secretary of War, Unbound (M-504), NA.

8. *OR* 5:249; E. J. Allen [Pinkerton] to McClellan, October 16, 1861, Pinkerton letterbook, Box 44, Pinkerton's National Detective Agency Collection, LC; Moore, *Rebellion Record,* 3:209–11; Haydon, *Aeronautics in the Union and Confederate Armies,* 123; Sears, *The Civil War Papers of George B. McClellan,* 109.

9. Burlingame and Ettlinger, *Inside Lincoln's White House,* 27–29; Meade, *Life and Letters,* 1:224; *Report of the Joint Committee,* 2:257.

10. *Report of the Joint Committee,* 2:259; Woodward, *Our Campaigns,* 44–45.

11. Hill diary, October 18 and 19, 1861, Mississippi Department of Archives and History; Fisher, "The Travels of the 13th Mississippi," 292; Silver, *A Life for the Confederacy,* 68.

12. "E. J. Allen" to "General," October 28, 1861, Reel 13, McClellan Papers, LC.

13. Hill diary, October 19, 1861, Mississippi Department of Archives and History; Fisher, "The Travels of the 13th Mississippi," 292; *OR* 5:349; Silver, *A Life for the Confederacy,* 68; "E. J. Allen" to "General," October 28, 1861, Reel 13, McClellan Papers, LC.

14. Silver, *A Life for the Confederacy,* 68–69.

15. Hunton, *Autobiography,* 45, 47; Richmond Howitzers Order Book, 47, VIIS; Flavius Alfred Osburn gravestone, Union Cemetery, Leesburg, Va.; Hamilton, *The Papers of Randolph Abbott Shotwell,* 1:111.

16. *OR* 5:292, 621; *Report of the Joint Committee,* 2:403; Stone to McClellan, 6:45[?] PM October 18, 1861, Reel 12, McClellan Papers, LC; Stone to McClellan 10:45 PM October 18 and 11 PM October 19, 1861, Reel 20, Telegrams Collected by the Secretary of War, Unbound (M-504), NA.

17. *Letter of the Secretary of War,* 32.

18. *OR* 5:349; Silver, *A Life for the Confederacy,* 68.

19. *OR* 5:292.

20. *Letter of the Secretary of War,* 32; *OR* 5:293. For the most detailed and insightful examination of the entire battle of Ball's Bluff, see Morgan, *A Little Short of Boats.*

21. *OR* 5:290–91, 293, 333, 361; Isaac Taylor to "Sis Alvina," October 20, 1861, Minnesota Historical Society; *Boston Journal,* October 25, 1861.

22. *OR* 5:360–61; Fisher, "The Travels of the 13th Mississippi," 292; Silver, *A Life for the Confederacy,* 69.

23. Special Orders No. 451, Reel 4, Beauregard Papers, LC.

24. Stone believed that the reconnaissance started late because Devens was out of camp at the time the order arrived. Quartermaster Howe testified that the order came later in the afternoon, and that it specified a dusk reconnaissance, but Howe's testimony included some obvious errors in remembering the timing of events: *Report of the Joint Committee,* 2:277, 375, 403.

25. Coco, *From Ball's Bluff to Gettysburg,* 39, 42; Walter Eames to "My Dear Wife," October 20, 1861, Murray Smith Collection, USAMHI; *Report of the Joint Committee,* 2:267, 375, 403, 405.

26. *Report of the Joint Committee,* 2:375; *OR* 5:299–300.

27. J. J. Schoolcraft to "My dear Father," October 27, 1861, Reel 42, Schoolcraft Papers, LC; *OR* 5:294.

28. Coco, *From Ball's Bluff to Gettysburg,* 39–40, 42; *Report of the Joint Committee,* 2:404–5; Caspar Crowninshield to "my dear Mother," October 22, 1861, Box 1, Putnam Papers, MHS. Crowninshield's letter also appears on Reel 7 of the Crowninshield-Magnus Papers, MHS.

29. Scott, *Fallen Leaves,* 67; *Report of the Joint Committee,* 2:405; Crowninshield journal, October "20," 1861, Boston Public Library.

30. Coco, *Ball's Bluff to Gettysburg,* 39–40; *Report of the Joint Committee,* 2:405.

31. *Report of the Joint Committee,* 2:405; *OR* 5:308. In his official report, written two

days later, Devens guessed that the footpath up Ball's Bluff lay "about 60 rods" downstream from their landing point, or about 990 feet; fourteen weeks later, in an apparent error in transcription, the stenographer of the congressional committee recorded his testimony on the distance as "some sixty or seventy yards, perhaps more."

32. Palfrey, *Memoir of William Francis Bartlett*, 20; *Report of the Joint Committee*, 2:405, 475–76.

33. *OR* 5:361; muster-in roll and "Record" of the Magnolia Guards, William L. Duff file, reel 253, Compiled Service Records, Mississippi (M-269), RG 109, NA; *OR* 5:361.

34. Burns diary, October 21, 1861, Save the Flags Collection, USAMHI; Vanderslice, *The Civil War Letters of George Washington Beidelman*, 44.

35. *OR* 5:308; *Report of the Joint Committee*, 2:405. The U.S. Naval Observatory calculates that "civil twilight" on October 21, 1861, would have begun at 5:59 AM, Eastern Standard Time, and sunrise at 6:26, but the concept of standard time had not yet been established, so individual watches varied widely.

36. *Report of the Joint Committee*, 2:375, 405; *Windham County Transcript*, November 7, 1861.

37. *Report of the Joint Committee*, 2:405-6.

38. *OR* 5:309; *Report of the Joint Committee*, 2:406.

39. Palfrey, *Memoir of William Francis Bartlett*, 20–21; muster roll of Company I, 20th Massachusetts, August 28, 1861, William R. Riddle service file, Records of the Adjutant General, RG 94, NA; Valentine, *To See My Country Free*, 51; *Report of the Joint Committee*, 2:475, 476. Colonel Lee testified that he thought the boats were all supposed to be carried over the island, but he did not know whether Revere had done so in the case of the big scow. Revere, who heard Lee's testimony, declined an offer to expand upon it (*Report of the Joint Committee*, 2:475, 486). The question is answered only by their regimental history, which records that transportation to the Virginia side "had been more than doubled by the addition of a scow, brought around the upper end of the island during the morning by Major Revere" (Bruce, *The Twentieth Regiment*, 32). Logically the scow came around under Revere's orders, rather than by his own hand, but so explicit a statement would presumably have been based on the submission of a contributor who had witnessed or participated in the actual movement of the boat.

40. Palfrey, *Memoir of William Francis Bartlett*, 21; Caspar Crowninshield to "my dear Mother," October 22, 1861, Charles Putnam Papers, MHS; N.M.J. Dale to Seth Williams, January 4, 1862, William R. Riddle service file, Records of the Adjutant General, RG 94, NA.

41. Four days later Riddle's captain wrote (Palfrey, *Memoir of William Francis Bartlett*, 21) that the shooting occurred "about sunrise," or 6:26 in modern terms. Lieutenant Colonel Isaac Wistar of the 1st California, waiting on the canal upstream from the island, heard "a scattering fire" that he took for the driving in of pickets, "about an hour before" an event that he timed at eight o'clock, while Colonel Lee remembered it as "half past seven o'clock (*Report of the Joint Committee*, 2:307, 476).

42. *OR* 5:363; Valentine, *To See My Country Free*, 47, 51, 147.

43. *OR* 5:309, 363; Valentine, *To See My Country Free*, 51, 148; *Windham County Transcript*, November 7, 1861; *Report of the Joint Committee*, 2:406.

44. Register of Appointments, and Jenifer to Josiah Gorgas, October 6, 1862, Walter H. Jenifer file, Reel 83, Compiled Service Records, Virginia (M-324), RG 109, NA; Heitman, *Historical Register*, 1:571; John Cheves Haskell memoir, 19–21, VHS; *OR* 5:368; Miller diary, November 21, 1861, Balch Library.

45. *OR* 5:309, 368.

46. *Report of the Joint Committee*, 2:376.

47. *OR* 5:335; William Barksdale to Nathan G. Evans, November 7, 1861, Reel 7, Confederate Casualty Lists (M-836), RG 109, NA.

48. *Report of the Joint Committee*, 2:462-63; *OR* 5:349, 368.

49. *Report of the Joint Committee,* 2:476–77; Palfrey, *Memoir of William Francis Bartlett,* 21–22.

50. *Report of the Joint Committee,* 2:376, 477.

51. *OR* 5:309; *Report of the Joint Committee,* 2:376. The original source for Ward's suspiciously self-exculpatory claim appears to be Ford's 1898 *Story of the Fifteenth Regiment,* 75, in which an alleged excerpt from Ward's October 21 diary entry is inserted; in it, Ward illogically insisted that "I told him [Howe] what General Stone's orders were," as though Howe were relaying contradictory instructions, when in fact it was Howe who had delivered those orders in the first place.

52. Coco, *From Ball's Bluff to Gettysburg,* 41–42; Charles H. Eager to "My dear Wife," October 28, 1861, Eager Letters, Lewis Leigh Collection, USAMHI.

53. Coco, *From Ball's Bluff to Gettysburg,* 42.

54. *OR* 5:295, 303; *Report of the Joint Committee,* 2:275, 434.

55. *Report of the Joint Committee,* 2:434.

56. Ibid., 376; *OR* 5:295–96.

57. *Report of the Joint Committee,* 2:376–77; Coco, *From Ball's Bluff to Gettysburg,* 42.

58. Valentine, *To See My Country Free,* 53, 148; Fisher, "The Travels of the 13th Mississippi," 292; *OR* 5:368–69.

59. *OR* 5:309–10; *Report of the Joint Committee,* 2:407; Coco, *From Ball's Bluff to Gettysburg,* 42.

60. Coco, *From Ball's Bluff to Gettysburg,* 42–43; Walter Eames to "Dear Father," October 23, 1861, Eames Letters, Murray Smith Collection, USAMHI; Charles H. Eager to "My dear Wife," October 22, 1861, Eager Letters, Lewis Leigh Collection, USAMHI.

61. Coco, *From Ball's Bluff to Gettysburg,* 43; Valentine, *To See My Country Free,* 53; *OR* 5:310, 369.

62. Scott, *Fallen Leaves,* 60; *Report of the Joint Committee,* 2:477.

63. *Massachusetts Soldiers, Sailors, and Marines,* 2:499–501.

64. Marriage certificate and original application, Jane Merchant widow's pension certificate 22,512, RG 15, NA; Melville, *Battle Pieces,* 28; *Massachusetts Soldiers, Sailors, and Marines,* 2:499–501; *Rebellion Record,* 3:216.

65. *Report of the Joint Committee,* 2:477; Scott, *Fallen Leaves,* 62; John J. Schoolcraft to Henry Rowe Schoolcraft, October 27, 1861, Container 54, Reel 42, Schoolcraft Papers, LC.

66. *OR* 5:364; Valentine, *To See My Country Free,* 53; J. J. Schoolcraft to "My dear Father," October 27, 1861, Reel 42, Schoolcraft Papers, LC.

67. *Report of the Joint Committee,* 2:307; *OR* 51(1):502.

68. *Report of the Joint Committee,* 2:258, 489; *OR* 51(1):499.

69. *Report of the Joint Committee,* 2:276, 490; *OR* 5:312, 320, 365; White, *History of the Battle,* 10.

70. *Report of the Joint Committee,* 2:307–8, 477–78; *Dedham Gazette,* November 23, 1861; *OR* 5:326.

71. *OR* 5:310; Burns diary, October 21, 1861, Save the Flags Collection, USAMHI; Coco, *From Ball's Bluff to Gettysburg,* 44; Wistar's report of November 7, 1861, published in his *Autobiography,* 364–65; *Report of the Joint Committee,* 2:308–9; 377, 478.

72. *Dedham Gazette,* November 2, 1861; *Report of the Joint Committee,* 2:309; *OR* 5:367, 370.

73. Coco, *From Ball's Bluff to Gettysburg,* 44–45; *Report of the Joint Committee,* 2:480.

74. *OR* 5:312, 320–21, 364; Valentine, *To See My Country Free,* 53–54.

75. *OR* 51(1):46–48; *Annual Report of the Adjutant General of the State of Rhode Island and Providence Plantations for the Year 1865,* 761.

76. *Report of the Joint Committee,* 2:310, 479; *OR* 5:365–67, and 51(1):47–48; administrator's petition and report of sick and wounded, E. R. Burt file, Reel 264, Compiled Ser-

vice Records, Mississippi (M-269), RG 109, NA; John Martin Steffan to "Dear Guss," October 23, 1861, Steffan Letters, Civil War Miscellaneous Collection, USAMHI.

77. *Report of the Joint Committee*, 2:479; Scott, *Fallen Leaves*, 62; Washington A. Roebling to unidentified recipient, undated but October 23 and 24, 1861, Reel 2, Roebling Family Papers, Rutgers University.

78. *Report of the Joint Committee*, 2:377; J. J. Schoolcraft to "My dear Father," October 27, 1861, Reel 42, Schoolcraft Papers, LC; *OR* 51(1):47–48.

79. Scott, *Fallen Leaves*, 62; Caspar Crowninshield to "my dear Mother," October 22, 1861, Box 1, Putnam Papers, MHS; Michael Donlon to "Dear Brother," October 23, 1861, Donlon Letters, Civil War Miscellaneous Collection, USAMHI; J. J. Schoolcraft to "My dear Father," October 27, 1861, Reel 42, Schoolcraft Papers, LC.

80. Barnes, *Medical and Surgical History*, 1(1): appendix, 11–12; Howe, *Touched with Fire*, 13, 23–24; Scott, *Fallen Leaves*, 62.

81. Barnes, *Medical and Surgical History*, 1(1): appendix, 12–13 and 2(2): 831; Scott, *Fallen Leaves*, 63–64; Howe, *Touched with Fire*, 25; Richard Cary to "My dear Helen," October 25, 1861, Cary Letters, MHS.

82. "List of Killed, Wounded, and Missing in Battle of Ball's Bluff fought 21st Oct 1861," Reel 5, Confederate Casualty Lists (M-836), NA; *Charleston Mercury*, October 26, 1861.

83. *OR* 5:357, 367; "List of Killed, Wounded, and Missing in Battle of Ball's Bluff fought 21st Oct 1861," Reel 5, and William Barksdale to Nathan Evans, November 7, 1861, Reel 7, Confederate Casualty Lists (M-836), NA; A. B. Wagner to "Col. Ballou," October 28, 1861, Ballou Family of Virginia Papers, LC.

84. *OR* 5:357, 367; William Barksdale to Nathan Evans, November 7, 1861, Reel 7, Confederate Casualty Lists (M-836), RG 109, NA; Clinton Hatcher to Mary Anna Sibert, May 29 and October 8, 1861, Evans-Sibert Family Papers, LOV; *Democratic Mirror*, October 30, 1861.

85. Acken, *Inside the Army of the Potomac*, 33–34.

86. Caspar Crowninshield to "my dear Mother," October 22, 1861, Box 1, Putnam Papers, MHS.

87. *Report of the Joint Committee*, 2:480–81.

88. *OR* 5: 358, 360, 367; White, *History of the Battle*, 10; Silver, *A Life for the Confederacy*, 69–70.

89. Coco, *From Ball's Bluff to Gettysburg*, 48; *Report of the Joint Committee*, 2:410–11; Thomas Compass to "Friend Cuttle," November 1, 1861, Lewis Leigh Collection, Book 4, USAMHI.

90. *OR* 5:322; Washington A. Roebling to unidentified recipient, undated but October 23 and 24, 1861, Reel 2, Roebling Family Papers, Rutgers University; Timothy O'Meara to John O'Meara, October 9, 1861, April 1 and November 23, 1863, and R. Sheridan to John O'Meara, Nov. 29, 1863, all in Mary O'Meara's mother's pension file, certificate 39332, RG 15, NA.

91. *Report of the Joint Committee*, 2:411–12; Charles H. Eager to "My dear Wife," October 22 and 28, 1861, Eager Letters, Lewis Leigh Collection, Book 15, USAMHI; Walter Eames to "My dear Wife," October 22, 1861, to "Dear Father," October 23, 1861, and to "Dear Mother," November 30, 1861, Eames Letters, Murray Smith Collection, USAMHI; *Fitchburg Sentinel*, November 15, 1861.

92. Coco, *From Ball's Bluff to Gettysburg*, 49–50; David Schambert to "Monsieur," November 1, 1861, Winthrop Family Papers II, MHS.

93. Palfrey, *Memoir of William Francis Bartlett*, 26–27; J. J. Schoolcraft to "My dear Father," October 27, 1861, Reel 42, Schoolcraft Papers, LC.

94. Palfrey, *Memoir of William Francis Bartlett*, 27–29; *Roxbury City Gazette*, November 28, 1861; J. J. Schoolcraft to "My dear Father," October 27, 1861, Reel 42, Schoolcraft Papers, LC; Valentine, *To See My Country Free*, 149.

95. Peirson, *Ball's Bluff*, 14.

96. *OR* 5:367; John Wampler journal, October 21, 1861, quoted in Kundahl, *Confederate Engineer*, 99.

97. Valentine, *To See My Country Free*, 54, 149; Silver, *A Life for the Confederacy*, 72.

98. *Report of the Joint Committee*, 2:487; *OR* 51(1):501–2; Stone to McClellan, 6:45 PM October 21, 1861, Reel 12, McClellan Papers, LC.

99. Stone to McClellan, 9:30 PM October 21, 1861, Reel 20, Telegrams Collected by the Secretary of War, Unbound (M-504), NA; *Report of the Joint Committee*, 2:487.

100. *OR* 51(1):500–501; *Report of the Joint Committee*, 2:490.

9. Shovel Them Under and Let Me Work

1. Harris, *Prison-Life*, 13–15; Acken, *Inside the Army of the* Potomac, 35–36; *Report of the Joint Committee*, 486.

2. *Democratic Mirror*, January 12, 1859 and May 8, 1861; muster rolls of September through December, 1861, William S. Pickett file, Reel 592, Compiled Service Records, Virginia (M-324), RG 109, NA.

3. Acken, *Inside the Army of the Potomac*, 38–40; Stowe journal, October 21–23, 1861, Civil War Times Illustrated Collection, USAMHI; Blackford, *Letters from Lee's Army*, 49–50.

4. A. S. Webb to "My dear Sister," October 24, 1861, Webb Family Papers, SHC.

5. Stowe journal, October 23–24, 1861, Civil War Times Illustrated Collection, USAMHI; Lanman, *The Journal of Alfred Ely*, 199–200; *Richmond Daily Dispatch*, November 4, 1861.

6. Acken, *Inside the Army of the Potomac*, 37; Silver, *A Life for the Confederacy*, 72; Valentine, *To See My Country Free*, 54; Scott, *Fallen Leaves*, 62.

7. McIntosh, "The Whole World Was Full of Smoke," 7; Neill A. Baker to his daughter, November 10, 1861, Lewis Leigh Collection, Book 41, USAMHI; M. D. King to "Dear Brother and Sister," October 30, 1861; BV 80, Fredericksburg and Spotsylvania National Military Park; *Daily Courier*, November 5, 1861.

8. *OR* 5:314, 350; *Daily Courier*, November 4, 1861.

9. Quaife, *From the Cannon's Mouth*, 274; *Report of the Joint Committee*, 2:425–17, 506; Burlingame and Ettlinger, *Inside Lincoln's White House*, 27–28.

10. *OR* 5:350, 354; Evans to Beauregard, October 23, 1861, Beauregard Papers, DU; Hill diary, October 23, 1861, Mississippi Department of Archives and History; Fisher, "The Travels of the 13th Mississippi," 293; Barksdale to Evans, November 7, 1861, Reel 7, Confederate Casualty Lists (M-836), RG 109, NA.

11. Theodore Compass to "Friend Cuttle," November 1, 1861, Lewis Leigh Collection, Book 4, USAMHI; *Report of the Joint Committee*, 2:254–55; Hill diary, October 23, 1861, Mississippi Department of Archives and History.

12. *Report of the Joint Committee*, 2:506; Evans to Beauregard, October 23, 1861, Beauregard Papers, DU.

13. *Report of the Joint Committee*, 2:506; Beauregard to Evans, October 23, 1861, Reel 2, Beauregard Papers, LC; Theodore Compass to "Friend Cuttle," November 1, 1861, Lewis Leigh Collection, Book 4, USAMHI. See Meade, *Life and Letters*, 1:226, for weather details.

14. Walter Eames to "Dear Father," October 23, 1861, Eames Letters, Murray Smith Collection, USAMHI; *War Letters, 1862–1865*, 247; Thomas Jordan to Jefferson Davis, October 22, 1861, Telegrams Received (M-618), RG 109, NA.

15. Burlingame and Ettlinger, *Inside Lincoln's White House*, 27; Taft diary, October 22, 1861, LC; Crawford, *William Howard Russell's Civil War*, 159. The reporter was Charles C. Coffin of the *Boston Journal*, a generally truthful observer prone to romantic prose (*Stories of Our Soldiers*, 12–13).

16. See, for instance, the optimistic ruminations that Brigadier General Samuel P. Heintzelman recorded in his journal on the very day of Ball's Bluff, Reel 7, Heintzelman Papers, LC.

17. *New York World*, October 29, 1861; Stedman, *Life and Letters*, 1:248, 251.

18. *New York Tribune*, October 23, 1861; *New York Times*, October 23–25, 1861; *New York Herald*, October 25, 1861; Taft diary, October 23, 1861, LC; Nevins and Thomas, *Diary of George Templeton Strong*, 3:189–90; Meade, *Life and Letters*, 1: 225–26.

19. *New York Tribune*, October 31, 1861; *War Diary and Letters of Stephen Minot Weld*, 31; Worthington, *A Cycle of Adams Letters*, 1:63, 65.

20. *Aegis and Transcript*, November 2, 1861; *Fitchburg Sentinel*, October 25, 1861.

21. Charles Eager to "My dear Wife," November 8, 1861, Eager Letters, Lewis Leigh Collection, Book 15, USAMHI; *Fitchburg Sentinel*, November 8, 1861; *Massachusetts Spy*, November 11, 1861.

22. Looby, *The Complete Civil War Journal and Selected Letters of Thomas Wentworth Higginson*, 224; Bartol, *Our Sacrifices*, 7.

23. *New York Herald*, October 28, 1861; *New York Examiner*, October 31, 1861; Worthington, *A Cycle of Adams Letters*, 1:65; Nevins and Thomas, *The Diary of George Templeton Strong*, 3:190. The *Examiner* article, which criticized Baker's performance in the battle, was written by one of Lincoln's private secretaries (Burlingame, *Dispatches from the White House*, 39–40), and another of his secretaries alluded to the offered commissions in his eulogy to Baker (Hay, "Colonel Baker," 108).

24. L. V. "Brieux" [illegible] to Benjamin Wade, November 1, 1861, Reel 3, Wade Papers, LC.

25. Richard Cary to "My dear Helen," October 25, 1861, Cary Letters, MHS; Morse, *Letters Written During the Civil War*, 25–29.

26. Gideon Welles to "My Dear Wife," October 24, 1861, Reel 19, Welles Papers, LC.

27. *Frank Leslie's Illustrated Newspaper*, November 9, 1861; *New York Herald*, October 28, 1861; *New York Tribune*, October 25, 28, and 31, 1861.

28. W. W. Burns to Charles P. Stone, November 2, 1861, Letters Sent and Received, Entry 3812, and November 6, 1861, Letters Received, Supplemental, Entry 3810, both in RG 393, Part II, NA; General Orders No. 2, file II600, Box 294, Court Martial Case Files, RG 153, NA; Basler, *The Collected Works*, 5:60; *OR* 5:327–29.

29. *New York Tribune*, October 25, 1861; Stone to George McClellan, October 27, 1861, Reel 13, McClellan Papers, LC; *OR* 5:329–30.

30. Scott, *Fallen Leaves*, 68, 70, 73; *Roxbury City Gazette*, November 7, 1861; Hammond, *Diary of a Union Lady*, 180.

31. *OR* 5:339–41.

32. Wilson Hix file, Reel 450, Confederate Papers Relating to Citizens or Business Firms (M-346), RG 109, NA.

33. Brownlow, *Sketches*, 249–55.

34. Harrison to Judah P. Benjamin, November 13, 1861, and indictment against George Ish, Abner Hixson, and William B. Atwell, Item 7585, Reel 15, and Evans to Benjamin, November 26, 1861, Item 7753, Reel 16, Letters Received by the Confederate Secretary of War (M-437), NA; Vote on Secession Ordinance, May 23, 1861, Miscellaneous Lists, Balch Library; Seventh Census (M-432), Reel 942, 171, RG 29, NA; Laas, *Wartime Washington*, 221.

35. Pinkerton to J. L. McPhail, October 17, 1861, to Andrew Porter, October 19, 1861, and to George R. Dodge, October 20, 1861, folder 11, Box 44, Pinkerton's National Detective Agency Collection, LC.

36. *OR* Series 2, 2:295, 298, 299, 302, 306, 308, 309, 665, 771–72, 801–2; Stone to "My Dear General," October 10, 1861, Letters Sent and Received, Entry 3812, RG 393, Part II, NA.

37. *OR* Series 2, 2:298–315.

38. *OR* Series 2, 2:298–315, 1021–23; Nevins and Thomas, *The Diary of George Templeton Strong*, 3:190.

39. *Maryland Union*, November 14, 1861; *OR* Series 2, 2:319.

40. *Maryland Union*, November 14, 1861.

41. Burlingame and Ettlinger, *Inside Lincoln's White House*, 29; William Sherwood to his wife, October 23, 1861, MDHS; *OR* Series 2, 1:608–16, and 2:103–4; *Baltimore Sun and American*, November 7 and 8, 1861.

42. Hancock, "The Civil War Diaries of Anna M. Ferris," 232; L. V. Brieux to Benjamin F. Wade, November 1, 1861, Reel 3, Wade Papers, LC; *Boston Journal*, October 5, 1861; *Richmond Daily Dispatch*, October 22, 1861.

43. *OR* 5:300–302.

44. Walter Eames to "My Dear Wife," November 5 and 6, 1861, Murray Smith Collection, USAMHI; Joseph J. Dimock to "My dear sister Jennie," November 9, 1861, Dimock Family Papers, Emory University; *New York Times*, November 10, 1861; *OR* 5:306–7.

45. Such images appeared in *Harper's Weekly* of October 26 and November 2, 1861.

46. Burns to Stone, November 2, 1861, Burns to Vaughn, November 6, 1861, and Thomas F. Vaughn to Stone, October 31, 1861, all in Letters Sent and Received, Entry 3812, RG 383, Part II, NA.

47. David Patterson to unidentified recipient, June 13, 1862, Rhode Island Historical Society; *Annual Report of the Adjutant General of the State of Rhode Island*, 789; Dyer, *Compendium*, 1397.

48. Joseph J. Dimock to "My dear sister Jennie," November 9, 1861, Dimock Family Papers, Emory University.

49. Church Howe to Stone, November 6, 1861, Letters Sent and Received, Entry 3812, RG 393, Part II, NA; *New York Tribune*, October 25 and 28, 1861.

50. P. R. Burdick to Stone, November 12, 1861, Letters Sent and Received, Entry 3812, RG 393, Part II, NA.

51. *OR* 2:351; G.W.B. Tompkins to Stone, with Stone's endorsement, October 2, 1861, Letters Received, Entry 3808, Stone to Tompkins, undated and December 26, 1861, and Stone to commanding officer, 2nd New York Militia, January 17, 1862, Letters Sent and Received, Entry 3812, all in RG 393, Part II, NA.

52. Dimock to Conkling, January 8, 1862, Reel 3, Wade Papers, LC.

53. Ben Wade to Caroline Wade, October 25, 1861, Reel 3, Wade Papers, LC. McClellan kept his headquarters at 19th and Pennsylvania that winter (Taft diary, October 28, 1861, LC).

54. Sears, *The Civil War Papers of George B. McClellan*, 111–12, 114–16, 122; Zachariah Chandler to Letitia Chandler, October 27, 1861, Reel 1, Chandler Papers, LC.

55. Russell, *My Diary North and South*, 320–21.

56. Zachariah Chandler to Letitia Chandler, October 27, 1861, Reel 1, Chandler Papers, LC; Burlingame and Ettlinger, *Inside Lincoln's White House*, 28, 30; Basler, *The Collected Works*, 5:9–10.

57. Sears, *The Civil War Papers of George B. McClellan*, 125–26, 128, 129, 130–32, 133–34.

58. Heintzelman journal, November 11, 1861, Reel 7, Heintzelman Papers, LC; Burlingame and Ettlinger, *Inside Lincoln's White House*, 32; Beale, *The Diary of Edward Bates*, 200.

59. Taft diary, November 20, 1861, LC; French, *Witness to the Young Republic*, 380–81; John G. Nicolay to Therena Bates, November 21, 1861, Nicolay Papers, LC; Sears, *Civil War Papers of George B. McClellan*, 137.

60. Burlingame and Ettlinger, *Inside Lincoln's White House*, 28, 29, 31–32; Basler, *Collected Works*, 5:34–35; Taft diary, November 24–29 and December 1–21, 1861, LC; Sears, *The Civil War Papers of George B. McClellan*, 143.

61. Pease and Randall, *The Diary of Orville Hickman Browning*, 1:512; Niven, *The Salmon P. Chase Papers*, 1:321–22.

62. Blight, *When This Cruel War Is Over*, 64.

63. *Congressional Globe*, 37 Cong., 2 Sess., 6, 16–17, 29–32, 52–55.

64. *OR* 5:474–76, 489, 490–94; *Report of the Joint Committee*, 1:67.

65. *Report of the Joint Committee*, 1:116, 120–21, 123–24, 182, 184.

66. Basler, *The Collected Works*, 5:88; Schleiden Dispatch No. 1, January 6, 1862, Schleiden Correspondence, Bremen Staatsarchiv, LC, translated in Trefousse, *The Radical Republicans*, 184.

67. Niven, *The Salmon P. Chase Papers*, 1:322; *Report of the Joint Committee*, 1:131–45.

68. *Congressional Globe*, 37th Cong., 2nd Sess., 162–66.

69. Taft diary, November 21–23, 1861, LC; French, *Witness to the Young Republic*, 375–76; U.S. Congress. House. *Loyalty of Clerks and Other Persons*, 1–92, but especially 28–29; Basler, *The Collected Works*, 5:25.

70. For a thorough analysis of the committee and its impact, see Tap, *Over Lincoln's Shoulder*.

71. *Report of the Joint Committee*, 2:5.

72. Ibid., 253–64.

73. *Report of the Joint Committee*, 2:265–80; Charles Stewart to Francis Palfrey, December 23, 1861, Letters Sent and Received, Entry 3812, RG 393, Part II, NA.

74. *Congressional Globe*, 37th Cong., 2nd Sess., 130.

75. Stone to Sumner, December 23, 1861, Sumner Papers, Harvard.

76. *New York Tribune*, December 21, 1861; *New York Times*, December 28, 1861; Greeley to Wade, December 29, 1861, Reel 3, Wade Papers, LC.

77. Stone to Seth Williams, December 28, 1861, Reel 14, McClellan Papers, LC; Stone to Simon Cameron, December 29, 1861, Reel 20, Telegrams Collected by the Secretary of War, Unbound (M-504), NA; Daniel Harvey Hill to his wife, December 7 and 13, 1861, Hill Papers, USAMHI; *Report of the Joint Committee*, 1:72–73.

78. *Report of the Joint Committee*, 2:279–80.

79. *Congressional Globe*, 37th Cong., 2nd Sess., 189–91, 193–94; Stone to James Hardie, January 7 and 10, 1862, Reel 15, McClellan Papers, LC; *OR* 51(1):517.

80. *Report of the Joint Committee*, 2:388–96.

81. Ibid., 289, 295–96; *OR* 2:351; Thomas T. Gantt to Stone, September 27, 1861, Army of the Potomac Letterbook, Reel 62, McClellan Papers, LC.

82. *Report of the Joint Committee*, 1:90; Basler, *The Collected Works*, 5:167.

83. *Report of the Joint Committee*, 2:442–43; Stone to Seth Williams, January 18, 1862, Reel 15, McClellan Papers, LC.

84. *Report of the Joint Committee*, 2:318–31; General Orders No. 2, file II600, Box 294, Court Martial Case Files, RG 153, NA; Basler, *The Collected Works*, 5:60. Although Young's testimony is dated January 16, 1862, the committee's minutes specify that no witnesses were examined that day; his testimony is instead noted under the minutes of January 17. *Report of the Joint Committee*, 1:75.

85. *Report of the Joint Committee*, 2:18.

86. Mansfield to Zachariah Chandler, January 21, 1862, Reel 1, Chandler Papers, LC.

87. Cameron to Lincoln, January 11, 1862, Reel 31, Lincoln Papers, LC; Lincoln to Cameron (two letters), January 11, 1862, Reel 8, Cameron Papers, LC. See also Alexander K. McClure to Gideon Welles, September 22, 1870, Welles to an unnamed recipient (probably Montgomery Blair), September 24, 1870, and Welles to McClure, September 30, 1870, all on Reel 25, Welles Papers, LC.

88. Chase to Willim Pitt Fessenden, January 15, 1862, with Fessenden's endorsement, quoted in the statement of Francis Fessenden, Reel 1, Stanton Papers, LC.

89. *Kennebec Journal*, January 13 and 15, 1862; *The Age*, January 30, 1862.

90. "Trumbull Correspondence," 103. The authority for the breakfast meeting is Cameron's endorsement of a February 2, 1862, letter in the Ward Hill Lamon Collection, cited (erroneously) in Thomas and Hyman, *Stanton*, 139, as in the Library of Congress. The Lamon Collection is actually in the Huntington Library.

91. *Report of the Joint Committee,* 1:75-76; Basler, *The Collected Works,* 5:155.

92. Snethen to Stanton, January 22, 1862, and Medill to Stanton, January 21, 1862, both on Reel 1, Stanton Papers, LC.

93. *OR* 5:41.

94. *Report of the Joint Committee,* 1:78 and 2:426, 502, 504; Stone to Benjamin Lossing, November 5, 1861, Schoff Collection, University of Michigan.

95. *Report of the Joint Committee,* 2:426-27; Stone to Benjamin Lossing, November 5, 1861, Schoff Collection, University of Michigan.

96. *Report of the Joint Committee,* 428-29; Stone to John Geary, December 12, 1861, Reel 20, Telegrams Collected by the Office of the Secretary of War, Unbound (M-504), NA.

97. Stone to Powell, January 28, 1862, Reel 32, Lincoln Papers, LC.

98. *Report of the Joint Committee,* 2:432-33.

99. Ibid., 1:79-80. Prior to the election of 1860 Covode chaired a committee that investigated the Buchanan administration for alleged corruption (without result); he also introduced the initial resolution to impeach Andrew Johnson in 1868. The only other committee Democrat seldom resisted the Republican majority.

100. Beale, *The Diary of Edward Bates,* 229.

101. Pinkerton to McClellan, February 6, 1862, Reel 16, McClellan Papers, LC; *Report of the Joint Committee,* 2:504.

102. Laas, Wartime Washington, 102; Thomas Kimber to McClellan, February 11, 1862, Reel 16, McClellan Papers, LC; Stone to Benjamin Lossing, November 5, 1866, Schoff Collection, University of Michigan; Lt. Charles Wood's prisoner receipt for Stone, February 9, 1862, C. P. Stone file, Box 5, Generals' Papers, Entry 159, RG 94, NA.

103. Charles H. Ross, John Coons, and M. D. McCullough to Frederick Lander, February 13, 1862, Schoff Collection, University of Michigan; Allan Pinkerton to George B. McClellan, February 15, 17, 24, and 25, 1862, Reels 16 and 17, McClellan Papers, LC.

104. D. H. Hill to "My Dear Wife," February 13, 1861, Hill Papers, USAMHI; Heintzelman journal, February 10 and May 22, 1862, LC; Simpson and Berlin, *Sherman's Civil War,* 225-26.

105. Kearny to Cortlandt Parker, February 15, March 4, and March 17, 1862, Kearny Papers, LC.

106. Ibid., March 4, 1862; Cogswell's belated report (*OR* 5:320-23) outlines his specific criticism of Baker. Notably, Cogswell served through the war without rising above the rank of colonel, and the U.S. Senate even failed to confirm his brevet promotions until 1869.

107. Basler, *The Collected Works,* 5:154, and 7:285; Stone to Lorenzo Thomas, May 8, 1862, Charles P. Stone Papers, Box 5, Generals' Papers, Entry 159, RG 94, NA; *Congressional Globe,* 37th Cong., 2nd Sess., 1662-66, appendix, 414.

108. E. D. Townsend to Martin Burke, August 16, 1862, Charles P. Stone Papers, Box 5, Generals' Papers, Entry 159, RG 94, NA; Moore, *The Rebellion Record,* 4:28 (diary of events).

109. Stone to Benjamin Lossing, November 5, 1866, Schoff Collection, University of Michigan.

110. *Report of the Joint Committee,* 1:108, and 2:486-502; *Washington Evening Star,* February 28, 1863.

111. *New York Times,* April 13, 1863; *OR* 26(1):660, 34(2):756, and 41(2):680; James C. Biddle to his wife, September 15, 1864, Biddle Papers, Historical Society of Pennsylvania; Basler, *The Collected Works,* 7:285-86.

112. James C. Biddle to his wife, September 15, 1864, Biddle Papers, and John Gibbon to his wife, September 18, 1864, Gibbon Papers, both in Historical Society of Pennsylvania; *OR* 41(2):372, 572, 665-66; Stone to Meade, September 11, 1864, Lucas Collection.

113. For more than a dozen years Stone served as chief of staff of the Egyptian army, with the rank of lieutenant general.

Epilogue

1. Even Stanton's rather flattering biographer, Harold Hyman, could not deny that "Stanton was closely involved in the persecution of General Charles P. Stone." Hyman nevertheless attempted to blame McClellan for Stone's plight, suggesting that in the middle of the Peninsula campaign McClellan, rather than Stanton, should have answered Stone's appeals for less stringent confinement, some hint of the accusations against him, and a court martial (*Stanton*, 260–61).

2. See, for instance, Lincoln's intercession in the case of an officer who had been dismissed when found guilty of spying on a married woman as she undressed (Basler, *The Collected Works*, 6:538–39). The Stone affair is conspicuously absent from William Lee Miller's *Lincoln's Virtues: An Ethical Biography*, and from Geoffrey Perret's *Lincoln's War*. In *The Presidency of Abraham Lincoln* (104–5) Phillip Paludan noted the Stone episode, among others, tentatively excusing it on the reasoning that Stone and the other injured generals had put themselves in jeopardy by revealing their politics. Stone had done nothing of the sort, however, except by obeying the existing laws regarding fugitive slaves.

3. For prominent examples see Nevins and Thomas, *The Diary of George Templeton Strong*, 3:95; Williams, *Diary and Letters of Rutherford Birchard Hayes*, 2:2, 4; John M. Botts to Edward Bates, Bates Family Papers, MOHS; "The Letters of Samuel J. Reader," 27.

4. See Lincoln's letter of September 22, 1861, to Orville Hickman Browning (Basler, *The Collected Works*, 4:531–33).

5. See, for instance, Fogel and Engelman, *Time on the Cross*, Goldin, *Urban Slavery in the American South*, and Aitken, *Did Slavery Pay?*, especially Robert Evans Jr's essay, "The Viability of Slavery," 197–205.

6. For a careful study of Confederate repression, see Neely, *Southern Rights*.

Bibliography

Manuscripts

Thomas Balch Library, Leesburg, Va.
  William Noland Berkeley Letters
  Civil War Letters
    Thomas McDermott Letter
    Mary E. Sangster Letter
  Civil War Lists and Registers
    Miscellaneous Lists
    Loudoun County Vote on Ordinance of Secession
    Membership of the Loudoun Guard
  Mary E. Lack Diary
  Loudoun County Historic Buildings
  Springwood File
  Loudoun County Tax Lists and Land Books
  Virginia J. Miller Diary
  Charles E. Paxton Daybook
  Elijah V. White Manuscript Address
  William Williams Narrative
Boston Public Library, Boston, Mass.
  Caspar Crowninshield Journal
Bowling Green State University, Bowling Green, Ohio
  Askew Family Letters
George Cleveland, Private Collection, Tamworth, N.H.
  Lewis Frederick Cleveland Letters
Dartmouth College Library, Hanover, N.H.
  Elmer Bragg Papers
  Arthur S. Nesmith Collection

Oscar D. Robinson Papers
Daniel Ruggles Collection
Duke University, Durham, N.C.
P.G.T. Beauregard Papers
William L. Broaddus Papers
C.S.A. Archives
Frederick W. Clark Papers
Lizzie Gill Papers
Marshall McDonald Papers
Mosby Monroe Parsons Papers
William Nelson Pendleton Papers
Gideon Johnson Pillow Papers
Daniel Ruggles Correspondence
James H. Wiswell Letters
East Carolina University Library, Greeneville, N.C.
J. Y. Joyner Library
George Duncan Wells Letterbook
Emory University, Atlanta, Ga.
Dimock Family Papers
Fredericksburg and Spotsylvania National Military Park, Fredericksburg, Va.
Chatham Hall
M. D. King Letter
Harvard University, Cambridge, Mass.
Houghton Library
Charles Sumner Papers
Historical Society of Pennsylvania, Philadelphia
James C. Biddle Papers
John Gibbon Papers
Indiana Historical Society, Indianapolis
Miriam W. Green Papers
Johns Hopkins University, Baltimore, Md.
Peabody Institute Library
John Pendleton Kennedy Papers
Huntington Library, San Marino, Cal.
Ward Hill Lamon Collection
Kansas State Historical Society, Topeka
John Stillman Brown Family Papers
James H. Guthrie Diary
Webster W. Moses Diaries
Luke F. Parsons Diary
Charles and Sara T. D. Robinson Papers
Alva Curtis Trueblood Diary
Library of Congress, Washington, D.C.
Ball Papers
Ballou Family of Virginia Papers
Edward Bates Papers

P.G.T. Beauregard Papers
Blair Family Papers
Breckinridge Family Papers
Bremen Staatsarchiv
    Rudolph Schleiden Correspondence
Simon Cameron Papers
Cartter Family Papers
Zachariah Chandler Papers
Daniel B. Conrad Diary
Samuel Wylie Crawford Papers
John J. Crittenden Papers
Cass Gilbert Papers
James J. Gillette Papers
Habersham Family Papers
Samuel P. Heintzelman Papers
Joseph Holt Papers
Frederick West Lander Papers
Abraham Lincoln Papers
Beriah Magoffin Letters
George B. McClellan Papers
John McEwen Papers
Edward McPherson Papers
Willie P. Mangum Papers
Montgomery Meigs Papers
Miscellaneous Manuscripts Collection
    F. A. Dick Papers
John G. Nicolay Papers
Franklin Pierce Papers
Pinkerton's National Detective Agency Collection
Prints and Photographs Division
    Alfred Waud Drawings
Henry Rowe Schoolcraft Papers
Edwin M. Stanton Papers
George Hay Stuart Collection
Horatio Nelson Taft Diary
Lyman Trumbull Papers
Benjamin F. Wade Papers
Gideon Welles Papers
John H. Wheeler Papers
Thomas L. Wragg Collection
Library of Virginia, Richmond
Evans-Sibert Family Papers
Executive Journal and Index
Executive Papers
Fairfax Family Letters
Isaac Hirsh Diary
Newlon Family Letters

Frank Potts Diary
Welsh Family Papers
Loudoun County Circuit Court, Leesburg, Va.
    Chancery Case Files
    Deed Books
    Land Books
    Will Books
Robert Lucas, Private Collection, North Wales, Pa.
    Charles Stone Letter
Maine Historical Society, Portland, Me.
    Marshall Phillips Correspondence
Manassas National Battlefield Park, Manassas, Va.
    Robert Grant Letters
    Richard B. Smart Letters
    Ai B. Thompson Letters
The Mariners' Museum, Newport News, Va.
    George Geer Letters
Maryland Historical Society, Baltimore, Md.
    Briggs-Stabler Papers
    David Creamer Diary
    Rebecca Dorsey Davis Papers
    Luther Van Buren Furber Collection
    Edward F. Jones Papers
    William Kirkwood Correspondence
    John Merryman Collection
    Philpot-Randall Family Papers
    William Sherwood Letter
    Daniel Murray Thomas Papers
    Isaac Trimble Papers
Massachusetts Historical Society, Boston
    Charles E. Bowers Papers
    Richard Cary Letters
    Crowninshield-Magnus Papers
    Charles H. Dalton Papers
    Nathan Hayward Letters
    George H. Johnston Papers
    Charles F. Morse Papers
    Otis Norcross Papers
    Charles Pickering Putnam Papers
    Paul Joseph Revere Papers
    Tufts-Robertson Papers
        John C. Robertson Letters
    Winthrop Family Papers II
        Daniel Schambert letters
Minnesota Historical Society, St. Paul
    Adam Marty Letter
    Isaac Taylor Letter

Mississippi Department of Archives and History, Jackson
    William H. Hill Diary
Missouri Historical Society, St. Louis
    Badger Collection
    Bates Family Papers
    Blair Family Papers
    James O. Broadhead Papers
    Civil War Collection
    Clark Family Papers
    Herbert S. Hadley Papers
    George B. Hunt Letter
    Lucy Hutchinson Letter
    Richard Marshall Johnson Diaries
    Knapp Family Papers
    Nathaniel Lyon Collection
    Euphrasia Pettus Letter
    Thomas C. Reynolds Papers
    Dr. John F. Snyder Collection
Montgomery County courthouse, Rockville, Md.
    Deed Books
Museum of the Confederacy
    John B. and Robert Royall Letters
National Archives, Washington, D.C.
    Record Group 15, Records of the Pension Office
        Pension Applications
    Bureau of the Census, Record Group 29
        Seventh Census of the United States (M-432)
        Eighth Census of the United States (M-653)
    Records of the Adjutant General, Record Group 94
        Case Files for Presidential Pardons, 1865–67 (M-1003)
        Letters Received by the Office of the Adjutant General, 1861–1870 (M-619)
        Returns from Regular Army Artillery Regiments, June, 1821 to January, 1901
            (M-727)
        U.S. Military Academy Cadet Application Papers (M-688)
        Generals Papers, Entry 159
            Box 5
                C. P. Stone File
                Charles P. Stone File
                Charles "B." Stone File
            Box 18
                John W. Geary Papers
                Individual Service Records
    Records of the Office of the Secretary of War, Record Group 107
        Register of Letters Received by the Office of the Secretary of War, Main
            Series, 1800–1870 (M-22)
        Telegrams Collected by the Office of the Secretary of War, Unbound
            (M-504)

War Department Collection of Confederate Records, Record Group 109
    Confederate Papers Relating to Citizens or Business Firms (M-346)
    Compiled Service Records of Confederate Soldiers Who Served in
        Organizations from the State of Mississippi (M-269)
    Compiled Service Records of Confederate Soldiers Who Served in
        Organizations from the State of Virginia (M-324)
    Compiled Service Records of Confederate General and Staff Officers, and
        Non-Regimental Enlisted Men (M-331)
    Confederate States Army Casualties: Lists and Narrative Reports, 1861–1865,
        (M-836)
        Reel 5, Virginia, Ball's Bluff, October 21, 1861, Consolidated Report
        Reel 7, 13th Mississippi, Edward's Ferry, Va., and Kephart, Md.
    Letters Received by the Confederate Secretary of War (M-437)
    Records of Confederate Movements and Activities (M-861)
    Telegrams Received by the Confederate Secretary of War (M-618)
Record Group 153, Records of the Office of the Judge Advocate General
    Court Martial Case Files, 1809–1894
Record Group 393, Part II, Records of U.S. Army Continental Commands
    Letters and Telegrams Sent, Corps of Observation, 1861–1862, Entry 3804
    Letters and Telegrams Received, Corps of Observation, August 28–October
        28, 1861, Entry 3808
    Letters and Telegrams Received, Corps of Observation, 1861–1862,
        Supplemental, Entry 3810
    Letters and Telegrams Sent and Received, Corps of Observation, Entry 3812
    General Orders, Corps of Observation, 1861–1862, Entry 3813
    General Orders, Corps of Observation, August 12–December 30, 1861, Entry
        3814
    Special Orders, Corps of Observation, August, 1861–January, 1862, Entry
        3816
New Hampshire Division of Records Management and Archives, Concord, N.H.
    Adjutant General's Records
    Executive Correspondence
    Miscellaneous Military Records
New Hampshire Historical Society, Concord
    Burnham/Stearns Family Papers
        Samuel Burnham Letters
    John Gilbert Letters
    John S. Godfrey Papers
    Thomas B. Leaver Letterbook
    George H. Sargent Letters
    Mason Weare Tappan Papers
Peabody Essex Museum, Salem, Mass.
    John Peirce Letters
Rhode Island Historical Society, Providence
    David B. Patterson Letter
Rutgers University, New Brunswick, N.J.
    Roebling Family Papers

State Historical Society of Missouri, Columbia
> Western Historical Manuscript Collection
>> William W. Branson Diary
>> Confederate Proclamation
>> Alexander Doniphan Letter
>> Draper-McClurg Family Papers
>> Randolph Harrison Dyer Letter
>> Isaac Hockaday Letter
>> Claiborne Jackson Letter
>> Nathaniel Lyon Letter
>> James S. Rollins Papers
>> Elvira A. W. Scott Diary
>> Avington Wayne Simpson Diary

U.S. Army Military History Institute, Carlisle Barracks, Pa.
> Civil War Miscellaneous Collection
>> Michael Donlon Letters
>> Graham Family Papers
>> John Holston Letter
>> John Marten Steffan Letters
>> Alfred Wheeler Letters
> Civil War Times Illustrated Collection
>> Jonathan P. Stowe Journal
> Lewis Leigh Collection
>> Neill A. Baker Letter
>> Thomas Compass Letter
>> Charles H. Eager Letters
> Save the Flag Collection
>> William J. Burns Diary
> Murray Smith Collection
>> Walter A. Eames Letters
> Wiley Sword Collection
>> Albert G. Bates Letters

University of Georgia, Athens
> Margaret Branch Sexton Papers

University of Michigan, Ann Arbor
> James S. Schoff Civil War Collection
>> Letters and Documents
>> Charles H. Ross Letter
>> Charles P. Stone Letter

University of Mississippi, Oxford
> Russell Jones Collection
>> Edwin C. Myers Letters

University of New Hampshire, Durham
> Adams Family Papers
>> Enoch Green Adams Letters
> Louis Bell Papers
> Charles E. Jewett Papers

University of North Carolina, Chapel Hill, N.C.
    Southern Historical Collection
        Bedford Brown Papers
        David Thomas Copeland Papers
        Platt K. Dickinson Papers
        Meta Morris Grimball Journal
        Kenton Harper Papers
        Alexander Cheves Haskell Papers
        Stephen D. Lee Papers
        Stephen Russell Mallory Papers
        Maurice Family Papers
        Henry Page Papers
        Benjamin Franklin Perry Papers
        Trusten Polk Papers
        Frank F. Steel Papers
        Meriwether Jeff Thompson Papers
        Sarah Wadley Diary
        Webb Family Papers
        John Taylor Wood Papers
University of Notre Dame, Notre Dame, Ind.
    Archdiocese of Cincinnati Papers
    John D. McMaster Papers
University of South Carolina, Columbia
    South Caroliniana Library
        E. A. Miller Letter
University of Virginia, Charlottesville
    Brooks Family Papers
    James Singleton Letter
Vermont Historical Society, Barre
    Daniel S. White Letters
Virginia Historical Society, Richmond
    Barbour Family Papers
    Dabney Family Papers
    John Cheves Haskell Reminiscences
    John Montgomery Holloway Papers
    Meade Family Papers
    Richmond Howitzers Order Book
Washington and Lee University, Lexington, Va.
    Leyburn Library
        Rockbridge Historical Society Collection
        McCutchan Family Papers
Wilson's Creek National Battlefield, Republic, Mo.
    John K. Hulston Library
        Horace Poole Diary
Wisconsin Historical Society, Madison
    Joseph Spencer Letters

Wyoming Historical and Geological Society, Wilkes-Barre, Pa.
  Hendrick B. Wright Papers
Yale University, New Haven, Conn.
  Beineke Special Collection Library
    M. Dulany Ball Papers
    Edward T. Crosby Diary
    Letters to Samuel Wolcott

Published Sources

Acken, J. Gregory, ed. *Inside the Army of the Potomac: The Civil War Experience of Captain Francis Adams Donaldson.* Mechanicsburg, Pa.: Stackpole, 1998.
"The Advantages of Defeat," *Atlantic Monthly* 8, no. 47 (September, 1861): 360–65.
Aitken, Hugh G. J. ed. *Did Slavery Pay? Readings in the Economics of Black Slavery in the United States.* Boston: Houghton Mifflin, 1971.
Anderson, Frederick, et al, eds. *Mark Twain's Notebooks and Journals.* 4 vols. Berkeley: University of California Press, 1975–1979.
Andrews, J. Cutler. *The South Reports the Civil War.* Princeton, N.J.: Princeton University Press, 1970.
Annual Report of the Adjutant General of the State of Rhode Island and Providence Plantation for the Year 1865. Providence, R.I.: E. L. Freeman and Son, 1895.
"A Page of Political Correspondence. Unpublished Letters of Mr. Stanton to Mr. Buchanan." *North American Review* 276 (November, 1879): 473–83.
Armstrong, George D. *"The Hand of God Upon Us": A Thanksgiving Sermon, Preached on the Occasion of the Victory of Manassas, July 21st, 1861, in the Presbyterian Church, Norfolk, Va.* Norfolk, Va.: J. D. Gheselin, 1861.
"A Texan at Wilson's Creek." *Civil War Times Illustrated* 17, no. 9 (January, 1979): 46–47.
Athearn, Robert G., ed. *Soldier in the West: The Civil War Letters of Alfred Lacey Hough.* Philadelphia: University of Pennsylvania Press, 1957.
Atlas to Accompany the Official Records of the Union and Confederate Armies. Washington, D.C.: Government Printing Office, 1891–1895.
"A Veteran of Two Wars." *Confederate Veteran* 22, no. 8 (August, 1914): 359.
Ayling, Augustus D. *Revised Register of the Soldiers and Sailors of New Hampshire in the War of the Rebellion, 1861–1866.* Concord, N.H.: Ira C. Evans, 1895.
[Bacon, Mrs. Georgeanna Woolsey, and Eliza Woolsey Howland]. *Letters of a Family during the War for the Union, 1861–65.* 2 vols. [New Haven, Conn.: privately printed], 1899.
Balicki, Joseph, and Walton H. Owen II. *Documentation of Eight Civil War Forts and Earthworks in the Vicinity of Leesburg, Virginia.* Alexandria, Va.: John Milner, 2002.
Baltz, John D. *Col. E. D. Baker's Defense in the Battle of Ball's Bluff, Fought October 21st, 1861, in Virginia.* Lancaster, Pa.: privately published, 1885.
Barnes, Joseph K. *Medical and Surgical History of the War of the Rebellion (1861–65).* 3 parts in 6 vols. Washington, D.C.: Government Printing Office, 1870–1888.
Bartol, Cyrus Augustus. *Our Sacrifices. A Sermon Preached in the West Church, No-

vember 3, 1861, being the Sunday after the Funeral of Lieut. William Lowell Putnam. Boston: Ticknor and Fields, 1861.

Barton, Randolph. "Stonewall Jackson." *Southern Historical Society Papers* 38 (1910): 268–87.

Basler, Roy P., ed. *The Collected Works of Abraham Lincoln*. 8 vols. New Brunswick, N.J.: Rutgers University Press, 1953.

Bates, Samuel P. *History of Pennsylvania Volunteers, 1861–5, Prepared in Compliance with Acts of the Legislature*. 5 vols. Harrisburg, Pa.: B. Singerly, 1869–1871.

Beale, Howard K., ed. *The Diary of Edward Bates*. Washington, D.C.: Government Printing Office, 1933.

———, ed. *The Diary of Gideon Welles, Secretary of the Navy under Lincoln and Johnson*. 3 vols. New York: Norton, 1960.

Beale, Jane Howison. *Journal of Jane Howison Beale, Fredericksburg, Virginia, 1850–1862*. Fredericksburg, Va.: Historic Fredericksburg Foundation, 1979.

Bek, William G., trans. "The Civil War Diary of John T. Buegel, Union Soldier." *Missouri Historical Review* 40, no. 3 (April, 1946): 307–29.

Blackford, Susan Leigh, comp. *Letters from Lee's Army*. New York: Scribner, 1947.

Blair, William Alan, ed. *A Politician Goes to War: The Civil War Letters of John White Geary*. University Park: Pennsylvania State University Press, 1995.

Blight, David W., ed. *When This Cruel War Is Over: The Civil War Letters of Charles Harvey Brewster*. Amherst: University of Massachusetts Press, 1992.

Bombaugh, Charles C. "Extracts from a Journal Kept During the Earlier Campaigns of the Army of the Potomac." *Maryland Magazine of History* 5 (1910): 301–26.

[Booth, George Wilson]. *Personal Reminiscences of a Maryland Soldier in the War Between the States, 1861–1865*. Baltimore, Md.: privately published, 1898.

Bowen, Ralph H., ed. *A Frontier Family in Minnesota: Letters of Theodore and Sophie Bost, 1851–1920*. Minneapolis: University of Minnesota Press, 1981.

Boyd, William H., comp. *Boyd's Directory of the District of Columbia* [annual]. Washington, D.C.: Wm. H. Boyd, 1882–1899.

Branch, Edgar Marquess, et al, eds. *Mark Twain's Letters*. 6 vols. Berkeley: University of California Press, 1988–2002.

"Brother against Brother: An American Heritage Original Document." *American Heritage* 12, no. 3 (April, 1861): 4–7, 89–93.

Brownlow, W[illiam] G. *Sketches of the Rise, Progress, and Decline of Secession; with a Narrative of Personal Adventures Among the Rebels*. Philadelphia: George W. Childs, 1862.

Burlingame, Michael. *Dispatches from Lincoln's White House: The Anonymous Civil War Journalism of Presidential Secretary William O. Stoddard*. Lincoln: University of Nebraska Press, 2002.

Burlingame, Michael, and John R. Turner Ettlinger, eds. *Inside Lincoln's White House: The Complete Civil War Diary of John Hay*. Carbondale: Southern Illinois University Press, 1997.

Cashin, Joan E., ed. *The War Was You and Me: Civilians in the American Civil War*. Princeton, N.J.: Princeton University Press, 2002.

Casler, John O. *Four Years in the Stonewall Brigade*. 1893. Repr., with an introduction by James I. Robertson Jr. Dayton, Ohio: Press of Morningside Bookshop, 1981.

Chapman, George T. *Sketches of the Alumni of Dartmouth College, from the First Graduation in 1771 to the Present Time, with a Brief History of the Institution.* Cambridge, Mass.: Riverside Press, 1867.

Clift, G. Glenn, ed. *The Private War of Lizzie Hardin: A Kentucky Confederate Girl's Diary of the Civil War in Kentucky, Virginia, Tennessee, Alabama, and Georgia.* Frankfort: Kentucky Historical Society, 1963.

Coco, Gregory A., ed. *From Ball's Bluff to Gettysburg . . . And Beyond: The Civil War Letters of Private Roland E. Bowen, 15th Massachusetts Infantry 1861–1864.* Gettysburg, Pa.: Thomas Publications, 1994.

Conrad, D[aniel] B. "History of the First Battle of Manassas and the Organization of the Stonewall Brigade." *Southern Historical Society Papers* 19 (1891): 82–92.

Coulter, E. Merton. *The Civil War and Readjustment in Kentucky.* 1926. Repr., Gloucester, Mass.: Peter Smith, 1966.

Correspondence between S. Teackle Wallis, Esq. of Baltimore, and the Hon. John Sherman, of the U.S. Senate, Concerning the Arrest of Members of the Maryland Legislature and the Mayor and Police Commissioners of Baltimore in 1861. Baltimore: 1863.

Crawford, Martin, ed. *William Howard Russell's Civil War: Private Diary and Letters, 1861–1862.* Athens: University of Georgia Press, 1992.

Cullum, George W. *Biographical Register of the Officers and Graduates of the U.S. Military Academy.* 3 vols. Boston: Houghton Mifflin, 1891.

Cutrer, Thomas W., and T. Michael Parrish, eds. *Brothers in Gray: The Civil War Letters of the Pierson Family.* Baton Rouge: Louisiana State University Press, 1997.

Cutrer, Thomas W., ed. *Longstreet's Aide: The Civil War Letters of Major Thomas J. Goree.* Charlottesville: University of Virginia Press, 1995.

Davis, William C. *Battle at Bull Run: A History of the First Major Campaign of the Civil War.* Baton Rouge: Louisiana State University Press, 1981.

———, ed. *Touched by Fire: A Photographic Portrait of the Civil War.* 2 vols. Boston: Little, Brown, 1985.

Dennett, Tyler, ed. *Lincoln and the Civil War in the Diaries and Letters of John Hay.* New York: Dodd, Mead, 1939.

Directory of Leesburg. Leesburg, Va.: William L. Stork, 1860.

Donnelly, Ralph W. *Biographical Sketches of the Commissioned Officers of the Confederate States Marine Corps.* Washington, N.C.: privately published, 1983.

Dumond, Dwight Lowell, ed. *Southern Editorials on Secession.* Gloucester, Mass.: Peter Smith, 1964.

Duncan, Russell, ed. *Blue-Eyed Child of Fortune: The Civil War Letters of Colonel Robert Gould Shaw.* Athens: University of Georgia Press, 1992.

Dyer, Frederick H. *A Compendium of the War of the Rebellion.* 1908. Repr., with an introduction by Lee A. Wallace Jr., Dayton, Ohio: Morningside Press, 1978.

Earle, David M. *History of the Excursion of the Fifteenth Massachusetts Regiment.* Worcester: Press of C. Hamilton, 1886.

Easley, Virginia, ed. "Journal of the Civil War in Missouri: 1861, Henry Martin Cheavens." *Missouri Historical Review* 56, no. 1 (October, 1961), 12–25.

Eby, Cecil D. Jr., ed. *A Virginia Yankee in the Civil War: The Diaries of David Hunter Strother.* Chapel Hill: University of North Carolina Press, 1961.

Eckert, Edward K., and Nicholas Amato, eds. *Ten Years in the Saddle: The Memoirs of William Woods Averell.* San Rafael, Cal.: Presidio Press, 1978.

Evans, Clement A., ed. *Confederate Military History: A Library of Confederate States History by Distinguished Men of the South.* 17 vols. 1899. Repr., Wilmington, N.C.: Broadfoot Publishing, 1987–1989.

Faley, Paul. "Cultural Aspects of the Industrial Revolution: Lynn, Massachusetts Shoemakers and Industrial Morality, 1826–1860." *Labor History* 15, no. 3 (Summer, 1974), 367–94.

Field, Ron, and Robin Smith. *Uniforms of the Civil War.* Guilford, Conn.: Lyons Press, 2001.

Fishel, Edwin C. *The Secret War for the Union: The Untold Story of Military Intelligence in the Civil War.* Boston: Houghton Mifflin, 1996.

Fisher, John E., ed. "The Travels of the 13th Mississippi." *Journal of Mississippi History* 45 (1983): 288–313.

Fite, Emerson D. *Social and Industrial Conditions in the North During the Civil War.* New York: Macmillan, 1910.

Ford, Andrew E. *The Story of the Fifteenth Regiment Massachusetts Volunteer Infantry in the Civil War, 1861–1864.* Clinton, Mass.: W. J. Coulter, 1898.

French, Benjamin Brown. *Witness to the Young Republic: A Yankee's Journals, 1828–1870.* Hanover, N.H.: University Press of New England, 1989.

Gallagher, Gary W., ed. *Fighting for the Confederacy: The Personal Recollections of General Edward Porter Alexander.* Chapel Hill: University of North Carolina Press, 1989.

"General M. C. Meigs on the Conduct of the Civil War." *American Historical Review* 26, no. 2 (January, 1921): 285–303.

Gerteis, Louis S. "'A Friend of the Enemy': Federal Efforts to Suppress Disloyalty in St. Louis During the Civil War." *Missouri Historical Review* 96, no. 3 (April, 2002), 165–87.

———. *Civil War St. Louis.* Lawrence: University of Kansas Press, 2001.

Goldsborough, W. W. *The Maryland Line in the Confederate Army, 1861–1865.* Baltimore: Guggenheimer, Weil, 1900.

Grant, U. S. *Personal Memoirs of U. S. Grant.* 2 vols. New York: Charles L. Webster, 1885.

Groat, James W. *Pages Clothed in the Plainest of Dress: The Groat Diary.* Anoka, Minn.: Anoka County Historical Society, 1988.

Hahn, Thomas F. *Towpath Guide to the Chesapeake & Ohio Canal.* Shepherdstown, W.Va.: American Canal and Transportation Center, 1985.

Hamilton, J. G. de Roulhac, ed. *The Papers of Randolph Abbott Shotwell.* 3 vols. Raleigh: North Carolina Historical Commission, 1929.

Hammond, Harold Earl, ed. *Diary of a Union Lady, 1861–1865.* 1962. Repr., with an introduction by Jean V. Berlin, Lincoln: University of Nebraska Press, 2000.

Hancock, Harold B., ed. "The Civil War Diaries of Anna M. Ferris," *Delaware History* 9, no. 3 (April, 1861), 221–64.

Harris, Robert F., and John Niflot, comps. *Dear Sister: The Civil War Letters of the Brothers Gould.* Westport, Conn.: Praeger, 1998.

Harris, William C. *Prison Life in the Tobacco Warehouse at Richmond.* Philadelphia: George W. Childs, 1862.

Hartman, McIntosh, ed. "'The Whole World Was Full of Smoke . . .': The Civil War Letters of Private John Alemeth Byers, 17th Mississippi Infantry." *Military Images* 9, no. 6 (May and June, 1988): 6–1.

Hassler, William W., ed. *One of Lee's Best Men: The Civil War Letters of General William Dorsey Pender.* 1965. Repr., with a new foreword by Brian Wills. Chapel Hill: University of North Carolina Press, 1999.

Hatcher, Richard W. III, and William Garrett Piston, eds. *Kansans at Wilson's Creek: Soldiers' Letters from the Campaign for Southwest Missouri.* Springfield, Mo.: Wilson's Creek National Battlefield Foundation, 1993.

——. *Wilson's Creek: The Second Battle of the Civil War and the Men Who Fought It.* Chapel Hill: University of North Carolina Press, 2000.

[Hay, John]. "Colonel Baker." *Harper's New Monthly Magazine* 24, no. 139 (December, 1861): 105–10.

——. "Ellsworth." *Atlantic Monthly* 8 (July, 1861): 119–25.

Haydon, Frederick Stansbury. *Aeronautics in the Union and Confederate Armies, With a Survey of Military Aeronautics Prior to 1861.* Baltimore: Johns Hopkins Press, 1941.

Haynes, Martin A. *A Minor War History Compiled from a Soldier Boy's Letters to "The Girl I Left Behind Me," 1861–1864.* Lakeport, N.H.: privately published, 1916.

Heitman, Francis B. *Historical Register and Dictionary of the United States Army, from its Organization, September 29, 1789, to March 2, 1903.* 2 vols. Washington, D.C.: Government Printing Office, 1903.

Henig, Gerald S., ed. "Give My Love to All: The Civil War Letters of George S. Rollins," *Civil War Times Illustrated* 11, no. 7 (November, 1972), 16–28.

Hennessy, John. *The First Battle of Manassas: An End to Innocence, July 18–21, 1861.* Lynchburg, Va.: H. E. Howard, 1989.

Hesseltine, William B., and Hazel C. Wolf. *The Blue and the Gray on the Nile.* Chicago: University of Chicago Press, 1961.

"Historickal Crotchets." *New York History* 82, no. 2 (Spring, 2001), 183–86.

History of the First Regiment Minnesota Volunteer Infantry, 1861–1864. Stillwater, Minn.: Easton & Masterman, 1916.

History of the 71st Regiment, N.G., N.Y. New York: Veterans Association, 1919.

Holliday, Joseph E. "Relief for Soldiers' Families in Ohio during the Civil War." *Ohio History* 71, no. 2 (July, 1962): 97–112.

Howard, McHenry. *Recollections of a Maryland Confederate Soldier and Staff Officer.* 1914. Repr., with an introduction by James I. Robertson Jr. Dayton, Ohio: Press of Morningside Bookshop, 1975.

Howe, Mark DeWolfe, ed. *Touched with Fire: Civil War Letters and Diary of Oliver Wendell Holmes, Jr., 1861–1864.* New York: Da Capo, 1969.

Huettel, William L., ed. "Letters from Private Richard C. Bridges, C.S.A., 1861–1864." *Journal of Mississippi History* 33 (1971): 357–72.

Hunter, Robert W. "Men of Virginia at Ball's Bluff." *Southern Historical Society Papers* 34 (1906): 254–74.

Hunton, Eppa. *Autobiography of Eppa Hunton.* Richmond, Va.: William Byrd Press, 1933.

Irwin, Ray W., ed. "Missouri in Crisis: The Journal of Captain Albert Tracy, 1861."

Missouri Historical Review 51, nos. 1, 2, and 3 (October, 1956, and January and April, 1957): 8–21, 151–64, 270–83.

Janney, Samuel M. *Memoirs of Samuel M. Janney.* Philadelphia: Friends' Book Association, 1881.

Johannsen, Robert W., ed. *The Letters of Stephen A. Douglas.* Urbana: University of Illinois Press, 1961.

Johnston, Terry A. Jr., ed. *Him on the One Side and Me on the Other: The Civil War Letters of Alexander Campbell, 79th New York Infantry Regiment and James Campbell, 1st South Carolina Battalion.* Columbia: University of South Carolina, 1999.

Jones, John B. *A Rebel War Clerk's Diary.* New York: Sagamore Press, 1958.

Jordan, William B. Jr., ed. *The Civil War Journals of John Mead Gould, 1861–1866.* Baltimore: Butternut and Blue, 1997.

Journal of the Honorable Senate and House of Representatives, June Session, 1861. 2 parts. Concord, N.H.: Henry MacFarland, 1861.

Journal of the House of Representatives of the State of Missouri, at the Called Session of the Twenty-first General Assembly. Jefferson City, Mo.: J. P. Ament, 1861.

Journal of the House of Representatives of the State of Missouri, at the First Session of the Twenty-first General Assembly. Jefferson City, Mo.: W. G. Cheney, 1861.

Journal of the Senate of Missouri, at the Called Session of the Twenty-first General Assembly. Jefferson City, Mo.: J. P. Ament, 1861.

Kimmel, Stanley. *Mr. Lincoln's Washington.* New York: Coward-McCann, 1957.

Kohl, Lawrence Frederick, ed. *Irish Green and Union Blue: The Civil War Letters of Peter Welsh.* New York: Fordham University Press, 1986.

Krug, Mark M., ed. *Mrs. Hill's Journal: Civil War Reminiscences.* Chicago: Lakeside Press, 1980.

Kundahl, George G. *Confederate Engineer: Training and Campaigning with John Morris Wampler.* Knoxville: University of Tennessee Press [2000].

Laas, Virginia Jean, ed. *Wartime Washington: The Civil War Letters of Elizabeth Blair Lee.* Urbana: University of Illinois Press, 1991.

Lanman, Charles, ed. *The Journal of Alfred Ely, A Prisoner of War in Richmond.* New York: D. Appleton, 1862.

Lawson, Melinda. *Patriot Fires: Forging a New American Nationalism in the Civil War North.* Lawrence: University Press of Kansas, 2002.

Larimer, Charles F., ed. *Love and Valor: The Intimate Civil War Letters between Captain Jacob and Emeline Ritner.* Western Springs, Ill.: Sigourney Press, 2000.

Lee, K. Y., and A. J. Froelch. *Triassic-Jurassic Stratigraphy of the Culpeper and Barboursville Basins, Virginia and Maryland.* U.S. Geological Survey Professional Paper 1472. Washington, D.C.: Government Printing Office, 1989.

Letter of the Secretary of War, Transmitting Report of the Organization of the Army of the Potomac, and of Its Campaigns in Virginia and Maryland, Under the Command of Maj. Gen. George B. McClellan, from July 26, 1861, to November 7, 1862. Washington, D.C.: Government Printing Office, 1864.

"Letters of Edward Bates and the Blairs, Frank P. — Sr. and Jr. — and Montgomery, from the Private Papers and Correspondence of Senator James Rood Doolittle of Wisconsin." *Missouri Historical Review* 11, no. 2 (January, 1917): 123–46.

"Letters of John and Sarah Everett." *Kansas Historical Quarterly* 8, no. 4 (November, 1939): 350–83.

Lewis, S. Joseph Jr., ed. "Letters of William Fisher Plane, C.S.A., to His Wife." *Georgia Historical Quarterly* 48 (1964): 215–28.

Livermore, Thomas L. "Patterson's Shenandoah Campaign." *Papers of the Military Historical Society of Massachusetts* 1 (1895): 1–58.

Lobdell, Jared C., ed. "The Civil War Journal and Letters of Colonel John Van Deusen Du Bois, April 12, 1861 to October 16, 1862." *Missouri Historical Review* 60, no. 4 (July, 1966), 436–59, and 61, no. 1 (October, 1966), 21–49.

Lomax, Elizabeth Lindsay. *Leaves from an Old Washington Diary.* [New York]: Books, Inc., 1943.

Longacre, Edward G., ed. *From Antietam to Fort Fisher: The Civil War Letters of Edward King Wightman, 1862–1865.* Rutherford, N.J.: Fairleigh Dickinson University Press, 1985.

Looby, Christopher, ed. *The Complete Civil War Journal and Selected Letters of Thomas Wentworth Higginson.* Chicago: University of Chicago Press, 2000.

Lutz, Ralph Haswell. "Rudolf Schleiden and the Visit to Richmond, April 25, 1861." *Annual Report of the American Historical Association for the Year 1915,* Washington, D.C. 1917, 209–16.

McGuire, Judith W. *Diary of a Southern Refugee during the War, by a Lady of Virginia.* New York, E. J. Hale, 1867.

McPherson, James M. *For Cause and Comrades: Why Men Fought in the Civil War.* New York: Oxford University Press, 1997.

Map of Loudoun County, Virginia, from Actual Surveys by Yardley Taylor. Philadelphia: Thomas Reynolds and Robert Pearsall Smith, [1853].

Marks, Bayly Ellen, and Mark Norton Schatz, eds. *Between North and South: A Maryland Journalist Views the Civil War.* Rutherford, N.J.: Fairleigh Dickinson University Press, 1976.

Marshall, Jeffrey D., ed. *A War of the People: Vermont Civil War Letters.* Hanover, N.H.: University Press of New England, 1999.

Marvel, William. "A Poor Man's Fight." *Historical New Hampshire* 43, no. 1 (spring, 1988): 21–40.

———. *Burnside.* Chapel Hill, N.C.: University of North Carolina Press, 1991.

———. "Fortnight as a Confederate: Mark Twain's Missouri Campaign." *Blue & Gray Magazine* 13, no. 3 (winter, 1996): 30–32.

Massachusetts Soldiers, Sailors, and Marines in the Civil War. 8 vols. Brookline, Mass.: Riverdale Press, 1931–1935.

Meade, George, ed. *The Life and Letters of George Gordon Meade.* 2 vols. New York: Scribner's, 1913.

Meagher, Thomas F. *The Last Days of the 69th in Virginia.* New York: Irish American, 1861.

Meltzer, Milton, and Patricia G. Holland, eds. *Lydia Maria Child: Selected Letters, 1817–1880.* Amherst: University of Massachusetts Press, 1982.

Melville, Herman. *Battle-Pieces and Aspects of the War.* 1866. Repr., with an introduction by Lee Rust Brown, [New York]: Da Capo, 1995.

Memorial of the Mayor and City Council of Baltimore, with Accompanying Documents. Baltimore, Md.: Wm. H. Innes, 1861.

Miller, William Lee. *Lincoln's Virtues: An Ethical Biography.* New York: Knopf, 2002.

Moe, Richard. *The Last Full Measure: The Life and Death of the First Minnesota Volunteers.* New York: Avon Books, 1994.

Moore, Frank, ed. *The Rebellion Record, a Diary of Events with Documents, Narratives, Illustrative Incidents, Poetry, etc.* 11 vols. New York: G. P. Putnam and D. Van Nostrand, 1861–1969.

Moore, John Bassett, ed. *The Works of James Buchanan, Comprising His Speeches, State Papers, and Private Correspondence.* 12 vols. New York: Antiquarian Press, 1960.

Morgan, James A. III. *A Little Short of Boats: The Fights at Ball's Bluff and Edward's Ferry, October 21–22, 1861.* Fort Mitchell, Ky.: Ironclad, 2004.

Morrell, Carl A. *Seymour Dexter, Union Army: Journal and Letters of Civil War Service in Company K, 23rd New York Volunteer Regiment of Elmira, with Illustrations.* Jefferson, N.C.: McFarland, 1996.

Morse, Charles F. *Letters Written During the Civil War.* Boston: privately published, 1898.

Myers, Robert Manson, ed. *The Children of Pride: A True Story of Georgia and the Civil War.* New Haven, Conn.: Yale University Press, 1972.

Neal, Mary Julia, ed. *The Journal of Eldress Nancy, Kept at the South Union, Kentucky, Shaker Colony August 15, 1861–September 4, 1864.* Nashville, Tenn.: Parthenon Press, 1963.

Neely, Mark E., Jr. *The Fate of Liberty: Abraham Lincoln and Civil Liberties.* New York: Oxford University Press, 1991.

———. *Southern Rights: Political Prisoners and the Myth of Confederate Constitutionalism.* Charlottesville: University Press of Virginia, 1999.

Nevins, Allan, ed. *A Diary of Battle: The Personal Journals of Colonel Charles S. Wainwright, 1861–1865.* New York: Harcourt, Brace, & World [1962].

———. *The War for the Union.* 4 vols. New York: Scribner's, 1959–1971.

Nevins, Allan, and Milton Halsey Thomas, eds. *The Diary of George Templeton Strong.* 4 vols. New York: Macmillan, 1952.

Niven, John, ed. *The Salmon P. Chase Papers.* 5 vols. Kent, Ohio: Kent State University Press, 1993–1998.

Norris, James D., ed. "A Northern Businessman Opposes the Civil War: Excerpts from the Letters of R. G. Dun," *Ohio History* 71, no. 2 (July, 1962): 138–47.

Norton, Sara, and M. A. DeWolfe Howe, eds. *Letters of Charles Eliot Norton.* 2 vols. Boston: Houghton Mifflin, 1913.

Official Army Register for 1861. Washington, D.C.: Adjutant General's Office, 1861.

Official Army Register for September 1861. Washington, D.C.: Adjutant General's Office, 1861.

Official Records of the Union and Confederate Navies in the War of the Rebellion. 31 vols. Washington, D.C.: Government Printing Office, 1894–1927.

Otis, George H. *The Second Wisconsin Infantry.* Dayton, Ohio: Press of Morningside Bookshop, 1984.

Palfrey, Francis W. *Memoir of William Francis Bartlett.* Boston: Houghton, Osgood, 1878.

"Papers of John A. Campbell, 1861–1865." *Southern Historical Society Papers* 42 (1917): 3–81.

Parrish, William E. *Turbulent Partnership: Missouri and the Union, 1861–1865*. Columbia: University of Missouri Press, 1963.

Patch, Joseph D. *The Battle of Ball's Bluff*. Leesburg, Va.: Potomac Press, 1958.

Pease, Theodore Calvin, and James G. Randall, eds. *The Diary of Orville Hickman Browning*. 2 vols. Springfield: Illinois State Historical Library, 1925 and 1933.

Peirson, Charles L. *Ball's Bluff: An Episode and Its Consequences to Some of Us*. Salem, Mass.: Privately printed, 1913.

Perkins, Howard Cecil, ed. *Northern Editorials on Secession*. Gloucester, Mass.: Peter Smith, 1964.

Perret, Geoffrey. *Lincoln's War: The Untold Story of America's Greatest President as Commander in Chief*. New York: Random House, 2004.

Petersen, William J., ed. "The Iowa Regiments." *Palimpsest* 40, no. 9 (September, 1959): 369–72.

Phillips, Christopher. *Damned Yankee: The Life of General Nathaniel Lyon*. Columbia: University of Missouri Press, 1990.

Phillips, Ulrich B., ed. "The Correspondence of Robert Toombs, Alexander H. Stephens, and Howell Cobb." *Annual Report of the American Historical Association for the Year 1911* 2: 53–743.

Porterfield, George A. "A Narrative of the Service of Colonel ———." *Southern Historical Society Papers* 16 (1888): 82–91.

Protest of the General Assembly against the Illegal Arrest and Imprisonment by the Federal Government of Citizens of Maryland. Frederick, Md.: Beale H. Richardson, 1861.

Quaife, Milo M., ed. *From the Cannon's Mouth: The Civil War Letters of General Alpheus S. Williams*. 1959. Repr., with an introduction by Gary W. Gallagher. Lincoln: University of Nebraska Press, 1995.

Quint, Alonzo. *The Potomac and the Rapidan, Army Notes, 1861–1863*. Boston: Crosby & Nichols, 1864.

Radigan, Emily N., ed. *Desolating This Fair Country: The Civil War Diary and Letters of Lt. Henry C. Lyon, 34th New York*. Jefferson, N.C.: McFarland & Company, n.d.

Reidenbaugh, Lowell. *27th Virginia Infantry*. Lynchburg, Va.: H. E. Howard, 1993.

Reid-Green, Marcia, ed. *Letters Home: Henry Matrau of the Iron Brigade*. Lincoln: University of Nebraska Press, 1993.

Report of the Joint Committee on the Conduct of the War. 3 vols. Washington, D.C.: Government Printing Office, 1863.

Report of Louis H. Steiner, M.D., Inspector of the Sanitary Commission, Containing a Diary Kept During the Rebel Occupation of Frederick, Md. New York: Anson D. F. Randolph, 1862.

Report of the Police Commissioners of Baltimore City, with Accompanying Documents. No place: House of Delegates, 1861.

Resolutions of the General Assembly in Regard to the Relations of the State of Maryland to the Federal Government. Frederick, Md.: Beale H. Richardson, 1861.

Rhodes, Robert Hunt, ed. *All for the Union: A History of the 2nd Rhode Island In-*

fantry in the War of the Great Rebellion as Told by the Diary and Letters of Elisha Hunt Rhodes. Lincoln, R.I.: Andrew Mowbray, 1985.

Richards, T.W.T. "Ball's Bluff." *Confederate Veteran* 12, no. 1 (January, 1904): 31–32.

Robertson, James I. Jr., ed. *The Civil War Letters of General Robert McAllister*. 1965. Repr. Baton Rouge: Louisiana State University Press, 1998.

Roelker, William Greene. "Civil War Letters of William Ames: From Brown University to Bull Run." *Rhode Island Historical Society Collections* 33, no. 4 (October, 1940): 73–92, and 34, no. 1 (January, 1941): 5–24.

Rollins, C. B., ed. "The Letters of George Caleb Bingham to James S. Rollins, Part IV." *Missouri Historical Review* 34, no. 4 (July, 1938): 484–522.

Rundell, Walter Jr., ed. "'Despotism of Traitors': The Rebellious South through New York Eyes." *New York History* 45, no. 4 (October, 1964): 331–67.

Russell, William Howard. *My Diary North and South*. New York: McGraw-Hill, 1988.

[Sangston, Lawrence]. *The Bastiles of the North, By a Member of the Maryland Legislature*. Baltimore: Kelly, Hedian and Piet, 1863.

Scarborough, William Kauffman, ed. *The Diary of Edmund Ruffin*. 3 vols. Baton Rouge: Louisiana State University Press, 1972–1989.

Schafer, Joseph, ed. *Intimate Letters of Carl Schurz, 1841–1869*. Madison: State Historical Society of Wisconsin, 1928.

Schlesinger, Arthur M. Jr. "The Causes of the Civil War: A Note on Historical Sentimentalism." *Partisan Review* 16 (1949): 969–81.

Scott, Robert Garth, ed. *Fallen Leaves: The Civil War Letters of Major Henry Livermore Abbott*. Kent, Ohio: Kent State University Press, 1991.

———, ed. *Forgotten Valor: The Memoirs, Journals, and Civil War Letters of Orlando B. Willcox*. Kent, Ohio: Kent State University Press, 1999.

Searles, J[asper] N. "The First Minnesota Infantry, U.S. Volunteers." In *Glimpses of the Nation's Struggles*. 6 vols. Minneapolis and St. Paul: Minnesota Commandery of the Military Order of the Loyal Legion of the United States, 1887–1909. Vol. 2, 80–113.

Sears, Stephen W., ed. *For Country, Cause & Leader: The Civil War Journal of Charles B. Haydon*. New York: Ticknor & Fields, 1993.

———, ed. *The Civil War Papers of George B. McClellan*. New York: Ticknor and Fields, 1989.

Sellman, Mrs. John P. "Experiences of a War-Time Girl." *Confederate Veteran* 35, no. 1 (January, 1927): 19–20.

Sherman, W[illiam] T[ecumseh]. *Memoirs of Gen. W. T. Sherman*. 2 vols. New York: Charles L. Webster, 1891.

Sigel, Franz. "The Flanking Column at Wilson's Creek." In *Battles and Leaders of the Civil War*, edited by Robert U. Johnson and Clarence C. Buel. 4 vols. New York: Century, 1884–1888. Vol. 1, 304–6.

Silver, James W. *A Life for the Confederacy, as Recorded in the Pocket Diaries of Pvt. Robert A. Moore*. Wilmington, N.C.: Broadfoot, 1987.

Silverman, Jason H., Samuel N. Thomas Jr., and Beverly D. Evans IV. *Shanks: The Life and Wars of General Nathan G. Evans, C.S.A.* New York: Da Capo, 2002.

Simpson, Brooks D., and Jean V. Berlin, eds. *Sherman's Civil War: Selected Corre-*

spondence of William T. Sherman, 1860–1865. Chapel Hill: University of North Carolina Press, 1999.

Smart, James G. *A Radical View: The "Agate" Dispatches of Whitelaw Reid.* 2 vols. Memphis, Tenn.: Memphis State University Press, 1976.

Snead, Thomas L. "The First Year of the War in Missouri." In *Battles and Leaders of the Civil War,* edited by Robert U. Johnson and Clarence C. Buel. 4 vols. New York: Century, 1884–1888. Vol. 1, 262–77.

Sparks, David S., ed. *Inside Lincoln's Army: The Diary of Marsena Rudolph Patrick, Provost Marshal General, Army of the Potomac.* New York: Thomas Yoseloff, 1964.

Speech of the Hon. Henry May of Maryland, on the Bill to Indemnify Executive Tyranny, and to Continue It by Suspending the Writ of Habeas Corpus. Washington, D.C.: Henry Polkinhorn, 1863.

Sprague, Dean. *Freedom under Lincoln.* Boston: Houghton Mifflin, 1965.

Stampp, Kenneth M. *And the War Came: The North and the Secession Crisis, 1860–1861.* Baton Rouge: Louisiana State University Press, 1950.

Starr, Louis M. *Bohemian Brigade: Civil War Newsmen in Action.* New York: Knopf, 1954.

Stearns, Amos E. *Narrative of Amos E. Stearns, Member of Co. A, 25th Regt. Mass. Vols.* Worcester, Mass.: Franklin P. Rice, 1887.

Stedman, Laura, and George M. Gould, eds. *Life and Letters of Edmund Clarence Stedman,* 2 vols. New York: Moffat, Yard, 1910.

Stone, Charles P. "A Dinner with General Scott," *Magazine of American History* (1884): 528–532.

——. *Notes on the State of Sonora.* Washington, D.C.: Henry Polkinhorn, 1861.

——. "Washington in March and April, 1861." *Magazine of American History* (1885): 1–24.

——. "Washington on the Eve of the War." *Battles and Leaders of the Civil War,* edited by Robert U. Johnson and Clarence C. Buel. 4 vols. New York: Century, 1884–1888. Vol. 1, 7–25.

Stories of Our Soldiers: War Reminiscences, by "Carleton" and by Soldiers of New England. Boston: Journal Newspaper Company, 1893.

Struve, Gustav. *Das 8 Regiment N.Y. Freiwilliger.* Washington, D.C.: John F. Niedfeldt [1862].

Sumner, Merlin E., ed. *The Diary of Cyrus B. Comstock.* Dayton, Ohio: Morningside, 1987.

Tap, Bruce. *Over Lincoln's Shoulder: The Committee on the Conduct of the War.* Lawrence: University Press of Kansas, 1998.

Tatum, Georgia Lee. *Disloyalty in the Confederacy.* Chapel Hill: University of North Carolina Press, 1934.

Taylor, F. Jay, ed. *Reluctant Rebel: The Secret Diary of Robert Patrick, 1861–1865.* Baton Rouge: Louisiana University Press, 1959.

"The Diary of James R. Stewart, Pioneer of Osage County." *Kansas Historical Quarterly* 17, no. 4 (November, 1949): 360–97.

"The Last Roll," *Confederate Veteran* 7, no. 4 (April, 1899): 171–81.

"The Letters of Samuel James Reader, 1861–1863," *Kansas Historical Quarterly* 9, no. 1 (February, 1940): 26–57.

"The Union. Its Benefits and Dangers," *Southern Literary Messenger* 40, New Series (January, 1861): 1–4.

Thomas, Benjamin P., and Harold M. Hyman. *Stanton: The Life and Times of Lincoln's Secretary of War.* New York: Knopf, 1962.

Thompson, Robert Means, and Richard Wainwright, eds. *Confidential Correspondence of Gustavus Vasa Fox.* 2 vols. New York: Naval History Society, 1918–1919.

Throne, Mildred, ed. "Iowa Farm Letters, 1856–1865." *Iowa Journal of History* 58, no. 1 (January, 1960): 37–88.

Tombaugh, Wendell C. and Jean C. *Fulton County, Indiana Newspaper Extracts, 1858–1864.* Rochester, Ind.: Tombaugh, 1982.

Trefousse, Hans L. *The Radical Republicans: Lincoln's Vanguard for Racial Justice.* Baton Rouge: Louisiana State University Press, 1975.

Trout, Robert J., ed. *With Pen and Saber: The Letters and Diaries of J.E.B. Stuart's Staff Officers.* Mechanicsburg, Pa.: Stackpole, 1995.

"Trumbull Correspondence," *Mississippi Valley Historical Review,* Vol. 1, no. 1 (June, 1914), 101–8.

U.S. Congress. *Congressional Globe.* 37th Congress.

U.S. Congress. House. *Loyalty of Clerks and Other Persons Employed by the Government.* 37th Cong., 2nd sess. H. Report 16.

Valentine, Clifton C., ed. *To See My Country Free: The Pocket Diaries of Ezekiel Armstrong and Joseph A. Miller.* Pittsboro, Miss.: Calhoun County Historical Society, 1998.

Vanderslice, Catherine H. [ed.] *The Civil War Letters of George Washington Beidelman.* New York: Vantage Press [1978].

Waite, Otis F. R. *New Hampshire in the Great Rebellion.* Claremont, N.H.: Tracy, Chase, 1870.

War Diary and Letters of Stephen Minot Weld, 1861–1865. Boston: Massachusetts Historical Society, 1979.

War Letters of William Thompson Lusk, Captain, Assistant Adjutant General, United States Volunteers, 1861–1863. New York: privately printed, 1911.

War Letters, 1862–1865, of John Chipman Gray and John Codman Ropes. Boston: Houghton Mifflin, 1927.

War of the Rebellion: A Compilation of the Official Records of the Union and Confederate Armies. 128 vols. Washington, D.C.: Government Printing Office, 1880–1901.

Welker, David A., ed. *A Keystone Rebel: The Civil War Diary of Joseph Garey, Hudson's Battery, Mississippi Volunteers.* Gettysburg, Pa.: Thomas, 1996.

Wheeler, William. *Letters of William Wheeler.* N.p.: privately printed, 1875.

White, E. V. *History of the Battle of Ball's Bluff, Fought on the 21st of October, 1861.* Leesburg, Va.: Washingtonian Print, [1902].

Wilkeson, Frank. *Recollections of a Private Soldier in the Army of the Potomac.* New York: Putnam, 1887.

Wilkie, Franc B. *Pen and Powder.* Boston: Ticknor, 1888.

Williams, Charles R., ed. *Diary and Letters of Rutherford Birchard Hayes, Nineteenth President of the United States.* 5 vols. Columbus: Ohio State Archaeological and Historical Society, 1914–1926.

Williams, Frederick D. *The Wild Life of the Army: Civil War Letters of James A. Garfield.* East Lansing: Michigan State University Press, 1964.

Winter, William C. *The Civil War in St. Louis: A Guided Tour.* St. Louis: Missouri Historical Society Press, 1994.

Wistar, Isaac J. *Autobiography of Isaac Jones Wistar, 1827–1905: Half a Century in War and Peace.* Philadelphia: Wistar Institute of Anatomy and Biology, 1937.

Woodward, E. M. *Our Campaigns: The Second Regiment Pennsylvania Reserve Volunteers.* 1865. Repr., Shippensburg, Pa.: Burd Street Press, 1995.

Worthington, Chauncey Ford, ed., *A Cycle of Adams Letters, 1861–1865,* 2 vols. Boston: Houghton Mifflin, 1920.

Wright, William C. *The Secession Movement in the Middle Atlantic States.* Rutherford, N.J.: Fairleigh Dickinson University Press, 1973.

Writ of Habeas Corpus. Speech of James A. Pearce, of Maryland, in the Senate of the United States, July 30, 1861. No place: no pub. [1861].

Younger, Edward, ed. *Inside the Confederate Government: The Diary of Robert Garlick Hill Kean.* Baton Rouge: Louisiana University Press, 1985.

Newspapers

Aegis and Transcript, Worcester, Mass.
The Age, Augusta, Maine
The American, Baltimore, Md.
Arkansas True Democrat, Little Rock
Baltimore (Md.) *Sun*
Baltimore Commercial Advertiser
Berkshire County Eagle, Pittsfield, Mass.
Boonville (Mo.) *Weekly Observer*
Boston (Mass.) *Evening Transcript*
Boston (Mass.) *Journal*
Boston (Mass.) *Post*
Central City and Brunswicker, Brunswick, Mo.
Central Republican, Faribault, Minn.
Charleston (S.C.) *Mercury*
Chelsea (Mass.) *Telegraph and Pioneer*
Christian Advocate and Journal, New York
Christian Recorder, Philadelphia, Pa.
Cincinnati (Ohio) *Daily Commercial*
Cincinnati (Ohio) *Daily Gazette*
Cincinnati (Ohio) *Daily Press*
Clay County (Mo.) *Flag*
Commonwealth, Frankfort, Ky.
Daily American, Manchester, N.H.
Daily Conservative, Leavenworth, Kan.
Daily Courier, Charleston, S.C.
Daily Exchange, Baltimore, Md.
Daily Messenger, Hannibal, Mo.
Daily Missouri Democrat, St. Louis

Daily Missouri Republican, St. Louis
Daily National Intelligencer, Washington, D.C.
Daily Picayune, New Orleans, La.
Daily Times, Leavenworth, Kans.
Daily Whig and Republican, Quincy, Ill.
Davenport (Iowa) *Daily Democrat & News*
Dedham (Mass.) *Gazette*
Delaware Gazette, Wilmington
Democratic Mirror, Leesburg, Va.
Democratic Standard, Concord, N.H.
Detroit (Mich.) *Free Press*
Dollar Weekly Mirror, Manchester, N.H.
Dover (N.H.) *Gazette*
Dubuque (Iowa) *Weekly Times*
Fitchburg (Mass.) *Sentinel*
Fort Scott (Kans.) *Democrat*
Frank Leslie's Illustrated Newspaper, New York
Frederick (Md.) *Herald*
Friend's Review, Philadelphia, Pa.
Gazette, Annapolis, Md.
German Reformed Messenger, Chambersburg, Pa.
Granite State News, Wolfeborough, N.H.
Harper's Weekly
Hartford (Conn.) *Courant*
Haverhill (Mass.) *Gazette*
Illinois State Journal, Springfield, Ill.
Independent, New York
Journal of Commerce, New York
Kennebec Journal, Augusta, Maine
Kentucky Yeoman, Frankfort
Laconia (N.H.) *Democrat*
Lawrence (Kans.) *Republican*
Loudoun Times-Mirror, Leesburg, Va.
Louisville (Ky.) *Journal*
Lowell (Mass.) *Courier*
Maryland Union, Frederick, Md.
The Massachusetts Spy, Worcester, Mass.
Mercury, Rochester, Ind.
Mirror, Manchester, N.H.
New Hampshire Patriot, Concord, N.H.
New York Examiner
New York Herald
New York Times
New York Tribune
New York World
North Carolina Standard, Raleigh
Pennsylvania Daily Telegraph, Harrisburg

Philadelphia (Pa.) *Inquirer*
Philadelphia (Pa.) *North American and United States Gazette*
Pioneer, St. Paul, Minn.
The Republican, Carthage, Ill.
Richmond (Va.) *Daily Dispatch*
Richmond (Va.) *Inquirer*
Rochester (Ind.) *Sentinel*
Rochester (N.Y.) *Union and Advertiser*
Roxbury (Mass.) *City Gazette*
St. Charles (Mo.) *Demokrat*
States and Union, Washington, D.C.
Smyrna (Del.) *Times*
South Danvers (Mass.) *Wizard*
Springfield (Mass.) *Daily Republican*
The Villager, Amesbury, Mass.
Washington (D.C.) *Evening Star*
The Washingtonian, Leesburg, Va.
Westliche Post, St. Louis, Mo.
Windham County Transcript, Danielson, Conn.
Winona (Minn.) *Daily Republican*

Miscellaneous

Headstone inscriptions, Green River Cemetery, Greenfield, Mass.
Headstone inscriptions, Henry Family Cemetery, Manassas, Va.
Headstone inscriptions, Loudoun County cemeteries, Loudoun County, Va.
Headstone inscriptions, Ossipee Village Cemetery, Ossipee, N.H.
Headstone inscriptions, Sherwood Episcopal Church Cemetery, Cockeysville, Md.

Acknowledgments

This book began with my interest in the melee at Ball's Bluff; I did not originally intend to treat anything beyond the characters and events of the battle
and the political repercussions that followed it. The deeper I delved into the
background, though, the more the aftermath of Ball's Bluff seemed to offer a
metaphor for the entire turbulent year between the creation of the Confederate States and the point at which the war against secession started swinging
toward a war of emancipation. The "era of suspicion" that Bruce Catton identified with Ball's Bluff, Charles Stone, and the McClellan tenure marked the
nadir in an epidemic of deteriorating distrust that began with the secession
crisis. Stone played conspicuous parts throughout that epoch — first as one of
his country's more prominent protectors and later as its most visible victim.

For the initial suggestion and subsequent encouragement to pursue Stone's
story I am most grateful to Stephen Sears, who first settled the issue of Stone's
competence and loyalty in *Controversies and Commanders: Dispatches from
the Army of the Potomac* (Boston: Houghton Mifflin Company, 1999). As has
been the case in previous projects that I have undertaken, his generosity with
notes and research tips constituted only a fragment of his ultimate assistance.
George Rable religiously forwarded pertinent material from his own research
projects, and Michael Parrish suggested numerous primary sources and sec-
ondary treatments of various subjects, particularly relating to the prelude to
the conflict.

Most of the Ball's Bluff battlefield, except around the bluff itself, was developed beyond recognition between my first hiking trek there in 1986 and my
second visit in June, 2003. My understanding of the battle improved considerably, though, as a result of meeting James A. Morgan III, of Lovettsville,
Virginia. Jim supplied me with a copy of his then-manuscript history of the
battle, *A Little Short of Boats,* and accompanied me in examining the bat-

tlefield, even providing the canoe in which we scouted Harrison's Island and the now-obliterated site of Smart's Mill. Murdoch Campbell and Neal Brown of the Harrison's Island Conservation Society arranged for us to visit the island, while Clark Brown graciously gave us a guided tour of the island and the house that served as one of the Union field hospitals. Paul McCray, of Sterling, Virginia, supplied me with copies of manuscripts and rare publications, and assisted me enthusiastically in researching Ball's Bluff and the men who fought there.

The archaeological work of Joseph Balicki and Walton H. Owen II proved useful in determining troop and earthwork locations around Leesburg. Equally as helpful in illuminating Loudoun County's antebellum society was Brenda E. Stevenson's *Life in Black and White: Family and Community in the Slave South* (New York: Oxford University Press, 1996).

Each aspect of this book naturally reflects a small library of other works that never made it into the footnotes, and especially Lincoln's handling of the Fort Sumter crisis. Taking the historiography of the episode from its most critical to its most generous, Lincoln has been characterized as (among other things) an aggressive instigator, a political gambler, and something of a misunderstood innocent. In a 1937 article in the *Journal of Southern History* entitled "Lincoln and Fort Sumter," Charles W. Ramsdell accused Lincoln of deliberately provoking the clash of arms at Sumter and maneuvering the enemy into firing the first shot. In a four-volume biography of the sixteenth president published eight years later, James G. Randall contradicted Ramsdell by arguing that Lincoln intended only "that the first shot would be fired by the other side *if a shot was fired.*" While that semantic defense does not seem particularly specious on its face, it ignores Lincoln's possession of overwhelming evidence that the provisioning of Sumter would be resisted by violence. In *And the War Came* (1950) and *Lincoln and the First Shot* (1963) Kenneth M. Stampp and Richard N. Current respectively articulated a more moderate interpretation that credited Lincoln with consciously risking war, rather than deliberately provoking it. After three more decades of study Stampp expanded even more precisely on that perspective in *This Imperiled Union* (1980).

Considering the apparent disintegration of Northern unity on the issue of secession by the end of March, and Lincoln's delay of action until the second house of Congress had adjourned, he appears to have decided to personally orchestrate a decisive confrontation within the fortnight before Sumter's rations ran out. Confederate authorities hardly lacked complicity in the crisis, but Lincoln should be judged for his own actions in relation to the alternatives available to him. Both law and logic recognize only a slight difference in culpability between the intentional infliction of violence and reckless conduct in the face of near-certain tragic consequences, and with that consideration my assessment falls somewhere between Ramsdell's and those of Stampp and Current. I therefore find myself in substantial agreement with

Jeffrey Rogers Hummel. In *Emancipating Slaves, Enslaving Free Men* (Chicago: Open Court, 1996) Hummel remarked that "it certainly strains credibility to suppose that such an astute politician did not realize that war would be a likely result" of the Sumter relief expedition.

The arbitrary abrogation of civil liberties and the institution of national conscription to support his effective choice of war further blighted Lincoln's performance, in my view, although he appears to have been accorded an interpretive deference that has discouraged adequate criticism of those points. This also brings me somewhat in tune with Hummel, whose work has been specifically criticized as a libertarian perspective. One need not be a libertarian, however, to recognize that Lincoln's unconstitutional excesses marked an important step in the sporadic but undeviating course of increasing federal and executive authority, and in the concomitant erosion of local control and individual liberties. Neither would one have to be a libertarian — or a pacifist, for that matter — to comprehend the irony of conducting a war against slavery by invoking the feudal concept of conscription, which imposed a temporary form of involuntary servitude of greater potential deadliness than the original evil.

The two books that best treat the federal manhandling of Maryland and Missouri are Dean Sprague's *Freedom under Lincoln* (Boston, Mass.: Houghton Mifflin Company, 1965) and Mark E. Neely Jr.'s *The Fate of Liberty: Abraham Lincoln and Civil Liberties* (New York: Oxford University Press, 1991). Both seem more forgiving of the Lincoln administration's constitutional transgressions than I am, although both clearly perceived the frightening potential of executive excess in time of war. Neely went on to a similar study of Confederate repression in *Southern Rights: Political Prisoners and the Myth of Confederate Constitutionalism* (Charlottesville, Va.: University Press of Virginia, 1999). Christopher Phillips has done much to reveal the situation in Missouri with his relentless biographies of Nathaniel Lyon, *Damned Yankee* (Columbia: University of Missouri Press, 1990) and, with William E. Foley, of Claiborne Fox Jackson, *Missouri's Confederate* (Columbia: University of Missouri Press, 2000). The most comprehensive and readable overview of Missouri at the outset of hostilities is the result of another collaboration. In *Wilson's Creek: The Second Battle of the Civil War and the Men Who Fought It* (Chapel Hill: University of North Carolina, 2000), William Garrett Piston and Richard W. Hatcher III provide an excellent social and political examination of not only the region but the early months of the war itself. Bruce Tap filled a long-neglected vacuum in Civil War historiography with *Over Lincoln's Shoulder: The Committee on the Conduct of the War* (Lawrence: University Press of Kansas, 1998), presenting a detailed and incisive treatment of that partisan body.

My quest for the details of Civil War battles relied heavily, as usual, on the knowledge of National Park Service personnel. John Hennessy, chief historian of Fredericksburg and Spotsylvania National Military Park and the author of his own book on the battle — *The First Battle of Manassas: An End to Innocence* (Lynchburg, Va.: H. E. Howard, 1989) — directed me to the site of the skirmish at Blackburn's Ford and gave me some useful tips on the terrain. Jim Burgess, Museum Specialist at Manassas National Battlefield Park, arranged an efficient research trip to the park library for me, and Librarian Jeffrey Patrick of the Wilson's Creek National Battlefield likewise assisted me most generously with material from that park's collection.

Any serious research depends upon an army of diligent manuscript curators and their assistants in repositories across the nation. As always, those included Michael Musick of the National Archives and Fred Baumann of the Library of Congress (both of whom, to my intense regret, retired as this manuscript neared completion), as well as Jennie Rathbun at Harvard University, Kathy Shoemaker at Emory University, Judith Ann Schiff of Yale University, and the eternally accommodating Dr. Richard J. Sommers of the U.S. Army Military History Institute.

I am also indebted to Dennis Northcott at the Missouri Historical Society, John C. Konzal of the State Historical Society of Missouri's Western Historical Manuscripts Collection, Steve Nielsen of the Minnesota Historical Society, Jennifer Ford and Leigh McWhite at the University of Mississippi's J. D. Williams Library, Bea Hardy at the Maryland Historical Society, Elizabeth Schaaf at the Peabody Institute of Johns Hopkins University, Mary Fishback of the Thomas Balch Library at Leesburg, Virginia, Sharon Defibaugh of the University of Virginia Library, Beth Bilderback at the University of South Carolina's South Caroliniana Library, Martha G. Elmore at the Joyner Library of East Carolina University, Sarah Hartwell of Dartmouth's Rauner Library, and Eric Frazier of the Boston Public Library's Special Collections Department. An assortment of staff members assisted me at the Massachusetts Historical Society, the New Hampshire Historical Society, the University of New Hampshire, the Kansas State Historical Society, the Southern Historical Collection at the University of North Carolina, Duke University, the Virginia Historical Society, and the Library of Virginia (the new name of which just doesn't seem to be catching on with veteran researchers). Special thanks is due an anonymous research assistant in the Mississippi Department of Archives and History, who went to the trouble of transcribing some light, almost illegible entries in the William H. Hill diary for me.

Blake Magner made his customary extra effort to produce clear and relevant maps for this book. There are good cartographers and there are careful students of Civil War history, but the overlapping population remains relatively small.

I am particularly grateful to Stephen Sears, George Rable, Alan Nolan, Kenneth Stampp, Jim McPherson, Nelson Lankford, and Jim Morgan for reading the entire manuscript, excerpted portions, or summative essays, and offering me their honest opinions. As I have always maintained, the best friend is also a cruel editor, and any praise this book merits is probably due to their influence; any failings likely come as a direct result of my decision not to take good advice from more accomplished historians.

Will and Maggie Greene of Petersburg, Virginia, also deserve special mention for giving bed and board to a wayfaring researcher with the customary hospitality of Casa Verde. Finally comes Ellen Schwindt, who, despite the demands of her alarm clock, bravely pretended to sleep through many a late night of clicking keys, shuffling papers, and the ill-muffled mutterings of a preoccupied pedant.

Index

abolitionists and abolitionism
  abolitionist congressmen, 261–62,
    264–65, 281, 284–85
  dismay at Lincoln's response to eman-
    cipation threat in Missouri, 191
  increasing sentiment for, 272
  inquiries by Joint Committee on the
    Conduct of the War, 266, 267, 269
  linking of Republican nationalism with
    antislavery cause, 191, 252, 262,
    266, 277, 285
  responses to Union defeat at Bull Run,
    151–52
  See also slaves and slavery
Alden, Henry, 259
Alexandria campaign
  Confederate army
    assumption of command by Taylor,
      63–64
    concern over Union advance on
      Leesburg and Harper's Ferry,
      89
    succession of Terrett to command,
      64
    Taylor's evacuation and retreat, 64
    Terrett's evacuation, 75, 77
  Union army
    capture of city, 77
    capture of Confederate flag,
      Ellsworth's death, 75–76
    demand for surrender, 75
    deployment of *Pawnee,* 74–75
    11th New York Fire Zouaves, 74
    14th New York State Militia, 74

    plan for invasion of waterfront, 72–
      73
    troop positions, 73–74
Anderson, Robert
  biographical sketch, 292
  in command of Kentucky, 189
  estimate of troop requirements at Fort
    Sumter, 14
  refusal to surrender Fort Sumter, 25–
    26
Andrew, John, 267
Arkansas
  provision of troops to Confederacy, 37
  2nd Arkansas Mounted Rifles, 179
Ashby, Turner, 217
Averell, William, 133, 152
Ayres, Romeyn, 117–18

Baker, Edward Dickinson
  Ball's Bluff engagement
    advance to bluff, 236
    blame for Union defeat, 252
    death, 242
    intention to advance to Leesburg,
      234
    mismanagement of command,
      238–39
    orders from Stone concerning
      crossing of river, 233
    position at Conrad's Ferry, 224, 226
  biographical sketch, 292
  command of California regiments, 211–
    12
  commissions offered by Lincoln, 252

friendship with Lincoln, 12, 250
hero's funeral, 252–53
recruitment of Union troops, 55, 211
Balkanization, xv–xvi
Ball, Burgess, 205–6
Ball, Dulany, 74, 77
Ball, Fayette, 205
Ball, George Washington, 205, 229, 234
Ballou, James, 242
Ball's Bluff engagement
  Confederate army
    assault on retreating troops, 241–42
    Beauregard's plan of attack, 249
    booty collected, 248
    casualties, 241, 242
    coordination of effort, 240–41
    Dailey plantation attack, 249
    decisive attack, 243
    observation of Union raiders, first exchange of gunfire, 227–29, 331n41
    positions, 201, 217, 218, 225, 234, 236, 240
    transport of captives to Richmond, 247–48
  geological features and estates in area, 203, 204–6, 225, 327n65
  Joint Committee on the Conduct of the War investigation, 265
  maps, 203, 228
  Northern reaction to Union defeat, 251, 257–58
  order of battle, 290–91
  post-battle accounts, 250–51
  responsibility for Union defeat
    Baker, 252
    McClellan, 253, 277
    Stone, 250, 253–54, 258–59
  Union army
    ascent of bluff, advance across fields, 225–26
    Baker, 224, 226, 233, 234, 236, 238–39, 242
    casualties, 241, 244
    confidence of troops, 213–14
    at Dailey plantation, 249
    deployment of James rifle, 239–40
    deployment of mountain howitzers, 236, 240, 242
    dissolution of front, 242
    establishment of Corps of Observation at Poolesville, 200–201
    inadequacy of weapons, 213
    lack of coordination, 237–38, 240, 242
    loss of weapons, 248
    massing of forces, 235–37
    positions, 200–201, 214, 222–24, 226, 231–32, 234–39, 243–44
    recovery of dead, 259
    retreat to Maryland, 249–50
    retreat to river, 243–44
    scouting expeditions, 223, 231
    Stone's plans and orders, 230–31, 233, 246, 261
    Stone's request for troops, 202–4, 206
    surrender, 245
Baltimore, Maryland
  arrest of city marshal and police commissioners, 103–5
  arrest of legislators to prevent secession vote, 42–43, 197–99, 285
  federal invasion, 67–68
  imposition of martial law, 104
  isolation of city to prevent passage of federal troops, 29–30, 34, 67
  monitoring of free elections, intimidation of voters, 94
  riot at passage of federal troops through, 28–29
  shutdown of newspapers, 196
  See also Maryland
Banks, Nathaniel P.
  arrest of Baltimore police commissioners, 104
  arrest of citizens suspected of disloyalty, 257
  arrest of Maryland legislators to prevent secession vote, 197, 198
  biographical sketch, 292
  imposition of martial law in Baltimore, 104
  positions near Ball's Bluff, 200, 249
  posting of military to supervise Baltimore elections, 94
  replacement of Patterson as Shenandoah commander, 126, 195
  in Richmond campaign, 286
  rumor of impending Confederate attack on Washington, 195
  selection of Stone as chief of staff, 279
Barksdale, William, 218, 219, 249
Barry, William F., 141
Bartlett, Francis, 244–45
Bartow, Francis, 136, 142, 143

Bates, Edward
    appeal to Stanton on Stone's behalf,
        275
    biographical sketch, 293
    demand for recall of Frémont from
        Missouri, 192
    on disarming of Missouri state troops,
        157
    justification of Lincoln's suspension of
        habeas corpus, 69–70
    recommendation to surrender Fort
        Sumter, 16
    support of Lincoln's use of military
        force, 28
battles. See specific engagements
Bayard, James, 19
Beauregard, Pierre Gustave Toutant
    assignment by Davis to protect Rich-
        mond, 87–88
    Ball's Bluff strategy, 217–18, 249
    biographical sketch, 293
    Bull Run engagement
        strategy, 132, 134, 137
        troop strength, 108–9, 129–30
    defection to Confederate army, 15
    plan to threaten Washington, 196
    preparation for Fort Sumter confronta-
        tion, 25
Bee, Barnard, 136, 142, 143
Benjamin, Judah, 255–56
Big Bethel engagement, 82–86
Blackburn's Ford engagement, 117–18, 128.
    See also Manassas campaign
Black Horse Cavalry, 143, 148
Blair, Francis P., Jr. "Frank"
    abandonment of regiment, assumption
        of seat in Congress, 172
    advocacy for Lyon, 157
    arming of Union regiments in St.
        Louis, 157
    biographical sketch, 293
    demand for dissolution of Missouri
        State Guard, 161
    meeting with Lyon on Price-Harney
        agreement, 164
    petition for removal of Harney from
        command, 163
    sponsorship of Clark's expulsion from
        Congress, 159
Blair, Montgomery
    advocacy for further offensive against
        South, 262
    appeal to Scott in Lyon's behalf, 171–72

biographical sketch, 293
    denial of mail service to anti-adminis-
        tration newspapers, 186
    recommendation of Frémont for Mis-
        souri post, 106, 192
    recommendation to defend Fort
        Sumter, 17
Blair, Preston, 17
Blenker, Louis, 111
Bonham, Milledge
    advance to Bull Run, 145
    command during Union invasion of
        Alexandria, 74
    defense of Fairfax Court House, 109
    evacuation of Fairfax Court House, 112
    pursuit of retreating troops at Bull
        Run, 147
    retreat from Centreville, placement of
        pickets at Bull Run, 114
Botts, John Minor, 28
Bramhall, Walter, 239–40
Breckinridge, John, 95
Broadhead, James, 157
Brown, George, 28, 29, 197
Buchanan, Frank, 16
Buchanan, James, 4, 9
Buckner, Simon, 193, 293
Bull Run engagement
    abolitionist responses to Union defeat,
        151–52
    assignment of blame for Union defeat,
        152–53
    Confederate army
        advances on Henry Hill, 138, 140,
            143–46
        casualties, 143
        confusion over diversity of uni-
            forms, 140, 143
        pursuit of retreating Union troops,
            146, 150
        troop strength, 137–38
    Joint Committee on the Conduct of the
        War investigation, 267
    map, 115
    order of battle, 289–90
    Southern response to Confederate vic-
        tory, 151
    Union army
        advances on Henry Hill, 141–45
        casualties, 146, 148
        confusion over diversity of uni-
            forms, 139, 142–43
        cowardice, 152, 261

delayed start of advance, 132–34,
318n39
fatigue and disorganization of
troops, 145
ignorance of Confederate line at
Henry Hill, 140
ineffective use of troops, 138, 140
retreat, 145, 146–48
Burns, William, 259–60
Burnside, Ambrose
Bull Run engagement
advance to Henry Hill, 145
delayed start of advance, 133
retreat, 146
troop positions, 135–36
selection of Stone to preside over court
martial, 278
Burt, Erasmus
advance to Ball's Bluff, 237
death, 240
encouragement of troops at Goose
Creek, 219
formation of Burt Rifles, 37
Butler, Benjamin F.
biographical sketch, 294
command of Fort Monroe, 79, 82
establishment of base at Newport
News, 79–80
liberation of Virginia slaves, 82
plan for raid on Big Bethel Church,
82–83
suggestion to Lincoln for arrest of
Maryland legislators, 42
unauthorized invasion of Baltimore,
67–68
value to Lincoln, promotion to major
general, 68
Buxton, Frank
biographical sketch, 294
estimate of Confederate strength at
Leesburg, 210, 216
report of disloyalty in Union army, 254
suggestion for capture of Leesburg garrison, 216

Cadwalader, George, 68–69
California troops
1st California Infantry, 211, 237
2nd California Infantry, 211
Pennsylvania volunteers in, 211, 259
Cameron, James (Simon Cameron's
brother), 127, 144
Cameron, Simon

appeal for three-month militia to extend service, 48, 127–28
arrest of Maryland legislators to prevent secession vote, 197
biographical sketch, 294
departure from cabinet, 272
order for shutdown of Baltimore newspapers, 196
promise to Hicks concerning deployment of Maryland militia, 28
recommendation to surrender Fort
Sumter, 17
Catton, Bruce, xviii
Chandler, Zachariah
advocacy for further offensive against
South, 261–63
biographical sketch, 294
efforts toward Stone's removal, 262
exploitation of Stone to further abolitionist cause, 281
request for Senate investigation into
Union defeats, 265
on Southern sympathies at West Point,
266
Chase, Salmon P.
appeal to Scott in Lyon's behalf, 171
biographical sketch, 294–95
facilitation of Stanton's appointment as
secretary of war, 272
as head of Treasury Department, 11
plan to divide Confederacy, 105
recommendation to defend Fort
Sumter, 17
civil liberties violations
arrest of Baltimore city marshal and
police commissioners, 103–5
arrest of Maryland legislators to prevent secession vote, 42–43, 197–99,
285
by Confederacy, 255–56, 285
free speech rights, 67, 68, 70, 103, 185–
87, 196, 255–57
habeas corpus rights, 42–44, 68–71,
105, 310n27
martial law, 104, 187, 191–92, 255–56
monitoring of free elections, 71, 94
Civil War
constitutional legality of, xv
death toll, xvi
map of theater of war, 1861, 7
Clark, Fred, 57
Clark, John B., 159
Clary, Robert, 8

Clay, Cassius, 26, 41
Clay, Henry, 188
Clemens, Samuel Langhorne
    account of war service, 323n31
    on Missouri State Guard recruits, 166
    as pilot of *Alonzo Child*, 35
    travel through Nevada, 185
Cocke, Philip St. George, 130, 134, 143–44
Cogswell, Milton
    Ball's Bluff engagement
        coverage of retreat, 243–44
        movement of troops from Harrison's Island, 239
        offensive plan, 242
    defense of Stone at expense of career, 277, 338n106
Confederacy
    calls for peaceful separation, 18–20
    defections to, 27–28, 37
    desirability of Kentucky's neutrality, 189, 190
    inception of Confederate States of America, 5–6
    relocation of capital from Montgomery to Richmond, 87
    suppression of civil liberties in Southern states, 285
    suspicions of disloyalty, 254–55
Confederate army
    call for troops, 36–38
    defections to, 15, 31
    establishment of, 5–6
    independent soldiers in, 212–13
    inexperience of troops, 106
    training and experience of officers, 85
    uniforms, 139–40, 179, 212
Congress. *See* United States Congress
Conkling, Roscoe, 261, 265, 269
contraband of war, 82, 191
Cooke, Philip St. George, 31, 295
Cooper, Samuel, 15
Corps of Observation, establishment of, 200. *See also* Ball's Bluff engagement: Union army
Covode, John, 275, 337n99
Crittenden, John J., 11, 189

Dailey, Aaron, 222
Davis, Alexander, 255
Davis, Garrett, 191
Davis, Jefferson
    assistance in Virginia's secession, 37

centralization of authority, 285
    pledge to honor Kentucky's neutrality, 192
    relocation of Confederate capital to Richmond, 87
Dennison, William, 48
Devens, Charles
    on poor quality of troops, 202–4
    positions and advances at Ball's Bluff, 222–24, 225–26, 229–30, 234–35, 330n24
    retreat from Ball's Bluff, 244
Dimock, Joseph J., 261, 269
District of Columbia
    arrest of citizens suspected of disloyalty, 256, 257
    arrival of Lincoln, 10
    arrival of troops, 4, 26, 34, 41–42, 45–46
    Beauregard's plan to threaten, 196
    Confederates supporting seizure of, 33–34
    fear of Confederate invasion, 3, 5, 150, 151, 195–96
    isolation of, by destruction of rail lines, 40, 41
    questionable loyalty of militia in, 8–9, 12, 15–16
Dix, John, 197, 199
Douglas, Stephen, 27, 155
Duff, William L.
    observation of Union movement at Harrison's Island, 227
    positions at Ball's Bluff, 225, 227, 229, 236
    raising of Mississippi regiment, 37
Duryée, Abram, 83, 85

Eager, Charles, 244
Eames, Walter, 244
economic issues
    consequences of blockade of Southern ports, 38, 58
    effect of recession on Union enlistments, 50–56, 58, 167, 248
    loss of work with boycott on Northern goods, 50
    new markets with creation of Confederate States of America, 5–6, 61–62
Edwards's Ferry
    assumption of command by Banks, 249

Ball's Bluff engagement
  Confederate army, 213, 222, 231, 233
  Union army, 200, 221, 246
  Manassas campaign
    Confederate army, 95, 96, 98
    Union army, 96
18th Mississippi Infantry, 218, 234, 237, 240, 241
8th New York State Militia, 138–39
8th Virginia Infantry, 89
  Ball's Bluff engagement, 217, 219, 231, 234, 235, 238, 241–42
  Bull Run engagement, 130, 144–45
Einstein, Max, 111
11th Mississippi Infantry, 139
11th New York Fire Zouaves, 46–47, 74, 139, 141–43, 148, 149–50
Ellis (Union spy), 219
Ellsworth, Elmer E.
  biographical sketch, 295
  capture of Confederate flag in Alexandria, 75–76
  death, 76
  martyrdom, 78
  raising of companies, 46
Elzey, Arnold, 146, 153–54
emancipation
  in event of peaceful separation, 283–84
  insignificance to Lincoln in start of war, xiv, 13, 282, 284
  Lincoln's plan for, in border states, 264
  See also abolitionists and abolitionism
Evans, Nathan G. "Shanks"
  Ball's Bluff engagement
    construction of Fort Evans, 213
    expectation of Union attack at Edwards's Ferry, 233
    forces under command, 201
    offer of parole to captive officers, 247
    positions, 217, 218, 219, 220–21, 231, 237, 249
  biographical sketch, 295
  Bull Run engagement, 130–31, 134–35, 136
  defection to Confederate army, 15
  experience and rank, 100
  imposition of undeclared martial law in Leesburg, 255–56
Ewell, Richard, 80–81, 113
Ewing, Charles, 158

Fairfax Court House
  Confederate picket at, 218
  Confederate retreat from, 112, 124
  Union raid at, 80–81
Featherston, Winfield Scott, 219, 243
federal call for troops
  alienation of citizens, increase in Confederate sympathy, 27–28, 43, 72, 154, 155, 159, 283
  expansion of service to three years, 47–48
  Maryland's reluctance to comply, 28
  Missouri's refusal to comply, 156
  Northern compliance, 33
  proclamations, 26–27, 45
  role in Union defeat at Bull Run, 153–54
  Virginia military buildup in response to, 32
federal government. See Lincoln, Abraham; United States Congress
15th Massachusetts Infantry, 202–3, 213, 222, 224, 232, 238
5th New York Infantry, 83–84
5th U.S. Artillery, 93
First Amendment rights. See free speech rights, abridgment of.
1st California Infantry, 211, 237
1st Iowa Infantry, 169–70, 175, 178, 180
1st Kansas Infantry, 170, 178, 180
1st Maryland Infantry, 154
1st Massachusetts Infantry, 114–17
1st Massachusetts Sharpshooters, 208, 213, 249
1st Michigan Infantry, 77, 144
1st Minnesota Infantry, 139, 142–43, 200, 213, 231
1st Missouri Infantry, 178, 180
1st New Hampshire Infantry, 101, 186
1st New York Infantry, 83–84
1st North Carolina Infantry, 82
1st Rhode Island Artillery, Battery B, 208
1st Rhode Island Militia, 46, 136, 139
1st U.S. Artillery, Battery I, 221
1st Virginia Infantry, 117
Floyd, John, 4
Forrest, Nathan Bedford, 190
Fort Ellsworth, 77–78
Fort Jefferson, 18
Fort Monroe, 82
Fort Pickens, 18, 20–21, 23, 26
Fort Sumter
  Confederate attack on, 4

Fort Sumter (*cont.*)
    Confederate batteries around, 14–15
    federal attempt to reinforce, provoking
        war, 20–25
    Northern patriotic response to attack,
        32
    opinions concerning federal resupply
        of, 16–18
    Seward's attempt to influence policy
        on, 16, 20, 21
    Southern response to resupply effort,
        25
    surrender of, 27
Fort Taylor, 18
42nd New York Infantry "Tammany Regi-
    ment," 201, 237, 243
14th New York State Militia, 74, 138–39,
    142, 144
4th Pennsylvania Infantry, 127–28, 137
4th South Carolina Infantry, 130
4th Virginia Infantry, 140
Fox, Gustavus V., 20
free speech rights, abridgment of
    arrest of citizens suspected of disloy-
        alty, 67, 68, 70, 103, 187, 255–57
    suppression of newspapers, 70, 185–87,
        196, 255, 256
Frémont, John Charles "Pathfinder"
    assignment to Department of the West,
        172
    biographical sketch, 295
    in Blair's plan for command of Mis-
        souri, 106
    in Chase's plan to divide Confederacy,
        105
    declaration of martial law in Missouri,
        187, 191–92
    order of troops to Kentucky, 192
    Richmond campaign, 286
    threat to emancipate slaves, 191
French, Benjamin Brown, 11, 13–14
French, Frank, 236
Frost, Daniel, 158
Furber, Luther, 50–51

Gaither, George, 96
Geary, John W.
    arrest of citizens suspected of disloy-
        alty, 257
    biographical sketch, 295–96
    excitability and paranoia, 202, 210
    position near Ball's Bluff, 201–2
    raid on Harper's Ferry, retreat to Mary-
        land, 217

Geer, George, 55–56
Georgia, enlistment in, 38–39
Gilbert, John, 56–57
Glenn, William Wilkins, 197
Gooch, Daniel, 269
Gorman, Willis, 208, 221, 231
Gosport, Virginia, Union seizure of navy
    yard at, 31–32
Grafton, Virginia, Union seizure of, 79
Grant, Ulysses
    censure of, for maltreatment of Stone,
        281
    order for arrest of anti-administration
        newspaper editor, 187
    position of troops in Kentucky, 192,
        193
    relief of Stone from command, 279
Greeley, Horace
    biographical sketch, 296
    campaign against Stone, 268
    "Go West" solution for poverty in
        northeast, 54
    role in Union defeat at Bull Run,
        153
Griffin, Charles, 141–43

habeas corpus rights, suspension of
    in arrest of Baltimore militia lieuten-
        ant, 68–69
    attorney general's defense of, 69–70
    concept and principles of habeas cor-
        pus, 42–43
    extension to Florida Keys, 68
    extension to New York City, 105
    Lincoln's casual attitude toward,
        310n27
    precedent of Andrew Jackson, 43
    repercussions, 71
    secret and unilateral suspension in
        Maryland, 42–44
    Taney's challenge of, 68–70
Hamlin, Hannibal, 12
Hampton, Wade, 130, 138, 141
Harney, William S., 157, 158, 159–62
Harper's Ferry
    Confederate army
        defense by blockade of canal, 89
        evacuation, 97
        garrison, 96
    geological features, strategic chal-
        lenges, 96
    Union army
        destruction of armory, 31, 34
        headquarters, 126

intention to feign attack against, 97
raid, 216–17
Harris, Thomas, 166
Harrison, Henry T., 204
Harrison, Matthew, 255
Hatcher, Clinton, 72, 219–20, 242, 313n18
Heintzelman, Samuel, 131, 137–38, 142
Henry, Judith, 138, 142
Hicks, Thomas, 20, 28, 29, 296
Hill, Daniel Harvey
    biographical sketch, 296
    command at Big Bethel, 82
    command at Leesburg, 268
    confidence in Stone's loyalty, 277
    experience and training, 85
Hitchcock, Ethan Allen, 16
Holmes, Oliver Wendell, Jr., 236, 241, 282
Holt, Joseph, 4, 12, 14–15, 296
Hooker, Joseph, 278
House Select Committee on the Loyalty of Clerks, 266
Howard, Frank Key, 197
Howard, Oliver Otis, 145–46
Howe, Church
    fire direction of mountain howitzers at Ball's Bluff, 240
    reports to Stone, relay of instructions, 227, 229, 230, 234
    spread of misinformation, 232
    transfer of troops to Harrison's Island, 222–23
Hunter, David, 131, 133, 135
Hunton, Eppa
    advance to Manassas, 130
    biographical sketch, 296
    burning of Edwards's Ferry freight cars, 96
    composition of command, 89
    movement between Edwards's Ferry and Conrad's Ferry, 98
    position south of Mason's Island, 234
    reinforcement of Evans for Ball's Bluff engagement, 201
Hurlbut, Stephen, 17–18, 20, 283

Illinois
    deployment of troops to Missouri, 166
    removal of Missouri arsenal ordnance to, 157
    support for Union invasion of Missouri, 167
Iowa
    recruitment of unemployed, 168–69

support for Union invasion of Missouri, 167
Iowa troops
    1st Iowa Infantry
        motives for enlistment, 169–70
        Wilson's Creek engagement, 175, 178, 180
Ish, George, 255

Jackson, Andrew, 43
Jackson, Claiborne Fox
    approval of Price-Harney agreement, 162
    biographical sketch, 297
    outward Union support, private secessionist views, 155, 156, 321n5
    peace offer to Lyon, 164
    refusal to comply with federal troop levy, 156
    retreat from federal invasion, 171
    training and mobilization of Missouri militia, 156, 159, 165
Jackson, James W., 76, 78, 79
Jackson, Margaret (formerly Peggy Stoneburner), 205, 235
Jackson, Thomas J. "Stonewall"
    advance to Manassas, 129
    Bull Run engagement, 139–40, 142, 143
    confrontation with Patterson at Falling Waters, 106
    service as military instructor, 96
Jacobin Club (abolitionist congressmen), 261–62, 264–65, 281, 284–85. See also Joint Committee on the Conduct of the War
Janney, John, 30–31
Jenifer, Walter, 230, 231, 234, 235
Johnson, Andrew, 275, 282
Johnston, Joseph E.
    advance to Manassas, 124–25, 129
    biographical sketch, 297
    command at Harper's Ferry, evacuation, 96–97
    endorsement of Beauregard's plan to threaten Washington, 196
    position of troops near Martinsburg, 106
    retreat from Fairfax Court House, 218
    troop strength at Winchester, 107, 120
Joint Committee on the Conduct of the War
    efforts to remove McClellan from command, 266, 267

Joint Committee on the Conduct of
    the War *(cont.)*
    formation and mission of, 261, 265–66
    interrogation of Stone, 268–69, 274–
        75, 278–79
    judgment against Stone, 275
    publication of report, 279
    request for arrest of Stone, 273–74
    witnesses against Stone, 267, 269–71,
        277

Kane, George P.
    arrest of, 103–4, 105
    biographical sketch, 297
    isolation of Baltimore, 29–30
Kansas
    drought and poor economy, Union re-
        cruitment and, 167–68
    Fort Leavenworth headquarters of De-
        partment of the West, 163
    support for Union invasion of Mis-
        souri, 167
Kansas troops
    deployment to Missouri, 170
    1st Kansas Infantry, 170, 178, 180
    2nd Kansas Infantry, 170, 180
Kearny, Phil, 277
Kelley, Benjamin, 81
Kemper, Delaware, 147
Kentucky
    ambivalent loyalties, 71, 188, 190, 191
    benefits of neutrality to Confederacy
        and Union, 189, 190–91
    Kentucky Resolutions, concept of
        Union, 188
    Lincoln's secret support of pro-Union
        militia, 189
    neutrality, 156, 189, 190
    Union foothold at Columbus, 192–93
Kentucky State Guard, 189–90
Keyes, Erasmus, 140–41, 147, 150

Lamon, Ward Hill, 17
Lander, Frederick West, 208, 249
Lane, James, 26, 41
Lee, Robert E.
    command of Provisional Army of Vir-
        ginia, 31, 63, 64–65
    defense of Leesburg and Harper's
        Ferry, 89
    estate of, 64, 74
Lee, William
    advances at Ball's Bluff, 223–24, 225

dispatch of scouts near Leesburg, 227
on futility of Ball's Bluff campaign, 232
retreat from Ball's Bluff, 242, 244, 245
Leesburg, Virginia
    confrontation at, escalation of hostili-
        ties, 100
    geological features and estates in area,
        204–6
    map, 203
    reinforcement by South Carolina
        troops, 99–100
    undeclared martial law in, 255–56
    Union intention to capture, 93
    See also Ball's Bluff engagement
Letcher, John
    activation of Virginia militia, 63
    biographical sketch, 297
    buildup of defenses against federal
        government, 32
    defense of Gosport navy yard, 31
    offer of Confederate commissions to
        federal officers, 31
Lincoln, Abraham
    arming of regiments against Missouri
        state militia, 157
    assassination threats against, 10, 11
    concern over anti-Union sentiment in
        Kentucky, 191
    constitutional violations, xiv, 70, 195,
        282 (*see also* civil liberties viola-
        tions)
    failure to intercede for Stone, 279, 281
    Fort Sumter
        deliberations concerning resupply
            of fort, 16–18, 20–21
        dispatch of supplies, provocation of
            war, 20–25
        initial inaction, 15
    friendship with Baker, 12, 250
    frustration with McClellan's inaction,
        263–64
    government and military appointees
        Chase as treasury secretary, 11
        conditional removal of Harney
            from Missouri command, 163
        dismissal of Cameron as secretary
            of war, 272
        Frémont as commander of Depart-
            ment of the West, 172
        Lander as brigadier general, 208
        offer of commissions to Baker, 252
        Seward as secretary of state, 11
        Stanton as secretary of war, 272

habeas corpus rights suspension, 42–44, 68–70, 71, 105, 310n27
illnesses of sons, 278
inauguration, 10–14
militia levy
    alienation of citizens, increase in Confederate sympathy, 27–28, 43, 72, 154, 155, 159, 283
    call for troops, 47–48
    Maryland's reluctance to comply, 28
    Missouri's refusal to comply, 156
    Northern compliance, 33
    proclamations for, 26–27, 45
    role in Union defeat at Bull Run, 153–54
    Virginia military buildup in response to, 32
mobilization of Missouri troops, 187
monitoring of Bull Run situation, 148–49
preservation of Union, refusal to consider peaceful separation, xiv, 13, 20, 282–83
President's General War Order No. 1, 273
secret support of pro-Union militia companies in Kentucky, 189
slavery
    insignificance of, in start of war, xiv, 13, 282, 284
    noninterference with, 13, 82, 265, 285
    plan for compensated emancipation, 264
Southern ports blockade, 35, 38, 44, 47, 58
Lomax, Lunsford L., 12, 297
Longstreet, James, 11
Louisiana Infantry, 3rd, 178–79
Lowell, James J., 241
Lowry, Reigart B., 75
Lyon, Nathaniel
    arming of federal volunteers against state militia, 156–58
    assumption of command in Missouri, 163
    biographical sketch, 298
    "declaration of war" against Missouri, 164
    massacre of civilians, 158
    Missouri invasion plan, 170

petition for removal of Harney from command, 163
removal of Missouri from command of, 163, 171–72
shortages of troops and supplies, 174
Wilson's Creek engagement
    advances, 172–74, 175, 177–78
    death, 180
    equivocation concerning withdrawal, 175–76
    establishment of headquarters at Springfield, 174
    plan of attack, 177
    victory at Dug Springs, withdrawal to Springfield, 175
Macgill, Charles, 199
Magoffin, Beriah, 188, 189, 298
Magruder, John Bankhead, 82, 84, 85, 299
Maine troops
    enlistments, 53–54
    2nd Maine Infantry, 141
Mallory, Stephen, 88–89
Manassas campaign
    Confederate army
        evacuation of Harper's Ferry, 97
        retreat from Fairfax Court House, 112
        rumored atrocities committed by, 128
        strategic encampment at Manassas Junction, 66
        troop strength, 97, 100, 108–9, 120, 126
    Southern response to Confederate victory at Blackburn's Ford, 118
    Union army
        Blackburn's Ford defeat, 117–18, 128
        capture of Confederate prisoners and flag, 113
        casualties, 116–17, 118
        discharge of three-month militia, 123, 125, 126–28
        diversity of uniforms, 110–11, 116
        looting and pillaging, destruction of Germantown, 112–13
        low morale, 126, 128
        mobilization of troops, 109–10, 111–12, 124
        Patterson's inaction and failure to communicate, 97–99, 120–26
        Poolesville headquarters, 95

Manassas campaign (*cont.*)
　　Scott's plan for advance, 98, 106,
　　　107
　　seizure of Centreville, 113–14
　　skirmish, exchange of fire, 114–16
　　strategy, 108, 129, 131–32
　　troop strength, 108, 120, 126
　　See also Bull Run engagement
Mansfield, Joseph K. F.
　　biographical sketch, 299
　　invasion of Alexandria waterfront, 72–
　　　73
　　rebuke of McDowell for practice of
　　　troop maneuvers, 140
　　return of runaway slaves, 271–72
Marcy, Randolph, 195–96
Maryland
　　anger at federal authoritarian rule, 94–
　　　95, 102, 104–5, 155, 194, 198
　　arrest of peace candidates and voters,
　　　257–58, 285
　　arrests for treason, suspension of ha-
　　　beas corpus rights, 67–69, 103–4,
　　　256
　　Baltimore, 29–30, 34, 42–43, 67–68,
　　　94, 103–5, 197–99, 285
　　Confederate infantry from, 101–2
　　difficulty in maintaining neutrality,
　　　156
　　1st Maryland Infantry, 154
　　Fugitive Slave Law, 267
　　legislative resolution on right of seces-
　　　sion, 43
　　maps, 65, 203
　　reluctance to comply with federal mili-
　　　tia levy, 28
　　slavery, 155, 267
　　Southern sympathy, Confederate vol-
　　　unteers, 28–30, 40, 101–2, 315n22
　　suspension of right of habeas corpus,
　　　43–44
　　weakening of secessionist faction, 68
Massachusetts
　　abolitionist sentiment, 50
　　panic and grief over Ball's Bluff defeat,
　　　251
　　recruitment of unemployed, 51–52
　　shoemaking industry in, 49–50
Massachusetts troops
　　1st Massachusetts Infantry, 114–17
　　1st Massachusetts Sharpshooters, 208,
　　　213, 249
　　2nd Massachusetts Infantry, 123
　　6th Massachusetts Infantry

　　arrival in Washington, 34
　　march through Baltimore, incite-
　　　ment of riot, 28–29
　　monitoring of Baltimore elections,
　　　94
　　15th Massachusetts Infantry, 202–3,
　　　213, 222, 224, 232, 238
　　19th Massachusetts Infantry, 208
　　20th Massachusetts Infantry
　　　advance to Ball's Bluff, 223, 224,
　　　　225
　　　arrival at Poolesville, 208
　　　composition of, 235–36
　　　malfunction of weapons, 213
May, Henry, 94, 95
McCall, George
　　advance toward Leesburg, 216
　　evacuation of Dranesville, 237
　　position at Dranesville, threat to Ev-
　　　ans, 218, 220
　　position near Ball's Bluff, 201
　　testimony concerning fugitive slaves,
　　　267
McClellan, George B.
　　Ball's Bluff engagement
　　　advance of McCall's division toward
　　　　Leesburg, 216, 218
　　　arrival at Poolesville, 249
　　　blame for Union defeat, 253
　　　denial of ordering troops across
　　　　river, 262
　　　maintenance of position at Ed-
　　　　wards's Ferry, 246
　　　misinformation concerning Mc-
　　　　Call's position at Dranesville,
　　　　220, 237
　　　order for retreat to Maryland, 249–
　　　　50
　　　promise of reinforcements at
　　　　Poolesville, 206
　　　report of Confederate abandon-
　　　　ment of Leesburg, 200
　　　selection of Stone as commander,
　　　　200
　　biographical sketch, 298
　　campaign against Scott, 262
　　commands
　　　addition of Missouri to Department
　　　　of the Ohio, 163
　　　bypass of, for command of Depart-
　　　　ment of the West, 171
　　　Division of the Potomac, 152
　　　as major general at Grafton, 79,
　　　　80

overall army command, 262–64
  removal from command, 266, 273
contraction of typhoid, 265
endorsement of conscription, 196
experience and ability, 86
failure to mount Southern offensive,
  262, 263–64, 266
Joint Committee on the Conduct of the
  War's case against, 266, 267
Maryland conspiracy rumor, arrest of
  legislators, 195, 197, 199
proposal of Kentucky neutrality agreement, 164
protection of Washington against rumored Confederate invasion, 196
Richmond campaign, 286
slavery views, 266
Stone, 262, 273–74, 275, 276, 281
McCulloch, Ben
  biographical sketch, 298
  establishment of headquarters at
    Springfield, 182
  plan for Missouri's secession, 187
  rumored as leader for Confederate raid
    on Washington, 24
  Wilson's Creek engagement
    advance division at Crane Creek,
      174–75
    combination of forces with Mis-
      souri State Guard, advance to-
      ward Springfield, 172, 174–75
    estimate of enemy troop strength,
      181
    fragmentation of units, 179–80
    troop strength, 174, 176
McDermott, Thomas, 55
McDowell, Irvin
  assumption of command, 86–87, 108
  biographical sketch, 298
  Bull Run engagement
    artillery advance onto Henry Hill,
      141
    delayed start of advance, 133
    discharge of three-month enlistees,
      127
    fatigue and disorganization of
      troops, 145
    ineffective use of troops, 138, 140
    low morale of troops, 128
    plan of attack, 129, 131–32
    retreat to Potomac, 148
    troop positions, 137
  in Chase's plan to divide Confederacy,
    105

experience and training, 86
Joint Committee on the Conduct of the
  War's preference for, as army commander, 266
leading of military parade, 263
plan for advance toward Richmond,
  108, 109–10
relief from command, 152
in Scott's plan to advance to Manassas,
  106–7
McGuirk, John, 222, 225–26
Medill, Joseph, 273
Meigs, Montgomery, 20
Melville, Herman, 236
Merchant, John, 236, 241
Merryman, John, 68–69, 70–71
mid-Atlantic confederation, 20
Miles, Dixon
  abandonment of positions at Bull Run,
    148
  assumption of command, 108
  position at Bull Run, 131, 137
  role in Union defeat, 152
militia levy
  alienation of citizens, increase in Con-
    federate sympathy, 27–28, 43, 72,
    154, 155, 159, 283
  call for troops, 47–48
  Maryland's reluctance to comply,
    28
  Missouri's refusal to comply, 156
  Northern compliance, 33
  proclamations for, 26–27, 45
  role in Union defeat at Bull Run, 153–
    54
  Virginia military buildup in response
    to, 32
Minnesota Infantry, 1st
  Ball's Bluff engagement, 200, 231
  Bull Run engagement, 142–43
  uniform, 139
  weapons, 213
Mississippi troops
  11th Mississippi Infantry, 139
  13th Mississippi Infantry
    attack at Dailey plantation, 249
    encounter with Union scouts,
      231
    positions near Ball's Bluff, 217, 218,
      234
  17th Mississippi Infantry
    collection of booty, 248
    decisive attack at Ball's Bluff, 243
    lack of uniforms, 212

Mississippi troops (*cont.*)
    positions near Ball's Bluff, 218, 219, 222, 225
    18th Mississippi Infantry, 218, 234, 237, 240, 241
    lack of uniforms, 212
    raising of Confederate regiments, 37
Missouri
    answer to Confederate call for troops, 37
    arrival of Union regiments in, 166, 167
    Civil War dead from, 323n27
    election of Jackson as governor, 155
    fear of Confederate invasion, 163
    1st Missouri Infantry, 178, 180
    flight of citizens in fear of federal repression, 194
    loyalties
        animosity toward Union, growing Confederate sympathy, 155–56, 159, 285
        neutrality, 156
        Union support, 67, 155, 157, 176, 181
    Lyon, Nathaniel, 156–58, 163, 164–65, 170, 171–72
    map, 160
    martial law, 187, 191–92
    poverty, difficult economic times, 167
    Price-Harney peace agreement, 161–63
    refusal to comply with federal militia levy, 156
    riots, massacre of civilians, 66–67, 158
    suppression of free speech, 185–86
    Union preparations for uprising of Southerners, 151
    See also Wilson's Creek engagement
Missouri Compromise, 11, 283
Missouri State Guard
    arrest of suspected secessionist militiamen, 66–67
    break from Confederate force, advance north, 187, 193–94
    Confederate supply of artillery to, 156, 157
    demobilization of, in accordance with Price-Harney peace agreement, 162–63
    Lyon's attack on, 157–58
    merger of forces with Confederacy, 174–75
    mobilization against Union invasion, 165–66
    removal of ordnance from arsenal, 157

reorganization of state militia, 159
retreat south, 171
shortage of ordnance and discipline, 173–74
state militia training, 156
Union discouragement of recruits to, 166
Union loyalty, 67, 157, 176, 181
wide position near border, 172
Mix, John, 231

National Rifles, 8
Nebraska Territory, enlistment in, 167
New Hampshire troops
    1st New Hampshire Infantry, 101, 186
    2nd New Hampshire Infantry
        Bull Run engagement, 135–36, 145
        casualties, 147
        uniform, 139
    recruitment of unemployed, 52
    reluctance to reenlist for three-year service, 48–49
Newport News, Virginia, Union seizure of, 79–80
newspapers, shutdown of, 185–87, 196, 255, 256
New York
    habeas corpus suspension, 105
    recruitment of unemployed, 55–56
New York troops
    1st New York Infantry, 83–84
    2nd New York State Militia
        charges against Stone, 260–61
        deployment of mountain howitzers to Ball's Bluff, 224, 236
        desertion of officers from, at Bull Run, 148
        disciplinary problems, misconduct, 207–8, 261, 270
        loss of morale, 200
    3rd New York Infantry, 84
    5th New York Infantry, 83–84
    7th New York Infantry, 41–42, 45
    8th New York State Militia, 138–39
    9th New York State Militia, 204
    11th New York Fire Zouaves
        Alexandria invasion, 74
        arrival in Washington, 46–47
        Bull Run engagement, 141–43, 148
        casualties, desertions, 149–50
        uniform, 46, 139
    12th New York Infantry, 45–46, 117–18
    13th New York Infantry, 145
    14th New York State Militia

Alexandria invasion, 74
Bull Run engagement, 138–39, 142, 144
uniform, 74, 139
27th New York Infantry, 138
34th New York Infantry "Herkimer Regiment," 201, 207
39th New York Infantry, 110–11
42nd New York Infantry "Tammany Regiment," 201, 237, 243
69th New York Infantry, 144–45, 151
71st New York State Militia, 45, 135–36, 140
79th New York Highlanders, 127, 144
19th Massachusetts Infantry, 208
9th New York State Militia, 204
North Carolina Infantry, 1st, 82

Ohio, enlistment in, 58
O'Meara, Timothy, 55, 243–44, 245
Osburn, Flavius, 39, 219–20, 242

Parsons, Monroe, 171
Patterson, Robert
advance across Potomac, 106
advance to Charles Town, 120–21, 124
advance to Martinsburg, 107
biographical sketch, 299
blame for Union defeat at Bull Run, 152, 267
confusion and shame of troops, 125–26
departure of three-month troops, 123, 126, 127
discharge from service, 126–27
failure to communicate with Scott, 98–99
failure to communicate with Stone, 98, 99, 100–101
inaction, 106, 107, 120, 121–22, 123, 125–26
miscalculation of enemy troop strength, 97, 100, 126
plan to advance to Martinsburg, retreat into Maryland, 97
in Scott's plan to bar Confederate advance to Manassas Junction, 106
troop strength, 107, 120
Peace Convention, 10, 11, 19
peaceful separation
calls for, 6, 18–20
emancipation, in event of, 283–84
Lincoln's refusal to consider, xiv, 13, 20, 282–83
Peirce, Ebenezer, 83, 85, 299

Pender, William Dorsey, 15
Pennsylvania troops
division under McCall, 201, 216
4th Pennsylvania Infantry, 127–28, 137
in Manassas campaign, 93, 97, 101, 106
Philadelphia recruits in Baker's California regiments, 211, 259
28th Pennsylvania Infantry, 202
Perry, Benjamin Franklin, 27–28
Pettus, Frank, 241
Pettus, John J., 37
Philbrick, Chase, 222–23, 225–26, 229–30
Philippi, Virginia, Union victory at, 81
Pillow, Gideon, 192
Pinkerton, Allan
arrest of citizens, violations of constitutional rights, 256
arrest of Maryland legislators to foil secession vote, 197
collection of testimony against Stone, 276
report of Confederate withdrawal from Fairfax, 218
search for evidence against Maryland public officials, 199
Polk, Leonidas, 192–93
Porter, Andrew, 133, 135, 136
Porter, Fitz John, 122
Porterfield, George A., 79, 81, 299
Potter, John, 266
Powell, C. H., 274–75
Price, Sterling
biographical sketch, 300
break from Confederate force, advance north in Missouri, 187, 193–94
in command of Missouri State Guard, 159
merger of Missouri State Guard with Confederate forces, 174–75
mobilization of Missouri State Guard against Union invasion, 165–66
Price-Harney peace agreement, 161–63
retreat south from Lyon's invasion, 170–71
shortage of ordnance and discipline, inability to take offensive, 173–74
Putnam, John, 241
Putnam, William Lowell, 241, 252

Radical Republicans (abolitionist congressmen), 261–62, 264–65, 281, 284–85

Radical Republicans (*cont.*)
  See also Joint Committee on the Con-
    duct of the War
Rains, James, 178
Ray, John, 178
Revere, Paul, 209, 227, 235, 244, 331n39
Reynolds, Thomas, 162
Rhode Island troops
  1st Rhode Island Artillery, Battery B,
    208
  1st Rhode Island Militia, 46, 136, 139
  2nd Rhode Island Infantry, 135, 139
Richardson, Israel, 114, 117–18, 131, 134
Richmond, Virginia
  consolidated Union campaign against,
    286
  establishment of Confederate capital
    at, 87
  state seizure of federal building at, 32
  Union captives in, 248
Richmond Howitzers, 201, 219
Ricketts, James, 141–42, 143
Riddle, William, 227–29
Ruffin, Edmund, 86
Russell, William, reports for London
    Times
  departure of three-month soldiers
    from Bull Run, 136–37
  destruction of Germantown by Union
    soldiers, 113
  observes support for Confederacy, 39–
    40
  suspicious of allegations of Stone's
    treason, 262
  Union defeat at Bull Run, 149
Rust, George, 205

Sandford, Charles W.
  in Alexandria invasion, 73–74
  biographical sketch, 300
  refusal of appointment, 200
  willingness to detain Johnston at Win-
    chester, 122
Schaeffer, Frank B.
  biographical sketch, 300
  gathering of militia, enlistment in Vir-
    ginia, 40–41, 130
  questionable loyalty of, resignation
    from federal service, 8–9
Schleiden, Rudolf, 44, 66
Schmitt, George, 241
Schurz, Carl, 32–33
Scott, Winfield
  Alexandria invasion plan, 72–73

  arrest of Baltimore police commission-
    ers, 103
  biographical sketch, 300–301
  defense of Washington, 4, 6
  extension of habeas corpus suspension
    to New York City, 105
  Leesburg advance
    confusing communications, 121
    frustration with Patterson's inac-
      tion, 98–99, 106, 122, 123–24
    instructions to Stone to capture
      Leesburg, 93
    joining of Stone's and Patterson's
      forces, 101
  Manassas advance plan, 107
  recommendation to surrender Fort
    Sumter, 16
  relief of Butler from command, 67–68
  removal of Missouri from Lyon's com-
    mand, 163, 171
  retirement, 252, 262
  Southern ports blockade plan, 107
  unconcern at start of Bull Run battle,
    149
secession
  call for peaceful separation, 6, 18–20
  constitutional legality of, xv
  economic considerations and conse-
    quences of, 50, 61–62
  Lincoln's refusal to consider peaceful
    separation, xiv, 13, 20, 282–83
  Maryland's assertion of right to secede,
    43
  Northern attitudes toward, 6
  popular support for, prior to attack on
    Fort Sumter, 283
  in response to Lincoln's election, 3–5
  in response to militia levy, 27
  of Virginia, 30–31, 36–37, 72
2nd Arkansas Mounted Rifles, 179
2nd California Infantry, 211
2nd Kansas Infantry, 170, 180
2nd Maine Infantry, 141
2nd Massachusetts Infantry, 123
2nd New Hampshire Infantry, 135–36,
  139, 145, 147
2nd New York State Militia, 148, 200, 224,
  236, 207–8, 260–61, 270
2nd Rhode Island Infantry, 135, 139
2nd Wisconsin Infantry, 144
2nd U.S. Cavalry, 80, 117
2nd U.S. Infantry, 156
17th Mississippi Infantry, 212, 218, 219,
  222, 225, 243, 248

17th Virginia Infantry, 117–18, 129

7th Michigan Infantry, 213

7th New York Infantry, 41–42, 45

71st New York State Militia, 45, 135–36, 140

79th New York Highlanders, 127, 144

Seward, William Henry
appointment as secretary of state, 11
arrest of anti-administration newspaper editor, 187
arrest of Maryland legislators, 197, 199–200
attempt to influence Fort Sumter policy, 16, 20, 21
biographical sketch, 301
fear of Confederate attack on Washington, 24
on McDowell's retreat from Bull Run, 149
surveillance of judge suspected of disloyalty, 257
unauthorized negotiations with Confederate officials, 21, 22–23

Sherman, William Tecumseh
at Bull Run, 144–45
on incompetence of Union soldiers, 152
on massacre of civilians in St. Louis, 158
on Stone's arrest for disloyalty, 277

Shorb, Jacob, 275–76

Sickles, Daniel, 33

Sigel, Franz
advance to Wilson Creek, 177–78
assumption of command following Lyon's death, 181
biographical sketch, 301
repulse by State Guards at Neosho, retreat to Springfield, 172–73
retreat from Wilson Creek to Rolla, 182

Simonds, Clark, 235

6th Massachusetts Infantry, 28–29, 34, 94

69th New York Infantry, 144–45, 151

slaves and slavery
contrabands of war, 82, 191
emancipation, in event of peaceful separation, 283–84
Fugitive Slave Law, 267
insignificance to Lincoln in start of war, xiv, 13, 282, 284
Lincoln's assurance of noninterference, 13, 82, 265, 285
Lincoln's election as threat to, 3–5

Lincoln's plan for emancipation in border states, 264
Missouri Compromise, 11, 283
Peace Convention, 10, 11, 19
return of fugitives by Stone, 207, 267, 269
See also abolitionists and abolitionism

Smart, John, 206

Smart's Mill, 225, 230, 245

Smith, Caleb B., 16–17, 301

Smith, Charles F., 24

Smith, Larkin, 38

Smith, William (Confederate commander), 144

Smith, William (Union lieutenant), 116

Smith, William F. (Union brigadier), 210

Snethen, Worthington
biographical sketch, 301
reports of treason in Baltimore, call for arrests, 102–3, 104
support of Stanton, 273

South Carolina volunteers
first shot at Fort Sumter, 4
4th South Carolina Infantry, 130
at Leesburg, 99–100

Southern ports, blockade of
economic consequences, 38, 58
equivalent to declaration of war, 44
expansion of navy for, 47
Lincoln's announcement of, 35
in Scott's strategy against Confederacy, 107

South Kansas-Texas Cavalry, 176, 180, 181

Speed, Joshua, 191

Sprague, William, 135

Stahel, Julius, 111

Stampp, Kenneth, xvii

Stanton, Edwin McMasters
appointment as secretary of war, 272
biographical sketch, 301–2
on Lincoln's initial inaction at Fort Sumter, 15

Stone
arrest order for, 273
demotion of, 279
denial of post to, 278, 281
failure to file charges against, 278
order to appear before Joint Committee on the Conduct of the War, 273
persecution of, 275, 281, 338n1

Stearns, Amos, 52

Stedman, Edmund, 250

Stephens, Alexander, 44–45

Steuart, George, 101
Stewart, Charles, 208, 231
Stimson, Eugene, 116
Stone, Charles Pomeroy
    Alexandria campaign, 73, 77
    Ball's Bluff engagement
        advance of troops to Harrison's Is-
            land, 222, 330n24
        apprehension concerning Geary,
            202
        bolster of force, arrival of reinforce-
            ments, 202–4, 206
        confidence of troops, 213–14
        establishment of headquarters at
            Poolesville, 200
        expansion of observation posts, 214
        feint at Edwards's Ferry, 221
        formation of Corps of Observation,
            200
        misbehavior of troops, 207, 214
        misunderstanding of orders from
            McClellan, 237
        orders to Baker concerning cross-
            ing of river, 233
        plan of attack on phantom enemy
            encampment, 223
        poor quality of weapons, 213
        positions at upper Potomac, 200–
            201
        report of Confederate abandon-
            ment of Leesburg, 220, 230–31
        withdrawal from Edwards's Ferry,
            246
    biographical sketch, 302
    commands and assignments
        commission as colonel, 8
        Department of the Gulf chief of
            staff, 279
        Egyptian army chief of staff, 302,
            338n113
        elevation to division command,
            206, 208
        field command of federal militia
            companies, 25
        inspector general for District of Co-
            lumbia militia, 8
        new Regular Army regiments, 47
        resignation, 280
    death of wife, remarriage, 279
    disloyalty charges
        arrest, 273–75, 276, 278
        blame for Union defeat, 250, 253–
            54, 258–59
        defenders of Stone against charges,
            277–78
        discharge from prison, 278
        interrogation by Joint Committee
            on the Conduct of the War, 267–
            69, 274–75, 278–79
        McClellan's role, 262
        testimony against Stone, 253, 259,
            260–61, 269–72, 275–76, 277
    education and background, 8
    intelligence concerning Confederate
        plan to capture Washington and
        Maryland, 24
    Leesburg campaign
        advance to Poolesville, 95, 97–98
        assignment by Scott to capture
            Leesburg, 93
        bluff by detachment at Edwards's
            Ferry, 101
        confrontation at Leesburg, escala-
            tion of hostilities, 100
        extension of position to Point of
            Rocks, 99
        joining with Patterson, 101, 107,
            120
    mistrust of militia loyalty in District of
        Columbia, 8, 12
    monitoring of Maryland elections, 94–
        95
    restoration of rail lines between Wash-
        ington and Annapolis, 41
    return of fugitive slaves, 207, 267, 269
    rumors of mental decline, 279–80
Stoneburner, Jacob, 204–5
Strong, George Templeton, 14, 182
Stuart, J.E.B., 31, 106, 141–42
Sturgis, Samuel, 170, 171, 180–81
Sumner, Charles, 265, 267–68
Surratt, Mary, 281
Swann, Thomas, 204
Sweeny, Thomas William
    advance to Missouri State Guard en-
        campments at Neosho, 172
    biographical sketch, 302
    election to brigadier general, 181
    position at Rolla, 170
    position at Springfield, 171
Sykes, George, 276

Taney, Roger Brooke, 13, 68–70, 302
Taylor, Algernon Sidney, 63–64, 302–3
Tennessee Infantry, 3rd, 154
10th Virginia Infantry, 154

Terrett, George Hunter
  Alexandria
    in command at, 64
    escape from, 77
    refusal to surrender, offer to evacuate, 75
    at Union invasion of, 74
    biographical sketch, 303
Terrill, James, 31
Terrill, William, 31
3rd Connecticut Infantry, 141
3rd Louisiana Infantry, 178–79
3rd New York Infantry, 84
3rd Tennessee Infantry, 154
13th Mississippi Infantry, 217, 218, 231, 234, 249
13th New York Infantry, 145
34th New York Infantry "Herkimer Regiment," 201, 207
39th New York Infantry, 110–11
33rd Virginia Infantry, 142
Thomas, Francis, 101–2, 143
Thomas, George, 5, 31, 124
Tompkins, George W. B., 261, 269–70
Trimble, Isaac, 29–30, 67
Trumbull, Lyman, 261–62
Trundle, Horatio, 205
12th New York Infantry, 45–46, 117–18
20th Massachusetts Infantry, 208, 213, 223, 224, 225, 235–36
28th Pennsylvania Infantry, 202
27th New York Infantry, 138
27th Virginia Infantry, 140
Twiggs, David, 9–10
Tyler, Daniel
    advance toward Vienna, 111–12
    assignment as division commander, 108
    delayed start of Bull Run advance, 132–34, 318n39
    deployment of artillery at Blackburn's Ford, 117, 118
    in McDowell's plan of attack at Bull Run, 131
    retreat from Bull Run, 146–47

Union army
    assumption of command by McClellan, reorganization, 262–63
    defections from, 15, 31
    Democratic sympathies of officers, 266
    diversity of uniforms, 46, 74, 83, 110–11, 116, 139, 142–43
  enlistment
    for adventure, 45
    financial incentives for, 56–61
    surge in, with Ellsworth's martyrdom, 78
    of unemployed, 50–56, 58, 167, 248
    incompetence and cowardice in, 152–53
    inexperience and poor training of officers, 85, 86–87
    shock of officers at Stone's arrest, 277
    soldiers' pay and benefits, 51, 58
    substitutes and bounty men, 50, 59–61
    teenagers in, 116
    three-month militia, 47–48, 93, 123, 125, 126–28, 136–37
    See also militia levy
United States Congress
    House Select Committee on the Loyalty of Clerks, 266
    imbalance created by secession, threat to remaining slave states, 4–5
    Joint Committee on the Conduct of the War
      efforts to remove McClellan from command, 266, 267
      formation and mission of, 261, 265–66
      interrogation of Stone, 268–69, 274–75, 278–79
      judgment against Stone, 275
      publication of report, 279
      request for arrest of Stone, 273–74
      witnesses against Stone, 267, 269–71, 277
    Radical Republicans (Jacobin Club) antislavery strategy, 261–62, 264–65, 281, 284–85
    release of army officers held without charges, 278
    request for evidence in arrest of Baltimore police commissioners, 105
United States troops
    5th U.S. Artillery, 93
    1st U.S. Artillery, Battery I, 221
    2nd U.S. Cavalry, 80, 117
    2nd U.S. Infantry, 156

Vaughn, Thomas, 260
Virginia
    areas under Union control, 86
    arrest of citizens suspected of disloyalty, 255

Virginia (*cont.*)
  Big Bethel engagement, 82–85
  Blackburn's Ford engagement, 117–18, 128
  expectations of federal invasion, 37, 63, 109
  Fairfax Court House
    Confederate picket at, 218
    Confederate retreat from, 112, 124
    Union raid at, 80–81
  Fort Ellsworth construction, 77–78
  Gosport navy yard seizure by Union, 31–32
  Grafton seizure by Union, 79
  Leesburg, 93, 99–100, 204–6, 255–56
  loyalties
    ambivalence, 88–89
    Confederate sentiment, 30–31, 39
    Union sentiment, 45, 109
  maps, 65, 115, 203, 228
  massing of troops in, from Confederate states and Kentucky, 37, 66–67
  military buildup in response to federal militia levy, 32
  Newport News seizure by Union, 79–80
  Philippi seizure by Union, 81
  Richmond, 32, 87, 248, 286
  Rich Mountain seizure, Union advance into state, 109
  secession, 30–31, 36–37, 72
  See also Alexandria campaign; Ball's Bluff engagement; Bull Run engagement; Edwards's Ferry; Harper's Ferry; Leesburg, Virginia; Manassas campaign; Richmond, Virginia; Virginia troops
Virginia troops
  1st Virginia Infantry, 117
  4th Virginia Infantry, 140
  8th Virginia Infantry
    assault and retreat at Ball's Bluff, 241–42
    Ball's Bluff positions, 201, 217, 219, 231, 234, 235
    at Bull Run, 130, 144–45
    composition of, 89
    skirmish at Ball's Bluff, 238
  10th Virginia Infantry, 154
  17th Virginia Infantry, 117–18, 129
  27th Virginia Infantry, 140
  33rd Virginia Infantry, 142
  Richmond Howitzers, 201, 219
von Steinwehr, Adolph, 111

Wade, Benjamin F.
  abolitionism, 261–62, 281
  advocacy for further offensive against South, 261–63
  attempts to remove McClellan from command, 267, 273–74
  biographical sketch, 303
  as chairman of Joint Committee on the Conduct of the War, 261–62, 265–66
  complicity with McClellan in removal of Scott, 262, 273–74
  interrogation of Stone, 274–75
  lack of interest in Stone's explanations, 277–78
Wallis, S. Teackle, 199
Ward, George, 232, 241
Washington City
  arrest of citizens suspected of disloyalty, 256, 257
  arrival of Lincoln, 10
  arrival of troops, 4, 26, 34, 41–42, 45–46
  Beauregard's plan to threaten, 196
  Confederates supporting seizure of, 33–34
  fear of Confederate invasion, 3, 5, 150, 151, 195–96
  isolation of, by destruction of rail lines, 40, 41
  questionable loyalty of militia in, 8–9, 12, 15–16
Weightman, Roger, 9
Welles, Gideon, 16, 20, 303
Welsh, Peter, 59
Wentworth, Albert, 116, 129
Wheeler, Alfred, 56
White, Elijah, 245
Whiting, William, 277
Wilkeson, Frank, 60, 312n79
Wilkeson, Sam, 215
Wilkie, Franc B., 169–70
Willcox, Orlando Bolivar, 77, 144
Williams, T. Harry, xiii
Wilson, Henry, 51
Wilson's Creek engagement
  casualties, 164, 180
  Confederate and Missouri combined forces
    decisive attack, 180–81
    fragmentation of units, 179–80
    position at Crane Creek, advance toward Springfield, 175
    resistance of Sigel's advance, 178
    troop strength, 174, 176

confusion over uniforms, 179
map, 160
New York reports of Union victory, 182
order of battle, 290
Union army
    advances, 172–74, 175, 177–78
    equivocation concerning with-
        drawal, 175–76
    establishment of headquarters at
        Springfield, 174
    flight from encounter in cornfield,
        178–79
    Lyon's death, assumption of com-
        mand by Sturgis, 180–81
    plan of attack, 177
    retreat, 181
Winans, Ross, 67

Winthrop, Theodore, 83, 84
Wisconsin Infantry, 2nd, 144
Wistar, Isaac, 236, 238, 241, 276
Wool, John, 87

Young, Francis G.
    biographical sketch, 303
    campaign against Stone, 250, 253–54,
        260
    desertion of post, relief of duty,
        253
    theft and reselling of government
        property, 214, 253
Young, Samuel, 204

Zouaves. *See* New York troops: 11th New
    York Fire Zouaves